Tourists and Tourism

Tourist encounters the ethnic Other in typical fashion, through the lens of a camera. (Photo by Toot Oostveen)

Tourists and Tourism

A Reader

Sharon Bohn Gmelch

Union College

WAVELAND PRESS, INC.

Long Grove, Illinois

For information about this book, contact:
  Waveland Press, Inc.
    4180 IL Route 83, Suite 101
    Long Grove, IL 60047-9580
    (847) 634-0081
    info@waveland.com
    www.waveland.com

Cover photo: Women rowers ferry tourists on the Ngo Dong River at Tam
              Coc, Vietnam. (Photo by Sharon Gmelch)

To my parents, Harold and Patricia Bohn,
who introduced me to travel and other
cultures from the earliest possible moment
and who instilled in me a curiosity
for which I am grateful.

Tourist photography outside the Sun Yatsen Memorial Hall in Guangzhou, China. (Photo by Sharon Gmelch)

Contents

Two: Marketing Culture and Identity

Three: When Tourists and Locals Meet

Four: The Impact and Implications of Tourism

Preface

This volume was inspired by the anthropology course I teach on tourism and by a desire to bring together a collection of engaging readings that capture the diversity and importance of tourism research. Although no collection can hope to cover everything, I have tried to achieve a balance between theory and recent case studies from different parts of the world. I have also sought articles from international specialists in a range of disciplines including anthropology, sociology, history, geography, and folklore as well as journalism. Although domestic tourism is discussed in several articles, the focus is on international tourism and—as befits my interests as an anthropologist—on the cross-cultural encounter and impact. Appendices provide information on the authors, recommended films, and examples of behavioral guidelines written for tourists.

I wish to thank the many contributors to this volume who made this collection possible. I also thank Union College librarians Donna Burton, Bruce Connolly, and Mary Cahill for their efficiency and good humor. Deb Ludke, Elizabeth Daigle, Amanda Haig, and Farida Siddiqi provided secretarial support and critiques on the essays. I also benefited from the suggestions of my colleague and husband, George Gmelch. Pat Mahoney and Morgan Gmelch, as well as the students in my past tourism courses, read many of the articles I considered for inclusion and gave their opinions. Emily Newman, Kaitlyn Richards, and Michael Mosall scanned and printed photographs. Lastly, I thank Tom Curtin of Waveland Press for his encouragement, good cheer, and shared desire to make this an appealing and valuable collection both for students and the specialists who teach them.

One:
Tourism and the
Tourist Experience

Travel and change of place impart new vigor to the mind.

— Seneca, Roman statesman, 4 B.C.–65 A.D.

So far as my experience goes, travelers generally exaggerate the difficulties of the way.

— Henry David Thoreau, U.S. writer and naturalist, 1849

Like all great travelers, I have seen more than I remember and remember more than I have seen.

— Benjamin Disraeli, British statesman and Prime Minister, 1804–1881

Student anthropologist with village friends, Barbados. (Photo by George Gmelch)

1

Why Tourism Matters

Sharon Bohn Gmelch

I became interested in tourism as a result of directing an anthropology field school for students in Barbados, a popular tourist destination.[1] Each year, this small Caribbean island "hosts" four times as many tourists as its 275,000 population.[2] The impact of tourism is visible everywhere, from the hotels with fantasy names like "Glitter Bay" that block much of the ocean view along the west and south coasts to the scantily-clad, sunburnt visitors who wield carts down grocery-store aisles or stand awkwardly in bank lines next to neatly-groomed and fully-clothed Bajans. Tourists often do seem out of place, if not "vulgar, vulgar, vulgar," as Henry James once wrote.

My students are always horrified when they leave the villages they live in and are mistaken for tourists. They are embarrassed by the insensitivity and ignorance tourists sometimes display and are eager to disassociate themselves. After all, they are in Barbados to work, not vacation. They are learning the culture and living with local people, not lying on the beach being served by them. Their experiences are deeper and obviously more valuable than those of tourists.[3] Ironically, tourists often draw similar distinctions amongst themselves: "*I* am a traveler, *you* are a tourist, *he* is a tripper" [emphasis added] (Waterhouse 1989). The reason students are classified as tourists (their foreign accent and, for most, white skin) and their reactions to this raise some initial questions about tourism. Where do most tourists come from? What kind of engagements with local people do they seek? What impact does their presence have on the people and places they visit?

3

Tourism's Global Reach and Economic Impact

Worldwide, tourism employs one in every 12 workers and accounts for 11 percent of global gross domestic product (GDP).[4] In some countries the figures are higher. In Barbados, for example, tourism employs 21 percent of the labor force and accounts for 15 percent of the island's GDP and 57 percent of its foreign exchange earnings.[5] Tourism is also the top foreign exchange earner in communist Cuba (Medea 1998). By 2020, growth in the tourism and travel industry is projected to reach 1.6 billion tourist arrivals a year with receipts of US$2,000 billion. Considering this, it is not surprising that many less developed nations view tourism as the road to development and prosperity.[6] Even Arab governments (besides the long-established destinations of Tunisia, Egypt, and Morocco) are now promoting tourism.

But international tourism is a fickle form of development. Nations have little control over events that can cut off the tourist flow overnight. Whether and where people travel depends largely upon economic factors, namely the cost of a trip and a person's ability to afford it. Eighty percent of international tourists are citizens of twenty rich nations. Citizens from just five—the United States, Germany, Japan, France, and the United Kingdom—account for five of every ten international trips and half of all global spending on tourism. They have the leisure time, discretionary income, and easy access to transportation to make this possible. This profile is changing, however.

Tourist boats, sporting Coca-Cola ads, on the sacred Ganges River in Varanasi, India. (Photo by Sharon Gmelch)

Before long Asia will dominate tourism due to the region's growing economies and population (Smith and Brent 2001).[7] By 2020, China will rank
fourth in terms of the number of its citizens who travel abroad as tourists and
first as an international destination (France currently holds this distinction).

Tourists demand not only affordable and appealing places (both "sites"
and "sights") to visit, they also demand safety. They need to feel confident
that their trip and chosen destination are not unacceptably more risky than
staying at home. Since 1970, international tourism has experienced several
precipitous, although short-term, declines during crises such as the oil crisis
of 1975, the global recession of 1981, the Gulf War in 1991, and the terrorist
attacks of September 11, 2001. Domestic and regional events can also keep
would-be tourists at home: the Chinese government's harsh reprisal against
prodemocracy demonstrators in Tiananmen Square in 1989, the murder of
tourists in Cairo and Luxor, Egypt in 1997, the terrorism in Bali in 2002, and
the outbreak of the SARS virus in 2003 are just a few examples.

Tourism has enormous social implications globally. It represents the
largest ever movement of people across national borders, eclipsing emigration and immigration, refugee flight, pilgrimage, business and educational
travel. In many locations, tourists significantly outnumber residents during
peak seasons. In the course of a year, they may nearly double the population
of a country (as in Ireland) or even quadruple it (as in Barbados).[8] In some
nations, like the United States and India, most tourism is domestic, that is, the
tourists are fellow Americans or Indians rather than foreigners. Regardless of
where they come from, however, any large influx of people to a particular
place has a significant effect on its population, its natural and built environment, its infrastructure and services, and—through the creation of tourism
attractions and venues—on its cultural and national identity. More will be
said about these later.

A Brief History

Tourism, defined broadly as temporary travel for the purpose of experiencing a change, is not new.[9] In Imperial Rome, for example, elites traveled
to the isle of Capri and to cities like Pompeii and Herculaneum for holidays.
Travel for pleasure is historically linked to other quests: the pursuit of profit
(trade and commerce), of spiritual renewal (pilgrimage), of knowledge (e.g.,
the "Grand Tour"), of adventure (early exploration), and of health. Most cultures have long-established traditions of hospitality: rules and etiquette on
how to treat the strangers who show up at your door (i.e., providing food,
shelter, and protection).

Much early tourism was linked to pilgrimage. For many of the medieval pilgrims in Chaucer's *The Canterbury Tales*, the trip to St. Thomas
Becket's shrine was as much a holiday as a pilgrimage. I became aware of the
connection between pilgrimage and tourism when I visited the shrine of

Knock in western Ireland, the site of an apparition of the Virgin Mary, Joseph, and St. John the Evangelist in 1879. I was unprepared for the causal jollity of the pilgrims on the train from Dublin and taken aback by the commercial bustle of Knock's main street as people who had finished their prayers jostled with vendors to buy all manner of sacred and secular souvenirs—from plastic Marys meant to be filled with holy water to tacky T-shirts. In pilgrimage we see important features of tourism: the welcome change of scene, the freedom from everyday routine and responsibilities, the excitement of the journey, and playful permissiveness of a "liminoid" experience (Turner and Turner 1978, Graburn this volume).[10] Today, many secular tourist sites are also, deep down, places of pilgrimage: from the nearly sacred, such as the Vietnam Memorial in Washington, D.C., and Dachau concentration camp outside Munich, to the completely secular like the Baseball Museum and Hall of Fame in Cooperstown, New York, and Tokyo Disneyland.

Touristic travel is also associated with health. Many spa towns developed throughout Europe during the eighteenth century. Barbados's salubrious sea breezes made it a popular health destination in the nineteenth century and even earlier; in 1751 George Washington brought his half-brother Lawrence there hoping he would recuperate from tuberculosis (he died on the voyage home). Tourist destinations boasting hot springs, pure mountain air, and warm seas are still linked to health and recuperation—both physical and mental (Löfgren this volume). When we think about tourism, we tend to forget this long history. The earliest form of tourism most of us are familiar with is the "Grand Tour" of the seventeenth and eighteenth centuries when young English elites, and some Americans, polished their education by exposing themselves to European architecture, geography, history, and culture. Visits to Paris and major Italian cities such as Florence, Venice, Naples, and Rome were especially important. Guidebooks and a fledgling tourism industry developed to meet the needs of these visiting elites and their tutors as they traveled across Europe.

The development of large-scale or mass tourism, however, only became possible with improvements in transportation. Many tourism destinations were promoted by railways and shipping companies in cooperation with private entrepreneurs. Thomas Cook, a British temperance worker turned entrepreneur, used the railways and later, steamships to take people on guided excursions first within England and later to the Continent and beyond (e.g., up the Nile and across the Holy Land). After the success of his first organized railway temperance excursion between Leicester and Loughborough in 1841, he realized people's fascination with railway travel and their need for a specialist agent who could organize complex journeys that covered several railway lines and issue tickets at favorable rates (Brendon 1991). This led to the formation of a travel agency that still bears his name. Tourism through the Inland Passage to southeastern Alaska was instigated by steamship companies in the late 1800s to fill their ships during the summer. Totem poles made by Northwest Coast natives were restored and new ones commissioned in order to market the region to tourists; the poles were positioned along railway lines and ferry routes and at ferry terminals to evoke the region's exotic Indian heritage and wildness (Jonaitis 1999). With the rise of jet travel in the 1960s (which dramatically cut travel times) and the increased use of private automobiles in North America and Europe—aided by higher salaries and more generous vacation times—both international and domestic tourism flourished. The age of mass tourism had begun.

The Study of Tourism

Tourism began to receive sustained academic attention from social scientists in the 1970s (Cohen 1974, 1979; MacCannell 1973, 1976; Smith 1978), following the development of mass tourism. But many academics at first appeared to regard the study of tourism as barely respectable.[11] One reason may be that tourism is basically about relaxation and play; it stands in marked contrast to work and therefore it seemed frivolous and not worthy of serious study. Sport as a subject of inquiry suffered from the same stigma and marginalization.[12] With tourism, there may also have been reluctance on the part of anthropologists to acknowledge that the "exotic" people they studied were also visited by other outsiders called "tourists." Fieldwork in a foreign culture is a rigorous rite of passage into anthropological "adulthood," and anthropologists may not have wished to acknowledge the extent of their group's outside contact or their own similarities to tourists (Crick 1995). Fredrick Errington and Deborah Gewertz discuss some similarities, but also the fundamental differences, between tourists and anthropologists in this volume.

In anthropology, research on tourism began to flourish at the same time a major paradigm shift was taking place (Gupta and Ferguson 1997), that is, anthropologists ceased treating cultures as bounded in place and time, cut off from outside influences and change. They became more interested in processes and in the encounters that link people. Today popular culture is disseminated globally by all sorts of media (e.g., Internet, television, film, and mobile phones) and has reached even the most remote people anthropologists study. Tourism is an increasingly important influence in this transmission. While it is still possible to visit a H'mong village in the northern highlands of Vietnam, watch people dressed in hand-dyed indigo clothing plant rice in terraced fields that have been maintained for generations, and focus on how different and timeless they seem, we know that the life of the H'mong is far from static. If we made the effort, we would soon learn that family members of the villagers we see live as far away as Los Angeles, and that the people working the fields are also engaged in setting up a sustainable tourism project.[13]

Why tourism is worthy of serious study (e.g., its scale, scope, and economic importance) should be clear from what has already been said. Another feature that makes it of particular interest to social scientists is the way it brings consumers (i.e., tourists) and producers (e.g., local providers, ethnic Others) into intimate contact with each other. In this regard tourism is very different from most modern industries. Think about what it is like to be a tourist compared to being a consumer who buys groceries at the supermarket or a pair of jeans at the Gap. When we buy bananas or Levis, we seldom even think about who produced them or where they came from. When we travel, in contrast, we meet and interact directly with the local people who make the products, services, and experiences we consume and, although we may not realize it, we probably also end up interacting with many of the people who produce the other products we purchase. Increasingly, the things we buy at home are made by the people we visit abroad—workers in Vietnam, Thailand, the Philippines, Indonesia, China, and Mexico. As tourists, we experience their local economies, observe their standard of living, and develop at least some empathy and interest in their lives.

Research on tourism has focused on two themes: its origins and impacts (Stronza 2001).[14] When examining origins, the focus has been on the reasons people travel and what determines where they go. People travel for many reasons including the desire for change or difference, the opportunity to relax on a cruise or experience the tactile pleasures of the beach, a craving for adventure by visiting distant and "exotic" peoples and locales, the wish to experience "wilderness" or pristine nature, an interest in history or culture, a search for meaning, the desire for sexual excitement, and thrill seeking and dan-

Tourists in the 1890s enjoy the sublime view above the Grand Canyon of Yellowstone National Park. (Photo by Elliott W. Hunter)

ger—from organized adventure tourism (e.g., white-water rafting, bungee-jumping) to visits to active war zones (Phipps this volume). A seldom mentioned motivation to travel is the desire of parents to interest their children in the world around them; many family trips are undertaken to expose children to interesting and significant places—historical, cultural, and natural (M. Estellie Smith, personal communication).

What determines where people travel is similarly complex. As mentioned earlier, cost and safety are important considerations for most tourists. After that, much depends on how effectively locations have been marketed by local resorts, tour operators, and government tourism boards (e.g., through brochures and Web sites). Destinations are advertised like any other "product" through photographs and language that create appealing images and fantasies (Moeran this volume). Tourists also have their own preestablished ideas about certain places. Many sites are famous for being famous. Others become attractive based on word-of-mouth recommendations or associations created by books, magazines, and films. Prince Edward Island is a popular destination for Japanese tourists, for example, because it is the fictional home of Anne Shirley, the beloved heroine of Lucy Maude Montgomery's 1908 novel *Anne of Green Gables* (and a more recent television miniseries). Anne's spunk and determination have made her a popular character in Japan ever since 1954 when the book was translated and introduced into the junior high curriculum. Tourists from all over the world visit Anne Frank's house in Amsterdam, the war-related site made vividly real in her published diary. When I was in graduate school, some American college students traveled to Mexico's Sonoran desert to find Juan Matus, the Indian *brujo* who was anthropologist Carlos Castaneda's spiritual guide in *The Teachings of Don Juan* and later books. Since 1989, baseball enthusiasts have traveled to a cornfield in Iowa to see the "field of dreams" made famous by the movie of the same name. Status considerations also play a role in where tourists decide to go: some destinations have more *cachet* than others within the tourist's home society. The reasons they have greater status may be based on distance, expense, associations with "high culture" or celebrities, and a host of other factors.

Tourism's Many Impacts

The Economic Impact

The economic impact of tourism on a country (or region or locality) depends on many factors including the scale of tourism, the size of the country, the complexity of its economy, and who controls and profits from the industry. Tourism can contribute significantly to local economies by creating jobs both during the development phase and in hotels and related businesses once it is established. It also provides opportunities for local people to become independent entrepreneurs (e.g., starting a guest house, making souvenir crafts, acting as unofficial guides). George Gmelch (2003) has examined work in tourism through oral histories and found that most Barbadians involved like their jobs, although they do not intend to stay in them long. At the regional and national levels, tourism can also bring improved infrastructure and services that benefit the local people, including better roads, water, and electricity.

But not everyone benefits equally from tourism development. Many locals have no direct economic involvement in their area's tourism industry. The formal sector jobs that are typically available to local people in tourism (e.g., maids, waiters, gardeners, bartenders) are low-paying and seasonal and provide little long-term security, benefits, or opportunity for advancement. Higher paid managerial positions are usually filled by foreign employees or expatriates. In the Galapagos Islands of Ecuador, for example, most of the labor force in tourism was recruited from the mainland. These newcomers benefit more from tourism than do locals and now outnumber them, creating social tensions. The jobs that local people create for themselves in the informal sector of the tourist economy—such as unlicensed tour guides, "taxi" operators, and street vendors—are even less remunerative and secure. Local elites generally benefit far more from tourism development than other citizens since they are far more likely to have the capital, connections, and know-how to take advantage of emerging opportunities (van den Berghe 1994, Smith this volume).

Most research on the impacts of tourism—whether by anthropologists, cultural geographers, sociologists, or activists—has, in fact, stressed the negative. Much of tourism's profits never reach destination countries due to the foreign ownership of tourism's key players. One study of "leakage" in Thailand estimated that 70 percent of all money spent by tourists left the country via foreign-owned tour operators, airlines, and hotels, and through the purchase of imported drinks and food.[15] Polly Pattullo (1996) estimates that the Caribbean as a whole loses from 70 to 90 percent of every dollar earned from tourism. All-inclusive resorts in developing countries that offer tourists a prepaid package of airfare, accommodation, entertainment, food, and other services pump even less money into the local economy; tourists have little reason to leave the resort since they have paid for everything in advance. Cruise ships, which are in essence floating all-inclusives, likewise contribute little to the local economy, and they are getting bigger and offering more onboard entertainment all the time. Cunard Lines' *Queen Mary II* is 377 yards long and as tall as a 21-story building and contains a planetarium, putting green, casino, skating rink, and rock-climbing wall in addition to the usual features.

Infrastructure developments such as international airports and deepwater harbors that are built by local governments to support tourism—often with loans from international organizations like the International Monetary Fund (IMF) and World Bank—siphon off money that could be used for other projects like schools and hospitals that would better serve the population. They must also be maintained largely through local taxes. Moreover, when services like water or electricity are in short supply, priority is usually given to guaranteeing the tourists' comfort (and future business) instead of that of the local population.

International airports, deep-water harbors, large-scale resorts, golf courses, and game parks and nature preserves often displace local people who may have been unwilling to move and have been unfairly compensated for their land and homes. Three percent of the island of Barbados is now devoted to golf courses used primarily by visitors; some of these also have attached gated communities that physically exclude the local population. Large tourism projects of this kind often remove important agricultural or grazing land and fishing grounds from use. Sally Ann Ness (2003) has documented the plight of the many Filipinos who were resettled in the 1990s to make room for the huge Samal Island Tourism Estate adjacent to Mindanao. The Philippine government projected the creation of thousands of jobs, but training programs fell far short of what had been promised to the local people and the actual development of the huge complex has been repeatedly delayed and scaled back. Most relocated residents have no new jobs, no access to their old agriculture land or fishing grounds, and have received few of the promised new services. As in this example, too often tourism's impact is asymmetrical.

Tourism and the Environment

Wherever the carrying capacity of the environment is exceeded by too many visitors or too much tourism development, the environment is damaged.

Visitor parking crowds the edge of an Austrian glacier. (Photo by Sharon Gmelch)

Because tourists generally seek the most beautiful or unique environments to visit—often the most fragile—the local environment can be degraded easily. For example, each year 300,000 tourists wearing shoes and hiking boots—compared to 500 Inca in bare feet or sandals—visit Machu Picchu in Peru, trampling the trails and causing land slippage of .4 inches a month according to Japanese geologists. Coral reefs are often damaged by diving boats and cruise ships. One study of the effects of a single cruise ship anchor dropped for just one day over a coral reef found that it destroyed an area half the size of a football field. Yosemite, one of America's most popular national parks, now has more than thirty miles of roads covering its small valley floor (7 miles by 1 mile) over which a million cars, trucks, and buses travel each year adding noise, pollution, and congestion to other environmental damage.

Tourism depletes natural resources. It takes an especially heavy toll on local water supplies (i.e., for use in hotel laundries, showers, pools, landscaping, and golf courses). Tourists easily use twice as much water as do locals. One golf course in a tropical country like Thailand requires 1,500 kg of chemical fertilizers, pesticides, and herbicides a year and can use as much water as can 60,000 rural villagers. Similarly, the wood needed to support one trekker for one day in Nepal equals that used by a Nepalese family of five for a week (Gurung 1992, Fisher this volume). In the Annapurna area, the forest is being cut down at an estimated rate of 3 percent per year to build hotels, lodges, and furniture and to provide fuel for cooking, hot showers, and campfires. In the Caribbean, wetlands, mangroves, and beaches are destroyed for hotels, yacht harbors, deep-water harbors for cruise ships, and other tourism infrastructure. Their loss destroys fish, crustacean, and bird habitats and damages shorelines and offshore corals, often with serious consequences during hurricane season (Pattullo 1996).

Tourism creates pollution, often in surprising ways and places. Oxygen canisters, food containers, and more debris now litter Mount Everest. Trekking groups in Nepal leave fields of human excreta, toilet paper, and litter behind. Cruise ship passengers produce about 3.5 kilos of garbage per day, compared to .8 kilos for the residents of the Caribbean countries they visit. Some cruise lines still dump garbage and oil illegally at sea. Tourists account for 60 percent of air travel and of the ozone depleting emissions that jets emit. Tour buses left idling in very hot or cold climates in order to keep air conditioning or heat flowing for tourists' comfort exacerbate air pollution. As a result of the noise pollution caused by scenic helicopter flights, natural stillness can be found in only one third of the Grand Canyon. So many visitors used snowmobiles in Yellowstone National Park in the winter of 2000 that researchers found that engine noise was heard fully 90 percent of the time at eight popular tourist sites, including Old Faithful geyser. Visual pollution occurs when tourist destinations are overbuilt or resorts are prominently situated on mountainsides and along coastlines with only tourists' and not the locals' views in mind.

Ecotourism is one of the newer developments in tourism. It refers to tourism in natural areas that contributes both to the conservation of the local environment and to an improvement in the lives of local people. According to Martha Honey (1999), ecotourism has several characteristics: it is small-scale, has minimal environmental impact, promotes environmental awareness on the part of tourists and their local hosts, financially benefits the local community, respects local culture, and supports human rights and democratic aspirations. Not all tourism destinations or ventures that bill themselves as ecotourism, however, meet all these criteria. Many tourism operators use the "green" label merely as a form of niche marketing (just as some food merchandisers intentionally misuse the "natural" label).

"Alternative" tourism is very similar to ecotourism in that it refers to tourism projects that are managed for the common good and place human and local ecological needs on a par with profits. Richard Butler (1992) offers a cautionary critique of alterative tourism, however, pointing out that it is not always or in all ways better than more conventional mass tourism. For example, even small-scale alternative tourism projects can result in fairly dramatic long-term change. Such projects usually place tourists and locals in more intense contact than mass tourism does, and their interactions usually occur in more sensitive areas such as the home and village vs. the beach and hotel lobby. Alternative tourists usually visit more fragile areas, placing pressure on vulnerable resources. Such projects usually take place the year round and thus can have a greater impact on local people and the environment than seasonal mass tourism even though the number of tourists involved is smaller. Although alternative tourists tend to stay in an area longer, they spend less than do mass tourists. Moreover, there is a limited market for alternative tourism, and visitors are not likely to return to the same destinations as mass tourists often do. Butler concludes that alternative tourism should only be considered as a complement to mass tourism; it can never replace it. Furthermore, it must be carefully planned and controlled and should be regarded only as one way to supplement the incomes of rural people in marginal areas.

"Responsible" tourism is an even newer concept that supports ecotourism and alternative tourism principles as well as the concept of sustainable tourism development (cf. Smith and Brent 2001). It encourages individual tourists to consider the ethics of their travel by examining their reasons for going and by taking responsibility for minimizing the negative impact they have (McLaren this volume).

The Social and Cultural Impact

Relatively little research has examined the effect travel has on tourists and their attitudes (G. Gmelch this volume); the bulk of the research has looked at the opposite side of the equation—the social impacts large numbers of tourists have on local people. These are diverse and not easily summarized. Clearly when too many tourists visit a destination, especially if they do so the year round and are not confined to certain areas (e.g., the beach), both tourists and local people can feel overwhelmed. Carrying capacity is about more than just the physical environment; it also has psychological and social dimensions. Once tourists feel that the quality of their experiences has deteriorated, they can vote with their feet by choosing new, less crowded destinations (often with serious economic consequences for the tourism-dependent populations they leave behind). Their hosts, however, do not have this luxury.

Local people react to tourists in many ways, not only in response to their numbers and behavior but also based on preconceived ideas. It is worth remembering that the images and stereotypes locals have of tourists can be as distorted as the tourists' ideas about them. After all, many ideas about foreigners come from film and television; *Baywatch,* reputedly the most watched television show in the world, hardly portrays typical Americans. I remember wondering some years ago, as I sat in a small rural pub in Ireland, what the somber farmers around me—dressed in dark work suits and mud-covered Wellington boots—thought about Americans as they watched *Dallas* with its depictions of ostentatious wealth, ruthless backstabbing, and casual sex. Most encounters between tourists and local people are short-lived and instrumental, usually involving the sale of a commodity or service or an exchange of information. Local people react differently to different kinds of tourists based to a large extent on their own role in the tourism industry. Villagers may appreciate the informality and adventurousness of backpackers, while most business people in cities and towns dislike them since they spend so little money compared to other tourists. Some locals seek tourists out, not only for economic reasons, but to practice their language skills. I was surprised by the English proficiency of many of the young people I met in Vietnam who had acquired it from tourists.

So-Min Cheong and Marc Miller (this volume) point out the power local tourism brokers and middlemen have to control what tourists do. In a very real sense, tourists—even though they come from powerful countries and usually have more wealth than most locals—are relatively powerless as visitors in a foreign country. When they wander into more private or "backstage" areas local people often attempt to elude them. Jeremy Boissevain (this volume) discusses some of the common strategies locals use, including hiding, fencing their property, keeping group or community events secret, and reacting aggressively as well as organizing protests against tourism. The Suri of Ethiopia are offended by much tourist behavior and treat tourists aggressively by taking their cameras, demanding payment, and sometimes threatening them physically (Abbink this volume). Other groups like the Pueblo Indians discussed by Louise Sweet (this volume) use humor, management strategies, and regulations (that are enforceable on their reservation with the help of Native police) to keep tourists in line and preserve their privacy.

In many parts of the world, tourists are increasingly being confronted by signs that explain local customs and lay out the rules for visiting. Examples include being told to remove one's shoes, not give candy to children, and not photograph sacred objects. Ads in newspapers produced for tourists in Barbados try clever jingles: "We value your business and we know that you're cool, but please leave exposed tummies around the pool" (Wirthlin 2000). Increasingly, organizations and ethnic minorities are publishing tourism guidelines that they distribute to visitors and post on their Web sites (see Appendix B). The Himalayan Tourist Code, for example, was developed by Nepalese tour operators and nongovernmental organizations (NGOs) working with the British-based NGO, Tourism Concern. Among other things, tourists are told to ask permission before taking photographs, to respect local etiquette by not wearing revealing clothing or kissing in public, and to never touch religious objects. The Kuna Indians of Panama's San Blas islands have drawn up a comprehensive "Statute on Tourism in Kuna Yala," which attempts to ensure Kuna control of tourism development and to define their own terms for interaction with outsiders (Snow 2001).

Tourism has been blamed for introducing or exacerbating many social ills: everything from drugs, crime, and prostitution to bad language, bad manners, and bad art.[16] In fairness, however, it is difficult to disentangle the social effects of tourism from other global influences, notably the spread of Western popular culture and consumer values through a largely American-owned and produced media (e.g., satellite television, films, music videos, Internet). Many researchers have discussed tourism's "demonstration effect"—the fact that it creates desire in local people of modest means for the lifestyle and possessions tourists have. By raising the expectations of people in less developed nations who do not yet have the resource base or opportunities to acquire what wealthy visitors have, tourism can contribute to feelings of deprivation and a search for ways to "get rich quick"—activities like street crime, drug dealing, hustling, and gambling. "Jinoterismo" in Cuba was coined to describe those who try to latch on to tourism dollars: beggars, freelance tour guides, hustlers, and drug dealers. Barbadian police report that the first four drug arrests on the island (for marijuana) occurred in 1971 just as mass tourism was getting underway; three of the four people arrested were tourists (Gmelch and Gmelch 1997:177). Today, in many parts of the world, drug traffickers use tourism's infrastructure—planes, ships, casinos, offshore banks, and hotels—to transport, launder, and invest drug money.

Some tourists' sexual taste for "exotic" others has fueled a demand in the developing countries tourists visit for young women and men and children, drawing local people into prostitution (Brennan this volume). Specialized tour operators in the tourists' home countries and abroad offer package tours for the purpose of exploiting erotic nightlife. Local governments are not innocent here; some like Thailand have marketed their population's beauty and availability.[17] Child prostitution is a growing problem in many tourist destinations. The Bangkok-based End Child Prostitution in Asian Tourism (ECPAT) estimates that a million children are involved. According to the World Tourism Organization (WTO), a study of 100 school children in Kalutara, Sri Lanka, found that 86 had their first sexual experience at ages 12 and 13, the majority with a foreign tourist. Recent legislation in the United States, Germany, Britain, Sweden, and other countries has made it a crime to travel abroad for the purposes of having sex with a minor, and prosecutions have been brought against tourists.

Some forms of sex tourism are arguably less exploitative then others, as when young Japanese and Western women travel abroad and explore their sexuality with men in the host society (Kelsky 1996, Pruitt and LaFont this volume). Much depends on the circumstances—the extent to which local people have real alternatives and give informed consent—and on the nature of the inequality (e.g., age, gender, economic) that exists within the relationship. On tourist beaches in many countries, local men actively seek out sexual partners from among tourist women who may have had no prior intention of having an "affair" or "romantic fling" while on vacation. In some situations, they manipulate racial stereotypes to their advantage and play on the tourist's desire not to appear prejudiced (Gmelch and Gmelch 1997).

To attract tourists, destinations have to differentiate themselves from other places. One way they do so is to market local heritage and culture and any visible cultural diversity that exists. New Orleans, for example, markets its African-American influenced musical heritage (Atkinson this volume). Barbadian businesses use images of dread-locked, spliff-smoking Rastafarians on T-shirts and other tourist goods to highlight and create a "no worries," feel-good image for the island. Vietnam highlights its 53 ethnic minorities in promotional literature to give it added exotic appeal and so do the many guidebooks that market the country: "To see them [the H'mong] in their traditional style of dress—layers of indigo-dyed, brilliantly embroidered cotton; elaborate headdresses; and silver adornments—is to feel yourself caught in a time warp," states a recent Fodor guide (Kaufman 2001:114). If the groups in question are still somewhat isolated; have interesting architecture, clothing, crafts, or art; maintain "exotic" traditions such as tattooing or lip plates; or practice dramatic courtship, initiation, marriage or funeral rituals, so much the better.

When local people become the objects of the "tourist gaze" (Urry 1990) and are watched and photographed while doing even the most mundane things, their lives are dramatically altered. The "love market" of SaPa in northern Vietnam provides one example; historically a Red Dao tradition, the market draws ethnic minority people from within a two-days walk of SaPa. They come to sell their wares, buy what they need, socialize, and for some, seek marriage partners. Courting couples who meet at the market serenade each other with impromptu and highly personalized songs that tell of their attraction for the other person, their domestic abilities, and strong work ethic. Today the market is losing its courtship function as couples feel too much on display, and now meet elsewhere in order to avoid tourists (Pham, Lam and Koeman 1999). Conversely, some people capitalize on the love market's fame, volunteering to perform their songs for tourists in exchange for money.

When local rituals and celebrations are marketed as tourist "spectacles" by local entrepreneurs or government tourism boards they can lose their importance to local people. When the Chambri of Papua New Guinea opened their initiation ceremony to tourists, they unwittingly turned it into a performance that was losing its meaning for initiates (Errington and Gewertz this volume). Davydd Greenwood (this volume) has reassessed some of his conclusions in a much cited work on the impact of tourism on the *alarde* celebration in Hondarribia, Spain. The ceremony reenacts the town's historic victory over the French in 1638 and reenforces its Basque identity and solidarity in a richly symbolic ceremony that once involved most of the population. After it was marketed to tourists by municipal authorities, local people's participation declined dramatically. Today, however, it has acquired a new political purpose and value.

Much has been written about the impact of tourism on cultural authenticity and the fact that societies frequently "stage" and "manufacture" culture for tourists. Edward M. Bruner (this volume) discusses the ways in which American popular culture and global media influence Maasai performances for tourists. New dances, songs, and festivals are created all the time to provide tourists with entertaining "cultural" or "folkloric" performances. A state-supported dance troupe entertained my students and me in a mountain village in Vietnam in 2002, performing "traditional" folk songs and dances that had just been created and that they were performing for the first time. Similarly, the Barbados Tourism Board created "Crop Over" (referring to the end of the sugarcane harvest) in 1974 as a national celebration to promote tourism in the slack summer season. While it is true that small-scale celebrations had taken place in the past on individual plantations at the end of the harvest, this was an entirely new and lavish festival modeled after Carnival in Trinidad. The medieval pilgrimage to Santiago de Compostella, the reputed burial place of the Apostle James, was revived in modern times by the Catholic Church, Spanish Tourism Board, and Council of Europe, which adopted it as a European Heritage Trail. Recently, a controversy broke out in Romania over a proposed Dracula theme park at Sighisoara, the medieval Transylvanian town that was home to the mid-fifteenth-century historical Vlad Dracul (not the mythical Dracula that Bram Stoker created in 1897). The debate was whether to mangle Romanian history (and seriously disrupt the local environment to provide needed tourism facilities) by promoting the fictional vampire or to leave things as they were and lose a moneymaking venture.

Terms like "authentic" and "traditional" are frequently used with reference to the aspects of culture marketed to tourists. Most tourists like to think that what they are seeing is "real" in the sense of being old and an internally generated part of local culture. The hula, for example, was once a sacred temple dance that celebrated the procreative powers of the Hawai'ian chiefly class. Today it has been thoroughly co-opted by and commodified for tourism and is performed in entirely secular contexts (Desmond 1999). Yet to tourists it is a signifier of authentic Hawai'ian culture—a real and unmediated dance that is "a genuine performance of an age-old tradition rather than something merely undertaken for the tourist" (Urry 2001:5). Some tourists are very concerned with authenticity. I have listened as visitors to the Sitka National Historic Park in southeastern Alaska question the Tlingit craftsmen who work there about the "authenticity" of the materials they use and the art they create; pointing out to the silversmith, for example, that his grandfather could not have used the metal carving tools he uses today and to the weaver that her ancestors could not have used the colored glass beads she works with. Western tourists often regard any change towards the modern—whether it occurs among ethnic minorities in their own society or in the less developed countries they visit abroad—as negative. As MacCannell (1999) has pointed out, however, authenticity exists whenever people have significant control over their lives and play an active role in determining what changes occur in their society. He provocatively asks which is more real or "authentic": the town that decides on its own to tear down historic buildings to build a golf course for tourists or the town that is prevented by the government from making any changes in order to artificially preserve its ancient townscape? Traditions and culture are constantly reworked and reinterpreted to fit the needs and reality of each generation. Tourism is now part of that reality in most parts of the world.

Of course, not all tourists care about tradition or authenticity. Many are perfectly happy with completely artificial environments and activities as long as they are clean and entertaining. Some prefer simulations like ethnic theme parks, living museums, and other reconstructions to the real thing (Mintz this volume). I'll never forget my surprise at the comment I overheard a middle-aged tourist make to her husband as we left the small submarine that had just taken us on a 100-foot dive on Barbados's outer reefs: "Sure, it was good. But the submarine at Disneyland was better." She preferred an artificial reef, fake fish, and a submarine that runs on a circular track in a few feet of water to the real thing. Some people ("post-tourists") actually seek out inauthenticity—the more glaring and kitschy the better. Las Vegas immediately comes to my mind (although many could argue that it is "authentically" American) but so do the roadside attractions that I call "folk tourism" like Carhenge in Nebraska—an imitation Stonehenge constructed out of up-ended cars. As suggested earlier, local peoples often don't care whether their performances are authentic (i.e., old and internally generated) or not. The Balinese, for example, often incorporate touristic performances into their culture; the "frog dance" created for tourists in the 1970s is now performed at Balinese weddings (Bruner this volume). Similarly, Barbadians have fully embraced the "Crop Over" festival.

Tourism has wide-ranging ramifications as indicated. It is also an important agent of globalization. However, in contrast to the popular understanding of globalization as a process that eliminates differences between cultures, tourism can have the opposite effect (Sofield 2001). Governments and the tourism industry's many agents work hard to highlight, if not create, local differences by aggressively reimaging, reconstituting, and appropriating heritage, culture, and place in order to present and emphasize a location's uniqueness and to distinguish it from other possible tourist destinations

(Sofield 2001:104). Thus, despite the uniformity that does occur as a result of applying international standards in accommodations, travel arrangements, and service, tourism does not necessarily destroy cultural differences. It also offers opportunities that many local people want. The essays in this collection provide many thought-provoking and detailed examples of the ramifications of this complex phenomenon called tourism.

Source: Written expressly for *Tourists and Tourism*.

Notes

[1] I have codirected an anthropology field school for Union College undergraduates every other year since 1983 with my colleague, George Gmelch. Most of these years we have run the program in Barbados, but it has also been held in Ireland and Tasmania.

[2] According to World Tourism Organization figures, Barbados in 2002 received 497,899 "stopover" tourists (−1.8 percent from the previous year) and 529,319 cruise ship passengers (up 0.3 percent).

[3] The exception might be the small number of tourists who are regular visitors to the island and have established long-term friendships with local people.

[4] Gross domestic product is the market value of all goods and services a country produces in a year. It is the standard measure of the overall size of an economy. Global GDP averages the gross domestic product of all countries. According to the World Travel and Tourism Council (WTTC), the travel and tourism industry generates US$4,495 billion in economic activity and provides 207,062,000 jobs globally.

[5] These are World Bank figures for 2000. The World Tourism Organization has adopted global standards for measuring the economic impact of tourism. This measure is referred to as the "tourism satellite account." It calculates tourism's contribution to a country's GDP and balance of payments, how many jobs it creates, and how much capital investment and tax revenue it generates.

[6] See *Vision 2020* (1998), a WTO publication.

[7] Among the most developed nations (MDCs), only the United States and the United Kingdom will have population increases over the next 50 years; the rest will decline. As Smith & Brent (2001) also point out, virtually all industrial nations, including China, now have adopted a maximum 40-hour workweek, encouraging more leisure time. The electronic technology that has created jobs and prosperity in Asia, the United States and Europe also provides more discretionary income. Increasingly, too, travel is recognized as a human right, which encourages still more travel.

[8] The figures for Barbados include both land-based tourists and those who visit the island abroad cruise ships.

[9] Valene Smith defined the tourist as "a temporarily leisured person who voluntarily visits a place away from home for the purpose of experiencing a change" (1989:1).

[10] Liminoid situations are those in which people's everyday obligations are suspended and a relatively unconstrained "communitas" or social togetherness is encouraged. Travel—whether for tourism or pilgrimage—creates a situation of relative anonymity and freedom from collective scrutiny during which the normal social conventions under which people live are relaxed (Turner and Turner 1978).

[11] Some of these earlier studies include Mitford 1959, Nunez 1963, Forster 1964, and Boorstin 1966 (cited in Cohen 1984).

[12] Furthermore, both are of the body, not of the mind and intellect.

[13] My students and I participated in such a sustainable tourism project in the fall of 2002 in the H'mong village of Sin Chai. It was introduced to the village and coordinated by The World

Conservation Union (IUCN), an NGO working out of Hanoi. We were the third small group of tourists to arrive in the village in which five families had opened their homes to two or three overnight guests. Other activities included tours through the village, a cultural performance, exchanges in which tourists and local people teach each other some language or clean up trash together, and guided nature hikes up Mount Fansipan (also spelled Phanxipan).

[14] Cohen's (1984) review article of the sociology of tourism identified eight conceptual approaches to tourism that largely hold true today. Research has looked at tourism as: (1) commercialized hospitality, (2) democratized travel, (3) a modern leisure activity, (4) a modern form of pilgrimage, (5) an expression of culturally specific meanings on the part of tourists from different backgrounds, (6) an acculturative process, (7) a type of ethnic relations, and (8) a form of neocolonialism.

[15] Thai Institute for Development and Administration, Bangkok, 1990. Quoted in WTO Web site.

[16] Tourism cannot be blamed for the introduction of prostitution in most countries, although it clearly increases the demand and changes its form. Jones (1982), in a study of Bali, found that most customers at brothels were Balinese and other Indonesians, while those who frequented women on the beach and call girls were tourists. He found that the physical relations prostitutes had with tourists differed from those they had with locals: with tourists, most of whom were Western, there was more foreplay, more mouth-to-mouth kissing, and more attention to the breasts as an erotic zone.

[17] Tourism has different impacts on the arts. It is blamed in many parts of the world for causing a deterioration in local crafts and arts by encouraging simplifications (e.g., in design and materials) in order to produce items more quickly and bastardized styles and performances (like the limbo) to appeal to tourist tastes. But tourism can also be credited with creating a demand for quality visual arts and for supporting the performing arts by providing more venues and work for local dancers, singers, and musicians.

References

Boissevain, Jeremy. 1996. "Introduction," in *Coping with Tourists: European Reactions to Mass Tourism*, ed. J. Boissevain, pp. 1–26. Oxford: Berghahn Books.

Brendon, Piers. 1991. *Thomas Cook: 150 Years of Popular Tourism*. London: Secker & Warburg.

Butler, Richard. 1992. "Alternative Tourism: The Thin Edge of the Wedge," in *Tourism Alternatives: Potentials and Problems in the Development of Tourism*, ed. Valene Smith, pp. 31–46. Philadelphia: University of Pennsylvania Press.

Crick, Malcolm. 1995. "The Anthropologist as Tourist: An Identity in Question," in *International Tourism*, ed. Marie-Françoise LaFant, John Allock, and Edward M. Bruner, pp. 205–23. London: Sage.

Cohen, Erik. 1974. "Who is a Tourist?: A Conceptual Clarification." *Sociological Review* 22(4): 527–55.

———. 1979. "A Phenomenology of Tourist Experiences." *Sociology* 13:179–201.

———. 1984. "The Sociology of Tourism: Approaches, Issues, and Findings." *American Review of Sociology* 10:373–92.

Desmond, Jane. 2001. *Staging Tourism: Bodies on Display from Waikiki to Sea World*. Chicago: University of Chicago Press.

Gmelch, George. 2003. *Behind the Smile: The Working Lives of Caribbean Tourism*. Bloomington: Indiana University Press.

Gmelch, George, and Sharon Bohn Gmelch. 2001 [1997]. *The Parish Behind God's Back: The Changing Culture of Rural Barbados*. Prospect Heights, IL: Waveland Press.

Gupta, Akhil, and James Ferguson. 1997. *Culture, Power, Place: Explorations in Critical Anthropology*. Durham, NC: Duke University Press.

Honey, Martha. 1999. *Ecotourism and Sustainable Development: Who Owns Paradise?* Washington, DC: Island Press.

Jonaitis, Aldona. 1999. "Northwest Coast Totem Poles," in *Unpacking Culture: Art and Commodity in Colonial and Postcolonial Worlds*, ed. R. Phillips and C. Steiner, pp. 104–21. Berkeley: University of California Press.

Jones, David. 1982. "Prostitution and Tourism," in *The Impact of Tourism*, ed. F. Rajotte Pacific. Trent University, Canada: Development in the Environmental and Resource Studies Programme.

Kaufman, Deborah. 2001. *Vietnam: Completely Updated Where to Stay, Eat, and Explore: Smart Travel Tips from A to Z*. New York: Fodor's Travel Publications.

Kelsky, Karen. 1996. "Flirting with the Foreign: Interracial Sex in Japan's 'International' Age," in *Global/Local: Cultural Production in the Transnational Imaginary*, ed. Rob Wilson and Wimal Dissanayake, pp. 173–92. Durham, NC: Duke University Press.

MacCannell, Dean. 1973. "Staged Authenticity: Arrangements of Social Space in Tourist Settings." *American Journal of Sociology* 79(3): 580–603.

———. 1999. *The Tourist: A New Theory of the Leisure Class*, 2nd edition. Berkeley: University of California Press.

McLaren, Deborah. 1998. *Rethinking Tourism and Ecotravel*. West Hartford, CT: Kumarian Press.

Medea, Benjamin. 1998. "Chasing the Good Life." *New Internationalist* 301:26.

Ness, Sally Ann. 2003. *Where Asia Smiles: An Ethnography of Philippine Tourism*. Philadelphia: University of Pennsylvania Press.

Pattullo, Polly. 1996. *Last Resorts: The Cost of Tourism in the Caribbean*. London: Cassell.

Pham Thi Mong Hoa, Lam Thi Mai Lan, and Annalisa Koeman. 1999. *The Impact of Tourism on Ethnic Minority Inhabitants of Sa Pa District, Lao Cai: Their Participation in and Attitudes toward Tourism*. Unpublished paper. Hanoi, Vietnam: The World Conservation Union (IUCN).

Sofield, T. H. B. 2001. "Globalization, Tourism and Culture in South East Asia," in *Interconnected Worlds: Tourism in Southeast Asia*, ed. Cheok Teo, Chang Chin, Chuang Tou, and K. C. Ho, pp.103–120. London: Butterworth Heinemann.

Smith, Valene, ed. 1989. *Hosts and Guests: The Anthropology of Tourism*, 2nd edition. Philadelphia: University of Pennsylvania Press.

Smith, Valene, and Maryann Brent. 2001. *Hosts and Guests Revisited: Tourism Issues of the 21st Century*. New York: Cognizant Communications.

Snow, Stephen. 2001. "The Kuna General Congress and the Statute on Tourism." *Cultural Survival Quarterly* Winter: 17–20.

Stronza, Amanda. 2001. "Anthropology of Tourism: Forging New Ground for Ecotourism and Other Alternatives." *Annual Review of Anthropology* 30:261–83.

Turner, Victor, and Edith Turner. 1978. *Images and Pilgrimage in Christian Culture*. New York: Columbia University Press.

Urry, John. 1995. *Consuming Places*. London: Routledge.

———. 2001. "Globalizing the Tourist Gaze." Department of Sociology, Lancaster University at www.comp.lancs.ac.ek/sociology/soc079ju.html.

———. 2002. *The Tourist Gaze: Leisure and Travel in Contemporary Societies*, 2nd edition. London: Sage.

van den Berghe, Pierre. 1994. *The Quest for the Other: Ethnic Tourism in San Cristobal, Mexico*. Seattle: University of Washington Press.

Waterhouse, Keith. 1989. *Theory and Practice of Travel*. London: Hodder & Stoughton.

Wirthlin, Karin. 2000. *Tourism and Barbados: An Examination of Local Perspectives*. Masters Thesis, Colorado State University.

2

Secular Ritual: A General Theory of Tourism

Nelson H. H. Graburn

Tourism, defined by the sentence "a tourist is a temporarily leisured person who voluntarily visits a place away from home for the purpose of experiencing a change" (Smith 1989:1), may not exist universally, but in many ways it is functionally and symbolically equivalent to other institutions—calendrical festivals, holy days, sports tournaments that humans use to embellish and add meaning to their lives. In its special aspect—travel—tourism has its antecedents in other seemingly more serious institutions such as medieval student travel, the Crusades, and European and Asian pilgrimages.

It is my contention that tourism is best understood as a *kind of ritual*, one in which the special occasions of leisure and travel stand in opposition to everyday life at home and work. This general theory applies to all forms of tourism. Therefore, we have to understand the nature of tourist travel and experience in terms of the *contrasts* between the special period of life spent in tourist travel and the more ordinary parts of life spent at home while working. Tourism experiences are meaningful because of their difference from the ordinary and they reflect the home life from which the tourists stem. Thus, any one kind of tourist experience (e.g., a week in Paris) can mean something very different in the life of tourists from, for example, urban New York, metropolitan Tokyo, or rural California. Indeed, for some people a week in Paris would be too ordinary and boring, whereas for other people, from very different social backgrounds, it might be too daunting and exciting and they would never undertake such a vacation. Thus, we can see that the tourists' gender, class, occupation, and life stage are all significant in determining where tourists choose to go and what they think of the experience when they have been there.

Tourism: Rituals of Reversal

The ritual theory of tourism proposes that the motivations and compensations of tourism involve "push" and "pull" factors. Tourists leave home because there is something that they want to get away from, and they choose to visit a particular place because they believe that they will experience something positive there that they cannot easily experience at home. This kind of explanation involves the "ritual reversal" or "ritual inversion" of some aspects of life. Simple examples would include the winter migrations of eastern Canadians to the Caribbean and of Scandinavians to the Mediterranean, when these northerners seek some warmth away from home, or when lower-middle-class Californians go to large hotels in Las Vegas or Reno at any time of the year and "live it up" by occupying large, well-appointed rooms and being served lavish meals (Gottlieb 1982). Middle-class Japanese who vacation in the hotels of Southeast Asia in the wintertime seeks both touristic goals: seasonal warmth and a luxurious style of life (Beer 1993)—inversions of their cramped lives in cold Tokyo.

The felt needs of tourists, the things that they look for and forward to in their travels, are never the complete opposites of their home class position and lifestyle. For instance, erudite people don't want to become ignorant, although they may want a relaxing break, and good athletes don't try to become physically incompetent. The felt needs are indeed the product of, or an inherent part of, the values of the home class and lifestyle. Scandinavians and Canadians value sunshine and warmth; American college professors value culture and history and may seek more of it on their vacations; many obese people value thinness and may visit a special reducing establishment; and gourmets may partake of simple foods in their travels, but never bad foods—not willingly! So the temporary reversal sought is rarely an antithesis of their values but is a product of their cultural background, and the promised reward is supposed to satisfy the need in a direction of further enhancement of these values, not turn the tourist into an entirely different kind of person.

The claim that tourism is a secular ritual, embracing goals or activities that have replaced the religious or supernatural experiences of other societies, was strongly suggested by a recent television advertisement in the San Francisco Bay area (1997). It showed exciting scenes of young, fit people diving off cliffs into the sea, skiing down steep slopes, bungee jumping, and so on. At the end of these came a voice-over, "If you want a religious experience, why don't you try a religious experience!" as the scene moved to a shot of the Protestant evangelist the Reverend Billy Graham, who was about to bring his crusade to the area.

Tourism, Ritual, and Time

Tourism in the modal sense emphasized here is but one of a range of choices or styles of recreation or vacation. All of these ritualized breaks in routine define and relieve the ordinary. There is a long tradition in anthropology of the examination of these special events and institutions as markers of the passage of time. Vacations involving travel (i.e., tourism) are the modern equivalent for secular societies to the annual and lifelong sequences of festivals and pilgrimages found in more traditional, God-fearing societies. Fundamental is the contrast between the ordinary/compulsory work state spent "at home" and the extraordinary/voluntary metaphorically "sacred" experience away from home.

The stream of alternating contrasts provides the meaningful events that mark the passage of time. English anthropologist Edmund Leach (1961) suggested that celebratory events were the way in which people without clocks and calendars used to measure the passage of time, implying that those who have scientific calendars and other tacit reminders such as newspapers, TV, and radio rely only on the numerical calendar. I believe that even "scientific, secular" Westerners gain greater meaning from the personal rather than the numeric in life. We are more satisfied and better recall loaded symbols marking the passage of time: for example, "that was the year we went to Rome" or "that was the summer our dog drowned at Brighton Beach" rather than "that was 1988," because the former identify the nonordinary, festive or sorrowful, personal events.

Our two lives—the sacred/nonordinary and the profane/workaday/at-home—customarily alternate for ordinary people and are marked by rituals or ceremonies as should be beginnings and ends of lives. For instance, after a period of work we celebrate with TGIF (Thank Goodness Its Friday), "happy hours," and going-away parties, to anticipate the future state and to give thanks for the end of the mundane. The passing of each year is marked by the annual vacation (or by Christmas or a birthday); something would be wrong with a year in which these events didn't occur, as though we had been cheated of time! These repetitive events mark the cyclical passage of time just as in traditional Christian societies weeks would be marked by Sundays and churchgoing and the year would be marked by Easter, Harvest Festival, Advent, Christmas, and so on. These rituals have been called rites of increase or rites of intensification in agricultural or forager societies (Durkheim 1912), but are generally better thought of as *annual cycle rites*. The types of holidays and tourism that fill these may be family occasions at home, but when they involve travel (e.g., weekends spent skiing or fishing, weeks spent on the beach or even longer trips traveling abroad), they are usually of the seasonal or "annual vacation" type, a form of re-creation, renewing us and making the world go round.

Life is not only cyclical with the same time-marking events occurring again and again, but it is also progressive or linear, as we all pass through life by a series of changes in status, each of which is marked by different but similarly structured rituals. These life-stage marking events are called *rites of passage* and were first analyzed by French folklorist Arnold Van Gennep (1960); it is his model that we shall follow in our analysis of tourism as ritual. Just as rites of passage (e.g., births, graduations, marriages, and funerals) are usually more significant rituals than ordinary cyclical events such as birthdays, Thanksgivings, or *Días de los Muertos*, so rites-of-passage-type tourist experiences may be unusually intense (e.g., semesters abroad, honeymoons, or retirement cruises). But in the relatively individualistic, informal lives of the contemporary Euro-Americans, many rites of passage as kinds of tourism may be purposely self-imposed physical and mental tests (e.g., college-aged people trekking across continents trying to go as far as possible with little expenditure) (Cohen 1973, Teas 1988) or when recently broken-up, divorced, or laid-off middle-class persons take "time off" for long sailing, walking, or cycling trips or other adventures (Frey 1998, Hastings 1988).

The Structure of Ritual and Tourism

For the present discussion our focus is consciously on the prototypical examples of tourism, such as long-distance travel to famous places or to visit exotic peoples, all in unfamiliar environments. However, even the most minimal kinds of tourism, such as a picnic in the garden, contain elements of the "magic of tourism." The food and drink might be identical to that normally eaten indoors, but the magic comes from the movement and the nonordinary setting. Conversely, a very special meal in the usual but specially decorated eating place may also, by contrast with the ordinary, be "magic" enough for a special celebration.

The alternation of sacred and profane states and the importance of the transition between them were first shown by the French sociologists Hubert and Mauss (1898) in their analysis of the almost universal ritual of sacrifice. They emphasized the sequential process of leaving the ordinary, that is, the sacralization that elevates the participants to the nonordinary state where marvelous things happen, and the converse of desacralization and return to ordinary life. "Each festival [each tourist trip, we contend] represents a temporary shift from the Normal-Profane order of existence into the Abnormal-Sacred order and back again" (Leach 1961:132–136). The flow of time has a pattern, represented in figure 1.

Each festive or tourist event is a miniature life, with a happy anticipation, A–B, an exciting middle, C–D, and a bittersweet ending, D–F. The peri-

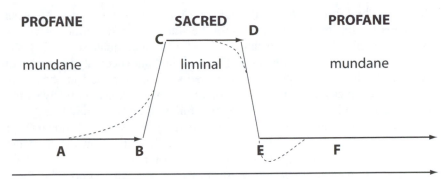

Figure 1: *The Ritual of Tourism* (modified from Feyerabend 1997:11)

ods before A and after F are the mundane, everyday life, expressed in "That's life." The period C–D, the metaphorically "sacred," the "liminal" (see below) out-of-the-ordinary period, is the time of pilgrimage, travel, and tourism. These holidays (formerly "holy days") celebrated in vacations and tourism might be expressed as: "I was living it up, really living . . . I've never felt so alive." These changes in moral and spatial states are usually accompanied by aesthetic changes and markers. This is most obvious in the case of religious rituals and rites of passage, where colorful dresses and strikingly decorated settings are accompanied by chanting, singing, and music. In tourism, too, there may well be aesthetic and sensory changes, in clothing, settings, and foods, and even in touch and smell in the case of tropical beach holidays or Japanese hot springs tourism (Graburn 1995b).

Entries and Exits

The experience of being away on vacation (or going on pilgrimage) has important effects on the life of the traveler *outside* of the actual time spent traveling. Just as there are rituals of preparation, cleansing oneself, changing garments, perhaps putting on perfumes, or getting into the right frame of mind before undertaking religious rites such as pilgrimages, sacrifices, or Christian communion, so for the tourist and travelers there are rituals of preparation. These routinely involve not only planning, booking, and getting new clothes, gear, or luggage, but also social arrangements such as getting someone to water the garden, to look after the house and pets, to collect the mail, to leave numbers for emergencies, and often having parties for saying goodbye.

All of these necessary actions produce the pleasure of anticipation in the period A–B and the weeks and months before the actual takeoff B–C, but the feelings are also ambivalent. There may be misgivings about having made the right decisions, having laid out so much money, or having chosen the right traveling companions. There is also the remote possibility that one is saying goodbye forever, especially for long journeys to more distant places for greater lengths of time, as well as for the elderly or infirm either as travelers or those left behind. [For instance, when I went to graduate school in Canada (by ship), my mother at home in England died unexpectedly before I had my first trip home.] Nevertheless, this period of anticipation is extremely important: the pleasure being looked forward to itself shines on many of the preparations and is often what people "live for" in their workaday lives.

Going home, the journey D–F, the reentry process coming down from the "high" C–D, is equally important and fraught with ambivalence. Most people are reluctant to end a vacation, to leave the excitement and new friends, and to have to go back to work. In fact, a desire to get home and end the vacation might be seen as an admission that it didn't turn out to be as good as expected—that the recreation did not recreate. Some travelers even have twinges of sorrow during the period C–D, for instance on reaching the furthest point away from home (Frey 1998), as they anticipate "the beginning of the end," the loss of new friends, or of the "paradise" visited.

The work of Berkeley undergraduate Amanda Feyerabend (1997) on the rituals and experience of the reentry and the reincorporation into normal society explains what is called *reverse culture shock*. The term is a corollary to the notion of *culture shock*—the feeling of strangeness and inability to cope—that travelers feel when first in unfamiliar environments, such as tourists at point C in figure 1. The reverse of this is the unhappiness felt when the tourist first gets back into his/her home and working environment (the period E–F in figure 1). Feyerabend's informants suggested that while their normal home and work lives might be quite satisfying most of the time, life suffered by comparison with the excitement, the out-of-the-ordinary special experiences that they had just left behind; thus, the lowered state of feelings at E–F is a relative measure of happiness.

Feyerabend also found that, in general, the length of time this ambivalent reverse culture shock lasted was approximately *half the length of time* the traveler had been away. For instance, after a two-day weekend of skiing in the nearby Sierra Nevada range, Berkeley students felt the next day (Monday) was a real letdown, but they would feel okay by Tuesday. On the other hand, a student who returned from a year abroad in a foreign country might feel ill at ease and not quite at home for the whole next semester back in the United States.

The Tourist Experience: Liminality and Communitas

Van Gennep (1960), building on the work of Hubert and Mauss, gave us the model commonly used for the analysis of rituals in general. While Hubert and Mauss emphasized the micro-rituals of preparation, separation, and reincorporation in their look at sacrifice, Van Gennep focused on the central period of the ritual, C–D, and the nature of the participants' experience. In his analysis he labeled the "sacred" out-of-the-ordinary period "liminal," meaning "on/over the threshold," following the European custom where a groom has to carry his bride over the threshold of their new home. At this liminal point the participants are neither in nor out, or as Victor Turner (1974) put it, they are "betwixt and between." In some societies this special period is likened to a temporary death; the person in their old status dies, then follows the liminal period where they are bracketed off from ordinary time (or their ordinary place in the case of tourism), out of which they are reborn with their new status, e.g.,

Bachelor → [groom at wedding ceremony] → husband
Single   → [bride at wedding ceremony] → wife

Victor Turner (1974) and Edith Turner (Turner & Turner 1978) further examined this period of liminality in African rituals and Christian pilgrimages, and they noted: "If a pilgrim is half a tourist, then a tourist is half a pilgrim" (1978:20). Turner stressed that for the participants (those to be transformed in the ritual or the travelers as pilgrims and tourists), the normal social structure of life, work, and family roles, age and gender differences, and so on tends to become looser or disappear. This leveling he called "anti-structure" though, of course, these participants are always surrounded by others carrying out their usual structured roles (e.g., priests or shamans at rituals, and guides, hoteliers, and food workers for pilgrims and tourists). Turner suggested that this leveling of statuses ideally sought outside of home and work structures produces a special feeling of excitement and close bonding among the participants, which he called *communitas*. This state is often signaled by a reduction in marked differences, with all pilgrims wearing the same clothes or all Club Med clients in their beachwear, and with people addressing each other as equals and sharing the same foods, drinks, accommodations, pleasures, and hardships. While consulting for Club Med, I explained this ritual model to a number of *chefs de villages* and GOs *(gentils organisateurs)* who replied with a flash of understanding: "Of course, and the hard part of our job is to keep our customers 'up' in the state of communitas for their seven days nonstop!"

This liminal state, this special human feeling of communitas, may be examined and understood in a variety of ways. In lay language, "going on a trip" usually refers to a journey but it can refer to an "altered state of consciousness" (ASC) brought on by drugs or alcohol, and a special religious or magic experience; "trip" literally means away from the ordinary. Such experience may be called a "high" after which there is a "letdown" or a "come down" (i.e., period C–D followed by D–F in figure 1), and a "high" is opposed to a feeling of depression or a "low," the negative ASC experienced in period E–F. The special state of consciousness experienced during a "trip" was illuminated when I was discussing Feyerabend's findings with my undergraduate class on tourism. Some students pointed out that the reverse culture shock (E–F), lasting half as long as the period of absence (C), paralleled the students' common belief that the time it takes to get over a serious love affair or a broken friendship is half as long as the relationship lasted, putting the "magic" of tourism and pilgrimage into the same emotional category as love and friendship!

Variations on a Theme: Different Strokes for Different Folks

Our analysis of tourism as ritual and the equation of the feelings and meaning of the trip with other human experiences does not mean that all tourism experiences are the same any more than all rituals are the same. Turner and others have characterized the state of communitas as being "high," "liminal" (or liminoid when not part of a truly religious experience), a state of homogeneity, equality, and humility among the participants, a period of transition, magic, or otherworldliness. For today's tourists, the vacation away from home might be described as above, but also may be described as "away," "timeless," a time of freedom, play, mindless spending, and attention to the past or the future (cf. Dann 1996).

The range of tourist experiences has best been outlined by Israeli sociologist E. Cohen in his "Phenomenology of Tourist Experiences" (1979a). Here he takes into account the equation I have suggested between today's tourism and more spiritual pursuits such as pilgrimage, by placing such serious pursuits at one end of his continuum. At this serious end, the traveler is seeking a very important or "sacred" experience or place "out of this world," a sacred center spiritually more important than anything at home. These "existensional" tourists or pilgrims are on a true exploration and many are so moved by the experience attained or the place visited that they stay there and never go home or, in a more practical sense, they never want to go home. Thus, American Jews, having visited Israel, may emigrate there; North American mainlanders may retire to Hawai'i or San Franciscans to the Mendocino County coast. The nature of such tourists' experiences may well be spiritual rather than patently religious; one may feel deeply moved by "communing with nature." Others, atheist or agnostic, might follow the old European pilgrimage way through northern Spain, the Camino de Santiago, and have profoundly moving, even life-changing experiences both along the way and on reaching the cathedral in Santiago (Frey 1998).

At the other end of Cohen's continuum are the mere diversionary or recreational tourists, who never seriously doubt their commitment to their home lifestyle, but just want a simple change—perhaps a change of climate or season, a temporary change of recreation or sports—and have very little desire to explore or seek new experiences. And in the middle of the continuum are the more exploratory tourists, who may make considerable efforts to go to out-of-the-way places, may try to learn foreign languages, or may live temporarily like foreign peoples. These "experiential" and "experimental" tourists are fascinated by difference, like to get close to others, and like to immerse themselves in different environments (e.g., jungle ecotourists, Middle Eastern *souks*, or visitors to remote Nepalese villages). Such people, often young adults without much money or work experience, but probably well educated by their home standards (Cohen 1973, Teas 1988), have the exploratory urge and the *cultural self-confidence* (Graburn 1983) to get out of their shell and experiment with different lifestyles.

Plus ça Change, Plus c'est La Même Chose (The More Things Change, the More It's the Same Thing)

This chapter claims that tourism is a manifestation of a need for a change, and that the change the tourist seeks depends on what perceived touristic attractions would satisfy something not fully met at home. In this concluding section, this general proposition is explored by some specific cases, pointing in particular to the social historical contexts.

In the contemporary Western world and in modern Japan, tourism is the opposite to work; it is one kind of that recent invention: re-creation. It is a special form of play involving travel and "getting away from it all" (i.e., from work, including homework and housework). There is a symbolic link between work + staying and play + travel. Most people feel they ought to go away when they have holidays, and never to go on a vacation might be an indication of sickness or poverty, or extreme youth or old age. Able-bodied adults who don't take holidays might be thought of as poor, unimaginative, or the "idle rich." For the middle classes, this going away on holiday is supposed to be a worthwhile, even a stimulating, creative, or educational experience (see below); for such people, staying at home can be "morally excused" by participating in some creative activity, such as remodeling the house, redoing the garden, or seriously undertaking painting, writing, or sports.

Sociologist Dean MacCannell (1989) has powerfully expressed another instance of this theory in *The Tourist: A New Theory of the Leisure Class*, claiming that the educated middle classes are the sector of our present population who are the most alienated, contrary to Marx's nineteenth-century assertions. MacCannell shows that the urban and suburban middle classes feel that their lives are overly artificial and meaningless, lacking deep feelings of belonging and authenticity. These are thought to exist elsewhere, especially in the simpler lives of other peoples such as family farmers, manual workers and craftsmen, and "primitive peoples." This missing authenticity is thought to lie, above all, in the past, as indicated by English geographer David Lowenthal (1985) in *The Past is a Foreign Country*. Thus, historical, cultural, and ethnic forms of tourism have become increasingly popular, all of them catering to one form or another of modernity's nostalgia for the pre-

modern (Graburn 1995b). MacCannell also shows us that the producers of
tourist packages and displays understand these longings and are capable of
"manufacturing" authentic Others and Pasts, so that the unfortunate tourists
are once more faced with the artificial and commercial in their quest for
"reality" and the untouched. One popular arena for getting in touch with the
true and the pure is Nature itself, which is often sought in its wilder forms by
Euro-American campers, backpackers, and ecotourists, and in more managed
versions by the equally alienated urban Japanese (Graburn 1995a). The
world's tourist industry, in its advertising and its packaged offerings, must
paradoxically create the illusion that the tourists are, by purchasing their services, getting satisfaction of their needs.

While MacCannell's work is a brilliant analysis of educated Westerners, it is not a universal theory. Many people in Europe and North America
are not necessarily seeking the particular ritual inversion from "fake to
authentic culture"; indeed, it has been shown that this "moral" concern with
authenticity correlates with years of education. This search for the pure and
the Other, which Urry (1990) has called the "Romantic" gaze, is supplemented by a more direct, communal, and, some would say, unsophisticated
(perhaps a better term is unpretentious) kind of enjoyment he calls the "Collective" gaze. The latter is typical of the "working classes," who are more
gregarious and derive as much pleasure from the company they keep as the
places they visit. Indeed, R. Campbell (1988) has shown that city bus drivers
often return to their places of work on their days off, just to socialize with
their coworkers. Similarly, Japanese *salarymen* and other groups of male
workers often go on trips together, leaving their families at home. Hence,
Japanese women often travel in single-sex groups, and children travel in
school groups.

The research focus on the "gaze"—the visual practice of sightseeing—
has also been challenged by those whose research shows that the changes
desired may be sensual or tactile. Selänniemi (1994) found that Scandinavians wintering in the Mediterranean or elsewhere in the "south" want a thoroughly Scandinavian vacation, but one in which they can soak up the sun, lie
on the beach, or play simple sports. Jokinen and Veilola (1994) have criticized tourism theorists in general for overemphasizing the visual, the sightseeing quest, because that is the touristic goal of the educated class to which
the tourism theorists themselves belong.

In conclusion, this chapter has taken care in using the ritual model not
to see all tourism as one individual might experience it, nor should it be
expected that ritual reversals are all-encompassing. In fact, tourists on holiday are seeking specific reversals of a few specific features of their workaday home life, things that they lack or that advertising has pointed out they
could better find elsewhere. Other than obtaining some straightforward
goals, whether they be warmth for northerners, weight loss for the overweight, history for the culturally hungry, or immersion in nature for bored

urbanites, tourists generally remain unchanged and demand a lifestyle not too different from that at home. Rarely do the timid become bold, the neat become messy, the educated become dumb, the monolingual be come polyglot, the frigid become sexy, or the heterosexual become gay, except when these are the specific goals of the trip. Gottlieb (1982) has shown how tourists may play "Queen [Peasant] for a Day" with temporary changes in life or class style, and E. Cohen (1973, 1979b) and Frey (1998) have described some of the more rigorous touristic choices for the young or the alienated moderns, but most tourists on their seasonal and annual vacations want to enjoy their own chosen pursuits and come back refreshed as better versions of their same old selves.

Source: From *Hosts and Guests Revisited: Tourism Issues of the 21st Century,* Valene Smith and Maryann Brent (eds.), 2001. Reprinted with permission of the author and Cognizant Communications.

References

Beer, J. 1993. *Packaged Experience: Japanese Overseas Tourism in Asia.* Doctoral dissertation, University of California, Berkeley.

Campbell, R. 1988. "Bushman's Holiday—or the Best Surprise is No Surprise." *Kroeber Anthropological Society Papers* 67/68: 12–19.

Cohen, E. 1973. "Nomads from Affluence: Notes on the Phenomenon of Drifter Tourism." *International Journal of Comparative Sociology* 14:89–103.

———. 1979a. "A Phenomenology of Tourist Experiences." *Sociology* 13:179–201.

———. 1979b. "Sociology of Tourism." [Special Issue] *Annals of Tourism Research* 1–2.

Dann, G. 1996. *The Language of Tourism.* Wallingford: CAB International.

Durkheim, E. 1912. *Elementary Forms of Religious Life,* trans. J. Swain. London: Allen and Unwin.

Feyerabend, A. 1997. "Coming or Going: An Examination of Reverse Culture Shock in the 'Tourism as Ritual' Theory." (unpublished paper) Berkeley: University of California.

Frey, N. 1998. *Pilgrim Stories: On and Off the Road to Santiago.* Berkeley: University of California Press.

Gottlieb, A. 1982. "Americans' Vacations." *Annals of Tourism Research* 9:165–187.

Graburn, N. 1983. "The Anthropology of Tourism." [Special Issue] *Annals of Tourism Research* 10.

———. 1995a. "The Past in the Present in Japan: Nostalgia and Neo-traditionalism in Contemporary Japanese Domestic Tourism," in *Changes in Tourism: People, Places, Processes,* ed. R. Butler and D. Pearce, chapter 4. London: Routledge.

———. 1995b. "Tourism Modernity and Nostalgia," in *The Future of Anthropology: Its Relevance to the Contemporary World,* ed. A. Ahmed and C. Shore, pp. 158–178. London: Athlone Press.

Hastings, J. 1988. "Time Out of Time: Life Crises and Schooner Sailing in the Pacific." *Kroeber Anthropological Society Papers* 67/68: 42–54.

Hubert, H., and M. Mauss. 1898. *Sacrifice: Its Nature and Functions,* trans. W. Halls. London: Cohen & West.

Jokinen, E., and S. Veilola. 1994. "The Body in Tourism: Touring Contemporary Research in Tourism," in *Le Tourisme International entre Tradition et Modernité,* ed. J. Jardel. Nice, France: Actes du Colloque International, Laboratoire d'ethnologie.

Leach, E. 1961. *Rethinking Anthropology.* London: Athlone Press.

Lowenthal, D. 1985. *The Past is a Foreign Country.* Cambridge: Cambridge University Press.

MacCannell, D. 1989. *The Tourist: A New Theory of the Leisure Class.* New York: Schocken Books.

Selänniemi, T. 1994. "A Charter Trip to Sacred Places—Individual Mass Tourism," in *Le Tourisme International entre Tradition et Modernité,* ed. J. Jardel, pp. 335–340. Nice, France: Université de Nice, Laboratoire d'ethnologie.

Smith, V. 1989. "Introduction," in *Hosts and Guests: The Anthropology of Tourism,* 2nd edition, ed. V. Smith, pp. 1–17. Philadelphia: University of Pennsylvania Press.

Teas, J. 1988. "'I'm Studying Monkeys; What Do You Do?'—Youth and Travelers in Nepal." *Kroeber Anthropological Society Papers* 67/68: 35–41.

Turner, V. 1974. *Dreams, Fields, and Metaphors: Symbolic Action in Human Society.* Ithaca, NY: Cornell University Press.

Turner, V., and E. Turner. 1978. *Images and Pilgrimage in Christian Culture.* New York: Columbia University Press.

Urry, J. 1990. *The Tourist Gaze: Leisure and Travel in Contemporary Societies.* London: Sage.

Van Gennep, A. 1960 [1909]. *The Rites of Passage,* trans. M. Vizedom and G. Caffee. Chicago: The University of Chicago Press.

3

The Global Beach

Orvar Löfgren

To the Beach

Once I found a postcard in a secondhand shop. It was manufactured in New York, probably in the fifties, and carried the simple text: "By the beautiful sea." It is a good example of the universalization of the beach experience, the making of a truly global iconography and choreography of beach life. It is one of those many postcards without any hint of the "local," just sand, sea, and carefully arranged groups of beach visitors. Pictures like these turn up in any card rack along the coasts of the world. No surprise that I found it in Sweden.

What is a beach, what can a beach be used for? In the 1990s the Lego toy producers developed a transnational holiday world called *PARADISA* in the Esperanto of the global toy industry. If you bought kit number 6410 (and were over the age of six) you would be able to construct your own beach, with the following basic ingredients: 1 palm tree, 2 bathing huts, 1 parasol, 2 deck chairs, 1 surfboard, 1 fishing rod, 1 speedboat, 1 portable cassette player, 1 beach bar (complete with waiter and exotic drinks), 1 male and 1 female vacationer in swimsuits. This bricolage of props and activities comes from different settings and epochs all around the world and now, integrated and globalized, becomes a familiar place to play at being a teenager, a grownup, a tourist.

The concept of beach covers a lot of territory and history. The range of beach life is amply demonstrated along a coast like that of California. In northern California there is the constant search for a beach of your own, a small cove, protected by cliffs and rocks. As the tide moves out, strings of small beaches suddenly become available to couples or single families—*nota bene*, if public access is possible. The idea of this kind of beach is that it belongs to nobody but you. Intruders are a provocation, they should move on to find their own beach. This beach is yours, you can collect shells and driftwood, build a castle in the sand, knowing that in a few hours it will be gone, washed away. The other end of the scale would be a beach like the famous Los Angeles beach studied in the 1970s by the sociologist Robert Edgerton (1979). This "Southland," as he labeled it, attracted 400,000 visitors on a fine summer day.

Beaches come in all forms and fashions, finding their position along this continuum from the Robinson Beach, where there is just you, sand, water, and maybe a couple of palm trees, to the lively holiday beach, à la Coney Island or Blackpool. But any of these beaches represents a sedimentation of cultural traditions, from the eighteenth-century history of seashore invalids to the 1990s cult of *Baywatch*. For the eighteenth- and early nineteenth-century pioneers the beach was mainly an access to the ordeal of sea bathing, getting a quick dose of the healthy sea breeze and saltwater. The beach served for quiet strolls or as a site for sunset watching, but the idea of the beach as a playground was still far away.

In this global history some beaches occupy a limited stretch of sand but take up a huge mental space. These are the famous beaches that less famous beaches often try to emulate. There is the early example of the Lido outside Rome, later on the Murphys' beach, La Garoupe, at Antibes. "Romantic Rio can be yours" is the headline of a 1946 ad from Pan Am, which shows two women leisurely resting in the sand. The text continues, "In Rio de Janeiro it is summer! And by clipper Rio's Copacabana Beach is just a weekend away from the United States."[1] For Mediterranean package tourists the beach of Las Palmas on the Canary Islands had a strong image, just like Miami Beach in Florida or Malibu in California.

The Tropical Dream

The props of the PARADISA beach have their own history. Already in the making of the Riviera, palm trees became a must, and this tropical plant has steadily expanded north. The collapsible deck chair was borrowed from the decks of ocean cruisers, while the bathing hut has many national variations.

But the whole concept of paradise relies above all on the romance of the South Pacific and the tropical beach. The global notion of the beach as paradise began in the cult of Hawai'i and Waikiki Beach next to Honolulu. The site of Hawai'i is special. For a very long period it continued to be a fantasyland. The first modern resort hotel was built in 1901, but as late as 1955 the yearly number of tourists barely reached 100,000 and it was only with the arrival of cheap jet flights that Hawai'i became a mass destination. Until the 1950s Waikiki remained a beach experience for a small, mainly American elite. The power of the Hawai'ian imagery above all had to do with the fact that this was the first really mass-mediated paradise: a landscape not only to experience through colored postcards and illustrated magazine features but also a landscape set to music. As early as 1915 the tune "At the Beach of Waikiki" was a great hit at the Panama-Pacific Exposition in San Francisco (Grant 1996:60). Tin Pan Alley versions of Hawai'ian sheet music started spreading around the world and their colorful covers established the image of the tropical beach, hula girls with flowers in their hair and palm trees swaying gently in the breeze, or just a pair of lovers admiring the silvery moon and the mountain silhouette of Diamond Head. Tropical nights on the beach became a new romantic fantasy, and as Hawai'ian music on gramophone records complemented sheet music, everybody could create their own Waikiki atmosphere at home in the living room or even down at the local beach. It was the ultimate romantic beach serenade, with mass-distributed landscape sound and images. During the 1930s Waikiki became the first radio beach; there were countless shows broadcast from "the beach at Waikiki," and mass-syndicated radio shows like "Hawai'i Calls" at times were heard on 750 radio stations worldwide (Grant 1996:68).

During the Second World War tourists vanished from the Waikiki Beach, which was taken over by the hundreds of thousands of soldiers stationed in Honolulu or passing through. Discussions of tourism rarely mention the fact that masses of working-class men got their first experience of the exotic during the war, albeit in rather strange circumstances. Most of the GIs in Honolulu never came closer to their Polynesian dream girls than the offer of "Two Pictures with Hula Girl" for 75 cents, and then the hula girls usually weren't local Hawai'ians but Puerto Ricans or mainlander girls. The local women did not live up to the fantasy images of slender hula bodies, which the men brought with them from back home (Bailey and Farber 1992:212).

Many of the GIs came back later to Hawai'i and the South Pacific with their families as tourists. During the 1950s active mass media marketing furthered the fantasyland of the Pacific beach as an appetizingly exotic Eden of sensual women with inviting smiles. "Every man's vision of delight," as the *National Geographic* aptly called a 1962 feature on Tahiti. During the postwar period this influential magazine consistently pictured the Pacific as a friendly and secure paradise (Lutz and Collins 1993:133).[2]

On Waikiki the Hollywood presence had been strong since the 1920s. Movie moguls and stars simply had to spend a vacation in one of the fashionable resort hotels, and the result was a strong Hollywood interest in Hawai'ian settings, which culminated in the 1950s with movies like *From Here to Eternity* and Elvis's *Blue Hawaii.* In those years the favorite prize on an American quiz show was often a romantic trip to Hawai'i for two (Grant 1996).

By the time the mass tourists started flying in with the firmly established romance of Waikiki Beach among their baggage, the actual beach experience with its jungle of high-rise hotels, overcrowded beaches, and traffic congestions had difficulties in living up to these images.

After Waikiki with its groves of coconut palms any serious beach had to have palm trees, like the *PARADISA* version. Another element on the *PARADISA* beach also had a Waikiki past: the surfboard, but it made the global beach through a detour to California (Grant 1996).

When the tourists started visiting Waikiki Beach, surfing was almost gone as local tradition, and mainland Americans helped revitalize it. Local surfers became one of the great sights at the beach. They produced all kinds of stunts, from surfing dogs to night surfing with torches, but they also brought the experience to the tourists. Visiting Hawai'ian teams took the sport to California in the early twentieth century, but since few tourist seashores have good surf, the sport's diffusion was slow. Until the 1950s surfers made up a relatively small subculture, mainly confined to southern California.[3] Wearing swimming shorts, T-shirts, and sandals, they spent most of their summer on the beach and out in the surf, often staying overnight in the car and having improvised beach parties in the evenings. They also went on "surfing safaris" to distant beaches with great surf.

Surfing went global through the media, but in rather unorthodox ways. In the late fifties and early sixties low-cost surfing films were made and shown in high-school auditoriums and similar places. Surfing attracted attention in novels and later Hollywood movies, but the big breakthrough came when "surfing music" was transformed into an international success by some southern California musicians. When the Beach Boys (named after the famous surfers on Waikiki Beach) had several surfing songs in the top ten during 1962 and 1963 the craze was already a fact. The number of surfers grew and, more important, a new image of teenage beach life spread around the world to the tunes of "Surfing Safari" and "California Girls": blond and tanned youth, jumping into their open cars to drive down to the beach for a summer of endless parties. Surfboards no longer had to be part of the surf scene, other than as a suitable backdrop, and the surf scene was no longer seen as a Hawai'ian but a Californian innovation.[4] In the 1960s it also produced another global export: why not arrange a real California beach party down at the local beach or in your own backyard? It became an avant-garde form of informal socializing.

Beach Basics

Three basic elements make up the global beach: sand, sun, and sea. What are their characteristics? How did these three ordinary elements turn beaches into a global phenomenon?

Sand is usually not a popular terrain for human activity. It is hard to walk in, it gets into your clothes, eyes, and food. It moves too easily in the wind. The early seashore visitors who used the beach mainly as a vista or for a slow walk avoided the sandy dunes and made only quick expeditions over the banks when going into the water. People who went for a serious swim preferred other kinds of beaches. Sand was a strange and alien material, difficult to shape and control.

It was only when the swimming and sunning beach developed that sand acquired its new qualities. It became an extremely sensual element, caressing the body. From now on a real beach should have sand, and preferably either white or golden yellow, it should also look clean, virginal. The sand combined the fluidity of water and the warmth of the sun.

Once vacationers started to make contact with this new element, they found that it had all sorts of uses. Already during the early twentieth century sand and children were well linked. In northern Europe the sandbox was developed for children. Children needed sand; sand was good for them. It turned into a medium for play, and in suburban gardens and urban playgrounds small sand dunes, fenced in by planks, materialized. At the beach the sand brought out the child in the adult. Grown-ups joined the kids in fooling around with sand, building sand castles, canals, sculptures, covering each other in sand. Digging became a favorite pastime and in some cases led to stranger activities.

The craze for sandy beaches had some far-reaching consequences. Above all it began a burgeoning export of sand, not any sand, but the kind of perfect beach sand that does not occur just anywhere. All over the tourist world beaches have been constructed with the help of truckloads of sand. One of the first experiments was made in Monaco, where Elsa Maxwell was hired to promote tourism and came up with the idea of a rubber beach to be spread with sand. It didn't turn out to be such a good idea (Blume 1994:75). Cannes and other resorts along the Riviera imported sand from the French west coast, where it had the right quality.

The discovery of water as a hedonistic element was also slow. Body motions changed from slowly lowering yourself into the water to "taking a plunge," from controlled restraint to childish euphoria. People started to run rather than walk into the sea. All new kinds of water movements developed. In the water you could float, glide, stroke, paddle, dive, crawl. Again it was a chance of returning to the simple pleasures of childhood. Exploring water was like entering a different universe:

> there is the wonder of buoyancy, of being suspended in this thick, transparent medium that supports and embraces us. One can move in water, play with it, in a way that has no analogue in the air . . . . One can become a little hydroplane or submarine, investigating the physics of flow with one's body. (Sacks 1997:45)

You could also enjoy water from land. Water made you mellow, as the visitors to Southland Beach put it. The languid movements, the rhythm of the surf had a calming, soothing effect, and the endless horizon proved to be a perfect medium for daydreaming. Its vastness opened up a wide space for wandering thoughts and fantasies. Out there, past a distant ship on its way to an exotic destination, are other worlds. The philosopher Bachelard sees a connection between the immensity of the seashore landscape and the depth of "inner space." Staring at the horizon, your eyes glaze—you are looking at nothing and at a hidden world at the same time (1994:205–09). Contemplating the ocean and trying to represent its magic also calls for a new language, as in the description of Waikiki Beach from 1929: "Far out to the opalescent horizon stretches the ocean in broad bands of jeweled color—turquoise, sapphire, emerald, amethyst; and curving around it like a tawny topaz girdle presses the hard, firm sand of the shore."[5] At midday, as at sunset and in moonlight, Waikiki offered the perfect tropical beach: new combinations of light and colors, in the meeting of sky and ocean.

After learning to handle the water in new ways, tourists took the next step. They cultivated the art of sunbathing. A tanned body was previously a sign of manual labor and vulgarity: only bodies exposed to the sun in outdoor labor were tanned. As late as the 1920s Swedish magazines carried ads for lotions that would help you to get rid of a tan and regain the white, fashionable complexion, but a few years later the new fashion of sunbathing had spread to most of the Western world. (In some cases the same lotions that once promised to whiten the skin now offered a safe way of getting "the brown, beautiful summer tan.")[6]

Sunbathing as a hedonist project originated in Germany, already in the late nineteenth century, but the great expansion came when a new generation of war-weary youth craved a new life after 1918. The Englishman Stephen Spender was attracted to this movement and described the sun as "a primary

"By the beautiful sea": in this postcard from the 1950s, the photographer has choreographed his models' posture to demonstrate the properly relaxed beach body. (Courtesy of Orvar Löfgren)

social force in Germany": "Thousands of people went to the open-air swimming baths or lay down on the shores of rivers and lakes, almost nude, and
sometimes quite nude, and the boys who had turned the deepest mahogany
walked among those people with paler skins, like kings among their court-
iers" (quoted in Fussell 1980:140).

Nudism and sunbathing were often linked in this pioneer period, as a
utopia of modern and natural living. In Germany "Free Body Culture"
(*Freikörperkultur*) camps started up, and from his experience in such a camp
Kurt Barthel was one of those who brought nudism to the United States. Here
the emphasis was to be more on tanning and informality than on athletics.
Sunlight was seen as the cure for everything. Nudist camps developed all
over the United States, often viewed with great suspicion (and curiosity) by
the surrounding society. A promotional movie was made in 1933, called *Ely-
sia Valley of the Nude.* "The Sunshine Park" in New Jersey became the headquarters of the American Sunbathing Association, where there were hopes
for developing a whole "Nude City," but nudism never really caught on.
"Nudists bodies are free, but their souls are in corsets," as one critic of the
movement put it, and nudists spent as much time fighting one another as bat-
tling the ignorance of the public.[7]

The cult of sunshine did catch on, though, transforming vacations and
beach life. Sometimes it made tanning rather than swimming the most important pastime on the beach. "Sunshine is healthy" was the new advice, but the
British writer Evelyn Waugh, as usual, was critical. In 1930 he wrote for the
London Daily Mail: "I hate the whole business . . . . All this is supposed to be
good for you. Nowadays people believe anything they are told by 'scientists,'
just as they used to believe anything they were told by clergymen" (quoted in
Fussell 1980:141).

The health arguments soon faded as the sun became a liberating force, a
highly sensual communion with nature. The sun warmed both your body and
your senses, you should be drenched in it. It made you both beautiful and
sexy. A new color scheme was developed, a cult of *bronzage* as the French
term was. The romance of Polynesia was part of the picture. Natives like hula
girls or surfing beach boys were not black, they were just perfectly tanned.

The skills of acquiring the perfect bronze tan developed into a more and
more complex art, comprising ointments, tanning hints, and the rituals of rub-
bing down. As an Australian newspaper advised its readers, "It turns out to
be all too easy to obtain the uneven coloration deprecatingly termed a
'farmer's tan.' It takes time and commitment to get the all-over allure of deep
and enduring brownness" (quoted in Fiske 1989:47). The term "sunbaking"
replaced "sunbathing" in Australia, to mark this commitment (still quite serious in 1982; and in the United States the comic strip *Doonesbury* mocked and
immortalized Zonker's quest for the perfect tan). At the beach you learned to
massage yourself and your partner with all kinds of lotions, developing new
forms of body consciousness as well as redefining acceptable and unacceptable forms of nudity.

No sooner was the art of tanning safely institutionalized than the first warnings appeared. In the 1980s cancer patrols started to patrol beaches over the world, offering to protect you from the dangers of the sun. In some sunny parts of the world tanning was no longer the thing, but on the whole pale Northern tourists kept working on their *bronzage*.

Beach Bodies

The beach is very much the site of the making of the modern body. Wherever you look there are bodies, all kinds of bodies, old and young bodies, fat and thin, swimming or sleeping bodies, running bodies, bodies doing somersaults or rolling in the sand. Life at the modern beach becomes body-work: exposing the body to sun, water, winds, and sand—as well as the critical eyes of others. On the beach you learn a lot about bodies, your own and others'. After three-quarters of a century of bodies in scant swimwear and various degrees of exposure we may have become so blasé that we don't realize what a revolutionary experience this has been.

One genre may help us recapture some of this early impact. It is what George Orwell called, in an essay from 1942, "the penny or two-penny postcards with their endless succession of fat women in tight bathing-dresses" (1968:183–94). He was thinking of a specific comic postcard tradition that developed in Britain and elsewhere with the focus on beach bodies and beach situations. Orwell had an eye for popular culture but found it hard to repress his middle-class reactions to these images:

> Your first impression is of an overwhelming vulgarity. This is quite apart from the ever-present obscenity, and also apart from the hideousness of the colors. They have an utter lowness of mental atmosphere, which comes out not only in the nature of the jokes but, even more, in the grotesque, staring, blatant quality of the drawings . . . every gesture and attitude, are deliberately ugly, the faces grinning and vacuous, the women monstrously parodied, with bottoms like Hottentots. (1968:183)

Of course Orwell is able to see these postcards as a cultural phenomenon that represents a different kind of humor and lifestyle from his own. The cards tell us something of the making of a new body-oriented beach culture, which certainly isn't one of middle-class constraint and decorum. First, there are all kinds of bodies parading here, fat, ugly bodies and broad backsides, as well as vulgar forms of bodily contact: the slapping of backs, the pinching of bottoms, unrestrained public kissing and hugging. Second, they draw attention to other bodily functions, such as gluttonous overeating, getting blind drunk, or frantically searching for the restrooms. So many activities that should occur in privacy go on here in the wrong place, at the wrong time. These are bodies lacking any form of moderation: loud laughs, large gestures, swelling forms. In some ways they represent guerrilla warfare against middle-class taste and self-control, and they do this in a liberating, shameless

"The water is so clear you can see the bottom quite distinctly."

Beach bottoms, backsides, buttocks, behinds, and bums—such was the dominating obsession in the British comic postcard tradition of the 1930s. (Courtesy of Orvar Löfgren)

way. These voluptuous ladies bending down to expose their enormous backsides and the men floating on their big bellies in the water are not hiding their "vulgar" bodies. They are on the beach to enjoy themselves: "Having a great time, wish you were here!" In this world backsides, buttocks, behinds, bums, and bottoms are always good for a laugh, as is any form of nudity. (The nudist camp jokes were among its basic ingredients.)

The point I want to make about the symbolism of this world is that it celebrates bodies enjoying themselves, bodies that definitely do not live up to the rigorous standards that later came to dominate beach culture.

Some bodies are there on the beach to enjoy themselves—other bodies are there to be judged. In the 1920s the concept of bathing beauties appeared, with an endless string of beauty pageants that chose the beach as their stage (Cohen, Wilk and Stoeltje 1995). Starlets and models posed for photographers against the blue sea, and women's magazines started running advice on getting bodies ready for the beach season. Stern dieting programs later became part of this regime, creating the terror of pre-beach flab. And ads for men urged them to start building bodies during the winter to make sure some hunk on the beach didn't try to steal their girlfriend or trip them up in the sand. "Hey skinny—yer ribs are showing!" was the catching start of the 1950's ads about beach humiliations, in which Charles Atlas promised to make you into a new man for next summer, in only fifteen minutes a day.

In some settings the monitoring of the perfect body became so strong that some people stayed away or found other, less demanding beaches. But beach bodywork was not only about exposing sand, sea, and sun as well as different forms of motion. The languidness of swimming also influenced body movements on land. People learned to walk and move very differently on the beach. There was some kind of magic and liberating transformation occurring the moment your feet hit the sand.

The new beach bodies also demanded beachwear, a term that first appeared in 1928 on the Riviera beaches together with the two novelties of beach pajamas and beach gown, while items like beach bags and beach sandals appeared a few years later.[8]

Beach Etiquette

JIM: Wenn man an einem fremden Strand kommt, ist man immer zuerst etwas verlegen.

JAKOB: Man weiss nicht recht, wohin man gehen soll . . .

JIM: When a person lands at a strange shore, he is always a bit embarrassed at first.

JAKE: He doesn't rightly know, where he is to go to . . .

Brecht's lines from *Mahagonny* on the awkwardness of coming to an unknown beach would hold very true for most large beaches of the world. They hold an astonishing mix of people. Southland Beach is a good example. Here groups of different ages and classes and cultural and ethnic identities mingle. Inner-city people and tourists who are new to the city, strangers, sit close together on the same strip of flat sand, in full exposure, with very little protective clothing. It is a mass confrontation that in many other settings would be volatile. But still the beach works. Even strangers soon make themselves at home.

The beach is supposed to be an arena of relaxation, of minding your own business, of doing what you want. But behind such notions of anarchy or individualism is heavily regimented behavior. The French sociologist Jean-Claude Kaufmann's (1995) study of topless bathing on French beaches illustrates this very clearly. Many of his beach informants stated strongly, "Here on the beach everybody does what they want," but a world of unwritten rules and regulations allowed them to do so. People knew exactly where the borders were, how to look, how to dress and undress, how to move their bodies.

The rules were especially clear in the sensitive field of topless bathing, where women turned out to have very precise ideas about the propriety of this French tradition: when, where, and how to let go of the top piece. Kaufmann's choice of topic may sound esoteric, but it unearthed a whole universe of ideas about privacy, individualism, social relations, and gender.

One of his main arguments is that the beach is a laboratory for the sophistication of the gaze. People he interviewed often said, "I don't spend any time looking around, I am in my own world." There is, of course, no way you cannot look. People on the beach are constantly testing different ocular techniques, consciously or unconsciously switching between different ways of seeing: watching, staring, glancing, scanning, looking from the corner of your eye, pretending not to look, making brief eye contact, looking away.

There was constant observation of how other people handled these techniques and very quick registration of those who broke the rules. Topless women in particular monitored the male gaze as well as that of other females. "When bodies are naked glances are clothed," as the sociologist Erving Goffman once put it.[9]

All this doesn't come naturally. The ways in which people observe at the beach have changed over time.[10] The colonizing gaze of the Victorians would today be considered most provoking and unsophisticated. The degree of learning ocular competence also becomes obvious when kids constantly have to be told, "Don't stare." You have to learn to discipline the ways you look at others in a suitably disinterested way: observing but never staring.

The beach was also the place for another important innovation: sunglasses, which developed new forms of hiding yourself and at the same time offered new opportunities for unobtrusive observation.

A beach is, as we have seen, a very special arena, often with clear boundaries. The kind of behavior that is okay down by the water is not okay in the parking lot or on the other side of the beach road. Beach life may seem banal, but these banalities express very basic conceptions about private and public, decent and indecent, individuality and collectivity. Most of the rules regulating beach behavior have never been written down, many of them can hardly be verbalized, and yet—down at the beach—people know.

Unlike many other arenas, beaches bring classes together, sometimes in an uneasy coexistence, sometimes in strikingly unproblematic ways. They offer the chance to observe, very close at hand, "those other people" at play. The history of British tourism emphasizes this role of the beach as one of the few "neutral grounds" that allowed the working class to enter the vacation scene much earlier than in many other nations. As the historian John K. Walton describes the situation in the late nineteenth century, "At the seaside rich and poor, respectable and ungodly, staid and rowdy, quiet and noisy not only rubbed shoulders . . . they also had to compete for access to, and use of, recreational space" (1983:190–91). He overstates the classlessness of the beach, but a striking theme in early twentieth-century beach life is the idea of make-believe. Music-hall songs talked about "Beach Sultans" and on the comic postcards you could see working-class girls exclaiming: "At home I might be nothing, but here I am at least something!" The seaside visit was that special place, "a geography of hope," which stood out as a highlight in the British working-class year (Sprawson 1993:19).

In a similar manner a place like Coney Island became an arena of social confrontations. In the middle of the nineteenth century it was still a desolate beach, visited by a few wealthy families in search of fresh air and solitude. By the 1870s it had developed into New York's leading resort. By 1900 up to a half million New Yorkers visited the beach and its amusement parks on summer weekend days. By then it offered what has been called a "linear visual study in American class structure" with different social groups distributed along the shore. While certain areas kept a middle-class focus, others catered for the working class. Some spots had a reputation as a hangout for underworld figures or attracted a socially mixed male audience of the "sporting" subculture (Towner 1996:211).

Beaches like Coney Island and Blackpool fostered endless debates about beach morals and beach rules as different lifestyles overlapped or clashed. On some global beaches debates take new, multicultural, forms.

Beach Blankets

> I grow up bathing in sea water
> But nowadays that is bare horror
> If I only venture down by the shore
> Police is only telling me I can't bathe anymore.
>
> (quoted in Pattullo 1996:83)

This Calypso text from Barbados is one of many comments on the conflicts about beach access in the Caribbean. Here, as in most other tourist regions of the world, beaches are public, but in reality local access has been constrained. Seaside resorts may try all sorts of tactics to monitor visitors. Tourists' complaints of being hassled by vendors or "beach boys" cruising for single female tourists led to an increased policing of beaches, as in the Barbados case, which opened up a discussion of who and what belongs on the beach. On many Caribbean islands, the natives feel that they have been forced out of the best beaches, or as a local paper put it, "The day could come when the ordinary Jamaican doesn't know what a good beach looks like" (Pattullo 1996).

So who owns the beach? A Canadian travel ad from 1958 says: "Want to own an ocean?" There is a picture of a family on a beach blanket in the middle of vast empty space, an image of perfect order and relaxation, but most tourist beaches tend to be crowded, though, which has led to all sorts of tactics for creating private space. When Robert Edgerton interviewed Los Angeles beachgoers, the vast majority argued that the first thing they did was to carve out space on arrival by rolling out their towel and arranging their private belongings: "I pick out my little plot of sand and set down my towel. For the next few hours that is my own little world; it belongs to me" (1979:150). To cross over this private territory or to sit down next to it was considered a provocation and rarely happened. Beach etiquette thus starts with the micro-rituals of installation, of making yourself at home, and at the same time marking a physical and mental distance from others.

Another common ritual of signaling privacy is to immerse yourself in some activity as soon as you have arranged your belongings, to bury yourself in a book or lie down in the sand. The strong sense of privacy even on a crowded beach also has to do with the techniques of daydreaming. By closing your eyes you are signaling that you are in your own private dream world, far away.

After such initial moves you can become more active later on. Some complain of beach life being too private, with people going to great lengths not to communicate with those close by. "It's like being in an elevator where nobody talks," one woman complained to David Edgerton. Those who consistently break these rules of privacy and noncommunication are small kids and dogs.

Against this complex regimentation of the private sphere the clash with beach vendors or beach boys on distant vacation beaches become more understandable. These are locals who don't know the rules the tourists have brought with them from back home. In Los Angeles many white middle-class visitors also complained about Chicano families: they did not understand the need to keep their distance.

On the whole, Southland visitors stressed how easy it was to be on the beach. "I feel so safe here, people are mellow, the environment makes people behave. . . . It may be one of the places a woman can go alone and yet feel safe," were some of the comments.

The ability of the beach to produce this mellowness is a statement that turns up again and again: "Waikiki at that time was a very, very healing place. You would come there because you instinctively knew that's where you needed to be if you wanted a rest, if you needed to get well. The waters were beneficent, the breezes were soothing, the whole vibration of the place was something that just drew you in" (quoted in Timmons 1986:34).

My Home Is My Sand Castle

On some German beaches you may spot a sign telling you that it is absolutely forbidden to build sand castles. This may, to an outside visitor, seem like a harsh attitude to a harmless occupation, but then you have probably not seen what a German sand castle may look like. We are not talking about miniatures here but the old tradition of building a secluded, circular wall around your beach territory, to protect yourself from the wind and the regards of others. These structures are nothing like the improvised shelters you might make out of a ring of stones, which appear on beaches all over the world. On a real German sand castle beach you may have to maneuver your way past castle after castle, and then it might also feel like walking through an art show, because the German tradition puts great emphasis on decoration, as Harald Kimpel and Johanna Werckmeister (1995) point out in their history of the phenomenon.

The tradition of placing yourself inside a sand castle was well established in the nineteenth century. It probably started as a way of claiming space on the beach and also as a protection against the often chilly winds of German beaches. The tradition soon triggered off competition and the idea of building a more perfect and more beautiful structure around yourself. Some of the structures had elegant patterns accomplished with shells or wreckage, and many had sand sculptures.

Subtexts underlined the ways in which sand castles became personalized statements: "Young ladies welcome," "The unfinished," "Kalifornien," or "Castle Sansoucie." Less poetically they could be called "Düsseldorf," announcing your hometown, or just presenting the occupants "Irmgard und Egon." The changing aesthetics and namings mirror different periods of beach life. The nastier ones are some of the sand castles from the 1930s, as the one with Hitler's portrait in sand and the title "Unser Führer." This sand castle is photographed surrounded with happy beachgoers in swimwear doing the Heil Hitler salute.

As I pointed out earlier, German tourists have often had a bad press, and the sand castle–building habit contributed to it. When German tourists after the Second World War started traveling abroad they brought along their building tradition, not always aware of the kind of signals they were sending. In countries like Holland and Denmark, where the same beaches had been occupied by Nazi troops, surprised Germans found their castles trampled down when they returned to the beach the next morning. Local youths had demolished them during the night.

An earlier source of conflicts was the tradition of putting up flags on the beach. This was a late nineteenth-century tradition, found not only in Germany, but in this young nation travelers often took along flags when they went abroad. The tradition led to international conflicts, as locals saw it as a symbol of aggressive Germanness, the quest for *Lebensraum.* On one of the beaches in Denmark where there were many German castles and flags, local Danes went out and removed the flags. German tourists protested, and in the end the two governments had to exchange stern notes.

Apart from its place in the stereotype of "typical German tourist," the sandcastle tradition had quite another aspect. One castle from 1913 bears the inscription in small shells: The Club of Work-Shy. This imposing artwork must have taken many hours of hard work to build, but the whole idea of the sand castle is that of nonwork, it is work for pleasure, where you work off a lot of childish energy and creativity. You invest hours in building something that the wind and the tide will wash away. As the German authors point out, the investment may have to do with the fact that relaxation at the beach often produces boredom and restlessness: let's do something!

Seasides and Poolsides

Time isn't the great healer.
Poolside seats are.

This 1997 slogan of an American resort chain is part of a move away from the beach.[11] In many coastal settings, sand and seawater have become less important. An appetizing destination must advertise its beach, but when you get there you often find out that there are very few people in the water: it is too cold, too windy, too polluted. The sand is sticky or full of cigarette butts. The tourists have withdrawn to the safer territory of the hotel pool, but they have brought with them all the necessary skills developed at the beach.

If you look up "swimming pool" in the *Encyclopedia Americana* you get "a tank constructed of cement, wood, steel, plastic, fiberglass or other material and used for swimming, or pleasure bathing." Behind this minimalistic definition lies a gradual development that has made the pool rather than the beach a focus of much vacation life. Pools have an impressive history, but in the Western world there is a long void from the Roman era to their reintroduction in the nineteenth century.[12]

Down at the old boardwalk of Santa Cruz, California, you may view the ruins of the old giant swimming pool building from 1907, but the first tank was built next to the beach in the 1860s. In nearby San Francisco the even bigger Sutro Baths were developed in the 1890s. They covered three acres on the western headlands of San Francisco, with saltwater and freshwater pools, palm trees, a tropic beach, restaurants, galleries, and an amphitheater. The baths could accommodate ten thousand swimmers a day and were in use until 1966, when they were dismantled (Croutier 1992:159, Sprawson 1993:268).

In other big cities like Chicago and New York public swim baths were often introduced to encourage working-class cleanliness, but the public pools soon became popular playgrounds. By 1911 Chicago's outdoor pools were so popular that groups were marched in by the hour, supplied with swimsuits and towels, and then ordered out of the water one hour later, to make room for the next group in line (Crantz 1982:72).

The waning popularity of these giant baths during the twentieth century had to do with the scale on which different groups and classes mixed. The future of the seaside pools turned out to be the more private hotel pools, often developed as alternatives to overcrowded beaches or polluted coastal waters. In the early 1950s a hotel developer at Waikiki surprised the world by developing a complex away from the high-cost beach locations but with its own hotel pool (Grant 1996:82). A new concept was born. Most hotel pools developed out of the Californian model, the testing ground not only for pool styles but also for pool etiquette. In southern California's roaring 1920s private pools became part of Hollywood stardom, but the real expansion came in the 1950s and 1960s, with new and cheaper techniques (Baldan and Melchior 1997, Elving 1972, and Spawson 1993).

During the 1980s hotel pools became more and more elaborate, as designers developed veritable water lands, with artificial sand beaches, waterfalls, slides, and lagoons. Water spectacles have become an increasingly important part of hotel aesthetics and entertainment.

The vacation pool culture shows an immense degree of standardization. The same azure blue nuance, imitating tropical beaches, similar pool shapes, springboards, chairs. We move our bodies according to a well-established choreography, pull our stomachs in before climbing onto the diving board, or nonchalantly rest one of our arms on the side of the pool as we make poolside conversation from the water, just the way we have seen in countless advertisements for Martini.

Today the pool is a condensation of the beach and seashore: a much better managed version, nice water temperature, no sand between the toes, close to the hotel bar. The restricted space makes for new kinds of conflicts. All over the world people sneak down to the pool in the early morning to wrap a towel around a chair in a good position for basking in the sun. During the day they move their chairs around, group and regroup them, and then leave them for dinner in a frozen sociogram of the day's interaction.

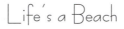

Life's a Beach

Maybe it is the mix of activities and possibilities with an aura of luxurious living that has made beach and poolside life such a vacation success. Here you oscillate between very different vacation modes. Frolic in the water, daydream with the help of the horizon or a Walkman, float on your back in sand or water, drink cold beer or cappuccino, fool around with the sand, mas-

Alone together: reading on a global beach. Nusa Dua, Bali, Indonesia.
(© 2003 Martin Benjamin)

sage your own body or that of your partner with suntan lotion, and not least important: who could have guessed that the beach or pool chair would become one of the most cherished reading places in the world? Everywhere people are buried in their books, magazines, mysteries, and thick paperback novels with sunscreen smudges. The beach has become a great read.

The fact that this is a territory for the pursuit of hedonism also means that it often becomes a place of boredom. Modes of awareness drift in and out: dozing, daydreaming, sitting up to take in the scenery, registering activities around you, reflecting on the behavior of others, becoming self-conscious when moving through the beach landscape or diving into the pool.

You learn so much at the beach without ever noticing that you're a vacationer in constant training. The global beach has an ability to detach itself from its immediate surroundings, which means that you can travel the world and usually feel quite at home on any beach. Changing beach aesthetics make the landscape more and more minimalistic, as two ads in the *New Yorker* from 1996 illustrate. The first for Australia shows a couple walking along a sandbank completely surrounded by water, a small island of sand, and nothing else. Apart from a small parked airplane, there is total stillness. Another ad for the Bahamas shows just a deck chair in the sunset, vast areas of sand, and a few palm trees in the distance. Nothingness, emptiness, seclusion, not a single soul, getting away from it all.

In his analysis of an Australian beach John Fiske (1989) focuses on the structuralist notion of the beach being in-between, an anomalous zone between nature and culture. But the old slogan from the 1968 Paris student revolt is more telling: "The beach is under the street!" Just start breaking up the tarmac and you'll find the world of sand. However great its distance from city life, the holiday beach keeps its polarity to city life and work. Urban culture's competence of handling privacy and communication in crowds of strangers makes the beach as a global project possible.

The global beach is a fact, but there are still the fine distinctions of class and ethnicity. People on Southland Beach complain of outsiders not sticking to the local rules and feel affronted at Chicanos who bathe with their clothes on, as well as at the Swedish woman who performs the classic Scandinavian tradition (and feat) of changing into swimwear with the help of a scanty beach towel. And in many settings the locals are still not very happy about the ways in which tourists expose their bodies on the beach. The tradition of going into the water fully clothed is still strong in many parts of the world.

There is a constant tension between the beach as an individual experience and the beach as a cultural arena, impregnated with rules, routines, and rituals. When Jean-Claude Kaufmann tries to sum up his beach observations he finds himself saying things like: the beach does this or that, the beach thinks, the beach prefers . . . There was an unconscious cultural collectivity of beach life to set against the fact that individuals often experience the beach as a liberating space, a space to break habits, not make them. This ambiguity catches rather nicely the cultural complexities of beach life.

The beach may seem to standardize vacation life, and yet the closer you look at beach experiences, the more personal they seem. Let me end the chapter with a quote from the Swedish novel *The Beach Man*, which travels between distant beaches:

> First down the stairs is as usual the old couple from Rotterdam . . . they unfold their piece of Balinese cloth, seventeen years old. *Got*, how time passes, and arrange sandals, clothes, water bottle, books, towels, bags, lighters, a pack of Salem, according to a choreography, which has been perfected and made permanent after—I don't dare to think—how many vacations at the beach together. . . .
>
> They bring out a tube of Piz Buin from a plastic bag and rub it on each other's backs, in silence and without gestures, as if they were taking turns to wipe the kitchen table, that's all. They look out toward the sea. He makes a short comment and gets a surprised smile back. They make themselves comfortable, getting the right angle to the sun. He puts two fingers on her hip and she gives his hand a brief pat: their parting ritual, because from now on they will be alone, each with their own sun. (Kihlgård 1992:7)

Source: From *On Holiday: A History of Vacationing*, 1999. Reprinted with permission of the author and University of California Press.

Notes

[1] The text goes on to assure you that personnel speaking both Portuguese and English will meet you at the airport and take care of your needs; quoted in Bilstein (1994:117).

[2] Over in Europe there was a similar craze for Pacific romance, a "polynesification" of European beach life, as the French sociologist Jean-Didier Urbain (1994:151) has called it.

[3] See the discussion in Finney and Houton (1996) and Timmons (1986:42).

[4] See the discussion in Irwin (1977:84).

[5] Frances Parkinson Keyes, "Hawaii Gets Under their Skin" (quoted in Timmons 1986:43).

[6] See Andolf, "Turismen i historien" in Löfgren et al. (1989:79) and Stilgoe (1996:355–58).

[7] For an overview of the nudism movement see Ilfled and Lauer (1964).

[8] See under "beach-" in the *Oxford English Dictionary*.

[9] Quoted in Edgerton (1979:152). See also Douglas, Rasmussen, and Flanagan (1977), which discusses nudity and privacy on a southern California beach.

[10] See the discussion in Snow and Wright (1976:960–75) and in Peiss (1987:115–38), where the gendering of the beach also is analyzed.

[11] Advertisement for Omni Hotels, *New York Times*, 15 June 1997.

[12] On the history of pools see Elving (1972) and Sprawson (1993).

References

Andolf, Göran. 1989. "Turismen i historien," in *Längtan till landet Annorlunda: Om turism i historia och nutid*, ed. Orvar Löfgren et al., pp. 355–58. Stockholm: Gidlunds.

Bailey, Beth, and David Farber. 1992. *The First Strange Place: Race and Sex in World War II Hawaii*. Baltimore: Johns Hopkins University Press.

Baldon, Cleo, and Ib Melchior. 1997. *Reflections on the Pool: California Designs for Swimming*. New York: Rizzoli.

Bilstein, Roger E. 1994. *Flight in America: From the Wrights to the Astronauts,* 2nd edition. Baltimore: Johns Hopkins University Press.

Blanchard, Gason. 1994. *The Poetics of Space.* London: Beacon Press.

Blume, 1994. *Cote d'Azur: Inventing the French Riviera.* London: Thames and Hudson.

Cohen, Colleen B., Richard Wilk, and Beverly Stoeltje, eds. 1995. *The Beauty Queens on the Global Stage: Gender, Contest and Power.* New York: Routledge.

Crantz, Galen. 1982. *The Politics of Park Design: A History of Urban Parks in America.* Cambridge: MIT Press.

Croutier, Alex Lyle. 1992. *Taking the Waters: Spirit, Art, Sensuality.* New York: Abbeville Press.

Douglas, Jack, and Paul K. Rasmussen, with Carol Ann Flanagan. 1977. *The Nude Beach.* Beverly Hills, CA: Sage.

Edgerton, Robert B. 1979. *Alone Together: Social Order on an Urban Beach.* Berkeley: University of California Press.

Elving, Phyllis. 1972. Sunset Swimming Pools, 4th edition. Menlo Park, CA: Sunset Publishing.

Finney, Ben, and James D. Houton. 1996. *Surfing: A History of the Ancient Hawaiian Sport.* San Francisco: Pomegranate Art Books.

Fiske, John. 1989. *Reading the Popular.* London: Routledge.

Fussell, Paul. 1980. *Abroad: British Literary Travelling between the Wars.* New York: Oxford University Press.

Grant, Glen. 1996. *Waikiki Yesteryear.* Honolulu: Mutual Publishing.

Ilfled, Fred Jr., and Roger Lauer. 1964. *Nudism in America.* New Haven, CT: College and University Press.

Irwin, John. 1977. *Scenes.* Beverly Hills: Sage.

Kaufmann, Jean-Claude. 1995. *Corps de femmes: Regards d'hommes.* Paris: Nathan.

Kihlgard, Peter. 1992. *Strandmannen.* Stockholm: Bonnier.

Kimpel, Harald, and Johanna Werckmeister. 1995. *Die Strandburg: Ein versandetes Freizeitsvergnugen.* Marburg: Jonas Verlag.

Löfgren, Orvar et al., eds. 1989. *Langtan till landet Annorlunda: Om turism i historia och nutid.* Stockholm: Gidlunds.

Lutz, Catherine A., and Jane L. Collins. 1993. *Reading National Geographic.* Chicago: University of Chicago Press.

Orwell, George. 1968 [1942]. "The Art of Donald McGill," in *The Collected Essays, Journalism and Letters of George Orwell,* pp. 183–94. London: Penguin Books.

Pattullo, Polly. 1996. *Last Resorts: The Costs of Tourism in the Caribbean.* London: Cassell.

Peiss, Kathy. 1987. *Cheap Amusements: Working Women and Leisure in Turn-of-the-century New York.* Philadelphia: Temple University Press.

Sacks, Oliver. 1997. "Water Babies: The Boundless Possibilities of Being in the Water." *New Yorker,* 26 May 1997:45.

Snow, Robert, and David Wright. 1976. "Coney Island: A Case Study in Popular Culture and Technical Change." *Journal of Popular Culture* 9:960–75.

Sprawson, Charles. 1993. *Haunts of the Black Masseur: The Swimmer as Hero.* London: Vintage.

Stilgoe, John R. 1996. *Alongshore.* New Haven, CT: Yale University Press.

Timmons, Grady. 1986. *Waikiki Beachboy.* Honolulu: Editions Ltd.

Towner, John. 1996. *An Historical Geography of Recreation and Tourism in the Western World.* Chichester: John Wiley and Sons.

Urbain, Jean-Didier. 1994. *Sur la plage: Moeurs et coutumes balnéaires.* Paris: Payot.

Walton, John K. 1983. *English Seaside Resort: A Social History, 1750–1914.* New York: St. Martin's Press.

4

Sightseeing and Social Structure: The Moral Integration of Modernity

Dean MacCannell

The Place of the Attraction in Modern Society

Modern society constitutes itself as a labyrinthine structure of norms governing access to its workshops, offices, neighborhoods, and semipublic places. As population density increases, this maze of norms manifests itself in physical divisions, walls, ceilings, fences, floors, hedges, barricades, and signs marking the limits of a community, an establishment, or a person's space.[1] This social system contains interstitial corridors—halls, streets, elevators, bridges, waterways, airways, and subways. These corridors are filled with things anyone can see. Erving Goffman has studied behavior in public places and relations in public for what they can reveal about our collective pride, shame, and guilt. I want to follow his lead and suggest that behavior is only one of the visible, public representations of social structure found in public places. We also find decay, refuse, human and industrial derelicts, monuments, museums, parks, decorated plazas, and architectural shows of industrial virtue. Public behavior and these other visible public parts of society are tourist attractions.

Sightseeing and the Moral Order

The organization of behavior and objects in public places is functionally equivalent to the sacred text that still serves as the moral base of traditional society. That is, public places contain the representations of good and evil that apply universally to modern existence in general.

A touristic attitude of respectful admiration is called forth by the finer attractions, the monuments, and a no-less-important attitude of disgust attaches itself to the uncontrolled garbage heaps, muggings, abandoned and tumble-down buildings, polluted rivers, and the like. Disgust over these items is the negative pole of respect for the monuments. Together, the two provide a moral stability to the modern touristic consciousness that extends beyond immediate social relationships to the structure and organization of the total society.

The tours of Appalachian communities and northern inner-city cores taken by politicians provide examples of negative sightseeing. This kind of tour is usually conducted by a local character who has connections outside of the community. The local points out and explains and complains about the rusting auto hulks, the corn that did not come up, winos and junkies on the nod, flood damage and other features of the area to the politician who expresses concern. While politicians and other public figures like Eleanor Roosevelt and the Kennedys are certainly the leaders here, this type of sight-seeing is increasingly available to members of the middle class at large. *The New York Times* reports that seventy people answered an advertisement inviting tourists to spend "21 days 'in the land of the Hatfields and McCoys' for US$378.00, living with some of the poorest people in the United States in Mingo County, West Virginia."[2] Similarly, in 1967, the Penny Sightseeing Company inaugurated extensive guided tours of Harlem.[3] Recent ecological awareness has given rise to some imaginative variations: bus tours of "The Ten Top Polluters in Action" were available in Philadelphia during "Earth Week" in April 1970.

This touristic form of moral involvement with diverse public representations of race, poverty, urban structures, social ills, and, of course, the public "good," the monuments, is a modern alternative to systems of in-group morality built out of binary oppositions: insider vs. outsider, us vs. them. Traditional societies could not survive unless they oriented behavior in a "we are good—they are bad" framework. Although some of its remains are still to be found in modern politics, such traditional morality is not efficacious in the modern world. Social structural differentiation has broken up traditional loyalties. Now it is impossible to determine with any accuracy who "we" are and who "they" are. The modern world cannot survive if it tries to orient behavior in a traditional "we are good—they are bad" framework. As we enter the modern world, the entire field of social facts—poverty, race, class, work—is open to ongoing moral evaluation and interpretation. This craziness of mere distinctions forces the modern consciousness to explore beyond the frontiers of traditional prejudice and bigotry in its search for a moral identity. Only "middle Americans" (if such people actually exist) and primi-tives—people whose lives are "everyday" in the pejorative, grinding sense of the term—may feel fully a part of their own world. Modern humanity has been condemned to look elsewhere, everywhere, for authenticity, to see if we can catch a glimpse of it reflected in the simplicity, poverty, chastity, or purity of others.

The Structure of the Attraction

I have defined a tourist attraction as an empirical relationship between a *tourist*, a *sight*, and a *marker* (a piece of information about a sight). A simple model of the attraction can be presented in the following form:

[tourist / sight / marker] attraction

Note that markers may take many different forms: guidebooks, informational tablets, slide shows, travelogues, souvenir matchbooks, etc. Note also that no *naturalistic* definition of the sight is possible. Well-marked sights that attract tourists include such items as mountain ranges, Napoleon's hat, moon rocks, Grant's tomb, even entire nation-states. The attractions are often indistin-

The Austin used by Thich Quang Duc, the first Buddhist monk in Vietnam to commit a protest suicide through self immolation in Saigon in 1963. It is kept at his home monastery at the Thien Mau Pagoda near Hue. A photograph of the incident is on the windshield. (Photo by Sharon Gmelch)

guishable from their less-famous relatives. If they were not marked, it would be impossible for a layperson to distinguish, on the basis of appearance alone, between moon rocks brought back by astronauts and pebbles picked up at Craters of the Moon National Monument in Idaho. But one is a sight and the other a souvenir, a kind of marker. Similarly, hippies are tourists and, at home in the Haight Ashbury, they are also sights that tourists come to see, or at least they used to be.

The distinguishing characteristic of those things that are collectively thought to be "true sights" is suggested by a second look at the moon rock example. *Souvenirs* are collected by *individuals*, by tourists, while *sights* are "collected" by entire societies. The entire United States is behind the gathering of moon rocks, or at least it is supposed to be, and hippies are a reflection of our collective affluence and decadence.

The origin of the attraction in the collective consciousness is not always so obvious as it is when a society dramatizes its values and capabilities by sending its representatives out into the solar system. Nevertheless, the collective determination of "true sights" is clear cut. The tourist has no difficulty deciding the sights he ought to see. The only problem is getting around to all of them. Even under conditions where there is no end of things to see, some mysterious institutional force operates on the totality in advance of the arrival of tourists, separating out the specific sights that are the attractions. In the Louvre, for example, the attraction is the *Mona Lisa*. The rest is undifferentiated art in the abstract. Moderns somehow know what the important attractions are, even in remote places. This miracle of consensus that transcends national boundaries rests on an elaborate set of institutional mechanisms, a twofold process of sight *sacralization* that is met with a corresponding *ritual attitude* on the part of tourists.

Sightseeing as Modern Ritual

Erving Goffman has defined ritual as a "perfunctory, conventionalized act through which an individual portrays his respect and regard for some object of ultimate value to its stand-in" (1971:62). This is translated into the individual consciousness as a sense of duty, albeit a duty that is often lovingly performed. Under conditions of high social integration, the ritual attitude may lose all appearance of coercive externality. It may, that is, permeate an individual's inmost being so ritual obligations are performed zealously and without thought for personal or social consequences.

Modern international sightseeing possesses its own moral structure, a collective sense that certain sights must be seen. Some tourists will resist, no doubt, the suggestion that they are motivated by an elementary impulse analogous to the one that animates the Australian's awe for his Churinga boards. The Australian would certainly resist such a suggestion. Nevertheless, modern guided tours, in Goffman's terms, are "extensive ceremonial agendas involving long strings of obligatory rites." If one goes to Europe, one "must see" Paris; if one goes to Paris, one "must see" Notre Dame, the Eiffel Tower, the Louvre; if one goes to the Louvre, one "must see" the *Venus de Milo* and, of course, the *Mona Lisa*. There are quite literally millions of tourists who have spent their savings to make the pilgrimage to see these sights. Some who have not been "there" have reported to me that they want to see these sights "with all their hearts."

It is noteworthy that no one escapes the system of attractions except by retreat into a stay-at-home, traditionalist stance: that is, no one is exempt from the obligation to go sightseeing except the local person. The Manhattan-ite who has never been to the Statue of Liberty is a mythic image in our soci-ety, as is the reverse image of the big-city people who come out into the country expressing fascination with things the local folk care little about. The ritual attitude of tourists originates in the act of travel itself and culminates when they arrive in the presence of the sight.

Some tourists feel so strongly about the sight they are visiting that they want to be alone in its presence, and they become annoyed at other tourists for profaning the place by crowding around "like sheep." Some sights become so important that tourists avoid use of their proper names: in the Pacific Northwest, Mount Rainier is called "The Mountain," and all up and down the West Coast of the United States, San Francisco is called "The City."

Traditional religious institutions are everywhere accommodating the movements of tourists. In "The Holy Land," the tour has followed in the path of the religious pilgrimage and is replacing it. Throughout the world, churches, cathedrals, mosques, and temples are being converted from reli-gious to touristic functions.

The Stages of Sight Sacralization

In structural studies, it is not sufficient to build a model of an aspect of society entirely out of attitudes and behavior of individuals. It is also neces-sary to specify in detail the linkages between the attitudes and behavior and concrete institutional settings.

Perhaps there are, or have been, some sights that are so spectacular in themselves that no institutional support is required to mark them off as attrac-tions. The original set of attractions is called, after the fashion of primitives, by the name of the sentiment they were supposed to have generated: "The Seven Wonders of the World." Modern sights, with but few exceptions, are not so evidently reflective of important social values as the Seven Wonders must have been. Attractions such as Cypress Gardens, the statue of the Little Mermaid in the harbor at Copenhagen, the Cape Hatteras Light and the like, risk losing their broader sociosymbolic meanings, becoming once more mere aspects of a limited social setting. Massive institutional support is often required for sight sacralization in the modern world.

The first stage of sight sacralization takes place when the sight is marked off from similar objects as worthy of preservation. This stage may be arrived at deductively from the model of the attraction

[tourist / sight / *marker*] attraction

or it may be arrived at inductively by empirical observation. Sights have markers. Sometimes an act of Congress is necessary, as in the official designation of a national park or historical shrine. This first stage can be called the naming phase of sight sacralization. Often, before the *naming phase*, a great deal of work goes into the authentication of the candidate for sacralization. Objects are x-rayed, baked, photographed with special equipment, and examined by experts. Reports are filed testifying to the object's aesthetic, historical, monetary, recreational, and social values.

Second is the *framing and elevation* phase. Elevation is the putting on display of an object—placement in a case, on a pedestal, or opened up for visitation. Framing is the placement of an official boundary around the object. On a practical level, two types of framing occur: protecting and enhancing. Protection seems to have been the motive behind the decision recently taken at the Louvre to place the *Mona Lisa* (but none of the other paintings) behind glass. When spotlights are placed on a building or a painting, it is enhanced. Most efforts to protect a sacred object, such as hanging a

Sight sacralization: Domestic and foreign tourists queue to see Ho-Chi-Minh's body in Hanoi, Vietnam. (Photo by Pat Mahoney)

silk cord in front of it, or putting extra guards on duty around it, can also be read as a kind of enhancement so the distinction between protection and enhancement eventually breaks down. Tourists before the *Mona Lisa* often remark: "Oh, it's the only one with glass," or "It must be the most valuable, it has glass in front." Advanced framing occurs when the rest of the world is forced back from the object and the space in between is landscaped. Versailles and the Washington Monument are "framed" in this way.

When the framing material that is used has itself entered the first stage of sacralization (marking), a third stage has been entered. This stage can be called *enshrinement*. The model here is Sainte Chapelle, the church built by Saint Louis as a container for the "true Crown of Thorns" that he had purchased from Baldwin of Constantinople. Sainte Chapelle is, of course, a tourist attraction in its own right. Similarly, in the Gutenberg Museum, in Gutenberg, Germany, the original Gutenberg Bible is displayed under special lights on a pedestal in a darkened enclosure in a larger room. The walls of the larger room are hung with precious documents, including a manuscript by Beethoven.

The next stage of sacralization is *mechanical reproduction* of the sacred object: the creation of prints, photographs, models, or effigies of the object which are themselves valued and displayed. It is the mechanical reproduction phase of sacralization that is most responsible for setting the tourist in motion on his journey to find the true object. And he is not disappointed. Alongside of the copies of it, it has to be The Real Thing.

The final stage of sight sacralization is *social reproduction*, as occurs when groups, cities, and regions begin to name themselves after famous attractions.

Tourist attractions are not merely a collection of random material representations. When they appear in itineraries, they have a moral claim on the tourist and, at the same time, they tend toward universality, incorporating natural, social, historical, and cultural domains in a single representation made possible by the tour. This morally enforced universality is the basis of a general system of classification of societal elements produced without conscious effort. No person or agency is officially responsible for the worldwide proliferation of tourist attractions. They have appeared naturally, each seeming to respond to localized causes.

Nevertheless, when they are considered as a totality, tourist attractions reveal themselves to be a taxonomy of structural elements. Interestingly, this natural taxonomic system contains the analytical classification of social structure currently in use by social scientists. A North American itinerary, for example, contains domestic, commercial, and industrial establishments, occupations, public-service and transportation facilities, urban neighborhoods, communities, and members of solitary (or, at least, identifiable) subgroups of American society. The specific attractions representing these structural categories would include the Empire State Building, an Edwardian house in Boston's Back Bay, a Royal Canadian mounted policeman, a Mississippi River bridge, Grand Coulee Dam, an Indian totem pole, San Francisco's Chinatown, a cable car, Tijuana, Indians, cowboys, an ante-bellum mansion, an Amish farm, Arlington National Cemetery, the Smithsonian Institution, and Washington Cathedral.

Taken together, tourist attractions and the behavior surrounding them are, I think, one of the most complex and orderly of the several universal codes that constitute modern society, although not so complex and orderly as, for example, a language.

Claude Lévi-Strauss claims that there is no such system in modern society. I think it is worth exploring the possible base of this claim, which is by no means confined to Lévi-Strauss's offhand remarks. Erving Goffman has similarly suggested that:

> . . . in contemporary society rituals performed to stand-ins for supernatural entities are everywhere in decay, as are extensive ceremonial agendas involving long strings of obligatory rites. What remains are brief rituals one individual performs for another, attesting to civility and good will on the performer's part and to the recipient's possession of a small patrimony of sacredness. (1971:63)

I think that the failure of Goffman and Lévi-Strauss to note the existence of social integration on a macro-structural level in modern society can be traced to a methodological deficiency: neither of them has developed the use of systemic variables for his analysis of social structure. In my own studies, I was able to bypass Lévi-Strauss's critique by working up the very dimension of modernity that he named as its most salient feature: its chaotic fragmentation, its *differentiation*.

Interestingly, the approach I used was anticipated by Émile Durkheim, who invented the use of systemic variables for sociological analysis and who named tourist attractions ("works of art" and "historical monuments") in his basic listing of social facts. Durkheim wrote:

> Social facts, on the contrary [he had just been writing of psychological facts], qualify far more naturally and immediately as things. Law is embodied in codes . . . fashions are preserved in costumes; taste in works of art . . . [and] the currents of daily life are recorded in statistical figures and historical monuments. By their very nature they tend towards an independent existence outside the individual consciousness, which they dominate. (1938:30)

Until now, no sociologist took up Durkheim's suggestion that "costumes," "art," and "monuments" are keys to modern social structure. The structure of the attraction was deciphered by accident by the culture critic Walter Benjamin while working on a different problem. But Benjamin, perhaps because of his commitment to an orthodox version of Marxist theory, inverted all the basic relations. He wrote:

> The uniqueness of a work of art is inseparable from its being imbedded in the fabric of tradition. This tradition itself is thoroughly alive and extremely changeable. An ancient statue of Venus, for example, stood in

a different traditional context with the Greeks, who made it an object of veneration, than with the clerics of the Middle Ages, who viewed it as an ominous idol. Both of them, however, were equally confronted with its uniqueness, that is, its aura. Originally the contextual integration of art in tradition found its expression in the cult. We know that the earliest art works originated in the service of ritual—first the magical, then the religious kind. It is significant that the existence of the work of art with reference to its aura is never entirely separated from its ritual function. In other words, the unique value of the "authentic" work of art has its basis in ritual, the location of its original use value. (Benjamin 1969:223–24)

Setting aside for the moment Marxist concerns for "use value," I want to suggest that society does not produce art: artists do. Society, for its part, can only produce the importance, "reality," or "originality" of a work of art by piling up representations of it alongside. Benjamin believed that the reproductions of the work of art are produced because the work has a socially based "aura" about it, the "aura" being a residue of its origins in a primordial ritual. He should have reversed his terms. The work becomes "authentic" only after the first copy of it is produced. The reproductions *are* the aura, and the ritual, far from being a point of origin, *derives* from the relationship between the original object and its socially constructed importance. I would argue that this is the structure of the attraction in modern society, including the artistic attractions, and the reason the Grand Canyon has a touristic "aura" about it even though it did not originate in ritual.

Attractions and Structural Differentiation

In the tourists' consciousness, the attractions are not analyzed type by type. They appear sequentially, unfolding before the tourists so long as they continue sightseeing. The touristic value of a modern community lies in the way it organizes social, historical, cultural, and natural elements into a stream of impressions. Guidebooks contain references to all types of attractions, but the lively descriptions tend to be of the social materials. Modern society makes of itself its principal attraction in which the other attractions are embedded. Baedeker wrote of Paris:

Paris is not only the political metropolis of France, but also the center of the artistic, scientific, commercial, and industrial life of the nation. Almost every branch of French industry is represented here, from the fine-art handicrafts to the construction of powerful machinery . . .

The central quarters of the city are remarkably hustling and animated, but owing to the ample breadth of the new streets and boulevards and the fact that many of them are paved with asphalt or stone Paris is a far less noisy place than many other large cities. Its comparative tranquility, however, is often rudely interrupted by the discordant cries of the itinerant hawkers of wares of every kind, such as "old clothes" men, the vendors of various kinds of comestibles, the crockery-menders, the "fontaniers" (who clean and repair filters, etc.), the dog barbers, and newspaper-sellers. As a rule, however, they are clean and tidy in their dress, polite in manner, self-respecting, and devoid of the squalor and ruffianism which too often characterize their class. (1990:xxix–xxx)

Georg Simmel began the analysis of this modern form of social consciousness which takes as its point of departure social structure itself. Simmel wrote:

Man is a differentiating creature. His mind is stimulated by the differences between a momentary impression and the one which preceded it. Lasting impressions, impressions which differ only slightly from one another, impressions which take a regular and habitual course and show regular and habitual contrasts—all these use up, so to speak, less consciousness than does the rapid crowding of changing images, the sharp discontinuity in the grasp of a single glance, and the unexpectedness of onrushing impressions. These are the psychological conditions which the metropolis creates. With each crossing of the street, with the tempo and multiplicity of the economic, occupational and social life, the city sets up a deep contrast with the small town and rural life with reference to the sensory foundations of psychic life. (Wolff 1950:410)

Simmel claims to be working out an aspect of the *Gemeinschaft Gesellschaft* distinction. It would be more accurate to say that he is describing the difference between everyday life impressions, be they rural *or* urban, and the impressions of a strange place formed by a tourist on a visit, a vantage point Simmel knew well.[4]

Baedeker's and Simmel's stress on the work dimension of society is also found in touristic descriptions of New York City, which is always in the process of being rebuilt, and the waterfront areas of any city that has them. Similarly, Mideastern and North African peoples have traditionally made much use of their streets as places of work, and tourists from the Christian West seem to have inexhaustible fascination for places such as Istanbul, Tangiers, Damascus, and Casablanca, where they can see factories without walls.

Primitive social life is nearly totally exposed to outsiders who happen to be present. Perhaps some of our love for primitives is attached to this innocent openness.

Modern society, originally quite closed up, is rapidly restructuring or institutionalizing the rights of outsiders (that is, of individuals not functionally connected to the operation) to look into its diverse aspects. Institutions are fitted with arenas, platforms, and chambers set aside for the exclusive use of tourists. The courtroom is the most important institution in a democratic society. It was among the first to open to the outside and, I think, it will be among the first to close as the workings of society are increasingly revealed through the opening of other institutions to tourists. The New York Stock Exchange and the Corning Glass factory have specially designated visitors' hours, entrances, and galleries. Mental hospitals, army bases, and grade schools stage periodic open houses where not mere work but good work is displayed. The men who make pizza crusts by tossing the dough in the air often work in windows where they can be watched from the sidewalk. Construction companies cut peepholes into the fences around their work, nicely arranging the holes for sightseers of different heights. The becoming public of almost everything—a process that makes all people equal before the attraction—is a necessary part of the integrity of the modern social world.

Tourist Districts

Distinctive local attractions contain (just behind, beside, or embedded in the parts presented to the tourists) working offices, shops, services, and facilities: often an entire urban structure is operating behind its touristic front. Some of these touristic urban areas are composed of touristic *districts*. Paris is "made up" of the Latin Quarter, Pigalle, Montparnasse, Montmartre; San Francisco is made up of the Haight Ashbury, the Barbary Coast, and Chinatown; and London of Soho, Piccadilly Circus, Blackfriars, Covent Gardens, the Strand. Less touristically developed areas have only one tourist district and are, therefore, sometimes upstaged by it: the Casbah, Beverly Hills, Greenwich Village. An urban sociologist or an ethnographer might point out that cities are composed of much more than their tourist areas, but this is obvious. Even tourists are aware of this. More important is the way the tourist attractions appear on a regional base as a model of social structure, beginning with "suggested" or "recommended" *communities, regions,* and *neighborhoods*, and extending to matters of detail, setting the tourist up with a matrix to fill in with discoveries of typical little *markets, towns, restaurants,* and *people.* This touristic matrix assures that the social structure that is recomposed via the tour, while always partial, is nevertheless not a skewed or warped representation of reality. Once on tour, only the individual imagination can modify reality, and so long as the faculty of imagination is at rest, society appears such as it is.

The taxonomy of structural elements provided by the attractions is universal, not because it *already* contains everything it might contain but rather, because the logic behind it is potentially inclusive. It sets up relationships between elements (as between neighborhoods and their cities) which cross the artificial boundaries between levels of social organization, society, and culture, and culture and nature. Still, the resulting itineraries rarely penetrate lovingly into the precious details of a society as a Southern novelist might, peeling back layer after layer of local historical, cultural, and social facts, although this is the ideal of a certain type of snobbish tourism. Such potential exists in the structure of the tour, but it goes for the most part untapped. Attractions are usually organized more on the model of the filing system of a disinterested observer, like a scientist who separates passion from its object, reserving passion entirely for matters of method; or like a carpetbagging politician who calculates his rhetoric while reading a printout of the demographic characteristics of the region he wants to represent. In short, the tourist world is complete in its way, but it is constructed after the fashion of all worlds that are filled with people who are just passing through and know it.

The Differentiations of the Tourist World

Functioning *establishments* figure prominently as tourist attractions. Commercial, industrial, and business establishments are also basic features of social regions, or they are first among the elements from which regions are composed. Some, such as the Empire State Building, the now-defunct Les Halles in Paris, and Fisherman's Wharf in San Francisco, overwhelm their districts. Others fit together in a neat structural arrangement of little establishments that contribute to their district's special local character: flower shops, meat and vegetable markets, shoe repair shops, neighborhood churches. Unlike the Empire State Building, with its elevators expressly for sightseers, these little establishments may not be prepared for the outside visitors they attract. A priest who made his parish famous had this problem, but apparently he is adjusting to the presence of tourists:

> For a time, in fact, St. Boniface became an attraction for tourists and white liberals from the suburbs. Father Groppi recalled that he had sometimes been critical of the whites who overflowed the Sunday masses at St. Boniface and then returned to their suburban homes.
>
> "But now I can understand their problems," he said. "They come from conservative parishes and were tired of their parish organizations, the Holy Name Society and that sort of nonsense."[5]

Under normal conditions of touristic development, no social establishment ultimately resists conversion into an attraction, not even *domestic establishments*. Selected homes in the "Society Hill" section of downtown Philadelphia are opened annually for touristic visitation. Visitors to Japan are routinely offered the chance to enter, observe, and—to a limited degree—even participate in the households of middle-class families. Individual arrangements can he made with the French Ministry of Tourism to have coffee in a French home, and even to go for an afternoon drive in the country with a Frenchman of "approximately one's own social station."[6]

A version of sociology suggests that society is composed not of individuals but groups, and *groups*, too, figure as tourist attractions. Certain groups work up a show of their group characteristics (their ceremonies, settlement patterns, costumes, etc.) especially for the benefit of sightseers:

> At an open meeting yesterday of Indian businessmen, government officials and airline representatives, Dallas Chief Eagle, spokesman and director of the new United States Indian International Travel agency, said the cooperative hoped to be able to offer low-cost group tours to German tourists by June.[7]

Other groups, even other Indian groups, militantly resist such showmanship, even though their leaders are aware of their touristic potential, because this kind of behavior *for* tourists is widely felt to be degrading.[8] Given the multichanneled nature of human communication, these two versions of the group (the proud and the practical) need not be mutually exclusive. The following account suggests that a member of one of our recently emergent self-conscious minorities can do her own thing and do a thing for the tourists at the same time:

> New Jersey, Connecticut, and even Pennsylvania license plates were conspicuous around Tompkins Square yesterday, indicating that the Lower East Side's new hippie haven is beginning to draw out-of-state tourists.

> "You go to where the action is," a blond girl in shorts said through a thick layer of white lipstick. The girl, who said her name was Lisa Stern, and that she was a freshman at Rutgers University, added: "I used to spend weekends in Greenwich Village, but no longer." However, Lisa didn't find much action in Tompkins Square Park, the scene of a Memorial Day clash between about 200 hippies and the police . . . Yesterday there was no question any more as to a hippie's right to sit on the grass or to stretch out on it.

> Some tourists from New Jersey were leaning over the guardrail enclosing a patch of lawn, much as if they were visiting a zoo, and stared at a man with tattooed arms and blue-painted face who gently waved at them while the bongo drums were throbbing. (Hoffman 1967:3)

Other groups—the Pennsylvania "Dutch," the Amanas, Basques, and peasants everywhere—probably fall somewhere in between resistance and acquiescence to tourism, or they vacillate from self-conscious showiness to grudging acceptance of it.

Perhaps because they have a human being inside, *occupations* are popular tourist attractions. In some areas, local handicrafts would have passed into extinction except for the intervention of mass tourism and the souvenir market:

> Palekh boxes are formed from papier-mâché and molded in the desired shape on a wood form. A single artist makes the box, coats it with layers of black lacquer, paints his miniature picture, adds final coats of clear lacquer and signs his name and the date. Each box represents two to three days' work. Some of Palekh's 150 artists work at home . . . I watched Constantine Bilayev, an artist in his fifties, paint a fairytale scene he might have been doing for his grandchildren. It illustrated the story of a wicked old woman with a daughter she favored and a stepdaughter she hated. She sent the stepdaughter into the woods to gather firewood, hoping harm would befall the girl. Instead, the stepdaughter triumphed over every adversity. (Chapman 1969:29)

In addition to this cute side of occupational sightseeing, there is a heavy, modern workaday aspect. In the same community with the box makers, there are *real* young ladies triumphing over adversity while serving as tourist attractions. The report continues:

But the main attraction of this city of 400,000 people is the Ivanovo Textile Factory, an industrial enormity that produces some 25,000,000 yards of wool cloth a year. The factory represents an investment of US$55 million. The factory's machinery makes an ear-shattering din. Ranks of machines take the raw wool and convert it into coarse thread, and successive ranks of devices extrude the thread into ever-finer filaments. The weaving machines clang in unison like a brigade on the march—Raz, Dva, Raz, Dva, Raz, Dva as an unseen Russian sergeant would count it out. The 7,500 workers are mostly young and mostly female. A bulletin board exhorts them to greater production in honor of the Lenin centenary.

Along with handicraft and specialized industrial work, there are other occupational attractions including glassblowers, Japanese pearl divers, cowboys, fishermen, Geisha girls, London chimney sweeps, gondoliers, and sidewalk artists. Potentially, the entire division of labor in society can be transformed into a tourist attraction. In some districts of Manhattan, even the men in gray flannel suits have been marked off for touristic attention.

Connecting the urban areas of society are *transportation networks*, segments and intersections of which are tourist attractions. Examples are: the London Bridge, the Champs Elysées, Hollywood and Vine, Ponte Vecchio, the Golden Gate, Red Square, the canals of Venice and Amsterdam, Broadway, the Gate of Heavenly Peace, the Rue de Rivoli, the Spanish Steps, Telegraph Avenue, the Atlantic City Boardwalk, the Mont Blanc tunnel, Union Square, and New England's covered bridges. Along these lines is the follow-

Gondoliers ferry tourists through the canals of Venice. (Photo by George Gmelch)

ing comment on an attraction that is not well known but for which some hopes have been raised:

> The city of Birmingham recently opened its first expressway. To do so it had to slice a gash through famed Red Mountain in order to complete construction and get people in and out of the city in a hurry. To the drivers of Birmingham the freeway means a new convenience, but to the thousands of visitors the giant cut at the crest of the mountain has become a fascinating stopping place . . . a new and exciting tourist attraction.[9]

In addition to roads, squares, intersections, and bridges, *vehicles* that are restricted to one part of the worldwide transportation network also figure as attractions: rickshaws, gondolas, San Francisco's cable cars, and animal-powered carts everywhere.

Finally, the system of attractions extends as far as society has extended its *public works*, not avoiding things that might well have been avoided:

> A London sightseeing company has added a tour of London's public lavatories to its schedule. The firm, See Britain, said the lavatories tour will begin Sunday and cost five shillings (60 cents). It will include lavatories in the city and the West End. A spokesman said visitors will see the best Victorian and Edwardian lavatories in the areas with a guide discussing the style of the interiors, architecture, hours of opening and history.[10]

The presentation of the inner workings of society's nether side is, of course, the Paris sewer tour.

Although tourists need not be consciously aware of this, the thing they go to see is society and its works. The societal aspect of tourist attractions is hidden behind their fame, but this fame cannot change their origin in social structure. Given the present sociohistorical epoch, it is not a surprise to find that tourists believe sightseeing is a leisure activity, and fun, even when it requires more effort and organization than many jobs. In a marked contrast to the grudging acquiescence that may characterize the relation of the individual to industrial work, individuals happily embrace the attitudes and norms that lead them into a relationship with society through the sightseeing act. In being presented as a valued object through a so-called "leisure" activity that is thought to be "fun," society is renewed in the heart of the individual through warm, open, unquestioned relations, characterized by a near absence of alienation when compared with other contemporary relationships. This is, of course, the kind of relationship of individual and society that social scientists and politicians think is necessary for a strong society, and they are probably correct in their belief.

Tourist attractions in their natural, unanalyzed state may not appear to have any coherent infrastructure uniting them, and insofar as it is through the attraction that the tourist apprehends society, society may not appear to have coherent structure either. It is not my intention here to over-organize the touristic consciousness. It exhibits the deep structure, which is social structure that I am describing here, but this order need never be perceived as such in its totality. Consciousness and the integration of the individual into the modern world require only that one attraction be linked to one other: a district to a community, or an establishment to a district, or a role to an establishment. Even if only a single linkage is grasped in the immediate present, this solitary link is the starting point for an endless spherical system of connections that is society and the world, with the individual at one point on its surface.

Source: From *The Tourist: A New Theory of the Leisure Class*, [1976] 1999. Reprinted with permission of the author and University of California Press.

Notes

[1] Detailed microstudies of social structure are provided by Hall (1969) and Sommer (1969).

[2] *New York Times*, 30 June 1969, p. 1.

[3] Ibid., 22 May 1967, p. 39.

[4] See Simmel's essay on "The Stranger" (Wolff 1950:410).

[5] *New York Times*, 12 April 1970, p. 34.

[6] From my fieldnotes.

[7] *International Tribune* (Paris), 26 March 1971, p. 7.

[8] Interestingly, behavior *for* tourists is only felt to be degrading by members of already exploited minorities. Middle-class hippies and radicals seem to enjoy working in front of the camera. Perhaps leaders of exploited minorities teach non-cooperation with tourists because this is one of the only areas in which members of these minorities can dramatize self-determination.

[9] News release dated 27 April 1970 from "Operation New Birmingham," a civic group, quoted in "Images of America: Radical Feeling Remains Strong in the Cities." *New York Times*, 24 May 1970, p. 64.

[10] "For Tourists Who Want to See All," *International Herald Tribune,* 4 November 1970.

References

Baedeker, Karl. 1900. *Paris and Environs*. 14th rev. edition. Leipzig: Karl Baedeker Publisher.

Benjamin, Walter. 1969. *Illuminations*, ed. Hannah Arendt, trans. Harry Zohn. New York: Schocken.

Chapman, Irwin M. 1969. "Visit to Two Russian Towns." *New York Times*, 23 February 1969, section 10.

Durkheim, Émile. 1938. *The Rules of Sociological Method*, trans. S. A. Solovay and J. H. Mueller. New York: Free Press.

Goffman, Erving. 1963. *Behavior in Public Places: Notes on the Social Organization of Gatherings*. New York: Free Press.

———. 1971. *Relations in Public: Microstudies of the Public Order*. New York: Basic Books.

Hall, Edward T. 1969. *The Hidden Dimension*. Garden City, NY: Anchor Books.

Hoffman, Paul. 1967. "Hippie's Hangout Draws Tourists." *New York Times*, 5 June 1967.

Sommer, Robert. 1969. *Personal Space: The Behavioral Basis of Design*. Englewood Cliffs, NJ: Prentice-Hall.

Wolff, Kurt H., ed. and trans. 1950. *The Sociology of Georg Simmel*. Glencoe, IL: Free Press.

5

Tourism and Terrorism: An Intimate Equivalence

Peter Phipps

Defending the (insert nation here) Way of Life

Since an earlier version of this essay was published in 1999, the connections between tourism and terrorism have been powerfully reinforced and intensified. The series of events and public gestures that the White House has successfully had defined in the endlessly repeated phrase "the war on terror" have brought this link to the forefront of global media consciousness. This has been epitomized by the (second) bombing of the World Trade Center in 2001, this time using commuter aircraft and their passengers as the explosive device, and the bombing of the Sari tourist nightclub in Bali in 2002. In addition, a host of related attacks on tourist aircraft (El Al in Kenya), foiled attacks, and the related renewal of security around all forms of transport have almost normalized a new level of intensification of the relationship between tourism and terrorism.

It has perhaps become even more important than previously to emphasize that there may be something amiss in the global distribution of mobility and wealth that tourism so overtly exemplifies. This un-homely state of things is increasingly evident in the state of public political discourse from George Bush Junior's aggressive oil war against Iraq "defending America" to the lesser mimicry of his international vassals. In the wake of the Bali bombing the Australian Prime Minister declared his determination to defend "The Australian Way of Life" of unrestricted, ostentatiously mobile leisure, while simultaneously keeping asylum seekers locked in concentration camps in the Australian desert and neighboring islands. The populist rhetoric of soft-authoritarian regimes of this nature—protecting borders from "them" and ways of life for "us"—has made border-crossing a central theme of political discourse. The sun, surf, and good-times tourists killed in Bali became martyrs of this national lifestyle cause, and asylum seekers approaching beaches in leaky boats a scourge slanderously associated with terrorism.

Tourorists

This concern with attacks on the sanctity of tourism is not just a very recent phenomenon. The news that a Norwegian backpacker was beheaded by members of the Al-Faran movement at an unidentified Himalayan hideaway in October 1995 had a powerful resonance in the Euro-American media. Media accounts of the execution portray an extremist, Islamic, Kashmiri-separatist terrorist group transgressing all bounds of decency, law, and order by beheading the very pinnacle of international innocence and neutrality: a Norwegian backpacker trekking through the Himalayas. This incident, and the threat to the four surviving foreign hostages, held the continued attention of the Western media as an attack on the assumed right of First World citizen-tourists to penetrate all corners of a world "made safe for tourism."[1] The indignity of this act is further compounded by the common sense assumption that tourists are, by definition, innocent of the implications of global geopolitics.

Anthropologist Valene Smith gives this truism a twist when she describes tourism as "the single largest peaceful movement of people across cultural boundaries in the history of the world" (Smith 1977:12). A militarized consciousness unfolds where tourism becomes noteworthy for being "non-war" while sharing some of the symptoms and anxieties of war: massive population movements, the crossing of cultural boundaries; a cheerful invasion.

That violent incident in Kashmir is just one among a litany of mishaps, murders, and hostage crises involving tourists that suggest a sustained consideration of the interrelations between the categories tourist and terrorist, and between tourism and violence more broadly, is in order. In the course of this project, originally just on tourist discourses, tourists have kept cropping up in the news media as victims of acts of anti-state, and less clearly explicable, terror. This chapter is a tentative exploration of the connections between these two things: tourist discourse and tourist death, and the logic that makes the representations of those events meaningful. I argue that tourist ideologies are implicated in the structuring of the violent times in which we dwell. Mentioning tourists and terrorists in the same tenor unsettles already-tenuous notions of guilt and innocence, citizen and criminal, consumer and killer, victim and perpetrator. While Said and others have challenged the discursive effects and political deployments of the laden term "terrorist" as opposed to "(our) freedom fighting allies," tourists, their unassuming doppelgänger, have escaped sustained attention while being at least as politically and morally charged a category. "Dead tourists" are a more significant trope than one might ever have expected.[2]

Interviews with backpackers and other tourists, their correspondence and photography, articulate a system of thought that could be characterized as extremist in its commitment to notions of authenticity and experience. The stridency with which many tourists have been willing to assert, or just assume, their right to experience the Other at any time and place resonates with an imperious arrogance that is almost militant. The underbelly of this logic is ironically expressed in a "discourse of touristic shame" (Frow 1991), a general condemnation of tourists by tourists for ruining that authentic Otherness that they have traveled so far to experience. Just as the supposed terrorist comes armed with extreme ideological commitments and powerful connections, so does the tourist; just as the ultranationalist/religious fanatic detests tourists, so do tourists; just as the terrorist craves anonymity in the crowd, so does the tourist. These strange equivalences are captured in a mainstream popular Hindi film by Mani Ratnam. Set in a Kashmir torn apart by insurgency, the local Kashmiri guide asks the hero and his girlfriend, "Tum tourist ho ya terrorist ho?" ("Are you tourists or terrorists?"), concluding that only the latter come here now.[3] The differences between tourists and terrorists, war and peace, may well be less than imagined.

Every traveler who has passed through the security cordon of an airport and been subject to the technologies of luggage x-ray and metal detectors, sniffer-dogs and customs interrogation, security cameras, and the ubiquitous question "did anybody else pack for you?" should know something of the connection between tourism and terrorism. Indeed these features of travel have become so common as to pass almost without question, a naturalized artifact of the tenuous relationship between travel and violence. These concentrated technologies of transition are designed largely to regulate the flow of travelers under the scopic control of the state, represented by its functionaries: customs, immigration, police. This is the point at which the State attempts to regulate the flow of citizens, aliens, commodities, narcotics, biological materials, firearms and other prohibited substances: symbolic or potential violations against its authority. These places are also the site of enormous potential damage directed against that authority by acts of terrorist violence, both directly and by extension, in an attack on "the people" whose protection is the official rationale for intrusive regulation.

Security cameras, x-rays, and random searches are designed to screen out these potential incendiary threats. Ironically, while the Western state is officially acting to protect mobility through this intense surveillance, it is simultaneously structurally threatened by mobility, even as it is bound to protect its sanctity (for its own citizens) and is utterly dependent on it. Governments express enormous anxiety about illegal aliens and immigration, smuggling, contraband ideas, diseases, politics, and so on. Ironically the "freedom to travel" was one of the key, and most seductive, distinguishing features of the "Free World" in the Cold War propaganda battles, and features as one of those much-ignored articles of the Universal Declaration of Human Rights. Deleuze and Guattari's "Nomadology" thesis articulates the structure of state ambivalence toward movement, equated here with the tireless movement of the "war machine," exemplified for them by (somewhat dehistoricized) Mongol hordes.

> One of the fundamental tasks of the State is to striate the space over which it reigns, or to utilize smooth spaces as a means of communication in the service of striated space. It is a vital concern of every State not only to vanquish nomadism, but to control migrations and, more generally, to establish a zone of rights over an entire "exterior," over all of the flows traversing the ecumenon. (Deleuze and Guattari 1986:59–60)[4]

Airports, train stations, and border crossing points are crucial markers of regulatory attempts to control movement. These are sites where the discipline and authorization of movement—stamping passports, searching bags, and so on—are always possibly about to be attacked in radical transgressions directed against that very logic of regulation—blowing up airplanes, taking hostages, smuggling contraband. The aim of the tourist, or legitimated traveler, is to pass through these points of surveillance and control as quickly and smoothly as possible with the authorization of all the authorities concerned. In a dark parallel, the terrorist or other illegitimates in transit (smugglers, illegal aliens) attempt to slip around or through this regulatory authority in the disguise of tourists; in the case of the terrorist to deliver to such legitimacy and omnipotence a mocking blow. Diller and Scofidio quote Freud as writing, "A great part of the pleasure of travel lies in the fulfillment of early wishes to escape the family and especially the father" (1994:41). At this end of the twentieth century, it is perhaps a great deal harder to "escape the father" as his capacity to police has become ever more sophisticated and insistent (though of course Deleuze and Guattari warn us in the tome mentioned above against such Oedipal reductions!).

The ever-expanding list of incidents involving dead tourists, most recently in Egypt, is a mark of the strategic importance of tourism in global and regional warfare and terror.[5] This significance extends beyond the fact that tourism has become the biggest single trade item in the global economy, but is located in the very logic at the heart of tourism itself. Tourists, particularly from the United States, have become acutely aware of their status as privileged targets of terror attacks, and the U.S. overseas travel industry is extremely sensitive to dramatic international conflicts. This was illustrated most clearly in the Gulf War when travel from Europe, but more especially the United States, came to a virtual standstill from a widespread fear of "terrorist" reprisals against First World soft targets. In this context it is little wonder that a Wexco publication, *The Complete Traveler's Guide*, which has such chapters as "Executive Targets," "Surviving a Hijacking," and "Fill the Bath; It's a Civil War" has been consistently reprinted from 1980 to 1994. Peter Savage's *The Safe Travel Book* recommends the following precautions when in countries with a "security problem":

> In public spaces, such as a restaurant, sit where you cannot be seen from the outside and try to sit on the far side of a column, a wall, or other structure—away from the entrance. You want to be inconspicuous, out of the line of fire and protected from any bomb blast. The same precautions should be taken at hotels, at clubs, and even sitting on the deck of a yacht in the harbor. (Savage 1993)

While something of a cliché, the construction and loathing of the loud, stupid, gringo stereotype (or Australian in Bali, English in Majorca, etc.) carries a different nuance in the light of the "savage" advice above. The loud and obvious tourist gives away the undercover operation of the "sensitive" cultural tourist (the fantasy of being invisible or undisturbing), reducing both of them to crass consumer. While this is often expressed as a nationality cliché, the issue is more one of class, which harks back to Wordsworth's condemnation of Cook's tours and the railway that brought working-class people tramping into his precious Lake District. It would be interesting to know if there was a similarly resentful response on the part of colonial officials at the instigation of Cook's tours to the Orient from the late 1860s (Mitchell 1991:21). It is reassuring for self-conscious tourists to displace their self-loathing, or at least their vague intuition of local hostilities, onto their "othered" fellow travelers. Kaplan (1996:62) quotes Kincaid describing her expatriate Antiguan perceptions and memories of tourists that confirm the very worst touristic anxieties of being "uncovered" by the perceptions of local people:

> An ugly thing, that is what you become when you become a tourist, an ugly, empty thing, a stupid thing, a piece of rubbish pausing here and there to gaze at this and taste that, and it will never occur to you that the people who inhabit the place in which you have just paused cannot stand you . . . That the native does not like the tourist is not hard to explain. For every native of every place is a potential tourist, and every tourist is a native of somewhere . . . But some natives—most natives in the world—cannot go anywhere . . . They are too poor to escape the reality of their lives; and they are too poor to live properly in the place where they live, which is the very place you, the tourist, want to go. (Kincaid 1988:17–9)

As the ideal operative works under cover, so too should the ideal tourist. Drawing attention to the presence of tourists, blowing their cover, can itself be an invitation to danger for tourist operations. The danger is in the very literal sense of making tourists a more obvious target for overcharging, intimidation, pickpocketing, and at the more extreme end of the spectrum, attack, murder, or hostage-taking. Just as immediate, though less obviously dramatic, is the danger that being conspicuous presents to the tourist fantasy of invisibility.

The tourist mission of penetrating the everyday life of the Other to observe and record their difference is disrupted when the tourist operative is uncovered: an army of touts selling souvenirs, offering everything from taxis to prostitutes, moves in to end the illusion of invisibility in an episode that causes tourists grief, confusion, anger, and very often acute embarrassment.

> Camouflage can be as tactical for the tourist as it is for the soldier. This is all the more difficult, however, in that the tourist and the soldier alike are "marked bodies, unable to blend into the crowd . . . These excluded figures—the tourist and the soldier—assume a similar representational role on foreign soil: they are both living symbols of another nationalism. Each one is seen as a performative body, measured against the image of its national stereotype." (Diller and Scofidio 1994:24)

As "a living symbol of another nationalism," tourists are perhaps more like an intelligence agent than an invading soldier. The "good" tourist who blends as much as possible with the crowd has a mission as firmly etched on the mind as any intelligence operative: seek the authentically Other; record it as experience, photography, souvenir, and written word; and return home to file a report as anecdote, recollection, and the personal transformation of having "been there." Like the intelligence operative or the foreign soldier, the tourist has passed out of the security of the relatively fixed identity of home and into a far less clearly defined liminal zone.[6] To leave home and journey to distant places as a tourist is to enter a symbolic limbo: not at home and yet partly still there; elsewhere but only passing through on an always-returning-home trajectory. The tourist in transit—and the tourist is always in transit—is at once nobody nowhere, as well as the bearer of certain nationalities, credit cards, and currencies. Just as the individual identity of the traveling subject is unsettled, a different set of more anonymous identifications come into play. Tourists become value in motion, both in their regular operation as consumers, and in their more rarefied symbolic values as exchange objects embodying another nationalism, for example as "normalizers of relations" (U.S. visitors to China post-Nixon) or as hostages, such as in the Kashmir situation.

Experience and the Real

> I went to get an authentic experience of another culture, to get away from my own usual experiences of Western life, things and tastes. (Backpacker in interview)[7]

"Experience" is an elusive quality that, regardless of its intangibility, is a powerful rationale for some of the otherwise inexplicably strange and dangerous pursuits of contemporary tourism, from bungee jumping to "disaster tours." Experience can refer both to an event of a particular kind, and can also be communicated as an air adhering to a particularly "experienced" individual. Bruce Robbins provides a critique of the "epistemological privilege of experience" as a "domain of direct truth," "a kind of pristine contact between the subject and the reality in which this subject is immersed" (Robbins 1986:148). Tourism is one of modernity's great compensations; it is the space where the fantasy of reforging that connection between the self and the world still tenuously hangs on.

For the most part, First World tourists share the modernist concern about the loss of a realm of authentic experience beleaguered by the extension of the market to touch the most basic aspects of social life. This "loss of innocence" is a familiar Romantic trope for representing the experience of other cultures, deployed by everyone from novelists to anthropologists and other travel writers. The astute tourist is constantly on guard to protect his or her travels, particularly their documentation in letters, postcards, journals, reminiscences, and the photographs that accompany them, from the taint of "inauthenticity" that invariably threatens where modern tourism is present. The primary fear here is that the tourist experience is fundamentally and irretrievably inauthentic. This is what cultural tourists, backpackers in particular, are concerned to avoid above all else in making the distinction between their own search for, and access to, "authentic" experience and "those other tourists," characterized as unable to pursue anything but the most banal and artificial forms of experience. The following quote illustrates this sense of "communion" or authentic experience of one backpacker in India:

> In Varanasi I would just sit by the Ganges, near the burning ghats, near a
> sadhu or a monk, or someone playing flute . . . I went into the Ganges for

Western backpackers walk the streets of Varanasi, India. (Photo by Sharon Gmelch)

> a bath and visited the temples there. Things were just so real there; life,
> death, pilgrims from the villages dressed in traditional clothes. I didn't
> feel like a tourist, I felt like another pilgrim. Nobody was hassling me or
> trying to get things . . . It was the India I came to experience, less artificial.

This fixation on the pursuit of authenticity finds expression in a slightly different form in discursive accounts of the "purity," or loss of it, of nature on the one hand, and cultures on the other. This notion of purity is set in opposition to that which is modern, capitalist, bureaucratized, and developed. Nature and folk culture were added to the tourist's multiple interests and motivations, which had already included notions of high culture, history, education, and physical rest and recreation, with the fashionable 1920s interest in nature and the authentically "ethnic" as repositories of the nonmodern (Graburn 1989:30–4). This theme crops up from time to time as the "untouched" tribe or village, or the hidden land, always on the verge of destruction by contact with modern, industrial societies and their values.

This concern with an authentic experience of the Other, untainted by the "modern" themes of alienation, mobility, and money, is not limited to the conceptual framework of backpackers alone. Professional travel writers, photographers, and social scientists are not immune to the allure of the possibility of "authentic" experiences of other cultures; indeed much anthropology is predicated on such assumptions. In her "Third World Landscapes," a discussion of tourism in India, Barbara Weightman assumes that an "authentic experience" of India is waiting to be uncovered: "communion with the ambience of Indian life worlds" (1988:232). She asserts that mass tourists miss out on these "real" experiences by being encapsulated in a "cultural bubble" in which they are shielded from any meaningful or spontaneous contact with local people. Weightman believes there is a "zone of authenticity" (1988:235) to be found in cities and villages. In Varanasi this zone is the Ganges and the Ghats, in Jaipur the pink city, in Delhi the old city. Her "zones" correspond remarkably closely to those depicted by travel brochures and guidebooks, uncritically reproducing the banalities of the romanticist travelogue.

Death and Danger

> What gives value to travel is fear. It breaks down a kind of internal structure . . . stripped of all our crutches, deprived of our masks . . . we are completely on the surface of ourselves . . . This is the most obvious benefit of travel. (Camus 1962:26)

The main feature that distinguishes backpackers from other tourists is the disproportionate value they place on the physical sufferings and dangers of travel on the cheap as a marker of value.[8] There is an extensive vocabulary of renunciative strategies and gestures that attach enormous status to poverty, hardship, and illness as signifiers of the authenticity of an experience. Backpackers engage in a competitive recounting of austerities undertaken and survived, be it a three-day train trip without a seat or a bout of typhoid. Every suffering is valuable because it can be reconstituted later in a powerful narrative strategy adding to a sense of true connection with alterity. This focus on the austerities of "authentic" travel (also described in Teas 1974), often leading backpackers to absurd extremes, is highlighted in this comment from the letter of a backpacker in India:

> You would not believe what an image trip the younger ones (travelers) are on. People going out of their way to check you out, to see if you're scumming it enough, or if you're staying at the "right" cheapie hotels, etc. . . . We mentioned to some people that we were flying from Varanasi to Kathmandu and you should have seen their faces, all snooty, looking down their noses at us. How dare we avoid the grueling thirty-hour bus trip!

The emphasis on self-testing can be seen as an example of voluntarily undergoing a "rite of passage," acting out a ritual space signifying a break from one life-stage to another, or proving to themselves that they have the strength to deal with a major crisis in their lives. Graburn takes up Van Gennep's *Rites of Passage* (1909), suggesting that his general framework of rites of separation from the ordinary, a period of marginality and rites of reincorporation, "is applicable to all forms of tourism" (Graburn 1983:13). By his account those most likely to engage in "rite of passage tourism" include young people deferring the responsibilities of adulthood, often in an intermediate stage between completing further education and embarking on a career or making commitments to a family, and those recently divorced, widowed, or making major career changes. It is characterized by prolonged absences from home, and often arduous travels and activities involving some form of self-testing, attributes that Graburn compares to the spirit quest of pre-invasion, North American indigenous societies.[9] This could be seen as a postcolonial context as a "Kiplingesque" quest to test the mettle of one's independence (whiteness) in the fire of the exotic, or one's national self in a space other than that nation.[10]

One of the sites of this distancing from ordinary life is the more conscious awareness of encounters with dangers or the possibility of some danger in exploring the unknown. In India the prime danger the traveler perceives is the risk of contracting some debilitating or even fatal disease. Most of the backpackers I have interviewed had experienced either fevers or diarrhea.[11] One claims to have been close to death from a serious infection and another from typhoid, despite the precautions available to the Westerner in the form of immunization (an activity that could be seen as a metaphoric blessing, protection, or granting of power by the home culture to the traveling individual). Travelers in India constantly discuss illnesses, symptoms, cures, and so on. These range from the frequent jokes, "When the bottom falls out of your world, come to Calcutta and watch the world fall out through your bottom" (reported in Hutnyk 1996:54), to discussions of the most appropriate forms of medication and treatment for particular ailments. Status is attached to those who have suffered the worst or most gruesome afflictions, lost the most weight, or come the closest to death. It is as if the very ill person has succeeded in moving as far as possible away from our everyday world that includes health as normal and a civic (bourgeois) duty. Unlike the "closed" hygienic environments of mass-tourists, backpackers valorize an openness to the environments they travel through, including the microbial.

This logic meets its penultimate expression in the significatory power of Death. There is, ultimately, nothing more indisputably "real" than the fact of death experienced either close at hand, or personally. Hutnyk (1996:63–4) confirms that in the early 1990s, a rumor spread like wildfire on the backpacker circuit that Tony Wheeler, editor and publisher of the ubiquitous *Lonely Planet* travel guide empire, had died violently in transit, either crushed by an elephant or in a bus crash. The rumor took hold on a collective imaginative theme: as his guides so meticulously reproduce backpacker ideologies and mark the limits of possibility, his imagined death confirms the authenticating power of his gritty guidebooks. There is a cult quality to these books, commonly referred to as "the Bible," which demands a sacrificial savior in the great Judeo-Christian tradition. Wheeler remains alive, well, and very rich.

Death itself becomes a macabre and fascinating tourist site. No trip to India is complete without a ghoulish visit to the burning ghats at sites along the Ganges River (in Irian Jaya/West Papua it is the preserved bodies of ancestors, in Borneo dried heads, etc.). This fascination is due in part to the state-regulated segregation and professionalization of death and dying in the overdeveloped world, which adds further fuel to the notion that death, or in this case the dead, are the ultimate signifier of the real. Ian Catanach (1997) described a collection of nineteenth-century British postcards sent from India during an outbreak of plague that show piles of corpses in one image, while another shows patients dying in a more orderly fashion in a specially constructed plague hospital.[12] While such a postcard would probably be regarded as in poor taste today, it does demonstrate a certain continuity of interest in "death elsewhere," which was far more likely to actually visit nineteenth-century travelers than it is today's.

In 1992 Italian travel agent Massimo Beyerle was offering clients visits to an unspecified (due to the obvious contingencies) "October war zone" (Diller and Scofidio 1994:136). He was offering to take tourists to the ultimate reality, "places shown on the television news" for US$25,000 per person. His services included armed guards, a doctor, flak jackets, and other necessities for visiting "the edge zones of combat." Possible sites included "the south of Lebanon, Dubrovnik or Vukovar; as close as possible to the places shown on the television news, so that our clients can see and speak with the people, and see for themselves the damages caused by the war." This is not a new phenomenon. Mitchell (1991:57) describes how, in 1830, entrepreneurs from Marseilles took tourists to Algiers to watch the colorful spectacle of the ongoing French bombardment of that city from the comfort of a large barge at sea.

The themes of death, the destructive forces of modern warfare, and the dangers of the road are an inescapable part of tourist thought. A recent edition of the women's magazine *Marie Claire* features three stories of luckless tourists who died on holiday. Titled "Trouble in Paradise," the article warns, "that long-planned trip to paradise can turn into a holiday in hell" (1995:55–8). Ironically, as the quote from Camus, above, reminds us, this threat of death and danger is something that tourism relishes so as to retain its imaginative power as a space for reconnection with that "real" that remains so elusive, and thoroughly denied, in the order of highly stratified, regulated and abstracted capitalist postmodern society.

Tourists and Commodities: On Exchange

For backpackers, their highly contested in-group status on the road is determined by a checklist of factors. High on the list are contact with the "authentic" Other, one's nonchalant relationship to time and disciplined work, the ability to live on very little money, distance from Western values and culture, a lack of materialism, and length of travels and stay in one place. Backpackers value those factors that can be seen to set them apart from the conventional experiences of tourism; their lack of availability to the mass tourist, their relative danger or lack of certainty of outcome, and the sincerely noncommercial nature of the exchange (this last being something the backpacker is never quite at ease about yet determined to assert). These are themes of the utmost importance in the backpacker status game; they authenticate experience. Ironically, experiences then become a kind of commodity, exchangeable for status in the travel subculture.

The language of exchange is an appropriate one for this encounter as it so much underlies the anxieties of tourists about being exploited in their ignorance of local conditions and values. Many tourists/backpackers complain of never feeling they had contact with locals outside of these commercial boundaries, some even feeling outright hostility toward all local hospitality workers as "exploitative rip-off merchants." The small army of touts, competitive rickshaw-wallahs and salesmen with which most tourists have to contend at some point, can leave those who perceive themselves as having come for more personal and "meaningful" interactions with locals (that is, outside the market) a little frustrated with the consistency of their hosts' capacity to see them primarily as the source of lucrative transactions (more so where tourism is one of the only means of supplementing local economies). Even where noncommercial motives are assumed in an interaction with locals, the backpacker tends to remain wary of any suggestion of a commercial or financial nature as a threat to her or his sense of engagement in an "authentic" friendship. Conversely, the market can be one of the main measures of authenticity, and the struggle to only pay the "local price" for a commodity or service can be seen as an achievement of the Real.

The relations of exchange are reversed somewhat in the situation where tourists are taken hostage, such as the European backpackers in Kashmir. It is precisely because of their high exchange value, in the image economy of the media and in the public relations economy of international diplomatic relations, that they are captured in the first place. Ironically the quest of these backpackers to add maximum value to their adventures, by traveling way off the beaten track and even into "dangerous" territory, sees their own bodies converted into a form of exchange value, in this case held by the militants against the Indian government.[13] The high anxiety of national governments, underwritten by national media attention in such instances, illustrates the significant resources that back up the itineraries of most backpackers. While they may often carry little money, holding certain passports has a real value on the ground that mostly confers an assumed protection; that harm done to a foreigner from a powerful country will make for terrible trouble.[14] This logic of course being reversed in the hostage situation, where the citizens of the most powerful nation, the United States, seem to carry the highest exchange value.[15]

In the recent case of the three backpacker hostages in Cambodia, it may well have been the fact of their national composition that caused their final demise. After a Khmer Rouge attack on a train traveling to a coastal town, the guerrillas rounded up all the foreign nationals on board. The Vietnamese passengers were summarily shot on the spot, one can only assume on the assumption that they were agents of the anti-Khmer Rouge Vietnamese government. The remaining foreigners, three unsuspecting male backpackers who had been headed south for famed marijuana and adventure on the frontier of anarchy, comprised an Australian, a Frenchman, and an Englishman. Consistent with backpacker logic, they had ignored the advice of their expatriates that it was too dangerous to travel where they planned. The first two carried particular value as subjects of neocolonial players in Cambodian politics: Australia and the country's former colonial ruler, France. Both countries were sponsors of the Cambodian peace accord, and were major sponsors of the Hun Sen regime after the breakdown of relations with the Khmer Rouge, supplying aid, weapons, and military training for government forces. The hostages were potentially powerful bargaining tools with the Cambodian government, which could be expected to pay dearly for the return of the citizens of its sponsor states. As it so happened they became pawns in a complex geopolitical game and were ultimately executed, arguably because the Cambodian government could extract more value from them dead than alive.[16]

Tourists are occasional targets of terrorist attacks and kidnappings primarily because they are available. However there is a more complex dynamic at work as well. The media value of tourists as hostages is not only based on their coming from a powerful or wealthy country, but also preys on common perceptions in media-saturated cultures of their apparent innocence. The tourist is almost by definition an innocent abroad; a consumer suckling infantlike at the great breast of the world. At the same time, by turning every-

Graffiti on a wall at base of Guell Park, Barcelona, reads "Tourist, you are the terrorist." (Photo by Danielle T. Furfaro)

thing around them into exchange value, tourists are necessarily guilty and undeserving in the terms of their own discourses of authentic and uncorrupted otherness. Tourists are caught in a dialectic of innocence whereby their very innocence as consumers propels them into being guilty participants, even agents, of global exploitation and corruption. This clearly seems to have been the combination that served as justification for the killing of tourists at Luxor, Egypt at the end of 1997.[17]

My interviews with tourists suggest that at least my youthful sample group traveling in Asia feel trapped within this dialectic. I suspect by imputation that tourists of all sorts feel guilty and anxious at some level about being tourists. Hostage taking and murder confirm this dramatic anxiety in a real and deadly way.

Tourist Shame, or Dealing with Homicide: A Conclusion

MacCannell (1976) analyzed the structure of tourist semiotics over two decades ago. Primarily, tourists are engaged in a quest for the real or authentic site. He pointed to the simple fact that this real could not be found without convenient markers to present it as such. He argued that the astute observer (theorist) would notice a productive apparatus behind this staging of the authentic that was in fact the "really real." This apparatus would in turn, in many cases, become a tourist site: the sewers of Paris tour, tours of Hollywood studio lots, tours of "real working life," and so on. The subsequent critiques of MacCannell's work have of course pointed to the privileged position he accords to the theorist (himself) who can somehow escape the world of artifice and show, and delve straight to reality itself: tourists are dupes and theorists are smarter than tourists.[18] The greatest irony is that MacCannell's theory repeats one of the primary motifs of late twentieth-century tourism: the claim of privileged access to the real shored up with the assertion of being different from the mass of other tourists. Obviously intellectuals, acutely status-conscious bourgeois creatures that we tend to be, suffer far more severely from this painful delusion than do those tourists more resigned to, or even celebratory of, or maybe even, as MacCannell would have it, oblivious to, their status as consumers of a staged authenticity.

Not surprisingly, it is the former, bourgeois intellectual, touristic sensibility that predominates in representations of tourist activity and consciousness: travel books, ethnographies, documentaries, postcards, and other technologies of dissemination. Two strategies are almost universal in these technologies:

1. Deny the presence of mass, or any other tourists, in the visited locale. This is most commonly practiced in photography where frequent attempts are made to erase other tourists, and any other signs of capitalist modernity, from the frame; a symbolic destruction of the signs of the self and its possible multiplication. Any challenge to the claim that being here in this place is a unique, unrepeatable event, any rupture that might shatter the aura of the real, must be denied, erased, and refused.

2. In those moments when the presence of other tourists is an undeniable and inescapable fact, the primary strategy is that of removal by distinction. Other tourists become "them": the uncouth, despised, insensitive, problematic, simplistic tourist, who threatens to give the whole game away and blow the "real traveler's" cover (he or she in search of the real, the intelligence officer of romanticism). This is a common strategy of travel writers from Paul Theroux through the more playful Pico Iyer or the ruggedly adventurist Robyn Davidson (1981). Indeed, the claim to be more than a tourist, to see that which could otherwise not be seen, to travel with the purpose of gathering intelligence to write a report is the very currency of travel writing.

Continuous with this logic, the ultimate tourist fantasy is to visit lands and people free from the blight of other tourists and modernity. Backpackers carry this theme with particular vigor and enthusiasm as the first wave of tourists to visit a region newly opened to touristic exploitation. These travelers tend to have an awareness of themselves as the vanguard of the hordes of tourists who would be responsible for the commercialization, and for the demise, of the very things that drew them there. As a consequence of this constant need for a touristic frontier, each few years a new country, beach, mountain, or desert place is reified in the travel pages of the *Times* and other petit bourgeois news-sheets, as the little-visited authentic place for the non-tourist traveler to explore. As its whereabouts and popularity spreads on the extensive word-of-mouth traveler's information network, the place becomes more and more touristed. By the time a small, well-institutionalized tourist industry has been established by locals or entrepreneurial outsiders the place will be "ruined" in the terms of the discourse that made it so popular. Bali has a particularly developed history of being subject to this discourse; it has been declared to be on the edge of devastation by crass tourists since the 1930s. In each case the declarations have been made by its self-appointed guardians of good taste and tradition.

All this leads to the conclusion that there is an underside of abject self-loathing, almost to the point of homicidal fantasy, in tourist ideologies. Tourist discourses consistently return to themes that deny, negate, or obliterate the presence of other tourists where this conflicts with their commitment to contact with the authentic Other. Erik Cohen (1982) has a brilliant illustration of this in his account of beach and hill tourism in Thailand. He describes how foreign tourists in Thailand go to the hills of the "Golden Triangle" to observe, photograph, and experience the tribal peoples, cultures, and costumes of the region. Cohen observes that when these same tourists go to the beach islands of southern Thailand they express and demonstrate almost complete indifference to the existence of "exotic" and vibrant village life a hundred meters inland from the beaches that so captivate them. In the first situation, discovering authentic cultural difference is the tourist's inspired mission; in the second, the experience of "nature" obliterates the local inhabitants as anything but service personnel. Cohen records a near-homicidal encounter between a tourist and a taxi driver on the island of Koh Sammui in southern Thailand. He saw this explosive conflict as a result of the consistent indifference to local sensibilities by tourists in the region, and predicted the inevitability of more such dangerous encounters.

This argument is not attempting to explain the motivations for the kinds of individual psychotic violence directed against tourists from the Port Arthur massacre (Tasmania 1996) to the Miami serial killer (Florida 1997), or the more clearly political violence of the Luxor massacre (1997)[19] or Bali bombing. It is, however perversely, suggesting that these acts resonate so powerfully in the Euro-Austral-American media, at least in part because they confirm the worst fears, anxieties, and fascination of tourists with their own destruction. Tourist ideologies include the notion that tourists are a scourge on the earth, and the fact that other people actually do violence to our fellow-tourists merely serves to confirm this half-submerged anxiety. The deaths of our fellow tourists brings us face to face with the ambivalent and death-driven horror of those formations that make us *Homo touristus*. As American Express advertising reminds us: "Don't forget to pack your peace of mind."

Source: Adapted from "Tourists, Terrorists, Death and Value," *Travel Worlds: Journeys in Contemporary Cultural Politics*, Raminder Kaur and John Hutnyk (eds.), 1999, Zed Books.

Acknowledgements

Thanks to John Hutnyk, Raminder Kaur, Nelson Graburn, Michael Dutton, William Mazzarella, Claudia Chambers, and David Martin for reading versions of this article and providing suggestions and corrections.

Notes

[1] Rephrasing of a cartoon strip theme by Chris Francis and John Hutnyk, Australia, 1991–3, which itself was quoting Fussel (1980:390). The cartoon strip extended this theme: "Making the World Safe for Bureaucracy," "Making the World Safe for Soft Drinks" and "Making the World Safe for Banks." Learn to like it. Thanks also to the Gnocchi Club.

[2] In many ways this project is perverse: it is, after all, an analysis of the structural significance of the murders, executions, and abductions of tourists. This assessment was vindicated and intensified when, a few days after proposing this chapter, a young "white" man in Tasmania, Australia, walked into a tourist kiosk at the former prison/concentration camp, now a tourist site at Port Arthur, and said, "Not many Japs here today, mostly WASPS," before opening fire and killing large numbers of tourists and employees of the tourist facility. In the perverse logic of media mediated violence, news consumers were constantly reminded that it was some kind of numerical record of deaths of this kind, setting a challenge that one assumes some other man crazed with the fantasies of power on which capitalist modernity runs will soon feel moved to surpass. Besides feeding a sense of guilty implication in the deaths of tourists everywhere, the repulsive coincidence of this writing and that violence made thinking about dead tourists (and the living over whom they cast their shadows) all the more serious a proposition. This writing has been pressed by its uncanny timing to take some responsibility for these deaths, or take some account for them in a different (cash/knowledge) register than the media's hyper-numeracy. The chapter is an attempt to speak of these horrors as if they were just another passing strangeness in the world, with some abstraction. I hope not to offend those who have known and loved "dead tourists," but only to offend assumptions about innocence and guilt, rationality and irrationality. While making no claim to explain the excess of violence in the world, aspects of it speak in a language that might be heard from a certain distance. I remember the shock of "meaninglessness" after the murder of one backpacker friend . . . no answers here . . . but some sense.

[3] Quote taken from Tejaswini Niranjana's critique of *Roja* (1994:81). Thanks to Raminder Kaur for bringing this article and film to my attention.

[4] The quotation continues:

> If it can help it, the State does not dissociate itself from a process of capture of flows of all kinds, populations, commodities or commerce, money or capital, etc. There is still a need for fixed paths in well-defined directions, which restrict speed, regulate circulation, relativize movement, and measure in detail the relative movements of subjects and objects. That is why Paul Virilio's thesis is important, when he shows that "the political power of the State is polis, police, that is, management of the public ways," and that "the gates of the city, its levies and duties are barriers, filters against the fluidity of the masses, against the penetration power of migratory packs, people, animals and goods. Gravity, gravitas, such is the essence of the State. It is not at all that the State knows nothing of speed; but it requires that movement, even the fastest, cease to be the absolute state of a body occupying a smooth space, to become the relative characteristic of a "moved body" going from one point to another in stri-

ated space. In this sense the State never ceases to decompose, recompose and transform movement, or to regulate speed." (Deleuze and Guattari 1986: 59–60)

The real border-crossing threat to the power of the State has been identified by one of the
world's main currency speculators, George Soros, as the movement of finance capital, both
as investment, and the much shorter-term movements of currency dealing and exchange rate
fluctuation that hold governments to ransom. Why not follow calls of the Left to allow labor
the same freedom as capital and let us all go where we please?

5 The following list of sites and incidents of violence directed specifically against tourists or
tourist destinations is a random, and far from exhaustive accounting of the ongoing litany of
violence: Aquile Lauro: hijacking . . . Beirut: "playground of the rich" to civil war . . . Tokyo:
subway gassing . . . TWA: mysterious explosion and crash . . . Lockerbie: bombing . . .
Manchester: bombing . . . Cambodia: hostages . . . London Docklands: bombing . . . Irian
Jaya (West Papua): hostages . . . Egypt: random attacks on foreign nationals . . . Charles
Sobraj: '70s tourist serial killing . . . Algeria: random attacks on foreign nationals . . . Gulf
War: travel angst . . . Uffizzi Gallery, Florence: bombing . . . Dubrovnik, World Heritage
listed city: destruction by shelling in Balkan war . . . Balangalow State Forest, New South
Wales: backpacker serial murders . . . Port Arthur, Tasmania: mass murder . . . World Trade
Building New York: bombing #1 and final destruction 2001 . . . Jerusalem tunnel: riots/civil
war . . . Sri Lanka: repeated hotel bombings and temple of the tooth bombing . . . Miami:
tourist serial murders . . . Empire State Building: mass murder . . . Kashmir: Al-Faran
hostages . . . November 1997: massacre of tourists at Luxor, Egypt . . . Bali: bombing 2002.

6 The Hollywood science fiction film, *Total Recall*, runs a nice parallel to this idea of the tourist
as secret agent. The hero, played by Arnold Schwarzenegger, takes a hi-tech holiday package
with Rekal Incorporated "where you can buy the memory of your ideal vacation cheaper,
safer, and better than the real thing." On this mind trip, or in reality, the plot obscures, Quail
discovers he is not an ordinary tourist, but in fact a secret agent who must now turn on his
evil, double-crossing Corporate-State employers (and his wife) and liberate the residents of
Mars from their oppressors while posing as an ordinary tourist. As undercover agent and tourist Quail becomes deeply confused about his true identity, and ultimately has to make a leap
of faith to identify who and what he really is in the unstable reality of his holiday to Mars.

7 All backpacker quotes are taken from interviews with international backpackers in Calcutta
1989, Melbourne 1990, and Delhi 1996, unless otherwise specified.

8 For a more detailed account of the tourist/backpacker distinction see Phipps (1991). Even the
apparently straightforward category "tourist" remains a troubled one in the social science of
tourism. To revert to a moment of legalism tourists are defined under the definition of the
U.N. International Travel and Tourism meeting in Rome in 1963 as: ". . . temporary visitors
staying at least 24 hours in the country visited and the purpose of whose journey can be classified under one of the following headings: (1) Leisure (recreation, holiday, health, study,
religion, sport); (2) Business, family, mission, meeting." (Quoted in Cohen 1974:530.) Obviously these categories are extremely general and permeable.

9 Diller and Scofidio (1994: 80) cite a wonderful, almost absurdist survey by S. Plog:
Travelers can be categorized according to psychographic segments distributed along a
spectrum extending, at one pole, from the "psychocentric" (inhibited, nonadventurous
travelers) to the "allocentric" traveler demanding change and adventure. The bulk of
travelers fit into the intermediate area, the "mid-centric." There are five basic motivations for leisure travel, with the following distribution: life is too short 35%, adds interest to life 30%, the need to unwind 29%, ego support 4%, sense of self-discovery 4%.

10 Thanks to Michael Dutton for this observation.

11 Hutnyk notes that while most budget travelers suffer from bowel-related problems (and have
frequent discussions of this over breakfast), they are less likely to suffer from serious afflictions as do the "poor" whom they go to visit (1996:40).

[12] Visvanathan points out an example where a terrible plague was promoted by British medical wisdom, testing a vaccine and forcibly preventing other measures to sour the experiment: "Haffkine's plague resulted in thousands dead and lasted 12 years, and it is not clear that his vaccine did much more than hurry along a declining epidemic in any case. Yet Haffkine is remembered as hero" (Visvanathan 1988: 264–5). Thanks to John Hutnyk for finding this text.

[13] I would like to thank Raminder Kaur for making these fascinating connections for me. Much of this paragraph is a simple paraphrase of an e-mail she sent me.

[14] Most passports carry a variation upon the following statement, this particular one being from an Australian passport and so bearing marks of that country's ongoing colonial legacy: "The Governor-General of the Commonwealth of Australia, being the representative of Her Majesty Queen Elizabeth the Second, requests all those whom it may concern to allow the bearer to pass freely without let or hindrance and to afford him or her every assistance and protection of which he or she may stand in need." Such documents have long played a role in the travel-emissary, diplomacy-threat gambit.

[15] The recent events in Peru are a brilliant variation on this theme, where the Tupac Amaru Revolutionary Army bypassed all symbolic intermediaries (such as tourists) and kidnapped the diplomats and ruling elite themselves. They wagered—in the end at some cost to themselves—on the fair assumption that the diplomats with whom they are negotiating have enormous concern for the welfare of diplomats. Similarly they bypassed all media intermediaries by publishing their plans, objectives, and press releases on an Internet site on the same day as their raid on the Japanese embassy.

[16] In the complexity of power in Cambodia, however, a country where the military had over 1000 generals at the time, some of whom operated as semi-independent warlords, or on behalf of differing government factions, the hostages were to become part of a still more complex game. Over the months of isolated reports of the hostages' whereabouts, some photos and tape recordings were smuggled (or sent as part of a media-savvy strategy) out of the jungle. In Australia the media ran the story as front-page news each time new information emerged. They were particularly responsive to the release of images of the hostages and their recorded voices, and from the start of the crisis developed a portrait of the Australian hostage, David Wilson, as an embodiment of the virtues of spirited Australian youth: independent, suspicious of authority, and brave. These representations reached a climax when images and recordings of the hostages became available that were interpreted to show Wilson as the leader and spokesperson for the group, as much by national as personal strength. Just as Australia had led the Cambodian peace process, and was the apparent leader of diplomatic efforts to free the hostages, the Australian national held hostage became the leader of the hostages in a poignant moment of symmetry. This image had still more emotive depth because of its association with Australia's official drive to "become part of Asia" on the one hand, and its resonance with deeply rooted memories of Australians as prisoners of war under the Japanese Imperial Army.

After months of intense confusion over the whereabouts of the hostages, their welfare, and who was conducting the negotiations for their release, there appeared to be an immanent breakthrough. The Khmer Rouge base where they were being held was identified and approached by government military forces. A price for the release of the hostages was negotiated, and as they were being brought toward the government forces, and being approached by the negotiator, the military opened fire on the Khmer Rouge in an intense bombardment and brought an immediate end to the exchange of money for hostages and weeks of careful negotiation.

It has since been surmised that there were elements in the Cambodian government who concluded that it would be more advantageous to fail to secure the return of the hostages than to succeed. If the hostages could not be returned, or were killed, it would increase Australian, French, and possibly British support for the corrupt and increasingly inept government, particularly in their war against the Khmer Rouge. This view was further encouraged in Australia by the extreme obfuscation by the Australian Foreign Affairs Ministry over the exact process of negotiations, what had gone wrong, who was responsible, and so on. In the months that followed, confused and contradicting reports emerged about the hostages' location and welfare, until finally their bodies were found by Cambodian soldiers led there by a Khmer Rouge defector. They had been killed in the method characteristic of the Khmer Rouge in their genocidal phase, with a blow to the back of the head by a mattock. In this instance it was the particular value of the national affiliation of the hostages that had determined their ultimate fate through such a complex chain of values and strategies. Had they been Indian, Kenyan, or Dutch, they may have been released without mishap, or perhaps have more rapidly met the fate of the Vietnamese nationals.

[17] Sheik Abdel-Rahman, an inspiration for Islamic militants in Egypt, was quoted in 1993 as saying of tourists, "They go to Egypt for transgressions such as fornication, drinking, intoxicants, gambling and usury. They transmit diseases such as AIDS to our land. To those lamenting what has happened to tourism, I say it is sinful . . . the lands of Muslims will not become bordellos for sinners of every race and colour." (*The Age*, Melbourne, Australia, November 22, 1997:19)

[18] See also van den Abeele (1980), Morris (1988), and Frow (1991) for ongoing discussion of this problematic.

[19] A similar phenomenon to that identified by Cohen occurs where Egypt is always pre-figured as "ancient," absenting contemporary Islam and Arabs from this European fantasy. The pyramids are known as a tourist site primarily for monumentalizing the dead. In the face of this the living can perhaps only pale into insignificance, though in the case of Egypt, tourist accounts are inclined to inscribe the local people as a kind of pestilence! This absenting hostility has ironically, and in some cases fatally, been returned recently by Islamic militants who find foreign tourists a disturbance of their reality, or as useful targets in a campaign to destabilize the "moderate" government of Egypt which generates substantial foreign exchange from tourism to its pre-Islamic monuments. These overdetermined relations of tourists to place and people are widely varied, but for the most part revolve around the well-worn themes of nature, culture, history, and nation. The theme that is perceived to hold the key to the authenticity of a place may vary over time, but the commitment to its pursuit remains militantly persistent. (This paragraph was written before the Luxor massacre, which unfortunately confirms its significance as a site of tension.)

References

Bureau of Tourism Research. 1995. Backpackers in Australia: Occasional Paper Number 20, BTR, Department of Sport, Recreation and Tourism, Commonwealth of Australia.

Camus, Albert. 1962. Carnets 1935–37. NRF/Gallimard (26).

Catanach, Ian. 1997. "Famine and Disease before and after 1947." Oral presentation at the South Asian Studies Association conference, *Translatings: Ideas of India Since Independence*. Sydney: Museum of Sydney.

Cohen, Erik. 1982. "Marginal Paradises: Bungalow Tourism on the Islands of Southern Thailand." *Annals of Tourism Research* 9:189–228.

Crick, Malcolm. 1985. "Tracing the Anthropological Self: Quizzical Reflections on Fieldwork, Tourism and the Ludic." *Social Analysis* 17:71–92.

———. 1988. "Sun, Sex, Sights, Savings and Servility: Representations of International Tourism in the Social Sciences." Melbourne University. *Criticism, Heresy and Interpretation* 1:37–76.

———. 1991. "Tourists, Locals and Anthropologists." *Australian Cultural History* 10:6–18.

Davidson, Robyn. 1981. *Tracks*. Granada: St. Martin.

Deleuze, Gilles, and Felix Guattari. 1986. "Nomadology: The War Machine," trans. Brian Massumi. New York: *Semiotext(e)*.

Diller, Elizabeth, and Ricardo Scofidio, eds. 1994. *Visite aux Armées: Tourismes de Guerre/Back to the Front: Tourisms of War*. Basse-Normandie, France: F.R.A.C.

Frow, John. 1991. "Tourism and the Semiotics of Nostalgia." *October* 57:123–151.

Fussel, Paul. 1980. *Abroad: British Literary Traveling Between the Wars*. New York: Oxford University Press.

Graburn, Nelson. 1983. "The Anthropology of Tourism." *Annals of Tourism Research* 10:9–33.

———. 1989. "Tourism: The Sacred Journey," in *Hosts and Guests: The Anthropology of Tourism*, 2nd edition, ed. Valene Smith, pp. 21–36. Philadelphia: University of Pennsylvania Press.

Hutnyk, John. 1996. *The Rumour of Calcutta: Tourism, Charity and the Poverty of Representation*. London: Zed Books.

Iyer, Pico. 1988. *Video Night in Kathmandu: And Other Reports from the Not-So-Far-East*. New York: Knopf.

Kaplan, Caren. 1996. *Questions of Travel: Postmodern Discourses of Displacement*. Durham, NC: Duke University Press.

Kincaid, Jamaica. 1988. *A Small Place*. New York: Farrar, Straus and Giroux.

MacCannell, Dean. 1976. *The Tourist: A New Theory of the Leisure Class*. London: Macmillan.

McGuckin, Eric. 1996. *Anthropologists and Other Tourists: Fieldwork and Tourism in Dharamsala, India*. Oral presentation, American Anthropology Association Annual Meeting.

Mehta, Gita. 1979. *Karma Cola: Marketing the Mystic East*. Britain: Fontana.

Mitchell, Timothy. 1991. *Colonising Egypt*. Berkeley: University of California Press.

Morris, Meaghan. 1988. "At Henry Parkes Motel." *Cultural Studies* 2:1–47.

Niranjana, Tejaswini. 1994. "Integrating Whose Nation? Tourists and Terrorists in Roja." *Economic and Political Weekly* 29(3) (January 15): 79–82.

O'Donoghue, Claire. 1995. "Trouble in Paradise." *Marie Claire* (September): 55–58.

Phipps, Peter. 1991. *Travelling Subjects: A Deconstructive Ethnography of Budget Travellers in India*. Honours thesis, Departments of Political Science and Anthropology, University of Melbourne.

Riley, Pamela J. 1988. "Road Culture of International Long-Term Budget Travelers." *Annals of Tourism Research* 15:313–328.

Robbins, Bruce. 1986. "Feeling Global: John Berger and Experience," in *Postmodernism and Politics*, ed. Jonathon Arac. Manchester: University of Manchester Press.

Savage, Peter. 1993. *The Safe Travel Book*. Lanham, MD: Lexington Books.

Teas, Jane. 1988 [1974]. "'I'm Studying Monkeys; What Do You Do?'—Youth and Travelers in Nepal." *Kroeber Anthropological Society Papers* 67/68: 35–41.

Theroux, Paul. 1975. *The Great Railway Bazaar: By Train through Asia*. London: Hamilton.

van den Abeele, George. 1980. "Sightseers: The Tourist as Theorist." *Diacritics* 10:1–14.

Visvanathan, Shiv. 1988. "On the Annals of the Laboratory State," in *Science Hegemony and Violence: A Requiem for Modernity*, ed. Ashis Nandy, pp. 257–288. Delhi: OUP.

Weightman, Barbara A. 1987. "Third World Tour Landscapes." *Annals of Tourism Research* 14:227–240.

Wexco Publications. [1980] 1994. *The Complete Travellers Guide*. London: Wexco.

6

Narrating the Tourist Experience

Orvar Löfgren

Memorable Experiences

We were waiting for our baggage, forming the kind of uneasy collectivity that marks any charter flight. As soon as the conveyor belt spat out our bags, we would disperse to the various hotels along the coasts of Cyprus, but now we glanced surreptitiously at the other families. When the conveyor belt started with a sudden pull, I heard a man next to me talking loudly to himself. Turning around I saw him eagerly filming the suitcases as they appeared on the belt, making a running commentary on the scene into the camcorder's microphone. It seemed a strange choice of subject. It was not until I saw him a week later as we gathered at the airport for the return flight that I understood what he was doing. Here he was again, directing the family as they disembarked from the bus. He was, of course, producing a vacation video complete with opening scene and happy ending.

Down in the basement I have an old holiday album, which I produced as a twelve-year-old. It describes a family trip across Sweden and starts with a pasted-in map where the route is carefully drawn. Snapshots, admission tickets, hotel labels, and picture postcards document each step, along with my running commentary. It documents a vacation *and* shows the project "our family," an institution that became very visible during those summer months of intensive interaction. Many children take vacations very seriously, and albums like these tell the story of learning to be a tourist.

I don't think I ever made another album like that, but my basement is full of relics and remnants of a tourist life. There are a few dusty boxes of slides and thirty reels of eight-millimeter film from the 1960s. Most of the slides are of landscapes, carefully selected and situated, while the moving pictures endlessly emphasize just this: movement. People always wave and clown around on these early reels. From later stages of my tourist career there are a few videotapes and box after box of snapshots in color, patiently waiting for placement in nice holiday albums. It'll never happen, though. A few early souvenirs have also made the downwardly mobile trip from the living room into the collection of basement junk. There are many basements or attics like mine all over the tourist world. The argument often runs thus: people are so obsessed by recording and documenting that they don't have time to experience what they see. When Germaine Greer (1995) travels on a group tour through China, she never stops complaining about her fellow passengers on the train. She calls them "the packages" and describes them as having one eye glued to the camcorder's sight and the other fixed on the guidebook as the fabulous Chinese landscape rolls by.

If that Cyprus tourist had let his camcorder stay in the bag, would he have devoted his energy to enjoying the landscape? Against the "must" of documentation he had to weigh the "must" of uncluttered attention. Tourist life is as always filled with unwritten rules and conflicting notions of the suitable. Those tourists who instead decide to buy the ready-made holiday videos of the sightseeing trip in Paris or the helicopter tour of Hawai'i risk another kind of criticism. If you insist on bringing a holiday video home, it should at least be one *you* made.

The critique of the urge to document misses an important point. The pleasure may not be in gathering mementos to display next winter but just in creating them: letting the video roll, jotting down a few lines on the back of a postcard, keeping a travel diary, clicking through a roll of Kodachrome. However much energy goes into the production of these narratives and whatever their fate, producing them was an experience in its own right.

Viewed from this angle, the phenomenon of tourist narratives over the last two centuries includes a range of artistic creativity that in other situations would be unthinkable. Here is an arena where nonartists and nonauthors do not hesitate to try their hand at producing a watercolor, a photo narrative, a travel diary, a video documentary, or a collage of shells or dried flowers. Here you may become your own director, scriptwriter, or scenographic.

In this history of representations there is a constant interaction between the tourist amateur and the professionals of the trade: travel writers, poets, landscape painters, filmmakers, and *National Geographic* photographers. The forms of this interaction and the genres emanating from it shift constantly as reproductive technologies or trends emerge or wear out, setting up hierarchies in modes of representation that label some souvenirs tacky or give them new life as kitsch. The new technology of watercolor sketching, easy to carry along and very suitable for amateurs, allowed pioneer tourists to dabble a bit in art. The snapshot trivialized the scenic landscape photograph; the oil-painted sunset was turned into a picture postcard. The photo album replaced the sketchbook and in turn yielded to the video library. Certain forms of representations have staying power, others disappear quickly, and still others make a comeback.

Wish You Were Here

Those who have been unfortunate enough to lose a roll of film in one of the biggest Swedish photo labs will receive a search list, which contains the most popular vacation motifs. You just have to tick off the ones that describe the content of your lost film. Two of the main headings run:

VIEWS (mountains, sea, meadow, forest, alps, lake)

ATTRACTIONS (church, ruin, monument)

Behind this laconic list of Swedish holiday sights lies a long process of selection and framing. Learning to reorganize the landscape into sights and views comes so naturally to most of us that we may find it difficult to understand the kind of relearning that went before it. There are many irritated comments on the Disneyland habit of putting up little flags to signal scenic photo spots, but most of us already carry those flags with us—more or less consciously. Our camera work is heavily preprogrammed. With the help of the nineteenth-century invention of the award system of one to three stars (later expanded into five) spread all over the world, tourists learned to look for attractions that demanded to be seen and photographed (Enzensberger 1971).

Nineteenth-century photography remained a relatively exclusive pastime, before the advent of cheap cameras and simple techniques. Photo prints, however, soon became a very important tourist medium, and by far the most important of these was the picture postcard.

Some claim that the first souvenir postcard was issued at the Paris Universal Exhibition of 1889 and depicted the Eiffel Tower. From then on the medium developed into a booming industry, and the decades around the turn of the century proved to be the golden age of the postcard. In 1904 the Swedish population of about five million people mailed over forty-eight million postcards. Exchanging and collecting picture postcards became a favorite hobby, and addicts could subscribe to special magazines for collectors.[1] Many attics still hold old postcard albums from that period. This collection mania may be difficult for us to understand, exposed as we are to all kinds of visual media, but at the turn of the century printed images were still a scarce resource. The picture postcard, as a cheap and attractive pictorial medium, filled a void, a hunger for images, and thus became a very important means to visualize the world. The Swedish term for picture postcards is *vykort* (literally, "a card with a view"), and the term reflects the complex relation between the new medium of photography and visual perceptions at that time.

Looking at a hundred years of Swedish postcards, we can follow very distinct subgenres and favorite motifs that developed rapidly. They became a condensation of the truly Swedish, an emotionalized territory. Photographers, many of them specializing in the new genre, learned the rules of composing attractive views, and mistakes were quickly corrected by the market. The tourists for their part got confirmations or redefinitions of ideas about beautiful or attractive views. The three-star prospects were not only listed in the guidebook but could also be bought in the form of postcards in the nearby souvenir shop. As a new mass medium, the postcard made sure you brought the view home or shared it with friends through the mail. The genre had a great influence on the development of amateur photography among tourists.

The motifs of picture postcards in many cases show great continuity, especially in the genre of landscapes. A couple of years ago I bought a standard set of slides in a Swedish souvenir shop, simply labeled "Sweden I" and "Sweden II." A number of its views had been scenographic "classics" even a century earlier. This gallery includes Lapland waterfalls, a little red cottage by the lake, timber floating (a trade long since gone), woodland farmers in folk costume rowing to church, Saami shepherding their reindeer down a mountain slope, and, of course, a midnight sun.

In an international perspective the sunset has been *the* most popular postcard motif over the last hundred years. This scenery has many local variations; a Swedish, a Moroccan, or an American sunset may be staged in different ways, but the basic structure is the same and is a product of tourist experiences as well as landscape painting.

In an account of her African fieldwork the anthropologist Manda Cesara recollects a remark one of the locals once made about his peculiar European friend who sat endlessly on the porch, sundowner in hand, waiting for the setting sun. "Why should anyone sit and watch the sunset?" he asked (Cesara 1982:55). The same bewilderment could be found among Swedish countryfolk who observed the first waves of urban middle-class tourists in search of scenic spots. Why go through all that work of climbing up the hillside just for a view?

The sunset panorama satisfied many emotional longings. Observing the view alone or with silent companions became a form of aesthetic worship, a profound experience of serenity and wholeness. The absolute stillness, the dying day, the landscape opening before you, all that could give a feeling of total belonging or quiet ecstasy. The experience often felt like "time standing still" or "natural time." It could work like a ritual of belonging, returning to a mythical past or a more authentic existence.[2] Feelings of nostalgia, of homecoming, of traveling back in time could also be part of it, as well as a feeling of closure.

The element of melancholy and longing could also take the form of a phrase that now seems rather worn. A Swedish sunset from 1909 bears the scribbled subtext: "If only you had been here this evening!" The definition of the sunset as an intimate or romantic situation intended for loving couples or close friends took the form of "Wish you were here." The sunset came to represent not only a specific scenery but a specific mood. From time to time this link has been made even more obvious by the addition of printed subtexts to the view, specifying the mood. In the early 1990s a popular Swedish sunset version carried the text "Missing you." The combination of picture and text could communicate moods and feelings that many found difficult to verbalize.

In nineteenth-century landscape painting the sunset was a favorite genre, which was gradually trivialized to the extent that it was redefined as vulgar—with too glaring colors. Filmmakers turned the sunset into a cliché as more and more heroes and heroines walked right into that happy or melancholy ending. Travel writers had their problems too:

> I do not think I shall ever forget the sight of Etna at sunset; the mountain almost invisible in a blur of pastel grey, glowing on the top and then repeating its shape, as though reflected, in a wisp of grey smoke, with the whole horizon behind radiant with pink light, fading into a grey pastel sky. Nothing I have ever seen in Art or Nature was quite so revolting.

As Martin Stannard points out, this piece from Evelyn Waugh's *Labels: A Mediterranean Journal* from 1930 can only be read as parody of one of his contemporary travel writers, Robert Byron's description of Stromboli from 1926—or a thousand other descriptions of Mediterranean sunsets (1982:111). Sunset representations became the icon of bad art and tired prose, but the more humble medium of the picture postcard could keep carrying this motif.

Sunset viewing is still a popular ritual for many of us. On the long sandy shores of the Danish west coast cars drive out on the beaches and people gather in small groups or remain inside their vehicles for silent communion with the sun. On California beaches you can experience a similar scene, and a really good sunset may also produce enthusiastic applause from the onlookers. But for really top-quality sunsets you have to go to Hawai'i:

> Visitors chasing the perfect sunset can find it in Wailea . . . . People become connoisseurs of Wailea sunsets. They rate them, collect them on film, discuss them as one might a vintage burgundy or a new car . . .

> The Renaissance Wailea Beach Resort has elevated sunset watching to an art form with the simple device of a few hammocks strategically hung among some palms. While your friends cuddle up with a mai tai in hand and romance in mind, you can shoot them against the setting sun. (Ariyoshi 1997:8–9)

Life Imitating Art?

The tourist postcard represents a powerful medium for organizing and presenting ideas about vacation preferences, tastes, and attractions. The same scenic preferences may confront you in the travel brochure you read at home, the guidebooks brought along, the stops made during the sightseeing trips for photo opportunities, and the cards available at the souvenir shops. There is a strong process of reinforcement here, which in part may account for the marked conservatism of scenic viewing.

An example from a booming scene of package tourism shows the process at work. One of the most reproduced images of Morocco comes from the colorful setting of "the Dyers' Lane" in the old artisanal section of the market in Marrakech, where bundles of yarn in all conceivable shades are draped across the lane. You will find this scene in tourist brochures, on travel posters, and in postcards racks. During the guided tours in the maze of this huge bazaar the guide will stop when you approach the lane and signal that here is a good spot for a photograph. The problem is that the mass tourist invasion to this part of the market has altered its look. Souvenir shops, as well as changes in production, have driven the dyers out of the lane, but in order to live up to tourist expectations, a few bundles of colorful yarn still remain draped across the walls.

In the background the water peddlers in their exotic red outfits wait with their brass cups, not to peddle water, for which the market in modern Marrakech is dwindling, but to act as a folkloristic backdrop in your photograph for the fee of a couple of dirhams. The sound of their brass bells is no longer a signal for the thirsty traveler but a reminder to the tourist that she or he is approaching a scenic spot. In Marrakech the water peddlers are a necessary cultural prop. Postcards and guidebooks immortalize their presence. The point to be made here is, of course, that once scenery has been institutionalized through various media it becomes in a way frozen and taken out of time. An element of mise en scène becomes necessary to make it stay that way, as local life changes. Here, as in many other situations, we observe the power of the representation as the norm of authenticity that reality will have to try to live up to.

The picture postcard is, however, not a stagnant genre, simply reproducing old images. It also makes fun of itself and tourists; the comic postcard, the ironic or kitschy postcard, the period postcard are all traditions with a rather long history. Anti-genres, discarding worn clichés in favor of new artistic or ethnographic traditions in professional travel photography, set up new norms, which mirror an urge to get away from anything that smells of the arranged, of fakelore, or of the classic sights. The fact that a dangling camera (photo opportunities!) has become the sign of the vulgar tourist poses a problem for those who feel a need to distance themselves: should they carry a camera at all? But otherwise, how can they bring back pictorial evidence of actually getting off the beaten track?

The Science of the Scenic

At least two centuries of scenic viewing thus condition our selections and evaluations of tourist settings and sights, but their work is not always conscious. A good example is the strange tradition of landscape evaluation measurement techniques that became very popular in environmental studies and planning for some decades, especially during the 1970s.[3]

Typical postcards: "Bridges on the Arno" Italy and "The Picturesque East Coast" Barbados.

Scores of studies appeared, with titles like "Eye Pupillary Measurement of Aesthetic Response to Forest Scenes" or "Modeling and Predicting Human Response to the Visual Recreation Environment" (Wenger and Videbeck 1969, Peterson and Neumann 1969). Hoping to create tools for natural resource management and planning, from wilderness aesthetics to scenic roads design, many of these studies put enormous amounts of energy and some pretty spectacular number crunching into what are good examples of social science trivia. They reflect a period in tourist and leisure management when hard facts, models, and clear taxonomies were in demand. How do we predict tourist preferences and measure visitor satisfaction? Studies like these demonstrate the prevailing strengths of the lessons of the picturesque. The most favored mountain scenes turn out to be those romantic artists would have preferred, like a grove of trees foregrounding a lake scene with a mighty mountain in the background or, in the words of the researchers, "the positive effect of a perimeter of immediate vegetation" (Shafer, Hamilton and Schmidt 1969:19). Other results announce that people with camping experience have higher emotional responses to woodland sceneries or that older people with a longer education prefer scenic natural beaches (Peterson and Neumann 1969:19).

Another study in the same tradition (which is still with us) asked 2,826 Danes to rank 52 different forest photos. The winner was a deer on a winding path in a sunlight forest clearing, but when a tractor replaced the deer, the same scenery ended up next to last (Koch and Jensen 1988).

This science of the scenic represents the ultimate pictorialization of nature experiences. Nature as a two-dimensional picture postcard, not to walk in or smell or touch or listen to but just to look upon. And obviously, the nineteenth century brought a focus on the power of vision with many new technologies, from the panorama and the stereoscope to the camera. But an increased ocularization of tourist life into the "tourist gaze" does not equate with the hegemony of the surveying or controlling (male) gaze. Rather there was a period of intense experimentation, juggling very different modes of seeing that came to coexist. Sightseeing elaborated the art of fixing, framing, and positioning a view, as well as the techniques of scanning, and it also explored the art of glimpsing and glancing—the furtive, disinterested, or distracted look. Later in the twentieth century the tourist industry learned to develop "eye candy" for the consuming gaze, which wants to touch and feel.

The abundance of pictorial (and increasingly affordable) representations, from the watercolor to the videocassette, also produced a materiality or concretion of the visible: this is what we experienced and remember. In our narratives we also depend heavily on the well-developed language for describing visual impressions that many of the other senses lack. And we are, of course, not just looking; other senses interact in this making of a vision. It is only that the other senses have not kept up with this verbalization and technologization of the visual.

Souvenirs

Mass-tourists ask little except the same sort of food that they eat at home; the English for example, scorn any meal that does not include potatoes—to hell with rice and spaghetti! And who wants wine, when he can get beer? They don't object to a little local color, especially fla-menco-strumming by pretended gypsies, and gaudy souvenirs; dolls in provincial costume, inlaid Toledo steel paper-knives, plastic castanets dangling colored ribbons, leather wine-bottles, olive-wood bowls and boxes, bullfighting posters with their own names printed between those of El Litri and James Ostos . . . But they shy away from any closer approach to the real Spain. (Graves 1969:16)

Robert Graves is commenting on the tourist scene in Majorca and the very touchy issue of souvenirs. This is a territory where different tastes and interests, as well as outspoken verdicts, continually clash. As a child I remember the meaningful glances passing between my parents when my sisters and I chose among the treasures of souvenir shops. Although nothing was said it was obvious that our taste was childlike and immature. Our grandmother, on the other hand, loved souvenirs too and had the dangerous habit of bringing home real bits and pieces from three-star attractions, stones from Bethlehem, marble fragments from the Parthenon. She followed the example of the young Englishman who wrote home to his mother in 1861 that he had been to see the Sphinx and had broken "a bit of its neck to take home with us,

Folk tradition and communist past: Maruska dolls and Lenin souvenirs will later help tourists remember and narrate their trip to Russia. (Photo by Sharon Gmelch)

as everyone else does" (Pemble 1987:5). We could not help worrying about our grandma's participation in this mass movement, which in the long run would clean the world of classical monuments.

Like many other children of my generation I loved souvenirs, and the ritual of acquiring one from each place was important. Pocket money for school excursions should preferably always include money for ice cream *and* a souvenir, and we always expected our parents to bring us home a token from their latest trip abroad. Growing older, I experienced how the genres of souvenir collecting change along the life cycle. Collecting tacky souvenirs was a student exercise in kitsch, and later on souvenirs became bottles of funny-smelling local liqueurs, a lucky stone from a memorable day at a beach, all kinds of objets trouvés. For me the magic of the souvenir still works.

A burgeoning souvenir market developed in the eighteenth-century world of the Grand Tour. Italian landscape paintings were popular, but there was also a great demand for archaeological finds, which soon tempted the locals to start forging them. Just like later generations of tourists these pioneers wanted to bring back something material: a piece of the landscape, and in Naples there was a brisk trade in pieces of lava (Towner 1996:137). Local artists and artisans started to work exclusively for the tourist market: new forms of "native crafts" constantly appeared.

At Niagara early tourists dug up bones from the battlefields of the 1812 war to bring home. Native Americans soon got caught up in the tourist trade, as providers of the authentic. Here as elsewhere the genres of "native crafts" and "local souvenirs" soon became blurred. In 1850 you could buy items cut from local rock and wood, beaded moccasins, bark trifles, baskets, leather cigar cases decorated with dyed elk's hair, and also miniature canoes (Jansen 1995:40, 50). At Niagara the tourists opened up a market for imported souvenirs, everything from prints to trinkets of all kinds. Here we may witness the start of the globalization of souvenir production. Instead of buying a piece containing the magic of local materials, you can buy an object made into a local souvenir by the magic of naming, from "Niagara Falls" in poker-work, produced in New York sweatshops, to the pens, ashtrays, or T-shirts from Taiwan of later periods.

Although souvenir shops have been denounced in every possible way over most of their history, they persist and thrive. Susan Stewart's (1984) classic study *On Longing* is one attempt to explain that popularity. She points out that souvenirs carry the magic of place, whether bought or found there, and this magic evaporates if they do not come from the faraway place—as in the devalued experience of receiving a friend's postcard mailed after the homecoming. She discusses the processes of fetishization and miniaturization, but the most convincing part of her argument is about their power to produce narratives.

The theme of miniaturization is equally absorbing. The tiny beaded canoe, the folklore doll, the Statue of Liberty piggy bank, they all hold, as Gaston Bachelard (1994) states, a strange attraction as a medium for daydreaming, as a way to experience what is large in what is small. Small things are easy to carry home, but they are also "good to think with," they often function as narrative coat hangers.[4] Their three-dimensionality is important in relation to the flatness of all the texts and pictures that otherwise make up our vacation leftovers.

The evocative power of souvenirs rests in their seeming unchangeability, all those objects that have no other function than to store memories. Cups that are not for drinking out of, painted cutting boards that never will come near a loaf of bread, funny hats that won't leave their pegs. But they are of course constantly changing, and their seductive thingishness may obscure the fact that they are vessels for travel in time and space. One of the best treatments of this theme is the folklorist Henry Glassie's text on Mrs. Cutler's kitchen dresser in the Irish village of Ballymenone. On the dresser there is a parade of souvenir plates, mugs, a doll in a kilt, a dippy duck, "a glass wee man with an ass and a cart," porcelain figures of saints, little brass ornaments, and much much more. Glassie describes Mrs. Cutler's running commentary on her souvenirs, her constant care and rearranging of them. They are always on the move: "their meaning lies less in their manifest content than in their magical capacity to bring events and human beings to life in the mind . . . . The art of ornaments does not lie in them, as part of their fabric. They become art in mind and manipulation" (1982:369).

These souvenirs may look trivial but the kinds of narratives and memories they trigger off are astounding, opening up this tiny kitchen to the world. So in answering the question, what is a souvenir—a fetish, nostalgia, an object without utility value, a narrative trigger? The answer is: maybe. To me the most striking characteristic of a souvenir is its openness, its readiness to carry the mind in all directions. There might be millions of tiny brass Eiffel Towers distributed over the globe, but no two of them carry the same meanings.

Déjà Vu

"Can I learn to look at things with clear, fresh eyes? How much can I take in at a single glance? Can the grooves of mental habits be effaced?" These are the classic questions of Goethe from his Italian journey in 1786–88, which tend to turn up again and again in reflections on tourism.

One of the grand narratives of tourism argues that we can never recapture the freshness of Goethe, Lord Byron, John Muir, or those other great pioneers. Our vacation experiences are hopelessly cluttered with sediments of associations, clichés, and images: "The problem is that life rarely feels real. If I am having a picnic with my friends out on the cliffs in the Åland archipelago, life suddenly disappears and I begin to think that everything we are doing is part of a beer commercial." This journalist's memories of the previous summer unfold against the backdrop of an immensely successful Swedish beer commercial. The TV spot plays seductively on the theme of the perfect summer memory in the archipelago. Young and tanned actors fool around in the waves, and stage an improvised picnic next to the boathouse. This is a nostalgic flashback to summer and fun, by a young couple who revisit the island in the melancholy of the autumn (Nordlund 1996).

The journalist's reflection on fiction invading life is the start of an interview with a Swedish author, who voices the often-heard standpoint that the basic definition of twentieth-century life is that we live in a world in which boundaries between reality and fiction are dissolved. Earlier generations did not have to face the problem, she argues, but the mix of reality and fiction has as long a history as the daydream, the flight of fantasy, or the religious vision. Vacationscapes develop out of the interplay between the physical and mental landscapes through which we move simultaneously.

The anthropologist Arjun Appadurai sets up "landscapes" to capture this interaction in the ways cultural flows help build new, transnational worlds, where fantasy and images are an important part of the everyday social practices. He talks of people on the move (ethnoscapes), of mobile capital (finanscapes), technologies (technoscapes), ideologies (ideoscapes) and finally the flow of information, images, and narratives (mediascapes) (1996:27). His approach is useful for a discussion of tourism. How are such different "scapes" produced and changed over time and integrated in everyday practices?

There is a constant play between experience and technologies of mediation here. Tourists always experiment with new forms of mediations and technologies of movement, perception, and sensing. On the Swedish west coast island I visit every summer, people still talk about how confounded the locals were by the visitors at the manor in the middle of the last century: Could you believe it? Those ladies with their hair let down sat in the grass down by the shore reading books!

"Those ladies" transformed the landscape into a multimedia space through other techniques of virtual reality than ours. Their flight of fantasy in reading novels blended with the experience of being out in nature, and a similar thought probably inspired the visitor to a Catskill lake in the 1830s who exclaimed: "What a place for music by moonlight!"[5] And a modern teenager with a Walkman can set music to the landscape she moves through.

We now consume music and texts out in the open and—paralleling the last decades' increase in our media consumption of images—we also carry with us a wider range of fore-sights, and increasingly so in the form of previsualizations. They may be everything from landscape paintings to scenes from vacation advertisements, to which we compare our actual landscape experiences, as well as all our past landscape experiences. The question is whether this massive pictorialization produces an overstimulation or just a wider range of possible associations.

The question of what we carry along into a tourist experience also produces the problem of wear and tear. The history of tourist experiences illustrates that many of the processes of change are more microprocesses of a somewhat cyclical nature. As new sights and attractions, new forms of tourist activities and leisure come into vogue, they run through processes of exploration, followed by institutionalization and sometimes commoditization, and may then appear worn and tired and trivialized. The intimate, picturesque view may grow stale or feel claustrophobic. Landscapes seen as barren and uninviting may take on a new aura as their very simplicity and nothingness become an asset. In all such developments we need to focus on the wear and tear. Why do we grow tired of experiences, how do souvenirs come to seem tacky, what makes a sight boring?

To answer this question, we need to ask another: what is an experience? If we look at the semantics of the word in different languages, there is a common emphasis on movement. Experience derives from experimenting, trying, risking, the German *Erlebnis* and the Swedish *upplevelse* from living through, living up to, running through, being part of, accomplishing. Again the focus is on personal participation, we have to be both physically and mentally *there*.

"To have an experience" calls for a situation with a beginning and an end. In the everyday flow of activity the experience stands out, it is marked and distinctive. It is something we enter and exit, and the production of experiences— especially out of the ordinary ones that can be furthered by rites de passage—is a situating that involves both time and space (Abrahams 1986). Experiences always take place, but in ways that combine the realities of both the grounds we are treading and the mental images present. We neither have nor can be given experiences. We *make* them in a highly personal way of taking in impressions, but in this process we use a great deal of established and shared cultural knowledge and frames. And yet we share experiences only through representations and expressions. Here is the famous hermeneutical circle: experience structures expression and expression structures experience. Our associations are culturally conditioned and so are our afterthoughts, the ways in which we reflect on and express consciousness. What is possible to express, how can it be expressed? The anthropologist Allen Feldman pushes this argument even further: an event is not what happens but what can be narrated (1991:14).

In the history of tourism there is a strong normative element in discussions of experiences. They are not only framed, localized, and memorized; they are also weighed, measured, and ranked. They can be described as rich and poor, deep or shallow, full or empty, strong or weak, to name some of the metaphors used. How do we know when we have had an experience or even a peak experience? Is it possible to prepare ourselves for it, to stage it or rehearse it, to open our senses to it? Or is it precisely the opposite way: rich experiences do not come prepackaged, they take us unawares, spontaneity is their hallmark? Questions like these seem to have always haunted both tourists and the tourist industry and they carry an element of catch-22. On the one hand, the wish for deeper or stronger experience means a focus on opening up the senses, being prepared, but on the other hand the peak experience should be spontaneous. It should sneak up, take us off guard, unprepared, like a sudden shiver running down the spine. How then is the cultural capital of preparation, of background knowledge to be weighed against the importance of freshness, the longing for a clean slate, an "unmediated" experience?

This dilemma may produce a tourist angst, which also has to do with the comparative framework of the narratives and experiences of those others: Goethe or the neighbors across the road? Will my holiday experiences live up to their standards? Cyril Connolly talks about that guidebook-produced "inadequacy of our feelings," when "the Acropolis just resembles a set of false teeth in a broken palate" (1984:25). In 1856 the American travel writer George Curtis wrote, "people love the country theoretically, as they do poetry. Very few are heroic enough to confess that it is wearisome even when they are fatigued by it." The reason for this was, he thought, the idea that "we ought to love it, and we ought to be satisfied and glad among the hills and under the trees."[6]

The history of Niagara and Yosemite demonstrate this anxiety, and the continuous mental wear and tear of our presence at tourist sites. As guidebooks and fellow travelers provide a wealth of subtexts to each panorama, we have to develop new strategies in order to make it into a strong and undisturbed personal experience.

A classic example is Nathaniel Hawthorne's sketch about the tourist who approached Niagara in 1834 and shut his eyes to avoid seeing the falls and instead hastened into his hotel room to build up the right mood, but his anticipations proved to be too much. When he stepped out to admire the falls, they turned out to be an anticlimax (quoted in Shepard 1967:146). Other travelers could describe their own disappointments or ironize about high-flying expectations.

In 1872 Isaac Bromley visited Yosemite and set out for the experience of the Grizzly Giant in the Mariposa Grove of giant sequoias. He had been "working up pretty carefully," supposing that he would be inspired to "soar on the wings of fancy, and all that sort of thing," only to find himself not inspired at all. There was nothing he could think of "except for lunch, and as for soaring, nothing in the world could make me soar except my unfortunate horse, and he had done it already so that I could hardly turn in the saddle" (quoted in Demars 1979:31).

Narratives of disappointments like these, as well as denunciations of "shallow experiences" or "tourist traps," tell us at once about tourist angst and about strategies of heightening the experience of a well-established attraction: intensification as a countermove to trivialization. One of its most striking examples is the nineteenth-century cult of concentration and stillness, so central in the sunset experience. Here is an emphasis on solitude and serenity, but also on focusing, which develops in many arenas of aesthetic consumption. During the early nineteenth-century people start hushing others in concert halls and art galleries. The focus of the senses should be directly forward, taking in the music, the acting, the artwork, without distractions. The ears must learn to absorb as well as the eyes.

James Buzard includes the cult of stillness in his discussion of strategies of intensification among nineteenth-century visitors to southern Europe. What he calls the "authenticity effect" can be furthered not only by stillness, but also by the elements of nonutility, saturation, and picturesqueness (1993:177). For the ambitious tourist intent on putting all the elements to work, the strategy calls for the timing of visits at propitious moments but also for the stillness of a spectator: allowing yourself to be drawn into the scenery. The emphasis here is on the dreamlike qualities of a strong experience. The nonutility element links the effect to an experience of unreality or the theatrical; a great tourist sight should not be contaminated by the everyday banality. The third element, saturation, is bound up with the two earlier and has to do with a situation or scenery that is "drenched" in significance, full of associations and reminiscences: a dense experience. And finally, the picturesqueness has to do with scenic qualities discussed earlier.

Buzard's discussion deals with a specific era and a specific narrative community of tourists and cannot be generalized, but some of these mechanisms of alterity are still important, although often in transmuted forms. And in certain settings the virtue of nonutility resembles its opposite, the authenticity of an undisturbed everyday reality: village and town scenes where the locals go about their daily business as usual. The picturesque faces competition from other aesthetic norms and so on. Today we find travel advertisements urging an involvement of all senses and activating the body.

Behind all these changing techniques of intensification there is, of course, a strong normative element present, namely, the idea that we ought to create experiences—they are good for us! Furthermore, we should be able to communicate them, represent them in words or images, drawing on available narrative genres for recapitulation, some of which are more tied to specific historic eras or cultural settings than others. Our own experiences are influenced by the narratives of others—other persons, other places, other moments. Sometimes in the midst of a landscape experience or at a tourist attraction I find my mind wandering to the questions of how this moment can be transformed into a memory, a souvenir, or a good story. As tourists we often devote a great deal of energy to the experiences of others, admiring or ridiculing them or even questioning their status as a "true" experience.

My argument is that tourism is a rewarding laboratory for exploring the production and transformation of experiences. Here we find the microritualizations of framing the right time and place, the turning of experience into event or occasion by markings, but also the demand to activate all senses.

It is the interaction between certain landscape characteristics, mindsets, and tourist technologies of movement and representation that produces a vacationscape. Some landscapes have special attractions for certain visitors because they carry a special potential of making room for mindscaping. The picturesque idyll contained all kinds of props to set thoughts flying, while a romantic like Thoreau appreciated landscapes uncluttered by human presence and local history, because they gave room for his imagination.[7] The mighty roar of Niagara could produce a special awe, a sense of liberation that set the mind working in other directions, just as the deafening stillness of the vast panoramas of Yosemite or the Grand Canyon helped to create a space for transcendence.

The grammar of landscape experiences includes all the different tourist forms of "taking in a landscape": to traverse it, pass through it or past it, to dwell in it, sense it, be part of it, or balancing at a viewpoint watching it unfolding in front of us. The tendency to talk about landscape in terms of settings and scenes, something to approach, enter, or look at, obscures the fact that landscapes are produced by movement, both of the senses and of the body.

A historical perspective can also show continuities and links backward in time, illuminating the didactic processes that help certain scenes convey specific cultural messages or moods; in other words, how they territorialize emotion. The way we react to a piece of landscape today is often the result of a long process of institutionalization, a development that has condensed a scene into a cultural matrix, an icon.

Because of this condensation, perhaps only a detail, the merest hint, can paint a landscape of the mind. A swaying palm tree or a tilted cocktail glass in a tourist brochure can be enough to conjure up a reader's whole world of holiday moods and carefree tropical dreams; the image of a single tree fills us with patriotic ardor or profound homesickness.

Any landscape experience blends the unique and personal with standardized preconceptions and cultural conventions. Here we are, tourists now, looking out over a beach, a meadow, or a mountain, enjoying particular tourist props with a swarm of earlier experiences, images, and associations we have collected. In this very moment history and the present collude in ways that are difficult to verbalize or even make conscious. We stand still in the same vacationscape with our feet firmly planted on the ground, but our minds travel far, in diverse confrontations between experiences past and present, daydreams, preconceptions, and afterthoughts. We follow the same beaten track and move through different mindscapes looking for different things. We may devote a lot of energy to deconstructing the conventions, associations, and cognitive frameworks of the tourist experience and still not be able to map it. In the ambition of the tourist industry to prepackage and market experiences this dilemma becomes very obvious. Experiences are hard to direct and predict. Their variability also prevents a unilinear narrative of the making of vacationscapes. What we get in such a narrative is often a normative history of what people ought to experience, which begs the question of who are setting the rules and who are supposed to live up to them in given situations.

Source: From *On Holiday: A History of Vacationing*, 1999. Reprinted with permission of the author and University of California Press.

Notes

[1] For a general discussion of the history of the picture postcard see Löfgren 1985.

[2] For comparative material on the panoramic view and the sunset, see Grossklaus and Oldemeyer 1983.

[3] See the discussion in Wilson 1992:46.

[4] See discussion in Löfgren 1998:114–25.

[5] Thomas Cole, "Essay on American Scenery" (1936), quoted in Shepard 1967:186.
[6] George William Curtis, *Lotus Eating* (1856), quoted in Shepard 1967:147.
[7] See the discussion in Ryden 1993:223–25.

References

Abrahams, Roger. 1986. "Ordinary and Extraordinary Experiences," in *The Anthropology of Experience*, eds. Victor Turner and Edward M. Bruner, pp. 45–72. Chicago: University of Illinois Press.

Appadurai, Arjun. 1996. *Modernity at Large: Cultural Dimensions of Globalization*. Minneapolis: University of Minnesota Press.

Ariyoshi, Rita. 1997. "Wailea–Sun and Sunsets." *Spirit of Aloha*, June:8–9.

Bachelard, Gaston. 1994. *The Poetics of Space*, trans. Maria Jolas. Boston: Beacon Press.

Buzard, James. 1993. *The Beaten Track: European Tourism, Literature and the Ways to Culture, 1800–1918*. Oxford: Clarendon Press.

Connolly, Cyril. 1984. *The Selected Essays of Cyril Connolly*, ed. Peter Quennell. New York: Persea Books.

Demars, Stanford E. 1979. *The Tourist in Yosemite, 1855–1985*. Salt Lake City: University of Utah Press.

Enzensberger, Hans Magnus. 1971. "Fine Theorie des Tourismus," in *Einzelheiten: Bewusstseins-Industrie*, pp. 179–205. Frankfurt am Main: Rowohlt.

Feldman, Allen. 1991. *Formations of Violence: The Narrative of the Body and Political Terror in Northern Ireland*. Chicago: University of Chicago Press.

Glassie, Henry. 1982. *Passing the Time in Ballymenone: Culture and History of an Ulster Community*. Philadelphia: University of Pennsylvania Press.

Graves, Robert. 1969. *The Crane Bag and Other Disputed Subjects*. London: Cassell.

Greer, Germaine. 1995. "Shanghai Express." *Granta*, 50:225–48.

Grossklaus, Gotz, and Ernst Oldemeyer. 1983. *Naturals Gegenwelt: Beitrage zur Kulturgeschichte der Natur*. Karlsruhe: von Loper Verlag.

Jasen, Patricia. 1995. *Wild Things: Nature, Culture, and Tourism in Ontario, 1790–1914*. Toronto: Toronto University Press.

Koch, N., and F. Sondergaard Jensen. 1988. *Skovernes Friluftsfunktion I Danmark: Befolkningens Onsker til Skovernes og det adne Lands Udformning*, vol. 4. Copenhagen: Statens Florstlige Forsogsvaesen.

Löfgren, Orvar. 1985. "Wish You Were Here! Holiday Images and Picture Postcards," in *Ethnologia Scandinavia*, pp. 96–108.

———. 1998. "My Life as Consumer," in *Narrative and Genre*, eds. Mary Chamberlain and Paul Thompson, pp. 114–25. London: Routledge.

Norland, Anna. 1996. "Fiktionen ar en del av Verkligheten." *Dagens Nyheter* (15 August). Stockholm.

Pemble, John. 1987. *The Mediterranean Passion: Victorians and Edwardians in the South*. Oxford: Oxford University Press.

Peterson, George L., and Edward S. Neumann. 1969. "Modeling and Predicting Human Response to the Visual Recreation Environment." *Journal of Leisure Research* 1(3): 219–37.

Ryden, Kent. 1993. *Mapping the Invisible Landscape: Folklore, Writing and the Sense of Place*. Iowa City: University of Iowa Press.

Shafer, Elwood L., John F. Hamilton, and Elizabeth Schmidt. 1969. "Natural Landscape Preferences: A Predictive Model." *Journal of Leisure Research* 1(1).

Shepard, Paul. 1967. *Man in the Landscape: A Historical View of the Esthetics of Nature*. New York: Knopf.

Stewart, Susan. 1984. *On Longing: Narratives of the Miniature, the Gigantic, the Souvenir, the Collection*. Baltimore: Johns Hopkins University Press.

Stannard, Martin. 1982. "Debunking the Jungle: The Context of Evelyn Waugh's Travel Books, 1930–39," in *The Art of Travel Writing: Essays on Travel Writing*, ed. Philip Dodd. London: Frank Cass.

Towner, John. 1996. *An Historical Geography of Recreation and Tourism in the Western World*. Chichester: John Wiley and Sons.

Wenger, Willy D. Jr., and Richard Videbeck. 1969. "Eye Pupillary Measurement of Aesthetic Response to Forest Scenes." *Journal of Leisure Research* 1(2):149–62.

Wilson, Alexander. 1992. *The Culture of Nature: North American Landscape from Disney to the Exxon Valdez*. Oxford: Blackwell.

Two:
Marketing Culture
and Identity

If the explorer moves toward the risks of the formless and the unknown, the tourist moves toward pure cliché.

— Paul Fussell, U.S. historian and critic, 1980

One of the most radical changes since, say, the 1950s is the degree to which leisure experience is commercially mediated to every conceivable individual taste.

— Ted C. Lewellen, U.S. anthropologist, 2002

7

Rereading the Language of Japanese Tourism

Brian Moeran

Although the Japanese had been going abroad since the end of World War II, it was not until 1964 (the year of the Tokyo Olympics) that the government began lifting its restrictions on foreign currency allowances and the international tourist industry, as such, got under way in Japan. Only fifteen years later, by 1979, more than four million people a year were traveling overseas on business and/or for pleasure. In that year, Japanese expenditure on international travel was US$4.8 billion (Sōrifu 1981:40), which made Japan the third largest tourist nation in the world after the United States and West Germany. A survey by the National Life Centre showed that international travel was the ambition of almost 38 percent of those living and working in Japan's major cities (Sōrifu 1981:12; see also Tamao 1980:130–1).

Since then, tourism has increased in scale, both within Japan and to international destinations. Following former Prime Minister Tanaka's push for "internationalization" during the mid to late 1980s, the number of Japanese traveling abroad reached ten million in 1990. A peak of nearly 18 million was reached in 2000. Foreign tourism has declined since to approximately sixteen million visitors a year (Kokudo Kōtsūshō 2002), of whom at least 45 percent are women. Japan now ranks fourth in the world in terms of foreign tourism expenditure (US$32.8 million), after the United States, Germany, and the United Kingdom, although its income from foreign tourism is only US$3.4 million (31st in the world rankings).[1] Japan's overall tourism expenditure amounts to 5.7 percent of its gross domestic production (Kokudo Kōtsūshō 2003).

What do the Japanese seek when they travel abroad? In the 1960s and 1970s, international tourism was basically geared to sightseeing, mainly by middle-aged Japanese who traveled in groups accompanied by a tour guide: yesterday the Acropolis, today the Coliseum, tomorrow the Eiffel Tower. These sightseers wanted not just to experience foreign cultures, but also to *compare* them with their own. International travel began to be possible for the Japanese just at a time when they were starting to search for their "roots" and when their interest in national "traditions" and "history" was at its height. Thus, the Japanese toured the Acropolis, the White House, and the Louvre, partly to see the monuments themselves and partly to judge how they compared with such Japanese monuments as the Tōdaiji temple, the National Diet, and their own state-run art museums.

In the 1980s, the Japanese started to travel alone or in small groups of friends or relatives. They now wanted to experience action, not sights, to "participate with their own skins" *(jibun no hada de sanka suru)* in sports, hobbies, and events such as the Knoxville Expo, the Dutch Floriade, or Aloha Week in Hawai'i.[2] It was this interest in sports in particular that seems to have marked the shift from the earlier emphasis on group travel and sightseeing to individual travel and "play." This tendency remains today, as can be

Japanese tourists from the same company enjoy a cruise down the Li River in China in 1989. (Photo by Sharon Gmelch)

seen in the proliferation of the tourist industry's offerings to independent travelers: *I'll*, *My Style*, *Free Stay*, *Slim*, and so on. This younger generation of Japanese tourists has altered the face of international travel and brought the goals of Japanese tourism more in line with those found in Europe and North and South America. The tourism industry now invites the Japanese to do what they want, where they want, as they want. The rigidly controlled era of the flag-bearing, uniformed guide leading a party of bewildered Japanese tourists across Trafalgar Square or up the Empire State Building has not entirely disappeared, but it is becoming rare.

The Language of Travel Brochures

The idea that life was to be enjoyed, particularly prevalent among people in their late twenties and early thirties in the mid-1980s, has had serious implications for the society and economy of Japan. According to research conducted by the Hakuhodo Institute of Life and Living, this so-called "new breed" *(shinjinrui)* seriously upset its grandparents' generation of "corporate greying warriors" by "demanding more time for themselves, taking longer vacations, cultivating friendships outside the companies in which they worked, even considering changing jobs" (McCreery 2000:54). Before discussing the implications of these changes, however, let us look at some of the concepts and phrases with which travel agencies sought to attract people to join their tours at the beginning of the 1980s. While some potential tourists already had heard about "thrilling" Waikiki Beach, "exotic" Bangkok, "glamorous" Monte Carlo, and so on from colleagues, friends, and family, they also read and were influenced by travel brochures. Tracing the language used in the travel brochures put out by tour companies allows us to track the aspirations of tourists and hence those of Japanese society as a whole (cf. Thurot and Thurot 1983).

In the early 1980s, the standard Japanese travel brochure (for a *Look* or *Jalpak* tour, for example) started out with an introductory page, followed by a list of tour variations and prices. It then devoted one section to hotels, another to food, and a third to the advantages of this particular tour (advantages that emphasized that Japanese-style service would be available). The brochure would then turn to a description of the sights to be seen and things to be done abroad. A study of brochure literature at this time suggested that the Japanese tourist was preoccupied with nature, food, and recreation—"nature tourism"—on the one hand, and with shopping, art, and culture—"culture tourism"—on the other (Graburn 1977:27). General themes that recurred were those of status and experience.

Contemporary brochures (Autumn 2002) reveal rather different emphases in their overall structure. For a start, they are more like catalogues that are packed full of information about how and where to travel, shop, eat, be entertained, and so on. In this, they resemble info-tainment magazines like *Orange*

Page, Lettuce Club, and so on that came on the market in the mid to late 1980s. As a result, less space is given to contextualizing tourist activities by describing their natural and/or cultural environment. Some cultural markers are still included—like *Verona, the scene of Romeo and Juliet,* or *Mont St. Michel, designated world heritage site by UNESCO,* or even *Belgium, the chocolate empire*—but for the most part Japanese now *know* everything there is to know about French and Italian designer brands, where to shop in London, and even that La Sagrada Familia was designed by the celebrated Spanish architect, Gaudi. They do not necessarily have to be told so by brochures, as in the past.

A second noticeable aspect of contemporary travel brochures is the way in which, following the overall pattern of consumer marketing (Moeran 1996:102–3), they have made tourism an inherent part of the tourist's lifestyle. Here, keywords are brought into play to emphasize practicality or experience. The *ANA Hallo Tour,* for example, emphasizes five advantages: the emotional security *(anshin)* of having safe travel arrangements, whose practicality *(benri)* is borne out by good connections to Narita international airport from all over Japan, as well as the savings *(otoku)* made by not having to pay airport tax. Then there are the services and comfort provided by the airline company *(kaiteki),* which provides further happiness *(ureshisa)* through its air miles system. Club Med, on the other hand—with boxed pictures of village accommodation, relaxation, food, sports, entertainment, communication, discovery, and kids—emphasizes first and foremost freedom of choice in its holiday offerings, which always stress superiority *(yū),* play *(yu),* and individual *(ji)* freedom *(yu).*

Nature Tourism

One of the major themes of Japanese tourism in the early 1980s was the appreciation of nature. This is hardly unexpected in view of the fact that the Japanese have long been famed for their interest in nature, and that the media regularly use nature images as part of the *lingua franca* of consumerism (Moeran and Skov 1997). In the early years the Japanese were not in general that concerned with the *physical* advantages to be gained from traveling somewhere with good weather; rather, nature was something to be spiritually experienced in its totality. It was depicted in minute detail in descriptions of a hotel garden in Singapore, the streets of Penang, or the gentle breezes of the Aegean.

Three comments might be made about Japanese tourists' attitudes toward nature. In the first place, their love of nature has, in part at least, been stimulated by the fact that post-war economic growth and industrialization within Japan led to overcrowded living conditions and to pollution of the environment. This is made clear in the brochures published for domestic tourism, where the contrast between the peace and quiet of Japan's countryside and the noise and bustle of city life is much more obvious.³ Secondly, although the Japanese liked to experience nature in its totality, by the early 1980s a new tendency emerged whereby Japanese tourists emphasized certain aspects of nature—in much the same way as Western tourists have done. They now wanted to make use of nature, and sun and sea rapidly came to be associated with and valued for the recreation they could provide. At the time, this appeared to be the result of the increase in the number of young tourists going abroad and of their interest in "experience" as opposed to mere "sightseeing." The Japanese, it seemed, were in the process of shifting from Graburn's "environmental" to "recreational" tourism.

In contemporary travel brochures, nature is highlighted primarily in literature on Asian destinations—Bali, Bintan, Borakai, Cherating Beach, and Phuket are now part of the Japanese tourist's playground. Particular aspects of the subtropical region are mentioned time and time again: Asian tropical gardens, ivory beaches, giant coconut palms, luscious bougainvillea flowers, and so on. There are still plenty of references to "grand nature" (daishizen), reflecting earlier Japanese tourists' interest in spiritually experiencing nature in its totality rather than gaining physically from good weather. Previously, nature had "grandeur" *(yudai)* and "art" *(geijutsu)*; it was "beautiful" *(utsukushii)*, "magnanimous" *(ōraka)*, "opulent" *(yutaka)*, and "unpolluted" *(yogore no nai)*. In more recent years, however, nature allows visitors to let both their minds and bodies relax *(yuttari to, kokoro mo karada mo relax)*. "Health" *(kenkō)* has become the new buzzword in connection with nature, and tourists are invited to engage in a rich variety of activities *(varietyi yutaka no)*: snorkel, windsurf, practice archery, get massages, and enjoy *"esthé"* salons and fresh foods.

Thirdly, the wealth of nature in foreign places has at times been directly contrasted with the naivety or "artlessness" *(soboku)* of the people living there. The first Japanese tourist I ever met was in Athens, Greece, in the summer of 1967. He, and all the other men in his party of 25, carried three pieces of hand baggage. Of these, two were filled with food! The first Japanese tourists abroad were wary of sampling foreign cooking and often took with them, as a precautionary measure, green tea, dried seaweed, pickles, instant noodles, and various other Japanese delicacies, in order to survive the perceived "rigors" of overseas travel. Those days are gone. The Japanese tourist has learned that foreigners can cook after all, and one of the pleasures advertised in brochures for international travel is the food: Macao is billed for its Portuguese cooking, Penang for its fresh fish, Vienna for its coffee, Paris for its raw oysters, Geneva for its fondue, even London for its fish and chips. Honeymooners are invited to sample "romantic" dinners with "tropical" drinks in Singapore, and food—from Alaskan salmon to Hawai'ian pineapples—is frequently advertised as one of the better gifts to bring back home. In short, food is also a means by which the Japanese are invited to experience "being abroad."⁴

Beginning in the 1980s, Japanese people traveling abroad also began to want to participate in the activities of their hosts, rather than merely see the sights of the countries they visited. This trend has continued and is probably connected with the fact that young people form a very large percentage of Japanese tourists overseas. Tourism advertising integrates young Japanese women tourists, in particular, into different exotic scenarios, by depicting them among flamenco or Balinese dancers, talking with a French woman in a Parisian café, walking through the streets of London as just one among many shoppers, and so on (Moeran and Skov n.d.). In an interesting take on "occidentalism" (Carrier 1995), Japanese tourists are thus naturalized in a foreign environment. It is young tourists who are invited to participate in "active," "sporty," and "thrilling" recreational activities. The travel brochures are filled with information on what to do where—fish, ski, and golf in Europe and roller skate, cycle, and sail in the United States.

Economic factors are partly responsible for this shift toward "activity" tourism, as well as for the tourist destinations people choose. As a general rule, recreational activities were not readily available to the average Japanese in the 1980s unless s/he was prepared to pay very large membership fees for the use of gymnasiums, tennis courts, or golf courses. Few young people could afford to pay US$2,000 for an American-style keep-fit class or US$5,000 for a golf membership without company or parental aid. Tourism thus provided an opportunity to indulge in the sort of activities that they could not regularly do at home. It also allowed them to try new sports that were not widely known or practiced in Japan. It is probably for this reason that Hawai'i and the West Coast of America were such popular targets of Japanese tourism during the 1980s to mid 1990s, and why Southeast Asian destinations are so popular now. Japanese tourists have brought these new sports back home. A lot of young Japanese go wind surfing during the summer months and some Tokyo satellite towns, like Zushi, have their own surfer subcultures. This integration of formerly "exotic" sports into Japanese life prompts tourist brochures to emphasize even newer activities like snorkeling, kayaking, and beach volleyball.

Tourism is basically a product of urbanization. Up to 1978, for example, almost one in four tourists came from Tokyo (Naikaku Sōridaijin 1979:73). In general, those who live in cities are the first who want to get away from what they see as the artificiality of their surroundings and go back to nature. It is they who want to eat something other than packaged food and to participate in activities other than those that confine them to milling around inside large palaces of glass and concrete. Hence the urban city dweller's desire to travel back "home" to the Japanese countryside (Ehrentraut 1993) and "old-village villages" (Robertson 1998), or far away overseas, where they can sample "natural" uncontaminated foods, in a "natural" environment, doing "naturally" healthy sports. In this respect, nature tourism becomes, perhaps especially for the Japanese, a "sacred journey" (Graburn 1977).

Cultural Tourism

The theme of shopping, which is emphasized in travel brochures, is very much part of the Japanese tourist's desire to compare life abroad with that back home. This penchant for comparison can lead to a degree of "ethnic" tourism: the traveler purchases Balinese *batik*, Hong Kong silk, or Eskimo arts and crafts as mementos of her trip abroad. But, in general, Japanese do not buy such products of ethnic tourism for themselves so much as to give them to others. Shopping abroad, therefore, is emphasized in the brochures because it gives the traveler some indication of the sort of gift she can bring home and present to family, friends, neighbors, and fellow workers. Souvenirs for the Japanese tourist do not so much remind the tourist that she has been abroad; they remind those in her immediate social network of this fact (Graburn 1983). Japan is famous for its "souvenir culture" *(omiyage bunka)*; the giving and receiving of presents is an important part of everyday social relations as well as of the Japanese economy.[5]

At the same time, one of the major preoccupations of the Japanese tourist has been that of status. Over the years, Japanese consumers were led by persuasive advertising to believe that quality was only to be found in certain "brand name" commodities and this led to a kind of "brand mania" during the 1970s and early 1980s. Thus one of the pleasures—and indeed for some one of the "musts"—of going abroad was, and to some extent still is, that of being able to purchase a brand name commodity in its country of origin. Japanese tourists still tend to use trips abroad to buy Burberry coats in London, Louis Vuitton bags in Paris,[6] or Royal Copenhagen porcelain in Denmark. It is this kind of commodity that the Japanese tourist keeps for herself, not just as a reminder of a trip abroad, but as a symbol of status that comes from having been abroad. "I bought my Philippe-Patek in Mitsukoshi Department Store" can thus be replaced by the ultra-casual "Oh! I got that the last time I was passing through Switzerland."

A second important aspect of Japanese culture tourism has been an emphasis on art and culture in the travel brochures. Just as Europeans and Americans have learned to equate Florence with the Renaissance, Egypt with the pyramids, and Mexico with Mayan and Aztec civilizations, Japanese tourist information is very specific in its use of "cultural markers" (MacCannell 1976:110). Thus Lausanne is where to find the headquarters of the IOC (International Olympic Committee); Geneva's university library houses a room used by Rousseau; the Rhine is noted for the poetry written about it by Heine and Byron; the Cotswolds and the town of Bybury in England are linked with William Morris; while the Piazza di Spagna is where "Hepburn walked in the film." This preoccupation with culture is also apparent in the travel brochures' frequent reference to cultural institutions such as palaces, cathedrals, ruins, and opera houses; to historical markers such as "baroque," "gothic," and "Islamic"; and cultural keywords—history *(rekishi)*, tradition *(dentō)*, art *(geijutsu)*, fine art *(bijutsu)*, fashion *(fasshon)*, civilization *(bun-*

mei), and to culture itself *(bunka)*. There is also a lot of emphasis on art and art institutions: Bali's shadow puppet theatre, Milan's *La Scala*; Carmel in California as an "artists' town," and New York's SoHo and Greenwich Village as the places artists gather (or used to gather). The Japanese are still extremely conscious of culture, and travel brochures are mines of foreign cultural information. This might seem paradoxical in view of Japanese tourists' new interest in "participation," but it needs to be remembered that a very large percentage of overseas tourists are women who are the prime consumers of art and culture (Skov and Moeran 1995).

Status and Tourism

The ability to avoid work and indulge in leisure activities such as tourism is often translated into status terms. When older people travel abroad it is an indication of their secure financial status and the newly found leisure that comes with retirement. When younger people "go abroad," status considerations are also important. This was especially true in the 1970s and 1980s. A large percentage of the young Japanese who then went abroad were honeymooners. Japanese wedding etiquette made it virtually essential that newly wedded couples went abroad for their honeymoons. Many couples also had second wedding ceremonies performed in churches in Hawai'i or on the West Coast of America. It was then fashionable and prestigious to get married according to Western and Christian styles in addition to traditional Shinto beliefs (cf. Goldstein-Gidoni 1997). This trend is dying now, although many Japanese honeymoon couples still go abroad.[7]

In the 1970s and 1980s, when a comparatively significant number of marriages in Japan were still arranged, a prospective bride's "character" was measured by her ability to perform the tea ceremony, arrange flowers, and cook Japanese style. To these accomplishments she added the status (or "social capital") of at least one trip abroad, since the "modern" housewife was expected to have something more than just traditional Japanese qualities.[8] Today things have changed. Many young women are not getting married until well into their 30s. For them, tourism is undertaken as a means to escape the drudgery of work in an employment system that usually fails to make the most of their skills. It is not so much going abroad or even *where* they go, but *how often* they can get away every year that counts in their peer-group status game.

As in Western nations, the Japanese now view group travel as having lower status than individual travel. One reason is that group package tours are now much cheaper. There also has been a growing emphasis within Japanese society on "personalization"—a form of individuation associated with the notion of elitism. Status now accrues from the way in which one travels, and this is reflected in the language of tourism. In travel brochures, facilities at hotels and sports clubs are "luxurious" and "gorgeous." Everything from shops to stage shows in resort areas are now described as "high class," "first class," or "deluxe." Hotel interiors, meals, and nightlife are "extravagant" and "elegant." The feeling a tourist should get from experiencing all of these is one of personal "richness." Luxury, and the status that is implied by luxury, is of course also found in the names of hotels (Royal, Regency, Imperial), the class of airline travel (Ambassador, Executive, Club), and in tour names (Special, Royal, Ace, Luxury).

Status is also derived from where Japanese tourists travel. Here three different criteria are brought to bear. In the first place, there is "destination elitism," in which the distance traveled more or less indicates a person's financial status. In the 1970s and 1980s it was much better for a Japanese tourist to go to Singapore than to Seoul, and to the United States or Europe than to Southeast Asia. Sometimes, however, it is possible for a country to rank high on the Japanese tourist's prestige list despite its proximity to Japan. Mainland China was a case in point during the 1980s, largely because Japanese tourists at the time had to pay more for their trips there than for an equivalent trip to, say, Hawai'i. This is not so today. Destination elitism depends not just on distance but on the general development of the tourism industry as a whole in the country a tourist wishes to visit.

Secondly, there is also "cultural elitism." The Japanese travel literature suggests that cultural elitism can be independent of economic status. Japanese travel brochures frequently compare tourist areas in Southeast Asia and America to their European counterparts. Thus, Pattaya Beach in Thailand has been likened to the south of France, Macao is described as "the Monte Carlo of the East," San Francisco is praised for its "Mediterranean mood," and Boston for its "European city mood." For the Japanese, it appears, Europe is still at the pinnacle of cultural prestige. The fact that Europe is also one of the most distant destinations, however, makes it difficult to prove that cultural elitism is entirely independent of destination elitism (cf. Gather International 1972–73).

One indication of the Japanese admiration for Western culture is found in the travel brochures' extravagant use of English and other European language loanwords in their descriptions of sights and amenities. Such loanwords are also used when the Japanese talk or write about Western culturally influenced topics like fashion and music. The Japanese tourist is invited in brochures to experience the "unique," "fresh," "nostalgic," "exotic," "thrilling," "romantic," "sporty," "happy," "active," and "modern"—all rendered in English. In this respect, the language of international tourism used in Japanese brochures stands in direct contrast with that of domestic tourism. Here, place and experiences are described with Japanese words: *dokutoku* (the unique), *azayaka* (fresh), and *natsukashii* (the nostalgic). Foreign loanwords are used in brochures for domestic travel when they describe urban tourism. Literature on a "Tokyo Graffiti" tour, for example, uses loanwords like "exciting," "crystal," "academic," "romantic," and "thrilling," which especially appeal to young people. Most domestic tourism, however, actually focuses on scenic or cultural spots and, for these, typically Japanese phrases are used.[9]

The last criterion brought into play in tourists' decisions about where to visit is "leisure elitism." In the early 1980s, Hawai'i and the West Coast of America met this criterion since their apparent free and easy lifestyle contrasted strongly with that of Japan. Today, after a decade-long recession has created considerable change for the better in most Japanese people's previously stressful, work-dominated lives, leisure elitism has shifted to an emphasis on health, sports, and play. Now the resorts of Southeast Asia attract Japanese tourists by the hundreds of thousands, offering them what they cannot find elsewhere. To some extent, the economic downturn of the 1990s, together with a strengthened dollar, placed leisure elitism at the center of the Japanese tourists' quest for status, replacing destination elitism. Precisely because many people can no longer afford expensive trips to the United States, they see their money being better spent in Southeast Asia.

The timing of travel is often closely connected with status in that there are "on" and "off" seasons for tourism. A holiday taken during the off-peak season is usually considered in the West to be "superior" to one taken during the summer vacation along with everyone else. There does not appear to be that much status or elitism attached to the timing of vacations for the Japanese, however. The resorts popular with them have good weather all year round. Also, Japanese salaried workers typically do not take annual vacations at a fixed time of year. This gives Japanese tourists considerable flexibility in their choice of when to travel. Moreover, today young Japanese women who have not been fully incorporated into Japan's male-focused employment system, readily give notice and go on extended vacations with their hard-earned savings. They then return to Japan, find new temporary employment with comparatively good pay, and work for several months before again giving notice in order to travel abroad. This freedom from the constraints of work has given young women a certain elite cachet that has become the envy of their male colleagues and friends. It should be noted, however, that even male Japanese salaried workers today are more inclined to take advantage of their annual holidays and to go away for two or three weeks—unlike the two or three days that was customary in the 1970s. As a result, more Japanese families are traveling and this coincides with school vacations. (The Japanese school year begins in April, not in September).

Identity and Japanese Society

Tourism is one means by which people living in contemporary societies "experience" life. Thus, one of the major themes in travel brochures is "discovery"; the tourist is invited to experience the thrill of being abroad.[10] "Discovery! Discovery! At every crossroad," says the blurb on Singapore. "Round one unknown country after another—that is the joy of travel," states the introduction to a tour of Europe. "A great experience awaits you: *I love New York*" is how the tourist to the east coast of America is greeted. The tourism literature suggests that the world is waiting to be discovered by you—and you alone.

It is also suggested that the tourist will not just be an outsider in his travels, he or she will be a party to the smells, the laughter, the fun of an evening in Taipei, Barcelona, or Los Angeles. She will "melt" *(tokekomu)* into her surroundings, "not just as a passing traveler, but in touch with the lives of the local people." The subjective experience that travel brochures and popular magazines generally offer is one of identification and naturalization. As the Japan Travel Bureau's catchphrase used to go: "Travel is contact" *(tabi wa fureai)*. With Club Med these days it is "Communication."

Although this invitation to experience "authenticity" is common to much tourism (cf. MacCannell 1976), it has been particularly important for the Japanese because of the way in which their society is organized, with its strong ideological emphasis on the importance of the collective over the individual; and on the necessity for every person to subordinate his or her interests to those of the group to which s/he belongs. When Japanese go abroad, they are temporally without a group affiliation, and can escape from collectively imposed restrictions; "Throw away shame while traveling" *(tabi no haji wa kakisute)*, goes a popular proverb. Today, however, the Japanese are being invited to identify with the people they visit and hence avoid that anomalous state of being an "outsider" *(yoso no mono)*. The idea of "discovery," therefore, seems to be used in the travel literature to help the Japanese feel that they will merge into their new surroundings even though they will be temporarily cut off from the embrace of family, office, or other primary groups. At the same time, however, the invitation to melt into a foreign society is couched in language that can only make a Japanese tourist aware of his or her isolation. The travel brochures use the direct vocative "you" *(anata)* in addressing the tourist and there is the persuasive idea that "you" are always *alone*, that the moods that you experience abroad are entirely your own, perhaps shared by a loved one or close friend but certainly not by a group of people on the same tour or by the crowds of people thronging the sites or resorts visited.

This use of the second person to appeal to the individual is not just a trick of the travel trade, but one of advertising in general. Advertising appeals to individual consumers; and the general trend in advertising has shifted from the mass to the niche or personal lifestyle markets over the past four decades. Travel brochures use such phrases and titles as "My Pace," "My Plan," *My Style,* and even *I'll* (all written in English), to make the Japanese tourist realize that she can do as she wants once she has escaped the confines of society. The tourist is invited to "enjoy" herself, to play *(asobu)*, and to be lighthearted *(kigaru)* when away from a society that still stresses the importance of work and seriousness. She is told to take it easy *(yukkuri)*, to be carefree *(nonbiri)*, to "relax," to make use of "free time," to do as she pleases *(kimama)* in a leisurely *(yuttari)*, self-composed *(ochitsuita)*, and easy *(yutori)* manner. In short, the tourist is invited to do all the things that Japanese society has not generally permitted her to do.

Conclusion

The tourist literature is an excellent guide to fundamental changes that have been taking place in Japanese society over the past quarter of a century. It points out contrasts between the tourist's own and other countries' cultures and the "organization of diversity" (Hannerz 1992:14) to which they contribute in the global ecumene. International tourism, therefore, in a way threatens the tourist's present social system. It is potentially revolutionary, for it invites the tourist to experience change and hence possibly to bring back such change to her own society. This we have seen in the development of sports like surfing and windsurfing and the communities or subcultures of young *aficionados* they engender.

What is especially interesting in Japan is the fact that it is young women who travel with such frequency and in such great numbers. Not only are they refusing to get married as early as they once did. They are not even paying lip service to the masculine Japanese work ethic, and are influencing their young male friends to think in a similar manner. In this respect, although excluded from politics and business, women may be compensated for their apparent subordination by manipulating their role as tourists and consumers. This may be a dangerously easy argument to make, given the general male:work::female:leisure equation, but it is worth taking into consideration (Skov and Moeran 1995:1–59).

In a number of important respects, then, tourism is a bane to the idea that every nation should maintain its own "cultural identity." Japanese ideologists—from politicians to academics, by way of businessmen (Yoshino 1992)—have long upheld the idea that Japan is "unique" and that its culture and traditions can never be fully understood by foreigners. By going abroad in such numbers and so often, most young Japanese now question this ideological assumption. One major barrier to an outsider's understanding of Japan is the Japanese language, which makes use of two thousand Chinese characters and three syllabaries *(hiragana, katakana,* and the Roman alphabet, *rōmaji)*. Japanese linguists have claimed, in addition, that their language is unrelated to other Asian language groups, giving suspect support to the view that the Japanese way of thinking is "unique" (cf. Dale 1986). But, as already noted, the language of "modernity"—of tourism, fashion, popular music, advertising, and the media in general—relies to a very large extent on the use of foreign loanwords, or *gairaigo*, for its appeal. Tourist language would seem, in this respect, to threaten the "inscrutability" of Japanese written forms and to make the language as a whole more accessible to outsiders: barriers can be broken down, thanks to the adoption of Western concepts.

Thus, the language of tourism, as the language of modernity, poses a threat to Japan's uniqueness and sense of difference. At the same time, however, the frequent use of foreign words in Japanese shore up the preservation of that which is culturally different and specifically "Japanese." The same is true of the Japanese tourist abroad. If she does not find what she is looking for in other cultures, her tourism can reaffirm the superiority of Japan's cultural identity.[11] Potentially revolutionary, the ideas and language of tourism could in fact end up by being "reactionary."

The wording of travel brochures shows that the concerns of the Japanese tourist *are* mainly those of the American and European tourist. This would suggest that industrialization, urbanization, and consumerism give rise to a similar type of "modern" person and that cultural differences between nations are disappearing in much the same way as they have done locally within more advanced nations. In this respect, as well as in its standardization and homogenization of sightseeing spots, souvenir shops, and promotional language (Löfgren 1999:277), tourism achieves a kind of "globalization"—a topic much discussed in political, business, and academic circles today.

One of the major indications of the merging of cultural identities between Japan and other industrialized nations is the emphasis on subjectivity *(kosei)* noted above. The travel brochures' emphasis on concepts of play *(asobi)* and contact *(fureiai)* are in fact invitations to the Japanese to disregard the hitherto propagated group ideology (cf. Moeran 1984). The man who "plays" is being asked to withdraw from all the moral and social restrictions connected with work. The woman who is told to value "heart contact" *(kokoro no fureai)* is being told to meet people and situations on her own, independent of group affiliations. And this is precisely what is happening in contemporary Japanese society where men have devoted themselves so single-mindedly to work, while young women have been known to queue up outside American bases in Guam and pick up soldiers and sailors for a night out on the town. If the language of tourism *is* the same as the language of other aspects of consumerism in (post-) industrial society then it is clear that a study of such language provides us with a clue to the "structure of modernity." MacCannell (1976:2) has said that the fragmented aspect of modernity is a mask. The study of tourism *per se* shares this fragmented aspect in anthropology's approach to the study of modern society.[12] The experience of tourism is, yes, the experience of society, but it is an experience of society that has in many ways been created by the media (McLuhan 1964).

Source: Adapted from "The Language of Japanese Tourism," *Annals of Tourism Research*, 1983, 10:93–108.

Notes

[1] Average expenditure, by Japanese traveling abroad, amounts to ¥371,000 (approximately US$3,000), compared with ¥61,320 for domestic travel. Of this, just over ¥100,000 is spent

within Japan in preparation for the trip. The remaining ¥257,000 (approximately US$2,000) is spent overseas.

2 A much-publicized aspect of "skin participation" at the time was the all-male sex tours around the capitals of Southeast Asia.

3 In her discussion of Japanese return to origins through travel, Marilyn Ivy (1995:42–3) notes that the famous *Discover Japan* advertising campaign for domestic travel in the early 1980s directly copied both the idea and graphic design of a similar campaign run in the United States, *Discover America*.

4 The tourist's ability to adapt during her temporary and brief trip abroad contrasts with the way in which Japanese company employees temporarily resident abroad tend to keep to their Japanese dietary habits (Cwiertka 2002).

5 In 1981, total expenditure on gifts by the Japanese amounted to US$6.5 billion. Of this amount, US$3 billion was spent on seasonal and US$2 billion on personal gifts. A further US$500 million was spent on company gifts and US$1 billion on premiums (Nishio 1982:5). By the year 2000, the gift market stood at approximately US$126 billion, more or less equally distributed between personal and corporate gifts, with seasonal gifts accounting for US$25 billion and occasional and memorial gifts US$61.2 billion. Sales promotion gifts (including premiums) amounted to US$52 billion (*Gekkan Gifuto* 2001:47). In 1982, Nishio (1982:5) was able to point to a 10–15 percent annual increase in gift economy turnover, regardless of whether the Japanese economy as a whole was going through a boom or recession. Although there has been a flattening out of the gift economy in the very last years of the 1990s, it has still registered a comparatively healthy growth during the past two decades. Souvenirs alone now amount to US$3.9 billion (*Gekkan Gifuto* 2001:47).

6 As one informant put it, if Louis Vuitton sales amount to US$150 billion worldwide, two thirds of these sales take place within Japan. Of the remainder, 20 percent, or US$10 billion, is purchased by Japanese travelers overseas. This means that sales of Louis Vuitton products *not* purchased by Japanese amount to a mere US$40 billion.

7 At one stage, a considerable number of such couples arrived back in Japan and separated at the airport—in what came to be called the "Narita divorce"—after they had discovered that they were not really compatible at all.

8 Playing the piano was another "modern" virtue much in demand of prospective brides in middle-class urban families.

9 On Japanese domestic tourism, see Graburn (1983).

10 Discovery has also been an element in domestic tourism: witness, the National Railways "Discover Japan" advertising campaign in 1970.

11 This may explain the simultaneous usage of both the imported loanword, *karuchā* (culture), and its Japanese equivalent, *bunka*, in one recent travel brochure. "Culture" is for foreign countries, but "Japanese culture" or "tradition" *(dentō)* exists only in Japan.

12 Since this paper was first written, a whole wave of books and learned articles has washed over academia discussing the relation between the fragmented nature of society and post modernity. In rewriting the paper, I have decided it better to let these—sometimes interesting, at other times pretentious, at all times complex—discussions lie where they have fallen in the ocean of intellectual fashions.

References

Carrier, James, ed. 1995. *Occidentalism*. Oxford: Clarendon Press.

Cwiertka, Katarzyna. 2002. "Eating the Homeland: Japanese Expatriates in the Netherlands," in *Asian Food: The Global and the Local*, ed. K. Cwiertka and B. Walraven, pp.133–52. Honolulu: University of Hawai'i Press.

Dale, Peter. 1986. *The Myth of Japanese Uniqueness*. London: Croom Helm.

Ehrentraut, Adolf. 1993. "Heritage Authenticity and Domestic Tourism in Japan." *Annals of Tourism Research* 20(2): 262–78.

Gather International. 1972–73. *A Study of Japanese Travel Habits and Patterns*. Washington, DC: United States Travel Service.

Goldstein-Gidoni, Ofra. 1997. *Packaged Japaneseness: Weddings, Business and Brides*. Honolulu: University of Hawai'i Press.

Graburn, Nelson. 1977. "Tourism: The Sacred Journey," in *Hosts and Guests: The Anthropology of Tourism*, ed. V. Smith. Philadelphia: University of Pennsylvania Press.

———. 1983. *To Pray, Pay and Play: The Cultural Structure of Japanese Tourism*. Aix-en-Provence: Centres des Hautes Etudes Touristiques.

Hannerz, Ulf. 1992. *Cultural Complexity: Studies in the Social Organization of Meaning*. New York: Columbia University Press.

Ivy, Marilyn. 1995. *Discourses of the Vanishing: Modernity, Phantasm, Japan*. Chicago: University of Chicago Press.

Kokudo Kōtsūshō. 2002. *Kankō Hakusho (White Paper on Tourism)*. Tokyo: Zaimushō Insatsukyoku.

Löfgren, Orvar. 1999. *On Holiday: A History of Vacationing*. Berkeley and Los Angeles: University of California Press.

MacCannell, Dean. 1976. *The Tourist*. New York: Schocken Books.

McCreery, John. 2000. *Japanese Consumer Behaviour: From Worker Bees to Wary Shoppers*. Richmond, Surrey, UK: Curzon Press.

McLuhan, H. Marshall. 1964. *Understanding Media: The Extensions of Man*. New York: McGraw-Hill.

Moeran, Brian. 1984. "Individual, Group and *Seishin*: Japan's Internal Cultural Debate." *Man* 19(2): 252–66.

———. 1996. *A Japanese Advertising Agency: An Anthropology of Media and Markets*. Honolulu: University of Hawai'i Press.

Moeran, Brian, and Lise Skov. 1997. "Mount Fuji and the Cherry Blossoms: A View from Afar," in *Japanese Images of Nature: Cultural Perspectives*, ed. P. Asquith and A. Kalland, pp. 181–205. London: Curzon.

———. "Images of Spain and Europe in Japanese Advertising." Paper presented at the JAWS (Japan Anthropology Workshop) conference, Santiago de la Compostela, May 1996.

Naikaku Sōridaijin. 1979. *Kokusai Kankō no Genjō to Tōmen no Naisaku*. Tokyo: Chief Secretary of the Cabinet's Committee.

Nihon Kōtsū Kōsha. 1982. *Nyūsu to Shiryō*, Volume 2. Tokyo: Japan Travel Bureau.

Nishio, M. 1982. *Gifuto Marketingu*. Tokyo: Bijinesu-sha.

Robertson, Jennifer. 1998. "It Takes a Village: Internationalisation and Nostalgia in Postwar Japan," in *Mirror of Modernity: Invented Traditions of Modern Japan*, ed. S. Vlastos, pp. 110–29. Berkeley and Los Angeles: University of California Press.

Skov, Lise, and Brian Moeran, eds. 1995. *Women, Media and Consumption in Japan*. Honolulu: University of Hawai'i Press.

Sōrifu. 1981. *Kankō Hakusho* (White Paper on Tourism). Tokyo: The Prime Minister's Office.

Tamao, T. 1980. "Tourism within, from and to Japan." *International Social Science Journal* 32(1): 128–50.

Thurot, Jean-Maurice, and Gaétane Thurot. 1983. "The Ideology of Class and Tourism: Confronting the Discourse of Advertising." *Annals of Tourism Research* 10(1): 173–89.

Yoshino, Kosaku. 1992. *Cultural Nationalism in Contemporary Japan*. London and New York: Routledge.

8

The Maasai and the Lion King: Authenticity, Nationalism, and Globalization in African Tourism

Edward M. Bruner

Early work on the anthropology of tourism documented a variety of tourist experience in terms of a typology of tourism, including ethnic, cultural, historical, environmental, and recreational tourism (Smith 1989:4–6), as well as a typology of tourists, including explorer, elite, mass, individual traveler, backpacker, and charter tourists (Cohen 1979; Pearce 1982; Smith 1989:11–14). All tourism and all tourists were not the same, but scholars in the field tended to reduce the variety by seeking the essence of the tourist experience, as a quest for authenticity (MacCannell 1976), a personal transition from home to elsewhere (Graburn 1989), a form of neocolonialism (Nash 1989), or a particular type of "gaze" (Urry 1990). The typologies of tourism and tourists ordered the data but yielded few insights. Exceptions to the generalizations were common, rendering questionable their usefulness; one was never sure when or where the general propositions were applicable.

More recent field studies of tourism among particular peoples have tended to avoid typologies and monolithic generalizations, but still there is a predilection to homogenize local tourist displays.[1] The Maasai are represented as male warriors (Bruner and Kirshenblatt-Gimblett 1994), the Pueblo

as female potters (Babcock 1990), the Balinese as living in a magical world
of dance and drama (Bruner 1996b; Picard 1996; Vickers 1989), and the
Tahitians as representing South Seas sensuality (Kahn 2000). In such cases, a
single form of tourism becomes associated with one ethnic group in a given
locality, similar to the effect that Appadurai (1988) observes for ethnography,
where the connection between topic and place becomes the defining characteristic of a people, to the exclusion of other perspectives, for example, caste
with India, lineage with Africa, or exchange with Melanesia. Tourism scholarship thus aligns itself with tourism marketing, in that scholars tend to work
within the frame of the commercial versions of their sites. Grand statements
about the nature of tourism in Bali or Africa or even more broadly in the
"Third World" are sometimes the result, to the neglect of more ethnographi-
cally based and nuanced analyses of the variety of tourist displays within any
one culture area.

My objective in this article is to open up the theoretical dialogue in
tourism scholarship, and I do so by applying a method of controlled comparison (based on Eggan 1954), showing how one ethnic group, the Maasai, are
exhibited for tourists at three different sites in Kenya. Although all three sites
present a gendered image of the Maasai warrior (the personification of masculinity), a controlled comparison enables me to describe three ways of producing this image. Accordingly, I demonstrate how the breadth of meanings,
ironies, and ambiguities in tourist performances emerges from a critical comparison of the processes of their production. For example, familiar concepts
in the literature (such as authenticity, tradition, and heritage) are relevant in
only certain touristic contexts. I emphasize the importance of the distinction—not fully appreciated in the anthropological literature—between
domestic and foreign tourism, as well as the wide-ranging impact of globalization on the staging of local tourism.[2] Further, I show that historically
forms of tourism are parallel to forms of ethnographic writing. Finally, I
examine the sites in terms of what I call the "questioning gaze," my reference
to tourists' expressed doubts about the veracity of what they are seeing and
the way their questions and skepticism penetrate the commercial presentation, undermining the producer's dominant narrative.[3]

Elsewhere I have offered humanistically oriented descriptions of tourist
performances privileging political complexities and local voices (Bruner
1994, 1996a, 1996b). My emphasis in this article is on the production and on
the tourists, not on indigenous perceptions. My intention is to discuss each of
the three sites so that the comparisons and juxtapositions between them
become grist for the theoretical mill. What I say about any one site is
designed to contrast with another.

By way of background, Kenya achieved independence from Britain in
1963 and has a population of approximately 30 million divided into about 42
ethnic groups. The tensions between these many ethnic groups have been
severe at times. Tourism is a major source of income, the main attraction
being safari runs to view the wild animals in the game parks. The Maasai,

presented at the three tourist sites I discuss, are a seminomadic pastoral group with a total population of about 400,000 in Kenya; Maasai also live in Tanzania (Spear and Waller 1993).

My three Kenyan field sites are Mayers Ranch (Bruner and Kirshenblatt-Gimblett 1994), a privately produced performance organized by local entrepreneurs; Bomas of Kenya, a public production developed by the national government; and what a tour agency calls an "Out of Africa Sundowner" party at the Kichwa Tembo tented safari camp near the Masai Mara national reserve.[4] A thumbnail sketch of each site follows.

Designed for foreign tourists, the production at Mayers staged Maasai dancing in their warrior compound, chanting and carrying spears, proud and aloof. The production hid all outside influences and manufactured objects, presenting Maasai as timeless and ahistorical. Mayers reproduced a nineteenth-century colonial narrative (Knowles and Collett 1989) of Maasai men as exemplars of an African primitive, as natural man. It depicted Maasai men as brave warriors, tall and athletic, men who, at least in the past, would raid for cattle, kill lions armed with but a spear, consume raw foods such as milk and blood, and (as "Lords of East Africa") instill respect and fear in others. The producers strived for tourist realism (the aura of authenticity), and the site was designed as a series of tableaux, set up for tourist photography. The tourists viewed the Maasai from a colonial subject position, as did early explorers and ethnographers. Mayers began in 1968 and flourished until the 1980s but was eventually closed by the government, as the colonial aspects were offensive to many Kenyans. I will discuss the relations between tourism and ethnography later, but I note here that the critique of colonialism within anthropology (Asad 1975; Hymes 1972; Marcus and Fischer 1986) was part of the same worldwide anticolonial movement that led to the closing of Mayers Ranch in Kenya. Mayers is presented here as a baseline, as a superb example of postcolonial tourism that eventually gave way to newer modes of production.

Bomas is a national folklore troupe that presents the dances of Kenyan ethnic groups, including the Maasai, primarily for an audience of modern urban Kenyans. The mechanisms of production are prominently displayed. The dances are staged in an auditorium, with rows of seats and a bar in the back for the sale of refreshments. The theme of the production is Kenyan nationalism, to show that all the ethnic groups of Kenya are equally valued. Representatives of Bomas say that their aim is the preservation of Kenyan heritage, as if each ethnic culture is in the past and has to be recuperated in a museum-like setting. Bomas is an ethnic theme park for domestic tourists, a genre now found in many areas of the developing world.[5]

The Sundowner presents Maasai men dancing in the context of an "Out of Africa" cocktail party near an upscale tented safari camp on the Mara reserve. The Maasai performers mix with the tourists, who are served drinks and hors d'oeuvres by uniformed waiters. Globalizing influences are apparent, as Hollywood pop culture images of Africa and blackness are enacted for these foreign tourists as they sip champagne, alternately chatting among themselves and dancing with Maasai, all the while on safari in the African bush. These are posttourists (Feifer 1985; Urry 1990:100–102), beyond traditional tourism, who want a gracious African experience, all the comforts and luxury of home, and a good show rather than staged authenticity.

At all three tourist sites, Maasai men perform for an audience, but there are important differences. These differences are evident in the modes of transportation taken by the tourists to each site, and I describe them here, as the journey to a tourist destination is itself an inherent part of the tourist experience. Mayers is located in the Rift Valley about fifty minutes by car from Nairobi. Most tourists reached Mayers over dirt roads as passengers in a van provided by a local tour company. Bomas is located on the outskirts of Nairobi along the public bus route, and a convenient way of going is to drive or to take a city bus. Kichwa Tembo safari lodge is located by the Masai Mara reserve. In 1999, to take one example in which I participated, a group of tourists on the Intrav agency "Out of Africa" tour first visited Ngorogoro Crater in Tanzania, then went by a small charter aircraft directly from Kilimanjaro Airport in Tanzania to the Kichwa Tembo private airstrip in Kenya. The planes did not stop in Nairobi or go through Kenyan immigration or customs.[6] They flew directly from Tanzania to Kenya, over nation-states, in a seamless journey from one game park to another, indeed a transnational experience. From the perspective of the tourists, there was no border crossing, as the "nations" of Tanzania and Kenya were not really experienced. The tour was above borders, traveling not just in airspace but in global space. Travel by van, public bus, and charter aircraft characterize the three tourist attractions.

First, I summarize briefly the material on Mayers and then contrast these data with Bomas and the Sundowner. The latter sites will receive most of my descriptive and analytic attention. Although this study deals with Kenya, I suggest that the different contexts of production may be replicated in many other areas of the world where tourism is prominent. For reasons I explain in the conclusion, my claim is that my approach in this article has relevance beyond Kenya.

Mayers Ranch

Mayers Ranch was built by the Mayers, a British family who became Kenyan citizens. The Mayers came to Kenya early in the twentieth century, eventually went into cattle ranching, drastically reduced their land holdings after Kenyan independence, and in 1968 established a tourist attraction on their land as a way of generating additional income. There have been four generations of Mayers in Kenya. Their current homestead, located in the Great Rift Valley 30 miles from Nairobi, is blessed with a natural spring and features a verdant lawn and English garden. The Mayers hired local Maasai, some from families who had worked on their cattle ranch as herders, to build a Maasai *manyatta* (compound) for young warriors who would perform their dances and enact selected aspects of their culture for tourists. After viewing the Maasai performance, the tourists would then go to the Mayers's lawn for tea and crumpets.

The transition from the mud huts and brown dust of the Maasai compound to the lush green lawn and garden adjacent to the Mayers's main house enacted a key theme in East African tourist discourse, the contrast between the primitive Maasai and the genteel British, which evokes the broader contrast between the wild and the civilized. The tourists at Mayers experienced vicariously the wildness of the Maasai and, by extension, the wildness of Africa, only to return at the end of the performance to the safety of the Mayers's cultivated lawn, to the veritable sanctuary of a British garden in the Rift Valley. The Maasai dancers never spoke directly to the tourists. They carried spears and clubs, wore a solid red cloth, covered their bodies with red ochre, and braided and decorated their hair. On the elegant lawn, the Mayers were gracious, socializing with the guests and telling stories about colonial times, while two black servants (not Maasai) dressed in white aprons and white chef's hats served tea and cookies. As white settlers, the Mayers themselves were part of the tourist attraction, nostalgic relics of a colonial era. The performance was a fastidious and carefully constructed combination of tribalism and colonialism, which the tourists told me they found fascinating and romantic.

The show at Mayers Ranch was carefully edited and produced. The Maasai performers (or actors) were not allowed by the Mayers (the directors

Maasai warriors with spears at Mayers Ranch. (Photo by Edward M. Bruner)

of the drama) to wear or display modern clothing, watches, or any industrial manufactured objects. The only souvenirs sold at Mayers were those hand-crafted by Maasai. The entire performance was produced to achieve tourist realism, an ambience of authenticity, and the appearance of the real. The Mayers directed the Maasai to act as if they were what the foreign tourists regarded as nineteenth-century tribesmen, the African primitive. The ritual performed at the Maasai village was made to seem natural, as if the Maasai were dancing for themselves and the tourists just appeared there by chance. The constructedness of the site was masked. Some of the Maasai dancers had been to school and spoke English, but during performance time they remained aloof and mute.

I first gathered data from Mayers in 1984; when I returned in 1995, I learned that the performance had been closed. During lunch at the Mayers's home, Jane and John Mayers explained to me why they had been put out of business, and they did so, of course, from their own subject position, as descendants of a white British colonial family. It was a combination of fac-tors, they said, but the primary reason was that the government felt they were exploiting the Maasai. The Mayers reported that an African-American tour group visiting the ranch to watch the Maasai performance had objected strongly, complaining about its colonial aspects—specifically that the May-ers lived in a big house whereas the Maasai lived in mud huts, and that the Mayers gave food to the Maasai as part of their compensation, which they felt was paternalistic. The Mayers's brochure said that the Maasai were a lin-guistic subgroup of the Nilotic, but other black American tourists objected strongly to the term *subgroup*, which they regarded as insulting. The key fac-tor, however, according to the Mayers and others in the tourism industry, was that many Kenyans felt the performance of Maasai warriors dancing in a European homestead was simply too anachronistic for modern-day Kenya.

After closing the tourist performance, the Mayers remained on their ranch and engaged in other income-producing activities. They missed the income from tourism, but Jane expressed a feeling of relief, saying they had felt "totally invaded" having 150 tourists come to their home on any given day. Jane agreed that a performance about tribalism and colonialism was indeed an anachronism in contemporary Kenya and felt it would be best if the Maasai were producing their own performance. Some of the Maasai who had worked at Mayers went to the hotels in Mombasa and the coast where they found employment as performers in Maasai tourist productions, and a few became involved in the sex industry, catering mainly to European women seeking a sexual experience with a Maasai man.

Rosaldo (1989) coined the phrase "imperialist nostalgia," noting that contemporary Western peoples yearn for the "traditional" cultures that the previous generation of Western colonialists had intentionally destroyed. Ros-aldo's concept is not entirely adequate for my purposes as it refers primarily to a feeling (a yearning). Cultural tourism goes far beyond this yearning, recreat-ing in performance idealized colonial images and other representations of the past, the pastoral, the original, and the unpolluted. Tourism frequently enacts imperialist nostalgia. Tourism performances, throughout the world, regularly reproduce stereotypic images, discredited histories, and romantic fantasies. The past is manipulated to serve the expectations of the tourists and the political interests of those in power, and because the Mayers, as ex-colonialists, had little power in modern Kenya, their operation could be closed. Mayers Ranch, a good example of tourism artfully produced in the postcolonial era for a foreign audience, catered to the darkest desires of the tourist imaginary, fixing Maasai people in a frozen past, representing them as primitive, denying their humanity, and glorifying the British colonialism that enslaved them.

Bomas of Kenya

The second attraction discussed in this article, Bomas of Kenya, constructs a different picture, for a different audience. Bomas, opened to the public in 1973, is a government museum of the performing arts, an encyclopedic presentation of the cultural heritage of a nation, performed by a professional dance troupe whose members are government employees.[7] Their Web site says Bomas "offers Kenya in Miniature" (Bomas of Kenya 2000). Like Mayers, Bomas has regularly scheduled daily shows. The patrons pay admission, move into a 3,500–seat auditorium for the performance, and then exit from the building to walk to the 11 traditional minivillages.[8]

Each village features the architecture of a particular ethnic group—Kikuyu, Kalenjin, Luhya, Taita, Embu, Maasai, Kamba, Kissii, Kuria, Mijikenda, and Luo—and consists of a few houses typical of that group, or as the Bomas Web site says "the original traditional Architecture . . . as built by the ancestors" (Bomas of Kenya 2000). Significantly, there is no claim that the houses are those of contemporary peoples. Handicrafts are available for purchase in each village. The crafts shown, however, are not restricted to those produced by the members of any one ethnic group but are representative of all Kenyan groups, comparable to the crafts that can be found in any souvenir shop in Nairobi. Nor are the sellers necessarily members of the same ethnic group as those in whose village the array is located. A Kikuyu seller, for example, might be found in the Maasai village. Further, no one actually lives in the villages; they are for display purposes only.

National dance troupes have been established in Uganda, Senegal, Mali, and most other African nations as part of government policy, just as performance troupes, ethnic village complexes, nations in miniature, and national museums have been established in many countries of the world. These sites differ, of course, but a general aim is to collect, preserve, and exhibit the art, culture, and history of a nation. To quote from a mimeographed information program distributed by Bomas of Kenya, "We specialize in traditional dancing and preservation of Kenya Cultural Heritage." The word *preservation* is a key. Whereas at Mayers the claim is that the Maasai are still living as they have for "a thousand years" and are essentially unchanged, Bomas talks of preserving, which implies that traditional ways no longer exist, that they are in danger of disappearing, that they belonged to the ancestors. Bomas makes a claim very different from the discourse directed toward foreign tourists. At Mayers, the Maasai occupy space in the ethnographic present; at Bomas they, and the other Kenyan groups, are in the traditional past.

At the top of the Bomas program one finds "REF: NO.BK/15/11," a reference number, typical of government documents everywhere. Other evidence of a nationalistic emphasis is easy to find. For example, the performance troupe calls itself the "harambee dancers." Coined by Jomo Kenyatta, the first president of Kenya, *harambee* is a powerful national slogan that means roughly "all pull together" (Leys 1975:75). In Kenya there are many harambee groups, sometimes called self-help or cooperative groups, and, indeed, there is a national harambee movement. The program distributed at Bomas consisted of six pages, including advertising, and described each act or scene in sequence—there were 22 in all. The last act, called the finale, was described as follows: "This is a salute in praise of His Excellency Hon. Daniel Arap Moi the President of the Republic of Kenya." Such statements render the performance of traditional dancing explicitly nationalistic.

The Bomas harambee dance troupe consists of members of many different ethnic groups, and any member of the troupe may perform the dances of any of the other Kenyan groups. At Mayers, Maasai performed Maasai dancing, but at Bomas a Kikuyu dancer, for example, could do the dances of the Maasai, the Samburu, the Kikuyu, or any group. Bomas creates an ensemble of performers from different groups who live together at Bomas as a residential community in a harambee arrangement, almost as an occupational subculture, apart from their extended families and home communities. The harambee dancers from Bomas are available for hire all over the world and have made overseas tours to the United States, the United Kingdom, Sweden, Japan, and other countries.

The troupe acts as a single functioning unit, detaching ritual dancing from its home community and putting it in a museum, a professional theater, or on the national or international stage. The troupe becomes an explicit model of the nation, melding diversity into a modern organization, disconnecting heritage from tribe. The implicit message of Bomas is that tribal dances belong to the nation. By separating cultural forms from tribal ownership, Bomas asserts that the multiethnic heritage of Kenya is now the property of all Kenyans. As an expression of nationalist ideology, Bomas speaks about tribalism as memory, in performance, where it is less threatening.

Bomas tells a story for Kenyans about themselves and appeals most to urban Kenyans. Their Web site states that visitors can see "rural Kenyan life" (Bomas of Kenya 2000). On Sunday afternoons, Bomas is crowded with local families who come with their children. Whereas the Mayers were hosts to foreign tourists and, on Sundays, to a resident expatriate British community, Bomas is host to a few foreign tourists but mostly to urban Kenyan families.[9] Businessmen meet there for conversation over beer or coffee. It is a

place for Kenyans to honor their ethnicity in an urban setting, to see dances
that they might not otherwise have an opportunity to witness. Bomas also
arranges special shows for schools and educational institutions in the mornings, two days a week, highlighting their educational function.

For purposes of this article, it is important to understand how Kenyan
tourist discourse uses such terms as *tribalism, traditional, modern, primitive,*
and *civilized.* The six-page program of Bomas does not once contain the term
tribal or *tribesmen*, and it uses the word *tribe* only twice, and then merely
descriptively, as the equivalent of people or group," in contrast, *tribal* and
tribesmen are crucial terms in tourist discourse for foreigners. The tourist brochures issued by private tour companies advertising trips to Kenya for an
American or European audience use *tribal* with the implicit idea that the people so characterized are primitive and representative of an earlier state of existence. Significantly, the term used in the Bomas program is *traditional*, which
contrasts with *modern*. The Kenyan audience at Bomas consists of modern
urbanites, and what they witness on stage are their own traditional dances, part
of a previous historical era, reflecting on their own present modernity in composite ways. Although sometimes used in the Kenyan media, the terms *tribal*
and especially *tribalism* have a negative connotation in contemporary Kenya,
as they have in many of the multiethnic nations of the world. The Kenyan government has long acknowledged deep-rooted ethnic identifications as a serious
national problem (Chilungu 1985:15; Okumu 1975).

In brief, *tribal* is a term for foreign tourists used at Mayers, *traditional*
is a term for domestic tourists used at Bomas, and *ethnicity* is a more neutral
term, used by some Kenyans and anthropologists alike to avoid the deroga-
tory or misleading connotations of *tribal* or *traditional*. The terms have different associations in touristic, ethnographic, and political discourse. Bomas,
in a sense, has taken the concept of the tribe, and put it in the archives or in
the museum, where hopefully, it will be safe and out of the way.

The language of the Bomas program is revealing. Here are excerpts
describing two of the Bomas acts:

> The background to this item is the assassination of Nakhabuka, a young
> and beautiful girl of Abamahia clan in Bunyala (Western Kenya). Her
> jealous boyfriend shoots her with an arrow at the river, because she has
> married someone else. Her great spirit enters the body of one of the vil-
> lagers and demands that a wrestling dance be performed occasionally in
> her memory.

> This item features a Giriama couple who are getting married. Unfortu-
> nately, the bride, having been bewitched just before the ceremony,
> threatens to refuse her man. It takes the skill of a famous medicine man
> to bring her back to agreement before the wedding can continue. The
> events of the wedding are heralded by the Gonda dance (performed
> mainly around Malindi on the Northern Coast of Kenya).

This is the genre of the folktale. Embedded in the Bomas program are
mini folktales, dramatic narratives about everyday life. The stories are cultur-

ally and geographically specific. They refer to the Abamahia clan or to a Giriama couple and to such actual places as western Kenya or the north coast. These are real places. There is none of the generalized language of much of the tourist discourse produced for a foreign audience with its vague references to the untouched African primitive.[10] The function of such generalized references to tribesmen or to primitives is to distance the object, to depersonalize, to separate the tourist from the African. The Bomas stories, on the other hand, tell about the heritage of specific groups, ones with which the Kenyan audience can identify. That the stories tell about being bewitched, about a famous medicine man, and about spirits is part of the magical language of the folktale, but it also reflects a reality of Kenyan cultural life (Geschiere 1997).

Mayers was performed in a Maasai compound, and all Western objects were hidden from the audience. Bomas is performed in a modern auditorium that contains a restaurant and a huge bar. Before, during, and after the performance, members of the audience can order drinks. Mayers was characterized by an absence of signs; at Bomas there are signs everywhere, including ones that give the price of admission, directions to the auditorium, directions to the traditional villages, even signs that advertise Coca-Cola. Each of the villages has its own sign.

Bomas is professionally produced with such technical virtuosity that it seems like a Kenyan Ziegfeld Follies, with professional lighting, sound effects, and with the performers in matching costumes. At Bomas, the performers are clearly on stage and they smile at the audience, whereas at Mayers the Maasai were preoccupied with their dancing. At Mayers, toward the end of the dancing, the audience was invited to come on to the outdoor stage to view the performers close up, and to photograph them, whereas at Bomas there is an unbridgeable gap between the actors and the audience. The audience at Bomas does not mix with the actors on stage. Bomas gives one the feeling of being at a concert or at a theatrical production, and, indeed, Bomas employed an American producer for a time.

Mayers had a close fit between the performance and the setting and that was part of the message. Bomas has a lack of fit between the performance and the setting, and that too is part of the message. The genre of Mayers was tourist realism. The genre of Bomas is nationalist theater. Although both are studiously produced, Mayers was made to seem underproduced, and Bomas overproduced. The aim at Mayers was to mask the artifice of production. The aim at Bomas is to expose the processes of production so as to create a discontinuity between the production and what it is designed to represent. Mayers denied change. Bomas highlights change. Bomas detaches culture from tribe and displays it before the nation for all to see and share, and in the process Bomas aestheticizes, centralizes, and decontextualizes ritual. Ironically, what Bomas represents is what British colonialism was trying to achieve, the detribalization of Kenya. The British tried, but eventually failed, to turn Kenyans into colonial subjects. Bomas succeeds, in performance, in turning Kenyans into national citizens. Disjunction at Bomas is a rhetorical strategy, whereas at Mayers the strategy was to stress continuity. Mayers was a Western fantasy. Bomas is a national wish fulfillment. Mayers and Bomas are equally political and each tries to present its own version of history. Mayers was not an accurate reflection of contemporary Maasai culture, neither is Bomas an accurate reflection of Kenyan traditionalism.

Out of Africa Sundowner

Kichwa Tembo Tented Camp is described in the brochure as "luxurious enough for even the most pampered traveler," with private sleeping tents, electricity, insect-proof windows, a veranda, and an indoor bathroom with hot showers.[11] So much for roughing it in the African bush. The camp is located near the Masai Mara National Reserve, which is an extension of the Serengeti. The main attraction at the camp is game viewing from safari vehicles, but the Maasai are also prominent. There are Maasai at the private airport welcoming the incoming tourists, Maasai dancing at the camp, a scheduled visit to a Maasai village, and a briefing on Maasai culture by a Maasai chief, who began his talk to the tour group I joined by saying in English, "I think all of you must have read about the Maasai." I choose, however, to discuss the Out of Africa Sundowner party held on the Oloololo escarpment on the bank of the Mara River.

This performance introduces a new note into ethnic tourism in Kenya. The Sundowner is basically a cocktail party with buffet on a river bank in the bush. The Kichwa Tembo staff set up a bar, with a bartender in red coat, black pants, white shirt, and bow tie. The attraction is called the Out of Africa Sundowner, from the 1985 Hollywood movie starring Robert Redford and Meryl Streep, based on Isak Dinesen's (1938) book about colonial days in Kenya. *Out of Africa* (1985) was also shown to the tour group on the airplane en route to East Africa. The brochure from the tour agency describing the Sundowner says, "Standing at the precipice of the escarpment, the sun setting low amidst an orange and pink sky, it is easy to see why Africa so inspired Karen Blixen and Dennis Finch-Hatton." The brochure invites the tourists to experience the Sundowner, not from the point of view of the movie or the actors, or the book or the author, but rather from the point of view of the main characters in the story. It is all make-believe. At the Sundowner, waiters serve drinks and food to the tourists standing in groups or seated together in clusters of folding chairs. Then the Kichwa Tembo employees form a line, singing and dancing for the tourists, and the Maasai men begin their chanting and dancing. The performance is remarkable in a number of respects.[12]

During the dance, individual Maasai dancers come among the tour group, take the hands of tourists, and bring them into the line to dance with them. The other Maasai dancers smile in approval and visibly express their appreciation of the dance steps now also performed by the tourists. The remaining tourists laugh and comment; most nod in sympathy and enjoyment. A few of the dancing tourists look uncomfortable but make the best of

Smiling Maasai dancing with tourists at the Sundowner. (Photo by Edward M. Bruner)

the situation, while others rise to the occasion, dancing away, swinging about wildly, improvising, introducing dance steps ordinarily seen in an American disco. After the dance, the Maasai again mix with the tourists, this time passing out free souvenirs—a necklace with carved wooden giraffes for the women and a carved letter opener for the men. These curios are given as if they were personal gifts, but actually the tour agency at the camp buys these items for distribution at the Sundowner. It is all smiles and politeness.

At the Sundowner, the Maasai warrior has become tourist friendly. Gone is the wildness, or the illusion of wildness, or the performance of wildness, to be replaced by a benign and safe African tribesman. In Mayers Ranch, the particular appeal was precisely the tension between the wild Maasai and the cultured Englishman, but at the Sundowner that binary opposition is dissolved. At the Mayers performance, the tourists moved between two distinct spaces, the Maasai manyatta and the Mayers's lawn, the African space and the English space, the wild and the civilized. The Maasai did not enter the Mayers's area, for to do so would be a violation and would destroy the touristic illusion. At the Sundowner, however, the two spaces have merged—there is no separation between the Maasai and the tourists, but only one performance space where the two intermingle. By breaking the binary, ethnic tourism in Kenya is structurally changed (Sahlins 1981).

During the dancing at the Sundowner, the camp employees begin to sing a Kenyan song called "Jambo Bwana," written in the mid-1980s by a musical group called "Them Mushrooms."[13] The song was first performed in a tourist hotel in Mombasa, became an instant hit, and is still known through-out Kenya. Them Mushrooms moved from Mombasa to Nairobi, established their own recording studio, and have performed abroad.

The message of "Jambo Bwana" is that tourists are welcome in Kenya, which is characterized as a beautiful country without problems. One tour agent in Nairobi said it is now the "tourist national anthem" of Kenya, as it is so popular with foreign tour groups. Prominent in the song is the Swahili phrase "Hakuna Matata," which in one version is repeated four times and means "no worries, no problem." The phrase itself has a history. In the 1970s, there was political turmoil in Uganda and in the states surrounding Kenya. During this time, "Hakuna Matata," although always part of coastal Swahili language, came to be widely used as a political phrase, to say that Kenya is safe; it was reassuring to refugees as well as to the citizens of Kenya. After Them Mushrooms wrote "Jambo Bwana" in the mid-1980s, the phrase "Hakuna Matata" became more associated with tourism.

"Hakuna Matata" is familiar to tourist audiences as the title song from the Hollywood movie *The Lion King* (1994), with music by Elton John and lyrics by Tim Rice. The lyrics repeat the phrase "Hakuna Matata," defining it as follows:

> Hakuna Matata!
> What a wonderful phrase
> Hakuna Matata!
> Ain't no passing craze
>
> It means no worries
> For the rest of your days
> It's our problem-free philosophy
> Hakuna Matata! [14]

The hotel employees at the Sundowner then sang "Kum Ba Yah," an Angolan spiritual, popular in the United States as a folk, protest, and gospel song. Despite its African origins, "Kum Ba Yah" is now established in U.S. popular culture and has taken on new American meanings. The phrase "Hakuna Matata" has been similarly appropriated and is associated with *The Lion King* (1994).

At the Sundowner, the performers present "Kum Ba Yah" with a Jamaican reggae rhythm, a musical tradition that, to many North Americans, equates good times, blackness, dancing, and Caribbean vacations.[15] In other words, Africans have taken a phrase and a song originating in Africa and have performed it for the tourists with a New World Caribbean reggae beat. This musical tradition and the songs themselves, "Hakuna Matata" and "Kum Ba Yah," have been widely interpreted in American popular culture as expressions of "Africanness" and "blackness," and then have been re-presented to American tourists, by Africans, in Africa. What is new is not that transnational influences are at work, that a song or an aspect of culture flows around the globe, as ethnographers are already familiar with these processes.

Nor is it new that a global image of African tribesmen is enacted for foreign tourists, as this is also the case at Mayers. What is new is that, at the Sundowner, the Americans, who have presumably made the journey in order to experience African culture, instead encounter American cultural content that represents an American image of African culture. The Americans, of course, feel comfortable and safe, as they recognize this familiar representation and respond positively, for it is their own.

This is globalization gone wild: Paul Gilroy's (1993) "Black Atlantic," transnationalism as a Lacanian mirror image, and Appadurai's (1991) "scapes" as a ping-pong ball, bouncing fantasy back and forth across the Atlantic. A reggae Lion King in the African bush. Points of origin become lost or are made irrelevant. Old binaries are fractured. The distance is narrowed between us and them, subject and object, tourist and native. Ethnography is transformed into performance, blurring the lines between genres in ways that go beyond Geertz (1983). What is left are dancing images, musical scapes, flowing across borders, no longer either American or African but occupying new space in a constructed touristic borderzone (Bruner 1996b; cf. Appadurai 1991) that plays with culture, reinvents itself, takes old forms and gives them new and often surprising meanings.

The colonial image of the Maasai has been transformed in a postmodern era so that the Maasai become the pleasant primitives, the human equivalent of the Lion King, the benign animal king who behaves in human ways. It is a Disney construction, to make the world safe for Mickey Mouse. Presented in tourism are songs that have African roots but that in North America and probably globally are pop culture images of Africa and blackness. Black Africa in the American imagination has been re-presented to Americans in tourism.

At the Sundowner, tourists receive drinks, food, a good show, an occasion to socialize, a chance to express their privileged status, an opportunity to experience vicariously the adventure of colonial Kenya, and a confirmation of their prior image of Africa. As posttourists in a postmodern era, they may also revel in the incongruity of the event, of dancing with the Maasai, of drinking champagne in the African wilderness. But what do the Maasai receive? The answer must be seen against the backdrop of what the Maasai received at Mayers and receive at Bomas. The Maasai performers at Mayers received a small daily wage for each performance in which they participated, a measure of ground maize, and a pint of milk a day. They derived additional income from the sale of their handicrafts and from the tips they received by posing for tourist photographs. They were wage laborers, as are the performers at Bomas.

The Maasai on the Mara, however, are part owners of the tourist industry and receive a share of the profits from safari tourism, but this is neither readily apparent nor ordinarily disclosed to the tourists.[16] The tourists see only what is exhibited to them in performance, but there is a vast behind-the-scenes picture. The Maasai receive 18 percent of the gross receipts of the "bed nights," the cost of accommodations at Kichwa Tembo per night per person. This can be a considerable amount as there are 51 units at the camp and the cost per night could be US$300 to US$400 in high season, or over US$100,000 per week with full occupancy (Kichwa Tembo 2000). There are a total of 22 camps and lodges on the Mara, some even more luxurious and expensive than Kichwa Tembo. The entrance fee to the Masai Mara Reserve is US$27 per person per day, and Maasai receive 19 percent of that fee. The percentages of 18 and 19 (odd figures) were the result of a long process of negotiation. The funds are accumulated and given to two county councils, and in one of these, the Transmara Council, where Kichwa Tembo is located, the funds are divided among the "group ranches," each based on one of the ten Maasai clans that own land on the reserve.

The Maasai ownership of most of the land on the reserve, as well as the land on which the camps and lodges are built, is the basis of their receiving a share of the gross receipts. Philip Leakey (a brother of Richard Leakey) reports that before the 1980s, Kenyan elite and foreign investors derived almost all of the income from international tourism (personal communication, February 19, 1999; see also Berger 1996). As a result, most Kenyans including Maasai were indifferent or even hostile to tourism, as they did not profit from it. Further, there was considerable poaching in the game parks. The depletion of the wildlife on the East African reserves posed a danger to the national heritage of Kenya and to the natural heritage of the world, not to mention that the deterioration of game threatened the entire tourism industry and with it a key source of foreign exchange. Things changed in the 1980s, as it was widely recognized that the way to gain the support of the Maasai for tourism development was to give them a stake in the industry, which the Maasai had argued for. Since then, there has been a drastic reduction in poaching on the reserve. The Maasai, who do not usually eat wild game, now have a financial interest in protecting the animals and in stopping poaching. Further, a new law was passed stipulating that anyone caught poaching in Kenya may be killed on sight.

The Maasai profit from tourism on the Mara in other ways. There are 170 park rangers on the reserve, and all are Maasai. The Kichwa Tembo package includes a visit to a Maasai village, where the villagers receive the US$10 per person admission fee as well as the profits from the sale of handicrafts. One day I counted 80 tourists, for a total income of US$800. When the Maasai perform their dances for tourists, they receive compensation. One group consisting of about 15 Maasai received US$163 per performance. Again, tourists are not usually aware of these financial arrangements. Some Maasai on the Mara are wealthy by Kenyan standards, but that wealth is not visible to the tourists. Most Maasai have used their income to increase their herds of livestock—cows, sheep, and goats—which are kept away from the tourist routes.

Maasai are employed at Kichwa Tembo not only as waiters, chefs, and security guards, but in management positions as well. Yet, the tourists do not "see" these employees as Maasai. In the hotel context, the Maasai waiters are reserved and deferential in their white uniforms, avoiding eye contact with tourists and speaking only when spoken to. If waiters were to overstep the bounds of appropriate service behavior they would be reprimanded, whereas if the same Maasai performing for tourists as warriors behaved deferentially, they would be a disappointment to the spectators. All parties understand the behavior appropriate in each position, for it is a mutually understood symbolic system, and each party to the drama performs an assigned role. Within the lodge, the tourists are usually polite to the waiters but are disinterested, for they are perceived as service employees. Kichwa Tembo camp is a space that provides the comfort, luxury, and safety on which upscale tourism depends.

In contexts in which the Maasai are performing as "Maasai," on display for tourists, it is tourist time. The Maasai men, adorned with red ochre, wearing red robes, beadwork, and sandals, and carrying sticks, change their demeanor—they become warriors. In performance, in these contexts, the tourists become voyeurs—there is a cornucopia of visualization, and the simultaneous clicking of many cameras. Ironically, in the same day a single individual might be a deferential waiter in the hotel during the serving of a meal, but a Maasai warrior, one of the "Lords of East Africa," during performance time in the evening.

The Maasai, of course, are well aware of the discrepancy between their own lifestyles and their tourist image, and they manipulate it, but there are many complexities in the situation. Some Maasai, who have in effect become performers in the tourism industry, display themselves for tourists, to be observed and photographed, and if asked, they reply that they do it for the money. They play the primitive, for profit, and have become what MacCannell (1992) calls the ex-primitive. This is the case for performers at all three sites, at Mayers, Bomas, and the Sundowner. Tourism for them is their livelihood, a source of income. On the other hand, I knew one Maasai business executive who assumed "ethnic" Maasai traits only during his nonworking hours. He dressed in Western clothing with shirt and tie during the work week in Nairobi, where he spoke English, but on most weekends, wearing jeans and a T-shirt, and speaking Maasai, he would return to his native village to become a pastoralist to attend to his extensive herd of livestock. On ceremonial occasions, he would wear traditional Maasai clothing and dance and chant in Maasai rituals. To put it another way, what touristic or ethnographic discourse characterize as Maasai "ethnic" traits, may, in tourism or in life, be displayed situationally, depending on the context, which is probably the case universally for all ethnicities. Identities are not given; they are performed by people with agency who have choices.

But boundaries are elusive. As de Certeau (1984) suggests, spatial patterns are not composed of rigid unbreakable regulations, flawlessly executed, but are spatial practices, characterized by transgression, manipulation, and resistance, as individuals appropriate space for themselves. I give two examples. While watching the dancing at the Sundowner, I noticed one man, a waiter in black pants and white shirt, who picked up a club and began dancing along with the red-robed Maasai. He was out of place, apparently a Maasai waiter who decided to join his fellow tribesmen, but it was a broken pattern.

At Kichwa Tembo, one of the tourists, an African-American woman, had taken an optional nature walk with Maasai guides. During the walk they came upon a pride of 12 lions. The woman reported that she had never been so scared in her life, but the Maasai guides urged calm and slowly moved the group away from the lions without incident. After that dramatic encounter, while resting and chatting, the woman showed the Maasai guides a picture of her grown daughter, a strikingly beautiful woman. One of the guides announced to the woman that he wanted to marry the daughter, but the woman passed it off and they continued on the nature walk. Later, back at the camp, the Maasai man came to the woman with his father, a marriage spokesman, and offered 25 head of cattle for the daughter, with the implication of a still larger offer, a huge bride-price. The father urged the woman to consult with her own marriage brokers, and then to meet again to negotiate—a Maasai practice. When the woman told me about this incident, I playfully suggested that the least she could have done would have been to transmit the offer to her daughter and let her make her own decision. But the woman replied that her daughter was finishing her studies at a prestigious law school in California, was very driven and ambitious, and would not want to be the second wife of a Maasai villager. Boundaries are not rigid—tourists and natives do move into each other's spaces.

Maasai then are incorporated into the safari tourism industry on the Mara in a dual capacity. First, they are part owners, possibly partners, and certainly beneficiaries. Second, they are also performers in a touristic drama, a secondary attraction to the wild animals on the reserve, but clearly objects of the tourist gaze. As the Maasai receive a share of the profits and a stake in the industry, the question may be asked, to what extent do they control the images by which they are represented? My observations suggest that if the Maasai now have economic and political power, they do not exercise it to influence how they are presented in tourism. As the Maasai say, they are in it for the money and are willing to play into the stereotypic colonial image of themselves to please their clients, the foreign tourists. As one Maasai explained to me, the European and American tourists do not come to Kenya to see someone in Western dress, like a Kikuyu. The Maasai put on the red robes and red ochre and carry clubs so the tourists will be able to recognize them as Maasai.

Who is producing the Sundowner Maasai? Kichwa Tembo tented safari camp was built by the tour agency Abercrombie and Kent, but was recently sold to another company, Conservation Corporation Africa. Regardless of the particular company involved, the Out of Africa Sundowner is produced by tour agencies and, by extension, by international tourism to meet a demand. Tourism is marketing, selling a product to an audience.

The production is skillful because the hand of the tour agency is masked in the presentation of the Maasai. It is the Maasai dancers who distribute gifts directly to the tourists at the Sundowner (with gifts provided by the tour agent), it is the Maasai chief who collects the $10 fee to enter the village (but it is the tour agent who selects the village), and it is a Maasai (hired by the tour agent) who provides explanations of Maasai culture. At Mayers, the entrance fee was given to the Mayers or to their staff, and the staff provided the commentary on Maasai lifeways. It was apparent at Mayers that white Europeans were explaining and producing Africans, with all its colonial overtones. At Kichwa Tembo, however, Maasai explain Maasai culture, but briefly, as most tourists are not really interested in a deeper ethnographic understanding. In Maasai tourism generally, at Mayers, Bomas, and the Mara, there is a master narrative at work, but it is usually implicit, a background understanding. On site, textual content is less prominent than evocative visualizations, songs, dance, and movement. In a sense, the producer is more important in Maasai tourist attractions than the writer. At the Mara, a casual observer might say that the Maasai are producing themselves, but I believe it more accurate to say that the tour agents are the primary producers, with the Maasai at best relegated to a minor role. The role of the tour agent is concealed, which is part of the production.

If the Maasai at the Mara are behaving in accordance with a generalized Western representation of Maasai and of African pastoralists, then tourism in a foreign land becomes an extension of American popular culture and of global media images. The startling implication, for me, is that to develop a new site for ethnic tourism, it is not necessary to study the ethnic group or to gather local data, but only to do market research on tourist perceptions. I know these statements are somewhat conjectural, but is it too speculative to contemplate that the Maasai will eventually become (rather than just appear as) the pop culture image of themselves? I do not believe in the homogenization of world cultures caused by globalization, for local cultures always actively assert themselves, and I would argue for the long-term integrity of the Maasai. But the issue is raised, how well will the Maasai continue to compartmentalize themselves and separate performance from life? The line separating tourist performance and ethnic ritual has already become blurred in other areas of the world with large tourist flows, such as Bali. The Balinese can no longer distinguish between performances for tourists and those performances for themselves, as performances originally created for tourism have subsequently entered Balinese rituals (Bruner 1996b; Picard 1996). Where does Maasai culture begin and Hollywood image end?

Writing Tourism and Writing Ethnography

To summarize thus far, Mayers presented the tourist image of the African primitive, Bomas presents the preservation of a disappearing Kenyan tradition, and the Sundowner an American pop-culture image of Africa. The tourists at Mayers sat on logs facing the performance area in a reconstructed Maasai village, at Bomas they sit in tiered auditorium seats facing the stage, and at the Sundowner on folding chairs on the escarpment as the performance evolves around them. The performance and the setting were concordant at Mayers; are detached at Bomas; and at the Sundowner, the most global message is delivered in the most natural setting, along a river bank in a game reserve. Mayers served English tea, Bomas serves drinks at the bar, while the waiters at the Sundowner pour champagne. The binary opposition at Mayers is between the African primitive and the civilized Englishman; at Bomas it is between traditional and modern Kenyans; and at the Sundowner, the binary is dissolved because the performance presents what the tourists interpret to be their own transnational media image of Africa. The master trope at Mayers was tourist realism, at Bomas it is undisguised nationalism, and at the Sundowner it is a postmodern image.

Mayers, Bomas, and the Sundowner differ in many respects but all three sites combine tourism, theater, and entertainment. All take simultaneous account of the prior colonial status, local politics, national forces, and global international requirements. I have emphasized globalization at the Sundowner site, but there clearly are global dimensions to Mayers and Bomas. Mayers (as tourist realism) and Bomas (as national theater) are examples of transnationalism, and both arose in Kenya as an extension of the postcolonial condition, one for foreigners and the other for locals, for as Oakes (1998:11) says, both authenticity and tradition are themselves modern sensibilities. In the 1960s, Mayers reworked a nineteenth-century colonial narrative for foreigners, and Bomas is a recent variant for domestic tourists of public displays of living peoples. Such displays have a history dating back to European folk museums (Horne 1992), World Fairs (Benedict 1983), and even earlier (Kirshenblatt-Gimblett 1998:34–51; Mullaney 1983). Bomas most resembles the ethnic theme parks of contemporary China (Anagnost 1993), Indonesia (Bruner 2000; Errington 1998; Pemberton 1994), and other nations (Stanley 1998).

Viewed historically, the three tourist sites parallel three different forms of ethnographic writing. Mayers Ranch can be likened to ethnographic realism—it strived for an aura of authenticity based on a prior image of what was believed to be the authentic African pastoralist. When Mayers was opened in 1968, colonialism was gone in Kenya, a thing of the past, but there were still many British expatriates and a worldwide longing for a colonial experience—an enacted imperialist nostalgia—that Mayers produced for the expatriate community and foreign tourists.

Authenticity has figured prominently in tourism scholarship since Boorstin (1961) and MacCannell (1976). Boorstin characterizes tourist attractions as pseudo-events, which are contrived and artificial, as opposed to the real thing. MacCannell sees modern tourists as on a quest for authenticity, which is frequently presented to them as "staged authenticity," a false front that masks the real back stage to which they do not have access. For both Boorstin and MacCannell, there is a real authentic culture located somewhere, beyond the tourist view. Contemporary anthropologists would not agree with the early work of Boorstin and MacCannell, for as anthropologists now know, there are no originals, and a single "real" authentic culture does not exist. Of course, all cultures everywhere are real and authentic, if only because they are there, but this is quite different from the concept of "authenticity," which implies an inherent distinction between what is authentic and what is inauthentic, applies labels to cultures, and values one more than the other. There is no one authentic Maasai culture, in part because Maasai culture is continually changing and there are many variants. If one were to identify, say, a nineteenth-century version of Maasai culture as the real thing, one could then look further, back to the eighteenth century or to a more distant region, as the locus of the really real Maasai. It is an impossible quest.

The same vision is apparent in ethnographic realism (Marcus and Fisher 1986; Rosaldo 1989; Tedlock 2000), the basic mode of ethnographic writing until the 1960s. The classic monographs in Africa (e.g., Evans-Pritchard 1940) did not describe what the ethnographers actually observed at the time of their fieldwork but were a construction based on the prevailing anthropological vision of a pure unaltered native culture. As in anthropology, where the hypothetical ethnographic present was discredited and colonialism criticized, so too was Mayers Ranch disparaged and eventually closed. Mayers existed historically before either Bomas and the Sundowner, but it was an anachronism, doomed from the beginning.

An effort to influence the political culture of Kenya, Bomas emerged in response to those forces that led to political activism within anthropology during the 1970s, the epoch of the civil rights movement and the emergence of new nations. The genre is ethnographic activism. Bomas depicts traditional Maasai culture as fast disappearing, requiring that it be preserved in museum archives or in artistic performance. As a collective past, Maasai culture as represented at Bomas becomes part of the national heritage of postindependence Kenya. Bomas is a response to the intense nationalism that characterized many newly independent multiethnic Third World countries. The basic problem for the nation was how to express ethnicity yet simultaneously to contain it, a problem not yet resolved in many African states.

The Sundowner is an outgrowth of global media flows, electronic communication, and pervasive transnationalism. It is for foreign post-tourists, produced in the style of postmodern ethnography. Unlike Mayers, it rejects the realist genre. Unlike Bomas, it rejects nationalist rhetoric. Postmodern ethnography describes juxtapositions, pastiche, and functional inconsistency, and recognizes, even celebrates, that cultural items originating from different places and historical eras may coexist (Babcock 1999). Contemporary ethnographers no longer try to mask outside influences, nor do they see them as polluting a pure culture (Bruner 1988).

In performance, the Sundowner is more playful. It intermingles elements from the past and the present, is less concerned about points of historical origin, and does not strive for cultural purity. The comparison is not quite that neat, however, as the Sundowner tourists do occupy a colonial position and do want to view "primitive" Maasai; nevertheless, there has been a shift in the stance of the audience. Post-tourists at the Sundowner are willing to dance with the Maasai and joke with them, and they are not that fastidious about authenticity. But postmodern tourists, and ethnographers, have not entirely overcome the contradictions of their modernist and colonial pasts. Many postmodern ethnographers, it must be recognized, still struggle with an inequitable colonial relationship and vast differentials in wealth and power between themselves and the people they study. Further, ethnographers, as those who write, control how culture is represented.

That the three sites correspond to different genres of ethnographic writing is not unexpected, as both tourism and ethnography are disciplinary practices, products of the same worldwide global forces. Ethnographers are not entirely free from the dominant paradigms of their times. As an ethnographer studying tourism, ethnographic perspectives are reflected back to me by the very tourist performances that I study. The predicament, of course, is not restricted to an anthropology of tourism; it is inherent in the ethnographic enterprise (Bruner 1986).

The Questioning Gaze

I use the phrase the "questioning gaze" to describe the tourists' doubts about the credibility, authenticity, and accuracy of what is presented to them in the tourist production. The key issue is that tourists have agency, active selves that do not merely accept but interpret, and frequently question, the producers' messages (Bruner 1994; Jules-Rosette and Bruner 1994). In Bomas, authenticity both is and is not an issue—it depends on which Kenyan is speaking, as there is no monolithic local voice. Some Maasai are illiterate, others have been educated at Oxford University; some live in the game parks, others in the city; some are pastoralists, others are doctors, lawyers, and businessmen; some have a stake in the tourism industry, others have not. Urban Kenyans I know have told me they enjoy seeing their native dances at Bomas, as they do not travel frequently to their home areas, and even when they do they are not assured of witnessing a dance performance. They respect the ethnic diversity exhibited at Bomas, and they appreciate the performance as well as the entire Bomas experience. In addition to the dancing, Bomas features picnic sites, a children's playground, football, volleyball, badminton, table tennis, and a swimming pool. In other words, it is more than a display of Kenyan ethnic culture for intellectuals, ethnographers, and foreign tourists; it is a family recreational site.

Yet not all local observers share this view. Originally from Uganda, Christine Southall (a scholar specializing in East Africa) suggested to me that many Kenyan intellectuals laugh at parts of the Bomas performance, criticizing the inaccuracies in its representation of tradition and regarding its characterization of the various ethnic groups as inauthentic. In 1999, Jean Kidula, a Kenyan musicologist who has worked with the Bomas performers, explained to me that Bomas is a failed project because the original objectives were not achieved. The aim in the early 1970s was to construct a national dance troupe that would accurately perform the ethnic arts of Kenya. She feels that the dances now performed are not authentic so that Bomas has become a tourist thing, folkloristic, and commercial. The difficulty was that once the dance troupe was formed the performers began to innovate, and over the years the original tribal dance forms were changed. Kenyan people, she says, understand this but keep going to Bomas primarily because it is entertaining. To these two scholars, authenticity is important, and they criticize Bomas for not achieving it.

Commenting to me on Bomas, Jane Mayers said that "it's not true in any respect," meaning that the Maasai dance at Bomas is not necessarily performed by Maasai, that no one lives in the villages, and that their dance troupe is professional. The questions become, what is seen as true, and how does a performance derive its authority? There are different meanings of authenticity (Bruner 1994), but from my perspective, Mayers, Bomas, and the Sundowner are not authentic in the sense of being accurate, genuine, and true to a postulated original.

Anthropologists, at least in the past, have tended to regard tourism as commercial, even tacky. From the perspective of realist ethnography, tourism is a disgraceful simplification, an embarrassment, like an awkward country cousin who keeps appearing at cherished field sites (Bruner 1989; de Certeau 1984). Some U.S. anthropologists, Kenyan intellectuals, and foreign tourists might experience Bomas as being superficial and inauthentic—but that would be to miss the point. At Bomas, traditional dances are placed in such a high-tech setting and the production is so professional that the dances become detraditionalized. The modern auditorium, the bar, the signs, and the commercialism are not necessarily experienced by Kenyan visitors as an intrusion, for they serve to remind the Kenyans that they are not in a tribal village but in a national folklore museum.

Although the issue for some Kenyan intellectuals is authenticity, the issue for many Kenyan tourists, based on my interviews, is doubt about the validity of the nationalistic message of Bomas. The message of the producers is not necessarily the one received by their tourist audience. Kenyan people from all segments of society are very well aware of the reality of ethnic conflict in Kenyan society, and hence those Kenyans who visit Bomas have their doubts about the ethnic harmony portrayed there. The understanding of Kenyans in this respect is similar to the Americans who celebrate the Abraham Lincoln rags-to-riches narrative that everyone can be president, yet they know that no American of African, Native, Asian, or Hispanic descent, and no woman or Jew, has been elected president of the United States.

In this sense, Bomas is like Lévi-Strauss's (1967:202–228) definition of a myth, in that it tries to resolve a contradiction between a vision of Kenyan national integration and the reality of ethnic conflict and separatism, just as in the United States the Lincoln myth tries to resolve a contradiction between an ideology of equality and an actuality of discrimination. The function and the promise of national myths is to resolve contradictions, if not in life, then in narrative and performance. Nor is it a false consciousness, as the Marxists would have it, for most Kenyans and Americans are aware of these discrepancies.

At Mayers Ranch, many tourists had their own doubts, which they expressed to me, for the performance was too picture perfect, too neat and well scheduled, and the back stage of the performance as well as the actualities of Maasai life were too well hidden. Tourists vary, for to be a tourist is not a fixed slot to be occupied but is a role to be fashioned and performed (Jules-Rosette and Bruner 1994). Some tourists willingly surrendered themselves to the experience of the Mayers performance. One tourist told me that he was on vacation in Africa to relax, and he simply accepted whatever was offered to him. For him, there was no questioning gaze, or at least it was suppressed. Others behave as if they are in a graduate anthropology seminar. They are obsessed with issues of authenticity and question the truth value of everything. They ask, "Are these Maasai for real?"

One American student at Mayers Ranch during my visit kept muttering to herself and to anyone else who would listen that the Maasai were being exploited, which may have been the case. The African-American tourists who complained about Mayers to the Kenyan government did not see the performance as the producers intended, as a story about the English and the Maasai, but focused on skin color, as an example of whites producing blacks. This is interesting as it exports an American political sensibility to an African context (Bruner 1996a). Tourists, however, like the rest of us, have the ability simultaneously to suspend disbelief and to harbor inner doubts, and sometimes to oscillate between one stance and the other. The questioning gaze may be pushed aside, so that tourists may delight in the excitement and danger of being with the Maasai and play, in their imagination (even temporarily and tentatively) with the colonial slot into which they are being positioned. For them, Mayers was good theater, and many made a conscious effort to engage the Mayers fantasy and to identify with the plot and the characters, at least during performance time, despite inner doubts.

The Intrav tour agency that took the group to the Sundowner was skilled and sophisticated in catering to upscale tourists. It was an "Out of Africa" tour not just in the sense of the Isak Dinesen book, but in the sense of being literally "out" of Africa, above Africa, so as to protect the tourists from hassles, waits, and crowds, and to shield them from experiencing the darker side of Africa—the poverty, starvation, brutality, disease, dirt, corruption, and civil wars. The Sundowner itself went smoothly but there was an earlier instance, a memorable occasion in Tanzania, when Africa broke through the bubble. The tourists I spoke with were very disturbed about it. On a trip from Lake Manyara to Ngorogoro Crater, over a two-hour ride, the cars carrying the tourists passed a number of painfully poor Tanzanian villages. As each village came into view, emaciated children dressed in rags ran after the cars with outstretched hands, hoping for a handout, and they continued running even after the cars had passed far beyond them. The drivers did not stop, but I saw many of the tourists continuing to look back along the dusty road at the desperate children. Afterward, with pained expression, one woman tourist commented on the shocking disparity of wealth between the members of the tour group and the Tanzanian villagers, noting the contrast between our luxury and their poverty. Another said she felt ashamed to have spent so much money on a vacation while these villagers had nothing. It was a fleeting but significant moment. The tourists talked about it for days and were obviously distraught. Its significance extended beyond that one specific incident to the entire tourist itinerary, raising the larger question in the tourist consciousness, what else was being concealed on their tour of Africa? The incident materialized an inner doubt. By carefully orchestrating the "Out of Africa" tour, the agency had tried to suppress and silence parts of Africa, but they did not entirely succeed.

The tourists' identification with Africans in this instance is reminiscent of the position of the character Dennis Finch-Hatton in Isak Dinesen's *Out of Africa* (1938). In that book, Finch-Hatton, a white colonialist, casts a critical eye on the institution of colonialism, identifies with the independent pastoral Maasai, and is ultimately buried in a Maasai grave. In structural terms, he was a bridge between the civilized and the wild, flying freely over the African landscape, with the ability to move back and forth between the two domains of the binary. The tourists on the "Out of Africa" tour who participated in the Sundowner may want to be accepted, even blessed, by the primitive Maasai, if only temporarily, as a kind of absolution for the privileged position that haunts the edges of their dreams. They may relish the gifts, smiles, and dancing on the Sundowner as evidence that they are liked, or at least welcomed, by the Maasai. The African-American woman on a walking tour with the Maasai who encountered the lions may retell that story, not only as a tale of unexpected adventure (always a source of good stories for tourists) but as a way of identifying herself with the Maasai.[17]

At Mayers, Bomas, and the Sundowner, there are always doubts among the tourists about what they are "seeing," doubts that differ from tourist to tourist, but that move beyond what has so artfully been constructed for them. The questioning gaze is a penetration of the constructedness devised by the producers, but it is also more, in a number of respects. First, there is always an unpredictability of meaning about any performance, for individuals attribute their own understandings to the event, which may not be predicted in advance, and these understandings may change over time. Second, some tourists apply a frame to the activity of sightseeing and to everything else that occurs within the tour. A well-traveled tourist, for example, once whispered to me as we were about to watch a performance, "Here comes the tourist dance." It made no difference to her what particular ethnic dance was on display, except that it was presented within a touristic frame. It was a tourist dance, period. For other tourists, more inclined to surrender, an immersion in the physicality of the dance activity itself was more important than any explanation or attribution of meaning. This verges on what Kirshenblatt-Gimblett

(1998:203–248) describes as an avant-garde sensibility, where the experience itself is more important than the hermeneutics. Further, in many cases tourists simply do not understand what they are seeing and make no effort to interpret Maasai dance and culture. Even to those tourists most willing to open up to the experience and to accept the producers' fantasy, there is still, in MacCannell's terms, "an ineluctable absence of meaning to an incomplete subject" (2001:34). It is what Kirshenblatt-Gimblett (1998:72) has called the irreducibility of strangeness. Urry's (1990, 1992) tourist gaze is too empiricist, too monolithic, too lacking in agency, and too visual to encompass these varied tourist reactions. The tourist gaze does not have the power of Foucault's (1979) panopticon, for it is not all-seeing and enveloping. It is variable, and there are seepages and doubts.

In this article, I have described how the Maasai of Kenya are displayed in three tourist sites originating in different historical eras and in disparate social milieus. I emphasize that touristic representations of a single ethnic group are multiple and even contradictory. I also discuss the parallels between tourism and ethnography especially evident in the concept of the questioning gaze. I demonstrate how ethnicity, culture, and authenticity gain and lose meanings in diverse touristic and world contexts. My approach has been to study local tourist performances by the methods of ethnography, to take account of tourist agency, and then to compare systematically the various sites with attention to the national and global frames within which they are located. Constructionism, my main theoretical thrust, is not an escape from history or ethnography. Such an approach enables the ethnographer to explore similarities and differences, to embrace complexity, and to open up new possibilities.

Source: From the *American Ethnologist*, 2001, 28(4):881–908. Reprinted with permission of the author and the American Anthropological Association.

Acknowledgments

Early versions of this article were presented at a conference on tourism in September 1999 at the Department of Anthropology, Yunnan University, Kunming, People's Republic of China, and in January 2000 at the University of Illinois workshop on sociocultural anthropology. I am indebted to the participants for helpful comments, to Alma Gottlieb, Arlene Torres, Nicole Tami, Richard Freeman, Bruno Nettl, the anonymous reviewers of *American Ethnologist*, and the University of Illinois Foundation and Ann and Paul Krouse for financial support enabling my wife and me to participate in the 1999 African trip. In all of my fieldwork, my wife, Elaine C. Bruner, has been an insightful and helpful partner.

Notes

[1] Recent works on tourism include Abram et al. 1997; Boissevain 1996; Castaneda 1996; Chambers 2000; Cohen 1996; Crick 1994; Dann 1996; Desmond 1999; Handler and Gable

1997; Kirshenblatt-Gimblett 1998; Lanfant et al. 1995; Lavie and Swedenburg 1994; Löfgren 1999; Nash 1996; Oakes 1998; Picard 1996; Rojek and Urry 1997; Schein 2000; and
Selwyn 1996.

[2] Adams 1998 and Cheung 1999 are exceptions.

[3] My "questioning gaze" was inspired by MacCannell's (2001) concept of the "second gaze,"
which he developed in opposition to Urry's (1990) "tourist gaze." I agree with most of Mac-
Cannell's critique of Urry. See also Kasfir 1999.

[4] When referring to the Maasai people, current scholarly practice is to use a double *aa*, derived
from the language group Maa. The game reserve Masai Mara, a proper name, is spelled with
a single *a*.

[5] In 1984, Barbara Kirshenblatt-Gimblett and I did fieldwork together at Mayers Ranch, which
we published, and at Bomas, which we did not publish. I returned to Kenya in 1995 and
1999, revisited old sites, gathered new data, and initiated fieldwork on Maasai tourism on the
Mara, including the Sundowner. For the past 15 years, Kirshenblatt-Gimblett has influenced
my work on the Maasai and on tourism.

[6] Members of the tour group had to obtain visas, but their passports were collected by the
Intrav tour guides who handled all the immigration and customs arrangements.

[7] Bomas of Kenya was initiated by the government in 1971 and opened in 1973 under the
Kenya Tourist Development Corporation, a part of the Ministry of Tourism and Wildlife.

[8] As there are 42 ethnic groups in Kenya, but only 11 traditional villages in Bomas, many
groups are left out, although some are represented in performance. There is no representation
of minorities such as the resident Indian population.

[9] It will be helpful to examine the charges for admission to the Bomas performance. At the
time of my visit, a Kenyan citizen paid about one-third the amount charged to a foreign tourist, and a resident child paid only about one-third of the amount paid by a Kenyan adult,
making it financially feasible for many Kenyans to come to Bomas for a family outing with
their children.

[10] The African Classic Tours (1986) brochure states:

> Here in East Africa, we can still view the world as our primitive ancestors saw it, in
> its natural state, without the influences of modern civilization. . . . Here are the living
> remains of prehistoric human cultures, people who still live by hunting and gather-
> ing: nomadic peoples living in small family groups. Here we can view the daily
> struggle for survival . . . and see people and wildlife living, for the most part, unaf-
> fected by our rapidly changing society.

[11] All quotes are from the brochure for the Intrav "On Safari in Africa" trip February 2 to 25, 1999.

[12] At this point, I must acknowledge the ambiguity of my subject position especially at the Sundowner, for I oscillated between being a tourist and being an ethnographer, on the one hand
enjoying the scene, talking with the tourists, avidly taking photographs, and on the other
hand studying the event, making ethnographic observations, and writing field notes (see
Bruner 1996b). All ethnographers occasionally experience a similar oscillation, between
being there as a participant in another culture (merging into the ongoing activity) and the
demands of being a scholar, striving for the distance and objectivity necessary to write for an
anthropological audience. I have felt this tension the most in my work on tourism rather than
in other ethnographic endeavors (cf. Bruner 1999).

[13] I am indebted to Mulu Muia, Duncan Muriuki, and to Jean Kidula for helpful information on
the musical scene in Kenya. I also note that data was gathered by modern electronic means,
by e-mail, and the Internet. Bomas, Kichwa Tembo tented camp, and Them Mushrooms all
have their own Web sites.

[14] I do not know the relationship between the use of Hakuna Matata in "Jambo Bwana" and in
the Elton John–Tim Rice song. Neither the lyrics nor music are the same, but the phrase,
Hakuna Matata, is equally prominent in both songs.

[15] Them Mushrooms also are known for reggae, and for fusions of reggae with local musical traditions. Them Mushrooms are credited with recording, in 1981, the first reggae song in East Africa, with CBS Kenya Records. Their inspiration was Bob Marley, the Jamaican reggae musician (Them Mushrooms 2000). Reggae also has a political meaning, connected to the Rastafarians.

[16] Wood (1999) reports that funds flow inequitably to the Maasai chiefs and politicians, and there have been many accusations of corruption. Berger (1996) discusses these inequities, offers solutions, and shows how the Maasai are being integrated into the tourism industry in Kenya. Kiros Lekaris, Stanley Ole Mpakany, Meegesh Nadallah, and Gerald Ole Selembo have helped me better to understand how the Maasai on the Mara do profit economically from safari tourism.

[17] I thank an anonymous reviewer for the *American Ethnologist* for many of the ideas in this paragraph.

References

Abram, Simone, Jacqueline Waldren, and Donald V. L. Macleod, eds. 1997. *Tourists and Tourism: Identifying with People and Places.* Oxford: Berg.

Adams, Kathleen M. 1998. "Domestic Tourism and Nation-Building in South Sulawesi." *Indonesia and the Malay World* 26(75): 77–96.

Anagnost, Ann. 1993. "The Nationscape: Movement in the Field of Vision." *Positions* 1(3): 585–606.

Appadurai, Arjun. 1988. "Putting Hierarchy in Its Place." *Cultural Anthropology* 3(1): 36–49.
———. 1991. "Global Ethnoscapes: Notes and Queries for a Transnational Anthropology," in *Recapturing Anthropology: Working in the Present*, ed. Richard G. Fox, pp. 191–210. Santa Fe, NM: School of American Research Press.

Asad, Talal, ed. 1973. *Anthropology and the Colonial Encounter.* London: Ithaca Press.

Babcock, Barbara. 1990. "A New Mexican Rebecca: Imaging Pueblo Women," in *Inventing the Southwest*, [Special Issue] *Journal of the Southwest* 32(4): 383–437.
———. 1999. "Subject to Writing: The Victor Turner Prize and the Anthropological Text." [Special Issue] *Anthropology and Humanism* 24(2): 91–73.

Benedict, Burton. 1983. *The Anthropology of World's Fairs: San Francisco's Panama Pacific International Exposition of 1915.* London: Scolar Press.

Berger, Dhyani J. 1996. "The Challenge of Integrating Maasai Tradition with Tourism," in *People and Tourism in Fragile Environments*, ed. Martin F. Price, pp. 175–197. Chichester, UK: John Wiley and Sons.

Boissevain, Jeremy, ed. 1996. *Coping with Tourists: European Reaction to Mass Tourism.* Providence, RI: Berghahn.

Bomas of Kenya. 2000. Bomas of Kenya Limited. Electronic document available at http://www.africaonline.co.ke/bomaskenya/profile.html [accessed July 2, 2001].

Boorstin, Daniel J. 1961. *The Image: A Guide to Pseudo-Events in America.* New York: Harper and Row.

Bruner, Edward M. 1986. "Ethnography as Narrative," in *The Anthropology of Experience*, ed. Victor Turner and Edward M. Bruner, pp. 139–155. Urbana: University of Illinois Press.
———. 1988 [1984]. *Text, Play and Story: The Construction and Reconstruction of Self and Society.* Proceedings, American Ethnological Society. Prospect Heights, IL: Waveland Press.
———. 1989. "On Cannibals, Tourists, and Ethnographers." *Cultural Anthropology* 4(4): 438–445.
———. 1994. "Abraham Lincoln as Authentic Reproduction: A Critique of Postmodernism." *American Anthropologist* 96(2): 397–415.

————. 1996a. "Tourism in Ghana: The Representation of Slavery and the Return of the Black Diaspora." *American Anthropologist* 98(2): 290–304.

————. 1996b. "Tourism in the Balinese Borderzone," in *Displacement, Diaspora, and Geographies of Identity*, ed. Smadar Lavie and Ted Swedenburg, pp. 157–179. Durham, NC: Duke University Press.

————. 1999. "Return to Sumatra: 1957, 1997." *American Ethnologist* 26(2): 461–477.

————. 2000. *Ethnic Theme Parks: Conflicting Interpretations*. Paper presented at the annual meeting of the American Anthropological Association, San Francisco, November 16.

Bruner, Edward M., and Barbara Kirshenblatt-Gimblett. 1994. "Maasai on the Lawn: Tourist Realism in East Africa." *Cultural Anthropology* 9(2): 435–470.

Castaneda, Quetzil E. 1996. *In the Museum of Maya Culture: Touring Chichén Itzá*. Minneapolis: University of Minnesota Press.

Chambers, Erve. 2000. *Native Tours: The Anthropology of Travel and Tourism*. Prospect Heights, IL: Waveland.

Cheung, Sidney C. H. 1999. "The Meanings of a Heritage Trail in Hong Kong." *Annals of Tourism Research* 26(3): 570–588.

Chilungu, Simeon W. 1985. "Kenya: Recent Developments and Challenges." *Cultural Survival Quarterly* 9(3): 15–17.

Cohen, Erik. 1979. "A Phenomenology of Tourist Experiences." *Sociology* 13(2): 179–201.

————. 1996. *Thai Tourism*. Bangkok: White Lotus.

Crick, Malcolm. 1994. *Resplendent Sites, Discordant Voices: Sri Lankans and International Tourism*. Switzerland: Harwood Academic Publishers.

Dann, Graham M. S. 1996. *The Language of Tourism: A Sociolinguistic Perspective*. Wallingford: CAB International.

de Certeau, Michel. 1984. *The Practice of Everyday Life*, trans. Steven Rendall. Berkeley: University of California Press.

Desmond, Jane C. 1999. *Staging Tourism: Bodies on Display from Waikiki to Sea World*. Chicago: University of Chicago Press.

Dinesen, Isak. 1938. *Out of Africa*. New York: Random House.

Eggan, Fred. 1954. "Social Anthropology and the Method of Controlled Comparison." *American Anthropologist* 56(5): 743–763.

Errington, Shelly. 1998. *The Death of Authentic Primitive Art and Other Tales of Progress*. Berkeley: University of California Press.

Evans-Pritchard, E. E. 1940. *The Nuer*. Oxford: Oxford University Press.

Feifer, Maxine. 1985. *Going Places*. London: Macmillan.

Foucault, Michel. 1979. *Discipline and Punishment: The Birth of the Prison*, trans. Alan Sheridan. New York: Vintage.

Geertz, Clifford. 1983. *Local Knowledge: Further Essays in Interpretive Anthropology*. New York: Basic Books.

Geschiere, Peter. 1997. *The Modernity of Witchcraft: Politics and the Occult in Postcolonial Africa*. Charlottesville: University Press of Virginia.

Gilroy, Paul. 1993. *The Black Atlantic: Modernity and Double Consciousness*. Cambridge, MA: Harvard University Press.

Graburn, Nelson. 1989. "Tourism: The Sacred Journey," in *Hosts and Guests: The Anthropology of Tourism*, 2nd edition, ed. Valene L. Smith, pp. 21–36. Philadelphia: University of Pennsylvania Press.

Handler, Richard, and Eric Gable. 1996. *The New History in an Old Museum: Creating the Past at Colonial Williamsburg*. Durham, NC: Duke University Press.

Horne, Donald. 1992. *The Intelligent Tourist*. McMahons Point, New South Wales, Australia: Margaret Gee.

Hymes, Dell, ed. 1972. *Reinventing Anthropology.* New York: Vintage Books.

Jules-Rosette, Bennetta, and Edward M. Bruner. 1994. "Tourism as Process." *Annals of Tourism Research* 21(2): 404–406.

Kahn, Miriam. 2000. "Tahiti Intertwined: Ancestral Land, Tourist Postcard, and Nuclear Test Site." *American Anthropologist* 102(1): 7–26.

Kasfir, Sidney Littlefield. 1999. "Samburu Souvenirs: Representations of a Land in Amber," in *Unpacking Culture: Art and Commodity in Colonial and Postcolonial Worlds,* ed. Ruth B. Phillips and Christopher B. Steiner, pp. 66–82. Berkeley: University of California Press.

Kichwa Tembo. 2000. Kichwa Tembo Tented Camp. Electronic document available at http://www.ccafrica.com/destinations/Kenya/Kichwa/default.htm [accessed June 20, 2001].

Kirshenblatt-Gimblett, Barbara. 1998. *Destination Culture: Tourism, Museums, and Heritage.* Berkeley: University of California Press.

Knowles, Joan N., and D. P. Collett. 1989. "Nature as Myth, Symbol and Action: Notes Towards a Historical Understanding of Development and Conservation in Kenyan Maasailand." *Africa* 59(4): 433–460.

Lanfant, Marie-Françoise, John Allcock, and Edward M. Bruner, eds. 1995. *International Tourism: Identity and Change.* London: Sage.

Lavie, Smadar, and Ted Swedenburg, eds. 1994. *Displacement, Diaspora, and Geographies of Identity.* Durham, NC: Duke University Press.

Lévi-Strauss, Claude. 1967. *Structural Anthropology,* trans. Claire Jacobson and Brooke Grundfest Schoepf. New York: Anchor Books.

Leys, Colin. 1975. *Underdevelopment in Kenya: The Political Economy of Neo-Colonialism.* London: Heinemann.

The Lion King. 1994. Directed by Roger Allersand and Rob Minkoff. Walt Disney Pictures.

Löfgren, Orvar. 1999. *On Holiday: A History of Vacationing.* Berkeley: University of California Press.

MacCannell, Dean. 1976. *The Tourist: A New Theory of the Leisure Class.* New York: Schocken.

———. 1992. *Empty Meeting Grounds: The Tourist Papers.* London: Routledge.

———. 2001. "Tourist Agency." *Tourist Studies* 1(1): 23–37.

Marcus, George, and Michael M. J. Fischer. 1986. *Anthropology as Cultural Critique: An Experimental Moment in the Human Sciences.* Chicago: University of Chicago Press.

Mullaney, Steven. 1983. "Strange Things, Gross Terms, Curious Customs: The Rehearsal of Cultures in the Late Renaissance." *Representations* 3:45–48.

Nash, Dennison. 1989. "Tourism as a Form of Imperialism," in *Hosts and Guests: The Anthropology of Tourism,* 2nd edition, ed. Valene L. Smith, pp. 37–52. Philadelphia: University of Pennsylvania Press.

———. 1996. *The Anthropology of Tourism.* Oxford: Pergamon.

Oakes, Tim. 1998. *Tourism and Modernity in China.* London: Routledge.

Okumu, John J. 1975. "The Problem of Tribalism in Kenya," in *Race and Ethnicity in Africa,* ed. Pierre L. van den Berghe, pp. 181–202. Nairobi: East African Publishing Company.

Out of Africa. 1985. Directed by Sydney Pollack. Mirage Enterprises Production.

Pearce, Philip L. 1982. *The Sociology of Tourist Behavior.* Oxford: Pergamon.

Pemberton, John. 1993. "Recollections from Beautiful Indonesia (Somewhere beyond the Postmodern)." *Public Culture* 6(2): 241—262.

Picard, Michel. 1996. *Bali: Cultural Tourism and Touristic Culture.* Singapore: Archipelago Press.

Rojek, Chris, and John Urry, eds. 1997. *Touring Cultures: Transformations of Travel and Theory.* London: Routledge.

Rosaldo, Renato. 1989. *Culture and Truth: The Remaking of Social Analysis.* Boston: Beacon Press.

Sahlins, Marshall. 1981. *Historical Metaphors and Mythical Realities: Structure in the Early History of the Sandwich Islands Kingdom*. Ann Arbor: University of Michigan Press.

Schein, Louisa. 2000. *Minority Rules: The Miao and the Feminine in China's Cultural Politics*. Durham, NC: Duke University Press.

Selwyn, Tom, ed. 1996. *The Tourist Image: Myths and Myth Making in Tourism*. Chichester, UK: John Wiley and Sons.

Smith, Valene L., ed. 1989. *Hosts and Guests: The Anthropology of Tourism*, 2nd edition. Philadelphia: University of Pennsylvania Press.

Spear, Thomas, and Richard Waller. 1993. *Being Maasai: Ethnicity and Identity in East Africa*. London: James Currey.

Stanley, Nick. 1998. *Being Ourselves for You: The Global Display of Cultures*. London: Middlesex University Press.

Tedlock, Barbara. 2000. "Ethnography and Ethnographic Representation," in *Handbook of Qualitative Research*, 2nd edition, ed. Norman K. Denzin and Yvonna S. Lincoln, pp. 455–486. Thousand Oaks, CA: Sage.

Them Mushrooms. 2000. Electronic document available at:
http://www.musikmuseet.se/mmm/africa/mushrooms.html [accessed June 15, 2001].
http://stockholm.music.museum/mmm/africa/mushroom.html [accessed June 27, 2003].

Urry, John. 1990. *The Tourist Gaze*. London: Sage.

———. 1992. "The Tourist Gaze Revisited." *American Behavioral Scientist* 36(2): 172–186.

Vickers, Adrian. 1989. *Bali: A Paradise Created*. Berkeley: Periplus Editions.

Wood, Megan Epler. 1999. Ecotourism in the Masai Mara: An Interview with Meitamei Ole Dapash. *Cultural Survival* 23(2): 51–54.

9

Culture by the Pound: An Anthropological Perspective on Tourism as Cultural Commoditization

Davydd J. Greenwood

Tourism is now more than the travelers' game. A few years ago, we could lament the lack of serious research on tourism, but now, like the tourists themselves, social researchers are flocking to tourist centers. This is necessary since tourism is the largest-scale movement of goods, services, and people that humanity has perhaps ever seen (Greenwood 1972). Economists and planners have been tracing the outlines of this industry and its peculiarities, and many anthropologists and sociologists have begun to chart the social effects of tourism on communities.

The literature generally points out that tourism provides a considerable stimulus to the local and national economy, but it also results in an increasingly unequal distribution of wealth. Tourism thus seems to exacerbate existing cleavages within the community. It is not, therefore, the development panacea that a few hasty planners proclaimed. This nascent critical literature is useful because it places tourism-related development in the analytical perspective from which a variety of different development strategies are being reviewed. The conclusion that tourism-related development tends to produce inequalities takes on added significance because it seems to parallel the inequalities produced by other development strategies like enclave factories, capital formation schemes, and the "Green Revolution." This serves as a needed corrective to overly exuberant dreams of an El Dorado paved with tourism receipts.

Tourism is not a monolith. It is an exceedingly large-scale and diverse industry, operating in a variety of ways under differing circumstances. Necessarily this means that we must differentiate between types of tourism and the range of impacts tourism can have on local communities.

This case study concentrates on the promotion of "local color" as a part of tourism merchandising and its impact on one community.[1] For clarity and to avoid any possible misunderstanding on this point, my analysis is not a general indictment of the tourist industry, but considers only the use of "local color" in tourism. The pros and cons of other aspects of tourism are weighed elsewhere in the literature generally.

Social researchers and moralists often speak critically of the uses and abuses of "local color" by the tourism industry. Spokesmen for local cultures decry the vilification of their traditions by tourism. Planners, too, feel vaguely uncomfortable about this but are quick to point out how little we understand the potential impact of these practices. Lacking well-documented research into the implications of the use of local color in tourism, it is not surprising that neither planners nor local people can decide just how to approach the problem. This study attempts, in brief compass, to analyze the commoditization of local culture in the case of Hondarribia,[2] Guipúzkoa in the Spanish Basque country.

Can Culture Be Considered a Commodity?

Logically, anything that is for sale must have been produced by combining the factors of production (land, labor, and capital). This offers no problem when the subject is razor blades, transistor radios, or hotel accommodations. It is not so clear when buyers are attracted to a place by some feature of local culture, such as the running of the bulls in Pamplona, an appearance of the Virgin Mary, or an exotic festival.

Economists and planners dealing with tourism have papered over this difficulty either by considering local culture a "natural resource" (that is, as part of the land factor) or simply by viewing local culture as part of the "come-on" and focusing their attention entirely on the number of hotel beds and the flow of liquor, gasoline, and souvenir purchases. Such a perspective is not very helpful because in ethnic tourism settings, local culture itself is being treated as a commodity sui generis.

A fundamental characteristic of the capitalist system is that anything that can be priced can be bought and sold. It can be treated as a commodity. This offers no analytical problem when local people are paid to perform for tourists. Like the symphony orchestra of economics textbook fame, they are being reimbursed for performing a service consumed on the spot. It is not so clear when activities of the host culture are treated as part of the "come-on" without their consent and are invaded by tourists who do not reimburse them for their "service." In this case, their activities are taken advantage of for profit, but they do not profit culturally. The onlookers often alter the meaning of the activities being carried on by local people. Under these circumstances, local culture is in effect being expropriated, and local people are being exploited.

We already know from worldwide experience that local culture—be it New Guinea aboriginal art and rituals, Eskimo sculpture (Carpenter 1972, 1973), Balinese dancing, bullfights, voodoo ceremonies, gypsy dancing, or peasant markets—is altered and often destroyed by the treatment of it as a tourist attraction. It is made meaningless to the people who once believed in it by means of a process that can be understood anthropologically. I think we have the social scientists' tools to understand the fragility of local culture and the humanists' responsibility to put these tools to use.

Anthropological Definitions of Culture and Public Ritual

To develop this view of local culture as a commodity, working definitions of culture and public ritual are needed. I will follow Clifford Geertz's views here. For Geertz, culture is an integrated system of meanings by means of which the nature of reality is established and maintained. His concept of culture emphasizes the authenticity and the moral tone it imparts to life experiences, as he calls attention to the fundamental importance of systems of meaning in human life. By implication, anything that falsifies, disorganizes, or challenges the participants' belief in the authenticity of their culture threatens it with collapse.

Public rituals can be viewed as dramatic enactments, commentaries on, and summations of the meanings basic to a particular culture. They serve to reaffirm, further develop, and elaborate those aspects of reality that hold a particular group of people together in a common culture (Geertz 1957, 1966, 1972).

As can be seen, the anthropological view of culture is far different from the economists' and planners' views of culture as a "come-on," a "natural resource," or as a "service." The anthropological perspective enables us to understand why the commoditization of local culture in the tourism industry is so fundamentally destructive and why the sale of "culture by the pound," as it were, needs to be examined by everyone involved in tourism.

The Alarde of Hondarribia

To analyze the process of cultural commoditization, I will use the specific case of a major public ritual in Hondarribia: the *Alarde*. The Alarde is a public ritual par excellence. It involves almost all the men, women, and children in the town during the preparations for it and includes a staggering number of them in the actual enactment.

The Alarde is essentially a ritual recreation of Hondarribia's victory over the French in the siege of A.D. 1638. This town was important from the fifteenth to the nineteenth centuries as a walled citadel standing almost on the border between Spain and France, where the Spanish and French crowns contested the rights to control the territory in the northeast corner of Spain. As a result, Hondarribia was besieged an immense number of times. Most famous was the siege of 1638, which lasted sixty-nine days and which the town successfully withstood, leading to the rout of the French army. Following this victory the town was accorded a number of privileges by the Spanish crown and was given an important honorific title to add to its official name.

But the Alarde does much more than simply commemorate a battle. Hondarribia is made up of the citadel, a fishermen's ward, and five rural wards, each with a corporate identity and responsibilities. The walled city and the six wards of the town each send a contingent of children who play Basque flutes and drums and march, dressed in the white shirt and pants, red sandals, sash, and beret symbolizing the Basques. They also send a contingent of men armed with shotguns. From among their young women, each ward elects a *cantinera* (water carrier) who is supposed to be the best flower of young womanhood in the ward. She dresses in a military-style uniform and carries a canteen. Various nonlocalized occupational groups are also represented. There is a contingent of *hacheros* (woodchoppers) dressed in sheepskin cloaks, with huge black beards and tall black fur hats. The mayor and the town council dress in military uniform and ride on horseback, leading the procession.

After an early mass, the groups form in the square outside the citadel gates. Each contingent of children marches through the gates and up the two-block street to the plaza where the somber fortress of Charles the Fifth is located, to the cheers and smiles of hundreds of relatives who crowd the streets and the overhanging balconies. The martial music is played with great fervor. The continual passing of each group, all playing a different tune, and the endless drumming have a profound effect on the bystanders.

Then the mayor and town councilmen on horseback ride in, symbols of leadership, valor, and nobility. They pass amidst general cheers and then dismount and move to the balcony of the town hall, which overlooks the main street about halfway up to the plaza, to review the parade. Led by its *cantinera*, each ward's group of armed men then marches up the street and stops under the town hall balcony. After saluting, they fire a unison shotgun salvo with deafening effect. The trick is to fire as if only one huge gun has gone off, and the audience continually comments on how well or badly each ward does this. Each group then marches on to the plaza and forms up there.

At the end of the parade, the mayor and town council rejoin the people, all now in the plaza. Together they fire a unison salvo that very nearly deafens all present. Everyone reloads and fires until he has run out of shells. With that the people begin to disperse. After rejoining their families, they walk down to the fishermen's ward for food and drink.

There are far too many elements in this ritual to permit a full commentary here. And *alardes* are not restricted to Hondarribia but are performed in many Basque and non-Basque towns. In each case, the details differ greatly (Caro Baroja 1968).

A few basic points about Hondarribia's Alarde should be made. The siege of Hondarribia was one in which wealthy and poor—men, women, and children, farmers, fishermen, and merchants—withstood a ferocious attack together. The Alarde reproduces this solidarity by involving all occupational groups, men, women, and children in the activity. The guns, by ward and then together, speak with one unified voice of the solidarity between the inhabitants that allowed them to survive. It is a statement of collective valor and of the quality of all the people of Hondarribia. It is an affirmation of their existence and identity at a time when most of the people earn money outside Hondarribia. It is a closing of wounds of gossip and bad faith opened up during the year of town life.

The mayor and town councilmen, often thought of as dishonest manipulators rather than as good men, are momentarily transformed into the embodiment of civic virtue and valor to the death. The fishermen and farmers, in much of their daily lives trying to free themselves of the rustic and working-class identity their trades give them, are for a moment the embodiment of the poor but free and noble Basques with whom they affirm an historical identity. Together these people, who most of the time are divided, vulnerable, and confused, are a single spirit capable of withstanding the onslaughts of the outside world as they once withstood the siege of 1638.

There is much more to it, but this suffices to provide the flavor of the event. What is most important is for whom the Alarde is performed. It is clearly not performed for outsiders; it is a ritual whose importance and meaning lies in the entire town's participation and in the intimacy with which its major symbols are understood by all the participants and onlookers (the latter often having spent months sewing costumes, directing marching practice, and teaching music to the children). It is a performance for the participants, not a show. It is an enactment of the "sacred history" of Hondarribia, a history by its very nature inaccessible to outsiders, even when equipped with a two-paragraph explanation courtesy of the Ministry of Information and Tourism. A few unrelated outsiders have always been present, especially members of the Spanish elite who have been summering in Hondarribia since the time of the monarchy (Greenwood 1972). They are welcome for they share some durable tie with the community. The presence of people who have no enduring relation to the community is much less welcome.

The Alarde is more than merely an interesting symbol of unity. As I am endeavoring to show in historical research on the Basques, the unique concept of Basque "collective nobility" is deeply involved here. By tradition, all people born in Guipúzcoa of Guipuzkoano parents were declared by that fact alone to have *limpieza de sangre* (no Moorish or Jewish blood), something that happened nowhere outside the Basque country. It gave rise to a unique situation: the Basques could assert that a cobbler, a farmer, a fisherman, a mayor, and a count were all equally noble. Though they recognized the differences in wealth and power, they asserted a common human equality by virtue of *limpieza de sangre* (Greenwood 1977).

Although the importance of *limpieza* is now gone, the equalitarian values arising from the idea live on in a Spain of stark class differences. To my mind, part of the importance of the Alarde is that it is the only occasion in which these ideas of equality and common destiny are given general expression. In this respect, the performance of the Alarde is a statement of their historical identity as Basques as well as an enactment of a particular moment in their history. The ritual is thus very important.

But the Alarde has the misfortune of taking place during the tourist season. The local population of Hondarribia is swollen fourfold; innumerable tourists drive in and out of town during the day to visit the beach, to watch boat races, to eat, swim, and take pictures of farms, old houses, and the city walls. The Alarde is listed by the Spanish Ministry of Information and Tourism in a national festival calendar that is given wide circulation. Tourism developers, a group including local politicians and contractors plus large national companies that specialize in tourism-related construction, have added the Alarde to their list of advertised features about Hondarribia. Posters and other publicity for the Alarde are circulated, as is anything else that makes the town attractive to the tourism consumer.

I do not wish to give the impression that the Alarde is singled out for this treatment. In fact, in the "come-on," the Alarde is relatively unimportant. It lasts only one day, and by comparison with tourist interest in the fortifications, the frequent boat races, and the other attractions of the town, the ritual is of only passing interest. The Alarde is simply part of the list of "local color" to attract tourist receipts; it is an offhand addition to the basic tourism package.

The Turning Point: The Alarde Goes Public

This offhanded treatment of the Alarde is not reflected in the effect its incorporation into the tourism package has had on the people of Hondarribia. Though the Alarde is still a going concern, it *is* in trouble. It has suddenly become difficult to get the people to show and participate in it.

The turning point occurred while I worked in Hondarribia during the summer of 1969. The town streets are narrow and all the balconies along the street belong to private houses. The plaza must be cleared of people to make room for the military formations. Thus, there is very little room for onlookers in the narrow streets of the old citadel.

In 1969, the Spanish Ministry of Tourism and Information finished remodeling the old fortress of Charles the Fifth in the plaza and opened it as a part of their well-known chain of tourist *paradores* (state hotel, restaurant, bar combination generally in historic buildings). It was personally inaugurated by Generalísimo Franco, an event commemorated on national television. Even a facsimile copy of Padre Moret's eyewitness account of the siege was published to add a note of "culture" to the occasion (Moret 1763). With the boost of national publicity, the municipal government felt obligated to resolve the problem of the onlookers. Not only should the people in the parador see the Alarde, but so should everyone else who wanted to. They declared that the Alarde should be given twice in the same day to allow everyone to see it.

In spite of the fact that the Alarde has not, to my knowledge, been given twice, the effect of the council's action was stunning. In service of simple pecuniary motives, it defined the Alarde as a public show to be performed for outsiders who, because of their economic importance in the town, had the right to see it.

The Aftermath: The Collapse of Cultural Meanings

There was a great consternation among the people of Hondarribia and a vaulting sense of discomfort. Soon this became the mask of cynicism that prefaces their attitudes toward the motives behind all business ventures in Hondarribia. Little was said publicly about it. But two summers later, I found that the town was having a great deal of difficulty in getting the participants to appear for the Alarde. No one actively or ideologically resisted, but in an event that depends entirely on voluntary compliance, the general lack of interest created serious organizational problems. In the space of two years, what was a vital and exciting ritual had become an obligation to be avoided. Recently the municipal government was considering payments to people for their participation in the Alarde. I do not doubt that they ultimately will have to pay them, just as the gypsies are paid to dance and sing and the symphony orchestra is paid to make music. The ritual has become a performance for money. The meaning is gone.

Conclusions: Culture by the Pound

This is undoubtedly a small event in a small place that few people will ever hear of, but its implications seem to be significant. By ordaining that the Alarde be a public event to attract outsiders into the town to spend money, the municipal government made it one more of Hondarribia's assets in the competitive tourism market. But this decision directly violated the meaning of the ritual, definitively destroying its authenticity and its power for the people. They reacted with consternation and then with indifference. They can still perform the outward forms of the ritual for money, but they cannot subscribe to the meanings it once held because it is no longer being performed by them for themselves.

I do not think this is a rare case by any means. Worldwide, we are seeing the transformation of cultures into "local color," making peoples' cultures extensions of the modem mass media (Carpenter 1972, 1973). Culture is being packaged, priced, and sold like building lots, rights-of-way, fast food, and room service, as the tourism industry inexorably extends its grasp. For the wealthy tourist, the tourism industry promises that the world is his/hers to use. All the "natural resources," including cultural traditions, have their price, and if you have the money in hand, it is your right to see whatever you wish.

As an analytical perspective has finally begun to develop with regard to the socioeconomic effects of mass tourism, it has become obvious that the increasing mal-distribution of wealth and resultant social stratification are widespread results of touristic development. Various remedies are proposed as an attempt to counteract these problems. While these problems are serious and must be remedied, I am terribly concerned that the question of cultural commoditization involved in ethnic tourism has been blithely ignored, except for anecdotal accounts. The massive alterations in the distribution of wealth and power that are brought about by tourism are paralleled by equally massive and perhaps equally destructive alterations in local culture.

The culture brokers have appropriated facets of a lifestyle into the tourism package to help sales in the competitive market. This sets in motion a process of its own for which no one, not even planners, seems to feel in the least responsible. Treating culture as a natural resource or a commodity over which tourists have rights is not simply perverse, it is a violation of the peoples' cultural rights. While some aspects of culture have wider ramifications than others, what must be remembered is that culture in its very essence is something that people believe in implicitly. By making it part of the tourism package, it is turned into an explicit and paid performance and no longer can be believed in the way it was before. Thus, commoditization of culture in effect robs people of the very meanings by which they organize their lives.

And because such a system of belief is implicit, the holders of it are hard pressed to understand what is happening to them. The people of Hondarribia only express confusion and concern about their Alarde; they know something is wrong and do not know exactly what it is or what to do about it. The Alarde is dying for them, and they are powerless to reverse the process. Making their culture a public performance took the municipal government a few minutes; with that act, a 350-year-old ritual died.

That is the final perversity. The commoditization of culture does not require the consent of the participants; it can be done by anyone. Once set in motion, the process seems irreversible and its very subtlety prevents the affected people from taking any clear-cut action to stop it. In the end, many of the venerated aspects of Basque culture are becoming commodities, like toothpaste, beer, and boat rides.

Perhaps this is the final logic of the capitalist development of which tourism is an ideal example. The commoditization process does not stop with land, labor, and capital but ultimately includes the history, ethnic identity, and culture of the peoples of the world. Tourism simply packages the cultural realities of a people for sale along with their other resources. We know that no people anywhere can live without the meanings culture provides; thus tourism is forcing unprecedented cultural change on people already reeling from the blows of industrialization, urbanization, and inflation. The loss of meaning through cultural commoditization is a problem at least as serious as the unequal distribution of wealth that results from tourist development.

Postscript (1977)

As this essay was going to press, I received word of the tragic consequences of the Alarde of 1976. The now "public" ritual became a major political event. In the context of the acute political tensions in the Basque country, the Alarde seemingly provides a means of political expression. Apparently the Alarde was celebrated this year amidst an atmosphere of considerable tension. Late in the evening in the fishermen's ward, a boisterous crowd confronted the police and a young worker from the nearby town of Irún was killed. The sense of shock and anger was intense and will probably play a role in the political future of Hondarribia. Perhaps the debasement of the Alarde set the scene for this event, and perhaps not. However, it is certain that, given the magnitude of the potential consequences, we cannot afford to merely guess at the political implications of cultural commoditization.

Epilogue (2004)

"Culture by the Pound" originally was written as an expression of both anger and concern. In the years since, I have returned to Hondarribia for only a few days at a time and have not again witnessed the Alarde. The creation of the Autonomous Community of the Basque Country after the passing of the Spanish Constitution of 1978, the ongoing terrorist movement, and the creation of a total of 17 autonomous communities in Spain have all moved history in new directions. I can only say that I understand that the Alarde has become much more a public event and is imbued now with contemporary political significance as part of the contest over regional political rights in Spain and also is involved in the struggle over gender equality as Basque women repeatedly have demanded the right to march in the parade in a capacity other than that of *cantinera*.

In 1989 I asked if tourism has unique effects that need to be understood separately from other forces for social and cultural change and if tourism's cultural manifestations are always negative and I expressed dismay at the bifurcation of the literature on tourism into two basic approaches. One focuses on political economy, making the case that tourism can have a substantial and disruptive impact on the local community. The other emphasizes cultural impacts and has had a strong tendency to view tourism as an alien and alienating force, typically in the form of a tragic narrative.

With these approaches went a relative lack of attention to the communities' alternative patterns of economic development and a rather homogenized view of government policy and the international tourist economy. The anthropological reaction to these developments was dominantly negative and fit generically with the anthropological critique of modernization already well developed in literature on the folk culture and urbanization. "Culture by the Pound" and my earlier article, "Tourism as an Agent of Change: A Spanish Basque Case" (Greenwood 1972) are examples of this.

Another part of the anthropological response to tourism focused on its cultural dimensions, or, specifically, on tourism as cultural exploitation. Here anthropological voices blended with those of journalists and cultural preservationists to a degree, though I tend to believe that anthropology had more challenging things to say. In this vein, many anthropologists, including myself, wrote of the cultural expropriation and demolition that tourism could impose on local cultures. This critique is still valid and there are enough examples to confirm both the analyses and predictions. However, this perspective provides only a partial view of the process.

The historical and ideological basis for this critique deserves analysis in its own right. Every generation produces moralists claiming that theirs is the epoch when culture has collapsed, when traditions have been destroyed and values lost. Though the anthropological critiques confidently announced this theme, it is troublingly difficult to separate this moral discourse, traceable in an unbroken genealogy back to Plato (Caro Baroja 1963), from other forms of intellectual and political conservatism, even though the rhetorical tone of the critique of tourism is politically left of center.

Lévi-Strauss put this worry quite eloquently in *Tristes Tropiques* when he wrote:

> The alternative is inescapable: either I am a traveler in ancient times, and faced with a prodigious spectacle which would be almost entirely unintelligible to me and might, indeed, provoke me to mockery or disgust; or I am a traveler of our own day, hastening in search of a vanished reality. In either case I am the loser—and more heavily than one might suppose; for today, as I go groping among the shadows, I miss, inevitably, the spectacle that is now taking shape. My eyes, or perhaps my degree of humanity, do not equip me to witness that spectacle; and in the centuries to come, when another traveler revisits this same place, he too may groan aloud at the disappearance of much that I should have set down, but cannot. I am the victim of a double infirmity: what I see is an affliction to me; and what I do not see, a reproach. (1970:45)

Fourteen years later, I find myself not only more troubled by my own judgments but also by the professional stance that they imply. It is not that my critique of tourism's cultural impacts seems wrong, but I now experience the way I researched and delivered this judgment to be professionally self-serving. I remember the feelings of righteous anger that I experienced in writing the original article and the sense of pride and satisfaction that I had in delivering an "anthropological" blow against tourism. I am hardly the only one to have done this.

In the Alarde, I found what I took to be an almost perfect microcosm of the destruction of all that is culturally good and authentic by the "state" and "world capitalism." My response was to denounce this from a position of professional anthropological authority—as an "expert" on culture. This denunciation took the form of two successive printings of an article in a collection of anthropological writings about tourism and a number of other reprintings. Though I know the article was widely read and so, in this way, it was somehow influential, here I invite you to consider the character of the professional posture of anthropology in the way this critique was delivered.

I did 18 months of fieldwork in Hondarribia and a few more summers after that, along with a great deal of archival research. I became an "expert" on the place in a way that has long been conventional for anthropologists. I delivered my arguments to an English-speaking audience of anthropologists and considered my professional duty to have been done with these publications.

In the interim, starting in the early 1980s, I became involved in the field of action research, a mode of research in which expert social researchers and local stakeholders together define problems to study, share their knowledge and methods, conduct research together, and design actions aimed at ameliorating situations that the local stakeholders consider unacceptable (Greenwood and Levin, 1998). Topic selection, analysis, action, and evaluation are collaborative and the role of the professional expert is as a process facilitator, coach on research methods, and team member.

How the tourism story might have been different had it been dealt with by an action research team? It is impossible to say at this distance, but I am sure it would not have been the same. What did the local stakeholders think about what happened at the Alarde? How did their views differ within this complex community by class, gender, locality, and ideological position? Given a chance to deliberate together about what happened and what should have been done, what would they have decided? How could they have negotiated with governmental officials about these matters and what would the reactions have been?

When I ask these questions, ones that are central to action research and to living up to a professional obligation to conduct research that matters to local stakeholders and not to treat them as mere objects of study, I realize that my mode of research in the 1970s gave me no basis for even guessing at the answers. I created a homogeneous image of the "culture" of Hondarribia and of a putative "community" reaction to the change in the Alarde. In effect, I now see that my research into this issue was superficial, a superficiality that was hidden well under the dramatic narrative I created.

This is not an apology. What I did in the 1970s was not only conventional anthropology then but it remains conventional anthropology now. We have rapidly growing anthropological literatures focusing on gender exploitation, racism, inequality, and human rights. Many of these narratives are as dramatic as mine and most of them are just as socially disengaged. I wrote passionately about cultural expropriation and now colleagues write with equal passion about sexual exploitations, human rights violations, terrorism, and environmental degradation.

Gradually, I have learned to ask for whom and to whom these narratives speak. The bulk are written to and for professional peers, showing the moral uprightness of the researcher but not contributing in any obvious way to the amelioration of the problems. Is it enough with issues like these to do the research on topics of our choosing, write about them in ways we and our colleagues like, reap the professional benefits, and move on?

I no longer think so. Not only does this constitute treating people like objects in a form of professional commodity production from which they benefit very little, but I think it also contributes to poor quality research. In reflecting back on my study of the Alarde from an action-research vantage point, what strikes me most is how simplified the view of Hondarribia had to be to make this into a neat moral tale. The deeper story might have been narratively less satisfying, but my subsequent experiences with action research suggest that the results might have been both better research and concrete benefits to someone other than me.

Source: Adapted from "Culture by the Pound: An Anthropological Perspective on Tourism as Cultural Commoditization," in *Hosts and Guests: The Anthropology of Tourism*, ed. Valene Smith, pp. 129–138. Philadelphia: University of Pennsylvania Press, 1977.

Acknowledgments

I am indebted to Pilar Fernández-Cañadas Greenwood for her editorial comments and the improvements she made in this manuscript when it was initially written. She is not responsible for the provocations that I have included in the epilogue. This article was first published in 1977 and reissued with an epilogue in 1989. I have retained the original article but have revised the epilogue for this volume.

Notes

[1] By "local color" I mean the promotion of a commoditized version of local culture as part of the "come-on," a widespread practice with little-understood consequences.

[2] Called Fuenterrabia in the original article, the name legally changed to Hondarribia after the creation of the Autonomous Community of the Basque Country.

References

Caro Baroja, Julio. 1963. "The City and the Country: Reflections on Some Ancient Commonplaces," in *Mediterranean Countrymen*, ed. Julian Pitt-Rivers. The Hague: Mouton.

———. 1968. "Mascaradas y Alardes de San Juan," in *Estudios Sobre la Vida Tradicional Española*, ed. Julio Caro Baroja, pp. 167–182. Barcelona: Ediciones Península.

Carpenter, Edmund. 1973. *Oh, What a Blow That Phantom Gave Me!* New York: Holt, Rinehart and Winston.

Geertz, Clifford. 1957. "Ethos, World View, and the Analysis of Sacred Symbols." *Antioch Review* 17:4.

———. 1966. "Religion as a Cultural System," in *Anthropological Approaches to the Study of Religion*, ed. Michael Banton, pp. 1–46. London: Tavistock.

———. 1972. "Deep Play: Notes on the Balinese Cock Fight." *Daedalus* 101:1–37.

Greenwood, Davydd. 1972. "Tourism as an Agent of Change: A Spanish Basque Case." *Ethnology* 11:80–91.

———. 1977. "Culture by the Pound: An Anthropological Perspective on Tourism as Cultural Commoditization," in *Hosts and Guests: The Anthropology of Tourism*, ed. Valene Smith, pp. 129–138. Philadelphia: University of Pennsylvania Press.

———. 1989. "Culture by the Pound," in *Hosts and Guests: The Anthropology of Tourism*, 2nd edition, ed. Valene Smith, pp. 171–185. Philadelphia: University of Pennsylvania Press.

Greenwood, Davydd, and Morten Levin. 1998. *Introduction to Action Research: Social Research for Social Change*. Thousand Oaks, CA: Sage.

Lévi-Strauss, Claude. 1970. *Tristes Tropiques*, trans. John and Doreen Weightman. Harmondsworth: Penguin Books.

MacCannell, Dean. 1976. *The Tourist: A New Theory of the Leisure Class*. New York: Schocken Books.

Moret, Rmo. R. José. 1763. *Empeños del Valor, y Bizarros, Desempeños, o Sitio de Fuenterrabia*, trans. Manuel Silvestre de Arlequi. Joseph Miguel de Esquerro, Impresor de los Reales Tribunales de Navarra. Originally written in 1654. Facsímile edition published by the Ministerio de Información y Turismo de España, Industrias Gráficas Valverde, San Sebastián, 1968.

10

Whose New Orleans?
Music's Place in the Packaging
of New Orleans for Tourism

Connie Zeanah Atkinson

For many places, music plays an important role in creating a distinct culture, and provides an important context for personal and collective identity. However, what happens when regional musics are commodified for tourism? Do traditional music practices and local identity change? And to what degree are musicians passive or engaged players in these activities? This essay looks at the New Orleans music community and its relationship to the tourist industry, focusing on the part music plays in the image and packaging of New Orleans as a tourist site. It also explores the consequences of tourism initiatives for the city's musical traditions and the musicians who live there.

New Orleans's Identification with Music—
Music and Place Images

New Orleans holds a unique place in the American landscape. Probably the most Africanized city in the United States (Hall 1994); about 60 percent of the population is black. With its French and Spanish, rather than English, colonial background, its Mediterranean culture and Catholicism, and its racial and ethnic diversity, including the early integration of Native Americans, it is part of, yet distinct from, the American South. Surrounded by water—the huge Lake Pontchartrain to the north, the Mississippi River to the west and south, and lakes and marshland to the east—New Orleans is also geographically separate from the rest of Louisiana and the South. Cultural activities brought in by the Africans, Italians, Spanish, and French have flourished unchecked in this relative isolation and merged with those of the indigenous population to produce rituals and cultural events—in which music plays a large part—that are unique to the United States, including second-line parades, jazz funerals, Mardi Gras Indians, and Carnival.

Visitors to the city's old French Quarter, the chief tourist area, can imagine themselves visiting another, more dangerous, more romantic time and place. The French colonial architecture of the Quarter, its narrow streets, iron-lace balconies, and lush courtyards reinforce this perception, as do the many Hollywood films that have portrayed New Orleans as the scene of unusual wickedness *(Blue Angel, Angel Heart, Walk on the Wild Side, Kid Creole)*. The infamous pirate Jean Lafitte's blacksmith shop lies just down the street from the strip joints and gay bars of Bourbon Street and just a few blocks from the Ursulines Convent; close by, Pirate's Alley runs alongside the oldest Catholic cathedral in the United States—iniquity and Catholicism sitting comfortably side by side. New Orleans' long history of racial and ethnic mixing gives the population an exotic look, contributing to the sense of

In the competition between cities, New Orleans' cultural activities, once considered "anti-business" by policy makers, are now encouraged as part of a strategy of distinctiveness in the tourism industry. (Photo by Connie Atkinson)

being in another country, another place in time. Visiting New Orleans, therefore, gives the white middle-class American tourist the chance to play out
fantasies of sin and danger from the safety of the balcony of a Holiday Inn, or
through the window of an air-conditioned tour bus.

The climate and festive inclinations of the city conspire to open up the
out-of-doors. Liberal drinking laws allow outdoor drinking; entertainment
spills outside buildings onto the sidewalks and courtyards of the French
Quarter, extending the tourist space to include the streets and *banquettes,* liberating the tourist, who can now "own" the entire space. Street bands can be
heard for blocks, and music clubs leave their doors wide open. "Private" cultural celebrations, such as neighborhood jazz funerals and parades, have no
boundaries between locals and tourists. Tourists watch and listen from door-
ways, out on the sidewalk, as well as inside the clubs. Music marks spaces
where revelry is permitted and serves as a signal that a space is open for
occupation. Where the music stops, tourists hesitate to venture.

In the mid-1980s, as the city government and private interests in New
Orleans began to take tourism more seriously, the riverfront was targeted as a
second tourist area. Port warehouses were torn down to create a park, and an
aquarium was built. Music is used to lure visitors to this new tourist space.
The riverboat *Natchez* blares out familiar tunes ("Waitin' for the Robert E.
Lee," "Way Down Yonder in New Orleans," etc.) on its steam calliope, creating a corridor of sound that tourists can travel, extending their space from the
Quarter to the river. Bands play on bandstands by the riverbank, street musicians serenade visitors on the "Moonwalk" that runs atop the levee, and concerts are held at the Spanish Plaza, using the river as a backdrop.

Music's Part in Packaging New Orleans— Music and City Tourism Policies

While a number of studies have looked at the impact on the way cities
and places are recognized and the influence of literary images on the portrayal and development of culture,[1] the role music plays has rarely been studied. Often overlooked, music is a powerful conjurer of places, as its use in
television, filmmaking, and advertising attest. Music is frequently thought of
as culture-specific, and sounds are often identified with place terms: an Irish
air, the Texas two-step, the Nashville sound, and so forth (John Skinner, personal communication).

New Orleans' image has been bound up with music from its founding,
with one of the longest histories of musical activity in North America. Early
visitors often commented on the abundance of music in the city. In 1802, a
visitor remarked, "New Orleanians manage during a single winter to exe-
cute about as much dancing, music, laughing and dissipation as would serve
any reasonably disposed, staid, and sober citizen for three or four years"
(Kmen 1966:6).

New Orleans' role in the evolution of jazz gave the city an international reputation that persists. However, for decades policy makers in New Orleans tried to dissociate the city from its jazz reputation because it was thought to hurt business and project an immoral, salacious lifestyle. In the 1940s, they reversed this strategy and adopted the romanticized image of the city as the "birthplace of jazz" to attract tourists. This early interest in the city's music, however, developed along limited lines. Promotion of the city's music was organized into "safe" cultural channels, such as traditional jazz museums, archives, newsletters, performance halls, and festivals, while the Franco-African performance activities, still alive in the black neighborhoods, went unsupported and ignored.

In the 1950s, the city regained the national musical spotlight, with stars such as Fats Domino, Lloyd Price, and Little Richard heralding the new age of R&B and rock 'n' roll. But despite their success, the local music industry remained small and fragmented, with little support from the city's business leaders or politicians. Meanwhile, music continued to be an integral part of the family and community life of many New Orleanians (Berry et al. 1990).

As late as the 1970s, in the midst of the offshore oil boom, the city's tourism initiatives remained confined primarily to the convention trade. New Orleans' musical reputation was considered "frivolous" and detrimental to attracting business. Instead, the city concentrated on building facilities (hotels, a convention center, and the 80,000-seat Superdome) and attracting national political and sports events.

This changed in the mid-1980s with the decline of the port and the oil industry. With the convention center only partially booked and new hotels standing half empty, the hotels passed a self-imposed $1/room tax to finance the New Orleans Tourism Marketing Corporation. Its brief was to market the city to discretionary tourists or nonconvention visitors. This commitment to tourism for urban regeneration placed New Orleans in competition with other cities in attracting people for entertainment and leisure activities. Research was commissioned to discover what distinctive quality of the city would be the most competitive. It found that discretionary tourists list "excitement" most often as the goal of their travels, and the images of New Orleans as a city of spontaneous celebration, sin, and so forth, fed into this. The tourism marketing board once again decided to exploit the city's music image. Their theme was "come join the parade" and all television and radio spots used New Orleans music. Tourists were invited to participate and join in the "New Orleans experience." From the airport where the only music played is by New Orleans artists, through the taxi ride into the city where the cab drivers (graduates of a city-run course in tourist relations) regale the visitor with stories about musical legends, to the Riverwalk shopping mall where again only New Orleans music is played, to the street musicians in Jackson Square, the visitor's experience is outlined and grounded in music.

Policy makers are often pushed reluctantly in the direction of arts and cultural industries as a base for economic regeneration, perhaps because of

A New Orleans street parade: private cultural activities in public spaces hold no boundaries between locals and tourists. (Photo by Connie Atkinson)

their unfamiliarity with the arts as compared to more traditional industries. However, the arts are often a substantial, if overlooked, economic force. The music industry in New Orleans, for example, contributed $1.45 billion to the city's economy in 1990 (Ryan 1990). The number of national and international visitors to the 25-year-old New Orleans Jazz and Heritage festival in 1993 exceeded 350,000. According to the U.S. Travel Data Service, almost 20 percent of total annual visitor spending is attributed to music.

Music-making in New Orleans

Andrew Kaslow has documented the many linkages within the New Orleans musical community through family ties and membership in social aid and pleasure clubs, carnival organizations, churches, and clusterings of other organizations and institutions (Kaslow 1981). Through individuals holding multiple memberships in widely different associations, these connections proliferate, revolving around charismatic leaders who maintain the continuity of the groups over time. The extensive kinship networks within the musical community of New Orleans are celebrated in Jason Berry's book *Up from the Cradle of Jazz* (Berry et al. 1990). In New Orleans, journalists and musicians commonly describe their music in terms of family relations. Kaslow wrote that music has ". . . enriched the lives of Orleanians in ways that have served to give a different focus to the meaning of 'community' than in other settings."

For the predominantly African-American musical community of New Orleans, music constructs social networks that shape notions of locality, reinforce family unity, and provide an important context for the issues of ownership and control of music and responsibility for the way music is used. Music is a locally valued activity in which the African-American community's leadership has been acknowledged by non-African-Americans. As Monson (1994) has pointed out, this is of extreme symbolic importance in African-American communities. Since this inversion of the usual relationship does not extend to the economic sector, however, conflicts can arise when dealing with ownership and representation. Tourism has been an important site of such conflicts.

Implications of Tourist Policies for Local Musicians and Residents

The city's attempts to attract discretionary tourists have been successful, and some businesses have prospered. What are the implications of these initiatives for local musicians and how do they affect the musicians' images of themselves and their city? Here some musicians and locals see tourism as contributing to increased employment opportunities, while others complain that distinctive music-making practices are changing because of tourism.

Gary, a 41-year old native New Orleanian, who, with his friends, often patronizes the small music clubs of his neighborhood, is bothered by changes that he has noticed since visitors have arrived.[2] In 1986, the Glasshouse was a tiny, run-down club in what is called the "back o' town" area of the city. Every Tuesday night, the Dirty Dozen (one of the most popular of the bebop-oriented brass bands) would play. Says Gary,

> At the Glasshouse, they don't charge to go in. It's just a neighborhood joint. But the man who owns it told them they could play there, pass the hat around, you know. They were just starting out.
>   For the Dozen, you see, their crowd, only the guys dance. The women sit and cheer them on. The dancing gets rowdy, you know, with the guys jumping up in the air and dropping to the floor and spinning around, twisting.

As the Dirty Dozen started getting popular, writers (including British DJ Andy Kershaw) "discovered" the Glasshouse, and, says Gary, "tourists started coming in cabs. They'd join in the dancing, women and men. Pretty soon, at the Glasshouse, the men and women dance together, just like everywhere else."

On the other hand, some musicians feel that the tourist industry fits uniquely into musical practices that already exist in New Orleans. Says one musician who has achieved a great deal of success both in the city and nationally:

> It's given musicians a place to play. Yeah, you can't usually make it as a full-time thing. But in New Orleans, music has always been a part-time

job. Louis Armstrong played all over town, yes, but he also had a job in a mattress factory. Lee Dorsey had all those hits, but he still had his car body shop, through it all. And where do you think Aaron Neville got those big ole arms of his? That was from the docks. He worked the docks until his music hit the big time.

The head of the city's music commission agrees:

Playing for tourists can be a way to prepare yourself for the general music industry, for recording purposes. It is a strategy that will work if it's done right. I tell people all the time, music in New Orleans, working with music in New Orleans is the best part-time job in the world. These people here are professional musicians, even though they may work at different jobs. They play music every Saturday and Sunday and then some of them are playing maybe two or three times a week. So they get an opportunity to mature a music style, they get a chance to be able to become much more at ease with what they're doing. Instead of playing for seven years and talking about it for the rest of their lives, or trying to regain that seven years for the rest of their life, or having that seven years kill them, here they play thirty years, and they're always playing, and that is just being honest. Who is one of the new stars of the New Orleans musical scene now? Harry Connick Sr. [district attorney of New Orleans, father of Harry Jr.], and he is in his sixties. The tourists love him, and he is still the D.A. He does gigs three or four nights a week now. And Frank Minyard [New Orleans coroner], he is still playing, playing all the time. They look for opportunities to play, and tourism provides those opportunities.

Donald, a 23-year-old horn player who has received a lot of local media attention, has recorded with local rock 'n' roll bands, played locally at clubs, and still works at a local radio station during the day:

It depends on what you think it's all about. On a Sunday I am playing in churches, in the mornings, and then I go over and play Commander's Palace [restaurant] for a brunch, and then I might have a gig laid on at night, and over the time period of the day, I've played music about eight to ten hours and I have made x number of dollars and that is fine. On Saturdays, I might play Saturday night at House of Blues with a rock band, or R&B band, or behind some big name who came to town and needs a horn player, or sometimes I might play Saturday nights with this guy Mickey Easterling and his orchestra and you know that is cool and we play for hours and I get the standard union scale and that's not bad at all. And then there may be a wedding in the afternoon. On Friday nights I am there playing a function, say a convention gig or at a gig at Tipitina's; they both pay, the tourist gigs pay more. I played the other Saturday afternoon at the airport. These people wanted a band to meet a plane. It all adds up. It's all music.

George, a musician who achieved quite a bit of fame in the 1960s, speaks from his experience:

If you don't watch out, trying to run around trying to be a great success [working full time] in the recording aspect of the music industry then

God, it'll run you insane. It'll drive your wife and family insane, to a point you can't have one. What you wind up doing is you lead this very disconcerting existence that really hurts you and your playing, because you don't have someone you belong to over and beyond your playing buddies, your fellow musicians. You don't have to come home, you don't have to get up and take the kids to school, you don't have to get to work at a certain time, you don't have to do all those things that ground you and keep you sane. You can kind of wallow in your self pity, and that's when your playing really gets bad. You need to have this grounding, this balance, to be a musician.

Can you make money in the tourism industry? Yes, but you have got to really work at being a part of what they're doing. You may be able to get to that point of say $50 an hour, which is not bad in New Orleans for any job, for a four-hour set on a Sunday playing from eight till twelve. You still got time if you want to go to church in the morning, to catch the Saints [professional football team] with your kids in the afternoon. Well if you do this on Saturday and Sundays every week that's four hundred dollars a weekend that you are making extra. So this is like an addition of 1600 dollars a month. The tourism stuff is over by midnight or 11 o'clock, they don't really go on late at night. So you could go on to a play club, since music starts so late in the clubs, or you could go home, and be home for 11 o'clock. That's the kind of thing a lot of people never realize, that tourism gigs end early. Believe me, 999 times out of 1000, in the long run it pays better than if somebody gets signed and goes off to Los Angeles, for sure.

The majority of musicians interviewed, however, confirmed the notion that the tourism industry requires the musicians to play a certain kind of music. One young musician who leads his own band put it this way:

They don't require that you do anything, they are just not going to hire you if you don't play what they want to hear. We have lots of bands, they can choose somebody else. So no, they are not going to tell you that they don't want you to play whatever, blues, rock, Irish ditties. They'll say they just want to hire your band. But if you don't play what they expect you to, you won't get hired again.

Another group leader:

It goes this way: They'll say, "I need a blues band, you are a jazz musician, I'm not telling you that you got to be a blues musician, I want to tell you I only hire blues bands. So I'm not telling you to change your life ambitions, I was just saying this is why you are hired." So yes, musicians do feel held back by the way they have to play. But that's also why most everybody plays most every way here, so you don't have those categories attached to you that can keep you from getting hired. You just let it out that you're a drummer, or a trumpet player, and you're ready to play. So the situation with tourism causes the musicians to have to be broad based.

There is general agreement that tourism provides opportunities for young people to play, but there are conflicting opinions about how this affects their future prospects. A music educator at the University of New Orleans:

Music requires discipline and especially commitment. It is very hard to be a young musician training to be a professional musician. There is that initial burst of talent, where people say a child is going to be great—well he may be very good at eight years old, but by 12, they have to move beyond the very good eight-year old status, to having to make a commitment. That's when the training comes in. Those who practice, they are better musicians. It becomes a thing of time, a thing of hours. It is a solo activity, it is an activity about developing the individual and it is an individual effort and that is what kids don't have anymore in this country, in lots of places; they run in packs. So music is a great social engineering tool for the city of New Orleans and it has always been a great social engineering tool. Here music has been used as a gang that kids got involved with, to develop a sense of who they are.

You also have to be able to improvise; New Orleans music is a music of improvisation, so at one point or other you have to step out from the crowd. You have to make your statement, inside of what is the overall group statement. So the tourism industry provides a place for all this to happen, and for young people, they can play on the streets, in the Quarter, and get that practice in, and also make a pretty good piece of change. You can get hired for these afternoon events, and on the weekend, while you're still in school, and make some pocket money. Look at Harry Connick, Jr. He was playing on Bourbon Street when he was 13, 14. But you have to be able to compete. You have to keep your level of musicmanship up or the tourist will just walk down to the next group. But playing, the more you play the better you are as a musician, and the tourist industry gives a lot of opportunity to play.

At the same time, there are doubts about the staying power of these opportunities afforded to young people. Teachers in local university music departments, including Ellis Marsalis, father of jazz giant Wynton Marsalis, worry that young musicians, given the opportunity to make a little money playing for tourists, will not continue their education, and that their talents may be stifled at a young age by their dropping out of jazz studies available in local institutions. "Yes, they're cute playing out there at 12, 15 years old. But how cute is that same musician at 35, when he hasn't progressed, and doesn't have a diploma because he dropped out of school to work for the tourists?" Others, including a member of the local public school board, disagree with this notion:

> It's easy for some people to say all children should go to college and all young musicians should take college jazz studies, but the reality is that college is not an option for many young New Orleanians, and playing music, at any level, is an honorable and fulfilling occupation especially with the limited options available to many young poor people in an urban area. And as a musician, I believe playing for years only improves musicians . . . . So just because a young person begins to play early, outside the institutions of learning, because of the opportunities given by tourism, that doesn't necessarily mean that that young person won't have a long and successful career. It happens all the time. That's a case of "let them eat cake." Well, "let them go to college to study jazz" may sound like an idea for everyone, but frankly, it's not.

The New Orleans and Liverpool Connection

As New Orleans opens ups its private cultural activities to the outside, the city is wrestling with questions such as what effect new tourism initiatives will have and whether these changes will, in fact, translate into economic regeneration and sustainable growth for the local music industry. Looking for balanced strategies that will facilitate control and ownership of representations and cultural products, and at the same time provide economic support for the community, New Orleans has looked to other localities for innovative ideas and information.

In the late 1980s, for example, New Orleans and Liverpool became "Sister Cities" (which officials in Liverpool City Council call "friendship-linked" since it doesn't involve international trips by city officials and exchanges of scrolls). Previous attempts to adapt similar programs from such "music cities" as Nashville, Tennessee, and Austin, Texas, proved impractical for New Orleans owing to what local policy makers described as "economic, social and historic differences" in the cities' experiences.

The predominantly African-American musical community of New Orleans felt little in common with the experiences of the predominantly white musical communities of Austin and Nashville. Despite the efforts of the New Orleans city government and a good relationship between the city's music business community and the annual South by Southwest Music Conference in Austin, few New Orleans musical groups attend the conferences, thereby missing opportunities to make links with the recording industry. When asked why they didn't participate New Orleans musicians said: "They aren't interested in our music"; "We don't play for free"; and most often "We can't afford to drive 500 miles to play for some record industry cat who came to hear some hillbilly punk band."

In contrast, the musical community of New Orleans views Europe as a site of possible business success. The popularity of New Orleans music in Europe creates opportunities for playing international festivals, and many New Orleans musicians have traveled to Europe who have never traveled within the United States. Musicians often mention "Europe" as a place of musical discernment where New Orleans music is appreciated, reaffirming their feelings of local difference and worth. An invitation to play overseas is seen as an endorsement of a group's talent and creativity.

Some informal links between New Orleans and Liverpool carried the news of initiatives in both places to boost their local music industries. Liverpool, it was felt, shared many common traits with New Orleans: historical trade links, a similar population size, heavy unemployment. Both cities have international musical traditions and reputations, yet neither had benefited in any substantial way from these. Both cities had been linked with crime and violence by their national media, and were looking for a way to overcome that image. Feelings of powerlessness and frustration with the music industry and belief that their contribution to popular music (jazz and R&B for New

Orleans, the Beatles and the many successful bands in the 1960s and 1970s for Liverpool) never resulted in adequate remuneration, together with a perception of lack of support from their own local and national governments, fed into common notions of being both geographically and economically isolated from the centers of power, creating a bond between the musicians in the two cities. The pairing of New Orleans and Liverpool demonstrates how music can generate notions of community that transcends national borders.

Conclusion

This look at New Orleans points out the often overlooked role of music in the way cities and places are recognized and the influence of musical images on the portrayal and development of culture. As towns and cities embrace tourism for economic development, decisions on how local cultural activities are commodified for tourist consumption could become important factors in the shaping of local identity. In addition, the way that New Orleans musicians relate to the tourism industry points up ways that economic pressures may affect local cultural products such as music and styles.

Source: Adapted from "Whose New Orleans? Music's Place in the Packaging of New Orleans for Tourism," *Fieldwork in Developing Societies*, S. Devereux and J. Hoddinott (eds.), 1993, Boulder, CO: Lynn Rienner.

Notes

[1] See, for example, Jan Nordby Gretlund, *Eudora Welty's Aesthetics of Place*, Odense, Denmark: Odense University Press, 1994; Leonard Lutwack, *The Role of Place In Literature,* Syracuse, NY, Syracuse University Press, 1984; David Kranes, "Space and Literature: Notes toward a Theory of Mapping," in *Where? Place in Recent North American Fictions*, ed. Karl-Heinz Westarp, Aarhus University Press, 1991; and Violet Harrington Bryan, *The Myth of New Orleans In Literature: Dialogues of Race and Gender*, Knoxville: University of Tennessee Press, 1993.

[2] Interviews with sources are drawn from research done in New Orleans, Louisiana, over the last decade, both as a doctoral candidate and as a journalist in the city.

References

Berry, Jason, Tad Jones, and Jon Foose. 1990. *Up From the Cradle of Jazz*. Athens: University of Georgia Press.

Esolen, Gary. 1994. Interview with the author, March 1994.

Floyd, Sameule. 1995. *The Power of Black Music: Interpreting Its History from Africa to the United States*. New York: Oxford University Press.

Hall, Gwendolyn Midlo. 1994. *Africans in Colonial Louisiana: The Development of Afro-Creole Culture in the Eighteenth Century*. Baton Rouge: Louisiana State University Press.

Kaslow, Andrew. 1981. "Oppression and Adaptation: The Social Organization and Expressive Culture of an Afro-American Community in New Orleans, Louisiana." Unpublished Ph.D. thesis, Columbia University.

Kmen, Henry. 1966. *Music in New Orleans: The Formative Years 1791–1841*. Baton Rouge: Louisiana State University Press.

Monson, Ingrid. 1994. "Doubleness and Jazz Improvisation: Irony, Parody, and Ethnomu-
    sicology." *Critical Inquiry* 20(2): 283–313.
Robins, Kevin. 1991. "Tradition and Translation: National Culture in its Global Context,"
    in *Enterprise and Heritage*, ed. J. Corner and S. Harvey. London: Routledge.
Ryan, Tim. 1990. *Economic Impact of Music on the New Orleans Economy: Report to the
    City of New Orleans*. New Orleans: University of New Orleans.
Wallis, R., and K. Malm. 1984. *Big Sounds from Small Peoples: The Music Industry in
    Small Countries*. London: Constable.

11

In a Sense Abroad: Theme Parks and Simulated Tourism

Lawrence Mintz

In British author David Lodge's novel, *Paradise News,* anthropologist Roger Sheldrake, a character described by one reviewer as a typical "theory-besotted professor," appears, in beige safari suit, en route to Hawai'i to continue his research on tourism. Sheldrake has become bored with the traditional subject matter of his discipline. He is on to something more interesting, more "hip." "Sightseeing," he enthuses, "is a substitute for religious ritual. The sightseeing tour as secular pilgrimage. Accumulation of grace by visiting the shrines of high culture. Souvenirs as relics. Guidebooks as devotional aids. You get the picture" (Lodge 1992:161).

Lodge's satire fails here only because the actual study of tourism approaches too closely his comic imagination. Scholarly writing about travel over the past decade has often compared it to pilgrimage. Titles such as John F. Sear's *Sacred Places* and Alexander Moore's subtitle for his discussion of Disney World, "bounded ritual space and the playful pilgrimage center," make the point unambiguously. Dean MacCannell, an important progenitor of this discussion, observed that the tourist seeks more than entertainment or amusement. Tourists are seeking more meaningful, even profound satisfaction, but what they actually experience is a "staged authenticity," an encounter that is essentially engineered both by the tourism industry that controls the plan of the visit and by the cultural expectations of each visitor. Cultural observers Daniel Boorstin, Jean Baudrillard, Umberto Eco, Jonathan Culler, and many others note that travel is itself in a sense a "pseudo-event," to use Boorstin's (1964) term, a "simulation" (Baudrillard 1988), a "hyperreality" (Eco 1986). Over a decade ago, Margaret J. King explained the management of experience at Walt Disney World, observing that "people have long 'understood' other cultures not through actual contact but through mediated experience and imagination" (1981:148). Such observations reflect the theoretical position that all reality is "socially constructed," that what we experience and understand is a result of decoding signs and symbols using cognitive tools (such as language) that are themselves cultural constructs.

It is the commercially designed and operated tourist simulations (i.e., theme parks) that particularly irk certain contemporary social philosophers. Critics such as Umberto Eco and Jean Baudrillard see them as disturbingly modern, or we should say postmodern, and as uniquely American phenomena. In an article on Colonial Williamsburg, critic Ada Louise Huxtable describes the restoration cum amusement environment as nothing less than the start of a "quintessentially American" process of replacing reality with "substitution." Huxtable is disturbed that it works all too well and detrimentally. She is also disturbed that theme park simulations are unabashed in their enthusiasm for the quality of the recreation: "nothing in it [the theme park] is admired for its reality, only for the remarkable simulation that is achieved; the selective manipulation of its sources is a deliberate expressive distortion that is its own art form" (1992:26).

Another source of criticism of theme park simulations is that they are "capitalist" or consumer-oriented ventures, expensive entertainments, and profitable endeavors. They are carefully planned, closely managed, technologically controlled—in short, industrialized and packaged. It is argued that they limit spontaneity, originality, individuality. In his study of Walt Disney World, Stephen M. Fjellman (1992) presents the park as a near perfect metaphor for America itself: prosperous, antiseptic, materialistic, narcissistic—powerful and controlling.

To apply a simulation of simulations to the discussion, we might note some dialogue from the popular novel and film, Michael Crichton's *Jurassic Park*, in which it is argued that real dinosaurs make lousy tourist exhibits because they move too fast to be appreciated by the human viewers. "Nobody wants domesticated dinosaurs, Henry. They want the real thing," John Hammond claims. "But that's my point," Wu responds. "I don't think they do. They want to see their expectations, which is quite different . . . You said yourself, John, this park is entertainment. And entertainment has nothing to do with reality. Entertainment is antithetical to reality" (Crichton 1990:122). Walt Disney himself understood that his park was not about "reality." Margaret J. King quotes the master as proclaiming, "I don't want the public to see the real world they live in while they're in the park . . . I want them to feel they are in another world" (1981:121).

The concerns about the meaning and effects of simulation are, of course, neither frivolous nor simple. What is the *effect* of the blurring of distinctions between original and copy, between old and new, and of radically reordering both text and context? Museums wrestle, for instance, with the problem of presenting exhibits that are composed exclusively of actual or authentic artifacts that might be incomprehensible as well as visually uninteresting; on the other hand, there are ethical and intellectual objections to offering recreations and restorations that might "work" artistically and educationally but are misleading and offensive in their "falseness." A legitimate question is raised as to whether the "real" can compete with the artificially enhanced, whether we are being conditioned to carefully structured, staged experience, with detrimental effects on our attention span, our patience for learning without amusement, our need for constant visual stimulation, our appetite for change and excitement, and so forth.

At the center of this debate lie attitudes about popular culture and its aesthetics. We have a hierarchy of tourist motives and activities that places various ambiguously defined spiritual and intellectual purposes at the top, and entertainment or amusement at the bottom. Travel that involves living and studying abroad, learning another language, making close contacts with the natives, and developing a mystical quality called "an appreciation" of the culture is deemed worthy, while various packaged tours and quick visits ("if this is Tuesday, it must be Belgium") are condemned. In a still lower circle of tourist hell is "armchair tourism," a term for media encounters (travel films, magazines, television tourism). Theme park simulations, of course, rank either just above or just below media-based travel, depending upon whether you add points because it is "live" entertainment or subtract some because they include rides and other "fun" activities.

Another cause for concern is the argument that the simulated theme park is "postmodern," disorienting in its dazzling, confusing, and facile mixture of tourist icons, parades, shows, multimedia attractions, rides, fast food, and service amenities. The food server wearing a Hollywood costume version of native dress while offering modern American fast food disguised as native fare, both of which are intended to be exotic while at the same time referencing other modern popular culture experiences, including other theme parks, leaves the visitor dangling somewhere between the excitement of new experience and the comfort zone of the familiar. Similarly, in the rapid changes of context as one moves from one attraction to another, covering a wide range of activity (touring exhibits, attending shows, enjoying rides, shopping, eating), audiences may become disoriented, overwhelmed. Such an assessment implies that the dazed spectator is therefore more vulnerable, controlled, manipulated. We need to know far more about the tourist experience, its various motives and functions, and its complex role in our society. One primary need is for more audience research, particularly qualitative, in which the participants themselves articulate their expectations and their sense of what it is they have experienced. However, it is a gross oversimplification to present the issues as one of the "real" versus "artificial" experience, or "learning" and/or "inspiration" versus recreation, amusement, or for that matter, of consumerism or leisure as a commodity. These distinctions are misleading and reductionist. Theme parks need to be explored and interpreted on their own terms, as contemporary popular culture, as participatory theater, as leisure environment, and as text.

The idea of recreating Europe or "the old country" in a nostalgic way is profoundly familiar in our culture from the accidental recreation of ethnic enclaves in our cities (e.g., Little Italys, China Towns, Little Polands, and many Irish and Jewish neighborhoods) to more consciously constructed tourist remakes such as the California Danish town of Solvang and the several Little Bavarias, Little Hollands, and Little Switzerlands dotting the landscape. We love to use European and other foreign motifs in our vernacular architecture, adding Spanish or Middle Eastern motifs to our shopping malls, gas stations, or just about anywhere we can find a place to anchor the iconic clues. Such simulations acknowledge the power of our attachment to our immigrant roots, the cultural significance we award to our parent nations, and our taste for the exotic; it coexists with our other simulations, of colonial America, of the Old West, and so forth, as means by which we establish and communicate our mythic personal, community, and national identities.

Theme parks that simulate the travel experience, most notably Walt Disney World Epcot's "World Showcase," but including such parks as Busch Garden's "The Old Country" near Williamsburg, Virginia, as well as other, less ambitious recreations of Europe, Africa, the Old West, and just about any other place a person might want to visit, present a special case of tourism. They are tours within tours, i.e., the tourist travels to the park to travel *within* the park. For that matter, in a visit to both World Showcase and The Old Country, one travels to the park, then travels within the park by cable car, boat, and monorail to reach specific destinations, and then "rides" each attraction by transport, which is either entertainment in its own right or a means of locomotion through an exhibit. In World Showcase's Norway attraction, for instance, a boat ride offers a rather tame version of a North Sea voyage while exhibiting that country's past and present through film and artifact displays. A particularly amusing case of the layering of travel within travel is provided by The Old Country's Marco Polo's journey, a ride with a Turkish motif within the Italy sector of the park. Only in America.

Perhaps the most disorienting thing about Busch Garden's "The Old Country" is its location in Williamsburg, Virginia, or as their promotional literature puts it, "surrounded by Colonial Williamsburg and Jamestown."[1] While a visit to Busch Gardens does not necessarily imply a visit to Colonial Williamsburg, it is assumed that many, if not most, tourists visit both attractions as part of the same trip. The two attractions were quite nervous about this "odd bedfellows" phenomenon when Busch Gardens opened in 1975. Colonial Williamsburg has a lot invested in its educational and inspirational potential and in the "authenticity" of its restoration and research programs.

However, they seem to have developed a comfortable relationship, fueled no doubt by the realization that they economically benefit one another. There may even be a growing if grudging acceptance by Colonial Williamsburg that in the areas of entertainment and visitor services, its functions are not really that different from those of its more clearly commercial neighbor.

Busch Gardens is one of several parks operated by Anheuser-Busch, brewers of Budweiser, Michelob, and other American mass-market beers. The first Busch Gardens, "The Dark Continent," opened in 1959 in Tampa, Florida. It was conceived as a botanical garden and zoo adjunct to the brewery, a private park built as a public service and community relations gambit. Success led to its growth into a naturalist-environmentalist theme park with an African motif, together with rides and other entertainments. The juxtaposition of the theme parks—a family ice cream and coke environment with active breweries offering brewery tours and beer samples—is potentially jarring. Unofficial amusements at the park are for teenagers to try and get a beer, and for adults to see how many free ones they can obtain.

Busch Gardens covers 360 acres, a little more than half a square mile, and serves some 2 million visitors yearly.[2] The park is divided into sectors: England's Banbury Cross and Hastings; Scotland's Heatherdowns; France's Acquataine; New France (so named so as not to violate the old country theme, but which is actually Canada); Italy's San Marco and Festa Italia; and Germany's Rhineland and Oktoberfest. Each sector uses clichéd architectural clues and familiar tourist icons to establish its national identity, thus Banbury Cross is represented by mock Tudor architecture and red London telephone booths, New France has log cabins, San Marcos has statues and fountains, and in a particularly amusing touch, France Acquataine is falling apart (e.g., artificial cracks in the sides of the buildings). Each sector offers its own selection of rides and attractions, including those for small children as well as more challenging roller coasters and other thrill rides. The rides' trappings are intended to contribute to the theme atmosphere, and names such as The Loch Ness Monster, Drachen Fire, Le Mans Raceway are used to remind revelers that they are indeed "abroad." Food options include pizza, burgers, barbeque, roast beef sandwiches, fried chicken, French fries, and other American commercial cuisine, presented as ethnic dining experiences in each country sections (pizza in Italy, barbeque in New France). Shopping for souvenirs and rather schlocky imported gifts is likewise given a national context by offering ordinary products such as cigarette lighters and coin purses decorated to appear as if they had been made in and are representative of the crafts of the "countries" in which they are purchased. Ironically, such theme park shopping might be seen as a realistic modern touch, as genuine native crafts become harder to find and to afford and are increasingly replaced everywhere by mass-manufactured junk. Rest amenities such as benches and scenic views, bridges, ponds, lakes, and pleasant park-garden settings are an important feature, and clean, efficient personal services for the comfort of the guests are readily available.

The shows at Busch Gardens have only the vaguest of themes, with the exception of Oktoberfest as discussed below. The Globe Theater offered a fascinating pastiche of Shakespeare's plays when the park first opened, became a blended magic show, light show, and extended skit, and has more recently degenerated into a variety show distinguished from others only by costume, badly rendered accent, and thinly applied motif. The concert and shows division of Busch Gardens is perhaps its weakest, though it is hard to say whether this is a failure on the part of the management or a concession to audience tastes for bland, light variety entertainment. The show in Italy, for instance, is a set of popular Italian-American classics like "That's Amore" with mercifully brief snatches of Bel Canto. The young performers are clean-cut and earnest in the classic American style.

Perhaps the most interesting attraction at Busch Gardens is Oktoberfest, an attraction reproduced from one created for the original Busch Gardens in Tampa, Florida. Oktoberfest, referring to the German harvest celebration in late September–early October that Americans tend to associate primarily with Munich and Bavaria, is held in Das Festhaus, a very large, barnlike building, nicely decorated with an attractive, gigantic stained glass window above an antique automated organ. Oktoberfesters file into a cafeteria area where they purchase platters of wurst with kraut and German potato salad or huge corned-beef sandwiches, topped off by slices of flavorless Black Forest cake and washed down by beer or soft drinks served in paper cups. They then take seats at large picnic tables encircling the stage and dance area. While dining, they are entertained by a rather authentic-looking German elder, dressed in lederhosen, drinking from a beer stein, feebly warbling "Edel-weiss" and other examples of the famed Teutonic musical genius. After a few minutes, an oompah-pah band and young dancers march in. As the band is installed in a circular bandstand that ascends into the heavens, a narrator informs the audience that they are about to experience "gemutlichkeit," the spirit of joy, abandon, and community spirit. Toward that end, visitors are encouraged to shake hands with everyone at their table within reach. After twelve minutes or so of waltzes and polkas, the audience is encouraged to participate as the dance troupe selects suitably cute partners from among the guests. Then the experience is over, and the next adventure begins.

For tourists, Busch Gardens is about having a pleasant day of varied amusements in a comfortable environment. As a place for relaxed visual stimulation, it is perhaps not as far from a European experience as it would first seem. Margaret King has observed that "in fact Americans go to Europe largely for the charming cities—for public spaces like the Italian piazza which is human and pedestrian in scale encouraging the outdoor stroll and public relaxation . . . and the sidewalk cafes which encourage 'people watch-ing'"(1981:121). Busch Gardens offers a safe, clean, comfortable simulation of the cosmopolitan ethos.

The park's diversity encourages family participation. There is some-thing for everyone from a very young child to grandparents, and it is safe to let reasonably young kids wander alone, checking in at designated times and places. Teenagers can travel in groups of peers; young couples can find privacy while surrounded by hundreds of others.

The Old Country does not overtly claim to be a learning experience or a pilgrimage. Indeed, in that sense it downplays its own theme of European travel. The various theme sectors of the park provide mild visual variety without disturbing the familiar rhythms, the comfort in formula and familiarity, and the realized expectations on which the genre depends. Visitors know what to expect in each area and from each activity, whether it is the rides or the shopping or the dining experience. Yet the park is successful in its suggestion of novelty, of variety rather than redundancy as one moves from England to Italy to France to Germany to Scotland. Though superficial, the environmental changes enhance the sense of adventure, of an escape from the ordinary world into a realm of vacation and recreation. That the same basic formula is repeated in each realm, disguised by the trappings and icons that simulate the local color, is an underlying popular culture verity. The experience is comfortingly familiar, unthreatening, immediately understood and appreciated, yet the illusion of freshness is maintained and apparently accepted. The references to the various ethnic and national identities confirm expectations; that is, they are based on familiar clichés and stereotypes. They are clearly intended to provide atmosphere rather than simulation in any active sense. At Busch Gardens the trip "abroad" is meant to be a vacation, an amusement, an opportunity for pleasure.

The "World Showcase" at Walt Disney World's Epcot is more ambitious and in a sense a more pretentious enterprise. A promotional flyer heads into the storm of simulation controversy with no quarter offered: "Situated around a 40-acre lagoon beyond Future World, the World Showcase nations are re-creations of landmark architectures and historic scenes familiar to world travelers. Built with infinite attention to detail, the mini-towns have buildings, streets, gardens and monuments designed to give . . . guests *an authentic visual experience of each land*" (emphasis added).

In any case, it is a more carefully constructed physical simulation than one would expect to find in any other theme park. The Disney organization put an enormous amount of effort and money into the materials, the design, and the construction of the World Showcase, and as Ada Louise Huxtable suggested of Colonial Williamsburg, the technological and artistic quality of the recreation might be in fact more significant than its content. The quality extends to the goods and services available. The shopping at World Showcase is of a higher order than at most theme parks, though merely by degree. It still involves souvenirs and gifts; just better quality. The fast food is also the same but better than one finds elsewhere. World Showcase's gourmet restaurants, however, claim to provide an "authentic" touristic experience. L'Originale Alfredo di Roma Ristorante, the Biergarten, Restaurant Marrakesh, Chefs de France, and Bistro de Paris lay claim to originality and top quality. The view of this writer is that while they do not quite make it, they come amazingly

China in Florida: part of Epcot's "World Showcase." (Photo by Walter Gmelch)

close considering the challenges they face. Any gourmet restaurant would be daunted by having to serve as many seatings with as many meals and by the time constraints posed by tourists with agendas and priorities other than the dining experience. There are also financial limits; while the restaurants are much more expensive than those at any other theme park, they are still considerably less expensive than most first-class gourmet establishments. As providers of "theme park fare," the restaurants at World Showcase are remarkably admirable.

World Showcase does not rely on exciting rides or participatory games and activities. Rather, it offers tours and exhibitions, in a most interesting way paralleling the definition of tourism that stresses information and inspiration as paramount goals. The tourist visiting the park's Mexico sector, for instance, is cast in the role of a tourist, given a brief and very superficial survey of that country's history, and an equally brief introduction to its tourist attractions, which are dwarfed by the enormous, adjacent Mexican bazaar. This creates the impression that Mexico's primary reason for existence is the revenue opportunity it provides for tourists to spend money. The presentation of the dominant national image in the other lands is generally less demeaning than it is in the Mexico sector, but the basic theme is that the countries of the world are places that are interesting for us to see—charming diversions for our shopping and dining pleasure.

Whatever lessons about native cultures are to be learned are self-gleaned from reading the annotations on some of the artifact displays. The films that are the highlights in several of the sectors are visual treats, especially the Circle-Vision 360 presentations "Wonders of China" and the "Impressions of France," but they too rely on the spectacular sensory effect rather than any significant social or cultural communication. We see the countryside, some of the landmarks, and faces of the people while listening to music and soothing narration. Despite the well-publicized fact that World Showcase employs natives of the various lands (who are issued special green cards by the U.S. Immigration Service toward that end), there is no real opportunity to engage in a serious encounter with the people or the culture of any of the simulated lands. The only sector where the visitor learns something about the culture, society, politics, or people to be encountered is the American Adventure. Although even here there is much less learning than in any *National Geographic* article, to say nothing of a more extensive stay abroad. (But as suggested earlier, the case may be made that the theme park experience is closer to the actual package tour experienced by many American tourists on a "trip of a lifetime" to Europe.) For all of its quality of detail, World Showcase is neither more informative, more stimulating, more inspiring, nor more fun than Busch Gardens. It seems a quiet respite from the more exciting Magic Kingdom or the newer MGM and Universal Studios parks and from the intellectual appeal made by Epcot's Future World. Here again tourism emerges as a pleasant, amusing vacation activity rather than anything invested with a higher purpose.

The question is: why should tourism be anything more than a pleasant, relaxing, entertaining experience? If we make some largely false assumptions about the value of tourism and then reason from them that theme park simulations fail to provide a "proper" tourist experience, and/or if we speculate that the simulations replace people's impulse for actual tourism or more extensive travel, we can conclude that the time spent at them is not well spent. If we wonder why trips to these parks, especially to Walt Disney World, nevertheless seem to be so highly valued, so prominent, and even monumental in the lives of American consumers, we will not find an answer by uncovering a hidden or overlooked profundity in the theme park formula. Indeed, evaluating the simulated tourism experience according to a false set of standards and assumptions about the meaning of tourism inevitably misleads. If instead we focus on what parks actually deliver, on their mildly stimulating, formulaic, predictable, safe, clean amusement; on the opportunity they provide for shopping for worthless but inexpensive goods and for eating convenient and comforting if mediocre food, we can properly understand the nature of simulated tourism. "It's the entertainment, stupid."

Source: Adapted from "Simulated Tourism at Busch Gardens: The Old Country and Disney's World Showcase, Epcot Center," 1998, *Journal of Popular Culture* 32(3):47–59.

Notes

[1] Most of the facts about Busch Gardens cited here come from the company's promotional literature, c. 1989. According to a spokesperson, they were still basically accurate as of 1993.

² Epcot provides a library and an information service office for educators, primarily for teachers using the park's resources for future-studies or for cultural studies rather than for study of the Disney parks per se. However, there are also some clippings and other general information, mostly from press releases, which provide useful materials on the history and details of the construction and operation of all of the Disney theme park enterprises.

References

Baudrillard, Jean. 1988. "On Seduction: Similacra and Simulations." *Selected Writings.* Stanford: Stanford University Press.

Boorstin, Daniel. 1964. *The Image: A Guide to Pseudo-events in America.* New York: Harper.

Crichton, Michael. 1990. *Jurassic Park.* New York: Knopf.

Culler, Jonathan. 1981. "Semiotics of Tourism." *American Journal of Semiotic* 1(1–2): 127–40.

Eco, Umberto. 1986. *Travels in Hyperreality.* San Diego: Harcourt, Brace.

Fjellman, Stephen J. 1992. *Vinyl Leaves: Walt Disney World and America.* Boulder, CO: Westview.

Huxtable, Ada Louis. 1992. "Inventing American Reality." *New York Review* 3 Dec: 24–29.

King, Margaret J. 1981. "Disneyland and Walt Disney World: Traditional Values in Futuristic Form." *Journal of Popular Culture* 15(1): 116–140.

Lodge, David. 1992. *Paradise News.* New York: Viking.

MacCannell, Dean. 1976. *The Tourist: A New Theory of the Leisure Class.* New York: Schocken.

———. 1992. *Empty Meeting Grounds: The Tourist Papers.* London: Routledge.

Moore, Alexander. 1980. "Walt Disney's World: Bounded Ritual Space and the Playful Pilgrimage Center." *Anthropological Quarterly* 53:207–18.

Sears, John F. 1989. *Sacred Places: American Tourist Attractions in the Nineteenth Century.* New York: Oxford.

Urry, John. 1990. *The Tourist Gaze: Leisure and Travel in Contemporary Societies.* London: Sage.

Three: When Tourists and Locals Meet

Travel is fatal to prejudice, bigotry, and narrow-mindedness.

— Mark Twain, U.S. writer and humorist, 1869

. . . when the natives see you, the tourist, they envy you, they envy your ability to leave your own banality and boredom, they envy your ability to turn their own banality and boredom into a source of pleasure for yourself.

— Jamaica Kincaid, Antiguan writer, 1988

12

Tourism and Anthropology in a Postmodern World

Fredderick Errington and Deborah Gewertz

As he drove from the airport in Wewak, Papua New Guinea, to his three-room guesthouse, Ralf warned us that with our arrival all fifteen beds would be filled. We were disappointed, for we had hoped to be largely alone there, as we occasionally had been in the past when we came from our Chambri Island field site to resupply in Wewak. Indeed, as we grumpily wrestled our heavy metal patrol boxes inside the door, his house seemed to be crawling with noisy, young tourists. Our annoyance was increased when one of them derisively asked us whether we always traveled so heavy, adding that he had just returned from two weeks of paddling from village to village along the Sepik River with only a small backpack. We promptly responded to this taunt. We said that we were anthropologists who had come not to travel but to stay; our boxes contained supplies sufficient for seven months of field research among the Chambri. Moreover, to ensure our victory in what was obviously a contest, we added that this was our fourth trip to Papua New Guinea during the past twenty years.

Thinking over the incident we were amused to see how easily these tourists had been able to pull us into competition over which, they or we, had had the more authentic experience with native people in Papua New Guinea. This had been a competition we had wanted to win, and we wondered whether we would have emerged triumphant if this had been our first trip.

After we had settled at Chambri, we might not have thought much more about these noisy young tourists—"travelers" they called themselves—with their search for the authentic and their competition with us—if it were not for the frequent arrivals of older and wealthier tourists. Although more easily accepting that we had surpassed them in their search for the authentic, the latter were largely unimpressed with our choice of a profession that was not only relatively poorly paying in their view but required the deprivation and discomfort of life in the jungles of Papua New Guinea. Unlike the travelers with their sporadic and low-budget arrivals, these tourists came to Chambri at regular intervals, transported in luxury on the Sepik in a cruise ship, the *Melanesian Explorer*. With their frequent visits, we realized that tourists now had a major role in Chambri life. Their presence, and that of the travelers— their reactions and those of the native people as members of each group observe and perform for the other—needs to be understood.

To this ethnographic focus, and prompted by our musings on our own relationship to these visitors, we add a more general theoretical discussion about the nature of anthropological authority. A number of contemporary writers would not have been surprised that we were so readily pulled into a comparison with these tourists (of both sorts). They have argued that, despite an ideology to the contrary, anthropologists are, in fact, little different from tourists (see Boon 1982; Dumont 1977; Hamilton 1982; Mintz 1977; and van den Berghe 1980). Perhaps the most forceful formulation of this view comes in a recent article by Crick (1985) who endorses and summarizes the recent critique that we have, as anthropologists, lost our authority because, like tourists, we do not reach an objective understanding of the other—what we do is for ourselves and in our own terms. (On the loss of ethnographic authority, see also Clifford 1988; Clifford and Marcus 1986; Crapanzano 1986; Strathern 1987, 1989; and Tyler 1986.)

Furthermore, Crick suggests, many field confessions reveal that anthropologists, far from immersing themselves and thereby acquiring competence in an alien culture, frequently spend much time avoiding interaction with native people by reading novels and dreaming of home (see Barley 1983). Semiotically if not linguistically maladept and chronically gauche, they both misunderstand what they are told and, in addition, annoy their informants who become little inclined to reveal themselves (Herzfeld 1983). And, often forced to employ interpreters and purchase information, anthropologists further distance themselves from the other.

Nor can anthropologists be readily distinguished from tourists since the former work and the latter play. According to Crick and others, tourists may be engaged in a modern secular ritual equivalent to a rite of passage or a rite of intensification. (See, for example, Cohen 1988; Graburn 1983; Lett 1983; and Pfaffenberger 1983.) Comparably, fieldwork may be a modern secular ritual for those seeking transformation from students into professional anthropologists.

Finally, at the most general level, it is argued that anthropologists, like tourists as products and agents of capitalist systems, objectify those they observe (Fabian 1983; Pratt 1986), regarding the other as available for their acquisition and use. In this process, the other, stripped of power and volition, becomes defined to meet Western standards of conceptual utility (Appadurai 1985; Asad 1973; Haraway 1985a; Spooner 1986).

Thus, according to this critique, the "I was there" of the anthropologist should carry little more ethnographic authority than that of the tourist. Ethnography, these writers contend, is like the tourist report; it is essentially self-interested fiction (Crapanzano 1986).

Although Crick allows that not all anthropologists or all tourists are the same (as we have indicated, many of the tourists in Papua New Guinea consider themselves not as "tourists" but as "travelers") and that there are differences between them, his general conclusion from this comparison is that anthropology, like tourism, is a game we play for our own purposes. This conclusion, however, does not disturb him particularly. Indeed, he thinks that the nature of anthropology as game has unfortunately been obscured by a scientism, which holds that social reality is an entity that may be perceived objectively through the application of value-free rules. (On misplaced scientism, see Bleier 1984; Haraway 1985b and 1986; Keller 1985; and Louch 1969.) Crick's is the postmodern perception that social life (including the disciplines that examine social life), in its fragmentation and multiplicity, is not *an* order produced by the enactment of *a* set of rules. Therefore, a much more accurate perception not only of anthropology but of social life more generally (including, of course, tourism) would be one that recognizes the importance in both of the continual negotiation of the rules in gamelike fashion. Freed from its pretenses, anthropology could itself become more ludic, he argues, and in so doing better convey the ludic in the game that constitutes social life.

We contend that one could regard social life as the product of continual negotiations and yet not share Crick's conclusion that anthropology should be more like play (no matter how important or pervasive play might be as a human phenomenon). We also contend that one could likewise reject scientism without accepting that anthropology be essentially ludic, simply one game of many, without substantial seriousness.

We doubt, in fact, that there can be much justification for anthropology if anthropologists are fundamentally like tourists. In this paper, therefore, while pursuing our ethnographic interest in the Chambri social field (which includes both tourists and anthropologists), we return to Crick's original comparison to examine the terms we share with those we met at Ralf's and elsewhere in Papua New Guinea, and those we did not. It will be our conclusion that, in a world in which it profoundly matters who controls the terms of the interactions—the negotiations—and who wins or loses, anthropology needs not a heightened sense of the ludic but of the political.

On Travelers

Ralf's guesthouse was inexpensive, costing PGK6.00 per night. (Kina is the currency of Papua New Guinea. In 1987, PGK1.00 = US$1.15.) In contrast, each of the three local hotels was by any standard expensive, costing approximately PGK100.00 per night. His guests were generally in their twenties, often on long-term excursions after they had completed university studies or military service. They stayed at Ralf's, not only because they rarely could afford the other accommodations, but also because they wished to distinguish themselves from those they regarded as tourists. They did not use money to insulate themselves from direct and significant experience—from the "real"—as did the "tourists." (On travelers, see, for example, Cohen 1989; Smith 1989; and Teas 1988.)

Ralf's accommodations were basic. Although he had electricity and running water, the shower was cold and the outdoor toilet, odorous. Strangers shared rooms with each other and with members of Ralf's family in what was his home. Ralf originally came from Germany to Papua New Guinea as a Catholic missionary. Although no longer a priest, Ralf had remained permanently in the country, as a citizen. He married a woman from a Sepik River village and was raising a family. Since Ralf had led an eventful life and seen much of Papua New Guinea, his guests felt that staying with him was memorable for it was in itself an authentic experience.

Most travelers arriving in the Sepik region brought with them a popular travel guide, *Papua New Guinea: A Travel Survival Kit* (Lightbody and Wheeler 1985), from which they learned, for example, that the Sepik is "the best known area of PNG for artifacts" (1985:44) and "has attracted little development and remains remarkably untouched by western influences" (1985:152). Nevertheless, Ralf's establishment was an important clearinghouse of information for them. In addition to the knowledge Ralf himself conveyed about where to go, how to get there, and what to take (he rented at low cost such absolute necessities for travel in the Sepik River area as mosquito nets), there was advice available from the other guests—especially those stopping at Ralf's as they returned from their trip on the Sepik.

Those returning furnished the new arrivals with accounts of recent adventures larded with travel tips. The new arrivals reciprocated in kind by telling of their own travel in other parts of Papua New Guinea or other remote parts of the world. In these accounts of adventure and advice there was a striving for verification. Virtually anyone who ended up at Ralf's could be recognized as intrepid, at least by comparison with the tourists. However, even among this relatively elite group, important distinctions were made about which among them was immersed most completely in native life. These preoccupations pervaded not only the conversation at Ralf's but also the observations that these guests wrote in notebooks Ralf provided for the edification of later visitors. As we shall see in the following excerpts from these notebooks, by recording what to visit and what to avoid, travelers conveyed the breadth of their experience, their fortitude, and their capacity to discriminate between the authentic and the inauthentic. Of particular interest to us are the criteria used in this discrimination.

1. An anonymous traveler wrote in April 1983:

> Watch out for Kanganaman and Parambei [villages along the Sepik] you might miss them. It is quite some paddling to get to Parambei. The *haus tambaran* [men's ceremonial house] in Kanganaman is sure worth seeing. They try to charge you for it. In both villages people are friendly because they are accustomed to the big spending Explorer tourist. Hardly any good carving left if you are looking for that. . . . Kapaimari, the Catholic school shortly after Kanganaman, you leave untouched. It is like other mission places—Timbunke, Ambunti. People very unfriendly; ready to rip you off. The smaller the village the better. Some places may get five white tourists a year. . . . Accommodation is no problem if you stay away from the tourist spots. Every village will put you up and sometimes even provide food free. Your visit is an honor for them—a change in everyday life . . .

This traveler assumed that tourist money and missionary activity spoiled local people by making them unfriendly and concerned only with acquiring money. Those so remote as to have escaped these pernicious Western influences retained a tradition of carving and hospitality. Moreover, they also recognized and appreciated the fact that this traveler was willing to leave the path beaten by the less enlightened members of his own European society to visit them. Such an encounter as an instance of intercultural communication was seen as reciprocally enriching traveler and villager alike.[1]

2. Two male travelers, one from Poughkeepsie, New York, and the other from Russian River, California, described villages along the Sepik in July, 1983:

> Japanaut: friendly; good resting spot. Yentchamangua: very friendly . . . free night. Korogo: very friendly; free night with Peter; his son is Ronny; one of the first houses up river; excellent haus tambaran; good for carvings . . . Yentchan: interesting haus tambaran; impersonal atmosphere; 5 PGKs [In 1983, PGK1.00 = $U.S.1.40] to sleep in haus tambaran . . . Kambrindo: friendly. Moim: uninteresting . . . ; no carvings, at least they don't offer to show us some. Also had clothes ripped off here. Important notes: . . . If you want to buy artifacts, do it last, or in the morning. Show you are interested in the villagers; they are interested in you. Be friendly and they will not treat you like a tourist. Explain difference between tourist and traveler. They are really good people. Show pictures. Tell stories. Ask questions . . . We met people who hated the Sepik. Be respectful of haus tambarans and culture. Bargain but don't degrade. Be a traveler, not a tourist. It makes a big difference . . . Don't leave things in canoe at night. Even grungy clothes will disappear—something belong "masta" [a colonial Pidgin English term for white man.] Food: bring plenty. No one really offered us food since we brought our own. They did let us use their pots, pans, fresh water and utensils. . . . By the way, we had a fantastic time. Go for it, yea, to the max, far-fucking out!

These travelers categorized villages according to whether social encounters had been friendly and nonmonetary or impersonal and commercial. In addition, they were alert to the presence of features of interest such as a haus tambaran or carvings and implied that since insensitive tourists were attracted to these features, local people had become cynical and indifferent. It was the travelers who could, because they were sensitive and caring, reestablish warm, human (and inexpensive) relationships and enable villagers to manifest their essential goodness. Although such a project of redemptive encounter might fail to reclaim those who coveted even grungy clothes, these travelers found their experience eminently rewarding.

3. A family traveling on motorcycles left their account anonymous but nonetheless included a photograph of themselves on their motorcycles. Writing in December, 1984:

As we travel as a family, two adults, two kids and two motorcycles, we had a different trip. Luckily for us we had got a Papuan friend here in Wewak and we went up to Ambunti [sub-provincial headquarters] with him in his motorboat free and slept in his house. Next day we borrowed his boat and went four hours up the Sepik River and turned up the April River to [the village of] Biaka where we lived with a family for two days free. The food we brought we gave to the wife and asked to have only native food during our stay. A bit hard to get sago down, but nice fish, taro and pumpkin and this was really an experience. Everything very "primitive." As gifts we had brought toys for children and these everybody enjoyed, adults as well as children. It was lots of fun. In return we got a grass skirt, pigs' teeth, a belt with tail and a cassowary knife, which we are really happy about. On way back we saw a witch doctor working in another village. A very outstanding experience.

These travelers had it all. They formed such a close friendship with a Papua New Guinean that he not only provided them with free accommodation but also loaned them his motorboat. They chose to spend their limited time in a single village where they developed reciprocal relations with a local family. Living under "primitive" conditions and encountering a witch doctor at work, they experienced Papua New Guinea life as it really was.

4. Two anonymous travelers wrote in July 1986:

The next morning half the village turned out to watch us spin out into the Sepik. The younger group amused, the older alarmed. After an erratic half hour in which the three of us simultaneously attempted to use our own steering methods, we calmed down and zigzagged semi-proficiently to the village of Korogo . . . The villagers are building a new haus tambaran. The carvings are interesting, but photographs [of the haus tambaran] cost an exorbitant 5 dollars [kina] . . . We stopped at Aibom village [in the Chambri Lakes] where they are carving a new haus tambaran to watch an old woman potter making the clay cooking pots for which the village is famous. The lakes are well worth a trip, beautiful islands with highlands in the distance. Many birds and fish, lilies in the water. The village of Chambri is huge [actually there are three villages on Chambri Island] with a large mission and interesting haus tambaran with oval windows. But it has become like a souvenir shop with chalked prices on the statues. There is a special house for visitors. No cooking facilities; two kina per person.

By lightheartedly demonstrating to a Sepik audience that they lacked competence in the basic skill of canoeing, these travelers showed themselves willing to establish relations of intimacy and equality with local people. Given their genuine interest in and appreciation of the people, it was lamentable that they, as if they were tourists, should be offered the culture—the haus tambarans and the artifacts—as commodities.

Ralf provided a place where travelers might appraise themselves and seek validation as unique, autonomous, and subjectively rich individuals. They were able to regard themselves as relatively unique and autonomous since few members of their society had either the desire or the self-reliance to travel in a place as distant and "undeveloped" as Papua New Guinea. Moreover, what they encounter there was experienced as further enhancing their already distinctive selves. For travelers, the encounter with what was seen as the "primitive"—the exotic, the whole, the fundamentally human—contributed to their own individuality, integration, and authenticity. Those who gathered at Ralf's also sought to affirm the extent to which they had embodied the values and the rewards of the successful traveler and, as we have seen, they competed as each tried to gain further distinction as being unique among this august body of fellow travelers. This competition concerned who had most fully encountered the most "untouched" people in Papua New Guinea. (In this competition, as we have noted, the anthropologist who lived for a major period in a remote village had the upper hand. Indeed, anthropologists are often drawn to the "remote" for many of the same reasons as are the travelers.)

The motives that impelled this competition frequently led to a politics that, while purporting to be (distinctively) radical in its rejection of conventional, materialistic Western values was—at least in the context of Papua New Guinea—relatively conservative. The principal value of Papua New Guineans to most of the travelers was that they be "untouched." (The radicalism at home and the conservatism abroad were experienced as consonant since travelers assumed that their own societies had become corrupt because earlier—more "primitive"—values were lost.)

Correspondingly, the principal lament of those travelers who found aspects of their trip disappointing was that the people had become spoiled. The social relationships between travelers and native people had become, like those in the West, essentially commercialized. The "primitives" they had expected to engage with had, in other words, become too much like us.

Those held most responsible for spoiling Papua New Guineans were "the big spending Explorer tourist[s]" (see account 1) who, representing the worse commercialism and superficiality of Western society, had through their insensitive use of money fostered the commercialization of social relations and the consequent development of a "souvenir shop" (see account five) atmosphere throughout the Sepik.[2] From the perspective of the travelers, the tourists not only reduced the value of the "primitives" by corrupting them, but also manifested their own corruption by remaining "content with [their] obviously inauthentic experiences" (MacCannell 1976:94).

On Tourists

Most tourists who visited the Sepik region had bought a packaged excursion that included four days on the river in the *Melanesian Explorer*. This was a relatively luxurious, air-conditioned tourist ship that cruised at 12–14 knots and contained European amenities, including in-room plumbing and showers, a full bar, a video recorder with tapes of Papua New Guinea peoples and a library with over 100 books on the country.[3] The Travel Corporation of America, which provided tours to the South Pacific that had the option of a swing through Papua New Guinea, furnished the *Melanesian Explorer* with most of its passengers. Their travel brochure described the Sepik River cruise as follows:

> Eighth thru 12th days—Tuesday thru Saturday—Sepik River Cruise: Board our cruise ship Tuesday evening and begin our journey to one of the world's most remote and fascinating areas, the Sepik River region. We cruise in air-conditioned comfort aboard the *Melanesian Explorer*. Our trip through the lower and middle Sepik visits villages such as Kamindimbit, Timbunke, and Tambanum. Off the main river, we use speedboats to travel the tributaries and the Chambri and Murik Lakes. Life along the Sepik has been virtually untouched by western ways.
>
> The villagers hew canoes from gigantic logs and set off on fishing and hunting trips, bringing back food, exotic feathers, shells, skins and animal bones to use as headdresses, adornments and ritual implements.
>
> You will have time to explore the many villages, and the House Tambarans, some of which are enormous and display a wealth of art. We are able to buy magnificent ritual masks, statues, and artifacts of these artistically gifted people. We will witness traditional sing-sings and get-togethers for joyous events or mourning, in the lives of these primitive people. (Travcoa n.d.:35)

This text promised an encounter with the "primitive." Tourists visiting the Sepik did wish to have this encounter although, as we will see, their reasons were somewhat different from those of the travelers. Most of the tourists from the *Melanesian Explorer* that we met, as they visited Chambri by speedboat or after we joined the ship itself for portions of two of its cruises, were prosperous middle-aged professionals—physicians, lawyers, scientists. Older and much better established in life than the travelers, they sought not the "pure primitive" but the "primitive" on the edge of change.

A tourist brochure promised: "You will have time to explore the many villages, the House Tambarans, some of which are enormous and display a wealth of art. We are able to buy magnificent ritual masks, statues, and artifacts of these artistically gifted people." (Photo by Deborah Gewertz and Frederick Errington)

An experienced guide on the *Melanesian Explorer* cautioned us that in the lectures we would give (in exchange for our board and room) we should be careful not to overemphasize the extent to which change had already taken place. For example, tourists interested in "black magic" should not be informed that old Chambri men had begun tape recording their magical spells so that these spells would not be forgotten when they died. The tourists "don't mind a little change," she said, "but would hate to know that the natives are sophisticated enough to tape their own chants."

One *Melanesian Explorer* tourist, a woman from New Jersey, told us that her Sepik trip had been wonderful although she had been, along with others, puzzled about how to characterize it. She said that it was "not a fun trip; not exactly educational; it was like stepping back in time, but there are modern things too." In a like vein, one physician from Chicago, in stating her reason for coming to Papua New Guinea, said that it was about as far away from her hospital as she could get, and that it is a place that "will be completely changed in ten years; one has to see it now as it really is." Another physician said that he was glad to have seen the Sepik "before," he added wryly, "people like us spoil it, as we have in so many other tourist places."

One group of these tourists told us with satisfaction of an unscheduled visit by the ship to a lower Sepik village where they came across a group of men trying to raise PGK4,000.00 to purchase what would be a collectively-owned truck. The PGK200.00 they had thus far raised was displayed on a mat around which the men sat. The tourists joined this group by contributing some PGK60.00. Their names, along with those of the native contributors, were duly recorded in a notebook. Then, probably in recognition that the tourists would not be able to make reciprocal claims for assistance, they were given two live chickens.

Because this stop was unscheduled, the tourists knew that these men were pursuing their own interests rather than engaging in a staged production. (See MacCannell 1976:91–107 for an interesting discussion of authenticity in tourist settings.) They found the mixture of old and new engaging: the villagers were cooperating in a traditional way to pursue nontraditional objectives, even though they were a long way from realizing their goal. (As one tourist commented to us, "My goodness, we contributed almost a third of what they had; they'll never get to where they want to go.") Certainly in the view of these affluent professionals, the villagers appeared naive: they were sadly naive in hoping to raise the money needed for their car[4] and charmingly naive in believing that a gift of live chickens was appropriate reciprocity to the Europeans. This naiveté marked these villagers as still on the edge of change and left them sufficiently open that they would reveal their real lives to the passing tourist.

We were told of another encounter by two members of a group that, before joining the *Melanesian Explorer*, had visited the home of "the daughter of a chief" in the Highlands of New Guinea.[5] She had been married to an Australian but had divorced him to return to her home territory and marry a Papua New Guinean. Now living on the outskirts of her natal village in a nice house, she had her own car in which she drove her children to school. Although well educated, having been trained as a teacher, she was not using her skills to help her people progress. The first tourist to tell us this story was incensed by the young woman's selfishness in not helping her people advance to her level of development. A different evaluation of this woman came from another tourist who was impressed by the attractiveness of her home, the clarity and precision of her English and the beauty of her mixed-race children. Both of our commentators agreed, though, that the sophistication of this woman relative to other Papua New Guineans must be the product of her special position as the daughter of a "chief" and as the former wife of an Australian. Although others would, and indeed should, follow in her path, she was in her cultivation still very unusual.

Another tourist we met, a physicist, saw himself as a catalyst for change. He had been impressed by the accuracy of what he regarded as the largely intuitive knowledge of physical principles possessed by Papua New Guineans. He commented to us with excitement and admiration that villagers had been able to modify their traditional canoes to accommodate the additional weight and speed provided by outboard motors in a way that duplicated the configuration of a Western-designed speedboat. He was impressed by certain projections internal to slit-gong drums, which, he said, served to amplify the sound in the same way as did the bridge of a violin. However, his dismay was apparent when he encountered some bamboo scaffolding surrounding a haus tambaran under reconstruction. This scaffolding did not employ triangular bracing. Speaking in English and describing the success of the Chinese in Hong Kong with high-rise bamboo scaffolding, he gestured toward the haus tambaran in an effort to convince a passing youth that this scaffold would have been easier to construct and safer to use if diagonal supports had been employed. He believed with obvious sincerity that he could significantly help Papua New Guineans in their further development by conveying to them an important principle of construction that they had not yet discovered for themselves.[6]

Of all the villages he and the other tourists on the cruise visited, Korogo was their favorite. They said that it was the first village they had seen in which the houses were ordered. By this they meant that the houses were laid out in a geometric lattice with a wide central avenue. There were also plantings of ornamental shrubs around a number of the houses. These the tourists referred to, only partly in jest, as "formal gardens." Many were particularly impressed by a house whose roof was under construction. Three-foot sections of sago-leaf thatch were stacked neatly in piles along the length of the house and adjacent to each section of roof. The concern with efficiency that this planning seemed to demonstrate was interpreted as indicating the advent of a "division of labor," a specialization of skills and work. In Korogo, the tourists thought that they had discovered a progressive community about to replicate Western patterns of development—a community on the edge of modernity.

The motives of the older and professionally successful tourists in coming to the Sepik were quite different from those of the young travelers who, as we have already noted, wished to engage with the "primitive" as a means of personal development. The tourists on the *Melanesian Explorer* wished to engage with the "primitive" partly to demonstrate that personal development had already successfully taken place. Whereas travelers wished for the "primitive" to remain frozen in time, tourists had a much more positive attitude toward change. Although many of our conversations with travelers concerned the extent to which Papua New Guinea had changed and was thereby spoiled, many of our conversations with the tourists focused on the obstacles that had to be overcome before change was possible. Tourists asked us whether college-educated Papua New Guineans would be able to reject beliefs in sorcery, and to persuade others to reject these beliefs. They urged us to persuade the Chambri to give up the "barbaric" practice of scarification during ceremonies of male initiation. They speculated about the marvelous transformations that could be made in Papua New Guinea, a country rich in natural resources, by people of vision and enterprise (such as the Israelis).

The view that Papua New Guinea should eventually develop was consistent with the interest of these tourists in validating the system in which they, as prosperous professionals, had achieved success. However, the tourists in addition wanted to be assured that they had come before this rapid transformation of the "primitive" world was complete: they viewed the "primitive" as an increasingly rare prize to be witnessed and captured before it was too late. But since they wanted to be among the last to do this, they also wanted assurance that they had come in time. They wished to use their money to enjoy life and see the out-of-the way portions of the world, and they wanted assurance that this world was still worth seeing.

The competition of most interest to these tourists was not with the other tourists who had chosen to visit the Sepik, but was with their peers at home where it would focus on efforts to display themselves as having led unusually full, interesting and successful—distinctive—lives (see Bourdieu 1984). Moreover, unlike the travelers, tourists—at least after the first sounding-out—did not find it important to compete with us as anthropologists. They did not envy our research conditions in Papua New Guinea—in a remote village without running water and plumbing—or our standard of living as academics at home. On those few occasions when we thought they were vying with us for distinction, the competition concerned the universities we were affiliated with as students and as teachers. (Thus, one tourist, after discovering that we were living at a Chambri Lake village as academic researchers rather than as missionaries, immediately volunteered how pleased she was that her daughter had just decided to attend M.I.T., an institution favored by members of her family for generations.)

It was not surprising that travelers felt antagonism toward the tourists: it was antagonism between the unformed and the well-formed and, we need add, between those who had time and energy and those who had money and experience. The older tourists were viewed by the younger travelers in what were perhaps Oedipal terms: the older tourists consumed and spoiled the "primitive" in such a way that it was difficult for those who were, in generational terms, their children to be nourished and to develop. Certainly the travelers took more notice of the tourists than the tourists did of the travelers. We did, though, hear occasional and somewhat wistful comments from the tourists about the enterprise of the youthful travelers: one anesthetist (who, perhaps significantly, had come to the Sepik as part of the affluent adventure of sailing around the world in a yacht) said that 20 years ago she and her husband would have been among those she had seen paddling along the Sepik River. An orthopedic surgeon and his wife, likewise, said that, if they didn't have the money to travel in comfort, they wouldn't, at their age, want to travel at all.

On Anthropologists

Many of these data would seem to substantiate Crick's case. Indeed, we recognized from our interaction with both varieties of tourists that we were motivated in some of the same ways as they. We readily understood the terms of comparison between us and the travelers concerning relative authenticity of experience and between us and the *Melanesian Explorer* tourists concerning relative professional status, earning capacity, and taste. And, of course, the outcome of these comparisons—more favorable in the first than in the second instance—was not a matter of indifference to us. Such could be expected. All of us were products of the same sociocultural system; all of us, despite differences in age, possessed largely comparable views of person, of self.

Yet, tourists (of both sorts) have little impetus or competence to go beyond self-reference: the significance of the other is largely in what it does for oneself. Although anthropologists may share some of the personal objectives that have led tourists to Papua New Guinea, the comparative data we have collected since the nineteenth century make us reject the epistemology on which the tourists rest their politics. Tourists are essentially unilinear evolutionists who find the world filled with chiefs and witch doctors, and their self-referential tales are based on—indeed require—partial, simplified, and often completely erroneous information. However ultimately incomplete the understanding anthropologists have of the other, we are, to judge by our Papua New Guinea experience, incomparably better informed.

We can use our superior understanding (and we really must emphasize that no tourist seriously attempts to understand a Papua New Guinea kinship, exchange, or cosmological system) to convey what the world looks like to the natives and how our world affects theirs. We can document and explicate moments of resistance, capitulation, confusion, and indifference. We can place their lives and ours in sociohistorical, cultural, and systemic context. Thus, if we cannot easily differentiate our personal motivation from that of tourists, we can differentiate our politics from theirs. What can distinguish anthropologists from tourists is that we can and must be political in terms, not self-referential and individualistic, but comparative and systemic.

Let us illustrate this argument that anthropologists do have something of distinctive importance to say by describing, as a modest example, an event in which anthropologists, tourists, and Chambri took part. As will be apparent, each had very different perceptions to report.

The Hazing

It was already mid-afternoon and the feast that Maliwan had arranged as part of the ritual to take place on the sixth day after his sons had received their initiation cuts had been over for some time. Everyone was waiting for the next ritual event. Maliwan was circulating inside the men's house, assuring an increasingly impatient audience of initiators that the tourists would be arriving soon. He was hoping to attract many tourists to Chambri during what would be a month-long course of events focused on the initiation. Indeed, he was counting on charging them admission fees of PGK10.00 per person or

PGK50.00 per group to defray a significant portion of his costs, expected to exceed PGK1,000.00.

Early in the initiation he had been disconcerted when a group of tourists from the Karawari Lodge (a luxury hotel set on one of the Sepik's tributaries) refused to pay. When their European guide translated Maliwan's policy to them, one exclaimed with tones of outrage, "Ten Kina! What a rip-off!" and the rest—clearly hot and tired—grumbled their agreement. When they left, claiming to have looked only at the artifacts in the men's house and not at the initiates, their guide had pressed PGK3.00 into Maliwan's hand. Maliwan was furious: he told us and other Chambri that he had been doing this tourist work a long time and was not to be tricked by a young man who gave him PGK3.00 rather than the amount he had set. He said that the tourists and the guide think they can treat those of us in Papua New Guinea as if we were of no importance. They spend lots of money to come here and take pictures that they will sell for large amounts of money. He simply did not believe them— staying as they were at the Karawari Lodge—when they claimed they could not afford to pay the PGK10.00 admission. If they don't want to pay, they can simply leave.

This unpleasantness was an exception: Maliwan usually had satisfactory encounters with tourists. Over the years, he had been especially careful to cultivate a good relationship with the owner and the guides of the *Melanesian Explorer*. And he had persuaded them to bring their tourists regularly to Chambri, where they could enter a traditional men's house (which Maliwan managed) and purchase artifacts. (Few of the 443 adults living at Chambri during the period of our most recent research were able or willing to subsist without money, and most saw tourism as the key to their postindependence economic viability. Although some money came into Chambri through the sale of produce, including crocodile skins, and in the form of remittances sent by relatives working in urban centers, most of the money acquired in the course of a year by men living at Chambri was derived from the sale of artifacts: the total from sales of artifacts comes to approximately PGK10,000, according to our 1987–88 data. Extensive as this contemporary reliance on money had come to be, the acquisition of money was, nonetheless, regarded as requiring the exercise of ancestral knowledge to "pull" tourists to Chambri and to impel them to purchase artifacts. Hence, the presence of tourists at Chambri was interpreted not as testimony to the transformation of Chambri tradition but to its persistence and strength.) In the present instance, Maliwan had even arranged with the *Melanesian Explorer* guide, who had guaranteed admission payment, to coordinate the major events of the initiation with the schedule of the ship. As a consequence, the ceremonies of the sixth day were to take place on the seventh, which meant that he had to convince members of the appropriate initiatory moiety to delay their hazing of the initiates for a day. Thus, as he circulated after the feast, he was anxious to reassure the other Chambri men that the delay had been justified, that the tourists were coming. But they were nowhere to be seen and clearly Maliwan was nervous.

Finally, to his evident relief the sounds of the two big speedboats that convey the tourists from the Sepik River anchorage of the *Melanesian Explorer* up the tributary to Chambri were heard.

Once the twenty-five or so tourists arrived in the men's house, many began to take pictures of the initiates who had been posed to show their partially healed cuts. Then the initiates, together with uninitiated clan brothers—some older and younger than they—were instructed to sit down in the middle of the men's house floor. As the tourists crowded around them, Maliwan asked us to advise the tourists that there was going to be a loud noise above them from the second story of the men's house. He did not want the tourists to be alarmed by the noise that would mark the awaking of Kwolimopan, the ancestral crocodile who had previously "eaten" the backs of the initiates.

As the four hazers approached the seated initiates, Maliwan instructed them to talk not in Chambri but in Pidgin English, which it was assumed the tourists could understand. Their performance, which consistently amused the Chambri audience and, periodically, even the initiates themselves, began when they offered fish and sago to the initiates but then pulled the food away and themselves ate portions. Next, they offered the initiates fish bones, fruit stalks, and other inedible scraps from a platter while shouting: "You don't know how to eat; you eat just like pigs, just like ducks; you don't have any shame."

While the initiates glumly contemplated their "food," there came the thundering from above as men jumped up and down on the floor of the second story, shaking loose a great cloud of dust. No sooner had the dust begun to settle, than water was poured through the floor, soaking the initiates and their platter of refuse, turning the dust covering the food into mud. The hazers walked among the initiates shouting "hurry up, hurry up" as they insisted that some of the water-soaked rubbish be consumed. (In fact, Kwolimopan's bull-roarer had been kept in this water and the water had thereby become filled with his power.)

Betel nuts were next offered the initiates and then taken away with the words, "You eat betel nut as if you were a woman, as if you were your little sister." Oversized spatulas covered with ashes instead of the lime normally consumed with betel nuts were shoved into their mouths. Burning banana leaf cigars—an inch in diameter and a foot long—were stuffed into their mouths and then pulled away, showering them with sparks, while the hazers harangued them: "You want to smoke; here, smoke! Your papa is giving this to you; smoke this big one, you rubbishman. You beg for cigarettes and betel nuts all the time, well here they are; take them; are you enough for them?"

Then a large female carving was brought out and was thrust on top of the initiates with the challenge: "Are you enough to make carvings and place them in the men's house for the tourists to buy?" Large pieces of firewood, including one with embers, were pushed down on them as they were asked: "Are you enough to bring firewood to the men's house?" A broom and a large bark dustpan were pushed down on the their faces with the words: "Are you enough to sweep out the men's house?" Several grass-cutting knives were pressed against them with the question: "Are you enough to cut the grass around the men's house?" Finally, the initiates were asked derisively if they had more than the understanding of their mothers—if they were enough to sire children.

All of these questions were meant to convey that the initiates should uphold Chambri custom. Chambri custom, especially as it concerned appropriate adult male roles within the men's house, was presented in a quite literal way as heavy, as not to be taken lightly. Such custom based on collective authority, an authority embodied by the four hazers, could be made to cover virtually all aspects of life. Thus, reference was made to a rule that men are not supposed to smoke or chew betel nuts until they have been scarified. Although this rule is normally ignored nowadays, it was presented as one that could be made binding if the assembled men chose to make it so.

This assertion of collective male power had lasted about twenty minutes when one of the hazers said in Pidgin: "The law is finished now; we will stand up and the tourists will take pictures of us." Then all four of the hazers moved behind the initiates and stood in a row, facing the tourists, who were then instructed: "Clap your hands. The rule of Kwolimopan is over; it's finished now; we have completed it. OK, you can take pictures of us now. Clap your hands." The tour guide informed the tourists in English that they should applaud and had been invited to take pictures.

The tourists did applaud, and most took a picture or two—although with some reluctance. They seemed somewhat annoyed and confused at this point. The hazers had suddenly defined the performance as staged, at least in part, for tourists rather than for the Chambri themselves and this called into question its authenticity. Moreover, by instructing the tourists to applaud and to take pictures of them, the hazers were extending to the tourists the same kind of control that they had exercised over the initiates: just as the initiates were not allowed to express their own autonomy with respect to activities that are usually defined as matters of individual volition—to smoke or chew betel nut—so too the tourists were commanded to express appreciation and interest. This occasion threatened to become for the tourists not simply a performance, but a performance out of control.

A fair number of tourists had left before this point in the performance and were outside photographing the Chambri women who were singing "take it, take it; listen, listen"—songs that enjoined the initiates to do as they were being told. It was very hot inside the men's house; with the shaking of the floor, it was very dirty—the tourists were anxious about their camera lenses after the dust had poured down. They seemed to find the hazing too violent, too aggressive, too prolonged; one woman looked askance at the cut that had opened on the initiate's arm when he had been pushed down by a burning piece of firewood.

By the end of the performance, those still remaining in the audience felt vulnerable, uncertain of their safety. Not only had the performance been violent, but they were no longer sure what the objectives and boundaries of the performance were. However, they were somewhat reassured when one of their number, an impressively large German man, asserted control by over-complying with the hazers' command to take pictures of them. He waded through the seated initiates, very much as the hazers had done, and took a series of extreme close-ups of each hazer's face.

The picture-taking concluded, Maliwan sent the initiates outside into an enclosure attached to the men's house. He was eager to clear the men's house so that the tourists could look at and purchase the carvings. Out in the enclosure, the hazers shook hands and talked with the initiates, some of whom were angry at the treatment they had received. One, for instance, was upset because several of his cuts had opened during the turmoil of the performance. He had enlisted the help of another initiate in cleaning up the blood so as not to further disturb the cut. Looking at them, a passing hazer said—in combined reassurance and disdain—that it was nothing to be worried about.

In this initiation, and in others we have seen with no tourists present, the initiates were made to appear not only ridiculous but impotent. Their escape was precluded; participants were forced to do as they were instructed yet nothing they could do was right. They were, in other words, placed in a multiplicity of double binds, a circumstance well designed to convey complete powerlessness—a powerlessness itself compounded in that they were unable to perform even the normal routines of life.

The hazing, however, was as well a means of conveying power to initiates. In particular, it was by having dirt and the water of Kwolimopan dumped on them and the garbage just served, and then being required to eat of that soggy garbage that the initiates incorporated into themselves important aspects of power—the power of Kwolimopan. As a result of this, they were released from most of the initiatory taboos—for instance, they might once more eat and scratch themselves in a normal manner, rather than with the use of tongs. In this Chambri version of what is a familiar theme of initiation throughout the world, the experience of powerlessness would seem to be an important step in the acquisition of adult status.

What was the effect of the presence of an audience of tourists—both men and women—on this ritual? Hazing, as we have described it, would be most effective when it completely precluded any escape on the part of the initiates. It seemed to us, though, that the presence of the tourists, by introducing another sort of audience, gave the initiates a partial escape from their double binds. Because the initiators were to some extent playing for another audience, the hazing was no longer a closed Chambri show.

Significantly, the hazers in this initiation were clearly trying to be funny, and that even the initiates frequently laughed. Certainly, based on our own and Chambri recollections of other initiations, hazing as an occasion for the display of virtually absolute power with respect to the initiates was not normally experienced or remembered by the initiates as funny. Moreover, on this occasion, there was a concern that the tourists might become frightened—they were warned, for instance, about the great thump that was to take place over their heads. Also, there is no doubt that the incorporation of the tourists into the proceedings made the hazing shorter—time had to be allowed for them to purchase artifacts. (As we have seen, the tourists thought even the modified performance was too frightening and lengthy.)

In addition, the distinction that the ritual of hazing imposed between those having and not having power—between those who could exercise adult volition and those who could not—and between those inside the men's house and those outside—between men and women—became somewhat blurred by the presence of the tourists, by the presence of these wealthy men and women from outside the Chambri system.

Thus, not only did the presence of the tourists dilute the display of absolute power and diminish the clarity of the distinctions that were made in terms of the social and spatial distribution of power, but their presence also reduced the duration and intensity of the hazing. The consequence, we think, of this partial leavening of ridicule was the emergence of comic elements.[7]

But this comic was not characterized by a complete amiability. Although the initiates found some humor in the double binds in which they were placed, they were, nonetheless, rendered substantially powerless. And if the presence of tourists had partially deflected the force of the display from the initiates, the tourists themselves became partial targets. They were transformed from spectator to performer and a portion of their volition (and distance) stripped from them, as they were commanded to applaud: they were required to assent, whether they had liked it or not, to a performance in which as the final act they too became victims.

Such a display of control over the tourists in an initiation staged in part as a tourist attraction would have especially appealed to Chambri. Certainly it would offset the vulnerability that Chambri might feel now that they were offering for sale not only artifacts but major cultural events such as the initiation itself.

Whether or not the Chambri were conscious of the sources of their satisfaction at turning the tables on the tourists, we do not believe they realized they were changing important elements of the initiation as it affected the initiates. To be sure, the world that these initiates were entering—a world in which adult capacities could now be measured through such activities as selling artifacts to tourists—was continually changing with respect to patterns of authority and valuation of Chambri custom. Yet, it seems to us that many of these changes had come about as the culmination of events like the initiation just described. An event of this sort had effects that, because they were unintended and unforeseen, were likely for some time to be unperceived. Understanding of what was in the process of happening was likely to be inhibited if there were no recognition that anything had happened. In particular, the Chambri did not understand that if they continued to sell their initiations (and perhaps other ceremonies) as tourist attractions, they would themselves no longer find them convincing and effective.

The tourists (including the travelers) were more aware than the Chambri that the tourist trade was an important component in change. They lacked, however, sufficient knowledge of both cultural particulars and cross-cultural patterns to understand in any sort of detail either the effect or the process of change. As far as we could observe, they understood practically nothing about the Chambri nor, significantly, did more than a very few want to learn from us anything except the most readily assimilated facts about the initiation or other aspects of Chambri life. Apart from knowing that the scars in some way marked manhood and that Maliwan was staging the initiation for his sons, the ceremony was, and remained, virtually opaque to them. They were, in most cases, uninterested in our simplified explanations of even the most noticeable events as the drenching of the novices and their "food" with Kwolimopan's water. But what is the importance of our having reported on this hazing? We have provided the most complete and accurate inscription this moment will probably ever have. The understanding of these moments in their contexts has political consequences because it enables us to talk knowledgeably about such intersecting matters as the nature of the world political economy, the reasons that tourists come to Papua New Guinea, and the effects on and the response of the Chambri—including their capacity to resist, adapt, transform. (Ortner 1984 and Fernandez 1985 make a similar point.) For anthropologists to work toward reaching *and* conveying an understanding of such matters (even when specific events have a ludic form) strikes us as serious, but not as value-free, business.

Anthropology in a Small Place

In a recent novel, *A Small Place*, Jamaica Kincaid writes a powerful critique of tourism and tourist economies. She does this by caustically (certainly nonludically) describing the postmodern malaise—the fragmentation of experience and relationships—that leads Europeans to visit places like Antigua.

> From day to day, as you walk down a busy street in the large and modern and prosperous city in which you work and live, dismayed, puzzled . . . at how alone you feel in this crowd, how awful it is to go unnoticed, how awful it is to go unloved, even as you are surrounded by more people than you could possibly get to know in a lifetime that lasted for millennia . . . I mean, your dismay and puzzlement are natural to you, because people like you just seem to be like that . . . But one day, when you are sitting somewhere, alone in that crowd, and that awful feeling of displacedness comes over you, and really, as an ordinary person you are not well equipped to look too far inward and set yourself aright, because being ordinary is already so taxing, and being ordinary takes all you have out of you, and though the words "I must get away" do not actually pass across your lips, you make a leap from being that nice blob just sitting like a boob in your amniotic sac of the modern experience to being a person vis-

iting heaps and death and ruin and feeling alive and inspired at the sight
of it . . . to being a person marveling at the harmony (ordinarily, what you
would say is the backwardness) and the union of these other people (and
they are other people) have with nature. (Kincaid 1988:15–16)

Kincaid does not specifically discuss anthropologists as among those
who are, in the words of another analyst of sightseeing in the postmodern
world, "striving for a transcendence of the modern totality, a way of attempting to overcome the discontinuity of modernity, of incorporating its fragments into unified experience" (MacCannell 1976:13). Presumably, she
would agree with Crick and others who have noted that Western anthropologists are products of the world economy and subject to the same influences as
the (Western) tourists. However, in her view, it would be the postmodern
nature of this experience that would make anthropologists similar to tourists
and, like them, pernicious influences and miscomprehending presences in
places like Antigua. As she objects to the tourists reading Antiguan lives as
the harmonious opposite of their own, she would, we think, object to anthropologists reading those lives as the fragmented equivalent of their own. Anti-
guans, in her presentation, are not postmodern: they are angry and oppressed.
Moreover, in Jamaica Kincaid, they have a powerful indigenous voice that is
able to combine intimate knowledge of Antiguan sociocultural particulars
with that of world systems.

Under circumstances as these, it seems to us, if anthropologists are
going to have anything of importance to say about these small places, we
need to move, not in the direction of indulging our own postmodern sensibilities of, as Crick puts it, "anything goes" (1985:86) but of developing an
anthropology of non-post-modern people: we need to develop an anthropology that has a voice as politically informed as that of Jamaica Kincaid. If she
had explicitly extended her critique to encompass anthropologists, it would
not have been to tell us to be more ludic, more poststructuralist, more self-
involved. Whatever our own feelings of malaise, of rulelessness, of anything
goes, we should not indulge them at the expense of the world, particularly as
we work in places (like Chambri) where such a voice as hers has not yet
emerged to correct and perhaps supersede our own.[8]

Source: From "Tourism and Anthropology in a Post-Modern World," *Oceania*, 1989, 60:37–54.
Reprinted with permission of the authors.

Acknowledgments

We wish to thank the National Endowment for the Humanities, the
American Council of Learned Societies and Amherst College for supporting
our most recent field trip to the Chambri during 1987. We also wish to thank
the Department of Anthropology of the Research School of Pacific Studies at
the Australian National University for sponsoring our field trip to the Chambri during 1983. Gewertz has made two previous trips. On the first, from

1974 through 1975, she was supported by the Population Institute of the East-West Center, the National Geographic Society and the Graduate School of the City University of New York. The second, during the summer of 1979, was paid for by the National Endowment for the Humanities and by Amherst College. Gratitude is expressed to each of these institutions, as it is to the Wenner-Gren Foundation for Anthropological Research, which allowed Gewertz to investigate archival material during 1981.

Notes

[1] To be sure, many anthropologists (including ourselves) have been influenced by similar expectations and assumptions. Indeed, anthropologists often minimize references to tourism, missionization, and other indications of "development" in their ethnographic accounts: these, it is thought, make "their" people and, by extension, themselves less distinctive and, hence, less valuable. Such elisions could, however, be regarded as obscuring the nature of the world system.

[2] Missionaries as well are regarded as a source of corruption but of quite a different sort.

[3] The owners of the *Melanesian Explorer* plan to replace their present ship with a far more luxurious one, equipped, for instance, with phones in each cabin that allow direct dialing worldwide.

[4] In fact, considerable sums of money, sufficient to buy large trucks, can be raised in this way.

[5] Perhaps basing their view of "primitives" on their stereotypes of Native Americans, many tourists, even when we attempted to explain the achieved leadership of big men, refused to change their views that Papua New Guinea social organization focused on chiefs.

[6] Although not used on this scaffolding, triangular bracing is common and was, for instance, employed on a small bridge we had crossed earlier that morning.

[7] In this analysis, the emergence of the ludic was something of an accident: it had not been the Chambri intention to allow the initiates respite from their double binds.

[8] The construction of ethnographies on the basis of dialogues might appear to be an anthropological responsibility under these circumstances prior to the emergence of an indigenous voice strong enough to command outside attention (Clifford 1986). However, we have argued that one of the difficulties in constructing such ethnographies is that, at least in the Sepik and in much of Melanesia, people wish the anthropologist to present not a dialogue—a plurality of voices—but a monologue, an inscription of a particular partisan view (Errington and Gewertz 1987). Although the voice of a Chambri comparable to Jamaica Kincaid might also promulgate a particular set of local interests, the politics expressed would under these circumstances be his or her responsibility, not ours.

References

Appadurai, Arjun. 1986. "Theory in Anthropology: Center and Periphery." *Comparative Studies in Society and History* 28:356–61.

Asad, Talal, ed. 1973. *Anthropology and the Colonial Encounter*. London: Ithaca Press.

Barley, N. 2000 [1983]. *The Innocent Anthropologist: Notes from a Mud Hut*. Prospect Heights, IL: Waveland Press.

Bateson, Gregory. 1946. "Art of the South Seas." *The Arts Bulletin* 2:119–23.

Bleier, Ruth, ed. 1984. *Science and Gender*. New York: Pergamon Press.

Boon, James. 1982. *Other Tribes, Other Scribes*. Cambridge: Cambridge University Press.

Bourdieu, Pierre. 1984. *Distinction: A Social Critique of the Judgment of Taste*. Cambridge, MA: Harvard University Press.

Clifford, James. 1986. "Introduction: Partial Truths," in *Writing Culture*, ed. James Clifford and George Marcus, pp. 1–26. Berkeley: University of California Press.

————. 1988. *The Predicament of Culture*. Cambridge: Harvard University Press.

Clifford, James, and George Marcus, eds. 1986. *Writing Culture*. Berkeley: University of California Press.

Cohen, Erik. 1988. "Traditions in the Qualitative Sociology of Tourism." *Annals of Tourism Research* 15:29–46.

————. 1989. "Primitive and Remote." *Annals of Tourism Research* 16:30–61.

Crapanzano, Vincent. 1986. "Hermes' Dilemma," in *Writing Culture*, ed. James Clifford and George Marcus, pp. 51–76. Berkeley: University of California Press.

Crick, Malcolm. 1985. "Tracing the Anthropological Self." *Social Analysis* 17:71–92.

Dumont, Jean-Paul. 1977. "Review of MacCannell." *Annals of Tourism Research* 4:223–225.

Errington, Frederick, and Deborah Gewertz. 1987. "On Unfinished Dialogues and Paper Pigs." *American Ethnologist* 14:367–76.

Fabian, Johannes. 1983. *Time and the Other*. New York: Columbia University Press.

Fernandez, James. 1985. "Exploded Worlds." *Dialectical Anthropology* 10:15–26.

Gewertz, Deborah, and Frederick Errington. 1990. *Twisted Histories, Altered Contexts: Representing the Chambri in a World System*. Cambridge: Cambridge University Press.

Graburn, Nelson. 1983. "The Anthropology of Tourism." *Annals of Tourism Research* 10:9–33.

Hamilton, Annette. 1982. "Anthropology in Australia," in *Anthropology in Australia: Essays to Honour 50 Years of Mankind*, ed. Grant McCall, pp. 91–106. Sydney: Anthropology Society of New South Wales.

Haraway, Donna. 1985a. "Manifesto for Cyborgs: Science, Technology, and Socialist Feminism in the 1980s." *Socialist Review* 80:65–108.

————. 1985b. "Teddy Bear Patriarchy." *Social Text* 4:20–64.

————. 1986. "Primatology is Politics by Other Means," in *Feminist Approaches to Science*, ed. Ruth Bleier, pp. 77–118. New York: Pergamon Press.

Herzfeld, Michael. 1983. "Signs in the Field." *Semiotica* 46:99–106.

Keller, Evelyn Fox. 1985. *Reflections on Science and Gender*. New Haven: Yale University Press.

Kincaid, Jamaica. 1988. *A Small Place*. New York: Farrar Straus Giroux.

Lett, J. W. 1983. "Ludic and Liminoid Aspects of Charter Yacht Tourism in the Caribbean." *Annals of Tourism Research* 10:35–56.

Lightbody, Mark, and Tony Wheeler. 1985. *Papua New Guinea: A Travel Survival Kit*. Victoria: Lonely Planet Books.

Louch, A. R. 1969. *Explanation and Human Action*. Berkeley: University of California Press.

MacCannell, Dean. 1976. *The Tourist*. New York: Schocken Books.

Mintz, Sidney. 1977. "Infant, Victim and Tourist: The Anthropologist in the Field." *Johns Hopkins Magazine* 27:54–60.

Ortner, Sherry. 1984. "Theory in Anthropology since the Sixties." *Comparative Studies in Society and History* 26:126–166.

Pfaffenberger, B. 1983. "Serious Pilgrims and Frivolous Tourists." *Annals of Tourism Research* 10:57–74.

Pratt, Mary Louise. 1986. "Fieldwork in Common Places," in *Writing Culture*, ed. James Clifford and George Marcus, pp. 27–50. Berkeley: University of California Press.

Smith, Valene. 1989. "Introduction," in *Hosts and Guests*, ed. Valene Smith, pp. 1–17. Philadelphia: University of Pennsylvania Press.

Spooner, Brian. 1986. "Weavers and Dealers," in *The Social Life of Things*, ed. Arjun Appadurai, pp. 195–235. Cambridge: Cambridge University Press.

Strathern, Marilyn. 1987. "Out of Context: The Persuasive Fictions of Anthropology." *Current Anthropology* 28:251–281.

————. 1989. *Partial Connections*. Maryland: University Press of America.

Teas, J. 1988. "'I'm Studying Monkeys; What Do You Do?'—Youth and Travelers in Nepal." *Kroeber Anthropological Society Papers* 67/68: 35–41.

Travcoa. n.d. *Tourist Brochure*. Travel Corporation of America.

Tyler, Stephen. 1986. "Post-Modern Ethnography," in *Writing Culture*, ed. James Clifford and George Marcus, pp. 122–140. Berkeley: University of California Press.

van den Berghe, Pierre L. 1980. "Tourism as Ethnic Relations." *Ethnic and Racial Studies* 3:375–392.

13

Tourism in the Balinese Borderzone

Edward M. Bruner

International tourism is an exchange system of vast proportions, one characterized by a transfer of images, signs, symbols, power, money, goods, people, and services (Lanfant et al. 1995; Smith 1989). The tourism industry is aggressive in ever seeking new attractions for its clients, so there are tours not only to Bali, which has been a tourist destination for over seventy years,[1] but also to places that formerly were difficult to access, such as Kalimantan, New Guinea, the Amazon, and even the South Pole. Tourism has no respect for national boundaries, except in those few countries that for one reason or another restrict tourism (e.g., Myanmar, Albania, Bhutan). Wherever ethnographers go or have gone, tourists have already been there or are sure to follow. And where tourism establishes itself, our traditional anthropological subject matter, the peoples and cultures of the world, becomes commercialized, marketed, and sold to an eager audience of international tourists.

International mass tourism has precipitated one of the largest population movements in the world, in which literally millions of temporary travelers from the industrialized nations seek in the margins of the Third World a figment of their imagination—the exotic, the erotic, the primitive, the happy savage. Bali, for example, is depicted in the tourist literature as a tropical paradise of haunting beauty, an unspoiled beach, an isle of mystery and enchantment, an exotic South Seas island of dreams, where the people live untouched by civilization, close to nature, with a culture that is artistic, static, harmonious, and well integrated.[2] We recognize the trope of the vanishing primitive, the pastoral allegory, the quest for origins (Bruner 1993; Clifford 1986). This romantic characterization not only suppresses the true conditions of Balinese life; it also depicts a culture that never existed (Boon 1977, 1990; Picard 1992; Vickers 1989). The excesses of the descriptions of Bali and many other Third World tourist sites echo Orientalist discourse and anthropological monographs based on a hypothetical ethnographic present. Indeed, the "happy primitive" image was a means of colonial control, one that was in part constructed by ethnography itself. It is ironic, however, that tourists are now chasing the ethnographer's discarded discourse, pursuing an ahistorical vision that anthropologists have long abandoned.

Tourism occurs in a zone physically located in an ever-shifting strip or border on the edges of Third World destination countries. This border is not natural; it is not just there, waiting for the tourists to discover it, for all touristic borderzones[3] are constructed. The parties involved are the tourists who travel from the industrialized nations with already formed images in their heads of the primitive peoples they will see; the "natives," or indigenous population, in their exotic setting; and the multinational travel companies, airlines, hotels, tour agencies, and government bureaucracies that construct and profit from building the touristic infrastructure.

The concept of borderzones used in this paper differs from the usage by Gloria Anzaldúa (1987), Guillermo Gómez-Peña, Emily Hicks (1991), and Coco Fusco (1989), who theorize based upon the U.S.–Mexican border, which is a site of migration between two national states. In touristic borderzones there are no immigrant tourists, almost by definition, but rather a recurring wave of temporary travelers, an ever-changing moving population. The tourists are always present and are always "there," but are always in motion, and they change constantly. The category and presence of tourists are permanent, but the actual individuals come and go; they flow across the border like each new freshman class in college, an ever-renewing source. The native or the resident population is more or less permanent, but as I visualize the touristic border, the natives have to break out of their normal routines to meet the tourists: to dance for them, to sell them souvenirs, or to display themselves and their cultures for the tourists' gaze and for sale. The touristic borderzone is like empty space, an empty stage waiting for performance time, for the audience of tourists, and for the native performers. The natives, too, then, move in and out of the touristic borderzone. But the perceptions of the two groups are not the same, because what for the tourists is a zone of leisure and exoticization is for the natives a site of work and cash income.

What is advertised as unspoiled and undiscovered in the touristic borderzone has been carefully manufactured and sold. The Balinese and other Third World peoples recognize the touristic thirst for the exotic and the unpolluted, so they present themselves and their cultures to conform to the tourist image. Tourists come from the outside to see the primitives; from the inside, paradoxically—from the native perspective—tourism is a route to economic development and a means of livelihood (Lanfant et al. 1995). The predicament is that the more modern the locals, the less interesting they are to the Occidental tourist, and the less their income is derived from tourism. Intellectuals and artists like Anzaldúa and Gómez-Peña theorize about the U.S.–Mexican border, but the situation is so different for those who are the object of the tourist gaze in the underdeveloped Third World, for peoples like the Balinese—if they step out of their assigned roles in exotica, they may lose their major source of income. What most native peoples do in this situation is to collaborate in a touristic co-production.

Professional anthropologists until recently had a very ambivalent attitude toward tourism (see Crick 1995). As intellectuals, anthropologists denigrated tourism as commercial, inauthentic, and tacky. Touristic culture, they felt, was simply a truncated version of a fuller, more authentic native culture located elsewhere. For ethnography, tourism was an embarrassment, an impostor. The stuff of ethnography, what we studied and wrote about in our monographs, was the real culture. Even with the questioning of ethnographic authority (Clifford 1983), anthropology as a profession still has not been entirely clear on what stance to take toward tourism and touristic culture.

Renato Rosaldo (1989:208) provides a theoretical key: "borderlands should be regarded not as analytically empty transitional zones but as sites of creative cultural production"—and, I would add, as sites of struggle. The touristic borderzone is a creative space, a site for the invention of culture on a massive scale, a festive liberated zone, one that anthropology should investigate, not denigrate. To ask how the culture presented for tourists compares with culture we ethnographers have traditionally studied is just the wrong question, one that leads to a theoretical dead end in the never-never land of essentialized nostalgia. The tourists are the ones who desire the uncontaminated precolonial past,[4] the so-called pure culture, so versions of that hypothetical past are invented and presented for tourist consumption. As scholars, anthropologists should study the recent construction of "authentic" culture for a tourist audience, not intellectualize it or judge it or criticize it as yet another Derridian instance of lost origins. Tourists do not travel to experience the new postcolonial[5] subject, the emerging nation in process of economic development; they yearn for their image of a precolonial past.

From the perspective of the geographies of identity, the Western elite travel to the margins of the Third World, to the ends of empire, to the borderzone between their civilized selves and the exotic Other, to explore a fantasyland of the Western imaginary. Curiously, the Other, the postcolonial subject, has already traveled in the opposite direction, for the Jamaican, the Pakistani, the Malay, the Algerian is already established in the centers of Western power (Buck-Morss 1987). Paradoxically, then, the Western elite spend thousands of dollars and travel thousands of miles to find what they already have.

Many Western peoples, of all social classes, make a desperate effort not to "see" the Third World presence in their midst, for they segregate themselves in safe and exclusive neighborhoods, or move to the suburbs if they can afford to do so, or insulate themselves by alternative means. When they do see the Third World peoples who surround them, it is with a very selective vision emphasizing poverty, drugs, crime, and gangs to the neglect of those Others who have become middle class; or the Other may be performers, entertainers, athletes, or servants. Western peoples enjoy ethnic restaurants and performances as long as they are in their proper "space/place."

Although the elite try to avoid the Other in First World cities, making a conscious attempt not to see, to overlook—an absence of sight—when they go to the touristic borderzones they do so with the specific objective of looking, for in tourism there is a voyeurism, an overabundance of seeing, a cornucopia of visualization—almost a pathology, a scoptophilia. The Other in *our* geography is a sight of disgust; the Other in *their* geography is a source of pleasure. In *our* place, the Other is a pollution; in *their* place, the Other is romantic, beautiful, and exotic. In *our* geography, the elite pay not to see the Other, keeping them distant or hidden, whereas in *their* geography, the Western elite pay for the privilege of viewing and photographing. There is a racialization at home and a primitivization over there, in exotica.

I have consciously exaggerated the differences for emphasis, but I do understand that First and Third World peoples intermingle and circulate in each other's spaces and I do understand that there is upward mobility. For a large segment of the Western elite, however, the essential paradox remains—in First World cities the Other is a social problem; in Third World places the Other is an object of desire. At home the industrialized peoples of the First World avoid the very peoples that they pay enormous sums to see and photograph in Africa or Indonesia. This is actually an old phenomenon, at least a century old in the United States, where Native Americans on their reservations become exoticized and romanticized, whereas the very same peoples as urban neighbors are considered drunks and undesirables.

The industrialized First World splits the Other into two spaces. Their space is made safe by the military, the government, and eventually by the tourist industry; the Other becomes domesticated, reworked for the tourists, frozen in time, or out of time, in past time or no time, performing a Western version of their culture, essentially as entertainers. In First World space the Other is dangerous, associated with pathology and violence, with bad neighborhoods and crime. Western peoples fail to see the joy and beauty of the Other in First World space, just as they fail to see the poverty and suffering of the Other in Third World space.

For the Western tourist, the Orientalist stereotype is dominant in Third World space, and tourists go there to collect souvenirs and photographs to show to their friends at home. They go for adventure, for experience, for status, for education, to explore and collect the image of the exotic Other. But the Other is already here at home, in the flesh, outside on the street, in a neighborhood across town, waiting for us. Tourists bring back a disembodied, decontextualized, sanitized, hypothetical Other, one they can possess and control through the stories they tell about how the souvenirs were acquired and the photographs taken. Tourists place the postcolonial subject in a new narrative frame, in stories in which the tourists become the traveling heroes and the Other, the objects of their search. Narrative mastery is the means to fix meaning, encapsulate, and control the Other, stop motion and time, and exert power.

Methodology

My project, in this essay, is to explore cultural production in the touristic borderzone, to learn how the Balinese and other Indonesian peoples respond to tourism, and to study how American tourists experience Indonesia. James Clifford (1989:183) asks the right questions, for we need to know "How do different populations, classes, and genders travel? What kinds of knowledges, stories, and theories do they produce? A crucial research agenda opens up."

In order to investigate these matters, I decided to become a tour guide to Indonesia, primarily for methodological reasons (Cohen 1985a).[6] Tour groups assemble in their area of origin—in, say, San Francisco or London—travel together, see the sights together, eat their meals together, become a tightly knit unit, and disband at the end of the trip. It is difficult to penetrate the tour group from the outside at midpoint in their voyage. Since the tour group is a traveling social unit, I felt that the best way to study tourism was to travel with the group and to share the adventures of a common journey. As a guide, I would be an insider, and would be there to observe and record the tourists' reactions, behaviors, and interpretations. I wanted to learn if tourists buy into the hyperbole of tourist advertising, or if they are really on a quest for authenticity, as MacCannell (1976) claims, or if they have given up the quest and have become posttourists (Urry 1990), or if tourists play at reality (Cohen 1985b). The approach is ethnographic. Standard ethnographic practice tells us to study cultural content in the social context of its reception, which in this case is the tour group, although as a guide/ethnographer my subject position was not that of a classical ethnographer.

Because there are many different forms of tourism, it would be appropriate to describe my particular tours to Indonesia. Briefly, the tours were an upscale version of what has been called cultural or educational tourism (see Graburn and Jafari 1991; Nash and Smith 1991). The agency advertised that their tours were led by "noted scholars," a reading list had been distributed in advance, and the front page of the tourist brochure for Indonesia presented a biographical sketch of my academic qualifications, stressing that I was an anthropology professor, had conducted three years of fieldwork in Indonesia, and spoke the language. One way to put it was that the tour agency was not only selling Indonesia, they were selling me, at least in my capacity as a scholar. Another way to put it was that tourism had co-opted ethnography. I was relatively straightforward with the tourists, telling them that I was an anthropology professor interested in Indonesia and also in tourism; I must admit, however, that I did not tell the tourists I was studying them. This was a tour with a tour guide professor and tourist students, ostensibly there to learn. University alumni associations and museums often organize such tours with faculty lecturers; indeed, the frequency of alumni tours is growing. Many anthropologists have led such tours, but few mention it and even fewer write about it or incorporate the experience into their academic discourse, a situation that poses the question, Why the silence? I suggest that tourism as a subject matter is perceived as somehow tainted: too popular, too commercial, and not worthy of serious scholarship. To become involved in the touristic enterprise is considered by the discipline to be in some sense unprofessional.

A sociological profile of those on the Indonesia tours shows that they were clearly older and more affluent than most tourists. The average age was about fifty. Almost half were retired, about one-third were divorced or widowed women traveling alone, all except one had a college education, everyone had taken previous tours, and most were business or professional persons. There were physicians, executives, a lawyer, an engineer, and two professors. If, as MacCannell (1976) says, tourists are alienated beings who lead such shallow lives that they have to seek authenticity elsewhere, one would never know it from these tourists. These were successful and affluent persons, quite secure about their identity, and they were traveling at a stage in their lives when they had the leisure and the income to do so. Tourism for them was consumption, and a tour to Indonesia was an expensive status marker (Bourdieu 1984).

I turn now to the analysis of several encounters between the members of the tour group and various Indonesians, as well as to the story of the confrontation of the tourists with Hildred Geertz in Bali in 1986. My point is to demonstrate innovation and creativity in the touristic borderzone.

An Incident in Bali

In addition to the standard *barong* and *kecak* dances that are on all the tourist itineraries, I had arranged to take the tour group to an *odalan* or temple festival, a ceremony that the Balinese enact for themselves. These events are not ordinarily on the tour schedule, for one is never entirely sure when they will begin, and the local tour agencies are reluctant to include them. I, however, had lived near the temple in the village of Batuan a few years previously and knew the area. We arrived at the temple about 4 P.M. The tourists, dressed in the appropriate ceremonial sash, sat together in a group along the temple wall and observed the scene, as I had instructed them to do. The Balinese do not appear to object to the presence of tourists at their temple ceremonies as long as they are respectfully attired and well behaved. We seemed to be the only tourists there except for one couple dressed very casually who stood off by themselves.

As the crystal sounds of the gamelan music pervaded the early evening glow, I looked across the temple compound and saw Hildred Geertz, the personification of Balinese ethnography, resplendent in full ceremonial Balinese dress.[7] I knew that Geertz was doing research in Batuan, for I had written to her in advance, informing her that after my work with the tour group was completed, I intended to return to Bali, and I looked forward to visiting with her at that time. Although I realized that Geertz was working in the area, I was nevertheless somewhat surprised to see her at this festival.

I crossed the compound to say hello to Geertz, whom I have known for over thirty years, and her response was an astonished "I didn't expect you until next month." I replied that indeed I was returning next month, and I offered to introduce her to the tour group. She responded, "Don't introduce me to those tourists, but after your tour is over, be sure to come to my house."[8] As Geertz later recalled the incident, she was "rather busy and didn't want to get involved in polite conversation with people [she] didn't know" (letter, August 5, 1991). As I interpreted the event, Geertz welcomed Ed Bruner, ethnographer, but chose to keep her distance from Ed Bruner, tour

Hildred Geertz at the Batuan festival. (Photo by Edward M. Bruner)

guide. After an awkward moment I went back across the compound to sit with the tour group. To ethnography, tourism is indeed like a poor country cousin, or an illegitimate child that one chooses not to recognize.

Unexpectedly, after a brief interval, Geertz came over to our group and asked if we would like to visit the studio of a nearby Balinese artist. I introduced everyone, and the tourists readily agreed. On the way to the artist's house, I asked Geertz why she had changed her mind. She replied that she was working on the life history of Ida Bagus Madé Togog, a Balinese painter, then an old man (and since deceased), who had been an artistic consultant for Gregory Bateson in the 1930s. Possibly Togog could sell one of his paintings to the tourists, she explained, and her reason for escorting us was to help the painter, not the tourists. The tourists didn't buy any of his paintings, but I did: a picture of the barong dance, which I have on the wall in my bedroom. It was Togog who suggested to Geertz that she should bring her "friends" to buy his pictures. She wrote, "I had already brought a California artist friend, a New York psychiatrist, several anthropologists, an Australian historian, an American composer, and a whole bunch of Harvard students, just to mention a few" (letter, August 5, 1991).

As we walked to Togog's house, I could not help reflecting that here was I, ethnographer qua tour guide, with a group of tourists, and all of us being guided by Hildred Geertz, tour guides guiding tour guides, to the home of a Balinese artist who in his youth had himself been involved with tourism, with anthropologist Gregory Bateson and the production of tourist art, and who now in his later years was even more involved with tourism. Togog was Bateson's research consultant, but in a sense Bateson was Togog's tourist. While walking to the painter's studio, Geertz pointed to the house that Gregory Bateson and Margaret Mead had occupied during their research in Batuan in the 1930s, and all of us, the tourists and I, stopped to take pictures.

This scene, I said to myself, is paradigmatic: Ed Bruner's version of a Balinese cockfight, a scene to be commemorated, a postmodern pastiche, a meeting of the First and the Third Worlds in the postcolonial borderzone, a site of in-betweenness, of seepage along the borders. In this event, how does one distinguish between ethnography and tourism, between the center and the periphery, between the authentic and the inauthentic? These faded binaries seem so dated, no longer relevant to the work that ethnographers are actually doing in the field.

What arises in ethnography enters into tourism, but the reverse is also true; what arises in tourism enters into and is legitimated by ethnography (Picard 1992; Vickers 1989). Balinese do paint and dance for tourists, but at a later date many of these creative expressions enter into Balinese social and cultural life. In Batuan in the 1970s, for example, a cultural performance called a frog dance was devised for tourists. At the time of its creation, there was no "authentic" counterpart of the dance located elsewhere in Balinese culture; the dance was a commercial invention specifically designed for a tourist audience. It was not a simulation of an original, for there was no orig-

inal (Baudrillard 1983). It was an example of cultural production in the borderzone. Over a decade later, in the 1980s, while I was living in Batuan, the
organizers of a Balinese wedding asked a dance troupe to perform the frog
dance at their wedding. What began in tourism entered Balinese ritual, and
might eventually be included in an ethnographic description of the culture.
Further, dance dramas and other art forms constructed by Westerners have
been adopted by the Balinese as their own and have been incorporated into
their artistic repertoire. When President Ronald Reagan visited Bali in 1986,
a kecak dance, one created by the German artist Walter Spies and some
Balinese dancers in the 1930s, was selected as emblematic of Bali and was
performed in Reagan's honor.

Balinese culture is performed worldwide, not just on the island of Bali.
Balinese dance dramas are exported to the concert halls of Sydney, Paris, and
New York, and have become part of the international art world. As early as
1931, a barong dance was performed at the Colonial Exhibition in Paris and
was probably seen by Antonin Artaud (Picard 1990:58). If the Balinese perform at a temple, it is traditional culture and is described in ethnography; at a
hotel, it is tourism; and on a concert stage, it is art, according to our Western
categories. From the Balinese perspective, however, these are not closed systems. The Balinese, of course, know if they are performing for tourists, for
themselves, or for the gods. They are very aware of the differences between
audiences, and indeed they have public debates about the impact of tourism
on their culture. The Balinese try to keep some sacred performances exclusively for themselves, but their language does not distinguish between sacred
and profane, and in practice, over time, there is slippage.[9] Ethnography, tourism, and art as discourse and practice are porous at the borders, and cultural
content flows from one arena to the other, sometimes in profound yet subtle
ways. Cultural innovation that arises in the borderzone as a creative production for tourists, what anthropologists formerly called "inauthentic" culture,
eventually becomes part of Balinese ritual and may subsequently be studied
by ethnographers as "authentic" culture.

For example, the barong and *rangda* performances involving trance
fascinated early Western visitors and residents more than any other Balinese
dance form (Bandem and de Boer 1981:148). Baum, in her novel *A Tale from
Bali*, explicitly documents this Western infatuation with the barong
(1937:282). The gifted group of intellectuals and artists who lived in Bali in
the 1930s, including Spies, Covarrubias, Belo, McPhee, Bateson, and Mead,
were captivated with the barong and, in collaboration with the Balinese, commissioned new forms of the barong dance. The famous Bateson-Mead 1937
film, *Trance and Dance in Bali*, which is usually regarded as an early photographic record of a Balinese ritual, was actually a film of a tourist performance for foreigners commissioned and paid for by Bateson and Mead. As
Jacknis (1988:167–68) and Belo (1960:97–98, 124–27) document, the barong ritual filmed by Bateson and Mead was not ancient but had been recently
created during the period of their fieldwork, and the story performed had

The *barong* from a tourist performance of the Denjalan group at Batubulan. (Photo by Edward M. Bruner)

been changed from the *Calon Arang* to the *Kunti Sraya*, a less dangerous form. The *Kunti Sraya* barong dance, after various transformations since the 1930s, is being performed for tourists to this day. Further, for the film, Bateson and Mead changed the dance by having women rather than men hold the krisses, and they commissioned the dance during the day, when the light was good for photography, rather than having the performance in the evening.

The interest of these influential foreigners enhanced the prominence of the barong performances in Balinese life to such an extent that the barong has become the preeminent tourist performance, and is now paradigmatic of Bali in Western discourse (Vickers 1989). The dance is so popular that it is performed for tourists by three different troupes simultaneously every day in the village of Batubulan and occasionally by other dance troupes as well (e.g., at Singapadu). The barong performance shaped by foreign fascination in the 1930s entered ethnographic discourse most prominently in the 1960s, in Clifford Geertz's influential "Religion as a Cultural System" (1966), which takes the barong and rangda as illustrative of his generalizations about religion. Balinese culture, after all, has been shaped for seventy years by performances for foreigners, so it is not unexpected that the barong dance that an earlier generation of ethnographers helped to construct is described by a more recent ethnographer as the incarnation of "the Balinese version of the comic spirit" (Geertz 1973:118) and as emblematic of Balinese religion. Even the Balinese themselves are not entirely sure what is "authentic" and what is touristic, and such scholars as Picard (1992) doubt if such a distinction makes any sense to the Balinese. To overstate the case for emphasis, the Balinese became what ethnographers studied, in that Western interest in the barong led the Balinese to modify their culture so that the barong became more prominent in their performances.[10]

The Tourist Response

To return to the meeting between the tour group and Hildred Geertz, we ask, How did the tourists react to this incident in Bali? One woman said it was "thrilling," and another that it was the high point of the Indonesia trip. I eventually saw color slide shows presented at home in America by two tourist families, and both included photographs of the Bateson-Mead house, which in itself is not very striking. Slide shows become an occasion for a narrative summary of the tour, a means to personalize a group experience, and an opportunity to tell stories of travel and adventure. From the perspective of these tourists, the presence of Gregory Bateson and Margaret Mead, and of Ed Bruner and Hildred Geertz—to them the pinnacle of scientific authority—gave them the validation that they, although mere tourists, were in the presence of professors who knew the "real" Bali.

In a sense, the decision of the tour agency to include an academic lecturer is a marketing ploy to have a built-in authenticator; thus I, and also Geertz, had become, like the Balinese, tourist objects (Morris 1995). Complexity is multiplied in a many-layered reflexive voyeurism, in a thick touristic description; the tourists were looking at the Balinese, the ethnographers were looking at the Balinese as well as the tourists; the tourists were looking at the ethnographers; and of course the Balinese were looking at everyone. One ethnographer, Bruner, was studying the other ethnographer, Geertz, who, after she had read a draft of this paper, stated, "This is the first time I've ever been an ethnographic object." The tourists were also looking at the other tourists, because the tour group for them was their basic social unit, the group they traveled with and discussed the sights with on a daily basis. What I want to emphasize here is not just the voyeurism, the tourist gaze, but also that all parties—the painter Togog, the ethnographer Geertz, the tour guide Bruner, and the tourists—were not just passive beings, looking or being looked at, but also were active selves interpreting their worlds.

I later learned that Geertz had selected Batuan as the site of her research precisely because the Balinese craft of painting for tourists began there in the 1930s (Geertz 1995). She was as much involved in the study of tourism and the borderzone as I was, and had a similar postmodern perspective. Geertz wrote to me in her letter of August 5, 1991:

> I was by no means "embarrassed" by the entry of your tourists into my Balinese world, for they were, and had been for some years, a common part of it. There was hardly a day in Batuan when foreigners had not

been around. I had long ago clarified to myself the presence of "other tourists" as a part of my own research or, at least, had learned to live with it. The Balinese never let me forget that I was just one more tourist among the others.

Geertz graciously gave me permission to write about our meeting in Bali, although she felt uncomfortable that she did not have more of an active voice in the presentation of her own views.

Between Tourism and Ethnography

I found aspects of the tour guide role uncomfortable and ambiguous (Bruner 1995). As ethnographer my aim was to study how the tourists experienced the sites, but as guide my assignment was to structure that experience through my commentary. My talk mediated their experience, so that in a sense I found myself studying myself. Like the Kaluli shamans who create the meaning they discover, I created the meaning of Indonesian sites for the tourists, and then I studied that meaning as if I had discovered it. This is not, however, especially unique in ethnographic research (Bruner 1986b).

"Tourist" and "ethnographer" are roles that one plays and manipulates. At times, when our tour group approached a new site, the Indonesians would behave toward me as if I were another tourist, and I could rupture that attribution by speaking the Indonesian language, which in effect said, "Don't confuse me with these tourists," or I could choose to remain silent and to accept the designation. At other times, by emphasizing my role as a working tour guide, I could identify with the Indonesian performers and locals, saying in effect, as guide and native, "We are in the same situation, catering to tourists, who are our source of income." I stressed to the Indonesians that we were on the same side, as it were, in opposition to the tourists, but I was never sure if the Indonesians accepted this alignment.

More disturbing was that during the journey, I would slip back and forth between the touristic and the ethnographic, for I could not always keep them straight. I truly enjoyed these hardy tourists who were, like me, older, college educated, and of either professional or business class. At times I felt myself becoming a tourist, gaping in awe at Borobudur, rushing from the bus to take photographs, enthralled by breathtaking scenery in Sulawesi, luxuriating in the hot showers but complaining about the meals at the hotel in the evening. At other times I felt myself as a straight ethnographer, making detailed observations of tourist behavior, dissecting their conversation and writing my field notes late into the night. Balinese barong performers wear masks, but so do ethnographers.

As a tour guide, I felt that what tourism needed was not another sojourn among the exotic savages of the mysterious East, not more clichés and stereotypes, so I tried to demystify traditional tourism, to deconstruct the romantic images of the Indonesians, to reveal the mechanisms of production of tourist performances. But the more I did so, paradoxically, the more I contributed to traditional touristic romanticism. For the tourists, I became the heroic ethnographer, a regular Indiana Jones, the "true" interpreter of the sites and enactments on the tourist itinerary. The tourists were proud that they had their own "authentic" ethnographer as tour guide, compared with those other more touristy tours, the superficial ones that didn't have their own professor as lecturer. I found myself in the position of "authenticating" the experience for the tourists at the same time I was deconstructing the Balinese cultural performances. The tourists saw me as providing the ultimate backstage, despite my protestations to the contrary.

Authenticity and Verisimilitude

In Yogyakarta, the heart of central Javanese culture, the tour agent scheduled a supper and performance at the home of "Princess" Hadinegoro, a relative of the sultan. We arrived in the early evening, the only tourists there, and were served drinks in the living room of the home. We then moved to the dining room, were seated at tables, and enjoyed a buffet supper as a gamelan orchestra played in the courtyard. After supper, we moved to the courtyard and watched a Ramayana ballet, a performance of the old Hindu epic. The performers were in colorful costumes, their bodily movements slow and controlled, and the presence of children peering over the courtyard wall added to the ambiance of the evening.

Afterward, when asked how they enjoyed the event, the tourists replied that it was absolutely lovely. I then explained that the invitation to the "home" of a Javanese princess was a gimmick, because it created the impression that they were "guests," which disguised the commercial nature of the attraction; actually they were paying customers, who had in effect gone to a restaurant. The princess ran a business to produce income, and had tour groups to her home an average of twenty days a month. Further, I explained, although the Ramayana ballet was presented as if it were an ancient classical dance, this was not the case. The ballet is not a Javanese genre, and the Ramayana ballet was created in 1961 as a performance for tourists (Laporan 1970), with support from the Indonesian central government of President Sukarno.[11]

The Javanese Ramayana, like the Balinese frog dance, was an example of new cultural production in the borderzone. At the time of its construction, it was somewhat of a theatrical event in Java because it brought together the best of the performing artists from Solo and Yogya and two distinct court traditions, and the ballet was performed at the Prambanan temple.[12] Since that time the artistic standards have declined, and the ballet has been shortened and adopted in a number of tourist settings. The Ramayana, as a dance for tourists, could not use the Javanese language because the foreigners could not understand it; the pace was made faster and the length was kept shorter to hold interest, and the gestures were exaggerated to communicate a story line across wide cultural chasms. Relative to other Javanese dances, the Ramayana was reduced and simplified so that it could be incorporated more readily into a Western system of meaning. In a sense, I told the tourists, the Ramayana is a caricature of a Javanese dance, a postmodern construction in the borderzone, an ancient Hindu epic reworked for foreign consumption.[13] Well, I asked the tourists, what do you think of the evening now, knowing that the setting and the dance were not as authentic as you had assumed? Their response, all of them, was that nothing I said had detracted from their enjoyment of the evening, that it was still absolutely lovely! "What did you like?" I asked. They replied that it was a good show, that they were the only persons present, that it was stimulating being in an Indonesian home and seeing all the old Dutch and Javanese pictures and memorabilia, that the food was fine, and that the performers were superb.

After this discussion the performers, dressed in their street clothes, came out to meet the tourists, as I had requested. We found that the male lead, a history major at Gajah Mada University, had joined the troupe as a part-time job. His wife of six months was a student at the Dance Academy of the university, and she hoped to become a professional dancer. The tourists asked questions about the dance and contemporary life, I translated, and the session ended with the taking of group photographs. My idea was to remove the performers from roles in the timeless Hindu past, and to show them as modern Indonesians who could interact with the tourists on a more direct and personal basis.

After leaving Java we flew to Bali, to stay at the Bali Hyatt Hotel, a large resort complex on the beach in Sanur that caters primarily to tour groups. The next evening the hotel advertised a *rijstafel* dinner with a performance of the Ramayana ballet, at a cost of twenty dollars per person plus service fees. I suggested that our group attend, as it was an opportunity to see the same performance in two settings on two different islands. Following the creation of the Ramayana ballet, the Balinese copied the dance drama in 1962 and adapted it to their own culture. After the dance, I asked the tourists how they enjoyed the evening. One replied that it was too much like Honolulu, then another corrected her and said it was more like Miami Beach. Everyone shared this negative view, and I inquired why. The answer was that they were in a room with three hundred or four hundred other tourists; one Hyatt hotel is like any other; it was too crowded; the buffet lines were too long; there was no feeling of intimacy; and they were too far from the performers to take good photographs. "But," I protested, "this is a Balinese version of the same Ramayana that you enjoyed so much in Yogya. The performers are a diverse group put together by a local producer, but they are good dancers, and the gamelan orchestra is hired as a troupe from one of the villages, so it is the same group that you might hear performing in a temple festival." Despite my arguments, they did not like the performance of the Ramayana ballet at the Bali Hyatt.

The next day in Bali was Nyepi, the one day in the calendrical cycle when all activity stops on the island, and the tourists could not leave the hotel. I felt it was an appropriate time for some extended discussion with the tourists, so I booked a seminar room for our meeting. Our topic was authenticity, and I rather liked the idea of holding a seminar on authenticity at the Bali Hyatt Hotel, a world-class hotbed of international tourism.

When I probed further into the differences between the Javanese and the Balinese versions of the Ramayana, it was apparent that the context was the crucial variable: the atmosphere of a home for just our group as opposed to a tourist hotel with many groups. In Java the audience, the gamelan orchestra, and the performers were on the same level, whereas in Bali there was an elaborate raised stage for the performers and another separate area for the orchestra. There was even a raised platform labeled "photo point," where the tourists could go to take pictures. Both the performances were commercial, but in the first the mercantile dimension was disguised, whereas in the second it was transparent.

These upscale tourists did not object to a performance constructed for tourists, but they demanded that it be a good performance, and they had their aesthetic standards. They were not romantics and were concerned with the artfulness of staged theatricality, not disguised issues of authenticity. What they wanted was a good show. Authenticity, they said, might be an issue in the literature on tourism, but it was not an important issue for them. They pointed out that the Ramayana ballet might be recent, but it was still Indonesian. They recognized that they might be responding to the "authenticity" of the setting, for the differences in context between the performances in a Javanese home and in a Balinese beach hotel were striking. They acknowledged that the Java version was more exclusive, more high-class, held in the home of Javanese royalty; and these tourists were, after all, trying to secure an exclusive tourist experience, of which I was a part. But the Java version was also a better show. The tourists appreciated my historical perspective on the dance and my data on the processes of its production, but my information did not detract from their enjoyment of the evening. I understood their position, and believe they accurately characterized the views of many other tourists.

We had seen a Balinese barong performance by the Denjalan group at Batubulan the previous day, and one woman volunteered that she immediately recognized it as the "sacred tourist dance," which she has come to expect on all her tours. Her comment elicited smiles of acknowledgment from the others. After all, if a dance performance begins at precisely 9 A.M. each day; if there are only tourists and no Balinese in the audience; if they charge admission and sell souvenirs; if it lasts for precisely one hour, after which everyone returns to the tour buses, it doesn't take much to figure out that this is a dance staged for tourists and not for Balinese. I said to the tourists, however, that the Denjalan group had two barongs, one of which was a consecrated barong with *sakti* (power); that the man in white sprinkling holy water on the stage, playing the part of a Balinese priest, was a Balinese priest, not an actor, and the water he sprinkled was holy; that they sacrificed a chicken on stage as an offering; that the performers recited mantras before the performance; and that the dancers reported that sometimes they did go into trance. For the Balinese the gods are always present. I agreed with the tour group, however, that this was a dance staged for tourists. The tourists, in turn, accepted what was presented to them and had no inclination to look beyond the "staged authenticity" of the Denjalan performance for the "real" barong.

The seminar convinced me that the basic metaphor of tourism is theater, and the tourists enter into a willing suspension of disbelief. The key issue for students of tourism then becomes the mechanisms by which a tourist production is made convincing and believable to the tourists, which in effect collapses the problem of authenticity into the problem of verisimilitude (Bruner 1994; Cohen 1988). What makes a theatrical or tourist production credible? This is the old anthropological question of how people come to believe in their culture (Crapanzano 1986). It is not just that the Ramayana in Java had fewer tourists and the Ramayana in Bali had more tourists, and was more touristy, which is the dimension that the tourism literature has emphasized. When there are fewer tourists, it is easier to suspend disbelief, to get into the event or site, or to imagine oneself as an adventurer or explorer in a distant land. The performance becomes more believable. Nor is it a question of the authenticity of a performance, which implies the presence of another performance that is more genuine or truer to life. The Ramayana ballet is not a simulacrum; it has no counterpart elsewhere in the culture, and there is no original. Even if there were an original, it would not be of primary concern to the tourists. The problem of focusing so narrowly on the quest for authenticity is that one is always looking elsewhere, over the shoulder or around the bend, which prevents one from taking the Ramayana and the barong as serious performances in themselves, ones that deserve to be studied in their own right.[14]

Clearly, what MacCannell wrote in 1976 in his classic book about touristic authenticity did not seem relevant for the tour groups I took to Indonesia, but his comments in 1990 on the ex-primitives and the postmodern tourists staging the touristic enterprise as a coproduction, as a kind of contract, seems very provocative, as do Erik Cohen's (1985b) view of tourist playful self-deception and Urry's (1990) notion of the post-tourist, although I have never known any other kind of tourist than the one Urry describes. The question emerges of whether what MacCannell, Cohen, and Urry now write seems relevant because the world has changed or because we are for the first time beginning to understand touristic phenomena. The results of my studies of Indonesian tourism suggest that the issue of authenticity in the tourism literature has been overdone, that tourists are not primarily concerned with authenticity, and that it would be more productive to pursue the metaphors of theater and of borders to study touristic verisimilitude.

Conclusion

This essay has tried to throw some light on what Taussig has called the epistemic murk of the anthropological predicament, what Geertz calls the great semiological swamp that we all live within. Postmodern complexities occur not only in the centers of Western power but also in postcolonial borderzones on the periphery, in what used to be the pure, authentic preserve of ethnographic science. Indeed, the border between ethnography and tourism is clouded, porous, and political. Tourism not only shapes Balinese culture but also is now part of Balinese culture—or it could even be said that tourism is Balinese culture (Errington and Gewertz 1989; Picard 1992). Balinese born since the 1930s have lived their entire lives as tourist objects, and in some areas, such as Batuan, any adequate ethnographic account of Balinese economy or ritual would have to take account of tourism.

Balinese performances are exported to the centers of Western power, and they are also enacted every day in a shifting touristic borderzone on the edge of the Third World, a zone of interaction between natives, tourists, and ethnographers. Tour agents are always looking for new products to present to their clients, for new temples or new islands to discover and to "touristify." The Balinese, the Javanese, and other Indonesian peoples in the tourist zone are themselves always experimenting, creating, and playing with new expressive rituals, constantly devising new performances for the tourists. But the new Indonesian culture does not necessarily remain forever fixed in the zone in which it was created. Old ceremonial forms are reworked for tourists, culture produced for tourists enters Balinese ritual, what arises in tourism or ritual may be exported to the concert stages of the West for an international audience, and what was at one historical period "touristic" at a later period becomes "ethnographic."

Anthropology has always recognized that peoples and cultures move, for concepts such as diffusion and migration have had deep roots in the discipline from the beginning, but we may not yet have taken account of the particular nature and the full extent of the movement of peoples and cultures in this postmodern world. The old anthropological metaphor of place, where one culture belongs to one people who are situated in one locality, is being challenged by the new metaphors of diaspora, travel, tourism, and borderzones (Appadurai 1988; Clifford 1989). I see the challenge as a continuation of the emphasis on practice, performance, movement, and process that has become so prominent in anthropology since the 1960s (Ortner 1984), and I welcome it. It makes ethnography more dynamic, more exciting.

Source: From *Displacement, Diaspora, and Geographies of Identity*, Smadar Lavie and Ted Swedenburg (eds.), 1996. Reprinted with permission of the author and Duke University Press.

Acknowledgements

An earlier draft of this essay was read at the Department of Performance Studies, New York University, and at the Departments of Anthropology at SUNY Buffalo and at Rice University. I wish to thank Barbara Kirshenblatt-Gimblett, Richard Schechner, Dennis and Barbara Tedlock, Bruce Jackson, George Marcus, and Hildred Geertz for their suggestions. Parts of an earlier draft were presented at the conference Tourism and the Change of Life Styles, Instytut Turystyki, Warsaw, Poland, in 1988. Helpful comments also were made following discussion of the paper at the Cultural Studies reading group at the University of Illinois.

Notes

[1] Specialists might argue about the precise date when tourism began in Bali, but by the time the KPM steamship line initiated weekly service in 1924, and opened the Bali Hotel in 1928, there was international tourism.

[2] See Picard 1992 and Vickers 1989. The same exuberant phrases are found in the Balinese travel brochures from the 1930s to the 1990s.

[3] In this essay, I use the concept of borderzones to better understand and conceptualize Western tourism to the less developed regions of the Third World. Although many tourist destinations are in First World countries, I focus on travel to the Third World.

[4] Other groups may seek an essentialized precolonial purity—for example, national liberation movements.

[5] I use the term "postcolonial" in the sense of "after the colonial era," but I realize that the term is problematic.

[6] See Bruner 1995 for the economic aspects of the tour guide role.

[7] For the Balinese, ceremonial attire at a temple festival is less an expression of individual identity and more a matter of respect toward others, especially the gods and demons who inhabit the ritual world. The Balinese would expect an ethnographer to dress respectfully.

[8] I did return to Bali the next month, and Geertz helped me gather data on Balinese tourism.

[9] This is best documented in Picard 1992.

[10] This thesis was presented at the annual meetings of the American Folklore Society in Cincinnati, 1985, by Kirshenblatt-Gimblett and Bruner in a paper titled "Tourist Productions and the Semiotics of Authenticity." See also the seminal work of Boon (1977); the scholarly work of Picard (1990); and the popular book by Vickers (1989).

[11] I wish to thank Edi Sedyawati for her help in understanding the Ramayana. I am also indebted to I Made Bandem for his help with Balinese performances.

[12] The local Javanese guide in Yogya complained in 1987 that there were now so many tourists at the Prambanan temple for the Ramayana performance that the Javanese could no longer attend. He had missed the point completely: that the Ramayana was constructed precisely for a tourist audience, and thus blurred the distinction between performances for tourists and for Javanese.

[13] The enactment of the Ramayana, from the performers' point of view, was more a rite of modernity, generating cash income in a market economy.

[14] In 1986, after the tourists had left, I saw a Ramayana ballet performed as part of a large, multiple-day temple ceremony, an example again of how a dance created for tourists becomes part of Balinese ceremonial. The Ramayana, however, was held the day following the major temple ritual. Such occurrences are commonplace in Bali.

References

Anzaldúa, Gloria. 1987. *Borderlands/La Frontera: The New Mestiza*. San Francisco: Spinsters/Aunt Lute Foundation.

Appadurai, Arjun. 1988. "Putting Hierarchy in Its Place." *Cultural Anthropology* 3(1): 37–50.

Bandem, I. Made, and F. de Boer. 1981. *Kaja and Kelod: Balinese Dance in Transition*. Kuala Lumpur: Oxford University Press.

Baudrillard, Jean. 1983. *Simulations*. New York: Semiotext(e).

Baum, Vicki. 1937. *A Tale From Bali*. Singapore: Oxford University Press.

Belo, Jane. 1960. *Trance in Bali*. New York: Columbia University Press.

Boon, James. 1977. *The Anthropological Romance of Bali, 1597–1972: Dynamic Perspectives in Marriage and Caste, Politics and Religion*. New York: Cambridge University Press.

———. 1990. *Affinities and Extremes: Crisscrossing the Bittersweet Ethnology of East Indies History, Hindu-Balinese Culture, and Indo-European Allure*. Chicago: University of Chicago Press.

Bourdieu, Pierre. 1984. *Distinction: A Social Critique of the Judgement of Taste*. Cambridge, MA: Harvard University Press.

Bruner, Edward M. 1986a. "Experience and Its Expressions," in *The Anthropology of Experience*, ed. Victor Turner and Edward Bruner, pp. 3–30. Urbana: University of Illinois Press.

———. 1986b. "Ethnography as Narrative," in *The Anthropology of Experience*, ed. Victor Turner and Edward Bruner, pp. 139–155. Urbana: University of Illinois Press.

———. 1993. "Epilogue: Creative Persona and the Problem of Authenticity," in *Creativity/Anthropology*, ed. Smadar Lavie, Kirin Narayan, and Renato Rosaldo, pp. 321–334. Ithaca, NY: Cornell University Press.

———. 1994. "Abraham Lincoln as Authentic Reproduction: A Critique of Postmodernism." *American Anthropologist* 96(2): 397–415.

———. 1995. "The Ethnographer/Tourist in Indonesia," in *International Tourism: Identity and Change*, ed. Marie-Françoise Lanfant, Edward M. Bruner, and John Allcock, pp. 224–241. London: Sage.

Buck-Morss, Susan. 1987. "Semiotic Boundaries and the Politics of Meaning: Modernity on Tour—A Village in Transition," in *New Ways of Knowing; The Sciences, Society, and Reconstructive Knowledge*, ed. Marcus G. Raskin and Herbert J. Bernstein, pp. 200–236. Totowa, NJ: Rowman and Littlefield.

Clifford, James. 1983. "On Ethnographic Authority." *Representations* 1:118–146.

———. 1986. "On Ethnographic Allegory," in *Writing Culture: The Poetics and Politics of Ethnography*, ed. James Clifford and George E. Marcus, pp. 98–121. Berkeley: University of California Press.

———. 1989. "Notes on Travel and Theory." *Inscriptions* 5:177–188.

Cohen, Erik. 1985a. "Tourist Guides: Pathfinders, Mediators, and Animators." [Special Issue] *Annals of Tourism Research* 12.

———. 1985b. "Tourism as Play." *Religion* 15:291–304.

———. 1988. "Authenticity and Commoditization in Tourism." *Annals of Tourism Research* 15:371–386.

Crapanzano, Vincent. 1986. "Hermes' Dilemma: The Masking of Subversion in Ethnographic Description," in *Writing Culture: The Poetics and Politics of Ethnography*, ed. James Clifford and George E. Marcus, pp. 51–76. Berkeley: University of California Press.

Crick, Malcolm. 1995. "The Anthropologist as Tourist: An Identity in Question," in *International Tourism: Identity and Change*, ed. Marie-Françoise Lanfant, Edward M. Bruner, and John Allcock, pp. 205–223. London: Sage.

Errington, Frederick, and Deborah Gewertz. 1989. "Tourism and Anthropology in a Post-Modern World." *Oceania* 60:37–54.

Fusco, Coco. 1989. "The Border Art Workshop/Taller de Arte Fronterizo, Interview with Guillermo Gómez-Peña and Emily Hicks." *Third Text* 7:53–76.

Geertz, Clifford. 1966. "Religion as a Cultural System," in *Anthropological Approaches to the Study of Religion*, ed. M. Banton, pp. 1–46. London: Tavistock.

———. 1973. *The Interpretation of Cultures*. New York: Basic Books.

Geertz, Hildred. 1995. *Images of Power: Balinese Paintings Made for Gregory Bateson and Margaret Mead*. Honolulu: University of Hawai'i Press.

Graburn, Nelson, and Jafar Jafari. 1991. "Introduction: Tourism Social Science." *Annals of Tourism Research* 18(1): 1–11.

Hicks, Emily. 1991. *Border Writing: The Multidimensional Text*. Minneapolis: University of Minnesota Press.

Jacknis, Ira. 1988. "Margaret Mead and Gregory Bateson in Bali: Their Use of Photography and Film." *Cultural Anthropology* 3(2): 160–177.

Kirshenblatt-Gimblett, Barbara, and Edward M. Bruner. 1985. "Tourist Productions and the Semiotics of Authenticity." Paper presented at the meetings of the American Folklore Society, Cincinnati, Ohio.

Lanfant, Marie-Françoise, Edward M. Bruner, and John Allcock, eds. 1995. *International Tourism: Identity and Change*. London: Sage.

Laporan, Seminar Sendratri Ramayana Nasional, Tahun 1970. Panitia Penjelenggara.

MacCannell, Dean. 1976. *The Tourist: A New Theory of the Leisure Class*. New York: Schocken.

———. 1990. "Cannibal Tours." *Visual Anthropology Review* 6(2): 14–24.

Morris, Meaghan. 1995. "Life as Tourist Object," in *International Tourism: Identity and Change*, ed. Marie-Françoise Lanfant, Edward M. Bruner, and John Allcock, pp. 177–191. London: Sage.

Nash, Dennison, and Valene L. Smith. 1991. "Anthropology and Tourism." *Annals of Tourism Research* 18(1): 12–25.

Ortner, Sherry. 1984. "Theory in Anthropology since the Sixties." *Comparative Studies of Society and Society* 26(1): 126–166.

Picard, Michel. 1992. *Bali: Tourisme culturel et culture touristique*. Paris: Harmattan.

———. 1990. "'Cultural Tourism' in Bali: Cultural Performances as Tourist Attractions." *Indonesia* 49:37–74.

Rosaldo, Renato. 1989. *Culture and Truth: The Remaking of Social Analysis*. Boston: Beacon Press.

Smith, Valene L., ed. 1989. *Hosts and Guests: The Anthropology of Tourism*, 2nd edition. Philadelphia: University of Pennsylvania Press.

Turner, Victor, and Edward M. Bruner, eds. 1986. *The Anthropology of Experience*. Urbana: University of Illinois Press.

Urry, John. 1990. *The Tourist Gaze: Leisure and Travel in Contemporary Societies*. London: Sage.

Vickers, Adrian. 1989. *Bali: A Paradise Created*. Berkeley: Periplus Editions.

14

Power Dynamics in Tourism: A Foucauldian Approach

So-Min Cheong and Marc L. Miller

From the perspective of Western society, tourism is usually understood as a product of the individual decisions made by tourists. The relationship forged between tourists and locals is routinely depicted as socioeconomic in character, with tourists and locals interacting either in a warm social milieu as "guests and hosts" or in the economic marketplace as "consumers and producers." Where a power differential between the two is perceived to exist, as between First World tourists and Third and Fourth world locals, the relationship is usually interpreted as colonial or imperialistic. Viewed from within such a framework, the influence of tourists on the social world of the places they visit is expected to be negative, at best benign. Tourism is, for example, blamed for commodifying the cultures of host societies and promoting materialistic consumerism among their populations. This paper questions how much power actually rests with tourists as opposed to other institutional actors in tourism and the populations of the societies tourists visit. To date, few studies have looked at the manner in which power relationships govern the behavior of the tourists themselves.[1] To address this oversight, we explore Michel Foucault's conceptualization of power, introducing four core features of Foucauldian power and discussing them in relation to tourism.

A small number of scholars in the overlapping fields of postmodernism and cultural studies have applied Foucault's concepts to the study of tourism.

Some researchers, for example, have concentrated on aspects of gaze (Hollin-shead 1994, Labone 1996, Rojek 1992, Urry 1990), the body (Veijola and Jokinen 1994), and resistance (Wearing 1995). These studies, however, have interpreted power in very generalized terms and have utilized Foucault's concept of power in oblique ways. Key features of Foucault's insights about power, however, seem to us to be especially pertinent to a consideration of tourism. To begin with, Foucault challenged what he saw as the dominant conceptualization of power as "a certain strength" with which people are endowed (1978:93).[2] Foucault also viewed power in a much more fluid way than what is brought to mind by an inventory of formal laws and rules or a view of power as something a dominant group exercises over another. Power for Foucault is a "complex strategical situation," consisting of "multiple and mobile field of force relations" that are never completely stable (1978:93–102). In viewing power as a relationship rather than an entity and in seeing power as something that flows in multiple directions, Foucault found common ground with most political scientists. Thirdly, Foucault insisted that power is so inextricably wedded to other knowledge that it cannot analytically be considered separately. In recognizing that "[t]he exercise of power perpetually creates knowledge and, conversely, knowledge constantly induces effects of power," Foucault often meshed the two concepts into "power-knowledge" in his writings (1980a:52).

Foucault saw power everywhere and all situations as embedding power relationships, including social relations between men and women and between family members. Power also exists in all kinds of institutions, not only those with economic significance. Thus, even seemingly nonpolitical institutions create power relations and mechanisms of power that often are useful for the general functioning of formal politics. According to Foucault, power is not a commodity or possession tied to a particular individual or entity. Instead it exists within networks of relationships: power is "circulating and never localized here or there, never in anybody's hands, never appropriated as a commodity or piece of wealth" (1980b:98). A variety of people can possess and dispossess power in varying circumstances and at different points in time and place.

In examining power relationships, the first task is to identify the *targets* (the subordinate actors in a relationship) and the *agents* that structure the differentiated positions people hold in a localized institution or system. Agents derive their power not from pure force but from tactics and strategies that induce targets to behave (or speak or think) in a certain way. Agents perform their power by constructing knowledge, that is, by creating normalizing discourses that define what is acceptable and not acceptable. They also exert power through an "inspecting gaze." (The concept of gaze is especially relevant to the discussion of power in tourism because seeing is so much a part of touristic experience and because the manipulation of the imagery is so important in the marketing of tourism.[3]) Agents construct the gaze as they observe the target. In the process, the target ends up internalizing the gaze to the point that he becomes his own overseer. Examples used by Foucault include the "parental gaze" and the "clinical gaze" by which agents (e.g., parents or clinicians and psychiatrists) compel their targets (i.e., children and patients) to see and to accept certain kinds of behavior as appropriate. At the same time, the supporting institutions of the agents grow and develop through the creation of such things as technical discourses, professional disciplines, and bureaucracies. The discourse on sexuality that developed during the Victorian era, for example, created standards for a healthy body, established school and public hygiene practices, and contributed to a general "medicalization of the population" (Foucault 1978:126). "What makes power hold good, what makes it accepted," Foucault observed, "is simply the fact that it doesn't weigh on us as a force that says no, but that it traverses and produces things, it induces pleasure, forms of knowledge, produces discourse" (1980:119).

Agents and Targets

Foucault's notion that power is omnipresent in human affairs clearly implies that tourism is no exception, although the many ways power operates may not be immediately obvious. Power relationships in tourism are commonly masked in everyday discourse by facts and statistics that draw attention to tourism's economic and social importance. The very complexity of a global tourism "industry" (with its service and manufacturing sectors and diverse ventures in entrepreneurship) interferes with an appreciation of its power relationships.[4] For the Foucauldian analyst, power relationships are located in the seemingly nonpolitical business and banter of tourists and guides, in codes of ethics, in the design and use of guidebooks, and so on. Tourism systems are sustained by the gaze at the individual level and by the productive effects of power at the institutional level.

Until fairly recently, the public and academics alike have tended to conceive of tourism as a two-part social system consisting of "hosts" in the destination and visiting "guests." This view has its roots in the first edition of Valene Smith's *Hosts and Guests: The Anthropology of Tourism* (1977). While many scholars continue to base their analyses on this distinction, the limitations of it as a framework are gradually being corrected. In this regard, many cultural anthropologists and sociologists have insisted that tourism is an activity substantially shaped by middlemen (Chambers 1997, Cohen 1985a, van den Berghe and Keyes 1984). Miller and Auyong (1991a, 1991b) have proposed a model of tourism comprising three standard elements: tourists, locals, and several categories of brokers. Brokers are people who derive a living from their involvement with tourism production. Hotel owners and employees, vendors, and guides who provide tourists with goods and services exemplify private-sector brokers. Public-sector brokers include city planners and politicians, those who work in government-operated tourism information centers as well as police and guards at tourism sites. Other broker variants include social movement brokers, academic brokers, travel media brokers, and consulting brokers.

Power relations in tourism systems are dynamic and constantly changing. The absolute numbers and ratios of tourists, locals, and brokers at particular destinations change throughout phases of development. Tourists themselves can become brokers by starting businesses or by assuming government positions as consultants or enforcement agents. They can also become locals by establishing permanent residency at a favored destination. Similarly, locals become brokers when they engage in the business or management of tourism; they can also become tourists. Brokers also can change their identity and become tourists or cease to be involved in tourism-related ventures and become locals. The shifting identities of tourists, locals, and brokers are largely dependent on contingencies, time, and place. Consequently, there is no one-sided, fixed flow of power from one individual to another.

Tourists are commonly seen as rational, independent, and powerful actors who initiate their touristic trips and are responsible for much of the consequences on local people and the environment. Tourists in the tripartite system described above, in contrast, are targets in the same way Foucault has described children, women, criminals, and madmen in their relationship to agents in their respective institutional systems. Yet, as we know, power flows in many directions and there are many cases in which locals and even brokers are told what to do by tourists. Indeed, this back and forth flow of power within tourism is often underestimated. For the purposes of this chapter, however, we are concentrating on tourists as targets.

Some might argue that a tourist trip is institutionally too different from a prison, a mental clinic, a school, or home to warrant any comparison. Designating tourists as the target of various agents (e.g., public and private sector brokers, locals, academics, market researchers, travel writers) also ignores the variety of tourist types. It could be pointed out, for example, that some tourists—the most affluent and privileged come immediately to mind—operate entirely on their own terms when traveling. Tourists are also much freer to wander around than are the incarcerated prisoners, mental patients, children, and women whom Foucault studied. And they are not subject to the same means of surveillance that constrains these other targets. Nonetheless, tourists qualify as targets because they operate from insecure positions. Once they reach their destination, tourists typically find themselves on unfamiliar political and cultural turf, and they often communicate at a distinct linguistic disadvantage. In the course of their sojourn, they are stripped of many of their cultural and familial ties and protective institutions, and are exposed to new norms and expectations. Their own culture, defined here as what "one has to know or believe in order to operate in a manner acceptable to its members" (Goodenough 1957:167), loses its supremacy if not its validity while in the tourist destination. Tourists must reconsider their political status and adjust to the situations they find themselves in, providing whatever justifications, behaviors, and gestures seem acceptable to those in command of the destination and its culture. Tourists are power-bound not by a mental clinic or prison, but by the trip.

How well does Foucault's model account for diversity among tourists? At first glance, for example, applying the model of controlling agents to "independent travelers" seems unworkable. However, no tourist can make *all* touristic decisions without outside consultation or advice. While Foucault would concede that the wealthy aristocrat (as well as the independent-minded ecotourist or professor on sabbatical) receives different treatment from guides, hotel concierges and staff, and other tourism agents than do tourists on an organized tour, it is still "treatment." The independent tourist may resist suggestions and planned itineraries more than other tourists, but the very act of resistance presupposes the position of the tourist as target. The flow of power in tourism can be negotiated, even mediated, but it cannot be denied.

Viewed in this light, all tourists are captives to a wide variety of agents, including brokers and guides. The package tour is the extreme case of constrained movement, the self-guided tour the least. In the former, tourists can find themselves quite literally imprisoned on buses and boats, and in enclave resorts. In these circumstances, they depend considerably on guides, among other agents. Even on self-guided tours the movements of tourists are limited and structured by the guidebook, the agent, or the signpost. To differing extents, then, tourists are power-bound and are influenced by Foucauldian agents from the time they first seek information and begin to make travel plans until they return home.

The Foucauldian agents of tourism power include the various tourism brokers as well as some categories of locals. Brokers drawn from the private and public sectors include government officials, tour guides, and hotel/restaurant employees, guidebooks, academics, and market researchers. They virtually compel tourists to function in certain ways. Viewed from a Foucauldian perspective, brokers are not weak intermediaries and providers of tourism-related services—as the customary view might suggest. They do not serve a neutral role. Rather, they intervene and constrain tourism activities for the sake of profit and public service (Cheong 1996).

In addition to participating in the formulation and implementation of tourism ethics, many types of brokers collaborate to develop strategies. At any given time, divergent brokers in different professions will align themselves around an issue. They discuss and negotiate how far development should proceed, what type of development is optimal, who should enter the area as tourists, and so forth. On-site brokers exercise enormous discretion in dealing with tourists. Park guards, for example, watch over tourists to see if they litter; guides protect, oversee, and educate them about how to act properly, and offer them interpretations of historic sites, cultures, and customs; restaurant employees instruct them in what and how to eat. Subsequently, brokers in a variety of guises constrain their movements, behaviors, and even thoughts, and act as a powerful force in the tourism system. In passing, it should be noted that off-site brokers—those who are not in direct contact with tourists—also manage tours and contribute to tourism plans and strategies.

Turning now to locals, the common view is that they exert the least control over what takes place in tourism. It is argued that they are the most oppressed and victimized participants in international tourism. Having the least control can mean having little involvement in tourism and being indifferent toward tourism activities. Since locals, as defined here, do not earn income from the tourism industry, unlike tourists or brokers, they have no immediate vested interest in its production. While the latter two groups are concerned with tourism ethics and conduct, locals—to the extent that they interact with tourists or witness tourism at all—conduct their daily lives according to a different set of cultural values and norms. Some locals, however, are Foucauldian agents. They behave as agents in power relations when they galvanize resistance (whether active or passive) to tourism or when they endorse it. If they oppose tourism, they can go to great lengths to inhibit and constrain it, as, for example, blocking the entry of tourists into certain regions or sabotaging the industry by refusing to act as "tourism objects." Such overtly political actions are unlikely to be approved of by brokers who need locals as willing unpaid labor in order to avoid charges of providing tourists with "staged authenticity" (MacCannell 1989). Experience in many resorts and destinations supports the idea that locals control the behavior of tourists in subtle but effective ways via informal face-to-face interaction. Here, the socialization of tourists to local traditions and manners is one outcome of social control.

The Touristic Gaze

In addition to the concepts of agent and target, the Foucauldian concept of gaze is useful in tracking the development and maintenance of power relationships in tourism. In using the term "tourist gaze," Urry borrows from Foucault focusing on what and how the tourist sees. Urry recognizes that the ability to gaze is afforded to tourists by a power relationship: ". . . this gaze is as socially organized and systematized as is the gaze of the medic. Of course it is of a different order in that it is not confined to professionals 'supported and justified by an institution.' And yet even in the production of 'unnecessary pleasure' there are in fact many professional experts who help to construct and develop our gaze as tourists" (1990:1). Urry is clearly alert to the fact that the tourist gaze exists together with the gaze of experts. But he establishes the tourist as the potent actor in these interactions. He concentrates on what tourists view and how they interpret it rather than on the techniques and strategies agents use to instruct tourists in how and what to see. Consequently, Urry places the tourist in the same category (agents) as Foucault's clinicians who have the medical gaze. This clashes with the argument being made here that the tourist is more a target than an agent, and that tourists' knowledge is constructed by surrounding brokers who define, constrain, and elicit a normalizing behavior for tourists. While tourists do acquire a gaze, agent-target power relations guarantee that it is the "touristic gaze" created by agents.

A major reason tourists are the primary objects of the gaze of brokers and locals has to do with their visibility, hence target-ability. They are not only conspicuous when in organized tours and because of documentation requirements, they are also often physically distinguishable from locals. Their style of dress, language, accent, and possessions contrasts with those of residents in the tourist destination. Although international tourists more clearly fit this profile, domestic ones also are exposed to similar experiences. A contrast between them and the people they visit frequently exists due to income differences, an urban versus a rural orientation, or an inland versus a coastal residence. These contrasting qualities can make tourists seem inherently threatening. Yet, because the contrast enhances their visibility, it situates them in a vulnerable position to be managed by agents of power.

In direct interactions with tourists, Foucauldian agents employ strategies that involve education, instruction, persuasion, advice, interpretation, surveillance, and coercion. At times, they act as buffers who protect tourists from the ethnocentrism of locals (and locals from the prejudices of tourists) by educating tourists about local cultural manners and mores. Agents also act as experts who shape the decisions tourists make when they purchase commodities and services and the conclusions they draw when appreciating (or devaluing) amenities and other features of the destination. Agents, then, transmit distinctions. They influence what tourists can and cannot do, where they can and cannot go, and what they select and reject. Agents not only focus the gaze, they also determine what is not to be seen or experienced. This is particularly evident in the actions and discourse of the travel agent, the guide, and the local. The flow of power is from the agent to the target and not vice versa.

The influence of the travel agent gaze on tourists is most apparent when they establish that they are not just *sources* of information or access, but are *experts*. Their "knowledge" and "competence" is legitimized by the tourist who accepts their recommendations on prices, airlines, hotels, and routes, and even full itineraries, destinations, and activities (Johnson and Griffith 1995). The travel agent gaze is typically supported by the technological features of the modern office, where interaction with the tourist is governed. They have exclusive control over computers that contain information and they have command over the dissemination of brochures, travel videos, hotel and destination reviews, and other materials. (Their exclusive control is now being challenged by online booking over the Internet, however.) Travel agents provide expert insights and personal opinions about the prevailing political climate, weather, and safety concerns at destinations, and other conditions subject to sudden change. While often forceful, they can also be subtle in the management of tourists. In all of this, travel agents create and limit opportunities for tourists.

Everyone who has traveled has encountered guides who dominate the touristic experience. Tourists see through their guides' eyes, as they choose the objects of interest to be viewed and steer attention to those selected objects (Cohen 1985b). An important implication is that tourists will not see what guides prefer they ignore. Of course, their success (and failure), like that of travel agents, lies in their ability to "read" tourists and to judge motivations and elicit attitudes. Guides are not always able to rely on repeat customers, but they do depend on the tips and word-of-mouth advertising of satisfied tourists. They construct the gaze through their special expertise, esoteric "local knowledge," and abilities. Thus, they demonstrate their worth by being able to converse with tourists in their language, by knowing popular trails and interesting flora and fauna, by recounting cultural and architectural histories, by knowing local customs, and so forth. Those who provide highly organized, scheduled, and expensive services show their prowess in museums and at ruins, on hikes and other eco-touristic treks, and on safaris, cruise ships, and bus tours. Many offer casually arranged impromptu services by taxis or on foot. Throughout the guided tour, tourists are socialized to the agendas of guides by the gaze. Results include tourists who change their way of thinking (and behavior) to incorporate cultural, religious, political, or ecological principles introduced by guides. Those sensitive to the stigmatized identity of the "Ugly Tourist/American" are candidates for transformations of this variety (Miller 1993). Guides also implement their own agenda when they orchestrate interactions with allied brokers employed at hotels, restaurants, retail shops, taxi stands, and the like.

Locals also contribute to the formation of the gaze. They share many power strategies with the travel agents and guides described above. Like them, they observe tourists, make inferences about their aspirations, and judgments about their behavior. The principal difference in their use of power is that locals have no short-term stake in forging relationships with tourists. Unlike agents and guides, they are not seeking clients and consequently have the option of behaving as a courteous host, becoming antagonistic, or exhibiting utter indifference to the presence of tourists. Many locals find themselves in the company of tourists at least intermittently in markets, on roadways, airplanes and boats, in churches, universities, and sports stadiums, and in myriad business establishments. In these brief encounters, they display the gaze toward tourists through their actions, gestures, insinuations, and other communications. The force of this gaze is multiplied when locals come together. Whether they direct their gaze as individuals or as participants in organized coalitions or in unorganized crowds, tourists are wise to take notice. The power of the local gaze on tourists (and their attending guides) can lead tourists to quickly understand where they might go and what they might do. For example, the local gaze has drawn tourists into homes and into the private spaces of locals. At other times it has prohibited the same

activities. There are many examples of tourists being enthusiastically welcomed by the local community, but plenty of examples of "tourist go home"
attitudes and violence.

Repressive and Productive Tourist Power

Tourists as individual Foucauldian targets have been both liberated and
constrained by the opportunities mediated by the gaze of brokers and locals.
As has been pointed out, this combined gaze consists of activities in which
agents (brokers and locals) instruct, educate, and reform tourists as well as
inspect, monitor, and otherwise manage them. These experiences both challenge and reward tourists precisely because they do not know in advance precisely how, or in how many different ways, they will be influenced. At the
institution level, the productive aspect of power is apparent in the numerous
professional specialties that have grown up around tourism, in the elaborate
structure of the tourism discourse, and in the great diversity of tourism commodities that these specialties and discourse require. In short, the productive
power is found in the rise of the tourism industry and the expansion of
knowledge around it.

Tourism has grown steadily since Thomas Cook invented the role of the
modern agent and broker in the last century. Its explosive growth since the
end of World War II is apparent in the legitimization of tourism "experts" in
the public, private, academic, and media sectors. The industry underwrites
multidisciplinary activity in design, marketing and sales, and many other
business specialties. Tourism has become an academic specialty in fields as
diverse as cultural anthropology, history, public affairs, planning, business,
political science, and sociology, to name but a few. The varied disciplines and
subdisciplines in academia find their counterparts in government and industry where tourism specialization has grown at a rapid rate. A vast inventory
of training and certification programs and regularly scheduled professional
and scientific meetings, trade shows, and conventions now exists.

Tourist knowledge includes the totality of ways in which tourism topics
are discussed in academic, industry, and everyday speech and texts, and also
the ways in which its operational symbols appear in advertising, the media,
and the arts. An organizing theme running through this composite discourse
is that of economic profit. Decisions made by tourists, brokers, and locals
that affect the quality and quantity of investments are discussed, interpreted,
and judged with great emotion and intensity. In this discourse, the costs and
benefits of policies are debated with reference to knowledge and theories
identified with the science and technology, with the aesthetic, and increasingly with the ethical establishments connected to tourism. This total knowledge informs both serious and casual discussions, including academic and
professional conversations as well as the ordinary chat about tourism memories, planning trips, and comparing experiences and impressions. Tourism has
emerged as a topic of real significance in society.

Conclusion

The principal goal of this paper has been to contribute to the emerging body of knowledge about power in tourism. By using the political ideas of Michel Foucault, we have sought to encourage a conceptual change in how analysts study power in tourism. We have highlighted dimensions of power in the industry that are often overlooked by the public and by researchers who are more accustomed to regarding tourism relationships and impacts as the outcomes of marketplace forces and the power of tourists. We make four main points. First, Foucauldian power is omnipresent in tourism as in virtually all other human affairs. Second, power relationships are conspicuous in the micro-interactions of brokers, locals, and tourists in a tripartite tourism system. While acknowledging that power works in many directions, we have emphasized the potentials for tourists to be Foucauldian targets and for brokers and locals (i.e., "hosts") to be Foucauldian agents. Third, the tourist gaze is a primary mechanism by which travel agents, guides, and some locals operate in a power relationship vis-à-vis tourists. Finally, the productive effects of power, evident in the proliferation of tourism studies and the formation of knowledge in this field, are emphasized.

This orientation to touristic power recommends that attention be shifted away from tourists and redirected toward agents who are prominent in the control of tourism development and tourist conduct. Ultimately, we suggest, the success or failure of "appropriate" or "sustainable" tourism programs lies more substantially in the power of brokers and locals than in the power of tourists. This understanding about power in tourism can assist in the rethinking of tourism development, and can contribute to the formulation of innovative tourism policies.

Source: Adapted from "Power and Tourism: A Foucauldian Observation." *Annals of Tourism Research*, 2000, 27(2):371–90.

Notes

[1] Textbooks promoting a multidisciplinary perspective on tourism have been compiled by specialists with backgrounds in tourism structure (Gee, Choy and Makens 1997), hospitality and business management (McIntosh and Goeldner 1990), state planning and marketing (Gregory and Goodall 1990; Gunn 1988; Rosenow and Pulsipher 1979), marketing (Fesenmaier, O'Leary and Uysal 1996; Plog 1991), and current issues (Shaw and Williams 1994). Compared to the substantial attention given to the practical business and marketing of tourism and its economic costs and benefits, very little about the political nature of tourism has been examined. Ritchie and Goeldner's (1987) edited handbook, *Travel, Tourism, and Hospitality Research*, is the only beginning text with a chapter that focuses on the industry's political dimensions. In recent years, the political study of tourism has slowly gained recognition as a subfield of its own. Most research has examined public policy and tourism planning which is often entangled with, or subordinate to, other policies and planning priorities. Some studies have advocated community solutions to tourism opportunities and problems (Elliott 1983; Farrell 1986; Murphy 1985; Reed 1997; Ringer 1993; Whittaker 1997). The appropriateness

of tourism development among planners, developers, and locals is a hotly debated issue in all this literature.

A second category of research on the political dimensions of tourism includes market-oriented studies of development policies that often focus on structural adjustments to the changing global economy. Researchers such as Hall (1994), de Kadt (1985), Lea (1988), Matthews (1978), and Poirier (1995) have documented the process of tourism development vis-à-vis other national/international development programs. Some research has examined the issue of unequal development and the hierarchical relationships that embody the hegemonic power of developed nations and transnational corporations. Britton (1989), Francisco (1983), Mowforth and Munt (1998), and Place (1995) and others have pointed out the continuing problem of dependency even in the age of new tourism designed to remedy the unequal balance of power between rich and poor. The one-sided flow of power delineated in some of these studies has been contested however. In making this case, some researchers (Cameron 1997; Milne 1998; Oakes 1995; Shaw and Williams 1998) claim that locals are not always passive when facing economic and social change. They can be proactive and resistant, as they negotiate and contest the direction of development in the pursuit of their rights and interests. With this perspective, power is seen to operate in both directions, and the assumption of the continual oppression of the locals is rejected.

[2] "By power, I do not mean 'power' as a group of institutions and mechanisms that ensure the subservience of the citizens of a given state. By power, I do not mean, either, a mode of subjugation, which, in contrast to violence, has the form of the rule. Finally, I do not have in mind a general system of domination exerted by one group over another, a system whose effects, through successive derivations, pervade the entire social body" (1978:9).

[3] The concept of gaze originates from the spatial arrangement of Bentham's Panopticon, an architectural model for a prison in the eighteenth century. The Panopticon was designed to that whomever was at the center could see everything, enabling one person to watch many. Anyone in the center of the edifice could operate the system. Hence, the idea that anybody can watch and be watched by somebody depending on where they are placed. Important in this spatial arrangement is the place of the individual.

[4] A recent report prepared for the World Tourism Organization (WTO) shows that domestic and international tourism in 1995 combined to create over 200 million jobs worldwide and made up 11 percent of the world's gross domestic product (Waters 1996:6). More people engage in pleasure and business tourism than ever before. WTO experts estimate that by the year 2020 roughly 1.6 billion of the world's 7.8 billion people will take a foreign trip (Crossette 1998:5).

References

Britton, S. 1989. "Tourism, Dependency and Development," in *Towards Appropriate Tourism: The Case of Developing Countries*, ed. T. Theuns and F. M. Go, pp. 93–116. New York: Peter Lang.

Cameron, C. M. 1997. "Dilemmas of the Crossover Experience: Tourism Work in Bethlehem, Pennsylvania," in *Tourism and Culture: An Applied Perspective*, ed. E. Chambers, pp. 163–182. Albany: State University of New York Press.

Chambers, E. 1997. "Introduction: Tourism Mediators," in *Tourism and Culture: An Applied Perspective*, ed. E. Chambers, pp. 1–12. Albany: State University of New York Press.

Cheong, S. 1996. "A Political Framework for Tourism Study: The Case of Cheju Island, Korea." Unpublished Master's Thesis. University of Washington.

Cohen, Erik, ed. 1985a. "Tourist Guides—Pathfinders, Mediators, and Animators." [Special Issue] *Annals of Tourism Research* 12.

———. 1985b. "Tourist Guides: The Origins, Structure and Dynamics of a Role." *Annals of Tourism Research* 12(1):5–29.

Crossette, B. 1998. "Surprises in the Global Tourism Boom." *The New York Times* April 12: Sec. 4 p. 5.

de Kadt, E. 1985. *Tourism—Passport to Development? Perspectives on the Social and Cultural Effects of Tourism in Developing Countries*. New York: Oxford University Press.

Dreyfus, H., and P. Rabinow. 1982. *Michel Foucault: Beyond Structuralism and Hermeneutics*. Chicago: University of Chicago Press.

Elliott, J. 1983. "Politics, Power, and Tourism in Thailand." *Annals of Tourism Research* 10:377–393.

Farrell, B. 1986. "Cooperative Tourism and the Coastal Zone." *Coastal Zone Management Journal* 14(1/2): 113–120.

Fesenmaier, D., J. O'Leary, and M. Uysal. 1996. *Recent Advances in Tourism Marketing Research*. New York: Haworth Press.

Foucault, M. 1975. *The Birth of the Clinic: An Archaeology of Medical Perception*. New York: Vintage Books.

———. 1977. *Discipline and Punish: The Birth of the Prison*, trans. A. Sheridan. New York: Vintage Books.

———. 1978. *The History of Sexuality: Volume I: An Introduction*. New York: Vintage Books.

———. 1980a. "Prison Talk," interview by J. Brochier, in *Power/Knowledge: Selected Interviews and Other Writings 1972–1977*, ed. C. Gordon, pp. 37–54. New York: Pantheon Books.

———. 1980b. "Two Lectures," in *Power/Knowledge: Selected Interviews and Other Writings 1972–1977*, ed. C. Gordon, pp. 78–108. New York: Pantheon Books.

———. 1980c. "Truth and Power," interview by A. Fontana and P. Pasquino, in *Power/Knowledge: Selected Interviews and Other Writings 1972–1977*, ed. C. Gordon, pp. 109–133. New York: Pantheon Books.

———. 1980d. "The History of Sexuality," interview by L. Finas, in *Power/Knowledge: Selected Interviews and Other Writings 1972–1977*, ed. C. Gordon, pp. 183–193. New York: Pantheon Books.

———. 1988a. "The Minimal Self," interview with S. Riggens, in *Politics, Philosophy, Culture: Interviews and Other Writings 1977–1984*, ed. L. D. Krtizman, pp. 3–16. New York: Routledge.

———. 1988b. "Critical Theory/Intellectual History," interview with G. Raulet, in *Politics, Philosophy, Culture: Interviews and Other Writings 1977–1984*, ed. L. D. Krtizman, pp. 17–46. New York: Routledge.

———. 1988c. "Politics and Reason," in *Politics, Philosophy, Culture: Interviews and Other Writings 1977–1984*, ed. L. D. Krtizman, pp. 57–85. New York: Routledge.

———. 1988d. "On Power," interview with P. Boncenne, in *Politics, Philosophy, Culture: Interviews and Other Writings 1977–1984*, ed. L. D. Krtizman, pp. 96–109. New York: Routledge.

Francisco, R. 1983. "The Political Impact of Tourism Dependence in Latin America." *Annals of Tourism Research* 10:363–376.

Gee, C., D. Choy, and J. Makens. 1997. *The Travel Industry*, 3rd edition. New York: Van Nostrand Reinhold.

Goodenough, W. 1957. "Cultural Anthropology and Linguistics," in *Report of the Seventh Annual Round Table Meeting on Linguistics and Language Study*, ed. P. L. Garvin. Washington, DC: Georgetown University Monograph Series on Languages and Linguistics No. 9.

Gregory, A., and B. Goodall. 1990. *Marketing Tourism Places*. London: Routledge.

Gunn, C. 1988. *Tourism Planning*. New York: Taylor & Francis.

Hall, C. 1994. *Tourism and Politics: Policy, Power, and Place*. New York: Wiley.

Hollinshead, K. 1994. "The Unconscious Realm of Tourism." *Annals of Tourism Research* 21:387–391.

Johnson, J. C., and D. C. Griffith. 1995. "Promoting Sportfishing Development in Puerto Rico: Travel Agents' Perceptions of the Caribbean." *Human Organization* 54(3):295–303.

Labone, M. 1996. "The Roaring Silence in the Sociology of Leisure." *Social Alternatives* 15:30–32.

Lea, J. 1988. *Tourism and Development in the Third World*. London: Routledge.

Leiper, N. 1992. "The Tourist Gaze." *Annals of Tourism Research* 19:604–607.

MacCannell, D. 1989. *The Tourist: A New Theory of the Leisure Class*. New York: Schocken Books.

Matthews, H. 1978. *International Tourism: A Political and Social Analysis*. Cambridge, MA: Schenkman.

McIntosh, R., and C. Goeldner. 1990. *Tourism: Principles, Practices, Philosophies*. New York: Wiley.

McNay, L. 1994. *Foucault: A Critical Introduction*. New York: Continuum.

Miller, M. L. 1993. "The Rise of Coastal and Marine Tourism." *Ocean and Coastal Management* 20:181–199.

Miller, M. L., and J. Auyong. 1991a. "Coastal Zone Tourism: A Potent Force Affecting Environment and Society." *Marine Policy* 15(2): 75–99.

———. 1991b. "Tourism in the Coastal Zone: Portents, Problems, and Possibilities," in *Proceedings of the 1990 Congress on Coastal and Marine Tourism*, vol. I and II, ed. M. L. Miller and J. Auyong, pp. 1–8. Newport OR: National Coastal Resources Research and Development Institute.

———. 1998. "Remarks on Tourism Terminologies: Anti-tourism, Mass Tourism, and Alternative Tourism," in *Proceedings of the 1996 World Congress on Coastal and Marine Tourism: Experiences in Management and Development*, ed. M. L. Miller and J. Auyong, pp. 1–24. Seattle: Washington Sea Grant Program and the School of Marine Affairs, University of Washington.

Milne, S. 1998. "Tourism and Sustainable Development: Exploring the Global-Local Nexus," in *Sustainable Tourism: A Geographical Perspective*, ed. C. Hall and A. Lew, pp. 35–48. New York: Longman.

Mowforth, M. and I. Munt. 1998. *Tourism and Sustainability: New Tourism in the Third World*. London: Routledge.

Murphy, P. 1985. *Tourism: A Community Approach*. New York: Methuen.

Oakes, T. 1995. "Tourism in Guizoh: Place and the Paradox of Modernity." Unpublished Ph.D. dissertation, University of Washington.

Pearce, D. G. 1989. *Tourist Development*, 2nd edition. New York: Wiley.

Place, S. 1995. "Ecotourism for Sustainable Development: Oxymoron or Plausible Strategy?" *GeoJournal* 35:161–174.

Plog, S. 1991. *Leisure Travel*. New York: Wiley.

Poirier, R. 1995. "Tourism and Development in Tunisia." *Annals of Tourism Research* 22:157–171.

Reed, M. 1997. "Power Relations and Community-Based Tourism Planning." *Annals of Tourism Research* 24:566–591.

Richter, L. 1989. *The Politics of Tourism in Asia*. Honolulu: University of Hawaii Press.

Ringer, G. 1993. "The Wilderness Begins at McCarthy: Perceptual Impacts of Tourism on Communities." Unpublished Ph.D. dissertation, University of Oregon.

Ritchie, J. R., and C. Goeldner. 1987. *Travel, Tourism, and Hospitality Research: A Handbook for Managers and Researchers*. New York: Wiley.

Rojek, C. 1992. "The 'Eye of Power': Moral Regulation and the Professionalization of Leisure Management from the 1830s to the 1950s." *Society and Leisure* 15:355–373.

Rosenow, J., and G. L. Pulsipher. 1979. *Tourism: The Good, the Bad, and the Ugly*. Lincoln, NB: Century Three Press.

Shaw, G., and A. Williams. 1994. *Critical Issues in Tourism*. Oxford: Blackwell.
————. 1998. "Entrepreneurship, Small Business Culture and Tourism Development," in *The Economic Geography of the Tourist Industry: A Supply-side Analysis*, ed. D. Ioannides and K. Debbage, pp. 235–255. London: Routledge.
Sheridan, A. 1980. *Michel Foucault: The Will to Truth*. New York: Tavistock Publications Ltd.
Smith, V. L., ed. 1989. *Hosts and Guests: The Anthropology of Tourism*, 2nd edition. Philadelphia: University of Pennsylvania Press.
Urry, J. 1990. *The Tourist Gaze*. London: Sage.
van den Berghe, P. L., and C. F. Keyes. 1984. "Introduction: Tourism and Re-created Ethnicity." *Annals of Tourism Research* 11:343–352.
Veijola, S., and E. Jokinen. 1994. "The Body in Tourism." *Theory, Culture and Society* 11:125–151.
Waters, S. R. 1996. *Travel Industry World Yearbook—The Big Picture: 1995–1996*. New York: Child & Waters.
Wearing, B. 1995. "Leisure and Resistance in an Aging Society." *Leisure Studies* 14:263–279.
Whittaker, E. 1997. "The Town that Debates Tourism: Community and Tourism in Broome, Australia," in *Tourism and Culture: An Applied Perspective*, ed. E. Chambers, pp. 13–30. Albany: State University of New York Press.

15

Coping with Mass Cultural Tourism: Structure and Strategies

Jeremy Boissevain

At present Europe is experiencing a massive influx of outsiders. New Others—migrant laborers/guest workers, political refugees, illegal immigrants and, to be sure, millions of tourists—are moving into established communities. The introduction of outsiders with widely differing customs into traditional, relatively homogeneous neighborhoods has brought about a confrontation with new ideas and habits. The presence of outsiders automatically creates new categories of "us" and "them," often generating suspicion, jealousy, and fear. Tourists are perhaps the least discussed "significant others" penetrating European communities. Many of these communities, in one way or another, increasingly depend on their presence. How do individuals and communities dependent on tourists cope with the commoditization of their cultural heritage and the constant attention of outsiders?

Tourists: Searching for the Other

Tourists come in many forms. A tourist has been defined as "a temporarily leisured person who voluntarily visits a place away from home for the purpose of experiencing a change" (Smith 1989a:2). They form a continuum that ranges from day-trippers to leisure immigrants who have more or less settled into their former holiday homes. Cultural tourists are interested in the lifestyle of other people, their history, and the artifacts and monuments they have made. This category also includes what some have called ethnic and historical tourism (Smith 1989a; van den Berghe 1994; van den Berghe and Keyes 1984; Wood 1984). Cultural tourism may be contrasted with recreational tourism—stereotypically focused on sun, sand, and sea—and environmental tourism. Obviously these categories overlap: mass recreational tourists often spend some time visiting monuments and local festivals, thus assuming the role of cultural tourists.

Certain general characteristics of tourists and tourism affect all destination communities in one way or another. To begin with, tourists are transients and their relations with locals are often unequal. Because they can afford to buy the services upon which the local economy depends and often come from more technologically advanced societies, tourists at times patronize and even abuse locals. The latter, on the other hand, because they monopolize local knowledge and services, can cheat and exploit the tourists. The visitor-host relation is thus potentially fraught with ambivalence and tension which, in turn, can exacerbate relations between state and civil society (also see Mac-Cannell 1984:387; van den Berghe and Keyes 1984:347; Wood 1984).

Another factor affecting relations between locals and tourists is the desire of the visitors temporarily to change their life situation. They seek escape from established routines, from the constraints of time and place, and from the behavioral codes that rule their daily lives. They believe this change will recharge their mental and physical batteries so that they will be better able to cope with the pressures of their daily commitments (see Graburn 1983, 1989; Leach 1964; Urry 1990). Becoming a tourist, however briefly, means shedding part of one's old identity and normal behavior. This involves adopting a new, temporary identity that necessarily incorporates some elements that are the opposite of habitual personality and behavior (Boissevain 1989; Graburn 1983; Lett 1983). This process is facilitated by the masking function that anonymity provides. Those being visited do not know the normal persona of the tourist. Tourists consequently can easily change their everyday behavior and, temporarily, become other persons and engage in extravagant if not illicit behavior (cf. Turner 1969:176). This change is often signaled by donning "leisure" clothes. These strange, often garish costumes unambiguously mark out the wearer as a tourist. This emblematic garb often amuses but can also offend locals going about their daily activities in bank, shop, or church. Strange dress and weakened inhibitions are not infrequently accompanied by behavior that would be quite unacceptable at home. Tourists can be loud, lecherous, drunken, and rude. In short, many tourists, for various reasons, are occasionally most unpleasant guests. Yet persons whose livelihood depends upon their presence must somehow come to terms with their difficult behavior and cater to their often bizarre habits.

Recent reports from the mass tourist resort of Ibiza illustrate the extreme form this can take.

Six girls decide to cool themselves down without the help of air conditioning by opting to drop their knickers and lift their skirts, for the pleasure of
those present. "This is nothing," says the owner of one of the most important bars in the area. "I've even seen men displaying their penises in the
street." This bar owner never ceases to be horrified by the spectacle. "Each
year gets worse. But let's just make some money and see if we can get
through the summer." (Quoted from *El Diario de Ibiza* in Sharrock 1998)

Cultural Tourism

Tourists in search of culture are generally welcomed as more discerning, and environment friendly. They are seen as more "sustainable." However, when the quest for the culture of the Other becomes an aspect of mass
tourism it can create problems. To begin with, cultural tourism is more intrusive. Not content to remain in (seaside) enclaves, visitors seek out the culture
and local customs they have been promised.

National and regional tourist authorities usually commoditize and market local culture or the environment without consulting the inhabitants (see
Greenwood 1989:180). This can lead to tension between, on the one hand,
tourists, who not surprisingly demand access to the sites and events they have
been promised and have paid for, and, on the other hand, local residents part
of whose cultural heritage, often unbeknownst to them, has been sold to the
visitors. This can lead to yet another characteristic of cultural tourism: the
loss of privacy. As tourists search for the culture they have paid to see, they
cross thresholds and boundaries to penetrate authentic backstage areas. Mac-
Cannell has discussed "back" and "front" regions in the context of tourism:
"The front is the meeting place of hosts and guests or customers and service
persons, and the back is the place where members of the home team retire
between performances to relax and to prepare" (MacCannell 1976:92). The
back region is normally closed to outsiders. Tourists view it as somehow
more "intimate and real" as against the front region's "show." It is consequently considered more "truthful," more authentic. The back region is where
the tourist can experience true authenticity and achieve a oneness with his
host (94–99). The desire to penetrate back regions in search of authenticity is
inherent in the structure of tourism. Cultural tourists consequently systematically attempt to penetrate domestic back regions or participate in private
events in order to sample authentic culture. In doing so they often discomfort
their unwilling "hosts."

Furthermore, excessive attention destroys the very resources that tourists come to examine: local inhabitants become entrepreneurs, traditional
tranquility is destroyed, the physical environment is eroded, and the local
population is slowly priced out of the area, transforming living communities
into open air museums and tourist entertainment areas. This is already occurring in the center of Prague, Kraków, and Weimar. It is occurring in many
other places, including Malta's Mdina, of which more will be discussed later.

A final characteristic of cultural tourism is a consequence of the fact that, unlike seaside tourism, for example, it is not necessarily a seasonal activity. The inhabitants of walled towns and historic city centers are exposed to the presence of tourists throughout the year. This exposure is steadily increasing as cultural tourism becomes more popular. The pressure on the inhabitants of such cultural destinations is often constant. Without the respite from the constant tourist gaze, characteristic of seasonal tourism, hosts become enervated and their behavior toward tourists increasingly hostile. Bus drivers, guides, hotel personnel, waiters, and shopkeepers are among the first to react. They become rude and off-hand, sometimes provoking outright aggression.

In short, cultural tourism has an unexplored dark side that particularly affects villages, small historic cities, walled towns, and islands. These are especially vulnerable to the overcrowding that mass tourism generates. The minuscule island state of Malta, inundated by waves of tourists for most of the year, has been particularly affected.

Malta

With a land area of only 120 square miles (316 km^2) and a population of 382,000, the Maltese archipelago makes up the most densely populated country in Europe. Situated in the center of the Mediterranean, the islands form something of a cultural bridge between Europe and Africa. Staunchly European and Roman Catholic, the inhabitants pray to Allah, for Maltese is a Semitic language. The islands have been densely inhabited since Neolithic times and occupied by the major Mediterranean powers. All have left a wealth of historic traces.

The development of tourism in Malta has been a relative success. Since mass tourism began in the 1960s, the volume of arrivals has grown steadily. In 1998, 1.2 million tourists visited this crowded micro-state. The infrastructure of hotels and places of entertainment developed mainly along the low northern and eastern coasts, in a few scenic inland locations, and in Gozo and Comino, Malta's smaller sister islands.

Government tourism policy has shifted in response to the growing pressure of mass summer seaside tourism and changing tourist tastes. The 1989 Tourist Master Plan recommended more seasonality, diversity, and quality. In the 1990s, government stimulated the construction of four- and five-star hotels and the National Tourist Organization of Malta (NTOM) began promoting cultural tourism and visits outside the peak summer season. It produced more brochures on the islands' heritage, targeting the more educated tourist. It promoted the advantages of winter visits. Instead of highlighting beaches, swimming, and nightclubs, as it had in the past, it promoted culture, learning, and specialized activities like walking, diving, and golf (Boissevain

1996b:223). In short, the NTOM has increasingly commoditized Malta's culture and physical environment without paying much attention to the impact of this commercialization on its citizens.

Mdina

The small, walled town of Mdina is a case in point (Boissevain and Sammut 1994; Boissevain 1996c). The islands' capital until the arrival of the Knights of St. John in 1530, it is now a major tourist attraction, vigorously promoted by NTOM. With a population of just under 300, it is visited by close to one million tourists annually. It houses the palaces of many of Malta's nobles, the cathedral, and a spectacular panorama. There are also some 25 commercial attractions that service tourist appetites for tea, food, antiques, jewelry, souvenirs, history, and horror. History is imparted via guidebooks, cassettes for hire, the Cathedral, and museums. "Cultural" experiences are touted via leaflets handed out at the town's entrance. These urge, among others, visits to the "Mdina Experience" *("Journey through time and re-live Mdina's tragedies and triumphs")*, the "Mdina Dungeons" *("Wander at your own pace and discover Horror, Drama and Mysteries from the dark past")*, and the exhibition on "Medieval Times" *("A spectacular recreation of 14th and 15th century life in Malta. Medieval Times is an entertaining and educational adventure—it is fun!")*.

For Maltese, the town has become the embodiment of their history. It is increasingly used for weddings, exhibitions of antique cars, prayer groups, concerts, and (re)invented historical pageants. It is no longer the "silent city" of the tourist brochures. The effects of constant exposure to hordes of curious visitors have created hostility to both foreign and local tourists among a growing segment of the town's residents. They resent being obliged to sacrifice their privacy and their tranquility for the national good. Many complain that tourists constantly peer and sometimes even sneak, uninvited, into their houses; that they leave a mess behind; that they block the narrow roads when residents try to drive home; that they are often indecently dressed; and that encroaching commercialism is spoiling the town's character.

While proud that their town is so popular, they are irritated by the behavior of tourists, tour operators, guides, and Maltese visitors. All take them for granted. This feeling of being used is exacerbated when the town becomes the site for special cultural events. In 1993 and 1994 the town became the venue of weeklong festival staged by the NTOM. The festival included animated guided tours, museum exhibitions, folkloric skits, street theater, puppet shows, evening concerts, and a richly costumed reenactment of the Grand Master of the Knights of St. John entering the town. It attracted tens of thousands of visitors, most of whom were Maltese. At times residents felt imprisoned by wall-to-wall crowds. Some residents trying to return home were even abused by tourist guides who accused them of joining their

tours without paying! One young woman summed up residents' attitude in
an emotional outburst:

> We are used as carpets! . . . The residents have a right to live. We want to
> live. When we air our views, outsiders tell us that Mdina is not ours but it
> belongs to the entire Maltese population. But we live here! We have a
> right to our city!

In 1994 local government was introduced and the first ever Mdina Local
Council was elected. It swiftly became involved with tourist related issues and
vigorously defended residents' interests. This ultimately brought the new
mayor into head-on collision with the special events director of the NTOM. He,
in turn, took the mayor to court for his alleged abusive conduct. The upshot of
the confrontation, however, was that the Local Council won the NTOM's assurance that future events would be coordinated with the Council. To the delight of
most local residents—except, of course, the tourist entrepreneurs, many of
whom are nobles who have opened tea rooms, restaurants, and boutiques in
their palaces—NTOM sponsored events now take place only every other year.

Reenactment of the
Grand Master of the Sov-
ereign Military Order of
St. John of Jerusalem
entering Mdina, spon-
sored by the National
Tourist Organization of
Malta. (Courtesy of
Malta Department of
Information)

Protecting Back Regions[1]

As the case of Mdina indicates, it would be a serious mistake to think that natives passively permit the tourism industry to destroy their culture. The inhabitants of most tourist destinations in time develop strategies to protect themselves from tourists bent on penetrating their back regions to stare, to undergo authentic experiences, and to photograph them. The strategies adopted include covert resistance, hiding, exclusion, aggression, and organized protest.

Covert Resistance

Values, rights, and customs threatened by tourism are often, and initially, defended by unspectacular means. Such everyday forms of resistance are diverse: "They require little or no coordination or planning; they often represent a form of individual self-help; and they typically avoid any direct symbolic confrontation with authority or with elite norms" (Scott 1985:29).

Those who work in the tourist industry in Malta, as elsewhere, depend on the goodwill of foreign visitors. Hence they are reluctant to confront them directly. The behavior of many Maltese who repeatedly deal with tourists exhibits forms of this everyday resistance: sullen waiters, rude bus drivers, and haughty shopkeepers. Denigrating stereotypes are also spread about difficult tourists. Stories about arrogant Germans, complaining Dutch, stingy Swedes, and Swiss who want nothing to do with local residents circulate freely in Malta.

Gentle parody, satire, and ridicule are also effective ways of covertly expressing discomfort, opposition, and hostility. Satirical Carnival songs in Andalusia are used to mock tourists (Nogués Pedregal 1996). Deirdre Evans-Pritchard (1989:95) presented a striking example of the way parody was used by a Native American silversmith:

> A lady was examining the silver balls on a squash blossom necklace. She turned to Cippy Crazyhorse and in a slow, over emphasized fashion intended for someone who does not really understand English she asked "Are these hollow?" Cippy promptly replied "Hello" and warmly shook her hand. Again the lady asked, "Are they hollow?" pronouncing the words even more theatrically this time. Cippy cheerily responded with another "Hello." This went on a few more times, by which time everyone around was laughing, until eventually the lady herself saw the joke.

Through self-parody Cippy was able to liberate himself from the dumb Indian ethnic stereotype and cajole the lady into seeing him as just as human as she.

Another form of covert activity directed against tourists is the sexual humiliation of female tourists by men structurally subordinated to tourists. Glenn Bowman (1996) recounts how Palestinian souvenir shopkeepers in Jerusalem "seduce" tourist women, whom they then insult. He explains their behavior by their subordinate status in geopolitical and local terms. Zinovieff (1991) found similar motives among the male "harpoons" who hunt foreign women in Greece.

Such covert acts of defiance enable persons subordinated by their dependence on tourists to retain their self-respect. Moreover, by these acts they keep alive the pilot light of resistance. Those who engage in such acts form a category of disgruntled persons. These, if the occasions arises, can be mobilized into more active protest, as will be discussed below (also see Davis 1975).

Hiding

Many communities, unenthusiastic about the presence of tourists, have taken to hiding aspects of their culture from visitors. Black (1996) discusses how her Maltese neighbors kept certain foods and spaces to themselves. They did not show their favorite swimming locations to tourists. Other communities hold celebrations at times and places that enable them to avoid the attention of outsiders (Boissevain 1992a, 1998). They are "insider-only" celebrations. They have a family resemblance to cast parties, when actors and (back)stage crew celebrate the end of a performance, well out of sight of the audience. Similarly, the inhabitants of tourist destinations withdraw to celebrate without tourists. In Malta, few tourists are present during the spectacular parades that take place under the scorching sun on the morning of the final day of the summer festas (Boissevain 1992b). Similar strategies have been noted in Spain and Greece (Crain 1996; Kenna 1992). This strategy of hiding certain aspects of their celebrations enables locals to continue expanding the major festivities that are important for their prosperity without sacrificing the intimacy of celebrating amongst themselves. These backstage rites of intensification are increasingly important for maintaining solidarity in communities that are both overrun by outsiders and tied to a work regime that limits socializing for months on end.

Exclusion

Another way of avoiding the tourist gaze is physically to exclude tourists from private areas and events. Many Lofoton islanders in northern Norway have fenced off their gardens to protect the privacy of sunbathing family members from curious tourists (Puijk 1996). The Kotzebue Eskimo of Alaska, annoyed by inquisitive tourists photographing them while they processed their seal catch on the beach, first erected screens to shield their work. When that proved ineffective, some hired taxis to haul the seals home so that they could process them in privacy (Smith 1989b:63–64).

In the Italian Val di Fassa village of Penia residents physically barred outsiders—neighbors from the lower valley as well as tourists—from the hall where their Carnival masquerade reaches its climax (Poppi 1992). In Malta, many residents who live in houses on Mdina's picturesque narrow dark streets have taken to closing their front doors to keep out curious tourists, instead of leaving them partly open to admit light, as they usually did. Some have also posted signs announcing that their house is "private."

Aggression

Occasionally people resort to violence to defend themselves against intrusive tourists. Some extreme cases have been recorded. A French tourist was stoned to death by the villagers of San Juan Chamula in Chiapas, Mexico, for photographing their Carnival (van den Berghe 1994:124). There was also the case of the furious Navajo who shot out the tires of the car of a tourist who barged into his dwelling to photograph his family eating together. The indignant tourist defended his action by arguing that his taxes supported the people on the reservation (Evans-Pritchard 1989). In the Andalusian seaside resort of Zahara, which for the previous five years has been suffering from drought, residents blamed tourists when the rationed water supply one day was cut off earlier than usual. The next day, shouting "The water has been cut, now we cut your way out," Zahareños sat down in the road, thus preventing tourists from leaving. They still proudly recall that many tourists missed their planes.[2]

In Malta, tourists, encouraged by government brochures to explore the countryside, are regularly menaced by hunters and bird trappers who object to foreigners invading territory they consider their domain. They believe that tourists threaten their hobby, since foreigners are usually critical of their shooting and trapping of migrating birds (see Fenech 1992). Recently, two Maltese police field inspectors were injured by bird shot pellets. The hunter, when asked by the magistrate why he had shot at a bird knowing that people were approaching, replied simply: "I thought they were tourists" (*The Times* [of Malta], April 26, 1996)!

Organized Protest

Local citizens occasionally organize action to protect their environment and culture against those commercializing it without their consent. Sometimes such efforts are successful, often they are not. For example, in Abbasanta, Sardinia, regional authorities expropriated a local monument, the *nuraghe* Losa. This Neolithic tower had for most of the century given inhabitants local, national, and even international recognition. They had felt no need to market it, or in other ways to exploit it as a moneymaking asset. The regional archaeological authorities, on the other hand, set about improving access to the site, enclosing it, and clearing "rubble," including, as it transpired, the complete Roman stratum of the site. The mayor promptly ordered the Carabinieri to stop the work. Irate regional authorities then retaliated and closed the site, denying locals access to their monument. The continuing conflict resulted in both the museum department and the local community abandoning Losa. Thus by converting the nuraghe from a community symbol into a commercial asset, the government destroyed its meaning for Abbasanta residents. They defended their honor by neutralizing the monument, at least temporarily, as a tourist resource (Odermatt 1996). The whole episode illustrates the consequences of commoditizing local culture without the consent of the participants (see also Greenwood 1989).

Maltese environmental NGOs have become increasingly active in combating the inroads of tourist developers. Sometimes they have been successful in halting developments, more often they have not (Boissevain and Theuma 1996, 1998). For example, despite their concerted efforts, NGOs were unable to halt the $122 million Hilton redevelopment project. This involved a new 300-bed hotel, 250 luxury apartments, a 16-story business center, the excavation of a marina, and the construction of a breakwater. In well-documented briefs the NGOs argued that a listed monument built by the Knights of Malta in 1770 would be destroyed; that the pollution caused by excavating the marina and its subsequent effluent would damage nearby seagrass meadows and pollute several popular swimming beaches; that the Environmental Impact Statement requested by the planning authority had not examined the project's socioeconomic consequences; that the public would be denied access to areas of the foreshore; and that the project's excavation, blasting, and building would subject residents in this densely populated neighborhood to five years of extreme inconvenience. They also organized a press campaign and various demonstrations. Finally, following a hunger strike by *Front Kontra il-Hilton* activists, the national ombudsman agreed to examine the way the land had been transferred and the prime minister granted them permission to examine the planning authority's Hilton case files.

The ombudsman concluded that while the original land grant conditions were not illegal, they clearly *"constitute a case of bad administration without due consideration to the national interest"* (Ombudsman 1997:13, his emphasis). The Front's report on the planning authority's files concluded that the project went against structure plan policies; the Environmental Impact Assessment was not correctly conducted, particularly in failing to assess the social and economic consequences; expert opinions were ignored without argument; there were many extraordinary and suspicious circumstances; the decision was rushed, which precluded proper study of all its consequences; no evidence was provided to support its claimed economic benefits (*Front Kontra il-Hilton* 1997a, 1997b). The planning authority branded the reports as simplistic (Planning Authority 1997) and the developers dismissed the Front as a handful of undemocratic fundamentalists (*The Sunday Times*, March 30, 1997).

Although the efforts of the NGOs were defeated and the Hilton redevelopment was approved and ultimately completed, they nonetheless accomplished a great deal. Their multipronged campaign illustrated the way powerful developers operate; displayed the laxity of government in dealing with such developers; showed the importance of extreme vigilance; demonstrated what could be achieved by determined nonviolent action; and put both planning authority and developers on notice that their future actions would be monitored and irregularities attacked.

In contrast to the Hilton case, NGO opposition to the $82 million Italian-Maltese plan to develop a hotel at Munxar Point was successful. Munxar Point, located alongside a quiet bay on Malta's southeast coast, had so far been spared the garish tourist-related developments that characterize most of the northern coastline. It is a favorite bathing, picnicking, and hunting area for inhabitants from inland villages, many of whom have small sheds and boat houses along the bay's foreshore. Opposition to the project began within days of the submission of the formal development application, in November 1995. Alerted by the local Friends of the Earth and a local counselor, *The Malta Independent* announced the proposed development with an article headlined "Tourist village plans for Marsascala beauty spot" (November 26, 1995). A week later a popular local priest wrote an emotional letter pleading for the preservation of the Munxar area. He then set up an action group to fight the application. In four months their activity generated over one hundred articles and letters to the press and a petition with 10,700 signatures. Faced with this massive opposition, the consortium withdrew its application in March 1996.

Why was the Hilton project approved and the Munxar consortium defeated? Was this a victory for the democratic process? The short answer is that much suggests that major political figures in both the Nationalist government and the Labour opposition backed the Hilton project. In a country as small as Malta, crosscutting ties are frequent and unavoidable and there were intimate links between the developer and leading figures in the two main political parties (Boissevain and Theuma 1998).[3] The Hilton developer had also spent several years honing the project with the planning authority.

The Munxar project, on the other hand, did not have the same local bipartisan political and financial backing. There were no major Maltese political and financial interests involved with the Munxar scheme and the developers had had little contact with the planning authority. NGO and public protest was allowed to run its course and the venture was withdrawn. The conclusion must be that if a project is backed by powerful financial and political interests, it will probably be approved by an ostensibly independent planning authority. On the other hand, if NGO protest is tolerated, well-organized action may sometimes be able to combat such projects successfully.

Conclusion

It is evident that where host communities perceive that their cultural and environmental heritage is threatened by tourism they often take protective action. Clearly such action is not always successful. It is usually undertaken by individuals or NGOs. Governments are rarely proactive. Initially, authorities usually take the part of the tourist industry. Although often defeated in the short run, there is evidence that sustained campaigning does achieve results in the long run. Maltese officials were quite rattled by the scale of support for the campaigns against the Hilton and Munxar projects.

After 30 years of extensive laissez-faire tourist development and three years of sustained NGO protests, the Ministry of Tourism in 1998 finally carried out a tourist carrying capacity assessment. Equally important, a representative of Friends of the Earth (Malta) was included on the board of experts supervising this research. This was the first time that the Ministry of Tourism included a representative of an environmental NGO on one of its advisory boards. Slowly but surely it seems that the efforts of civil society to cope with mass tourism is obliging government to consider its dark side.[4]

Source: From *Dziedzictwo a Turystyka (Heritage and Tourism)*, 1999. Reprinted with permission of the author and The International Cultural Centre in Cracow, Poland. This chapter was originally presented as a paper at the 1998 "Heritage and Tourism" conference sponsored by the Centre.

Notes

[1] This section is largely based on Boissevain 1996a:14–20.

[2] Personal communication from Antionio Miguel Nogués Pedregal, 1.5.97.

[3] What we found particularly interesting was the degree of cooperation, even intimacy, between planning authority experts and the developer (Boissevain and Theuma forthcoming). Perhaps this is not surprising since they had been working together on the project for several years. But still it was most instructive to discover that the developer's legal advisor was also the legal advisor of the planning authority (*Front Kontra il-Hilton* 1997a:6)— although the planning authority maintained it had not consulted him on the Hilton project (Planning Authority 1997:32)—and to learn that the developer had added the following personal note to a fax he sent to the planning authority case officer handling the project who at the time was chairman of the Fund Raising Committee of the Malta Hospice Movement (*Front Kontra il-Hilton* 1997a:7–8): "Dear Chris, I gladly (sic) enclose a donation of LM 2,000 for the Hospice movement which is so close to your heart. George."

[4] "Almost all of the most significant environmental issues, global or domestic, were crystallized first not by governments responding to or using 'science,' but by poorly resourced NGOs and sundry individual environmentalists" (Grove-White 1993:20).

References

Black, Annabel. 1996. "Negotiating the Tourist Gaze: The Example of Malta," in *Coping with Tourists: European Reactions to Mass Tourism*, ed. Jeremy Boissevain, pp. 112–142. Providence/Oxford: Berghahn Books.

Boissevain, Jeremy. 1989. "Tourism as Anti-Structure," in *Kulturanthropologisch. Ein Festschrift für Ina-Maria Greverus*, Notizien Nr. 30, ed. C. Giordano, et al., pp. 145–159. Frankfurt: University of Frankfurt.

———. 1992a. "Introduction: Revitalizing European Rituals, in *Revitalizing European Rituals*, ed. Jeremy Boissevain, pp. 1–19. London: Routledge.

———. 1992b. "Play and Identity: Ritual Change in a Maltese Village," in *Revitalizing European Rituals*, ed. Jeremy Boissevain, pp. 136–154. London: Routledge.

———. 1996a. "Introduction," in *Coping with Tourists: European Reactions to Mass Tourism*, ed. Jeremy Boissevain, pp. 1–26. Providence/Oxford: Berghahn Books.

———. 1996b. "'But We Live Here!' Perspectives on Cultural Tourism in Malta," in *Sustainable Tourism in Islands and Small States: Case Studies*, ed. Lino Briguglio et al., pp. 220–240. London: Pinter.

————. 1996c. "Ritual, Tourism and Cultural Commoditization: Culture by the Pound?" in *The Tourist Image: Myths and Myth Making in Tourism*, ed. Tom Selwyn, pp. 105–120. Chichester: Wiley & Sons.

————. 1998. "Hidden Rituals: Protecting Culture from the Tourist Gaze." in *Roots and Rituals: The Construction of Ethnic Identities*, ed. Ton Dekker, John Helsloot, and Carla Wijers, pp. 733–747. Amsterdam: Het Spinhuis.

Boissevain, Jeremy, and Nadia Sammut. 1994. *Mdina: Its Residents and Cultural Tourism: Findings and Recommendations*. (Report) Malta: Med-Campus Euromed Sustainable Tourism Network, University of Malta.

Boissevain, Jeremy, and Nadia Theuma. 1996. "Contested Space: Tourism, Heritage and Identity in Malta." Paper for the workshop, *Development, Identity Creation and Sentiments*. Biennial EASA Conference, Barcelona, July 12–15, 1996.

————. 1998. "Contested Space: Planners, Tourists, Developers and Environmentalists in Malta," in *Anthropological Perspectives on Local Development*, ed. Simone Abram and Jacqueline Waldren, pp. 96–119. London: Routledge.

————. 1999. "Jak sibie radzic z turystami? Stragie dzialania (Coping with Mass Cultural Tourism: Structure and Strategies)," in *Dziedzictwo a tyrystyka*, ed. Jacek Purchla, pp. 65– 79. Kraków: Miedzynarodowe Centrum Kultury.

Bowman, Glenn. 1996. "Passion, Power and Politics in a Palestinian Tourist Market," in *Chasing Myths: Essays in the Anthropology of Tourism*, ed. Tom Selwyn. New York: John Wiley.

Crain, Mary M. 1996. "Contested Territories: The Politics of Touristic Development at the Shrine of El Rocío in Southwestern Andalusia," in *Coping with Tourists: European Reactions to Mass Tourism*, ed. Jeremy Boissevain, pp. 27–55. Providence/Oxford: Berghahn Books.

Davis, Natalie Z. 1975. *Women on Top: Society and Culture in Early Modern France*. London: Duckwork, pp. 125–151.

Evans-Pritchard, Deirdre. 1989. "How 'They' See 'Us': Native American Images of Tourists." *Annals of Tourism Research* 16:89–105.

Fenech, Natalino. 1992. *Fatal Flight: The Maltese Obsession with Killing Birds*. London: P. Quiller.

Front Kontra il-Hilton. 1997a. *Report on the files relating to the granting of Planning Permission to Spinola Development Co. Ltd. for the Hilton Project*. Malta: Front Kontra il-Hilton, March, 1997.

————. 1997b. *Reply to the Planning Authority's comments on our report of 23rd March 1997 regarding planning permission given to Spinola Development Co. Ltd. for the Hilton Project*. Malta: Front Kontra il-Hilton, 29 March, 1997.

Graburn, N. 1983. "The Anthropology of Tourism." *Annals of Tourism Research* 10:9–33.

————. 1989. "Tourism: The Sacred Journey," in *Hosts and Guests: The Anthropology of Tourism*, 2nd edition, ed. V. Smith, pp. 21–36. Philadelphia: University of Pennsylvania Press.

Greenwood, Davydd. 1989. "Culture by the Pound: An Anthropological Perspective on Tourism as Cultural Commoditization," in *Hosts and Guests: The Anthropology of Tourism*, 2nd edition, ed. Valene Smith, pp. 171–185. Philadelphia: University of Pennsylvania Press.

Grove-White, R. 1993. "Environmentalism: A New Moral Discourse for Technological Society," in *Environmentalism: The View from Anthropology*, ed. K. Milton. London/New York: Routledge.

Kenna, Margaret E. 1992. "Mattresses and Migrants: A Patron Saint's Festival on a Small Greek Island over Two Decades," in *Revitalizing European Rituals*, ed. Jeremy Boissevain, pp. 155–172. London: Routledge.

Leach, E. 1964. *Rethinking Anthropology.* London: Athlone Press, University of London.

Lett, J. W. 1983. "Ludic and Liminoid Aspects of Charter Yacht Tourism in the Caribbean." *Annals of Tourism Research* 10(1):35–56.

MacCannell, Dean. 1976. *The Tourist: A New Theory of the Leisure Class.* New York: Schocken Books.

———. 1984. "Reconstructed Ethnicity: Tourism and Cultural Identity in Third World Communities." *Annals of Tourism Research* 11:375–391.

Nogués Pedregal, Antonio Miguel. 1996. "Tourism and Self-Consciousness in a South Spanish Coastal Community," in *Coping with Tourists: European Reactions to Mass Tourism,* ed. Jeremy Boissevain, pp. 56–83. Providence/Oxford: Berghahn Books.

Odermatt, Peter. 1996. "Case of Neglect? The Politics of (Re)presentation: a Sardinian Case," in *Coping with Tourists: European Reactions to Mass Tourism,* ed. Jeremy Boissevain, pp. 84–111. Providence/Oxford: Berghahn Books.

Ombudsman. 1997. *Land Development by Spinola Development Co. Ltd. (The Hilton Project). Report on Case No. 1398.* Malta: Office of the Ombudsman, February 1997.

Poppi, Cesare. 1992. "Building Differences: The Political Economy of Tradition in the Laden Carnival of the Val di Fassa," in *Revitalizing European Rituals,* ed. Jeremy Boissevain, pp. 113–136. London: Routledge.

Planning Authority. 1997. *Hilton Redevelopment Project: Response to Report from "Front Kontra il-Hilton."* Malta: Planning Authority.

Puijk, Roel. 1996. "Dealing with Fish and Tourists: A Case Study from Northern Norway," in *Coping with Tourists. European Reactions to Mass Tourism,* ed. Jeremy Boissevain, pp. 204–226. Providence/Oxford: Berghahn Books.

Scott, James. 1985. *Weapons of the Weak: Everyday Forms of Peasant Resistance.* New Haven: Yale University Press.

Sharrock, David. 1998. "Tourist Louts Force Consul to Quit." *The Guardian,* G-2 (August 31): 2.

Smith, Valene L. 1989a. "Introduction," in *Hosts and Guests. The Anthropology of Tourism,* 2nd edition, ed. Valene L. Smith, pp. 1–17. Philadelphia: University of Pennsylvania Press.

———. 1989b. "Eskimo Tourism: Micro-Models and Marginal Men," in *Hosts and Guests. The Anthropology of Tourism,* 2nd edition, ed. Valene L. Smith, pp. 55–82. Philadelphia: University of Pennsylvania Press.

Sweet, J. D. 1989. "Burlesquing 'The Other' in Pueblo Performance." *Annals of Tourism Research* 16:62–75.

Turner, Victor. 1969. *The Ritual Process: Structure and Anti-Structure.* Ithaca: Cornell University Press.

Urry, John. 1990. *The Tourist Gaze: Leisure and Travel in Contemporary Societies.* London: Sage.

van den Berghe, Pierre L. 1994. *The Quest for the Other: Ethnic Tourism in San Cristobal, Mexico.* Seattle: University of Washington Press.

van den Berghe, Pierre L., and C. F. Keyes. 1984. "Introduction: Tourism and Re-created Ethnicity." *Annals of Tourism Research* 11:343–352.

Wood, R. E. 1984. "Ethnic Tourism, the State, and Cultural Change in Southeast Asia." *Annals of Tourism Research* 11:353–374.

Zinovieff, S. 1991. "Hunters and Hunted: *Kamaki* and the Ambiguities of Sexual Predation in a Greek Town," in *Contested Identities: Gender and Kinship in Modern Greece,* ed. Peter Loizos and E. Papataxiarchis, pp. 203–220. Princeton: Princeton University Press.

16

Tourism and Its Discontents: Suri-Tourist Encounters in Ethiopia

Jon G. Abbink

Tourism as an "Avant-garde" of Globalization

The tourism "industry" is the largest business in the world, and has, apart from its economic significance, a growing social and cultural impact on the local societies and places visited. The transformative role of tourist activity in society and culture deserves closer attention. In its present form, tourism is the expression of a particular kind of consumer identity with a notable globalizing impact. It emanates largely from societies that are relatively powerful and wealthy. Communities and places visited by tourists undergo unforeseen changes due to these foreign visitors' unrelenting presence. While both positive and negative aspects can be recognized, in most cases a process of skewed or unequal exchanges between tourists and locals is evident, though these need more extensive empirical study in emerging contexts of globalization (which is here defined as a transformative process of intensified contacts—via mass and electronic media and migration—between human collectivities and communities in the economic, political, and cultural domains, forging new and more pervasive interrelations and dependency between social and cultural units of varying scale).

This article is a reflection on the encounter of foreign tourists with the Suri or Surma[1] people of southern Ethiopia, a relatively small ethnic group only recently "discovered" by the tourist industry. Next to describing the encroachment of tourism among these people, I intend to give a cultural critique of tourism, developed on the basis of Suri views. Seeing tourists at work was a phenomenon that initially rather disturbed me while doing field research.[2] The first question, of course, might be why an ethnographer should at all feel disturbed. Some critics will jump in to say: "Because there are "hidden similarities" between tourists and anthropologists, as affluent Westerners or uninvited guests, among a culturally different group—similarities that generate some kind of guilt and insecurity about the epistemological basis of the latter's research activities." We can respond to such a remark with a qualified yes: there is, on one level, indeed a similarity in that the tourist visit and the ethnographic praxis are both strategies for "framing the exotic" (Harkin 1995:667). But on this trivial level anthropologists can also be said to share characteristics with pilgrims, businessmen, or missionaries, or anybody entering for him/her a new social setting—a not uncommon experience for people also in their own society. Furthermore, this argument leaves us little wiser about *what is actually happening* in such "intercultural encounters," about their different shapes, or about their historicity.[3] An anthropological understanding of tourist-"native" interactions needs to aim at explaining the preconditions, the structure and meaning of the tourist encounter, with reference to the interests and cultural models that are articulated in that setting.

In many respects, tourism imposes itself as a dominant global "exotopic strategy" (Harkin 1995) to deal with cultural difference. Due to its ubiquitous presence in the media, in advertising, and in international business, the discourse of travel and tourism tends to exclude or push away other viewpoints. It can be said to be a hegemonic system of representation that may function as part of an (unconscious) *ideology* of globalization. As such, tourism deserves much more empirical and theoretical exploration, as Nash (1996:179) has suggested in a recent overview. However, in contrast with previous tourism studies ". . . the voice of the other [i.e., those visited by the tourists] needs to be given its due" (196). In this article, responses of the Suri people toward tourists will be developed.

The Suri, an agropastoralist group of about 28,000 people in the utmost southwest of Ethiopia, are an interesting case because of the fact that not their geographical area or natural setting (rivers, forests, mountains, game parks, etc.) but *they themselves* are the prime attraction for the tourists:[4] as a "real primitive, untouched tribe." This is how they are advertised. The Suri are indeed a marginal group in Ethiopia, and, although faced with manifold problems, retain a high degree of sociocultural integrity. But any idea of their being untouched or isolated is incorrect. They have been involved in wide-ranging regional trade-flows of cattle, gold, arms, ivory, and game products at least since the late nineteenth century and have, for the past two decades, been affected by the Sudanese civil war and by Ethiopian state efforts to incorporate them politically, economically, and socially. The production of their reputation of "primitiveness" and "remoteness" is in the first instance a phenomenon or problem to be explained from the perspective of the tourists, since they are the consumers of images of "authentic experience" and of "exoticism" that are carefully screened and constructed. These images function as commodities like any other and a growing part of the tourist industry is thriving on them. In exploring some aspects of the tourist encounter, this article will contend that especially when people instead of nature or buildings are the object of such commoditized images, tourism often leads to friction or conflict.

The Semiotics of Tourism

Theorizing on tourism has been done within a variety of frameworks, among them, neo-Marxism (MacCannell, 1976, 1984), semiotics (Culler 1981; Harkin 1995; Urry 1990), and cultural psychology. It is less interesting to present a list of possible motives of tourist behavior, such as nostalgia, quest for the unknown, breaking the daily routine, rediscovery of the self, etc.,[5] than to inquire into some of its formal, systematic aspects. Recognizing that there are several different types of tourists or "modes" of tourist experience (cf. Cohen 1979:183), it might be possible to identify some of these formal aspects. In this respect we follow some leads of Michael Harkin's very interesting semiotic approach (Harkin 1995).

In a semiotic perspective one can say that tourist experiences, especially of tourists of the type discussed in this paper, are initially marked by an ". . . anxiety about authenticity" (653). Tourists expect a kind of credibility and genuineness about the objects, places, and people they visit. Tourists expect the latter to be contained in a system . . . "whereby a set of signs marks the object as authentic," so that their attention can be focused (653). The tourists can thus be given an orientation vis-à-vis their own framework of familiarity related to their own society. In other words, the alterity of the other landscape or the other people should be appropriated (655). This implies a hegemonic strategy, domesticating the exotic (656). This semiotic enterprise, of course heavily supported by photography (see below), is evidence of the search of tourists for predictability in a context of new meanings. Culture difference as such is not problematic in such a scheme, but it should be marked clearly. The tourists expect such a minimal semiotic frame wherever they go.

Identity and Difference in the Contested Field of Global Encounters

In the encounter of Suri and tourists, extremes meet. Suri have always been at the margins of the Ethiopian state, even though they nominally have belonged to it since 1898. They were wary of outsiders—Ethiopian soldiers, traders and administrators, Italian colonizers, and visiting white tourists. A politically and economically largely self-sufficient society, they always tried to assert their way of life and group identity toward others. Questions of identity and difference have thus been a vital issue in all their relations with non-Suri.

In the past decade, the Suri have been visited not by mass tourism but by a "select" crowd of tourists who have seen all the regular mass-tourist destinations and who like to think of themselves as "adventurers and explorers." In the 1980s, a few travel agencies in Italy, the United States, and Germany (and several expatriate Italian and American travel agents with an office in Addis Ababa) started advertising the Suri as a destination for this category of "explorer"-tourists. This attracted small groups of Western and later also Japanese and other tourists for an adventurous or exotic vacation "off the beaten track." In the case of the Italians, one travel agency used a slogan indicating that the tourists could retrace the historical routes of some nineteenth-century Italian explorers of southern Ethiopia (like Cecchi, Vannutelli, Citerni, and Bottego). The reputation of the remarkably informative 1938 *Guida dell'Africa Italiana Orientale*, the publication of which was one of the first acts of the Italian occupation force in the country to legitimize and "normalize" its presence there, also played a significant role in creating Ethiopia as an Italian "tourist destination" (Consoziazione Turistica Italiana 1938). Tours were booked on which the visitors could take a plane to the grass air-strip near the small capital of the southwestern Maji district (the airstrip marked with a sign saying "The Wonderland Route," put there by a tourist agency) and then make a walking excursion with pack-mules and native porters into the Suri area. There the tourists lodged in tents, looked at the local people, took photographs of them, and engaged in some typical tourist bartering for material objects (the Suri lip-plates and ear-discs) as souvenirs. After spending a few days they left as they had come.

As we can see, the tourist interest in the Suri is undoubtedly based in part on "exoticism," the idea of going to a remote, isolated wilderness area "where hardly any whites had set foot" and where people are assumed to live in "pristine conditions of nature." This may go back to the renewed fascination in the (post) modern industrial world with the "radical others" outside industrial culture—and this time, due to the techno-economic conditions of globalization, it can be pursued as a mass-phenomenon. There is also a lingering heritage of the colonial gaze. As Bruner and Kirshenblatt-Gimblett note: "Tourism gives tribalism and colonialism a second life by bringing them back as representations of themselves and circulating them within an economy of performance" (1994:435). In the early eighties—before the tourist influx—the Suri were already known to a wider public, through folklore and tourist-guide texts,[6] as an exotic, strange, primitive people at the ends of Ethiopia (which was in itself a relatively unknown tourist destination). The Suri appearance was also fascinating: the women and girls wore big clay or wooden discs in their pierced lower lip and earlobes, and the virtually naked males had fine physiques and remarkable body scarifications and decorations made with bright natural paints.[7]

The coffee-table book and *National Geographic* article by photographers Beckwith and Fisher of 1990 and 1991 summarize this image of difference in a telling way. Their work contains a series of excellent photographs of the Suri, albeit only on some aspects of their way of life. The pictures evoke the impression of a very out-of-the-way and self-contained "happy" culture of complete African "others," in a somewhat romanticized way. The shots also appeal to the image of a remote, well integrated, and proud culture—almost the "noble savage" of old—and indeed, they help to *create* this

Young Suri woman with clay lip plate in Korum, Ethiopia. (Photo by Jon Abbink)

image. We see here a typical contemporary representation of a "tribal group" for the public eye of modern-industrial society, the genre of the exoticist, postcolonial photography of "natives." Needless to say, apart from granting that they may contain useful information and evoke fascination, what the pictures convey to us is incomplete.[8] They are not meant to be informative and analytic, but primarily evocative and aesthetic. We see that the image created by them is—as always with visual representations—in large part a reflection of the preoccupation or selective interests of the observers. As the photographic evocation of the Suri makes clear, both in professional and tourist form, difference and contrastive identity are essential elements in the encounter of opposites. Indeed, there is no effort, or indeed intention, by either Suri or tourist to come to a "mutual exchange" or an "understanding" between tourist and "native" except a purely businesslike one, even if the wish thereto may on occasion be rhetorically expressed (the photographic act is a major ingredient of the touristic appropriation of the Suri, a point further discussed below).

The inherent bias in the representation of the Suri, and of the tourist-Suri relationship (particularly acute in their case, as we shall see) is of course neither new nor surprising. It is rooted in the very encounter of "whites and natives" in non-Western parts of the world, conditioned as it is by tacit epistemological canons of colonial experience or a still in essence colonializing gaze. The Horn of Africa is no exception. A brief historical retrospect makes this clear.

The Image of the Suri Since 1897

Following the various, scarce descriptions of the Suri in travel and colonial literature, one sees that the image of "primitiveness" was an inherent ideological element of the colonial penetration of the Sudan-Kenya-Ethiopia borderlands from the start.

The first to mention the Suri was the Russian officer A. K. Bulatovitch who was traveling with a contingent of Ethiopian emperor Menilik II's army on a campaign in the Southern Käfa area in January–April 1898 (see Bulatovitch 1900, 1902). There they met a people resembling, he said, the "Sciuro" (in reality they were the *Me'en*, a neighboring agropastoral people).[9] However, the author notes that the natives extracted their lower incisors, and the inserting of lip and ear discs by the women he described is even now a distinctive custom of the Suri.

After Bulatovitch, the Suri are mentioned again in an article by a member of the British border demarcation commission in 1909. C. Gwynn met someone he called the "chief of the tribe" at Turmu, an escarpment north of Mt. Naita, a big border mountain between Sudan and Ethiopia. He described the tribe's women as wearing "indescribably hideous" wooden or leather discs in the lower lip (Gwynn 1911:127). Like all travelers after them, these two European observers felt the need to comment on the lip-plate custom and its, for them, unaesthetic appearance. This physical detail overrides all other information on this group, and emphasizing it has set a pattern reflected in all popular articles and tourist brochures written about them since, including the article and book by Beckwith and Fisher (1990; 1991).

From 1936 to 1941, Fascist Italy occupied Ethiopia and reports on the Suri came from Italian visiting travelers/businessmen or researchers.[10] The mining engineer C. Viezzer was probably the first to describe them and to publish photographs.[11] He pictures the Suri as a group living in very "primitive conditions," without cattle, cultivating poorly with primitive tools (Viezzer 1938:424–425). He praises their colorful body-painting and general physique, but predictably abhors the female custom of inserting wooden or clay lip-plates in the lower lip. He was one of the first to take photographs of this decoration, thus initiating the act so often repeated by visitors and tourists today. Viezzer also describes some rituals he observed, such as the spectacular burial of the wife of a chief. The language of the Tirmaga strikes him as primitive: ". . . suoni gutturali, animaleschi, assolutamente incomprehensibile" (425). His picture of the Tirmaga-Suri is, of course, very incomplete and characterized by a predominantly negative or condescending evaluation of their way of life, fed by the author's own ignorance of how such a society works.

F. Rizetto (1941) also stayed among the (Tirmaga-) Suri, but for a longer period. His report contains more factual information on the group and adds some qualifications about their character as a people. One can frequently hear an echo of his remarks on "Suri character" among their present-day highland neighbors. For example, Rizetto notes, perhaps echoing local highland dwellers' opinion, that they are "ignorant, violent, thievish, arrogant and revengeful" (1204). But, he says, they are also proud of their country and their freedom. They go naked, but are generally of good build and health (1204). They live isolated, in blissful ignorance of the world outside, and on a primitive, timeless level (1205, 1209).

In 1938, the Suri were studied by M. Marchetti, an Italian working for a private company at the time. He passed four months in the Suri area and describes their three original subgroups, then known as Tirma, T'id, and Zilmamo, in fairly detailed terms. Marchetti, though no social scientist, is the first to try to present a more balanced, matter-of-fact survey of Suri society, refraining from extreme evaluative statements about their character or level of cultural or intellectual development. He gives information on settlement patterns, cultivation practices, material culture, ornaments, food consumption, supernatural beliefs and customs related to marriage, burial, and, what he called, the "stick fight." Nevertheless, toward the end the author concludes his description with remarks about the "low level of social life" of the Suri, who are also ". . . assolutamente infantile come mentalità ed intelligenzia" (e.g., their counting system "was underdeveloped") and they have ". . . una lingua assai semplice," their speech accompanied by expressive mimic, and often repeating words (Marchetti 1938:71). They are said to lack an oral his-

torical tradition transmitted from parents to children—they only retain memory of the most recent events (71). Despite a good start, we again see the
account ending in questionable, evaluative statements on the basis of outsider
values, not very informative about Suri culture itself.

After 1941 there were few foreign or Ethiopian visitors in the Suri
area. The Ethiopian government had a nominal presence until 1988 (when
the few police and soldiers left the area), some intermittent tax collection,
and a short-lived American mission post in the 1960s with an elementary
school (up to fourth grade) and a small clinic. None of these episodes left
any lasting imprint on the local society, and no reports are available from this
period up to 1990.

The Suri have been part of a neglected and marginal region of Ethiopia,
without roads, facilities, and government services. The area was viewed as a
poor and unhealthy malarial lowland, where no Ethiopian would go of his
own free will. The Suri people were considered to be "uncivilized nomads"
without fixed abode. The Maji area served as a place of internal exile. Under
the Mengistu-government (1977–1991), army commanders who had failed in
the civil war were sent there to spend their days as civil servants. In the wider
regional context, however, the Suri were never isolated. In the early decades
of this century, they were connected to the cattle, game, and ivory trade in
Ethiopia and Kenya. In the 1980s they smuggled in automatic weapons from
Sudan and got involved in the gold trade (panned in rivers in southern Ethiopia) and in a network of Sudanese and Ethiopian traders. During the past

A ceremonial stick duel in progress among the Chari Suri. (Photo by Jon Abbink)

decade, a closer involvement of Suri with the Ethiopian authorities is notable (Abbink 2002).

In the early 1980s the Suri were "rediscovered" as a piece in what was stereotypically known as the "museum of peoples" of Ethiopia.[12] Some tourist agencies started organizing individual or small group trips to the Maji area, including the Suri country. Some of the tourists came with a guide of the Ethiopian National Tour Operators (NTO, a state agency), some with a personal guide from a private travel agency. Recent travel guidebooks on Ethiopia make mention of the "colorful" Suri people, describing their primitive material conditions but also their body paintings, lip- and ear-plates, and their spectacular ritual stick-dueling contests. Practical conditions for the tourists were difficult, but this was part of the attraction: to chart an allegedly unexplored culture at the margins of civilized society.

In fact, tourist trips regularly had to be cancelled due to security reasons. Until this day, foreign visitors, upon arrival in the area, may be officially forbidden by the local authorities to go down to the Suri due to fear of disturbances.[13] Nevertheless, during the 1990s, several hundreds of tourists visited the Suri, and this flow will continue in the near future.

The Suri and the Tourist: Exchanges and Confrontations

The interaction of Suri and tourists is more of a "confrontation" than normal social interaction. Obviously, the language difference is the first problem. The Suri are monolingual, and the Ethiopian guides do not speak the Suri language. "Conversation" is carried out by means of gesticulation and shouting. Prior to contact with tourists, the Suri had only known white foreigners in the shape of Italian soldiers in the 1930s and American missionaries in the 1960s. Their experience with them was much better than with the tourists, basically because, as some Suri said, ". . . they were there for a long time" [several years] and ". . . tried to get along with us. They traded things, like food-stuff, cattle, sheep, and tried to talk with us." However, the Suri quickly found out that the tourists of today were quite different from these earlier foreigners. Below, we look at the interaction from the two ends of the dyad.

The Suri View

The response of Suri, both men and women and the older and the younger generation, is remarkably similar. No doubt, the tourist presence will, in the near future, create a subgroup of Suri youngsters that can make a living on it and thus will suppress any feelings of disdain. But at present, the Suri are rather uniform in their display of bewilderment and irritation toward the foreign visitors. Two kinds of behavior strike the Suri as most characteristic of the tourists: their taking photographs all the time, and their behaving in a childish, rude, and incomprehensible way, to the point of being bizarre.

Photography is of course a quintessential activity or posture of a tourist. It was noted by Susan Sontag in her pioneering book *On Photography,* that from the point of view of the tourist, the ". . . very activity of taking pictures is soothing, and assuages general feelings of disorientation that are likely to be exacerbated by travel. Most tourists feel compelled to put the camera between themselves and whatever is remarkable that they encounter" (1977:10). While this is true in a general sense for all sorts of tourists, in the case of the explorer-tourists among the Suri, there is the desire for "authentic documentation" of the otherness of these people (and occasionally for commercially marketable pictures).[14] However, Sontag has definitely hit on a defining element of the tourist: as a traveling person s/he wants to make sense of his/her experience, and needs to "frame" it in some way, and to relate it to his/her own world. This calls to mind Harkin's analysis (see above) of the tourist experience as a quest for framing and structuration of meaning through the management of a set of signs rooted in the tourist's own life-world.

One aspect of the photographic act is especially pertinent to the Suri case. As Susan Sontag has noted: "To photograph is to appropriate the thing photographed. It means putting oneself into a certain relation to the world that feels like knowledge—and therefore, like power" (1977:4). The Suri being photographed are aware of this more than any other people and act accordingly: they say that no one should have this power over them, or if so, it should be compensated for by means of an appropriate monetary transaction.

Sontag also made the by now very familiar point that there ". . . is an aggression implicit in every use of the camera" (7). This is easy to observe in Suri-tourist exchanges. If an argument comes up over a specific photographing act, as is often the case, reactions very often take on an aggressive form: people are manhandled and those photographed try to get hold of the camera. In the case of one Japanese tourist group visiting in 1989, cameras were forcibly taken from them, thrown on the rocks, and destroyed. Suri irritation at cameras and photographing has nothing to do with the fear often ascribed to non-Western people that their "soul" or "well-being" is being taken away. Nothing of the kind. In this as in other things, the Suri are rationalists; they are well aware of how a camera works and what comes out of it. They only resent being "turned into an image or a souvenir" (9) that is taken away, and being limited in their interaction as adult humans with tourists they thought were other adult humans.

During fieldwork, observing interactions between tourists and Suri—always stunted because of translation problems and the insecure interpretation of gestures—I often noted Suri responses like the following: "You are not going to shoot me just like that, first give me the green leaves! [money]."[15] "For every one of us in the picture you pay us one note, now!" Turning toward me they said: ". . . Are they all like that, bothering us before they have done their duty and given us things? Tell them to cooperate!" "What is their aim, what is it they do? If we are being fooled, we will not allow any picture taken here!" "Can we deal with people who behave unfair?"

Such remarks illustrate the Suri dislike of the absence of equal exchange with the tourists. The apparent value tourists attach to taking pictures of them, but not taking their time and not communicating to them bred deep irritation. Suri often forbade tourists outright from taking pictures or even sitting in their village; they also asked what they knew were outrageous prices for some of their cultural items (lip plates, wooden stools, leather decorations, calabashes) when tourists expressed any interest to buy them. In doing so the Suri also ridiculed the tourists' wish to have everything. For instance, some tourists even wanted the special ivory bracelets worn by male members of the chiefly clan, but did not know that these can never be sold, and even if they heard about this would not desist.

Similar abrasive responses have been noted among the Mursi, the people neighboring the Suri, who are culturally very much alike. For instance, in response to his question of what they thought that tourists were doing, the anthropologist D. Turton quotes the following remarks from Mursi friends: "*You* tell us: why do they shoot [photograph] us? . . . They can't speak our language so we can't ask them why they are doing it. . . . They come with Ethiopian guides who just sit in cars. When the tourists have taken their photos they drive off. We say: 'Is it just that they want to know who we are, or what?' We say: 'They must be people who don't know how to behave.' Even old women come and totter about taking photos. 'Is that the way whites normally behave?' That's what we say. Goloñimeri [the Mursi name for Turton], what are they doing? Do they want us to become their children, or what? What do they do with the photographs?" Finally: "This photography business comes from your country—where the necklace beads grow. You whites are the culprits. Give us a car and we'll go and take pictures of you" (Turton 1994:286).[16] The only difference between Mursi and Suri is perhaps that the latter are in general more annoyed and aggressive in actually demanding money for the photographs, and also actively obstruct their being photographed if the tourists try to duck payment.

Photography is an essential element of the tourist gaze (cf. Urry 1990:140)—it expresses the token appropriation of the objects, landscapes, or people. The photographic act thus illustrates the underlying tourist concern with the visual, the aesthetic representation of experience. Here lies the link with the characteristic tourist desire for the consuming of ever-new images and experiences and that makes him/her the quintessential expression of postmodern consumer identity. As Sontag already noted, ". . . Needing to have reality confirmed and experience enhanced by photographs is an aesthetic consumerism to which everyone is now addicted" (1977:24). In semiotic terms, for the tourist the picture becomes not only the visual sign of "having been there" but also of having captured the "reality" of the signified.

In the literature it has often been remarked that tourist behavior exemplifies license, a release from everyday obligations and norms—"liminal" behavior (cf. Urry 1990:10). The manners and "civilizational standards" of tourists sometimes may or may not be greatly at variance with local mores, especially in very divergent cross-cultural settings. But the very structure of the encounter is a determining factor in bringing out behavior among tourists that is beyond "normal" bounds. The temporality, displacement, language difference, and perception of "distance" seem to cancel out the need for meaningful or respectful social contact, or some element of reciprocity. In the tourist game, a relationship is a commodity, and as the fleeting encounter of people will not ever be repeated, freedom from reciprocal norms seems guaranteed. Restraint or respect according to the local norms is secondary. The people visited are, so to speak, just part of the landscape, not meaningful social partners: a landscape cannot (and should not) have an opinion about people, as Nietzsche once said. But what is usually not treated in much detail in the literature on tourist-native interaction is the *actual* behavior of tourists in their contacts with locals and the effect this has on the latter.

From numerous interviews and observations I noted that the Suri and other local people neighboring them (Dizi and village people, who usually act as guides and porters for the tourists) are always amazed if not shocked by the "dirty," "uncontrolled," and "shameless" demeanor of the tourists. For example, they fart in public without inhibition, they urinate and defecate in plain sight of the porters and the local people, males and females demonstratively kiss and embrace each other in public, others frequently argue and shout to each other, often the couples. They also quickly show anger and other emotions, like children. This is all contrary to local standards of decent or adult behavior. Perhaps this kind of behavior is in principle still unacceptable, or at least questionable, in the tourists' own society as well. But the point is that here, in the "liminal phase" that trekking represents, tourists think they can afford to dispense with ordinary standards and manners because they suppose the natives have no such manners either. These "natives," however, were offended time and again, and their former image of the "polite" or "developed" foreigner became seriously dented. As a result, scorn and disdain are becoming the dominant feelings toward foreigners. Originally, Suri (and Mursi) approached white foreigners with some kind of awe or respect, expressed in their using the term *barári*, which means "having power" or "being hot," in the sense of "dangerous."[17] Today, this word is never used for any tourist.

The Tourist View

The other end of the dyad, the point of view of the tourists, must also be looked at. Here, the effect of the encounter is also upsetting. The main reason is that the Suri do not behave as the tourist frame of reference would expect them to behave. If the tourist encounter is seen as a kind of ritual, i.e. as a form of "scripted play" with some predictability or at least markedness, then the Suri do not give evidence of wanting to recognize that script. Numerous incidents illustrate this pattern. I take a few from observations and interviews with tourists in 1990–1994. The baseline in all these stories is the feeling of deception, indignation, and anger.

- In 1994 one group of Italian tourists came to a village to meet the Suri but was sent back after refusing to pay money for photographs and the daily "tourist tax." They claimed they had already paid that money (and money for their visas) to the NTO. They were adamant, but so were the Suri. As the latter had automatic rifles, the Italians did not insist and went back without having taken any pictures.

- In another incident in 1994, a small group of German tourists were threatened at gunpoint to give money, medicines, clothes, and razor blades. Some girls in the group panicked and dramatically started begging the Suri men not to shoot. Others started crying. In a state of shock they left the area.

- One elderly American couple with a private guide whom I met shortly after their return from the Suri area in 1995 told me about their utter disappointment and indignation about having been subjected to constant shouting and pushing by the Suri, who incessantly demanded money and other things. They said that they had cut short their visit among them, and that they ". . . had never met such impolite and rude behavior anywhere in the world."

- A Belgian tourist who was in the area in late 1994 was asked to pay huge sums of money because of his desire to take hundreds of photographs. His main interest was, as he phrased it to me, ". . . to see and photograph naked tribesmen in their original state, untouched by outside civilization." He stated that he loved the country and people, and would stay long among them. But finally he just had to pay up, and only then could move through the area. Afterward, he expressed to me his disappointment and his indignation at the efforts and financial sacrifices that he had to make to get his pictures. He said he loathed the Suri for their extreme monetary greed, and would never visit them again.

- In 1990, a group of about twenty Japanese tourists were bathing in the Kibish River in Suri territory. When they came out, they found that all their clothes, cameras, and bags had been stolen. Great indignation. No Suri claimed to have seen the thieves. After long deliberations with some local Suri spokesmen, some of the things were recovered. The tourists quickly left the Suri area, baffled and disturbed.

In Ethiopian terms, the Suri are exceptional in their response to tourists. Indeed, no group in Ethiopia routinely demands a sum of money from foreigners who come to visit them. In 1996, the Suri asked 150 *birr* (about

US$25) per tourist per day to be paid to their newly founded local "Surma Council," in addition to the money to be paid for individual photographs.[18] Nor do they mind being assertive, even aggressive, in their dealings with foreigners who come there for a few days. They say that this is their own country, so the people who visit them should pay just for being there, and they do not trust the motives of the tourists. Few local populations harass or threaten the tourists during their actual "meeting": in most places the "realist illusion" is somehow kept up because of the material benefits that accrue. Obviously, Suri also want the material benefits, driven by a logic introduced or made acutely relevant by the tourist presence, but underneath their attitude lies a deep irritation about the perceived power difference and arrogance of tourists not wanting to engage in meaningful contact and behaving like children. Their tactic is not one of terrorism, but it is one of intimidation; my own impression is that they would be even more violent if their religious leaders did not restrain them.

It is interesting to note that the travel agents who sell these trips do not warn their customers about such problems (except in very general terms, so as to make them appear part of the attraction of the trip): they do not intend to disturb the illusion of realism before they have dispatched their clients and cashed their checks.

In analyzing staged Maasai performances for tourists on the farm of the British-Kenyan Mayer family, Bruner and Kirshenblatt-Gimblett remarked that ". . . the Maasai and the Mayers are merely players in a show written by international tourist discourse" (1994:467). The Suri are an example of the opposite. They give clear evidence of a refusal to be incorporated as actors in the triadic tourist game (Suri–state agents/guides–foreign tourists). In a radical way they *refuse to act as a party in the relationship*, rejecting its terms and thus their inclusion into a system of meaning of others. In contrast to peoples who have been exposed for longer periods to external contacts and who are willing to see the advantages of an encounter with tourism—cf. the Balinese, the Maltese (Boissevain 1986), the Toraja (Volkman 1990), or the Maasai (Bruner and Kirshenblatt-Gimblett 1994)—the Suri consciously intend to keep the visitors at bay. If they do respond to them, it is in a remarkably exploitative way; for them, tourists are the last in a long line of visitors who intend to incorporate them into their scheme of things, be it the state administration, the colonial structure (the Italians), the army, tax gatherers, and so on. They resist them like they have resisted the latter: by militant and aggressive self-assertion.

The Clash of Identities and the Reinforcement of Group Boundaries

The meeting of Suri and tourists described above refers to a relatively new contact situation: before about 1988, the Suri were simply not visited by tourists, and they were not familiar with such a category of people. But the

friction is probably common at all locations where tourists are now an established feature of the social landscape. A study of such a situation in its "pristine form" reveals an ultimately irreconcilable clash of cultural interests
between the locals and the tourists, despite all the compromises and accommodations that are developed later when it has become clear that the tourists
will not leave the place alone.

We might also say that in the encounter of Suri and tourists, "violence"
is produced (cf. Mudimbe 1994): both symbolic (because of imposition and
power difference) and physical (pushing and hitting, stealing of property, and
threats, sometimes at gunpoint). The second could be seen as a response to
the first. The tourists—though equipped with plenty of money and material
goods—feel very tense, and come to see their being there as indeed having an
element of force. The conditions of discourse and "exchange" are imposed,
meaningful contact is precluded, and they are obliged to constantly and
unpleasantly negotiate on commercial values: money for pictures and for
objects, gifts of razors, soap, cloth, and so on. There are no reciprocal terms
of exchange known in advance but only exploitative ones, realized in what
both parties know is a, not to be repeated, one-off encounter.

All this inhibits and structurally precludes normal social exchange and
enhances antagonism. What the tourists do not immediately see is that this
clash is *predicated upon the very motive of their coming there*, as adventurous would-be explorers with their "social centre" (Cohen 1979:183) elsewhere but who come to discover the unknown other, a "remote primitive
tribe." This explorer-experience goes back to an old Western trope and still
functions as an ideological trapping cultivated by the travel agencies that
market such trips. It may or may not be related to the cultural ambiguity of
modern industrial society with its lingering nostalgia for a lost past (Graburn
1996:166) and its residual feelings of alienation (MacCannell 1976). But
more importantly it must be seen as part of the great tourist game of producing "realism" in an unambiguous, marked domain where people from both
sides are expected to "follow the rules."

From the point of view of the tourists, their encounter with the Suri is a
case of "failed framing": due to Suri resistance against the social model of
subordinate exchange and the rendering of "services," most (though not all)
tourists feel disoriented. They, as white visitors, are pushed back to their elementary identity as "intruders" and are confronted with the limited power of
their resources (money) and status (as "white, developed" people). Their illusion of authentic realism is punctured, and their image of a pristine tribe with
its own codes and customs happily and generously shared with outsiders,
shattered. One could say that the Suri have become so "authentic"—with
their very original "rude, savage, and uncontrolled" behavior—that they defy
the tourist script to the point of breaking it up.

The Suri example shows once again that the confrontation of "otherness"—both for the tourist and for the local people visited—can reinforce
group consciousness (see also MacCannell 1984). Increased contact between

ethnocultural groups does *not* automatically produce mutual understanding or the management of difference: more often it leads to the opposite.[19] In this case, of course, this is enhanced by the fact of spatiotemporal remoteness reproduced in the very encounter of locals and tourists: the latter will go back and are there *because* they cherish the fact that they are on the verge of going back to their social peers, which allows them to gaze at the differences separating them from those who will stay there in their full "otherness."

For the Suri, the encounter initially produces a redrawing of their group identity as "strangers" to the visitors. As remarked earlier, they are acutely aware of this fact. Their group consciousness—traditionally already characterized by high self-esteem, by a strongly shared normative culture centered on cattle, and by a tacit contempt for all others—is also reinforced by their actual dealings with tourists. Their disdain for them has underlined their conviction that only they themselves are what they call "real adult people" (in Suri: *hírí mú*). While they appreciate the ingenuity of some of the material culture items that the tourists bring and do not reject the money to be gained, they cannot take them seriously as persons. Inadvertently, therefore, their exposure to tourists may have brought about a revaluation of their own way of life.

Suri, Tourism, and Development

Above, we noted that Suri resist their unquestioned annexation into the tourist discourse, and in their encounter with tourists develop more self-consciousness about the value of their own ethnocultural tradition. They do not aspire to "become like them." This phenomenon underlines Cohen's conclusions about the mixed effects of "commoditization" in tourism: some local cultural values may be negatively affected but others may be redefined or reinforced (1988). It has to be noted, however, that much will depend on the extent and manner of outside interventions.

The relative autonomy and independence of the Suri way of life, and their ability to "resist" or "contest" the tourist challenge, will gradually erode, and social transformations will occur. Tourists will keep coming; there has been a foreign missionary station among them since 1990, and government political interference has become stronger since 1991.

The Suri will also find themselves increasingly connected to the global economy. This is most obvious in the recent National Parks Project. The European Union has financed a large, five-year development project in Ethiopia (of some 16 million ECU) to upgrade and redevelop the national parks and game reserves in the south of the country, with the underlying aim of stimulating wildlife tourism from the EU to Ethiopia (on the basis of the example of Kenya). These plans, fuelled by global concerns about wildlife diversity and conservation as well as by the long-term commercial interests of the tourist sector, did not initially consider the position of the Suri and other local groups. Of course, the Suri experience with future game park tourism may have some tangible benefits, certainly in the short-term: for example, the influx of cash. In the project plans, roads, clinics, schools, and the drilling of water holes[20] were also promised. Some of these have been realized. However, when the EU project that provided finances and manpower receded after some years (the project was phased out in 1999), the Ethiopian government was not able to uphold the level of local services or infrastructure, and the improvements are withering away. Moreover, a largely nonlocal elite from the capital are profiting from the proceeds of tourism, not the average Suri.

In the EU plans, the park areas were seen as an "impressive wilderness" (the tourist image), with the implication that human populations had always been marginal to their existence—although the park areas had known human existence for thousands of years and indeed owed their state to prolonged human activity (Turton 1996:107). In this context we see two rather different views of what is "real." There was little detail in the plans about the effective integration of local people's (underestimated) knowledge about ecological management, or their need for living space, or the importance of cultural values; the globalist model of top-down planning aimed at "conservation" and "tourist management" seems to have taken precedence. It might be advisable for development-oriented people (government agents, NGO people, and those in the Game Park Project) not only to take into effective account the presence, attitudes, and sociocultural aspirations of local people but also to recognize their right (as the most ancient and most knowledgeable inhabitants of the area) to have their identity as active local *subjects* respected.[21] In view of the increasing global flows, local identity in general is becoming more and more fragile (cf. Appadurai 1995). If these local interests and sensibilities are not recognized in such globalist schemes, drawn up largely on the basis of a Western approach, problems will arise. If a real role for local populations is not envisaged, the latter can easily resort to ways of undermining game park tourism, for instance by killing the animals in the park and causing security problems for tourists and others.

Conclusions: Globalization, Exotopy, and Suri Identity

While tourism itself is a phenomenon of considerable antiquity, by the early twenty-first century global conditions allow a large portion of the postmodern industrialized world to indulge in it. The existence of diverging values will always cause tensions in the tourist-"native" encounter, and this holds not only in Ethiopia but in any other country, the developed West included (see the studies in Boissevain 1996).

The Suri experience tourism as a disturbance and as a hegemonic strategy to be resisted. They refuse to be "signs" (of primitiveness, backwardness, tribalism, etc.) in a system of meaning of tourists that allows no reciprocity. The tourist effort toward inclusion is resisted by radical self-assertion and obstruction, whereby the Suri subvert the script of tourist realism. They refuse to be wrapped and taken home. So far, tourism among the Suri has not undermined their society but reinforced local values and self-esteem. At the same time, they are introduced to the charged symbolism of material exchange through money: money is the new means by which their group culture and artifacts are commoditized and expressed. Lacking another means of meaningful communication in the encounter with tourists, they capitalize upon money and thus are drawn into the idiom of "consumerism" themselves.

Contemporary tourist identity is a characteristic global consumer identity that has far-reaching implications in a socioeconomic and also moral sense. Tourism is an inevitable phenomenon, enhanced by conditions of modern technology and travel facilities, which diminish the costs of mobility and strengthen notions of virtual "simultaneity" of place and of experience. In view of the reactions tourism initially seems to evoke in the local settings it penetrates, it is also *inherently* problematic and conflictual, despite its highly ritualized character. The impact, role, and motivations of tourists need to be reevaluated continuously. For instance, at the present historical juncture, it is highly questionable whether tourists really search for authenticity that they are said to lack in their own daily lives. This claim, made by MacCannell in his landmark book, *The Tourist* (1976), has been challenged by Cohen (1979, 1988) and Urry (1990), among others. My interpretation is also that postmodern consumer tourists are much more cynical, and are very conscious (not to say arrogant) about the unassailable advance they, as members of a developed industrial/information-age society, have over people of the not so wealthy, or as they see it, not well organized—or worse, "primitive" or "chaotic"—societies they visit. That tourists go there is a result of the commoditization of local culture or landscape in tourist discourse on the home front: a discourse of status competition that structurally negates initial personal motives of a "sincere interest in the other." Tourists' exploration of these other societies and people is thus primarily to be seen as an act of self-confirmation or congratulation among social peers in their own society, and not of seeking "lost values" or an authentic or affectively rewarding life in the exotope, the visited locations outside one's own familiar sociocultural space.

Tourism is another act in the politicocultural drama of hegemonic strife between the global poles variously defined as rich and poor, north and south, developed and underdeveloped. As we saw in the case above, the Suri will be "made safe" for mass tourism through the noble aim of wildlife protection. The question remains whether a local society like the Suri, subjected unwillingly to tourists, can marshal its few resources of "counter-discourse" to enhance its interests and collective identity in this political arena where the local and the global meet, *or* can only resist temporarily before the onslaught of globalizing consumer patterns. Of course, the latter scenario seems more likely, however much one might regret it.

Source: Adapted from "Tourism and Its Discontents: Suri-Tourism Encounters in Southern Ethiopia," *Social Anthropology*, 2000, 8:1–17.

Acknowledgements

For support of research work in southern Ethiopia, I am grateful to the Royal Netherlands Academy of Science (KNAW), the Netherlands Organisation for Scientific Research in the Tropics (WOTRO, WR 52-601), and the African Studies Centre (Leiden). I also am much indebted to the former directors of the Institute of Ethiopian Studies (Addis Ababa, Ethiopia), Dr. Taddesse Beyene and Prof. Bahru Zewde, for their support. I thank Wim van Binsbergen and Azeb Amha for their critical comments on an earlier version of this text.

Notes

[1] Especially among neighboring groups they are known as *Surma*. Most commonly used self-names are Chai and Tirmaga (two sub-groups).

[2] Ambivalence toward tourists is of course not uncommon among social science researchers. Middleton considers the tourists on the Swahili coast as "cultural illiterates" (1991:vii) and sees the tourist trade as ". . . a final form of colonialism" and as ". . . the most degrading exploitation of the Swahili coast" (1991:53).

[3] Neither would the persistent ambivalence of the tourist enterprise be explained: why do tourists get irritated by other tourists, and why is the general image of the tourist so invariably negative? (Cf. the quotes on the first page of Urry's 1990 book.)

[4] In contrast to, for example, coastal tourism in Kenya (see Peake 1989, Sindiga 1996).

[5] As treated in, for example, Cohen 1979, MacCannell 1976, or Urry 1990.

[6] One of them an Ethiopian one: see N. Donovan & J. Last, 1980, *Ethiopian Costumes*. Addis Ababa: Ethiopian Tourism Commission, p. 24–25 (reprinted 1991).

[7] Perhaps one can recognize here something of the "Riefenstahl syndrome."

[8] Good explanatory text might have helped here, but G. Hancock's chapter on the Surma and related groups (Beckwith and Fisher 1990) leaves much to be desired. The Beckwith-Fisher article of 1991 contains very little text.

[9] For a brief survey, see Abbink 2002.

[10] Marchetti 1939, Rizetto 1941, Viezzer 1938.

[11] Although Arnold Hodson, British consul in Maji in the early 1920s, published a photograph of the "Kachubo"-Surma (these are the Kachepo or Balé-Surma, living on the Boma Plateau in Sudan) in 1929 (see Hodson 1929:207).

[12] The Italian scholar C. Conti Rossini was the first to call Ethiopia ". . . un museo di popoli" in his book *L'Abissinia* (Rome 1929, p. 20).

[13] When I was in the field in 1994, a group of German tourists was called back by the authorities and had to fly back to Addis Ababa without having seen the Surma. Similar incidents were recorded in recent years.

[14] This was the case with the Beckwith-Fisher expedition of 1988, and of one Belgian tourist-photographer of my acquaintance, who toured among the Surma in 1994. Both came back with pictures that they used in publications, or which they were about to sell or publicly exhibit.

[15] The Ethiopian one-birr notes given are green.

[16] See also the Granada TV ("Disappearing Word") film on the Mursi, called *Nitha* (1991). The most recent film on the Mursi is *Fire Will Eat Us,* Granada TV for Channel 4 Television (U.K.), 2001.

[17] This term is also applied to the innate "power" of their religious chiefs and to certain ritually important plants.

[18] That no Surma outside this council benefits from it, is of secondary importance.

[19] The conditions under which exposure to and experience with cultural differences *reinforce* group boundaries, generate antagonistic images or actual conflict are not yet well addressed in globalization studies (cf. Sindiga 1996:431).

[20] These were announced in the first (1993) program-document of the Agriconsulting Group which made a feasibility study for the project.

[21] This argument is forcefully made in a very interesting, unpublished paper by David Turton (1995).

References

Abbink, J. 2002. "Paradoxes of Power and Culture in an Old Periphery: Surma, 1974–98," in *Remapping Ethiopia: Socialism and After*, ed. D. Donham et al., pp. 155–72. Oxford: James Currey/Addis Ababa: Addis Ababa University Press; Athens: Ohio University Press.

———. 2002. "Me'en," in *Encyclopedia of World Cultures, Supplement*, ed. C. R. Ember, M. Ember and I. Skoggard, pp. 200–4. New York: Macmillan Reference USA; Farmington Hills, MI: Gale Group.

Appadurai, A. 1995. "The Production of Locality," in *Counterworks. Managing the Diversity of Knowledge*, ed. R. O. Fardon, pp. 204–25. London/New York: Routledge.

Beckwith, C., and A. Fisher. 1990. *African Ark*. London: Collins-Harvill.

———. 1991. "The Eloquent Surma of Ethiopia." *National Geographic Magazine* 179(2): 77–99.

Boissevain, J. 1986. *Tourism as Anti-structure*. Amsterdam: Anthropological-Sociological Centre (Euromed Working Paper).

Boissevain, J., ed. 1996. *Coping with Tourists: European Reactions to Mass Tourism*. Oxford/Providence, RI: Berghahn Publishers.

Bulatovitch, A. K. 1900. "Dall'Abessinia al Lago Rodolfo per il Caffa," *Bolletino della Società Geografica Italiana* 38:121–42.

———. 1902. "Les Campagnes de Ménélik," *Journal des Voyages et des Aventures de Terre et Mer*, 2me série, nos. 297–307, pp. 186–9, 206–7, 226–7, 241–3, 255–6, 274–5, 294–8 (Traduit et adapté par Michel Delines).

Bruner, E., and B. Kirshenblatt-Gimblett. 1994. "Maasai on the Lawn: Tourist Realism in East Africa. *Cultural Anthropology* 9:435–70.

Cohen, Erik. 1979. "A Phenomenology of Tourist Experiences." *Sociology* 13:179–201.

———. 1988. "Authenticity and Commoditization in Tourism." *Annals of Tourism Research* 15:371–86.

Consoziazione Turistica Italiana. 1938. *Guida dell'Africa Orientale Italiana*. Milano: CTI.

Culler, J. 1981. "The Semiotics of Tourism." *American Journal of Semiotics* 1:127–40.

Graburn, N. 1995. "Tourism, Modernity, Nostalgia," in *The Future of Anthropology: Its Relevance to the Contemporary World*, ed. A. Ahmed and C. Shore, pp. 158–78. London: Athlone Press.

Gwynn, C. 1911. "A Journey in Southern Abyssinia." *Geographical Journal* 38:114–36.

Harkin, M. 1995. "Modernist Anthropology and Tourism of the Authentic." *Annals of Tourism Research* 22:650–70.

Hodson, A. W. 1929. *Where Lion Reign*. London: Skeffington & Son.

MacCannell, D. 1976. *The Tourist: A New Theory of the Leisure Class*. New York: Schocken Books.

———. 1984. "Reconstructed Ethnicity: Tourism and Cultural Identity in Third World Communities." *Annals of Tourism Research* 11:375–91.

Marchetti, M. 1939. "Notizie sulle popolazioni dei Tirma, Tid e Zilmamo." *Archivio per l'Antropologia e l'Etnologia* 69:59–76.

Middleton, J. 1991. *The World of the Swahili: An African Mercantile Civilization.* London/ New Haven, CT: Yale University Press.

Mudimbe, V. 1994. "Race and Science." *Transition* 64:68–76.

Nash, D. 1996. "Prospects for Tourism Study in Anthropology," in *The Future of Anthropology: its Relevance to the Contemporary World*, ed. A. Ahmed and C. Shore, pp. 179–202. London: Athlone Press.

Peake, R. 1989. "Swahili Social Stratification and Tourism in Malindi Old Town." *Africa* 59:209–20.

Rizetto, F. 1941. "Alcune notizie sui Tirma." *Annali dell'Africa Italiana* 4:1201–11.

Sindiga, I. 1996. "International Tourism in Kenya and the Marginalization of the Waswahili." *Tourism Management* 17:425–32.

Sontag, S. 1977. *On Photography.* New York: Delta Books.

Turton, D. 1992. "Anthropology on Television: What Next?" in *Film as Ethnography*, ed. P. I. Crawford and D. Turton, pp. 283–99. Manchester/New York: Manchester University Press.

———. 1995. "The Mursi and the Elephant Question." Paper, Participatory Wildlife Management Workshop, Ministry of Natural Resources and FARM Africa, Addis Ababa, 16–18 May 1995, 29 pp.

———.1996. "Migrants and Refugees: A Mursi Case Study," in *In Search of Cool Ground: Flight and Homecoming in Northeast Africa*, ed. T. Allen, pp. 96–110. London: James Currey.

Viezzer, C. 1938. "Diario di una carovana di missione geo-mineraria di Bonga-Magi-Tirma nell'Ovest Etiopico." *Rassegna Mineraria Mensile* (Materie Prime d'Italia e dell'Impero) XVII: 404–25.

Urry, J. 1990. *The Tourist Gaze: Leisure and Travel in Contemporary Societies.* London/ Newbury Park/New Delhi: Sage.

Volkman, T. 1990. "Visions and Revisions: Toraja Culture and the Tourist Gaze." *American Ethnologist* 17:91–110.

17

"Let 'em Loose": Pueblo Indian Management of Tourism

Jill D. Sweet

The Pueblo Indians of the American Southwest have developed creative and assertive techniques for interacting with tourists. Embedded in specific historic and cultural circumstances, these techniques help the Pueblo Indians survive the pressures of tourist contact, fortify their cultural boundaries, and exercise a degree of power over individuals who are, in most other situations, defined as the more powerful.[1] In this paper I examine two of the techniques that are central to Pueblo tourist management and Pueblo cultural maintenance.

Although there is considerable literature examining host/guest dynamics in situations of tourist contact,[2] only recently have researchers regarded indigenous hosts as powerful players in the process.[3] An intriguing analysis of host/guest dynamics offered by Evans-Pritchard (1989) treats the indigenous hosts as "subjects" initiating action, rather than merely "objects" acted upon and ultimately doomed by tourism. Although the issue of host control in these interactions is not her focus, Evans-Pritchard does examine Native American/tourist encounters and notes that, "armed with stereotypes of tourists, and aware of touristic stereotypes of Indians, Indians can exercise more control over frequently uncomfortable situations" (1989:102). She also observes that many Native Americans have much more experience dealing with tourists than tourists have dealing with Native Americans; this gives the latter an advantage in host/guest interactions (1989:99).

Using Evans-Pritchard's observations as a point of departure, I will focus specifically on the ways the Pueblo Indians control the tourists who enter their world. In particular, this paper examines the Pueblo/tourist interactive techniques of secrecy and regulation. I also regard the techniques of burlesque and exportation as practices of tourist management, but these latter two techniques will not be dealt with here, since I have discussed them at length elsewhere.[4] An examination of the Pueblo situation will help researchers understand both host/guest dynamics and an important dimension of cultural maintenance. It also will contribute to a better understanding of the reasons why some indigenous communities survive and even benefit from tourist contact while others experience only cultural disruption.

Research for this paper was conducted primarily at the villages of Acoma, Santo Domingo, San Ildefonso, and San Juan, New Mexico, during several field sessions between 1973 and 1989. The first two villages are Keresan-speaking pueblos, and the latter two are Tewa-speaking pueblos. All of these villages currently are visited by tourists.

The Pueblo Indian and Tourism in the Southwest

Long before tourists first arrived in the Southwest, the Pueblo Indians already had considerable experience with cultural others, including Navajo, Apache, and other nomadic tribes; Spanish explorers, colonists, and missionaries; Anglo traders, settlers, entrepreneurs, missionaries, and military personnel. Although many of these early contact situations were extremely difficult and often tragic for the Pueblo people, they prepared these Indians to be forthright and clever in their response to outside domination.

By the turn of the nineteenth century, the time was right for tourist interest in the Native American. Spicer observes,

> In most cases, after the native peoples were subjugated, strong sentiment grew up in the conquering nation regarding the injustice of the original conquest. The native survivors assumed a symbolic significance as reminders of a ruthless past and as representatives of a lost and better way of life, pre-urban and pre-industrial. Associated with this symbolism strong feelings developed for preservation of the native peoples and their ways . . . (1962:1–2)

The sentiments described above developed among some Anglo-Americans and encouraged visits to surviving native communities. Anglo tourists began "discovering" Pueblo Indians in the 1890s (Eickemeyer and Eickemeyer 1895), and by the 1920s a tourist industry was flourishing in this region, with Pueblo people and villages regularly advertised as tourist attractions. Large touring cars with Anglo female guides dressed in Southwest Indian garb began bringing groups of tourists to the Pueblo villages. Hotel lobbies, town plazas, and train stations became sites where Pueblo Indians displayed and sold their arts and crafts to travelers (Weigle 1989). The types of tourists who were and who continue to be attracted to the Pueblo people are what researchers call participants in "ethnic tourism."

Ethnic tourism is travel for pleasure that features activities such as visiting native villages, observing ceremonies, and shopping for indigenous arts and crafts (see Smith 1977). Swain defines ethnic tourism as "the marketing of tourist attractions based on an indigenous population's way of life" (1989:85). Van den Berghe and Keyes characterize ethnic tourism as fostering "the most complex and interesting types of interactions between tourists and natives. The native is not simply 'there' to serve the needs of the tourist; he is himself 'on show,' a living spectacle" (1984:343).

Ethnic tourists in the Southwest want to see, experience, and interact with the native inhabitants. They want to take pictures of Indians and purchase their pottery, jewelry, and textiles. Some ethnic tourists are satisfied by seeing Indians selling their wares in the Santa Fe plaza or by viewing a theatrical performance of Pueblo dance at a staged, commercial ceremonial, while others want to visit a reservation where they will see Indians doing "whatever they normally do," or where they might even catch a glimpse of a ritual that is still a vital part of the native religious calendar. Those who find the exotic experiences they seek may try to learn when the rituals are most likely to be held and may return to the reservation villages repeatedly. These more frequent visitors sometimes develop friendships with Pueblo families and are invited to share in the domestic feasting that occurs during village rituals. This is not a rare occurrence; many Pueblo families have what they call "Anglo friends" or "white friends" who regularly come to the open village rituals. While some of these friendships are lifelong and anything but superficial, Anglo friends never become fully accepted or formally adopted members of a Pueblo community. Most Anglo friends fit Evans's description of the "resident" tourist who retires, resides seasonally, or vacations regularly in one area (1978:43–44). These frequent visitors, as well as other tourists who come to the Pueblo reservations, typically do so by private automobiles and in small groups. Although bus tours occasionally stop at some pueblos, mass tourism is not yet common, and one-to-one contact between host and guest still occurs.

It is when the ethnic tourist comes to the reservation that the Pueblo Indians are able to control their visitors most effectively. This is possible primarily because of the Pueblo communities' history and political status. That is, through rights established by land grants, legislation, and legal cases, the Pueblo Indians maintain considerable independence and control over their communities and lands. In the mid-1930s, the United Pueblos Agency, the centralized federal administration of all New Mexico pueblos, acknowledged "that matters of purely internal nature were the exclusive jurisdiction of Pueblo officials" (1979:217). Relevant to tourism, Pueblo officials have the right to exclude visitors and to set the rules for acceptable behavior. They have the right to close the village to outsiders at any time. They also have the right to police their reservations and enforce their regulations. In short, the Pueblo communities determine what tourists may do or see while on the reservation and whether or not tourism will be encouraged, simply tolerated, or discouraged.

The fact that the reservations are still relatively isolated and removed from cities, towns, hotels, restaurants, and shops also permits control. Most villages remain out of the way, with considerable land surrounding them, which serves as a buffer. This makes the villages appealing to the ethnic tourist who enjoys adventure "off the beaten path," but, more importantly, it keeps the Pueblo communities from being engulfed by tourist facilities.

The Pueblo Indians' position on reservation tourism is clearly reflected in the Pueblo rejection of a 1975 nationwide American Indian Movement call to boycott the tourist industry. Typical of the Pueblo position, the governor of Santa Clara Pueblo, Lucario Padilla, announced that his village, where 50 percent of the residents depend on tourism for at least a portion of their livelihood, would not support the A.I.M. boycott. He explained,

> We realize the tremendous impact of the tourist trade upon the economy of the people within our pueblo . . . But, we must reiterate that anyone entering our pueblo as visitors must be aware of the responsibilities that accompany their roles as guests and act accordingly.[5]

With their long history of contact with others, their established independence, and their spatial isolation, Pueblo Indians were able to develop specific techniques for interacting with and ultimately controlling the behavior of visitors. The first of these techniques to be considered here is the Pueblo practice of withholding information. Secrecy is one way the Pueblo people protect their privacy, influence the behavior of visitors, and maintain the advantage in host/guest encounters.[6]

Secrecy

Many anthropologists who have worked within Pueblo Indian communities have noted the importance of secrecy. One scholar even suggested that "the central problem confronting any Pueblo scholar is secrecy" (Brandt 1980:123). While Pueblo secrecy has been discussed as an external device for the protection of the traditional religion and as an internal device for Pueblo leaders to maintain political control, Pueblo secrecy has not been analyzed until now as an advantage in host/guest interactions or as a vehicle for controlling tourists.[7]

Pueblo secrecy involves privacy and the protection of what is considered sacred space. There are sections of some Pueblo villages that are strictly off-limits to all visitors. Kivas—Pueblo sacred ceremonial chambers—are always closed to tourists in all but the Hopi and Zuni villages. As a result, most kiva rituals remain private. In addition, streets or sections of a village may be temporarily blocked off during the day because of funeral rites or the activities of the native religious societies. There are also days when an entire village is closed, with Pueblo males guarding the entrances and turning away any outsiders who might try to enter. Finally, some villages are closed routinely to all Anglo friends and other visitors after dark.

The rules of secrecy also control information concerning village rituals, which are either closed, open but unannounced, or open and announced. The closed rituals may be held in one of the kivas or in a temporarily closed village. The open but unannounced performances are held in the village plazas. If outsiders arrive, they are permitted to stay and watch as long as they are respectful and do not get too close to the action. Anglo friends may learn of these open but unannounced rituals from their Pueblo friends, who will offhandedly mention that "something is going on in the village tomorrow."

Village performances that are open and announced are those native events that have become associated with the Catholic calendar. For example, each village holds native dances in honor of its patron saint. Because these events are now part of the public Catholic calendar, their occurrence is predictable and local chambers of commerce, newspapers, magazines, radio stations, and even some Pueblo governors' offices announce them to the general public.

The inquisitiveness of Anglo tourists may pose problems for the Pueblo Indians, who have been taught since childhood that it is rude to ask questions directly. Furthermore, Pueblo Indians believe sacred knowledge may lose its power if it is openly discussed; therefore, it must be protected from the uninitiated. If an Indian is seen talking to outsiders in public, especially during a ritual performance, he may be ridiculed by his neighbors or accused of giving away sacred information. As a result of these attitudes and methods of internal social control, Pueblo people learn to distance themselves when confronted with questions. A question posed by a tourist may be met with a polite but very short response or a claim of ignorance, after which the Pueblo individual may quietly turn away from the visitor. Eye contact is usually avoided throughout the exchange; if the questioning persists, some Pueblo Indians will simply refuse to acknowledge the tourist's presence. Pueblo families often teach their Anglo friends that direct questions make them uncomfortable and probably will go unanswered, particularly if the questions are personal or concern native religious practices.

There were countless times that I observed Pueblo Indians withholding information from inquisitive tourists. I observed such an exchange, for example, at a February Basket Dance at the village of San Juan. About thirty members of the village were dancing in the plaza as other villagers and a few tourists watched. One male tourist asked a Pueblo woman, "Why are you [generic 'you'] dancing today?" She kept her eyes on the dancers and did not acknowledge that she heard the question, but the man repeated it. She then responded as if she did not understand the generic use of the word you: "I'm not dancing today." Hearing this subtly sarcastic response, several other Indians standing nearby began to smile and quietly chuckle. Next, the man said, "I mean, why is the village dancing today? Why are they dancing?" and he pointed to the dancers. "Oh," she said, not lifting her eyes from the dancers in front of her, "I think they must want it to rain." "Is that what this is?"

responded the man. "A rain dance?" Without waiting for a confirmation, he continued, "What do the baskets symbolize then?" "I don't know," she said. After a few minutes, he asked, "What about the songs? What are they saying?" But by now the woman had moved slightly away from the man and was ignoring his last questions. After a few minutes of waiting for a response, he gave up his quest for meaning.

This example not only illustrates the Pueblo Indians' reluctance to share information about native religious practices but also reveals how they often use a tourist's ignorance to make him appear foolish. MacCannell observed that host/guest relationships are inherently unequal (1984). The nature of this inequality, however, depends on whether one considers economics or local knowledge. In terms of economics, the native host often holds an inferior position to that of the tourist, but, as the above example illustrates, the native host has the advantage in terms of local knowledge. By withholding information, the Pueblo people have control over something ethnic tourists want—exotic cultural knowledge and experiences.

Controlling the desired knowledge and access to coveted experiences gives the Pueblo people a considerable advantage over tourists; they can choose to tell or not tell these visitors when and where Indian cultural events will be held. Further, they can decide just how far they will permit their visitors to enter the private regions of their villages.[8] Controlling knowledge and access also gives the Pueblo Indians an edge in interactions, because they are the ones "in the know." They can decide whether to translate and share any of the meanings contained in these events and whether the information given will be truthful. In addition, they can make ignorant tourists look foolish because of their lack of knowledge.

An example from Evans-Pritchard illustrates this last point further. During Indian Market, an annual event held in Santa Fe,

> . . . a lady was examining the silver balls on a squash blossom necklace. She turned to Cippy Crazyhorse [Cochiti Pueblo artist] . . . and in the slow, over-emphasized fashion intended for someone who does not really understand English, she asked "Are these hollow?" Cippy promptly replied "Hello" and warmly shook her hand. Again the lady asked, "Are these hollow?" pronouncing the words even more theatrically this time. Cippy cheerily responded with another "Hello." This went on a few more times, by which time everyone around was laughing, until eventually the lady herself saw the joke. (Evans-Pritchard 1989:95–96)

In addition to the interactional advantages gained by withholding information from outsiders, some Pueblo Indians keep certain information to themselves because they fear that breaking rules of secrecy will not only be met with disapproval by their neighbors and families, but may also result in supernatural misfortune. An incident at Santo Domingo Pueblo illustrates this dimension of Pueblo secrecy.

On an afternoon in May a number of years ago, a non-Indian companion and I decided to take a canoe trip down a portion of the Rio Grande. We chose a section of the river that flows through the Santo Domingo Reservation, with the idea that we would stop at the village and take some of the children out in the canoe. When we neared the back side of the village, we heard muffled singing, as if the singers were wearing masks. Knowing that in this village all masked performances are closed to outsiders and considered extremely private events, I decided we should continue on down the river rather than enter the village. The following day, I talked to a Santo Domingo friend about this river trip and my decision not to enter the village. She was relieved that we had not come up from the river, not only because I would have been in trouble with the authorities, but, more importantly, because something very bad would have happened to all of us. She kept asking me, "Weren't you terribly afraid?" and hinted that if I was not afraid, I certainly should have been. Fifteen years later, this Santo Domingo woman as well as other members of her family still bring up this incident, referring to it as a potentially dangerous situation.

The people of Acoma Pueblo have gone to great lengths to control where visitors can go, what they can see, and what they can learn when they visit the village. Acoma is located on top of a mesa; since the early 1980s, tourists have been directed to park their cars at the base of the mesa. Then they must purchase a ticket to ride a shuttle bus up the steep road to the mesa top. On reaching the village, the visitors are guided in small groups by one of several Acoma women who talk about the settlement's history and culture. Along the way, the guests are given several opportunities to purchase Acoma pottery. This arrangement permits the Acoma people to control their visitors while benefiting economically from tourism. Nevertheless, Acoma is closed for certain ritual events, and visitors are simply turned away at the base of the mesa.

Controlling what outsiders may see and know are important to Pueblo cultural survival. Key aspects of Pueblo Indian tradition are reserved exclusively for the Pueblo people. To be Pueblo is to share in these private domains. Furthermore, withholding information from visitors puts the Pueblo Indians in a position of power, since they hold what their guests desire. This control of knowledge distances us (the Pueblo people) from them (the Anglo tourists) and is central to the socially supported and ongoing maintenance of the culture. Pueblo secrecy is not simply a cultural quirk, but rather a deeply embedded technique for cultural survival.

Regulations

When tourists enter a Pueblo village, they find one or more signs providing them with information about village regulations. These range in quality and content from crudely painted signs that simply state restrictions on photography, sketching, notetaking, driving speeds, and a curfew for visitors to more sophisticated and professionally printed signs such as the one at the entrance of the Acoma Reservation. The Acoma sign reads,

PUEBLO OF ACOMA OFFICIAL NOTICE

You are entering the Pueblo of Acoma. All lands herein are governed by statutes enacted and/or adopted by the Acoma Tribal Council. Continued entrance beyond this point constitutes a knowing and voluntary consent on your behalf to abide by the laws of Acoma and to be held accountable to the Acoma judicial system for any violation of Acoma law.

As visitors get closer to the Acoma village, they find another sign; this one hand painted and titled "Pueblo Etiquette." Advice here is informal but certainly to the point:

Do not be loud or obnoxious. Keep a low profile at all times . . . When attending dances or ceremonies stay clear of dance performers . . . Stay off old structures like kivas and ladders . . . Hope you enjoy your tour and visit here at the Pueblo of Acoma. Thank you and come again.[9]

In each case, the message is clear: visitors must accept a new set of rules and obligations if they want to venture onto the reservation.

But posting village regulations is not the only way that Pueblo hosts attempt to control the behavior of tourists. An open and announced ritual event held at San Ildefonso Pueblo exemplifies other forms of control. Every January, San Ildefonso holds a Buffalo/Game Animal Dance for snow, health,

Managing tourists through regulations. (Photo by Roger Sweet)

hunting success, and to honor the pueblo's patron saint. This event includes an evening prelude dance on 22 January, followed by a dawn ceremony and a full day of dancing on 23 January. Because the village is only a twenty-minute drive from Santa Fe and since the dance is held on the same date each year, this event has become a popular activity for residents of Santa Fe and winter tourists interested in native culture.

The 1988 Buffalo/Game Animal Dance was particularly revealing in terms of village regulations and the control of tourists. That year, there were approximately thirty tourists and one hundred Indians waiting in the plaza for the evening prelude performance. As soon as the singers and dancers appeared, a female tourist began taking notes in a small notebook. She was very open about what she was doing, recording details of the performance and talking to her companion about the numbers of dancers and their regalia. One Indian man mentioned to her that she should not be taking notes, but she ignored the warning. Soon an assistant war captain approached the woman, asked her what she was doing, and took her notebook away.[10] As he examined the pages by the light of the nearest bonfire, the woman became indignant, claiming that her rights were being violated. In minutes, there were four

Buffalo/Game Animal
dancer at San Ildefonso
Pueblo, New Mexico.
(Photo by Roger Sweet)

tribal police, one war captain, and two of his assistants surrounding the woman. The war captain spoke to her calmly but firmly and confiscated the notebook. Throughout the incident, other tourists and Indians whispered, criticizing the woman's behavior. No one came to her defense. After all, there was a sign at the entrance to the village stating that sketching, notetaking, and photography were not permitted. Furthermore, rather than apologize or plead ignorance, the woman argued with the authorities. While incidents like this are rare, they communicate to all present that Pueblo communities are absolutely serious about their regulations.

While the number of tourists attending the 1988 prelude performance was typical of past years, the dawn ceremony on the following day attracted approximately 250 tourists—more than twice the number I had observed in previous years. The increase was probably due to the fact that in 1988 the event fell on a Saturday and the weather was relatively mild. Apparently, the village officials were prepared for the increase with an elaborate system of control. As car after car entered the pueblo, drivers were directed to park by the church on the west side of the village. There the tourists sat waiting; a village official with a megaphone repeatedly told them they must remain in their cars. Through a series of signals from the performers in the eastern hills, the message was relayed to the church lot that the ceremony was soon to begin and the tourists could now leave their cars. I could hear officials calling to each other, "OK, let 'em loose, let 'em loose!" In moments, all the tourists were out of their cars and walking to the east side of the village. When they reached the base of the eastern hills, they were directed to stand at one side of the road while all the San Ildefonso Pueblo people stood on the other side. Surprisingly, although a few tourists found the entire situation amusing and some commented on feeling like cattle being herded to pasture, I did not hear any serious complaints about these measures taken to control them.

When the dancers neared the village, the war captain insured that the tourists stayed back from their path. This was accomplished through subtle but dramatic intimidation. Wrapped in a large blanket and wearing symbolically transforming face paint over a very serious expression, the war captain appeared powerful, even superhuman. An occasional quiet request from him was all that was required to keep the crowd back.

After the dawn ceremony, the officials became more relaxed about the festivities. The sign prohibiting photography was removed, and camera permits were sold to many of the hundreds of tourists who arrived throughout the day. As this event illustrates, however, the Pueblo people make the rules and enforce them. It is their decision which events will be open to the public and if and when camera permits will be sold.

Village regulations are designed to minimize potential conflicts between hosts and guests and serve as reminders that the Indian hosts are in charge. They set the limits and ultimately define the nature of the contact. Pueblo officials enforce their regulations in several ways. Visitors may be denied entrance or escorted out of the village. They also may be fined, their film or notebooks confiscated. The regulations and methods of enforcement communicate clearly that tourists must abide by Pueblo rules if they want to visit. The regulations also distinguish insiders from outsiders, since the rules often are not the same for both groups. For example, at San Ildefonso before the game animal dancers appeared, tourists had to stay in their cars and wait, while village members could move through the pueblo freely or gather by a bonfire at the base of the hills.

While Pueblo regulations have the potential of annoying or offending some tourists, the ethnic tourists often are intrigued, because, by following these rules, they gain access to a "backstage" region—a small price to pay for authenticity. Furthermore, many Southwest ethnic tourists feel that, by cooperating, they are participating in Pueblo culture, faithfully following the "when in Rome . . ." principle. Most Southwest ethnic tourists accept the Pueblo rules and even applaud them, for they suggest that the Pueblo people have not "sold out."

Controlling members of the wider society represents a reversal of the usual power structure. This reversal surely gives the Pueblo people a welcome sense of strength and pride. Not only are they aware that non-Indians travel great distances to see them and their villages, arts, crafts, and rituals, but they know that as long as these visitors are on their reservation lands, the hosts are in charge and the non-Indians can be made to conform to village policies and Pueblo notions of proper behavior. The regulations also serve to protect and underscore Pueblo ways of life while distancing the non-Pueblo from the Pueblo. Hence, along with secrecy, the regulations control outsiders and contribute to cultural maintenance.

Discussion

Overall, the Pueblo Indians participate in the tourist industry with considerable success.[11] They have been able to control tourists who come to their reservations and keep important aspects of their culture private, while benefiting financially from tourism. By contrasting themselves with the tourists, the Pueblo Indians also have strengthened their definitions of themselves and their cultural boundaries. The significant factors in their success have been time, space, type of contact, and level of self-determination.

Compared to many other areas of the world, the transition to tourism came slowly in the Southwest, giving the Pueblo people time to adjust to their most recent invaders. There has been no sudden onslaught of mass tourism; the number of tourists increased gradually throughout the twentieth century. Slow growth in numbers of tourists has given the hosts a chance to develop techniques for tourist management (M. E. Smith 1982).

Space is another important factor in the Pueblo case. The Pueblo communities have a significant land base, with established villages that are still isolated and protected from tourist development. The Pueblo Indians secured ownership rights over much of their territory soon after first contact with Europeans. Formal land grants were established under Spanish rule and later were recognized by the United States government. Unless a Pueblo community decides on development, the Pueblo villages are not going to be surrounded by hotels and restaurants catering to tourists. As long as the villages remain isolated, aspects of Pueblo culture will be private and protected. The ability to keep at least some of the host's culture private has been cited as critical to host survival during tourist contact (V. Smith 1977:2).

The type of tourist contact—one-to-one rather than the more impersonal mass tourism—is also an important factor in assessing the Pueblo situation. When one-to-one contact is positive, genuine cultural exchange and mutual respect is possible. These positive encounters sometimes have resulted in the establishment of genuine friendships between Pueblo and Anglo families. Many Pueblo village rituals remain open, in part because Pueblo families like to invite their Anglo friends. Sometimes Anglo friends have acted as cultural brokers, helping Pueblo individuals with difficult situations involving unfamiliar aspects of the wider Anglo-American society. Nolan and Nolan observe that independent travelers who engage in one-to-one contact with native hosts "may serve as positive agents of cultural exchange rather than as individual hammer blows in an assault on the host culture. These visitors and their hosts may benefit from the traditional broadening aspect of travel" (1978:43–44).

While time, space, and type of contact are important in shaping the Pueblo case, the most significant factors are independent authority, self-determination, and a degree of power. Within the limitations set by the larger society, these indigenous people are influencing the behavior of visiting members of that larger society. Through the control of knowledge and the establishment and enforcement of specific rules, the Pueblo Indians are defining their world in their own terms and actively shaping their relationship with their visitors. By controlling those visitors, the Pueblo people are directing their cultural destiny and contributing to their own faith in the Pueblo way of doing things—a faith essential for Pueblo cultural survival.

Source: From *American Indian Culture and Research Journal*, 1991, 15(4):59–74. Reprinted with permission of the author.

Acknowledgements

Thanks go to the many Pueblo Indian families who welcomed me into their homes and permitted me to experience their moving and symbolically rich ritual dramas. Thanks also are due to colleagues Donileen Loseke and William Fox for reading and commenting on earlier drafts of this paper.

Notes

[1] Power is defined here as the ability to influence the behavior and/or thoughts of other individuals.

[2] See, for example, Farrell (1979), Forster (1964), Greenwood (1977), and Huit (1979).

[3] See, for example, Adams (1990), Johnston (1990), Chapin (1990), McKean (1989), and Swain (1989).

[4] Burlesquing tourists is an extension of the ancient Pueblo clowning tradition. Ritual clowns and other village comics burlesque tourists and even draw them into their plaza skits, making the visitors the fools. For more on this form of tourist management, see Sweet (1989). Another interesting technique is the exportation of dance segments away from the villages. By presenting dance segments in cities, arts and crafts fairs, state fairs, or commercial ceremonials, the Pueblo Indians satisfy the curiosity of large numbers of tourists without having to host these visitors in their villages. For more on exploration, see Sweet (1983, 1985).

[5] *The Santa Fe New Mexican*, 13 June 1975.

[6] One reviewer of this paper expressed a concern that the following discussion about Pueblo secrecy might be actually disclosing Pueblo secrets. I can only respond by stating that the Pueblo people are not secretive about being secretive. On the contrary, given the opportunity, they try to educate outsiders about their secrecy principles with statements such as, "We don't [won't or can't] talk about that" or "We like you because you don't ask questions" or "We can't talk now because they will think you are asking questions." I hope the following discussion of Pueblo secrecy will promote respect for and understanding of the Pueblo reluctance to share certain kinds of cultural information.

[7] For a discussion of Pueblo secrecy as external control, see Dozier (1961) and Spicer (1962). For secrecy as an internal device, see Brandt (1980).

[8] For a discussion of the "frontstage" and "backstage" behavior, see Goffman (1959).

[9] This hand-painted sign was noted in 1988. In 1989 it had been replaced by a printed sign, and the request that visitors "not be loud or obnoxious" had been omitted.

[10] War captains are village officers who, among other duties, oversee public ritual activities.

[11] I am not claiming that tourism among the Pueblo communities has been without problems. Occasionally, obnoxious tourists offend the Indians. Recently, there has been a controversy over the rights of Indians to sell native arts and crafts in the urban centers. For information on this controversy, see Sweet (1990).

References

Adams, Kathleen. 1990. "Cultural Commoditization in Tana Toraja, Indonesia." *Cultural Survival Quarterly* 14:31–34.

Brandt, Elizabeth. 1980. "On Secrecy and the Control of Knowledge: Taos Pueblo," in *Secrecy: A Cross Cultural Perspective*, ed. Stanton K. Tefft. New York: Human Sciences Press.

Chapin, Mac. 1990. "The Silent Jungle: Ecotourism among the Kuna Indians of Panama." *Cultural Survival Quarterly* 14: 42–45.

Dozier, Edward. 1961. "Rio Grande Pueblos," in *Perspectives in American Indian Culture Change*, ed. Edward Spicer, pp. 99–186. Chicago: University of Chicago Press.

Eickemeyer, Carl, and Lilian Eickemeyer. 1895. *Among the Pueblo Indians*. New York: The Merriam Company.

Evans, Nancy. 1978. "Tourism and Cross-Cultural Communication," in *Tourism and Behavior: Studies in Third World Societies*, ed. Mario Zamora, Vinson Sutlive, and Nathan Altshuler. Williamsburg, VA: College of William and Mary.

Evans-Pritchard, Deirdre. 1989. "How 'They' See 'Us': Native American Images of Tourists." *Annals of Tourism Research* 16:89–106.

Farrell, Bryan. 1979. "Tourism's Human Conflicts: Cases from the Pacific." *Annals of Tourism Research* 6:122–36.

Forster, John. 1964. "The Sociological Consequences of Tourism." *International Journal of Comparative Sociology* 5:217–27.

Goffman, Erving. 1959. *Presentation of Self in Everyday Life*. Garden City, NY: Doubleday.

Greenwood, Davydd. 1977. "Culture by the Pound: An Anthropological Perspective on Tourism as Cultural Commodification," in *Hosts and Guests: The Anthropology of Tourism*, ed. Valene Smith, pp. 127–38. Philadelphia: University of Pennsylvania Press.

Huit, Groupe. 1979. "The Sociocultural Effects of Tourism: A Case Study of Sousse," in *Tourism: Passport to Development?*, ed. Emmanuel de Kadt. New York: Oxford University Press.

Johnston, Barbara. 1990. "Save Our Beach Dem and Our Land Too!" *Cultural Survival Quarterly* 14:30–37.

MacCannell, Dean. 1984. "Reconstructed Ethnicity: Tourism and Cultural Identity in Third World Communities." *Annals of Tourism Research* 11:387–88.

McKean, Philip. 1989. "Towards a Theoretical Analysis of Tourism," in *Hosts and Guests: The Anthropology of Tourism*, 2nd edition, ed. Valene Smith, pp. 119–38. Philadelphia: University of Pennsylvania Press.

Nolan, Sidney, and Mary Lee Nolan. 1978. "Variations in Travel Behavior and the Cultural Impact of Tourism," in *Tourism and Behavior, Studies in Third World Societies*, ed. Mario Zamora, Vinson Sutlive, and Nathan Altshuler. Williamsburg, VA: College of William and Mary.

Simmons, Marc. 1979. "History of the Pueblos Since 1821," in *Handbook of North American Indians*, vol. 9, ed. Alfonso Ortiz. Washington DC: Smithsonian Institution.

Smith, M. Estellie. 1982. "Tourism and Native Americans." *Cultural Survival Quarterly* 6:10–12.

Smith, Valene. 1977. "Introduction," in *Hosts and Guests: The Anthropology of Tourism*, ed. Valene Smith. Philadelphia: University of Pennsylvania Press

Spicer, Edward. 1962. *Cycles of Conquest: The Impact of Spain, Mexico, and the United States on the Indians of the Southwest, 1533–1960*. Tucson: University of Arizona Press.

Swain, Margaret. 1989. "Gender Roles in Indigenous Tourism: Kuna Mola, Kuna Yala, and Cultural Survival," in *Hosts and Guests: The Anthropology of Tourism*, 2nd edition, ed. Valene Smith, pp. 83–104. Philadelphia: University of Pennsylvania Press.

Sweet, Jill. 1983. "Ritual and Theater in Tewa Ceremonial Performances." *Ethnomusicology* 27: 253–69.

———. 1985. *Dances of the Tewa Pueblo Indians*. Santa Fe, NM: School of American Research Press.

———. 1989. "Burlesquing 'The Other' in Pueblo Performance." *Annals of Tourism Research* 16:62–75.

———. 1990. "The Portals of Tradition: Tourism in the American Southwest." *Cultural Survival Quarterly* 14:62–75.

van den Berghe, Pierre, and Charles F. Keyes. 1984. "Introduction: Tourism and Re-created Ethnicity." *Annals of Tourism Research* 11:343–52.

Weigle, Marta. 1989. "From Desert to Disney World: The Santa Fe Railway and the Fred Harvey Company Display the Indian Southwest." *Journal of Anthropological Research* 45:115–37.

18

When Sex Tourists and Sex Workers Meet: Encounters within Sosúa, the Dominican Republic

Denise Brennan

There is a new sex-tourist destination on the global sexual landscape: Sosúa, the Dominican Republic. A beach town on the north coast, Sosúa has emerged as a place of fantasy for white European male tourists willing to pay for sex with Afro-Caribbean women. But European men are not the only ones who seek to fulfill fantasies. Dominican sex workers also arrive in Sosúa with fantasies: fantasies of economic mobility, visas to Europe, and even romance. For them, Sosúa and its tourists represent an escape: women migrate from throughout the Dominican Republic with dreams of European men "rescuing" them from a lifetime of foreclosed opportunities and poverty. They hope to meet and marry European men who will sponsor their (and their children's) migration to Europe. Yet, even though more and more women and girls migrate to Sosúa everyday, most leave the sex trade with little more than they had when they arrived.

This article explores this paradoxical feature of sex tourism in Sosúa, and examines why women continue to flock to Sosúa and how they make the most of their time while there. Through the sex trade in this one tourist town, we see how globalization affects sex workers and sex tourists differently. In this economy of desire, some dreams are realized, while others prove hollow. White, middle-class and lower-middle class European visitors and residents are much better positioned to secure what they want in Sosúa than poor, black Dominican sex workers. Globalization and the accompanying transnational processes such as tourism and sex tourism not only open up opportunities but also reproduce unequal, dependent relations along lines of gender, race, class, geography, and history.

Why the Sex Trade? Why Sosúa?

Dominican women who migrate to Sosúa and its sex trade are seduced by the opportunity to meet, and possibly marry, a foreign tourist. Even if sex workers do not marry their clients, Sosúa holds out the promise of maintaining a transnational relationship with them, using new transnational technologies such as fax machines and international money wires. Without these transnational connections, Sosúa's sex trade would be no different than sex work in any other Dominican town. By migrating to Sosúa, women are engaging in an economic strategy that is both very familiar and something altogether new. I argue that they try to use the sex trade as an *advancement* strategy, not just a *survival* strategy. In short, these marginalized female heads-of-household try to take advantage of the global linkages that exploit them.

Though only a handful of women regularly receive money wires from ex-clients in Europe—and even fewer actually move to Europe to live with their sweethearts—success stories circulate among the sex workers like Dominicanized versions of the movie *Pretty Woman*. Thus, Sosúa's myth of opportunity goes unchallenged and women, recruited through female social networks of family and close friends who have already migrated, keep on arriving, ready to find their "Richard Gere." Yet what the women find is a far cry from their fantasy images of fancy dinners, nightclubs, easy money, and visas off the island. One disappointed sex worker, Carmen,[1] insightfully sums up just how important fantasy is to constructing the image of Sosúa as a place of opportunity: "Women come to Sosúa because of a big lie. They hear they can make money, and meet a gringo, and they come.... They come with their dreams, but then they find out it is all a lie."

Work choices available to poor Dominican women are determined not only by local factors, but by the global economy. Internal migration for sex work is a consequence of both local economic and social transformations and larger, external forces, such as foreign investment in export-processing zones and tourism. Just as international investors see the Dominican Republic as a site of cheap labor, international tourists know it as a place to buy cheap sex. In sex tourism, First-World travelers/consumers seek exoticized, racialized "native" bodies in the developing world for cut-rate prices. These two components—race and its associated stereotypes and expectations, and the economic disparities between the developed and developing worlds—characterize sex tourist destinations throughout the world. What do white men "desire" when they decide to book a flight from Frankfurt, for example, to Puerto Plata (the nearest airport to Sosúa)? I turned to the Internet for answers. Any exploration of the relationship between globalization, women's work choices in the global economy, and women's migration for work must now investigate the role the Internet has in producing and disseminating racialized and sexualized stereotypes in the developing world. The Internet is quickly and radically transforming the sex trade in the developing world, since online travel services make it increasingly easy for potential sex tourists to research sex-tourist destinations and to plan trips. I looked at Web sites that post writings from alleged sex tourists who share information about their sex trips.[2] In the process, they advertise not only their services but also Dominican women as sexual commodities. One sex tourist was impressed by the availability of "dirt cheap colored girls," while another boasted, "When you enter the discos, you will feel like you're in heaven! A tremendous number of cute girls and something for everyone's taste (if you like colored girls like me)!"[3] There is little doubt that race is central to what these sex tourists desire in their travels.

International Tourism: Who Benefits?

International tourism has not benefited poor Dominicans as much as many had hoped. Although development and foreign investment have brought "First-World" hotels and services to Sosúa, the local population still lives in Third-World conditions. The most successful resorts in Sosúa are foreign owned, and even though they create employment opportunities for the local population, most of the new jobs are low-paying service jobs with little chance for mobility. What's more, the multinational resorts that have moved into Sosúa have pushed small hotel and restaurant owners out of business. One such restaurant owner, Luis, comments on the effects of these large "all-inclusive" hotels (tourists pay one fee in their home countries for airfare, lodging, food, and even drinks) on the Sosúa economy:

> These tourists hardly change even US$100 to spend outside the hotel. Before the all-inclusive hotels, people would change between US$1000–2000 and it would get distributed throughout the town: some for lodging, for food and entertainment. Now, not only do any of the local merchants get any of the money, but it never even leaves the tourists' home countries—like Germany or Austria—where they pay for their vacation in advance.

Foreign ownership, repatriation of profits, and the monopolistic nature of these all-inclusive resorts, make it difficult for the local population to profit significantly. Tourism is one of the largest industries in the global economy (Sinclair 1997), and it is not unusual for foreign firms to handle all four components of a tourist's stay: airlines, hotels, services, and tour operators. I interviewed the general manager (an Italian citizen) of a German hotel, for example, whose parent company is a German airline company. Eighty percent of the hotel's guests are German, all of whom paid for their airfare, lodging, and food in Germany. Furthermore, this German company imported most of its management staff from Europe, as well as the furniture, fabrics, and other goods necessary to run the hotel. So much for opportunities for local Dominicans.

Marginalized individuals in the global economy frequently turn to migration and more recently to tourism as an exit from poverty. Both migration and transnational relationships with foreign tourists are perceived as ways to access a middle-class lifestyle and its accompanying commodities. A several decades-old history of migration between the Dominican Republic and New York (Georges 1990; Grasmuck and Pessar 1991) and the transnational cultural, political, and economic flows between these two spaces, have led many Dominicans to look *fuera* (outside) for solutions to their economic problems. A preoccupation with goods, capital, and opportunities that are "outside" helps explain how sex workers and other Dominican migrants can view Sosúa as a place of opportunity. These women would go to New York if they could, but they do not have the social networks (i.e., immediate family members in New York) to sponsor them for visas, nor the contacts to underwrite an illegal migration. Migrating internally to Sosúa is the closest they can get to the "outside." Without established contacts in New York, they have a greater chance to someday get overseas by marrying a tourist (no matter how slight a chance) than they do of obtaining a visa. In many ways, hanging out in the tourist bars in Sosúa is a better use of their time than waiting in line for a visa at the U.S. Embassy in Santo Domingo. Carla, a first-time sex worker, explains why Sosúa draws women from throughout the country: "We come here because we dream of a ticket" (airline ticket). But without a visa—which they could obtain through marriage—Dominican sex workers cannot use the airline ticket Carla describes. They must depend on their European clients-turned-boyfriends/husbands to sponsor them for visas off the island. They are at once independent and dependent, strategic and exploited.

A question I routinely posed to sex workers (and others have asked me, as an anthropologist working with women who sell sex) is why they decide to enter sex work rather than other forms of labor? The majority of these women are mothers with little formal education, few marketable skills, limited social networks, and minimal support from the fathers of their children. They are poor Dominican women who have few means to escape from poverty and the periodic crises they find themselves in. Within this context, sex work appears as a potentially profitable alternative to the low wages they could earn in export-processing zones or in domestic service—the two most common forms of formal employment available to poor women.[4] Many poor Dominican women must find work within the insecure and even lower-paying informal sector. Felicia and Margarita, two friends who had migrated to Sosúa from the same town, found that the employment opportunities available to them at home (e.g., hairstylist, waitress, domestic) did not sufficiently provide for their families. They summed up their dilemma this way: "If you have a husband who pays for food and the house, then you can work in jobs like hairstyling. Otherwise it's not possible to work in jobs like this." Maintaining the view that women's earnings are "secondary" or "supplementary," these women nevertheless became the primary breadwinners once they separated from their "husbands."[5]

Women can choose to enter the sex trade in other Dominican towns, so by choosing Sosúa they are choosing to work with foreign rather than Dominican men. The selection not only of sex work over other work options but also of Sosúa, with its foreign tourist clientele, over other Dominican towns demonstrates that sex work for these women is not just a survival strategy but rather a strategy of advancement. This "choice" of the sex trade *in Sosúa* presents an important counter example to depictions of sex workers (who are not coerced or forced into prostitution) as powerless victims of male violence and exploitation. Yet, without protection under the law, sex workers are vulnerable to clients' actions once they are out of public spaces and in private hotel rooms. They risk battery, rape, and forced unprotected sex. Sex workers in Sosúa, however, often discount the risks of violence and AIDS given what they see as the potential payoffs of financial stability or a marriage proposal. Recently, however, so many women have migrated to Sosúa from throughout the Dominican Republic that sex workers outnumber clients in the bars. Thus, in order to understand why women place themselves in a context of uncertainty and potential violence, we need to explore fully Sosúa's opportunity myth. How reliable are the payoffs and how high are the risks? Why might or might not women achieve "success" through sex work in Sosúa? Can these poor, single mothers benefit from globalization?

Sex Work: Short- and Long-term Strategies

Working with foreign tourists can represent considerable long-term financial gains for a sex worker and her extended family—far more than she could gain from factory or domestic work. Yet, not all women who arrive in Sosúa to pursue sex work want to build long-term transnational ties. Some have different long-term strategies, such as saving enough money to start a *colmado* (small grocery store) in their yard in their home communities. Others use sex work simply as a way to make ends meet in the immediate future. Those who hope to pursue long-term relationships with foreign tourists are often disappointed. Relationships go sour and with them their extended family's only lifeline from poverty disintegrates. For every promise a tourist keeps, there are many more stories of disappointment. Even the success stories eventually cannot live up to the myths.

Sex work yields varying levels of reward. Some women open savings accounts and are able to build houses with their earnings, while others do not have enough money to pay the motorcycle taxi fare from their boarding houses to the tourist bars. Why are some sex workers able to save, despite the obstacles, while most continue to live from day to day? Success at sex work in Sosúa depends both on a planned strategy and a real commitment to saving money as well as luck. I cannot emphasize enough the role chance plays in sex workers' long-term ties with foreign clients. Whether or not clients stay in touch with the women is out of their control. One sex worker, Carmen, was thus skeptical that the Belgian client with whom she spent time during his three-week vacation in Sosúa actually would follow through on his promises to marry her and move her to Europe: "I don't absolutely believe that he is going to marry me. You know, sure, when he was here he seemed to love me. But you know people leave and they forget." In fact, months later, she still had not heard from him. I helped Carmen write him a letter, which I mailed when I got back to the United States. It was returned to my address, unopened. Had she gotten the address wrong or did he give her a false address along with his proclamations of love and commitment to their living together?

Adding to the uncertainty and fragility of transnational relationships are other logistical obstacles to "success." Women must find ways to save money despite the drain on their resources from paying police bribes and living in an expensive tourist town where prices for food and rent are among the highest in the country. All of this combined with increased competition among sex workers for clients increases the likelihood of having to leave Sosúa with little or no money saved. Furthermore, the majority of women who arrive in Sosúa do not know what they are getting into. They have heard of police roundups and know that they must vie with countless other women like themselves to catch the attention of potential clients, but like most migrants they are full of hopes and dreams and believe that "it will be different for them." In gold-rush fashion, they arrive in Sosúa because they have heard of Sosúa's tourists and money, and they plan, without a specific strategy in mind, to cash in on the tourist boom. It only takes a few days in Sosúa to realize that the only hope they have to quickly make big money is to establish a transnational relationship. New arrivals see veteran sex workers drop by the Codetel office (telephone and fax company) every day, vigilantly looking for faxes from clients in Europe or Canada. If they want to receive money wires or marriage proposals from tourists overseas, they learn that they must establish similar ongoing transnational relationships.

Sex Workers' Stories

In order to explore how sex workers' time in Sosúa measures up to their fantasy images, I turn to three sex workers' divergent experiences. Their stories call attention to the difficulties of establishing a transnational relationship, as well as to its fragility. Through sex workers' accounts of their relationships with foreign men, we get a sense of just how wildly unpredictable the course of these relationships can be.

Elena and Jürgen: Building and Breaking Transnational Ties through Sex Work

This story begins with Elena's release from jail. After being held for two days, twenty-two-year-old Elena went to the beach.[6] When I saw her, back at her one-room wooden house, she was ecstatic. At the beach she had run into Jürgen, who had just returned to Sosúa from his home in Germany to see her. They had been sending faxes to one another since he had left Sosúa after his last vacation, and he had mentioned in one of his faxes that he would be returning. He did not know where she lived, but figured he would find her that evening at the Anchor, Sosúa's largest tourist bar and a place tourists go to pick up sex workers. He brought her presents from Germany, including perfume and a matching gold chain necklace and bracelet. Elena was grinning ear to ear as she showed off her gifts, talking about Jürgen like a smitten schoolgirl: "I am canceling everything for the weekend and am going to spend the entire time with him. We will go to the beach and he will take me to nightclubs and to restaurants."

Elena began preparing for the weekend. Her two sisters who lived with her, ages fourteen and sixteen, would look after her six-year-old daughter, since Elena would stay with Jürgen in his hotel. She chose the evening's outfit carefully, with plenty of help from her sisters, daughter, and friend, a young sex worker who also lives with them since she has very little money. Elena provides for these four girls with her earnings from sex work. They all rotate between sharing the double bed and sleeping on the floor. Spending time with a tourist on his vacation means Elena would receive more gifts, maybe even some for her family, and would make good money. So they helped primp Elena, selecting billowy rayon pants that moved as she did and a black lycra stretch shirt with long sheer sleeves that was cropped to reveal her slim stomach. She was meeting Jürgen at the Anchor, where I saw her later on, and she stood out in the crowd.

As soon as Jürgen's vacation ended, he went back to Germany with a plan to return in a couple of months. Since he was self-employed in construction, he could live part of the year in the Dominican Republic. Elena was very upset when Jürgen left and could not stop crying. Maybe Jürgen represented more than just money, nice meals, and new clothes. I had often heard sex workers distinguish between relationships with tourists *por amor* (for love) or *por residencia* (for residence/visas) but Elena's tears broke down that distinction.

Unlike Carmen's relationship with her Belgian client, Jürgen kept his word to Elena and wired money and kept in touch through faxes. Even more surprisingly, he returned to Sosúa only two months later. Within days of his return, he rented a two-bedroom apartment that had running water and an electrical generator (for daily blackouts). He also bought beds, living room furniture, and a large color television. Elena was living out the fantasy of many sex workers in Sosúa: she was sharing a household with a European man who supported her and her dependents. Jürgen paid for food that Elena and her sisters prepared and had cable television installed. He also paid for Elena's six-year-old daughter to attend a private school and came home one day with school supplies for her. Occasionally, Jürgen took Elena, her daughter, and her sisters out to eat at one of the tourist restaurants that line the beach where the tourists sun themselves.

Elena had moved up in the world: eating in tourist restaurants, sending a daughter to private school, and living in a middle-class apartment were all symbols of her increased social and economic mobility. As a female head of household who had been taking care of her daughter and sisters with her earnings from sex work, Elena was now able to quit sex work and live off of the money Jürgen gave her. Sex work and the transnational relationships it had built altered Elena's life as well as the lives of those who depended on her. But for how long?

Jürgen turned out not to be Elena's or her family's salvation. Soon after they moved in together, Elena found out she was pregnant. Both she and Jürgen were very happy about having a baby. He had a teenage son living with his ex-wife in Germany and relished the idea of having another child. At first, he was helpful around the house and doted on Elena. But the novelty soon wore off and he returned to his routine of spending most days in the German-owned bar beneath their apartment. He also went out drinking at night with German friends, hopping from bar to bar. He was drunk, or on his way there, day and night. Elena saw him less and less frequently, and they began to fight often, usually over money.

Eventually he started staying out all night. On one occasion, a friend of Elena's (a sex worker) saw Jürgen at the Anchor talking with, and later on leaving the bar with, a Haitian sex worker. Elena knew he was cheating on her. But she did not want to raise this with Jürgen, explaining that men "do these things." Instead, she focused her anger on the fact that he was not giving her enough money to take care of the household. Ironically, Elena had more disposable income before she began to live with Jürgen. Back then, she could afford to go out dancing and drinking with her friends—not to look for clients, but just to have fun. Now, without an income of her own, she was dependent upon Jürgen not only for household expenses but also for her entertainment.

On more than one occasion I served as interpreter between the two during their attempts at "peace negotiations" after they had not spoken to one another for days. Since Elena does not speak any German or English, she asked me to help her understand why Jürgen was mad at her as well as to communicate her viewpoint to him. In preparation for one of these "negotiations," Elena briefed me on what she wanted me to explain to Jürgen:

> I want to know why he is not talking to me? And why is he not giving me
> any money? He is my *esposo* [husband—in consensual union] and is
> supposed to give me money. I need to know if he is with me or with
> someone else. He pays for this house and paid for everything here. I need
> to know what is going on. You know I was fine living alone before, I'm
> able to do that. I took care of everything before, this is not a problem.
> But I need to know what is going to happen.

Since they were living together and Jürgen was paying the bills, Elena
considered them to be married. To Elena and her friends, Jürgen, as an
esposo, was financially responsible for the household. But Jürgen saw things
differently. He felt Elena thought he was "made of money" and was always
asking him for more. He asked me to translate to her:

> I'm not a millionaire. I told Elena last week that I don't like her always
> asking for money. She did not listen. She asks me for money all day
> long. I don't want to be taken advantage of.

One day, without warning, Jürgen packed his bags and left for Germany for business. Elena knew this day would come, that Jürgen would
have to return to Germany to work. But she did not expect their relationship
would be in such disarray, and that he would depart without leaving her
money (although he did leave some food money with her younger sisters
who turned it over to Elena). In Jürgen's absence, Elena took her daughter
out of the private school once the tuition became overdue and she started
working part-time at a small Dominican-owned restaurant. When Jürgen
returned to Sosúa from Germany a couple of months later, they split up for
good. Elena moved out of their apartment back to the labyrinth of shanties
on dirt paths off the main road. Her economic and social mobility was short-
lived. She had not accumulated any savings or items she could pawn during
her time with Jürgen. Jürgen never gave her enough money so that she could
set some aside for savings. And all the things he bought for the apartment
were his, not hers. When they vacated the apartment, he took all of the furniture and the television with him.

Elena's relationship with Jürgen dramatically changed her life; she was,
after all, having his child. But her social and economic status remained as
marginal as ever. Even though she was living out many sex workers' fantasies of "marrying" a foreign tourist, she still lived like many poor Dominicans, struggling day to day without access to resources to build long-term
economic security. When she and Jürgen fought and he withheld money from
her, she was less economically independent than she was as a sex worker,
when she was certain to earn around 500 pesos a client. Although sex workers take on great risks—of AIDS, abuse, and arrest—and occupy a marginal
and stigmatized status in Dominican society, Elena's status as the "housewife" of a German resident was fragile and constantly threatened.

Jürgen now lives, Elena has heard, somewhere in Asia. Elena is back
living in the same conditions as before she met Jürgen. She has not returned

to sex work and makes significantly less money working in a restaurant. Her older sisters now help take care of their younger sisters, and Elena sends what money she can, though less than in her sex work days, to help out her parents.

Luisa's Money Wires

Luisa is an example of a sex worker whose transnational connections were those other sex workers envied, but her "success," like Elena's, ended without warning. She, quite remarkably, received US$500 every two weeks from a client in Germany, who wanted her to leave sex work and start her own clothing store. She told him she had stopped working the tourist bars, and that she used the money to buy clothes for the store. Yet, when he found out that she was still working as a sex worker, had not opened a store, and was living with a Dominican boyfriend, he stopped wiring money.

At this juncture, Luisa was in over her head. She had not put any of the money in the bank, in anticipation of the day when the money wires might dry up. She was renting a two-bedroom apartment that was twice the size and rent of friends' apartments. And she sent money home to her mother in Santo Domingo, who was taking care of her twelve-year-old son. She also supported her Dominican boyfriend, who lived with her and did not have a steady job. Other sex workers called him a *chulo* (pimp) since he lived off of Luisa's earnings and money wires. They saw Luisa as foolish for bankrolling her boyfriend, especially since he was not the father of her son. She began hocking her chains and rings in one of Sosúa's half-dozen pawnshops.

As lucky as Luisa was to meet this German client at the Anchor, most of the women working the Anchor night after night never receive a single money wire transfer. Those who do generally receive smaller sums than Luisa did, on a much more infrequent and unpredictable basis. And as Luisa's story demonstrates, a sex worker's luck can change overnight. There is no guarantee that money wires will continue once they begin. Luisa had no way of knowing that she would lose her "meal ticket," nor can she be certain that she will ever find another tourist to replace him. Furthermore, women cannot count on earning money in sex work indefinitely. Luisa is in her early thirties and knows that over the next few years it will be increasingly difficult to compete with the young women in the bars (some are as young as sixteen and seventeen, most are between nineteen and twenty-five). Yet, once women make the decision to leave Sosúa and sex work, they face the same limited opportunities they confronted before they entered sex work. They are still hampered by limited education, a lack of marketable job skills, and not "knowing the right people." In fact, obstacles to economic and social mobility might have increased, especially if they are rumored to have AIDS. They might have to battle gossip in their home community and the stigma associated with sex work. After years of working in bars they might have a substance-abuse problem. And they return to children who have grown in their absence.

Carmen's Diversification Strategy

Carmen's story, compared to Elena's, is one of relative success, in which her relationship with Dominican clients figures prominently. In fact, supplementing uncertain income with foreign tourists by working with Dominican clients, as well as establishing long-term relationships with Dominican *amigos/clientes fijos* (friends/regular clients), supplies Carmen with a steady flow of income. Another sex worker, Ani, explains the function of *amigos*:

> You don't always have a client. You need *amigos* and *clientes fijos*. If you have a problem, like something breaks in your house, or your child is sick and you need money for the doctor or medicine, they can help.

For Carmen, working with Dominicans has proven much more reliable than establishing ties with foreign men. Carmen has saved enough money from four years in sex work to build a small house in Santo Domingo (the capital city five hours away where she will retire to take care of her mother and children). She has managed to save more money than most sex workers. I asked her why she thinks she was able to save money, while many of her friends don't have an extra centavo, and she answered,

> Because they give it to their men. Their husbands wait at home and drink while their women work. Not me. If I'm in the street with all the risks of disease and the police, I'm keeping the money or giving it to my kids. I'm not giving it to a man, no way. If women don't give the money to the men, they (the men) beat the women.

She is careful not to let the men in her life know how much money she has saved in the bank (unlike Luisa), or the sources of the money. She has a steady relationship in particular with Jorge, who is her economic safety net, especially in times of crises. She describes their relationship:

> He is very young [she scrunched her nose up in disapproval of this point]. He lives with his mother in Santiago and works in a *zona franca* [factory in an export-processing zone]. He gives me money, even though he does not make a lot. He bought me furniture for the new house.

At times, the money Jorge gives Carmen is the only money she has. By establishing a relationship with a Dominican man, she has been able to supplement her unpredictable income from sex work. Though the money he gives her is in smaller sums than transnational money wires other sex workers receive, like Luisa, it is money she can count on, on a regular basis.

Carmen not only has diversified her clients, focused on achieving one specific goal (building a house), but she also has clear personal limitations working in a dangerous trade. Since she has a serious fear of the police, she refuses to work when they are making arrests outside of the tourist bars where many of the sex workers congregate to talk, smoke, or greet customers entering the bars. At one point when the police seemed to be making more arrests than usual, Carmen quit going to the tourist bars altogether. Instead, she took a bus to a small Dominican town about thirty miles away to work in a bar that caters to Dominican clients. Thus, she developed an alternate plan to working in Sosúa when necessary.

By pursuing local Dominican clients as well as trying to establish transnational connections, sex work is paying off for Carmen in the long term. Carmen refused to be seduced by the promise of a tourist enclave and the sweet talk of foreign tourists. Instead, she treated Sosúa as any other Dominican town with "brothels" and set up a roster of local regular clients. Carmen's gains have been slow and modest. Nevertheless, she saved enough money to begin constructing a small house, though thus far it has taken her four years, and she still needs enough money for windows. But she will leave Sosúa with her future, and her family's, more secure than when she first arrived. Stories about modest successes like Carmen's are not as glamorous as those with transnational dimensions. Rather, stories of transnational relationships and quick, big money circulate among the sex workers, like those of Elena and Luisa. Their more immediate and visible ascension from poverty are regaled and fuel the illusion of Sosúa as a place to get rich quick.

Conclusion

Foreign sex tourists clearly benefit from their geographic position in the global economy, as they travel with ease (no visa is needed to enter the Dominican Republic) and buy sex for cheaper prices than in their home countries. Dominican sex workers, in contrast, face innumerable constraints due to their country's marginal position in the global economy. Sosúa's sex trade is but one more site where, broadly, we can observe globalization exacerbating inequality and, more specifically, we can situate tourism and sex tourism as both relying on and reproducing inequalities in the global economy.

Like most prospectors in search of quick money, few sex workers who rush into Sosúa looking for a foreign tourist to solve their problems find what they were hoping for. It is of little surprise, however, that women, despite the obstacles to fulfilling their "fantasies" continue to arrive everyday. Women from the poorest classes have no other work options that pay as well as the sex trade with tourists in the short term. Nor do most other work options offer the opportunity to establish long-term relationships with foreign men. Although most transnational relationships are unlikely to alter sex workers' long-term economic and social status, they make far more financial gains than most women in the sex trade or other accessible labor options (such as domestic service or factory work).

Sex workers also slowly can make gains without transnational connections. Though difficult to achieve, these gains might prove more durable than those resting on a transnational relationship. Carmen's transnational ties never paid off, and consequently she did not come into a lot of money all at once. But she still managed to save what she could over time. Her house represents security, but it does not catapult her out of *los pobres* (the poor). Her "success" is not on the same level as women with ongoing relationships with European men. But while these ties could dissolve at any time, Carmen's house will still be there. She looks forward to the day she completes her house and leaves Sosúa and its sex trade: "When I leave here I want to sit on the front porch of my new house with my mother and my children and drink a cold glass of juice. I want a peaceful life. No Sosúa, no men giving you problems."

Source: Adapted from "Globalization, Women's Labor, and Men's Pleasure: Sex Tourism in Sosúa, the Dominican Republic," *Urban Life: Readings in the Anthropology of the City*, 4th ed. George Gmelch and Walter Zenner (eds.), 2002, Waveland Press.

Notes

[1] I have changed all names.

[2] I did not join any of these sites, however. But, rather, looked at "satisfied customer" testimonials the sites post to try to entice new paying members.

[3] For more on the Internet and the sex trade see Brennan, Denise (2001), "Tourism in Transnational Places: Dominican Sex Workers and German Sex Tourists Imagine One Another," *Identities: Global Studies in Culture and Power* 7, 4 (1/01):621–63.

[4] These jobs, on average, yield under 1000 pesos a month, whereas sex workers in Sosúa charge approximately 500 pesos from foreign clients.

[5] Poor Dominicans are more likely to enter consensual unions than legal marriage. In fact, unless I specifically mention otherwise, sex workers are not legally married to their husbands. Yet since the women I interviewed referred to the men in their lives as "husbands" *(esposos)*, I also use this term.

[6] She paid 500 pesos (US$41.00) for her release—the standard bribe to the police.

19

Romance Tourism: Gender, Race, and Power in Jamaica

Deborah Pruitt and Suzanne LaFont

The United Nations identifies tourism as the world's fastest growing industry. It is the heart of development strategies in many less developed nations. Jamaica is one of the countries that has embraced the tourism industry as a path leading to economic prosperity and has focused on its growth and development for the past two decades.

Global economics means that most tourists are from the highly developed countries. The tourist's destination is often to poorer countries such as Jamaica that offer high value for their money and seemingly exotic locales. In contrast to these privileged travelers, most people in the world will never leave their native countries because poverty and/or visa restrictions preclude such luxuries as vacations. While the governments of the less-developed countries actively lure tourists, hoping to profit from the vast travel industry, many of the local people in these "tourist destinations" also try to benefit directly from tourism, either formally or informally, by offering a host of services to vacationers.

In recent years the contact between local peoples and tourists have received a great deal of attention (Altman 2001; Kempadoo and Doezema

1998). In Jamaica, these interactions are often between single women travelers and local men. Since the 1960s when the feminist movement fostered women's independence, expectations of freedom and mobility, and economic self-sufficiency, large numbers of single women have been traveling in pursuit of their own adventures—adventures that sometimes include sex, romance, and experimentation with new gender roles and power. Particular features of Jamaica and its image as a place to be "free" makes it a popular destination for such women.

Foreign women on the arms of local men in resort areas of Jamaica (and other parts of the Caribbean) are a regular part of the social landscape (de Albuquerque 1999). In this small-scale society, sufficient numbers of young men are involved in this activity that it is widely discussed and has recently become an issue for the media and the government-industry complex. It has been institutionalized to the point that the label "rent-a-dread" has been coined to refer to the men who get involved with foreign women. There are T-shirts, postcards, and cartoons making jokes about them. Popular songs also comment on these relationships. Such tourism liaisons are sufficiently common as to encourage at least one American tour operator to consider creating a promotional brochure complete with pictures of Jamaican men available as companions so she could broker the relationships from the United States before the women leave home. German women embark on these ventures frequently enough that an expression has developed in Germany that "The men go to Thailand and the women go to Jamaica" (Pruitt 1993).

But the interaction of foreign women and local men does not always end in Jamaica. In the small-scale tourism center where one author lived for two years, hundreds of local men have "gone foreign" with women who were vacationing. In fact, virtually all of the young men who sought their livelihood from informal tourism work during that period had or have gone to foreign countries with their tourist girlfriends at least once. Many of them are still living in Europe and all of them have ongoing relationships with foreign women.

Romance Tourism

Sexual tourism liaisons are diverse and multifaceted. Some are very short lived and could be termed superficial. We also see in Jamaica a particular kind of engagement between local men and tourist women that involves a complex set of desires, hopes, and fantasies that include romance, love, and the possibility of a long-term relationship in addition to sex. We use the term romance tourism to denote these particular qualities and to distinguish them from those of sex tourism.

Much more common and frequently studied are the sex-for-money exchanges that occur between male tourists and local women around the world. A survey of the Internet revealed hundreds of Web sites featuring travel agencies promising "sexual adventures" with women in Southeast Asia, Thailand, Russia, Eastern Europe, Central America, South America, Japan, and the Philippines. In contrast, none of the sites offered the sexual services of men to women (LaFont 2003). Although there is no doubt that some women travel to countries such as Jamaica specifically to engage in casual sexual relations with local men (Taylor 2001), sex tourism is primarily geared toward men and is quite formalized and widespread. It is often simply referred to as prostitution.

In Jamaica it is significant that neither actor in romance tourism relationships consider their interaction to be prostitution, even though others label it so. The actors place an emphasis on courtship rather than the exchange of sex for money. The purpose here is not to debate whether these men are prostitutes, but rather to convey the distinctive meaning these relationships hold for the partners and to acknowledge their definition of the situation. To refer to these relationships as prostitution and say that the participants are in "denial" (as some other authors have done) is to obliterate their reality and miss the subtle interplay of gender, money, and power. Gender is constitutive of these relationships, not ancillary to it. Gender roles are not simply being reversed. The nature of these relationships are shaped and defined by the fact that it is women who have the power, freedom, and money to engage in these liaisons. Romance is a dominant theme in Western culture and a central aspect of feminine sexuality. Not surprisingly, it is also a central aspect of many women's tourism relationships.

Romance tourism liaisons are constructed through a discourse of courtship and long-term relationship; an emotional involvement usually is not present in sex tourism. Both parties often share the ideal of a sustained relationship, though the meanings of such relationships are diverse. However, the framework of romance serves both parties as they seek to maximize the benefits they derive from the tourism relationship.

Tourists of Romance

The women who engage local men in romantic relationships span a wide range of nationalities, age, social, and economic backgrounds. The relationships are most often, though not always, cross-racial as well as cross-cultural in that the vast majority of tourists are classified as white, while the majority of the Jamaican population is of African descent. The duration of the women's stay is usually extended, lasting anywhere from a few weeks to a few months, and many are repeat visitors (Pruitt 1993). European women who often travel for periods of two to three months and come from countries with more relaxed immigration practices than those in North America are more likely to take local men back home with them. The women are seeking an "enriching" travel experience. They shun exclusive resorts in favor of locally owned guest houses, frequent local hang-outs, and socialize with the

local people. The milieu of romance tourism in Jamaica is in part a consequence of Jamaica's fame as the country that gave birth to the international
reggae counterculture. The burgeoning of adventurous travel and the global
spread of Jamaican reggae music has created a social environment within
which many tourists want to become more closely involved with local people, including having intimate relations with local men.

The desire for the "cultural" experience that the tourist woman seeks,
coupled with prolonged exposure to local society, demonstrates a readiness to
embrace, however superficially, the local culture. Such involvement contrasts
with the sexual liaisons of sex tourism. The Jamaican man is not merely a
sexual object, but rather becomes a woman's personal cultural broker. He
serves to ease her experience in his society and provide her with increased
access to local culture.

A foreign woman in Jamaica is assumed to be on vacation. If she is
without a male companion, it is often believed that she wants or needs a local
man to enhance her tourism experience. The frequency with which Jamaicans
have observed foreign women becoming involved with local men supports
this belief. It also relates, in part, to Jamaican notions of companionship and
pleasure and has resulted in what one local writer has called "the sexualization of routine encounters between a female tourist and a local Jamaican
male" (Henry 1988). Consequently, foreign women are frequently inundated
with offers from local men for companionship and a "bodyguard." One Canadian woman told the authors, "Guys at home are so confused, they don't
approach women directly very much. But you come down here [Jamaica] and
the men are dropping out of the trees like mangoes." The result is that many
women unexpectedly find themselves accepting the flattering offers they
receive. This might be the female traveler's opportunity to indulge fantasies
or explore a new aspect of herself by engaging in behavior that is unacceptable or unavailable at home.

Adding to the allure of the vacation romance are Caribbean ideals of
beauty. Light skin, straight hair, and Caucasian facial features are highly valued, and women who are considered overweight in their own cultures are
appreciated by many Jamaican men. Thus, foreign women who may not meet
Western standards of beauty find themselves being the object of amorous
attention by appealing local men.

Some women travel seeking companionship because they are unsatis-
fied with their relationships or the lack thereof at home. They travel with the
hope of finding an ideal mate and perhaps staying in Jamaica or returning
home with a partner. These women often express a frustration with men from
their own cultures as inattentive, preoccupied with careers, unemotional, or
confused about their male role (Pruitt 1993). However, many women are
unable or unwilling to establish permanent relationships with Jamaican men.
They sometimes settle for long-distance and part-time romances, returning to
the island year after year, while maintaining relationships through letters,
phone calls, and gifts of money and consumer goods.

The Caribbean man, who highly values proficiency at "sweet talk" (Abrahams 1983, Hubbard 2000), finds that his gender script for romancing women connects with her desire for romance. Ardent declarations of love, praises of beauty, and the like, which are a common part of a Jamaican man's repertoire, are seen as refreshing or passionate by the foreign woman who does not understand the culture. In the words of a Jamaican woman who runs a small guest house, the men "appeal to her emotions with flattery and compliments and do things for her to make her stay in Jamaica easier and more pleasant. They appeal to her sensual side by saying, 'Daughter [woman], if you come to Jamaica and never sleep with a Rastaman, the true, natural man of Jamaica, you never really experience Jamaica and yourself.'"

Courtship eases the interaction between local men and tourist women. It serves those women who are seeking "forbidden" experiences, romance idealism, or believe that sex should be linked to love. Western women draw from their cultural and gender script, assuming that Jamaican men hold the same ideals for intimacy. This pattern of social consumption also lies at the heart of romance tourism. The men are successful at elaborating on the tourist's imagination and thereby offering the promise of realization of her dreams.

Most Western tourist women in Jamaica are exposed to levels of poverty that are absent from their daily reality at home (Harrison 1997). "Third World poverty" is often perceived as noble in contrast to their hometown slums. Rural shacks may appear quaint, whereas ghettos are frightening. Reactions to poverty range from guilt and pity to the desire to help. This often brings people together despite striking socioeconomic differences. Fraternizing with local individuals of dramatically different social and economic status is seen as less threatening than at home. They develop a rapport and attempt to cross the boundaries of socioeconomic inequality. Consequently, many women romanticize their local lovers and hope to help him escape poverty. This tends to hasten the pace of the romance and add a "humanitarian" dimension to the relationship.

Racial, educational, age, and economic differences that constrain tourist women at home are often diminished or ignored during romance tourism. Thus, a rural, African-Caribbean man with little education and scant livelihood is often the companion of a foreign professional woman many years his senior. When necessary, the women pay for the man of their choice to accompany them to dinner, stage shows, discos, or trips around the island. In the light of obvious poverty, she frequently views her financial contribution to the relationship as relatively insignificant.

Women are also able to explore more dominant roles in the tourism relationship. The economic and social status the women enjoy provides them with security and independence that translates into power and control in the relationship. Some of the women say they enjoy the control they have in these relationships and express a preference for keeping a man dependent on them (Pruitt 1993). This ensures that he will be fully available to meet their needs and will not become distracted or otherwise occupied like the men in her own society.

Love and Money

The men hold their own ideals about the potential for emotional intimacy in relationships with foreign women. Many believe foreign women to be more tender and emotional than Jamaican women and imagine that they can experience an emotional and sexual intimacy in these relationships that is lacking in their lives, particularly as they are increasingly rejected by local women for their activities with foreigners.

Those men who desire a broader experience than that available in their immediate situation believe that a relationship with a foreign woman could also provide them with a way out of their limited circumstances. It has proven to be a successful strategy for many young men who seek opportunities and prosperity unavailable in the local society. The hope for economic benefits intertwines with emotional longing and fuels the men's romantic ideals for a relationship with a foreign woman.

Most of the men involved with female tourists can be seen as taking advantage of one of the few opportunities available to them. They generally come from that group of rural young people with little education and few social and economic prospects. The deprivation of opportunity in rural areas has led many young men to seek their livelihood directly from tourists (commonly referred to as hustling) by taking the role of guide or informal entrepreneur in the hopes of obtaining a few of the dollars tourists often spend liberally.

A steady flow of these young men who want to get out of rural areas move into the tourist developments and seek ways to make their living "hustling the tourists." In those regions where it is concentrated, tourism dominates the economy and has been billed as "The Answer" to Jamaica's economic future (Pruitt 1993). Yet, uneducated and unskilled young men living near resort areas are effectively cut off from formal jobs in the tourism industry. The prevalence of romance tourism has meant that increasing numbers of young men routinely view a relationship with a foreign woman as a meaningful opportunity for them to capture the love and money they desire. It is not uncommon to hear young men who come into the tourist areas from deep rural villages talk about their interest in "experiencing a white woman." The following is an excerpt from field notes.

> . . . It was a slow day, not many tourists were in town and none had ventured to Sunrise Beach that day. The guys were chatting about how slow things were.
>
> "Nothing's going on. No money is flowin'," Scoogie complained.
>
> "That's right. Nothing is happening around here. I just want to get me a white-woman and get out of here. Go to America and make real money," said Driver.
>
> "Yeah, you have to link up with a white-woman and get her to fall in love with you if you want a break . . ."

"Yeah man, you have to hook up with a white-woman. I mean look at
Decker, Jah Red, Collin, even Punkie. All gone foreign just since this
year," said Scoogie. . . . (Pruitt 1993:147)

The ability to earn a prosperous living has significance for the young
Jamaican man far beyond basic needs for survival. Brodber describes the
"pressure to establish one's maleness through the abilities to disperse cash"
(1989:69). The Jamaican man's aspirations to the status of a "big" man
(Whitehead 1992) involve money in each of the three elements—moral character, respectability, and reputation—which comprise that status. Evaluations
of moral character are based in part on a man's generosity. Expectations of
respectability include maintaining a household, while the reputation factor
central to achieving status as a "big" man is based partially on virility displayed by sexual conquests and fathering many children (Handwerker 1989,
Pruitt and LaFont 1997).

LaFont (1992:196) describes the expectations most Jamaican women
hold of financial remuneration from men in exchange for sex and domestic
duties by the woman with the result that "much of their [men's] role fulfillment is dependent on job opportunities and the economy." "No money, no
talk" is a common expression in Jamaica. Here, the word "talk" refers to intimate relations between a man and a woman. Women expect that a man with
whom they are having an intimate relationship will contribute financial support and that he will display an ability and willingness to do so early in the
courtship. Thus, the road to women and reputation that verifies a young
Jamaican male's manhood, and the status that follows, is constrained for the
man with uncertain income opportunities.

In contrast, while his finances are important in his native culture, relations with foreign women do not depend on his ability to provide income.
Her interests in him are not predominantly financial. Thus, he is able to
acquire the desirable "reputation" of being successful with women without
the financial outlay necessary in his own culture. This empowers the men's
relations with foreign women while at the same time changing his experience
of power and dominance.

While tourism acts as a catalyst for these men to manipulate gender
identity as a strategy for economic access, it also places them in a subordinate
role to women that is in conflict with their own gender ideals of male dominance. The independence and power the foreign woman enjoys from her
financial means yields a control in the relationship that is inappropriate for
Jamaican male aspirations. He chafes against her seemingly dominant position because, despite the discussions of male marginality (Chevannes and
Brown 1998) and matrifocality (Gonzalez 1970), which refer to men's relationship within the domestic domain, his desire to be dominant in gender
relations is intense. To maintain his reputation and avoid the appearance that
the woman controls him, the Jamaican man without economic means continually seeks new ways to exhibit his dominion over women. During the tourist
woman's holiday in Jamaica, the man has the power of local knowledge. He

can control much of his female companion's circumstances in Jamaica, generally without her awareness. He actively acts as buffer between her and others who might influence her; he makes it clear that he "controls that thing" and a hands-off message is relayed to the other male hustlers. This, along with controlling the car she has rented and getting her to buy him material goods, all exhibit his dominion over her.

In order to compete in his community for the status associated with a reputation for success with women, young men play off the features of masculinity available in their culture that have the greatest appeal to foreign women. For most foreign women these are associated with the male Rasta.

The Rasta Appeal

The connection a Western woman develops with a Jamaican man is generally based on her idealizations of his embodiment of manhood, idealizations fueled by the discourse of hegemonic relations constructed through "race" in which the exotic and the erotic are intertwined (Said 1978). The exotic Other has been constructed as more passionate, more emotional, more natural, and sexually tempting. Stereotypes of black men and their sexuality, of non-Western peoples, and on real differences between the tourists' cultures and Jamaican culture promote the belief that Jamaican men represent the archetypal masculine. This is augmented by the men's displays of machismo drawn from their cultural gender scripts. These beliefs are held by Western women considered black as well as white, though black women may not be adhering to stereotypes of black men in general, but rather the black man who stands closer to his African heritage, in this case embodied in the Rasta identity.

Though by no means exclusively, those men with dreadlocks who are assumed to be Rastafarian receive substantially more attention from foreign women than do Jamaican men without locks. Dreadlocks, "locks," or "dreads," are the result of letting hair grow naturally without cutting or combing.

In Jamaica, dreadlocks developed as a symbol of the spiritually based Rastafarian culture of resistance. Since the 1930s, they have represented "stepping out" of the dominant cultural and social system that enslaved the African and continues to denigrate that identity. Dreadlocks are symbolic of the strength of the lion, and signify pride in African heritage and represent strength, anything that is fearful. As such, dreadlocks represent a power source for the Rastafarian. They also symbolize a commitment to a natural way of life, unmediated by Western standards and vanities. Dreadlocks are but one element of a system of symbols that includes a distinctive use of the Jamaican language, images of the lion, and displaying and wearing of the colors of red, gold, and green. Each of them is a "reflection of a form of resistance, linking these symbols to some concrete struggle among African peoples" (Campbell 1987:95).

Rastafarian wearing dreadlocks, symbolic of the strength of the lion. (Photo by Ellen Frankenstein)

Reggae music developed in this same manner as an expression of the Rastafarian spirituality and a vehicle for spreading the message of resistance with an exhortation to the international community to "live up" to standards of interracial justice and peace. The penchant foreign women have for men with dreadlocks is fueled by the mystique associated with the dreadlock singers of the international reggae music culture who project an image of the Rastaman as a confident, naturally powerful, and especially virile man. During the late 1970s, Rastafarian musician Bob Marley was the first to achieve international recognition and subsequently succeeded in capturing the attention of countercultural people across the world. Reggae music, dreadlocks, and Rastafari became synonymous for much of the international community so that, following the model of Marley's success, reggae musicians increasingly grew their hair in locks and adopted the presentation of the powerful Rasta "lion." Through the years, the music has attracted millions of Westerners disaffected by their own culture's systems of inequality and materialism, and enticed them to Jamaica. The pilgrimage to the roots of Rasta resistance climaxes each year in July with the music festival called Reggae Sunsplash.

Whether due to an agreement with the Rasta political philosophy and a desire to demonstrate lack of prejudice, or an attraction to the powerful masculinity projected by the Rastas, or both, men who assume the Rastafarian identity have proven to be a particularly popular with the female European and American tourists with a lust for the exotic. Since the 1970s, young men living in the tourist areas who grew their hair in dreadlocks have attracted special attention from foreigners in general and women in particular. Therefore, those men interested in trading with foreigners, whether selling handicrafts or marijuana (associated with Rastas and an important tourism commodity), or generally acting as companion to ease the way for foreigners through the largely informal society, have increasingly styled themselves as Rastafarian. They "locks" their hair, speak in the Rasta dialect, and develop a presentation that expresses the Rastafarian emphasis on simplicity and living in harmony with nature, in effect, constructing a "staged authenticity" (MacCannell 1973). The man with locks picks up and elaborates on aspects of the stereotype of the exotic Other, enhancing the contrast between himself and Western men, thereby strengthening his appeal to the Western women.

In turn, because these men with locks have increased contact with tourists, they become familiar with the foreign cultures, perhaps learning to speak a little German, or developing an expertise for guessing what types of experiences the specific tourists are seeking. Hence, they become more accessible to the foreigner. Those foreigners in search of an authenticity associated with nonindustrialized society (MacCannell 1976; Cohen 1979) are attracted to the Rasta images and impressions of unity associated with them. The Jamaica Tourist Board reinforced these impressions by using images of dreadlock musicians singing Bob Marley's song "One Love" in the 1991 television advertisement for Jamaica.

Leed (1991:218) describes travel as a "stripping away of the subjectivity rooted in language and custom, allowing travelers to become acquainted with a common nature, fate, and identity that persist beneath the diversity of cultural types and ideals." That motivation for travel intersects in Jamaica with the philosophy of Rastafari, which has at its foundation an emphasis on common identity and unity of spirit. The dread who approaches the tourist appears to offer travelers to Jamaica just that experience of "oneness."

A Rasta identity is attractive to the Jamaican man involved in the tourist hustle because it provides a model of masculinity that is not dependent upon disbursing cash. Rather, it developed around an articulation of the forces that prohibit the African-Jamaican man from achieving economic success. No one expects a Rastaman to be rich. He traditionally emerged from the ghettos of Kingston or the rural areas, and eventually took to the airwaves and concert stages to spread the Rasta message of African liberation. This is the chord Rasta has struck with thousands of men in Jamaica and throughout the African Diaspora, whether rural or urban: its capacity to represent his experience and provide a definition of manhood in Afrocentric terms, thereby providing an alternative to the dominant ideology that places Eurocentric achievement of occupational success and money at the center of the status system. The political philosophy that developed out of the Rastafarian movement of the 1930s through the 1970s included in its critique of the system of oppression of Africans the manner in which the African man's identity is obscured by the Eurocentric ideology of gender and race. The Rastas went on to develop a response by articulating an identity that affirms the black man's dignity and provides a language of opposition to a social system that denies his experience and seeks to obliterate his reality.

Local Consequences

While Rastafari appeals to many rural and urban young men, those who hustle tourists also see the opportunity for parlaying that identity into an opportunity to secure his fantasy of an emotional relationship and perhaps a more comfortable way of life. As Matthews (1977) noted, "Why should a young man in Barbados, for example, work long hours in agriculture when he can triple his income by hustling female tourists on the beaches? The fringe benefits of sex, good food, and night club entertainment are hard to resist."

Such relationships offer the young man with no economic means the avenue to the status associated with success with women, particularly amongst his new peer group of other hustlers. Those men who circulate through the tourist spots—those who work with tourists and those who hope for the opportunity to talk to one—become the community that accords status and prestige to the young men whose ambitions are frustrated by a system of inequality. This peer group becomes increasingly significant for the hustler as many locals shun him for dealing with foreigners, and he faces the generalized and institutionalized discrimination of those with dreadlocks.

While gaining reputation for success with women, the hustler forfeits the respect of the larger community. Anyone who chooses to spend much time with foreigners is subject to criticism and censure from the broader community for being "too much with white people." These men then become embroiled in a further opposition to cultural norms that hold that a man is not supposed to take money from a woman and are subject to persecution and shaming from others in the community. Locals ignore the nuances of the romance tourism relationship and consider the men prostitutes who are too lazy and irresponsible to work for a living. They are resented by many locals who work hard for measly wages while they watch the hustlers living luxuriously with tourist women.

The hustler's claim to be Rastafarian is viewed as superficial as he appropriates Rasta symbols for personal gain, yielding to the individualism of Eurocentric culture and failing to enter the spirituality of Rastafari that repudiates material accumulation and participation in the system of exploitative lifestyles. His internalization of the material ethic that Rasta rejects and his willingness to achieve it by trading in his sexuality with foreign women places him in opposition to the Rastafarian critique of the political economy of Western civilization.

Young men who sport dreadlocks while living amongst tourists have created ambiguity around the Rastafarian identity and the meaning of dreadlocks. As stated earlier, the term "rent-a-dread" evolved in Jamaica to refer to those men who are said to locks their hair in order to appeal to women tourists. When asked how one identifies a rent-a-dread, most locals will say something similar to, "Rasta is known by his works, his livity [manner of living]. If you see the guy around with a different white woman every week or so, then he is a rent-a-dread." The man responds from his cultural gender script for courting multiple women and, by professing his love for his companion, distinguishes himself from a prostitute.

The hustler draws on the language of resistance of the Rastafarian culture to generate a response to his critics. He criticizes non-Rastas for not repudiating the dominant system and ideology by becoming Rasta. The internal contradiction in this position reflects the ambivalence and multiple realities these men confront daily. Criticism from Rastas presents a more formidable challenge for the tourist hustler. His response will usually consist of an argument that Rasta means "One Love," and that Rasta does not subscribe to racial or color discriminations.

What the tourist generally does not understand is the context of origin of her particular dread. Anyone with dreadlocks represents Rastafari for many foreigners who are unaware of its unique history and culture, or who fail to see its symbols as signifiers rather than the thing itself and who have had contact only with those who hustle tourists and claim the identity. Whereas to "locks" one's hair was formerly a dramatic declaration of opposition to the Western system of exploitation, it now can mark an intention to maximize one's position within that system.

Nurturing this possibility requires making the most of the opportunities available so that some men maintain relationships with numerous women from different countries for years until one comes through with an airline ticket, or perhaps makes the decision to move to Jamaica herself and set up a household with her boyfriend.

Beyond Romance

Those who make a commitment to the romance tourism relationship find that romance turns the corner down the path of the hard work of getting along day after day in an intimate relationship between two people whose ideals and expectations have been formed in different cultures. If the women stay in Jamaica or take their boyfriends home with them, typecasts break down to personalities in the minutiae of everyday life. The relationship that extends beyond the casual vacation romance often loses its bloom and leads to disappointment and conflict. The fact that each partner has come to the relationship with a different agenda becomes more apparent as the economic dependency within the relationship becomes more evident.

The women, ignoring or ignorant of the conflicting purposes arising from such disparity of financial means, education, and exposure, are initially unaware of many of the dynamics underlying their relationships. Those who seek their ideal relationships eventually often feel used and disappointed by their partners who likely do not share their Western ideals of sexual equality. The following remarks by a German woman to her Jamaican boyfriend illustrate this attitude. "I came to meet you half-way to help you but you are still caught up in the resentment of the past between blacks and whites and you are not ready to meet me half-way."

Cast in the role of financial provider, the women may become enmeshed in an exchange relationship that did not define their initial impulses. These women often face insecurities about the man's commitment to her, fearing he might get involved with another woman who is in a better financial position to take care of him. Furthermore, if the woman decides to remain in Jamaica, unless she is independently wealthy, she may lose the financial advantages she brought to the relationship or grow weary of the economic demands placed on her. She will also learn that her "Rasta's" alienation within the community extends to her.

The challenges become even greater if the relationship moves to the tourist's country of origin where the man has little of the cultural capital needed to achieve the success he desires in Western society. The rural Jamaican man with little formal education is ill prepared for the demands of making a living in the postindustrial society. With the man's role as culture-broker and tour guide no longer necessary, educational, age, and racial differences that seemed inconsequential in the host country are magnified. His ability to contribute to the relationship in many ways has been diminished, and his difficulty in acculturation, learning the language and bureaucratic systems, as well as making a living, place further strains on the relationship. His "natural" persona may seem incongruous with the demands of life in the "artificial" North, and he will be judged by her family and friends without, or perhaps because of, his exotic backdrop.

Furthermore, by traveling to the woman's country, the man loses what independence he had in his homeland, and he leaves the peer group that verifies his exploits and provides him with reputation and status. Thus, he simultaneously loses the cultural rewards for his deeds while entering a greater dependency on the woman.

The economic relationship conjoined with an emotional one sometimes backfires on the man. While the relationship between a local man and a tourist woman may at first involve a substantial element of economic venture for the man, it also springs from his desire for his ideal emotional relationship with a "tender" woman. It is an intimate relationship involving all the inevitable issues of identity, connection, and power, compounded in this case by racial issues, cultural differences, and economic dependency. Unlike the sex/money prostitutes, the Jamaican male hustler whose own culture idealizes romantic love may be caught in his own emotional web. Emotional attachments develop; hopes and desires are at work. While the man may be seeking a way out through a foreign woman, he is also vulnerable to being a mere instrument in her search for authenticity.

Tourist women often seem fickle, turning from one man, met early in their stay in Jamaica, to another man they later meet and find more desirable. These Jamaican men must cope with the insecurity of the status of one who represents an ideal type. The premise of the initial attraction is often feigned. To the extent that he has modeled himself to match an ideal, the relationship is not based on her choice of him in particular.

Many of the men describe feeling used by foreign women, only important to them so long as the desire for an exotic liaison lasts, or merely the instrument for her to have a "brown baby" to display her liberal ideas. The instances of children from these liaisons are noticeable but not easily quantified. The men are subject to being left behind as the woman returns home or moves on to new adventures. One interviewee expresses this sentiment succinctly: "I don't like the influence of tourism and being chased by white women. I realize that I can be used by these women. They go home and after a few months you are nothing. You never hear from them again." One of the authors heard a man say to his foreign girlfriend, "You are too emancipated. You think because you have money and education, you can come down here, buy everything and control man. But it can't work that way." When these resentments build, it is not uncommon for the man to resort to a common feature of his gender script for control over a woman and react with violence against the woman. This widespread use of the threat of violence by Jamaican men to maintain dominance is expressed in these lyrics of a popular song in Jamaica.

> Me, me, no woman can rule me.
> Now me is a man and me have me woman.
> But if she try to rule me, me have contention.
> She could get a broke foot and get a broke hand.
> And me rule she, she no rule me.
> If me tell her say A, she can't tell me B.
> And if me lift up me hand you know she feel it.
> (Shabba Ranks 1990)

Relationship between the tourist and local resident is generally based on stereotypes, each having preconceived but not well-formulated notions about the other and often dealing with each other not only as types, but as objects (Kempadoo 1999). Over time, the subjectivity of the partners overwhelms the simple objectified models each holds of the other. The disappointment from the failure of stereotypes to deliver their promise intrudes. The women often become dissatisfied with a partner with different ideas about loyalty and fidelity and who proves to aspire to the deluxe lifestyle that she believed him to refute as a Rastaman. The Jamaican who assumes that all tourists are wealthy may be disillusioned when he discovers that the object of his attentions is spending money freely in order to have a special vacation but is neither rich nor extravagant once the holiday is over.

Conclusion

Dissatisfied with the confines of cultural norms and expectations, people are willing, even eager, to experiment with and rewrite gender scripts. The constraining nature of gender ideologies (Gilmore 1990) invites response and resistance. Tourism creates a social space ripe with possibilities for change through the interplay between conventional scripts and new ideas. In a unique conjunction of need, hope, and desire, the romance relationships between tourist women and local men serve to transform traditional gender roles across cultural boundaries, creating power relations distinctive from those existing in either native society.

Travel has always offered a unique opportunity for self-discovery and potential transformation. Face-to-face contact with the Other and its concomitant challenge to cultural beliefs inevitably involves a confrontation with one's self qua self. While historically the purview of men and a "medium of peculiarly male fantasies of transformation and self-realization" (Leeds 1991:275), travel can now serve as a medium of female "self-realization." Travel has become part of the gendering activity of women as they seek to expand their gender repertoires to incorporate practices traditionally reserved for men and thereby integrate the conventionally masculine with the feminine.

Yet many women who seek more control in their relationships are simultaneously drawn to conventional notions of masculinity. Ideas about masculine power are central to women's attraction to local men, in particular the "natural" Rasta. Women's own gender scripts include a sense of appropriateness of the dominant male from a dualistic conception of man/woman constructed on hierarchical power relations. The farther women push the boundaries of feminine conduct to incorporate qualities conventionally defined as masculine, the more they confront internalized ideas about masculine power. The need for contrast through which to construct their identity draws them to the aspect of masculinity most closely associated with dominance, partially reproducing the dichotomy of gender from their cultural scripts. Thus, many women are drawn to the strength and potency of the masculine even as they experiment with the power they acquire through relative wealth.

Though not motivated by the search for a new gender identity per se, the men in these relationships manipulate their identity by expanding on features from their own cultural repertoire. The local men who associate with tourists, in many ways, enter into a new tourism culture and distance themselves from their society's normative authority. These men then are also free to explore new gender roles while they pursue social and economic mobility and the freedom to experience a new kind of intimate relationship. However, the demands of the role they have adopted put them in contradiction with their gender ideals. Western women bring economic superiority and ideas of female liberation that interact in complex ways with Jamaican men's tolerance of female economic independence, a tradition in their own culture (LaFont 2000, Safa 1995). Despite Jamaican women's economic independence, the predominance of female-headed households and notions of matrifocality (Prior 2001, UN 2000), men are perceived to be dominant in Jamaican culture (Barrow 1998, LaFont 1996, Stolzoff 2000). The Jamaican man's tolerance of female economic independence differs significantly from the subordinate position the man has entered into with the "affluent" tourist woman. While their cultural scripts include a model for the independence of women, the Jamaican woman does not control the man's economic opportunities. However, the men involved in romance tourism are faced with new gendered power relations in which the women control access to the financial success the men want.

While both individuals have the capacity to exert their influence over the relationship in a given circumstance, the woman possesses the disproportionate power to define the situation. Such a situated, contextual analysis (Rhode 1990) as presented here verifies that "it is in these contexts of inequities of wealth and power that one finds transformations of the native self" that incorporate the "evaluation of the West" (Bruner 1991:247). The potential for that transformation and the extent of its accommodation to Western fantasies and expectations is exhibited by these men as they manipulate their identity to fit the tourist's desire for a "natural" man. The consequence of the tourists' power is the commodification of Rastafarian culture and gender itself. Thus, romance tourism recapitulates the patriarchal structure of tourism (Enloe 1989) by reproducing the dominance relation in the tourism encounter wherein tourism functions to fulfill desires of the tourist by subordinating local culture and interests even while the women seek to challenge patriarchal power.

This situation serves to illuminate the significance of economic status for dominance and refutes conventional notions of male hegemony. Control of economic resources provides both genders the opportunity for dominance, for holding little regard for the Other's experience, needs, and feelings. Rather than the purview of men, dominance is rooted in various attributes such as economic power, physical strength, and personality characteristics that may reside with the man or the woman. Gender studies have shown that gender power is not necessarily sex-linked. This study contributes to a reconception of gender by further disentangling power and dominance from sex (Butler 1999).

The dynamics of these relationships also demonstrate that dominance and power are not static but shifting and situational, constantly negotiated and contested, a process at once global and personal. As the partners in these relationships play off traditional social and gender repertoires as well as the immediate circumstances of finance and cultural capital, the power in the relationship fluctuates between them "in relation to opposed sets of cultural values and established social boundaries" (Conway, Bourque, and Scot 1989:29).

Travel offers new opportunities for women to liberate themselves from patriarchal authority relations and redefine "woman." Feminists might celebrate as women break free of conventional constraints and gain power over their lives. However, the personal nature of these relationships may at first mask the social and historical dynamics of racial and economic hegemony embedded in them. Those social and economic inequities, as well as beliefs and stereotypes each partner holds about the Other, work to construct a relationship uncomfortably similar to the power relationship between the partners' respective societies. The agency has shifted from the characteristic nation-state and its transnational corporations to the intimately personal arena.

Breaking taboos and challenging tradition open uncharted territories of social relations. The outcome is never certain and carries with it the possibility of reproducing much of what is being challenged.

Source: Adapted from "For Love and Money: Romance Tourism in Jamaica," *Annals of Tourism Research*, 1996, 22(2):422–40. When we published the original version of this article, it drew criticism for "romanticizing" the relationships between tourist women and Jamaican men. We hope this new version will clarify our ethnographic findings and conclusions.

Acknowledgments

Although it is not possible to name them, the authors wish to acknowledge the numerous men and women in Jamaica whose kind assistance made this article possible. Winsome Anderson made invaluable suggestions on an earlier draft.

References

Abrahams, Roger D. 1983. *The Man-of-Words in the West Indies*. Baltimore: Johns Hopkins University Press.

Altman, Dennis. 2001. *Global Sex*. Chicago: University of Chicago Press.

Anderson, Patricia. 1986. "Conclusion: Women in the Caribbean." *Social and Economic Studies* 35(2): 291–325.

Barrow, Christine. 1998. "Caribbean Masculinities, Marriage and Gender Relations," in *Gender and the Family in the Caribbean*. Mona, Jamaica: Institute of Social and Economic Research.

Bond, Marybeth. 1992. "For Women Only." *justGO* 2(2).

Brodber, Erna. 1989. "Socio-cultural Change in Jamaica," in *Jamaica in Independence*, ed. R. Nettleford, pp. 55–74. Kingston, Jamaica: Heinemann Caribbean.

Bruner, Edward M. 1991. "Transformation of Self in Tourism." *Annals of Tourism Research* 18(2): 238–250.

Butler, Judith. 1999. *Gender Trouble: Feminism and the Subversion of Identity*. New York: Routledge.

Campbell, Horace. 1987. *Rasta and Resistance*. Trenton, NJ: Africa World Press.

Chevannes, Barry, and Janet Brown. 1998. *Why Man Stay So: An Examination of Gender Socialization in the Caribbean*. Kingston: UNICEF.

Cohen, Erik. 1979. "A Phenomenology of Tourist Experiences." *Sociology* 13:179–201.

Conway, Jill K., Susan C. Bourque, and Joan W. Scott. 1989. *Learning About Women: Gender, Politics and Power*. Ann Arbor: University of Michigan Press.

Davidson, Julia O'Connell, and Jacqueline Sánchez Taylor. 2002. "Fantasy Islands: Exploring the Demand for Sex Tourism," in *Sexuality and Gender*, ed. Christine L. Williams and Arlene Stein. Oxford: Blackwell Publishers.

de Albuquerque, Klaus. 1999. "In Search of the Big Bamboo." *Transition* 77, available online at www.cofc.edu/~klausda/bamboo.htm (accessed July 24, 2003).

Enloe, Cynthia H. 1989. *Bananas, Beaches and Bases: Making Feminist Sense of International Politics*. London: Pandora.

Gilmore, David G. 1990. *Manhood in the Making: Cultural Concepts of Masculinity*. New Haven: Yale University Press.

Handwerker, W. Penn. 1989. *Women's Power and Social Revolution: Fertility Transition in the West Indies*. Newbury Park: Sage Publications.

Harrison, Faye V. 1997. "The Gendered Politics and Violence of Structural Adjustment," in *Situated Lives: Gender and Culture in Everyday Life*, ed. Louise Lamphere, Helena Ragon, and Patricia Zavella. New York: Routledge.

Henry, Ben. 1988. "The Sexualization of Tourism in Jamaica." *The Star* (September 3).

Hubbard, Akintola E. 2000. "The Burden of Anansi: Caribbean Sexual Politics and the Problem of the Trickster." Unpublished paper presented at American Anthropological Association Meeting.

Keller, Evelyn Fox. 1989. "Women Scientist and Feminist Critics of Science," in *Learning About Women*, ed. J. Conway et al., pp. 77–91. Ann Arbor: University of Michigan Press.

Kempadoo, Kamala, and Jo Doezema, eds. 1998. *Global Sex Workers: Rights, Resistance, and Redefinition*. New York: Routledge.

Kempadoo, Kamala, ed. 1999. *Sun, Sex, and Gold: Tourism and Sex Work in the Caribbean*. New York: Rowman & Littlefield Publishers, Inc.

LaFont, Suzanne. 1992. *Baby-Mothers and Baby-Fathers: Conflict and Family Court Use in Kingston, Jamaica*. Ph.D. dissertation, Yale University.

———. 1996. *The Emergence of an Afro-Caribbean Legal Tradition in Jamaica*. Maryland: Austin & Winfield Press.

———. 2000. "Gender Wars in Jamaica." *Identities: Global Studies in Culture and Power* 7(2).

———. 2003. *Constructing Sexualities: Readings in Sexuality, Gender, and Culture*. Upper Saddle River, NJ: Prentice Hall.

Leed, Eric J. 1991. *The Mind of the Traveler*. New York: Basic Books.

MacCannell, Dean. 1973. "Staged Authenticity: Arrangements of Social Space in Tourist Settings." *American Journal of Sociology* 79(3): 589–603.

———. 1976. *The Tourist: A New Theory of the Leisure Class*. New York: Schocken.

Matthews, Harry G. 1977. "Radicals and Third World Tourism." *Annals of Tourism Research* 5:20–29.

Nash, Dennison. 1981. "Tourism as an Anthropological Subject." *Current Anthropology* 22(5): 461–481.

Prior, Marsha. 2001. "Matrifocality, Power, and Gender Relations in Jamaica," in *Gender in Cross-Cultural Perspectives*, ed. Caroline B. Brettell and Carolyn F. Sargent. Upper Saddle River, New Jersey: Prentice Hall.

Pruitt, Deborah J. 1993. *A Foreign Mind: Tourism, Identity and Development in Jamaica*. Ph.D. Dissertation, University of California at Berkeley.

Pruitt, Deborah J., and Suzanne LaFont. 1997. "The Colonial Legacy: Gendered Laws in Jamaica," in *Daughters of Caliban: Women in the 20th Century Caribbean*, ed. Consuelo Lopez. Springfield, Bloomington: Indiana University Press.

Rhode, Deborah L. 1990. *Theoretical Perspectives on Sexual Difference*. New Haven: Yale University Press.

Robinson, Jane. 1990. *Wayward Women: A Guide to Women Travelers*. New York: Oxford University Press.

Roberts, George W., and Sonja A. Sinclair. 1978. *Women in Jamaica: Patterns of Reproduction and Family*. New York: KTO Press.

Safa, Helen I. 1995. *The Myth of the Male Breadwinner: Women and Industrialization in the Caribbean*. Boulder: Westview Press.

Said, Edward W. 1978. *Orientalism*. New York: Pantheon Books.

Smith, Raymond T. 1956. *The Negro Family in British Guiana: Family Structure and Social Status in the Villages*. London: Lowe and Brydon, Ltd.

Stolzoff, Norman. 2000. *Wake the Town and Tell the People: Dancehall Culture in Jamaica*. London: Duke University Press.

Taylor, Jacqueline Sánchez. 2001. "Dollars Are a Girl's Best Friend? Female Tourists' Sexual Behavior in the Caribbean." *Sociology* 35(3): 749–764.

United Nations. 2000. *The World's Women 2000: Trends and Statistics*. New York: United Nations Publications.

Whitehead, Tony L. 1992. "Expressions of Masculinity in a Jamaican Sugartown: Implications for Family Planning Programs," in *Gender Constructs and Social Issues*, ed. Tony L. Whitehead and Barbara V. Reid, pp. 103–141. Urbana: University of Illinois Press.

Four:
The Impact and
Implications of Tourism

The industry . . . is primarily concerned with the blatantly unnatural construction and production of scenic destinations. . . . Life is governed on these landscapes, not by the laws of nature but by the semiotics of market forces.

— Sally Ann Ness, U.S. anthropologist, 2003

The common goal must be to develop and promote new forms of tourism, which will bring the greatest possible benefit to all participants—travelers, the host population and the tourist business, without causing intolerable ecological and social damage.

— Jost Krippendorf, Swiss academic, 1987

20

Sailing into the Sunset: The Cruise-ship Industry

Polly Pattullo

The first journeys across the Caribbean Sea were made by Amerindian canoeists who settled the island chains, paddling north from the river systems of the Orinoco and the Amazon. Hundreds of years later the Spanish explorers arrived, and when other European powers joined the fight for control of the Caribbean, it was the sea, not the land, that saw their greatest battles. The sea became an economic highway for slavers, traders, buccaneers, and fishermen; then it became a passageway for escaped slaves, indentured laborers, and settlers; and later still, it was a watery flight path for emigrants and boat people. These shipping channels (except for those traditionally used by Caribs and fishermen) were linked with the economic and political power blocs of Europe and North America rather than with each other, for each harbor was a juncture of imperial arrival and departure.

Caribbean ports are still working places. Container ships arrive with imports from tableware to tractors, mostly from the United States, or cars from Japan, and they depart with bananas from Martinique or St. Vincent for Europe. Now, however, by far the biggest vessels in port are cruise ships, also from the United States, on pleasure journeys that no longer pay attention to those old colonial lines. Crisscrossing the Caribbean Sea, these great white whales come and go more quickly than the banana boats loading up alongside them. There is time, though, for seven hours or so on land—arriving in the morning and departing in late afternoon.

Down the gangway come the cruise-ship passengers, straight into a purpose-built, duty-free shopping mall, or into streets packed with tourist shops. Just like at the last port of call, most terminals have pizza joints, ice cream parlors, souvenir shops, perhaps a casino or two, and hoardings [billboards] with familiar transnational names: Dollar Rent A Car, Colombia Diamonds, Benetton, Gucci, and Little Switzerland. There is time to fit in shopping, an island tour, or a trip to a beach or to the cruise line's private island. Ranks of minibuses line up to whisk the tourists away on their prebooked, prepaid tours arranged by the cruise lines with chosen ground operators. Those who have failed to book can take their chances and get a cheaper deal with the many freelance taxi drivers and tour guides.

The most popular ports of call are the ones with the best duty-free shopping and casinos. The shops are ice-cold and imitate Fifth Avenue: the gifts, under glass, are much the same whether in Ocho Rios or Antigua—jewelry, perfumes, or china figurines of pastel-colored cottages or simpering milk maids. Each destination is in competition with the next to provide a shoppers' paradise. St. Kitts, for example, with its modest duty-free mall in Basseterre, must try to compete with St. Maarten, its flashy Americanized neighbor, stiff with shops and casinos. "We would like to see a greater turnover so we are upgrading our duty-free outlets," said an official from the St. Kitts division of tourism. Armed with leaflets on shops recommended by the cruise ships, cruisers know which are the best and cheapest destinations. Not St. Kitts, for sure, and even Antigua is not a star attraction. A young couple in Antigua's duty-free Heritage Quay did not plan to spend much money there. They were saving it for St. Thomas, in the U.S. Virgin Islands (USVI). "We might as well go back on board and get some breakfast." They had heard that shopping was better in St. Thomas where the average expenditure in 2000 was US$259.80 compared to US$27.70 in Antigua.[1]

By afternoon, the passengers drift back to the ship, with their purchases, to eat (food is included in the cruise price) or to join those who have never left, preferring to glimpse the island from the rails. The last somewhat drunken stragglers, with T-shirts reading "Drink Till You Sink," are scooped up the gangway. Soon, the quayside will be almost empty, as shopkeepers count their takings and taxi drivers give up for the day. Only beggars and scavenging dogs remain as the ship disappears over the horizon, lights twinkling on its way to another sunset at sea.

The Cruise Boom

The Caribbean cruise business is booming; it grows still larger as the numbers and sizes of ships visiting ever-bigger terminals increase. "The untapped potential in the Caribbean—where we're putting more tonnage over the next several years—is vast," claimed Julie Benson of Princess Lines, a subsidiary of P&O Cruises, in the mid-1990s.[2] A decade later that boast seemed well founded with the industry running at a remarkable capacity of more than 90 percent, far higher than land-based tourism. The 1990s saw particularly spectacular growth. At least 28 new ships were delivered to the cruise companies; most were destined for the Caribbean. The biggest companies, Royal Caribbean Cruise Line (RCCL), Carnival Cruise, Holland America, and Princess, led the way. RCCL had three ships on order, all with a capacity for more than 1,800 passengers; Princess had spent almost US$1 billion on three ships, one, *Grand Princess* at 105,000 tons, was the biggest liner ever. Carnival also had added eleven ships to its fleet by 1996, and spent US$400 million on the Italian-built boat, *Tiffany*. Disney Corporation also entered the cruise market, with its first ship in operation in 1999. Even the smaller companies had increased their fleets, building vessels for three hundred or so luxury-market passengers or for those in the even more select sail-ship market.[3]

The emphasis, however, is on size—and the bigger the better. Of the new ships built between 1995 and 2001, nearly 80 percent had 1,500 or more berths. The largest, *Mariner of the Sea,* built for Royal Caribbean International at a price of US$520 million, has a tonnage of 140,000, and a capacity for 3,835 passengers and more than 1,000 crew. Another giant, *Carnival Glory,* which launched its seven-day cruises in mid-2003, boasts fourteen passenger decks with twenty-two bars and lounges, a 15,000-square-foot health club, four swimming pools, and three restaurants, including an upscale "steakhouse-style" supper club serving prime U.S. beef.[4]

The Caribbean has nearly half of the world capacity of cruise "bed days." However, its share of the cruise business has declined from a peak of 60 percent of all bed days out of North America in 1991 to 48 percent in 2000. According to the Caribbean Tourism Organization (CTO), this is because the cruise industry has "sought to add itineraries for the burgeoning capacity." Even if its share has decreased, its awesome volume of business continues to expand. In the Caribbean itself, cruise tourism has grown much faster than land-based tourism—from 7.8 million passenger arrivals in 1990 to 14.5 million in 2000, an increase of 8.6 percent per year, compared to an average annual increase of 4.7 percent for stay-over arrivals. The Bahamas, a traditional cruise destination close to Florida, was the busiest port of call, with 2.5 million cruise passenger arrivals in 2000. The next most popular destination was the U.S. Virgin Islands (1.7 million), followed by Cozumel (1.5 million) on the Mexican coast, Puerto Rico (1.3 million), the Cayman Islands (1 million), and Jamaica (907,000).[5]

Many destinations have recorded spectacular growth. St. Lucia, for example, had 58,000 cruise arrivals in 1986 but nearly half a million in 2000, when Dominica recorded 239,000, up from 11,500 in 1986. Other islands with an expanding cruise-ship market were St. Kitts & Nevis, Aruba, and Curaçao.[6] Belize and the Dominican Republic were late, but expanding, entries and even Haiti, abandoned by the cruise-ship industry in 1993 when sanctions against its military regime were announced, was back on the itinerary by 1995. Only Trinidad, perhaps, with an industrial rather than a tourist base to its economy, has not seen a massive rise in cruise visitors, along with some of the very small islands that do not have cruise facilities, such as Anguilla, Saba, and St. Barthelemy.

Most cruises begin in either Miami or Port Everglades in Florida or in San Juan, Puerto Rico. Of non-American bases, Aruba, Antigua, and Martinique also play their part, all being significant airline hubs for the European market. From these starting points, the ships crisscross the Caribbean Sea, dropping into islands here and islands there as they see fit, depending on the duration of the cruise and the range of attractions that the destinations can muster.

Rocking the Boat

Yet while the cruise lines steamed ahead, unloading more and more passengers off bigger and more luxurious ships on to the docksides of small Caribbean states, fundamental questions began to be asked by the mid-1990s about the benefits of the cruise industry to the Caribbean and its people, and its long-term effect on the region's own land-based tourism.

Taxation has been a thorny issue. Departure taxes for both airline and cruise passengers have traditionally been set by individual governments. This head tax is one way in which the cruise industry contributes to the expenses involved in providing appropriate port or airport facilities. In the case of the cruise tax, this ranged in 2000 from US$1.50 in Guadeloupe and St. Maarten (an increase from zero in the mid-1990s) to US$15 in Jamaica and the Bahamas. Intercountry rivalry and what are considered to be differences in the quality of facilities offered to cruise ships by each destination were said to explain such a discrepancy.[7]

To eliminate such discrepancies, in January 1992 the Organization of Eastern Caribbean States (OECS) agreed to adopt a standard head tax of US$10 to take effect in October of that year. The decision did not please the cruise lines. "To solve the hotel problem by raising taxes on cruise ships is stupid and punitive," said Bob Dickinson, president of Carnival Cruise Lines.[8] Retaliation was not long in coming. The RCCL announced that it would drop St. Lucia, one of the seven OECS states, from its itinerary; the *Nordic Prince,* which had made eighteen calls to St. Lucia in 1991, also decided to go elsewhere. The boycott of St. Lucia resulted in calls of solidarity from other CTO members, but in the end they were empty promises.

The OECS position was, however, strengthened when Caricom, the wider regional organization, also came up with a plan to adopt a unified tax (Jamaica had already taken the lead). It was to be set at US$5 in April 1994, to be raised to US$7.50 in October of that year, and to US$10 by 1995.[9] For the Caribbean this was a major step forward, since earlier discussions about increasing the head tax had only taken place bilaterally, giving the cruise operators the built-in advantage. The operators could play one country against another by threatening to skip one destination for another with a lower tax.

This time the region as a whole seemed to be flexing its muscles. As Jean Holder said: "The concept of the minimum tax, set at a reasonable level, was intended to enable the weak destinations to earn a little much-needed revenue, to create some Caribbean solidarity and thus effect an adjustment to the strategic advantage that is held largely by the cruise lines. Its success is dependent entirely on each country keeping the agreement."[10] Caricom's move raised the possibility of a regional approach, not just about the head tax but also about other important issues surrounding the cruise industry. St. Lucia's prime minister, John Compton, expressed the opinion that the region would "no longer accept mirrors and baubles for the use of its patrimony."[11]

The tax issue was symptomatic of the tensions between the cruise ships and the region's land-based tourist industry. Those on the side of the cruise ships expressed barely disguised contempt for the Caribbean's hotel industry. Without the cruise industry, said Joel Abed in *Travel Trade News*, "to both promote and present its attractions and facilities to potential vacationers, the Caribbean resort industry, as we know it today, would all-too-quickly become a virtual tourist desert."[12] Bob Dickinson of Carnival expressed his position only marginally less aggressively. "They're not only biting the hand that feeds them, they're yanking off the whole arm."[13]

The tax row provoked similar outbursts of passionate rhetoric from the region. There was a general distrust of what was considered to be imperious behavior by the cruise lines. Yet despite this, and the agreement made at the highest level in Caricom, the unified passenger head tax was not achieved within the agreed time span. (St. Lucia even aborted its decision to raise the head tax in 1994 according to the OECS decision.) Indeed, as has been seen, it has yet to be achieved.

Royston Hopkin, then president of the Caribbean Hotel Association, conceded in the wake of the row: "The cruise-ship lobby is very strong and the governments have been very weak. The cruise lines sweetened the governments who were not united. We gave our best shot, but by the time the heads of government got to it the three-tier system was introduced and this weakened our position." The Caribbean's failure dismayed many sections of its tourist industry. It demonstrated the inability of the region to take a unified stand and also showed just how powerful the cruise industry's grip was. Peter Odle, then president of the Barbados Hotel Association, was another aggrieved hotelier. "I was against cruise ships from the beginning," he said. "The Caribbean will not realize the cruise business is a disservice until it's nearly too late. The cruise ships are using our most precious asset—the sea—polluting it like hell and not making any significant contribution to our economy. And instead of taking a firm stand, the governments are all over the place; there is a lack of political will." Similar sentiments were expressed by Allen Chastenet, a former director of the St. Lucia Tourist Board: "If anyone is sucking the Caribbean dry it is the cruise ships."

A further row developed in 1997 when the Organization of Eastern Caribbean States, representing seven islands in the eastern Caribbean, decided to impose an environmental levy of US$1.50 per capita on all visitors, including those from the cruise ships, entering its member countries. The fee would help pay for a waste management project, partly financed by the World Bank and aimed at improving the collection of waste from sources such as cruise ships. The Florida-Caribbean Cruise Association (FCCA) objected, saying that its ships had "zero discharge" and that each vessel "usually" had "about US$10 million worth of waste disposal facilities, including incinerators, pulpers, and compactors." It argued that an across-the-board levy was not needed. Finally, the FCCA agreed to pay. It was a rare victory for regional unity.[14]

The CTO has continued to take the position that Caribbean governments have the right to take action to make the competition between land and sea tourism more equitable.[15] On the other hand, it has also recognized that the Caribbean doesn't hold many cards in relation to the cruise industry. "The cruise lines have the ability to move their ships and they do move them when they are not happy," said Jean Holder in 2000.[16] From the shore, foreign cruise lines are seen as having built-in advantages over land-based tourism—cruise ships generate greater local revenue and employment per passenger—but these advantages are used, it is argued, at the expense of the Caribbean, in a particularly rapacious manner.

Despite the row over head taxes, cruise ships do not pay as many taxes as the land-based industry, where taxation either doubles the price of many purchases or restricts the hotelier to buying regional products only. Hotels must also pay corporation tax and casino tax profits. In contrast, cruise ships are seen as moveable feasts that sail away into the sunset, their bars and casinos untaxed. Raising money to build hotels is problematic even though construction work employs local labor and supports local financial institutions. In contrast, cruise-ship contracts go to overseas shipyards largely in Europe, where long-term, low-interest loans are also available. Furthermore, more and more hotels are now owned by Caribbean nationals; no cruise ships are owned by Caribbean nationals.

The contrast continues. Caribbean hotels provide jobs for locals, with work permits required for the employment of non-nationals. Cruise lines operating in the Caribbean, on the other hand, are free to employ whom they wish. Their ships are not registered in the United States, their home base, but use flags of convenience to avoid U.S. labor laws, taxes, and regulations. Thus, as the president of the Carnival Corporation, whose ships are registered in Panama, wrote in his book, *Selling the Sea*: "Of course, ships registered in these flag-of-convenience nations pay lower wages and taxes on an aggregate basis than those registered in the United States (or Norway or Italy for that matter). But that makes it possible for them to offer cruises at much lower cost than if their ships were registered in countries with restrictive hiring policies" (Dickinson and Vladimir 1997).

Many lines employ European officers, with North American and western European staff in areas like business and entertainment, supported by a Third World crew. Around fifty countries may be represented as cruise employees. The officers on the Carnival's *Fantasy,* for instance, are Italian, while what is called its "international" crew is drawn from Latin America, India, and the Philippines. Crew members, often from the poorest parts of the Third World, are paid low wages, work in shoddy conditions, and endure an authoritarian management code, according to a 2002 study. "Conditions for workers below deck haven't improved in decades," said Tony Sasso, a Miami-based inspector with the International Transport Workers Federation. "Many are reluctant to come forward and complain. To most people, workers on cruise liners are nonentities. They have an almost invisible existence." In contrast, work in the land-based industry may seem more attractive with many employees being paid union rates and benefiting from trade union representation. This may be one reason why so few Caribbean nationals have jobs on cruise ships. Meanwhile, other nationals—from the Philippines or Bangladesh, for example—find the wages better than at home.

The proportion of Caribbean products purchased by cruise lines also remains small. Caribbean supplies to the cruise industry are estimated at between 1 and 5 percent of total requirements. According to the FCCA, member cruise lines spent US$51.2 million on Caribbean supplies in 1993. Technical inputs such as petroleum products, parts, and chemicals represent US$30 million (59 percent of the total expenditure), while handling services such as warehousing and stevedoring at ports account for US$7.1 million, or 14 percent of the total expenditure. Just over a quarter of the cruise lines' expenditure in the Caribbean was on food and drink (US$13.8 million), of which half was on beer and liquor. Foods included fruit and vegetables, dairy products, bread, water, spices, seafood, coffee, and sugar.[17] If this figure is at all accurate, only US$6 per passenger was spent on food and drink grown and produced within the Caribbean.

The list of significant Caribbean suppliers is short: Bico Ice Cream and Pine Hill Dairy, both of Barbados; Dominica Coconut Products; Commonwealth Brewery of the Bahamas; Tropical Beverages of Trinidad and Desnoes & Geddes; Red Stripe Beer, Jamaica.[18] Toilet paper from Trinidad and Tobago also joined the list after what the managing director of Savvy Traders Ltd. called "a long and frustrating battle." The result is that not only are most cruise ships supplied by U.S. companies, but that fresh produce from outside the region is also flown or shipped into the Caribbean during a cruise. Thus, in one ludicrous example, a barge from Venezuela filled with bananas was seen to supply the cruise ships in St. Lucia, one of the Caribbean's major banana producers. Since the tax row, however, the FCCA has been seen to play a more sensitive role. There have been opportunities for purchasers and Caribbean producers to talk to each other at trade shows and conferences. Such meetings, said the FCCA, enabled these companies "to strengthen their contacts within individual cruise lines, make new contacts and learn from other successful suppliers of cruise lines."[19]

The difficulties (quantity, quality, regularity of supply, delivering on time) faced by Caribbean producers are similar to, and even greater than, those they face in supplying the land-based industry. In a commitment to high standards, the cruise lines make tough demands on their suppliers. Part of the RCCL's mission statement, for example, pledges "to locate, buy, and deliver the highest quality of specified goods and services at the fairest overall cost possible in a timely manner."[20] The supplies must be competitive with products from Hong Kong and Taiwan; they must be on time and they must be delivered in an appropriate condition. They must also fit U.S. tastes. According to RCCL's head of purchasing, American cruise passengers expect steak from grain-fed cattle and products, such as yogurt and cereal, that have familiar brand names. Such demands are beyond most Caribbean producers.

From this low base, selling Caribbean goods to the cruise lines has proceeded painfully slowly. It began in the early 1990s with a CTO initiative that, according to Jean Holder, brought together the Caricom Export Development program and cruise lines to discuss their needs. Even the successful and efficient Dominica Coconut Products, now a Colgate-Palmolive subsidiary, took three years to sign a contract with the RCCL to supply three million bars of soap a year.[21] Most producers and tourist boards have been only vaguely aware of the needs of the cruise lines and even less able to deal in the quantity and the quality required. The small scale of many producers and the lack of developed regional exporting and marketing groupings have further limited the opportunities.

One successful link-up between producers and cruise ships shows just how small—and rare—such occasions are. In 2001 up to 10,000 tons of tomatoes from St. Kitts-Nevis found their way each week onto the dining tables of Royal Caribbean International ships. The contract was the result of collaboration between the producers, shippers, cruise lines, and the Republic of Taiwan's agricultural mission on St. Kitts-Nevis. It was trumpeted as a major achievement, with further opportunities for other crops to reach the cruise shippers sometime in the future.[22] Yet the cruise lines have always made it clear that servicing their ships is "no easy task "and "cannot be taken lightly." "This is a very price competitive business, often with very little differentiation in price. The key difference is who has what we need and who can deliver it 100 percent accurately," said the director of purchasing for Carnival Cruise Lines in 1998.

Despite what appears to be an uneven match between sea and land tourism, regional governments continue to give the cruise ships their blessing, boasting of the increase in passenger arrivals over the years. Responding to the needs of bigger ships, for example, the host countries have to expand and improve port facilities. The FCCA is in no doubt as to its requirements: "Ports must be welcoming, modern, and comfortable in order to effectively accommodate upwards of 3,000 guests and crew arriving at the same time. Services must be first-class, and ground excursions must be efficient, dependable, and offer visitors the best of the destination," is the FCCA's line. In an article, "Keeping up with the Megaships," it continued: "When the passengers disembark they should receive the same seamless attention and service that they do on board the cruise ship."[23]

Cruise-ship passengers disembark during a brief visit to Dominica. (Photo by George Gmelch)

The ships tie up at ports that have been especially deepened, widened, and modernized by local governments. To be able to offer a home porting facility (using a cruise destination as an arrival and departure point, as in San Juan, Puerto Rico, for example) is another reason behind port improvements. But San Juan has faced criticism from the cruise industry. While Puerto Rico had spent money on land-based facilities, similar developments had not taken place at the port, the FCCA complained. The cruise industry had been treated with "an astonishing indifference" with the infrastructure lagging behind the needs of the ever-increasing size and numbers of cruise ships, and San Juan had become "unappealing." This remained the case until early in 2001 when a new administration had, according to the FCCA, decided to stop the drift to indifference and to begin a "new sense of welcome" for all those future cruise-ship visitors.[24]

This sort of criticism from the FCCA makes both old and new cruise destinations scramble to invest millions of dollars on new facilities. In the eastern Caribbean, all the islands have sprung into action to improve their cruise facilities. Dominica spent US$28 million on a dock extension at its Roseau port and on a wharf and terminal building at the Cabrits, a national park on the north of the island, to boost its cruise-ship arrival figures. The facilities opened in 1991, and in that year alone cruise arrivals increased from 6,800 to 65,000. St. Kitts, too, has sought to expand its cruise business. In 1994, a US$16.25 million loan agreement was signed with the Bank of Nova

Scotia to construct a new cruise-ship berth, separate from the dust and cargo of the old port.[25] In 2002, it opened later than planned, the construction twice having been demolished by hurricanes. In 1995, St. Vincent also announced a cruise-ship berth development at its capital, Kingstown, to be funded by the Kuwaiti Fund and the European Investment Bank.[26] The latest destination to publicize a major upgrade of what is called its "cruise-tourism product" is the USVI. A US$30 million expansion of its second pier was announced in 2002. "If it is not built, St. Thomas, which is now number 4 in the world in cruise-ship destinations, within a decade will drop to number 10," said Gordon Finch of the Virgin Islands Port Authority.[27]

Even larger islands with established cruise-ship facilities sometimes have to run to keep up. The logistics of providing such facilities and service for these megaships is an enormous challenge. Ocho Rios in Jamaica, a popular cruise-ship destination, was, by the beginning of the twenty-first century, considered to have an inadequate port for the forthcoming mega-liners. A lack of cleanliness at St. Vincent's capital, Kingston, and harassment of visitors led to cruise cancellations; similarly, the Princess Line decided to drop Jamaica from its itineraries in the 2001–2002 season citing "very poor comments from visitors." The Caribbean is constantly addressing such problems—many of which require massive investment to overcome. It's not easy being a host to the cruise-ship industry.

Big Spenders?

The cruise lines also have another winning card: their very own islands. Cruise lines can reduce the number of days in port by buying or leasing their own island or by anchoring off a deserted stretch of beach. As *Caribbean Travel News* noted: "Increasingly, the trend is for cruise lines to go one step further from taking their passengers around the Caribbean islands—and to give them one all to themselves."[28] This policy was begun in the early 1980s by Norwegian Cruise Line, which owns Great Stirrup Cay in the Bahamas, now "remodeled" with a wider beach, a barbecue area, and water sports. Part of the point is that the islands are uninhabited. Holland America's 1997 brochure about Half Moon Cay, also in the Bahamas, paints an appropriate picture for the cruisers: "Half Moon Cay recalls the idyllic Caribbean of 30 years ago. There are no hassles. It's just you and a balmy island with a white-sand beach, coral reefs, and a clutter-free arrangement of attractive facilities designed for casual roaming." One inference is that it's desirable because it has no inhabitants—no needy locals to get in the way of the fantasy. By the end of the twentieth century, six out of the eight major cruise lines operating in the Caribbean owned their own private islands (Wood 2000).

On these islands, the cruise lines show off their private beaches, where what is called "cruise-style service" is on hand with barbecue and bar provided by cruise staff. Princess Cruises own Princess Cay on Eleuthera, Bahamas, ("For total tropical tranquility, it's hard to beat this land of lotus-eaters") and Saline Bay, Mayreau, in the Grenadines ("every castaway's first choice"). The RCCL owns Coco Cay, also on the Bahamas, and leases Labadee in Haiti, an isolated promontory on the north coast where tourists spend a day on a beach surrounded by a high wall patrolled by guards. When cruise lines create their own version of paradise, they avoid port fees and passenger head taxes while protecting their customers from the less than paradisical reality of much of Caribbean life.

Desert-island days, days at sea, island tours booked through the cruise ship: all are ways in which cruise lines can persuade customers to buy their services and thereby control the quality and quantity of the holiday experience. Another way is to attract customers to spend money on board in the shops, boutiques, and bars, available at all times (except when the ships are in port) and often at competitive prices compared to goods sold on land. The Princess line brochure states: "There's no need for you to be in port to go shopping. Both *Canberra* and *Sea Princess* carry a remarkably comprehensive selection of goods . . ." As an Economist Intelligence Unit (EIU) report on the Caribbean pointed out: "Onboard shopping, which by definition is duty-free, is being promoted increasingly aggressively as a means of maximizing their share of a passenger's overall holiday expenditure."[29] This continues to affect the land-based duty-free outlets, which find that the outlets on the cruise ships can outbid them.

The *Fantasy* of Carnival Cruise Lines is a typical giant cruise ship that provides its customers with just about everything they could desire. Sailing out of Cape Canaveral bound for Nassau and Freeport, its 2,634 passengers have paid as little as US$249 in 2002 for a three-day cruise. It has two dining rooms, nine bars and lounges, including Cleopatra's Bar (decorated with hieroglyphics and Egyptian statuary) and the Cat's Lounge with its tables in the shape of bottle tops and cats' eyes glinting from the ceiling. There is a casino and concert hall for "Las Vegas-style revues," and 1,022 "accommodation units," most of which convert to "king-size beds," while twenty-eight have bathtub whirlpools. There are three outdoor swimming pools, a 500-foot banked and padded jogging track, and a health club. The belly of this gleaming ship boasts two glass elevators that surround the Spectrum, a twirling lump of colored geometric kitsch.

The cruise industry continues to introduce more elaborate and more unusual attractions in its ships. Appealing to a broader market of cruisers—away from the stereotypical image—cruise ships have introduced ice-skating rinks, rock-climbing walls and basketball courts. No Caribbean island can compete with such an array of delights. "This is a tremendously dynamic industry. It's great value for money; everyone can afford a cruise. Everything is done for you and the marketing is tremendous. The passengers see the ship as the destination," claimed Robert Stegina of the *Fantasy*. Or as a Carnival spokesman said: "People do not come to us to visit the Caribbean, but to be on our boats."[30] If this is so, what then is left for the land destinations? How much do customers spend on land if the ship becomes the economic center-piece of the holiday?

Cruise lines argue that they make a major contribution to the economic well-being of the region. Their reasoning is affirmed in periodic reports commissioned by the FCCA. The latest report, "The Economic Impact of the Passenger Cruise Industry on the Caribbean," drew its material from surveys of passengers and crew undertaken in the first quarter of 2000. It reported that passengers and crew accounted for a total annual economic impact of $2.6 billion throughout the Caribbean of which $1.4 billion was in direct spending and $1.2 billion indirect. It estimated that a typical ship, carrying 2,000 passengers and 900 crew members generated almost $259,000 in passenger and crew expenditure during a port visit. In a survey of ten ports, average spending per passenger per call totaled $104 ranging from $173.24 in the U.S. Virgin Islands to $53.84 in San Juan, Puerto Rico. Crew members spent an average of $72 per port and were similarly most attracted to goods and services in the USVI. Other figures showed that cruise-related indirect expenditure generated 60,000 jobs throughout the Caribbean.[31]

The CTO's own figures for what passengers spent at various ports in 2000 shows a different pattern. While the USVI scored highest in passenger spending, the estimate here is $259.80 in the U.S. Virgin Islands. At the bottom of the CTO's scale is St. Vincent with a passenger spending of $16.20. Whatever the statistics, most of passenger onshore expenditure was on duty-free shopping, with much less on tours and attractions and little on food. In 2000, however, the CTO reported on "the gradually increasing economic contribution from the cruising sector." It commented that while cruise passenger expenditure was just under 6 percent of all visitor expenditure at the beginning of the 1990s, this had increased to 12 percent in 2000. Statistics threw up an infinite variety of claims in that decade; the EIU similarly plumped for a total cruise-ship contribution of 6 percent in 1990.[32] The Bahamas, the largest of the cruise destinations, put the industry's contribution at 10 percent in 1993, while Jamaica's 1994 OAS report concluded that cruise-ship passengers contributed 3.6 percent of tourist expenditure, "more than a quarter of which was for goods at in-bond stores that contribute little to the economy."[33]

Big Business

Conflicting statistics, major leakages of spending, especially of duty-free goods, and a generally low contribution to the overall income generated by tourism in the Caribbean are themselves indicators of the economic limitations of the cruise industry. But even more fundamentally, who earns the money spent by the cruise industry? Who benefits from the government's expenditure on port and shopping facilities and such expenses as extra police security?

The cruise-ship disembarkation points, with their car rentals, taxi services, helicopters, and tour-operator booths all under one roof, are largely controlled either by transnational chains, by local elites, or by established expatriates. These groups make private contracts with the cruise lines to act as their agents; they also own many of the retail outlets. The Bridgetown Cruise Terminal, for example, which opened in January 1994, is a joint venture between the port authority, three local companies (Cave Shepherd, Harrison's, and Beer & Beverage Ltd.), and the public (25 percent of the shares). Its financial structure was criticized by commentators, including Professor Hilary Beckles of the University of the West Indies at Cave Hill, who commented: "Those three companies have used their position to franchise to the duty-free outlets. They have restructured the white corporate structure of Broad Street [the capital's main shopping area] and duplicated it at the cruise terminal." Indeed, there are replicas of local streets and a chattel-house village—all accessible without leaving the terminal. While the chairman of the Port Authority, Edmund Harrison, denied any such monopolization of the terminal, opportunities for the smaller entrepreneur appear to be limited.

The extent of the interlocking of interests between cruise ships and local big business at the expense of local small business is at the heart of the debate about the cruise industry's economic contribution to the region. Complaints by small businesses in the Cayman Islands, for instance, illustrate this issue. In 1994, taxi drivers, water-sports businesses, and tour operators threatened to hold demonstrations against cruise ships if their grievances were not addressed. The main complaint of the Committee against Cruise Ship Abuse of Local Water Sports/Taxi Owners was that cruise lines prebooked passengers on island and water-sports tours with a few, foreign-controlled companies. "Small operators like us do not have the financial resources, marketing infrastructure, or contacts to approach the cruise lines in Miami," said the committee's chairman, Ron Ebanks. Cruise passengers were charged US$30 by the cruise ships for a snorkeling trip that was minutes from the cruise dock, where equipment could be rented at the site from local suppliers for US$8. Ebanks also charged that cruise ships told passengers not to use local taxis but to take a tour sold on board.[34]

There have been similar complaints from small retailers in Nassau and Freeport in the Bahamas, where T-shirt sellers claim that cruise-ship staff accompany cruisers on shopping trips, recommending certain stores that pay for advertising space or are big enough to offer concessions. The retailers allege that shopping is controlled by the few large outlets that have made financial deals with the cruise lines. Such difficulties, together with occasional insults and patronizing behavior from some cruise officials, have further reinforced suspicions that the cruise industry is a foreign-controlled body that seeks to make deals to its own advantage rather than in partnership with the Caribbean. While the immediate bitterness sparked off by the tax row has simmered down, even the CTO's diplomatic Jean Holder remarked that while some cruise lines seek a partnership in cooperation, others "seem to see the Caribbean simply as an area of exploitation for profit."[35]

On the other hand, many of the islands now have a population that has come to depend on the cruise-ship visitors. In Dominica, for example, where by the end of the 1990s the banana industry was in disarray, many people in the informal economy had turned to finding a source of income in tourism, and, in particular, the cruise ships. The CTO recorded average spending per cruise visitor to Dominica of $27.10 in 2000, the third lowest of all reported destinations after St. Vincent and Grenada. During the tourist season, four boats a week tie up in the capital, Roseau. Across the road, at the converted old marketplace, the place is crammed with vendors' booths selling crafts that vary little from one booth to another. If the tourists only buy sporadically, it is better than nothing and "better than staying at home," according to one vendor. For other vendors, like the Rastafarian who sells attractively printed T-shirts and incense sticks, every little dollar counts as it does for the women who provide the ice for the vendors at the entrance to one of the island's main sites. Whatever the tourist brings, however little, makes a difference.

Whatever the temperature of the relationship, cruise companies remain fierce and powerful competitors. They also spend large sums in promoting themselves. In 1993 alone, the two giant companies, Carnival and Royal Caribbean, spent almost US$82 million. (Compare this to the US$12 million spent on the CTO's first regional U.S. ad campaign in 1993.) Behind the campaigns is the "concept," spelled out by Bob Dickinson of Carnival Cruise Lines, when he listed six aspects of the cruise "product" that, he said, were superior to a land-based holiday: value for money; a "trouble-free" environment; excellent food; the "romance of the sea"; superior activities and entertainment; "an atmosphere of pampering service" (1993:118).

These factors are emphasized in cruise advertising, a constant presence on North American television and in magazines and newspapers. Indeed, cruise-ship brochures dazzle with descriptions of a life of luxury on board. "Sail with us in 1994, and you'll discover a world of attentive service and courtesy you simply cannot find ashore," boasts a P&O brochure. As the FCCA's executive director, Michelle Paige, told *Caribbean Week,* the passengers require excellent service on land because they are accustomed to the high standards on board. The Caribbean, she said, "could do a better job of providing a better service."[36] The Princess brochure, for instance, exudes self-congratulations: pampering includes a "fluffy white bathrobe" and "delicious petit fours to welcome you to your cabin and a foil-wrapped chocolate left on your pillow each night." Then there is the gala buffet, which, according to the same brochure, is an "ingenious display of gastronomic artistry that's a tribute to the skills of ice-carving and sugar-sculpture . . . But for sheer flamboyance, nothing can match the Champagne Waterfall, a glittering pyramid of 600 glasses with bubbly cascading from top to bottom. Magnifique! And the perfect introduction to the night ahead." Such flourishes have little to do with the Caribbean but if the ship is the destination, the Caribbean itself loses relevance except as a vague and shimmering backdrop. Or, as Carnival's Bob Dickinson, put it: "The limited number of countries and ports offered is not a deterrent to Carnival customers; after all the ship is the attraction, not the port of call" (Dickinson 1993).

Both the covert message of the cruise industry and its upfront promotional material compare cruise tourism favorably to land-based tourism. "Should anyone be in doubt that the cruise ships are in competition with us, the attached photocopy of a Royal Caribbean advertisement should set their mind at rest," was the curt memorandum sent by John Bell, executive vice-president of the Caribbean Hotel Association, to his board of directors and member hotel associations. The advertisement was headed "Why a Hotel Should Be Your Last Resort," and the introductory blurb began:

> There's not a lobby on earth that can stack up to the Centrum on a Royal Caribbean ship. Now compare all that a Royal Caribbean cruise offers versus a typical resort and you'll stop pretty quickly. There just is no comparison . . . A Royal Caribbean cruise ship is a resort of the very first order. Choosing anything less should be your last resort.

The cruise lines combine that sort of aggressive promotion with a hard-sell system to retailers. Nearly all cruises in the U.S. market are sold through travel agents who are visited by armies of sales representatives. The commission on sales paid to the agents tends to be higher than that paid for hotel-based holidays. At the same time, the cruise business has been offering discounts, anxious to fill the berths and so maintain its high occupancy rates. Carnival's pricing strategy is budgeted for an amazing 100 percent occupancy, which means that for the moment prices can be kept down. Caribbean hotels are unable to respond.

While some cruise analysts have pondered the wisdom of the rampant expansion in ships and berths, the big cruise lines continue to report healthy figures. In the third quarter of 2002, for example, Carnival announced profits of $500.8 million. Increasingly the giant lines are becoming an oligarchy as economies of scale push out the smaller operators. The second and third largest cruise operators, Royal Caribbean and P&O Princess Lines, were discussing a merger in 2002; this would make them the biggest single cruise line overtaking Carnival Cruise Lines—with its forty-three ships and five in construction (at an estimated value of $2.3 billion). And the passengers, mainly American, keep on coming, and no longer just the old and the rich. The market is changing: the young are being targeted by advertising and are responding. Cruises now attract honeymooners and families, and other "niche" markets; there are conference cruises; theme cruises around sports, music, and education; and so on. The populist Carnival Cruise Line announces in its online information that around 30 percent of its passengers are under 35, with 40 percent between 35 and 55, and 30 percent over 55.

The cruise lines argue that they market the Caribbean as well as the ship. A cruise, they say, provides an introduction to the region, a floating showcase for the charms of the Caribbean. One study suggested that up to 25 percent of stay-over tourists had first sampled their holiday choice from the rails of a cruise ship. Another survey indicated that 40 percent of cruise passengers would like to return to the Caribbean for a land-based holiday. The

Caribbean often misses opportunities to entice cruisers back to dry-land holidays, say the cruise lines. According to the FCCA's Michelle Paige, destinations do not package themselves as well as they could or advertise their attractions. "If we don't make the passengers feel comfortable, they are going to get right back on the ship."[37] The FCCA's 2000 survey also asked the tourists whether they would be likely to return to ten named destinations on a cruise or on a land-based holiday. The answers showed that the passengers were more likely to return on a cruise than on a land-based holiday. Between 59 percent (Bahamas) and 90 percent (USVI) wanted to return on a cruise. Only Jamaica and the USVI (and Cozumel in Mexico) scored above 60 percent as places where the passengers would be likely to return as stay-over visitors, with only 39 percent, for example, likely to return to St. Kitts.[38] The CTO's strategic plan of 2002 calls for an increase in the conversion of cruise-ship tourists to stay-over tourists.

Possibilities of partnership, stressed by both the CTO and the FCCA in their more conciliatory moods, have begun to be explored in marketing, employment strategies, sourcing, and so on. There is also much talk within the region of a more concerted approach towards the unresolved problems presented by the cruise industry. These more conciliatory tones, perhaps born of desperation, were made official at the end of the Caricom tourism summit in 2001 when a further attempt to ease the tensions between the sea and land industries was launched. A Caribbean cruise committee, cochaired by the tough-talking Paige and the equally robust figure of Butch Stewart, was formed in an attempt to promote "effective collaboration" and to maximize benefits to the region. Yet the introduction of some sort of licensing system for cruise ships, in which contracts and guidelines would be observed on both sides, seems far away. In the meantime, the cruise lines are often perceived as using the Caribbean islands as a chain of low-charge parking lots, coming and going as they see fit. The problem is that without them there would be more hardship and less opportunity for those hundreds and thousands of people who watch for the great white whales to appear over the horizon each morning.

Fishing, Sailing, and Water-sports Tourists

Of course, the cruise lines are not the only users of the Caribbean Sea. There is a growing group of tourists who also use the sea as the focus of their holiday for water skiing, surfing, windsurfing, fishing, sailing, and diving or snorkeling. Fishing and sailing, chartered and bareboat, remain the up-market pursuits. Fishing, in particular, has been a sport for tourists from the early days, and it remains particularly popular in the Bahamas where record catches are made in deep-sea game fishing, while in the shallows, fishing for barracuda and bonefish is popular.

The British Virgin Islands, one of the region's largest water-sports destinations, stresses the attractions of its unspoiled islands and cays. "One can imagine no better holiday for a fisherman than cruising in a motorboat among the islands, with a tent for shore at nights, with food and conversation enriched from the day's catch," enthused a circular from the West India Committee in 1921. Then, there was no mention of sailing, but by 1958, *McKay's Guide* mentioned that the islands had "wonderful sailing in the waters off their coasts" and advised: "With time on your hands in St. Thomas and a liking for the sea, you couldn't do better than to charter one of the many boats available for the purpose, and cruise among these islands for as many days as you can spare." Ten years later, another guidebook commented that "this part of the Caribbean is becoming known as a yachtsman's paradise." The British Virgin Islands has forbidden obtrusive development, but encourages marinas and secluded luxury resorts. The main focus of development has been the yacht charter business, which began in 1967. There are now more than 500 yachts for hire out of the British Virgin Islands, which makes it one of the largest bareback [self-skippered] charter fleets in the world. Charter yacht tourists outnumber hotel tourists and spend more money than them (Lett 1983:35–36). Much of the business is in flotillas where beginners in groups of 12–15 sail in small dinghies under expert supervision.

Modern-style marinas now dot the Caribbean, hangouts for a largely young, American clientele, who pay handsomely for a week's charter. For the yachties, the Caribbean is the fashionable place to be in the winter months, when the sailing elite of the world converges on Martinique after the Route du Rhum transatlantic run or on St. Lucia for Christmas following the Atlantic Rally for Cruisers. The regatta season then moves on to St. Maarten, Puerto Rico, and the Virgin Islands before ending in April, with Antigua's Sailing Week at English Harbor, where Nicholson's Yachtyard, an expatriate stronghold, was one of the first charter bases in the Caribbean in the 1940s. Marinas are big business, and Jamaica has a new project on hand: a marina at Port Antonio, one of the oldest tourism locations in the Caribbean. Promoted as a "megayacht destination," it will, according to the Port Authority of Jamaica, "compare favorably with any waterfront tourism development in the world." It will accommodate the range of craft: from "boutique" cruise ships to the megayachts of the megarich. The argument is that Port Antonio will benefit from such upscale visitors. "The last yacht that came here for a week bought £670 [US$1,120] worth of flowers every day," said Noel Hylton, the president and chief executive of the Port Authority.[39] The opportunities—for linkages into the local economy—are there.

Fishing, sailing, and windsurfing tourists are different from the beach-based tourists. They tend to be more upscale, and are traditionally socially and racially a select group (in an island like Barbados, this is still the case). However, at another level, they are more informal than other tourists. On Bequia, for example, the yachties, who cultivate a lotus-eating manner, hang around St. Elizabeth Bay and its bars, owned by bare-footed expatriates. While the tourist establishment eyes the boat people with some suspicion (they may be rich but they are scruffy) the yachties themselves appear less affronted by authentic Caribbean life than nervous package tourists. And they can make a significant, and direct, contribution to island economies, depending on local suppliers for provisions. In many cases, farmers supply direct to sailors at the marinas. In the British Virgin Islands two types of trading go on: There is the merchant who supplies the flotillas with fruit and vegetables from the United States, shipped in on containers from Florida. The alternative is to buy from individuals who provide Caribbean fruit and vegetables to the more discerning boat captains and owners from a boat-to-boat shop. In Grenada, a small farming cooperative relies on business with sailors for its success and expansion, while for the yachties at the uninhabited Tobago Cays in the Grenadines, young men from Union Island arrive by boat to sell whatever service is required.

Much of the ownership of water-sports businesses, however, remains in expatriate hands. This is partly because of the capital expenditure involved and partly because of the ambivalent nature of the relationship of Caribbean peoples to the sea. While the sea is all around them, and while as fishermen and boatbuilders they are linked to it, they have not traditionally seen it as a place to be exploited for sport. Hence, water-sports tourism has originally been run by and for white foreigners; with some exceptions this remains largely the case, along with such subsidiary businesses as ships' chandlers and marine supermarkets. In the water-sports s business, outsiders dominate both as employers and employees. The yacht charter owners tend to give jobs to other expatriates, often well-connected young men who spend the winter seeking work around Caribbean marinas. So says Jeremy Wright, who owns Boardsailing BVI and is chairman of the Caribbean Windsurfing Association: "My business employs outsiders due to the skills required in looking after the tourists who arrive with differing abilities. I occasionally employ locals yet find that they generally do not get that excited in the teaching and the beach operation side of things. This is the opposite to the outsider who, of course, loves the chance to work in this environment."

Diving and snorkeling have also emerged as an important niche market, for the Caribbean has some of the best diving in the world. Islands like Bonaire and the Cayman Islands, for instance, are both long established and have promoted themselves almost exclusively as dive destinations. New destinations, like Dominica, are also beginning to gain reputations. Divers, like yachties, are adventurous, relatively wealthy and, most important, conscious of the environment. In the Bahamas, the Exuma National Park, administered by the Bahamas National Trust, has developed a "support fleet" of yachties, who each contribute US$30 a year to its upkeep. Nick Wardle, of the National Trust, says that the well-being of the park, the first in the Bahamas, relies on goodwill and that the scheme is a strong replenishment exercise. "The Park is remote; we want to keep it like that. No one is allowed to take anything from it." The Exuma National Park has become a model of its kind and prompted the Bahamas government to announce the protection of 20 percent of the Bahamian marine ecosystem in 2000.

The Caribbean Sea is the resource of all who use it. Yet it is under threat from a range of environmental problems, from dumping to sewage disposal and the destruction of reefs, and all its users, whether cruise ships or jetskiers, are to some extent to blame. The only way to regulate the operations of cruise ships and to protect the marine environment would be to create regional regulatory bodies embracing every state. The CTO has, on many occasions, appealed to the region "as a matter of urgency" to put together a joint environmental plan to regulate behavior, enforce regulations, and punish offenders. Other organizations have also called on the region to establish a body to safeguard the marine environment. Meanwhile, the use of the Caribbean Sea for transporting nuclear waste has made the region even more aware that its waters are a vital component of its patrimony. As Jean Holder points out, the Caribbean has "few resources left that give us any real bargaining power."[40] One of those is the Caribbean Sea.

Source: From *Last Resorts: The Cost of Tourism in the Caribbean*, 2003. Reprinted with permission of the author and the Latin American Bureau.

Notes

[1] Caribbean Tourism Organization, 2000.

[2] Associated Press, London, 25 December 1994.

[3] *New York Times*, New York, 15 June 1994.

[4] Florida-Caribbean Cruise Association, *Caribbean Cruising*, Second Quarter 2002.

[5] Caribbean Tourism Organization, *Caribbean Statistical News*, Barbados, 2001.

[6] Ibid.

[7] Ibid.

[8] *Trade News Edition*, 7 June 1993.

[9] Jean Holder, "Getting the Most from Cruise Tourism for the Caribbean," address to conference at Coopers Lybrand International, Barbados, 1993.

[10] Ibid.

[11] *Caribbean Week*, Barbados, 26 June 1993.

[12] Ibid.

[13] Holder, op. cit.

[14] Caribbean Insight, December 1997.

[15] Ibid.

[16] IPS agency, November 2000.

[17] Florida-Caribbean Cruise Association (FCCA) Newsletter, July 1994.

[18] Ibid.

[19] Ibid.

[20] Edward Bollinger, Vice President of Purchasing, Properties and Logistics, RCCL, address given to the CTO, San Juan, Puerto Rico, 9 July 1992.

[21] *Caribbean Week*, 12–25 November 1994.

[22] Florida-Caribbean Cruise Association, *Caribbean Cruising*, second quarter 2001.

[23] Florida-Caribbean Cruise Association, *Caribbean Cruising*, second quarter 2002.

[24] Florida-Caribbean Cruise Association, *Caribbean Cruising*, second quarter 2001.

[25] *The Democrat for St. Kitts*, 25 March 1994.

[26] *Caribbean Insight*, London, January 1995.

[27] *Daily Nation*, Barbados, 15 April 2002.

[28] *Caribbean Travel News Europe*, Summer 1993.
[29] Economist Intelligence Unit (EIU), *Tourism in the Caribbean*, London, 1993.
[30] *Santo Domingo News*, 25 August 1995.
[31] Florida-Caribbean Cruise Association, *Caribbean Cruising*, second quarter 2002.
[32] EIU, op. cit.
[33] Organization of American States, *Economic Analysis of Tourism in Jamaica*, Washington, DC, 1994.
[34] Caribbean News Association (CANA), 5 November 1994.
[35] Holder, op. cit.
[36] *Caribbean Week*, 12–25 November 1994.
[37] CANA, 26 May 1994.
[38] Florida-Caribbean Cruise Association, *Caribbean Cruising*, second quarter 2002.
[39] Focus on Jamaica, *The Times*, 6 August 2002.
[40] Jean Holder, "Regional Integration, Tourism and Caribbean Sovereignty," mimeo, 1993.

References

Dickinson, Robert. 1993. "Cruise Industry Outlook in the Caribbean," in *Tourism, Marketing and Management in the Caribbean*, ed. Dennis Gayle and Jonathan Goodrich, p. 188. London.

Dickinson, Robert, and A. Vladimir. 1997. *Selling the Sea: An Inside Look at the Cruise Industry*. New York: Wiley.

Lett, James W. 1993 "Ludic and Liminoid Aspects of Charter Yacht Tourism in the Caribbean." *Annals of Tourism Research* 10.

Wood, Robert. 2000. "Caribbean Cruise Tourism: Globalization at Sea." *Annals of Tourism Research* 27(2).

21

The Role of the Elite in the Development of Tourism

M. Estellie Smith

Through the entire range of First- to Fourth-World locales, there is growing faith in tourism as a tool of development. This paper examines the rationales and role played by the indigenous elite who use their material and nonmaterial capital to expand tourism. It argues that tourism development serves the national elite by stabilizing (at least in the short term) their dominant position and more importantly by encouraging and even requiring socio-economically "divergent" groups to adopt lifestyles geared to the commoditization for tourism process.[1]

Tourism is still a little understood phenomenon despite the explosion of research across a wide range of disciplines. A recent review article on the "Anthropology of Tourism" lists fourteen questions that "urgently need investigation and analysis" (Stronza 2001:261–62). Stronza emphasizes "the need to pose" new kinds of questions . . . especially as we begin to consider the social, economic, and environmental merits . . . of tourism" (2001:263). She is not only interested in investigating "the differential affects of certain kinds of tourism on guests' attitudes and behavior" (both while touring and once they return home), but also in the factors "that can explain particular kinds of local involvement in tourism" (2001:263). She notes that a past focus on the factors that motivate tourists to travel has led to the neglect of examining the conditions under which people in host destinations decide to become involved in tourism. Finally, she stresses that "our understanding would improve if we examined the extent to which hosts act as decision-makers in shaping the kinds of tourism that will take place in their own communities" (2001:267).

Stronza is correct in stressing the need to look at the extent to which hosts shape the kinds of tourism that develop, but it must be noted that "there are hosts and then, there are hosts." In one sense, the entire destination country is the tourists' host community. At another level, there are the hoteliers (ranging from local managers for international chains to local bed and breakfast owners), the restauranteurs, the recreational fishing boat captains, the casual acquaintance who invites you to his or her home, the local participants in a festival, and so on. Clearly, they are not all the same; the variability within the category "host" is typical of the bewildering array of types within almost every category whether "tourist" or "development project."

This paper examines the question: "What role do internal elites—the rich, the powerful, the taste makers, and the influence brokers in a destination country—play in tourism given their critical role in the national and, often, the international arenas in which global tourism takes place?" These are the "hosts" with whom the vast majority of tourists, as well as those who study tourism, have little or no contact and thus little knowledge.

The Good and the Bad News of Tourism

Since the 1960s, development in economically marginal regions and countries has been a major concern of most countries, whether donor or recipient. Though some identify tourism development as simply a new kind of colonialism (e.g., Nash 1989),[2] most tourism development plans differ from classic colonialism primarily in their claim to being designed with input from, and with the altruistic aim of directing benefits to, the locale targeted for capital investment.[3]

For obvious (and some not so obvious) reasons, tourism has been an important component of most "modernization" projects, but this form of development exhibits distinctive features—what Bond and Ladman have termed the "peculiar characteristics of tourism as an export product" (1980:232). For example, instead of the modernization process involving a small number of alien or quasi-residential personnel such as foreign technicians, civil servants, and military, medical, educational, or religious professionals, tourism as a form of development depends on massive numbers of usually foreign and essentially transient consumers who visit the area for periods ranging from a few hours to a few weeks. Tourism is ". . . a service-oriented operation that may entail a great deal of face-to-fact contact . . ." (Pi-Sunyer 1977:151). It also relies on a full range of external decision-makers, from personnel in small firms in the leisure travel market (e.g., travel agents and writers) to media personnel and family-run hoteliers. Most importantly, tourism brings locals into continual and large-scale contact with outsiders whose selection of where to travel instills locals with feelings of "pride of place," a sense of strangeness in observing what they rarely if ever noticed before, as well as new aspirations.

Tourism involves foreigners in both the production and consumption sectors, leading to a great deal of concern with the extent, degree, type, and effect that they will have on the host population. First, and by no means insignificant, is the desire of those involved in tourism development to disassociate themselves from any suggestion of discredited colonialism, even if operating in a context that makes it difficult to avoid charges of neocolonialism. Second, because of the need to involve massive numbers of foreigners as initial service producers as well as ultimate consumers, "Tourism is not a sector in which an autarkic [autarky—national economic self-sufficiency and independence] approach is feasible" (Green 1979:88). This leads to the third reason why studies of tourism have emphasized the extent of foreign involvement, namely, the dramatic results of what has been labeled "the demonstration effect." Here, primary concern is on the extent to which the needs of providing tourists with what First World people see as everyday necessities (e.g., hot showers, high sanitary standards relative to food, water, and toilets, comforting and appealing surroundings) encourages local populations to emulate the affluent lifestyle of the visitors (never mind that such affluence is often spurious and that the locals may know it).

Much of the research on tourist development has focused on its pitfalls and the desirability of not imposing the homogenizing influence of the global economy on less-developed countries (LDCs). One of the great difficulties in development work, however, is the frequency with which—regardless of intent and training that has sensitized planners to the subtleties and potential pervasiveness of the commoditization process—it does become an agent of homogenization and a promoter of the interests of the local elite who seek to direct and benefit from it. Despite a considerable body of data on the role played by internal elite, this aspect of development is often trivialized when analyzing the effects of tourism development.

As a poignant example of how one can unintentionally serve to further the very processes one wishes to resist, let me draw from the description of a West African project in which a key player, a Canadian ethnologist, wished to avoid the kind of development that would deny tourists the opportunity "to discover what lies beyond the beach and come into contact with the real Africa" (Saglio 1979:321). It appears that by the time he wrote the paper, he was serving as technical advisor to the Senegal Department of Tourism and, he stresses, he was sensitive to the kind of development that lends itself to the host population being subject to "feelings of alienation" resulting from an "abandonment of certain traditional values . . ." (1979:322). He designed a "discovery tourism" project that encouraged visitors to travel to and reside in remote Senegalese bush villages whose inhabitants still followed a subsistence mode of production. It was deemed essential to the success of the program that the visitors' residences be "organically integrated dwellings" that were architecturally consonant with the housing and existing ambience of the permanent population and that provided an authentic context for visitor and host.

My own reading of the description of the attempts made to engage the villagers in the process, however, leads to the conclusion that the operation actually educated the Senegalese bush people in the basics of the commoditization process and the market system. Saglio tells us, for example, that:

> One purpose of the project was to restore the value of the traditional Diola dwelling by reproducing it as faithfully as possible. Construction of these houses required a collective effort of a type that until then had never involved a monetary transaction and no standard existed for estimated costs. Many meetings were held with the villagers to take account of such elements as the price of palm slats, the rate for cutting and clearing, the price of roof straw, and average income [to be derived from tourism]. (1979:325)

In short, people who had once deemed the cooperative creation of a dwelling to be an act of social exchange—whether in obtaining the materials or through the act of construction itself—learned through the "discovery tourism" project all about the monetized calculus of market exchange. They were taught how to commoditize the production, exchange, and consumption of their everyday activities and the social relations in which such activities are grounded.

The literature on tourism development is rife with such examples, and the dynamics involved are commonplace. This paper explores how such commoditization meshes with the aims of the internal elite. Indeed, it is likely to be a calculated and deliberate part of their programmatic goals for most development projects. (It has long been held that workers have to be educated to understand concepts such as "time is worth money" if they are to become motivated to be reliable, industrious wage laborers). For the remainder of the paper, I will present the various ways in which internal national elite in tourist destinations benefit from tourism both in terms of goods, that is, greater material affluence and money, as well as in "Good," meaning increased nonmaterial prestige, power, and authority.

To begin with, landlords often control the initial resource—land. My own work in the Mediterranean indicates that internal elite—local and national—are heavily involved in tourism development, especially in the initiatory or pre-development stages when transnational financing negotiations take place, the locales to be developed are chosen, primary contacts with external agents are made, and the critical decisions about necessary infrastructural foundations are set in motion. For example, prior to the development of tourism on Cyprus (pre-1960), "land . . . was either for agricultural use or composed of sand dunes" (Andronicou 1979:261). By 1973, however, the market value of a third acre of seaside land in what was to become the tourist center of Famagusta jumped from US$4,000 to US$375,000 even though the price of dry-farming agricultural land only increased from US$250 to US$400 per acre.[4] Similarly, Louis Perez notes that in the West Indies, "soaring land values limit ownership of land to all but national elite and foreigners" (1980:252). The control of land makes outsiders aware that they must go to the elite if the project is to succeed; this in turn enhances the access of the elite to networks of negotiation.

Second, the elite have a greater capacity to "manage" the production of laws that enhance their potential for profit at less risk. Elites profit not only from their control of land. When they perceive that they can make more money at less risk by investing at home, they will redirect their investment capital to internal development projects like tourism.[5] In his research on tourist development in the Philippines during the Marcos regime, Robert Britton tells us that:

> Elite self-interest has been amply documented . . . in tourism . . . it is undoubtedly a powerful force. An extreme example comes from Manila, where fourteen international hotels with a total capacity of about 13,000 rooms were built to meet a predicted shortage during the 1976 World Bank conference. Construction firms with ties to the . . . family [of then President Marcos] harvested large profits, and other friends and relatives of Marcos [owned] the properties. Financing came from various state sources and it was reported (*New York Times*) that 12% of the Philippines Development Bank's funds were committed to the projects. (1980:243)

In this scheme, the selling or leasing of land for high returns is only the first step to profit and is usually implemented at low risk by the passage of laws such as zoning and environmental rulings that direct tourist developers to target specific areas while excluding (in the name of "protecting") others. Laws that mandate a majority investment by nationals often end up creating new firms or force investment in established firms owned by private nationals. Their profits are derived directly from overcharging for shoddy materials and labor as well as from opportunities for graft and bribery and patronage obligations that come with their control of subcontracts and other local employment. Bonds used to finance tourism developments often pay high interest because of the weak credit rating of many of the issuing units. Further, any real risk to the capital of the national elite can be relatively low because, on one hand, international development agencies make their loans to the national government and, on the other hand, high-risk development is judiciously allocated to foreign investors.[6]

Third, tourism development not only enhances the ability of the elite to control dissident voices within their country but creates new aspirations and provides avenues for achieving them that makes elite control cheaper and their capital investment more profitable. Green noted that in central Africa, ". . . from 1965 to 1980 on the order of US$150 million has been or will be spent on 'tourist-oriented' airport construction or extension at Nairobi, Kilimanjaro, Mombasa, Kisimu, Dar es Salaam, Entebbe, and Gulu" (1979:97). Such large sums expended on infrastructure—notably jumbo jet airports— are clearly in excess of the needs of the existing or even a foreseeable expanded tourism sector.

In addition to the profits just outlined, such seemingly irrational investment of a nation's capital has two ancillary effects: first, such monumental architecture (e.g., infrastructure like airports) has, for millennia, enhanced the prestige of the elite, serving as visible representations of the progress and prosperity (and power) they have brought. These may be hollow symbols for some, but there is abundant evidence that, whether First World or Third World airports ("if you build them [business] will come"), they carry a positive spin for many citizens as markers of and hope for better times to come. (Think of the broad repercussions of a new stadium.) Second, and, more pragmatically, infrastructural projects often aid in crowd control. New, impressively wide urban avenues and superhighways that crisscross the country and airports with super-sized runways not only enhance a country's capital city and make further trade possible; they aid in controlling civil unrest and allow major troop and arms movements. Likewise, immense sports stadia not only offer venues for international sporting events; they can also serve to house large numbers of political detainees rounded up in massive sweep operations.

Lastly, tourism development is often earmarked for economically marginal geographic areas hitherto neglected by the governing elite because of their minimal economic role in the national accounts and their paucity of investment opportunities. The low priority given to the needs of the generally impoverished population by the central authorities prior to development is bad. However, on the good side, this same neglect gives such populations a fair degree of autonomy. The mechanisms of the State as well as the elite have little effect on the daily round of life in such regions. Negligence, incompetency, or insufficiency of funds on the part of national and even regional governing elite necessarily fosters local patterns of self-sufficiency (although the locales also serve as breeding grounds or sanctuaries for unrest and challenges to the State). The development of tourism brings, for better or worse, the intrusion of the State. Not infrequently, civil unrest escalates either because of rising expectations or a rejection of aspects of State management. Since unrest has a dampening effect on tourism, the State's or the ruling regime's repression gains legitimacy in the international arena. Both will be hailed for "restoring order" and "protecting the safety and property" of area residents, businesses, and tourists. Britton, for example, notes that during the last days of the Marcos regime "a prominent U.S. travel trade paper . . . wrote that Manila's streets were safe, 'thanks to martial law'" (1980:244–5).

One last benefit can be derived by the elite when divisions arise among the ranks of those hostile to the current regime (e.g., national devolutionists). Some elites may be willing to cooperate with proposed change and development, while others continue to resist them and wish for independence in order to more fully exert their own control over the path development takes and the potential wealth it is expected to bring (cf. the membership split in the Corsican and Spanish Basque nationalist movement).

One example incorporates several of the points just made. In a study of tourism development in the state of Guerrero, Mexico, the population lived along a thin margin of the coast where income was derived from the harvesting of copra and sesame seeds, fishing, and some livestock production (Reynoso y Valle and de Regt 1979). The region, however, overwhelmingly consisted of what Reynoso y Valle and de Regt describe as "totally unworked" mountain range.[7] Indeed, the inequities and frailties of the economy were such that, in the 1960s, portions of the region were marked by "guerrilla disturbances."[8] In the late 1960s, plans were made to develop tourism in the region. Actual work on the project (localized in Zihuatanejo) did not begin until September 1972 when, by an interesting coincidence, "construction was also begun on an iron and steel complex in Lazara Cardenas, only 120 kilometers from the tourist site" (Roynoso y Valle and de Regt 1979:115). The industrial project was totally separate from the tourism development and was financed by private capital from a consortium of internal elite. Unlike the tourist project, the industrial project was subjected to little genuine oversight, say, of the plant's potential for environmental damage. Yet the plant was so massive a project that analysts have maintained "it had a clear-cut effect on the entire national economy . . ." (Roynoso y Valle and de Regt 1979:116). Not surprisingly, the plant benefited from the infrastructural development (e.g., highways, electrical plants, airports) that was initiated for and funded by the tourist project.

Together, the two projects produced a profitable synergy, although it is debatable how the profits were distributed. For one thing, support for the guerillas shrank and the strength of the unrest they had helped create was considerably reduced. Second, the populace generally perceived that the State was responding to its needs. Third, the tourist project—which had an announced aim of "densifying" populations in the development loci—led to a population concentration that not only allowed for the more efficient delivery of services to the people but also made it easier to control them should unrest again emerge.[9] Finally, the densification process also assured a readily available worker population for both projects and also drained some surplus labor from other urban centers and a wide area of rural locales.[10]

Once the local population was settled, their labor became a more stable resource. Firstly, people were required to seek wage labor to pay for their hitherto uncollected taxes and rents as well as mortgage payments for the new homes to which the State directed them. Second, new zoning rules regarding the use of house plots forbade the production of vegetables or livestock and the populace became totally dependent on buying food from markets—added insurance for a steady labor supply (Reynoso y Valle and de Regt 1979: 130).[11]

What is worthy of special note is that the juxtaposition of industrial park and tourist development is not uncommon. Nancy Evans (1979) reports the same linkages in her study of development in the Mexican state of

Jalisco, including the same strenuous efforts to move the population into newly constructed housing with the same kinds of zoning restrictions.[12] The array of advantages to the national elite is obvious. At the least, by synchronizing the development of an infrastructure that services what is generally perceived as an environmentally cleaner tourist industry (supported with international funding), with that of a more socially and environmentally hazardous industrial development (internally financed), their capital investment opportunities were enhanced.

Lastly, the successful exercise of power generates future success. Decisions are often made about development at the national level with little if any input from the local population who are usually minimally apprised of the programs only after the operation makes its appearance in the local area, months into the development process. De Kadt notes "Rather fewer will interfere when nationally powerful groups bend [existing] regulations to their own advantage," behavior so regularly occurring that it does much to "reinforce existing inequalities" (1979:24). In Puerto Vallarta, for example, local authorities proved "impotent in the face of the activities of economically powerful groups from Mexico's large cities," a lack of control that is an example of what Pablo Gonzalez Casanova identifies as "internal neocolonialism." In this case, even though there was a local planning authority and there were local representatives on the board, input from this source was minimal; some members maintained that they were "too intimidated by the power, status, and presumed expertise of outside officials to be forceful in presenting their views" (de Kadt 1979:24).

The process by which the elite cultivate (in every sense of the word) current resources for enhanced future returns[13] may be extremely subtle; explicitly stated rationales and aims may bear little relation to their covert and real intentions. Laws may be passed that, on the face of it, work to the public good but, in reality, are of greater benefit to those who control wealth, power, and authority.

An example of this is reported by Boissevain and Inglott (1979) for Malta. A political shift in 1971 from the right-of-center National Party to the left-of-center Malta Labor Party appears to have only minimally affected the course of the development of tourism. To be sure, the Labor government—which rode to election victory on the crest of a wave of agitation about the inaccessibility of housing especially for young couples—established an excellent record in building new housing[14] and introduced measures to curb land speculation (although the measures were initiated too late to curb the traditional elite, including the Church, from extraordinary profit-taking during the previous political regime). The new government established watchdog agencies and minimum levels of employment for Maltese nationals in foreign-owned enterprises, which also opened new avenues for traditional patronage. However, it did not address the issue that much of the land used in development remained in the hands of the rich since it was only leased to developers rather than sold to them outright.[15]

Further, private water firms sharply increased the price of fresh water, while benefiting from the jump in consumption resulting from the massive amounts of water utilized by tourists in hotels with their attached swimming pools and other amenities (e.g., highly water-consumptive golf greens) required to attract visitors. Finally, a system of hotel classification was initiated on the grounds that it would aid tourists and package tour planners in selecting hotels and also would encourage small and medium hotels to upgrade their facilities. The classification, however, was more often detrimental to small and medium hotels and more beneficial to the large hotels in which wealthy Maltese were invested in a variety of ways. Furthermore, there was only a token response from the government to calls for reinforcing "existing measures to control building and clean up beaches and other public recreation areas" (Boissevain and Inglott 1979:279).

The tax structure is seemingly tangential to all the activities surrounding the expansion of tourism. Boissevain and Inglott call attention to the fact that "The wealthiest classes are . . . [still] favored by the income tax laws, for the maximum tax of 60% is applied annually to all incomes over MTL2500 [c. US$7000]!" (1979:276).[16] "Since prominent members of the two major political parties as well as the politically important General Workers Union are heavily involved in tourist-related activities," the authors conclude (ironically) that, "it is not likely that tourism will ferment class-based political conflict in the foreseeable future."[17]

All this indicates, as supported by recent evidence from Eastern Europe and China, that one would be naive to expect political rhetoric to be related to the actual behavior of the governing elite. Rather, one should focus on the crucial question cui bono—who benefits and how? In the commoditization of leisure through tourism development (and all of the other forms of commoditization that it engenders), the internal elite play a major role. In not a few cases, they also appear to be the major beneficiaries, not the least because of the role tourism plays in establishing a context that leads ordinary citizens to aspire to the goals of the elite. The elites then derive benefits from a consensual ideology that informs and guides everyone's behavior and articulates itself in a coherent and systematic fashion that comes to be seen as "natural" or at least "common sensible" because it is seemingly the road to a better life. In sum, it is the elite who write the script, design the stage settings, and even fix the price of admission for the unfolding drama of global tourism.

Source: Adapted from "Hegemony and Elite Capital: The Tools of Tourism," *Tourism and Culture: An Applied Perspective*, Erve Chambers (ed.), 1997, SUNY Press.

Notes

[1] There are numerous definitions of "commoditization." I will simply repeat the one that appeared in Smith: "It is the process of transforming goods and services once produced for self-use into products for exchange in markets. Any product produced and distributed via the

market has a price (determined by supply and demand), and this is the major, sometimes even the sole consideration for the characteristics of the product in production, exchange, and consumption" (2000:193).

[2] It might be argued that modern development differs by relying on and channeling funds either directly through agencies of the donor states or indirectly through contribution of such states to international lending agencies such as the World Bank or the International Monetary Fund. A close examination, however, seems to indicate that private capital is as critical in the process as previously, the new twist being that substantial amounts of the risks previously borne by the private sector now rest in the public sector.

[3] So that the texts themselves as well as additional data would be readily available to readers I have deliberately placed my chief reliance on two publications of collected papers, one by de Kadt (1979), the other by Vogeler and de Souza (1980). Both have been adjudged substantive contributions to tourism research and are readily accessible through most academic libraries. Although these were written more than two decades ago, the problematics of the issues they (and I) raise have not become outdated but, on the contrary, have intensified.

[4] Andronicou admits that some speculators got wealthy but argues that others recognized the potential value and sold for handsome profits sooner or later. He does not, however, note what portion of the land was exchanged freehold versus leasehold. In the latter, it is the land-lord and his heirs who derive enormous benefits, though it may take some years—during which the land will probably continue to appreciate considerably.

[5] As Marx pointed out, "If capital is sent abroad, this is not done because it absolutely could not be applied at home, but because it can be employed at a higher rate of profit in a foreign country" ([1894] 1962:251).

[6] Further, the employment brings prosperity and this helps stabilize the positions of those who control the government. It also offers them opportunities to increase their power by the patronage they exercise over subcontracting and employment opportunities ranging from the lowest unskilled day laborer to prestigious positions in the expanded bureaucratic structure that development requires. Changes in the government—even revolutions—do not necessarily alter the process; the new regime is sometimes little more than a change of the palace guard. In the Philippines, for example, following the overthrow of the Marcos regime, the same charges of nepotism and corruption were continually filed against members of the government of President Aquino (though the offenses were said to be of less magnitude—or at least more subtle). In any case, the Aquino family as well as its most powerful political rival are old and leading aristocratic lineages in the national elite system.

[7] Curiously, however, in a discussion of the nature of the work force that aggregated during the period of intense construction development, we are told that ". . . the majority of [construction] workers . . . seem to have come . . . primarily from the mountains" (p. 128). One is led to wonder how these people existed if the mountains were "totally unworked."

[8] Government development documents included the argument that development in these marginal areas would create employment opportunities that would stem the flow of migrants to already overburdened urban centers. There is no evidence that a cost/benefit analysis was done to determine if the same amount of funds directed to urban problems would not have offered greater benefit and dealt more effectively with issues of greater urgency.

[9] Reynoso y Valle and de Regt note (p. 123) that since development and the strict codes for land use, "Poorer families are now moving into the hills, beyond the reach of utilities they cannot afford, where they can keep goats and grow subsistence crops to eke out a living"—and, or course, formulate strategies for resisting the two projects.

[10] Reynoso y Valle and de Regt (p. 127) point out that at times during the initial period of intense new construction, ". . . there were as many as 35 construction companies on site with at least 4000 unskilled laborers and perhaps 1000 skilled workers and professionals."

[11] The authors emphasize that the new zoning regulations combined with the newly enforced land ownership rules. Among other changes, the villagers found that they were required (many for the first time) to pay taxes on their property—taxes that included the costs of electricity, water, sewage systems, etc. "Women, especially in the lower class, were pushed to look for work outside the home . . . the single mother [was] hit the hardest." Given that most construction workers were "single" males, forces conspired to expand both prostitution and impoverished single mothers with growing numbers of offspring. Thus, in addition to the commoditization process per se (e.g., food must be purchased in markets instead of grown for self-consumption), there was added pressure for villagers to become dependent on a wage economy.

Finally, citing a study by J. Kennedy, A. Russin and A. Martinez (1977), Reynoso y Valle and de Regt note "Opportunities . . . increased in the informal labor market for . . . washing clothes, renting rooms . . . selling food, and petty vending" (1979:116). It is clear that the "penny capitalism" of the informal economy was imposed by external factors. (For discussions of the various dynamics of the informal economy, see Smith 1989:292–317 and 1990.) One must wonder if the women preferred such tasks to the household production they formerly practiced. That the populace was not blind to the long-term consequences of the unfolding scenario is indicated by Reynoso y Valle and de Regt remarking (p. 116) that some villagers labeled those of their neighbors who favored development as "harmful persons" who were "selling out."

[12] Evans (p. 316) notes that the 4% interest rate on mortgages attracts buyers despite "long and complicated paper work that discourages anyone with little education from applying." A minimum wage employee, who is entitled to pay US$6400 for a 3-bedroom house, has a mandatory 18% (c. US$20.66) deducted from an average monthly paycheck of US$114.75 (based on a 25-day month at the minimum daily wage of US$4.50). It is perhaps overly cynical to question who ultimately profits from the construction and funding that underwrites such housing—and who pays the most. One may note, however, that in the context of remarks relative to problems created by "internal neocolonialism"—an urban form of paternalism—Evans (p. 309) reports that, according to a (1974) government brochure, 75% (28,364) of the Puerto Vallarta project investors were Mexican nationals—though we are not told how the dollar amount was spread relative to national vs. foreign investors or how the investment holdings were distributed.

[13] This is in line with my definition of "capital" as "resource-producing resources" (Smith 1991:51), a definition designed to make it possible for, especially, anthropologists to examine the role of capital in non-capitalist societies—i.e., in societies that pre-date the introduction of the modern market system (or possess dual economic systems, one of which employs capital but is not embedded in it).

[14] But it might be asked who owned the firms that got the contracts for the new housing and who gained power in the labor unions?

[15] Boissevain and Inglott (1979:273) call attention to a pilot project in the development of Maltese tourism that was initiated in 1963 by the privately owned Malta Developments, which leasehold purchased a thousand acres of church-owned farmland for an annual ground rent of MTL5000. The Santa Maria Project was developed into a "first-class garden estate with chalets and villas" which, by 1970 was bringing the developers an annual ground rent of MTL30,000. Ground rent increases were equally spectacular in other parts of the island: "A plot of land with an original ground rent in 1962 of 250, in 1967 yielded 6500 a year . . ." (p. 274). "Private fortunes skyrocketed—to MTL30 million in the extreme case of the Pace family Bical enterprise" (p. 276). Though in some cases those who sold lands leasehold saw the ground rents jump spectacularly one should be reminded that such "sales" are temporary in that, at the end of the specified lease period, the land and any buildings (with their improvements) revert back to those who made the original leasehold sale. Freeholders, on the other

hand, have borne no expenses (for improvements or taxes) but, at the expiration of the lease-hold, the property reverts to those who hold the freehold, at which time they are free to lease-hold again—and again, and again—or sell freehold. It might also be added that a colleague who is knowledgeable about Malta tells me that, although the Bical Enterprise ultimately went into liquidation, indications are that the Pace family seems to enjoy continued affluence and apparently was careful to divert large sums of money out of the enterprise before this process began. Whatever the case, Boissevain and Inglott (p. 276) remark that the economic potential in this process are considerable: ". . . the building boom did create in the space of a few years a truly wealthy class."

[16] MTL is the official international code for Malta's currency, the lira. At the time this article was written, MTL1.00 = US$2.80.

[17] Indeed, Boissevain and Inglott stress (p. 279) that "there has been a marked lack of success . . . in influencing government policy (or its enforcement) . . . . There are no orga-nized protest groups—potential members fear victimization if they criticize government. In a small country run by a powerful government there is basis for such fear. Protest is thus nei-ther open nor sustained . . . [and most] is limited to private grumbling and anonymous letters to the editors of the major newspapers."

References

Andronicou, A. 1979. "Tourism in Cyprus," in *Tourism: Passport to Development? Per-spectives on the Social and Cultural Effects of Tourism in Developing Countries*, ed. Emanuel de Kadt, pp. 237–65. New York: Oxford University Press.

Boissevain, J., and P. Serracino. 1979. "Tourism in Malta," in *Tourism: Passport to Devel-opment? Perspectives on the Social and Cultural Effects of Tourism in Developing Countries*, ed. Emanuel de Kadt, pp. 265–84. New York: Oxford University Press.

Bond, M. E., and J. R. Ladman. 1980. "International Tourism: An Instrument for Third World Development," in *Dialectics of Third World Development*, ed. I. Vogeler and A. de Souza, pp. 231–40. Montclair, NJ: Allanheld, Osmun.

Britton, R. 1980. "Shortcomings of Third World Tourism," in *Dialectics of Third Word Devel-opment*, ed. I. Vogeler and A. de Souza, pp. 241–47. Montclair, NJ: Allanheld, Osmun.

Casanova, Pablo Gonzalez. 1965. "Internal Colonialism and National Development." *Studies in Comparative International Development* 1(4) [as cited in de Kadt 1979:24].

Crick, Malcolm. 1989. "Representations of International Tourism in the Social Sciences: Sun, Sex, Sights, Savings, and Servility," in *Annual Review of Anthropology* 18:307–44.

de Kadt, Emanuel, ed. 1979. *Tourism: Passport to Development? Perspectives on the Social and Cultural Effects of Tourism in Developing Countries*. A joint World Bank-UNESCO Study. New York: Oxford University Press.

Evans, N. 1979. "The Dynamics of Tourism Development in Puerto Vallarta," in *Tourism: Passport to Development? Perspectives on the Social and Cultural Effects of Tourism in Developing Countries*, ed. Emanuel de Kadt, pp. 305–20. New York: Oxford Univer-sity Press.

Green, R. H. 1979. "Toward Planning Tourism in African Countries," in *Tourism: Pass-port to Development? Perspectives on the social and cultural effects of tourism in devel-oping countries*, ed. Emanuel de Kadt, pp. 79–100. New York: Oxford University Press.

Higley, J., G. L. Field, and K. Groholt. 1976. *Elite Structure and Ideology: A Theory with Applications to Norway.* New York: Columbia University Press.

Kennedy, J., A. Russin and A. Martinez. 1977. *The Impact of Tourism Development on Women: A Case Study of Ixtapa-Zihuatanejo, Mexico.* A restricted circulation report to the World Bank.

Marcus, G. E. 1983. "The Fiduciary Role in American Family Dynasties and Their Institu-tional Legacy: From the Law of Trusts to Trust in the Establishment," in *Elites: Ethno-*

graphic Issues, ed. G. E. Marcus, pp. 221–56. Albuquerque: University of New Mexico Press (A School of American Research Book).

Marx, K. 1962 [1894]. *Capital III*, ed. F. Engels. Moscow: Foreign Languages Publishing House.

Nash, D. 1966. *Anthropology of Tourism*. New York: Pergamon Press.

Perez, L. A., Jr. 1980. "Aspects of Underdevelopment: Tourism in the West Indies," in *Dialectics of Third World Development*, ed. I. Vogeler and A. de Souza, pp. 249–55. Montclair, NJ: Allanheld, Osmun.

Pi-Sunyer, Oriol 1977. "Tourists and Tourism in a Catalan Maritime Community," in *Hosts and Guests: The Anthropology of Tourism*, ed. Valene L. Smith, pp. 149–56. Philadelphia: University of Pennsylvania Press.

Reynoso y Valle, A, and J. P. de Regt. 1979. "Growing Pains: Planned Tourism Development in Ixtapa-Zihuatanejo," in *Dialectics of Third World Development*, ed. I. Vogeler and A. de Souza, pp. 111–34. Montclair, NJ: Allanheld, Osmun.

Saglio, C. 1979. "Tourism for Discovery: A Project in Lower Casamance, Senegal," in *Tourism: Passport to Development? Perspectives on the Social and Cultural Effects of Tourism in Developing Countries*, ed. E. de Kadt, pp. 321–35. New York: Oxford University Press.

Smith, M. Estellie. 1989. "The Informal Economy," in *Economic Anthropology*, ed. S. Plattner, pp. 292–317. Stanford: Stanford University Press.

———. 1991. "The ABCs of Political Economy," in *Early State Economics*, ed. H. J. M. Claessen and P. van de Velde, pp. 31–74. New Brunswick, CT and London: Transaction Publisher (Political and Legal Anthropology Series).

———. 2000. *Trade and Trade-Offs: Using Resources, Making Choices, and Taking Risks*. Prospect Heights, IL: Waveland Press.

Smith, M. Estellie, ed. 1990. *Perspectives on the Informal Economy*. Society for Economic Anthropology Monographs in Economic Anthropology No. 8. Lanham, MD: University Press of America.

Smith, V. L., ed. 1977. *Hosts and Guests: The Anthropology of Tourism*. Philadelphia: University of Pennsylvania Press.

Stronza, Amanda. 2001. "Anthropology of Tourism: Foraging New Ground for Ecotourism and Other Alternatives," in *Annual Review of Anthropology* 30:261–83.

Vogeler, I. and A. de Souza, eds. 1980. *Dialectics of Third World Development*. Montclair, NJ: Allanheld, Osmun.

22

Sherpa Culture and the Tourist Torrent

James F. Fisher

Tourists come to Khumbu not only because they want to see and experience Mt. Everest and the Himalayas but also because they like the Sherpas or like what they have heard or read about them. Khumbu offers tourists the rare opportunity (rare because, in Blake's phrase, "men and mountains meet" so much more closely there than elsewhere in the Himalayas) to experience culture and nature, and their combination—high human adventure at the top of the world.

A kind of mutual admiration society exists between Sherpas and Westerners, and just why this should be so is an interesting question in itself. What is involved is the set of stereotyped images each group has of the other. Westerners have developed a positive image of Sherpas: that of an egalitarian, peaceful, hardy, honest, polite, industrious, hospitable, cheerful, independent, brave, heroic, compassionate people. This image begins on the basis of literary evidence, which has by now assumed epic proportions, and is reinforced, when everything goes well, by personal experience in the course of a trek.[1] Of course, the image captures only one side of the Sherpa personality.

This image reflects not only what Westerners think about Sherpas but also what Sherpa culture itself values in human beings. So far as it goes, the image captures one side of the Sherpa personality—but only one side. Like all people, Sherpas wear masks. They have a public, onstage side that they want the rest of the world to see, and a private, backstage side that is more unadornedly true to themselves. Although the qualities that characterize the public side are also present—and are in fact rooted in the private side—so are other, less praiseworthy, types of behavior.

One of the difficulties Sherpas experience when working on a tourist trek—a twenty-four-hour-a-day job—is maintaining the onstage image full-time, a task that would vex a saint. Successful trekking Sherpas realize that they are, in part, paid professional actors and entertainers. Their stories and dances and songs are genuine enough, but they are also what clients want. And what clients pay for, they get. Only when the trek is over and the back-stage self can be safely unveiled at home do the Sherpas engage in the drinking binges and general hell-raising that may go on for days.

In addition to alcoholism there are other less salutary sides to Sherpa character. For example, because of their international mobility Sherpas can easily smuggle contraband such as gold and drugs. This activity can provide money to support lifestyles of ever-escalating luxury, comfort, and ease. It can also land the Sherpas in foreign jails. But none of this backstage behavior is included in the official image so ubiquitously brandished.

The original image Sherpas held of Westerners, before the airstrip was built at Lukla in 1964, was one of technologically sophisticated, generous, wealthy, irrationally adventurous, egalitarian, and well-intentioned, if not always physically strong, people. This more or less coherent image was formed on the basis of contact with a small number of relatively homogeneous people, mostly mountaineers and the occasional hardy trekker. But in post-Lukla times this image has given way to a less clearly focused one that has emerged out of the Sherpas' experiences with thousands upon thousands[2] of tourists—everyone from the psychotic French woman who had to be strait-jacketed and evacuated to the American who has taken the vows of a lama to the German divorcee in search of romance. Although the original positive image still holds, foreigners are now equally likely to be thought crude, stumbling, demanding, arrogant, unpredictable, and cheap. Where foreigners are concerned, Sherpas have learned to have no stable expectations. So much for unitary images.

Westerners are enchanted with Sherpas because the qualities the Sherpas are thought to possess are not only those Westerners admire but also precisely those they feel they should embody but conspicuously lack or do not adequately measure up to. So Sherpa society, or the Western image of it, represents a dramatic realization of what Westerners would like to be themselves, hence their frequently breathless enthusiasm for the Sherpas. There is also probably a measure of admiration for what Westerners regard as the liberal Sherpa sexual ethic.

Although the causes, strength, and justification of the mutual admiration may be debated, there is clearly an affinity between Westerners and Sherpas, as evidenced by the high rate of intermarriage. As of the mid-1980s there had been forty or so cases of marriage between Westerners and Sherpas, almost all relatively uneducated villagers from Solu or Khumbu (Fürer-Haimendorf 1985). And there have been many more informal liaisons, primarily between Sherpa trekking leaders *(sardars)* and their Western female clientele. (Similar liaisons occurred in the Alps in the nineteenth century.) These liaisons reverse the more typical tourist situation elsewhere in the world, where single tourists are apt to be males traveling in pursuit of interests both exotic and erotic.

Mountains and Mountaineering

Although it is the environment of Khumbu that attracts Western tourists, their perception of that environment, ironically, is fundamentally incompatible with that of the Sherpas. The most general Sherpa term for beautiful *(lemu)* can apply to the physical features as well as the personal qualities of human beings, both men and women. It can also apply to inanimate objects and to the environment as a whole. But while a field or forest might be lemu,

The Himalayas as near Khumbu. (Photo by James Fisher)

the giant snow peaks towering in every direction over Khumbu are never considered lemu. Their lack of color (their whiteness) is seen as uninteresting (though religiously significant)—not a surprising judgment in view of the Sherpa preference for vivid colors evident in such disparate contexts as religious paintings and women's aprons. A snow peak elsewhere might be admired for its shape, and Pertemba, one of the foremost Sherpa sardars of his time, says that one of the pleasures he derives from climbing is the beauty of the different views from high on a mountain. But in general, familiarity has bred indifference rather than awe, and the shape of the Khumbu snow and ice peaks is just too boring to be considered lemu. Even the dramatic setting of Tengboche Monastery is said to have been selected without regard to its beauty. It was chosen by name, sight unseen, because the footprints of Lama Sangwa Dorje, a seminal figure in Sherpa history who was born about 350 years ago, had been embedded in rock when he stopped there.

Sherpas pay close attention to their environment nonetheless, and not just to those features of it that are economically important. They often find familiar shapes in mountains or villages, much as Westerners find them in clouds. To Sherpas, Phortse looks either like a *damar*, a percussive rattle lamas use during rituals, or like an animal hide stretched out to dry. And together the villages of Khumjung and Khunde resemble a horse whose rider is Khumbi Yul Lha, the peak that rises above them.

Sherpas are generally mystified that Westerners come to Khumbu at such great expense and in such great numbers, whether to trek or to climb. Even the most experienced sardars admit they cannot fathom why Europeans climb, though they make guesses. One hunch is that they climb for fame, since the books they write always include plenty of pictures of themselves. But Sherpas also know that books are bought, so a second hypothesis is that people climb to make money. One sardar, for example, thought this was the case with the British mountaineer Chris Bonnington since he has written (and presumably sold) so many books; but the same sardar believed that fame drives Reinhold Messner (the first climber to ascend all fourteen 8,000-meter peaks) to the summits. Another sardar wondered whether science was not the prime motivation, while still another held that climbers climb to clear their minds from the worries of office work. If he were an office worker, this sardar told me, he might well need to clear his mind too, but if so he would do it by going on a weekend picnic rather than by climbing.

Eight of Khumbu's most experienced and illustrious sardars unanimously agreed that virtually the only reason they climb is that they need the high income they cannot earn any other way. As one put it, if he had the education to qualify for a good office job, he would unhesitatingly choose that line of work. Sherpas see no intrinsic point in climbing: neither fame (though that is welcome since it helps them get their next climbing job more easily; it also accounts for the multiple ascents of Everest), nor challenge, nor adventure. Climbing is simply a high-paying job. None of the eight sardars expressed much enthusiasm for a hypothetical all-Sherpa expedition because they could not imagine any earnings accruing from it. Even though they enjoy the camaraderie and the scenic views and take pride in a job well done, these reasons alone would never motivate them to move up a mountain. The "First Sherpa Youth Mt. Everest Expedition" of 1991 suggests contrary sentiments, but the participation of skilled Sherpa climbers who were paid for that expedition corroborates the view of the eight sardars.

Women are for the most part left behind during a climb with the difficult task of managing the household, but those affected see the inconvenience as a relatively minor one, for which they are compensated by the pay earned by their husbands. Sherpas see danger as by far the most negative feature of climbing. Their friends' deaths, one after the other over the years, make them vividly aware of the risks. Their wives and parents, although they welcome the earnings, universally oppose expedition work because of the danger. But the climbing Sherpas' view is that danger comes with the territory; they just hope they can learn enough from the deaths of their friends to avoid their mistakes. They judge that climbing is a hard but good job in which the benefits balance the risks—a view probably shared by Nepal's other big foreign exchange earners, the Gurkha soldiers who are paid to fight and die for Britain and India. Climbing Sherpas compare deaths on a mountain favorably with those of soldiers and taxi drivers, whose lives are not insured, unlike their own. Those who feel that the difference in pay and the perks do not justify the greater risks of climbing choose trekking, although many do both, depending on the vagaries of opportunity and their own fluctuating financial needs.

Sardar Pertemba, like many climbing/trekking Sherpas, abandoned his studies and started working earlier than he might have because of the English he had learned at his village school (he also points out that knowing English will not get you to the top of the mountain). Although Pertemba likes both climbing and trekking, the work he enjoys most is the teaching he has done at the government mountaineering school in Manang. Most Sherpas learn to climb not from foreign mountaineers but from other Sherpas, usually between base camp and camp 1 on their first expedition. Pertemba thinks Sherpas need a mountaineering school in Khumbu to train young Sherpas properly and systematically in mountaineering techniques. Such a school would also generate income locally for experienced climbing Sherpas.

Although Sherpas do not consider mountains aesthetic monuments, they are not indifferent to all peaks. Some, like Khumbi Yul Lha, rising behind Khumjung-Khunde, are sacred by virtue of the deities that reside on them. Sherpas were reluctant to climb Karyolang, because of its sacredness, during the first all-Nepal expedition to that peak in 1975. They had no such compunctions about Kwangde, the second objective of the expedition, and proceeded to the top, as it turned out, of the east peak, which they mistook for the summit. Whether for spiritual reasons Sherpas would have been reluctant to attempt the summits of Khumbu in 1907, when they first began climbing in Sikkim, is an interesting but unanswerable historical question. Certainly no such general reluctance exists today. Not only the mountains but also some of their spirituality may have eroded over the years.

Khumbu must now be one of the most thoroughly mapped regions on the face of the earth,[3] with vernacular names for virtually all prominent features of the landscape, but this detailed nomenclature is often a creation of foreign cartographers. When I visited Everest base camp in 1964, Kala Pathar (Nepali for "black ridge"), now one of the most popular trekking destinations in Nepal, was unnamed.

All this increasing specificity of geographical detail is evidence of the reversal of values that historically made Solu, with its lower elevation, more fertile fields, and more salubrious climate, the more highly valued land. According to one account, the earliest Sherpa pioneers settled first in the more hospitable climate of Solu, and the latecomers or impoverished Solu Sherpas had to settle for the harsher, more rugged landscape of Khumbu. Now, however, Khumbu is the center of prosperity, thus demonstrating that a "natural resource" acquires worth only when it is culturally constituted—i.e., when technology, values, and a market for it simultaneously converge.

Social Implications

Sherpa and Western concepts of pollution constitute yet another example of cultural incompatibility. The Sherpa concept of pollution, called *tip* (see Ortner 1973), has nothing to do with the environmental effects of discarded tin cans and plastic bottles that concern so many Westerners—porters and Sherpas are responsible for the bulk of non-toilet paper litter. Sherpas do not care one way or the other about this Western-style pollution because their concept of pollution concerns only the self, or human creations and artifacts, such as houses. *Tip* is a feeling, a moral state of mind, and is not generated ultimately from empirical observation of the natural world. For example, pollution can have religious causes, such as an imbalanced relationship with deities or contact with supernatural beings. Or it can be induced socially by contact with certain kinds of people, such as low-caste Nepali blacksmiths *(K mis)*, of whom there are a few families in Namche and one in Khumjung, or members of the Tibetan butcher class, another low-ranked group. Westerners would surely, if they were aware of these discriminations, moderate their views of egalitarian Sherpa society. They would be even more likely to modify their views if they realized that they themselves are a source of tip and that at least until very recently Thame Sherpas returning from an expedition had to be purified before they were allowed back in their houses. But since all Westerners must come to the Sherpas via the far more obviously hierarchical Hindu societies to the south, they are lulled into ascribing an egalitarian ideology to the Sherpas that simplifies, if it does not downright distort, the ethnographic facts.

But I do not want to leave the impression that Sherpas and their clients pass like ships in the night, completely misperceiving one another. The Sherpa-trekker relationship is, as these things go in the world of tourism, an unusually long and intensive one. Even though, as in any person-to-person interaction, only behaviors relevant to the encounter are exhibited—we never play all our roles at the same time. Nevertheless, Sherpas and their clients get to know one another over an extended period of time, rarely less than a week, often a month or more.

Exigencies of living break down what might otherwise be a formal, distant relationship: the Sherpas are in their element, perfectly acclimatized, doing well what they have always done naturally—walking, carrying loads, enduring cold weather. The Westerners, by contrast, are usually out of shape, tired, plagued by sore muscles and blisters, and gasping for air. Sherpas are paid to be helpful under these conditions, and they are. They are even heroic, as the many stories of Sherpas who have died trying to rescue their clients on high peaks attest. And they are cheerful, hardworking, and eager to please, so in the end a relationship of trust and respect is built that would be impossible with a guide on a half-day tour of Kathmandu.

Westernization

Are Sherpas being Westernized? By many visible indexes they are. First, they wear Western-style clothing—pants, shirts, down jackets, and climbing or hiking boots. (Women's clothes have not changed from the indigenous Tibetan style, thus conforming to the female sartorial conservatism that has generally been the rule all over South Asia.) It is significant, however, that Khumbu Sherpas wear either Sherpa clothes (even the best-equipped mountaineering Sherpa wears the traditional Tibetan coat on ceremonial occasions, such as weddings) or Western dress but never the Nepali national dress. When His Majesty King Birendra visited the government yak farm at Syangboche in 1974, the *pradhan panchas* (mayors) of both the Khumiung and Namche *panchayats* (village councils) greeted him with sport coats and neckties, not *daura-suruwal*, the national dress. (At a formal reception in Kathmandu for members of the Nepal-China-Japan Everest Expedition in 1988, attended by the king, however, Sherpas did wear daura-suruwal.)

Similarly, although Sherpas recognize the importance and desirability of mastering the national language in both its spoken and written forms, a Sherpa who uses too much Nepali in an otherwise purely Sherpa conversation in Khumbu is felt to be putting on airs.

Through association with trekkers as well as extensive travel abroad in the lands from which the trekkers come, Sherpas have gained a wide knowledge of modern hygiene, several Western languages (and Japanese), and material culture generally. The tradition of drinking Tibetan salt-and-butter tea has largely disappeared in Sherpa homes (because of the high price of butter and the uncertain supply of Tibetan tea). Western ways are admired because Western contacts have opened new channels of mobility and access to power, wealth, and prestige. Sherpas honor the West because their experience of it has been so overwhelmingly positive financially.

My own view is that such matters as clothing styles and diet are relatively superficial; much more important is the Sherpas' success in maintaining a cultural identity that is strongly and exclusively Sherpa. Sherpas tend not to be self-deprecating; whatever they are, they are mostly proud of it. Even those Sherpas who have achieved the greatest success, through mountaineering accomplishments or university educations, think of themselves primarily and uncompromisingly as Sherpas.

Part of the reason for this tenacious cultural identity is the mutual admiration of Westerners and Sherpas that I have already mentioned. Sherpas are so massively reinforced at every point for being Sherpas that they have every reason not only to "stay" Sherpa but even to flaunt their Sherpahood. One might say that tourists pay Sherpas in part for being Sherpa, or at least for

By 1988 Lama Sarki (pictured here with his wife) had married and opened a lodge in Phakding, a few hours' walk up the valley from Lukla. Although he has not followed his religious calling, he is still regarded as a reincarnate lama as indicated by his name. (Photo by James Fisher)

performing the role that accords with the popular image of Sherpas. The term "Sherpa" has now become a label for anyone who helps manage a trekking group, regardless of ethnic background. Even ethnicity has become a prize to be claimed, and the advantages of Sherpa status is not lost on other groups in Nepal. Tamangs, for example, frequently try to pass themselves off as Sherpas in an ethnic, not just job category, sense. This process of "Sherpaization" counters the momentum of the much-vaunted Sanskritization (emulation of high Hindu caste behavior) that has absorbed the upward-mobilizing energies of the subcontinent for centuries.

As evidence of the reinforcement Sherpas have received for their pride and independence, a number of the more successful among them in recent years have dropped the honorific suffix *saheb* and address their Western clients by their first names—something no house servant, hotel servant, or tour guide in Kathmandu would dream of doing. Westerners often react favorably to being treated as equals, even by someone waiting on them hand and foot. But some of them, accustomed to or expecting more traditional hierarchical relations between servant and master, are taken aback by the I'm-just-as-good-as-you Sherpa personality.

Because the "tourist Sherpas" still identify themselves very much as Sherpas, no class of marginal people—neither fully Sherpa nor Western—has developed, as it often does in such contact situations. The sexual differentiation that exists between Sherpa men and women is largely being maintained by differential access to education and jobs: there are occasional Sherpani [Sherpa women] "cook-boys" but only one Sherpani sardar so far. On the other hand, the three Sherpanis who have summitted Everest in recent years have shattered the traditional separation of high-altitude male Sherpas from low-altitude female Sherpas. The "tourist Sherpa" is not marginal to his society at all but fully accepted within its fold. Even Sherpas who live ten months of the year in Kathmandu keep their houses and fields and often their families in Khumbu. One Sherpa who has lived in Kathmandu for more than fifteen years, ten months of the year, now holds a high and trusted position (as *chorumba*) in the civil-religious hierarchy in his village. He is able to return to his village during the *Dumje* festival, in early summer, when his presence is essential. Even though he is hardly ever in his village, his status there does not diminish. On the contrary, his success in the travel business in Kathmandu has endorsed and enhanced it.

Intensification

Rather than becoming Westernized or nationalized, then, Sherpa culture has been intensified. That is, Sherpas have come to value some of their traditions even more than they did prior to the advent of tourism. For example, although nowadays Sherpas rarely commission the carving of prayers on stones to be placed on the prayer walls at the entrance of villages, there seems to be no lessening of faith in Buddhist doctrine, and interest and participation in the many Buddhist rituals are as strong as ever. Some Sherpas claim that interest in religion has deepened, and some of the most successful and "Westernized" Sherpas are among the most devout.

Certainly the most educated Sherpas are still committed Buddhists who believe in and rely on their lamas' liturgical and ecclesiastical powers. The Tengboche rimpoche was able to raise US$20,000 in two days, a considerable sum in 1981, for a new *gompa* (Buddhist temple) in Kathmandu. Kalden Sherpa, owner of a flourishing trekking company, considered himself a Christian in 1963 (Hillary 1964) after two years in a Catholic boarding school, but he is now one of the most generous supporters of Tengboche Monastery; he personally financed the higher studies of four *thawas* (novice monks) at this Kathmandu gompa.

Sherpas not only have maintained their cultural identity and intensified it but also have contributed to making generally Tibetan lifestyles respectable in Nepal among Hindu and Hinduized Nepalese. In the first place, the status of hero is accorded anyone who has climbed Mt. Everest—recognition in the press, praise by the prime minister, and an audience with the king, thus turning the job of high-altitude porter into a distinguished and honorable occupation. Through spring of 2002, 244 Nepalese Sherpas had climbed Everest (some with multiple ascents, including one who has climbed the peak twelve times—without ever using oxygen), along with 14 non-Sherpa Nepalese (nine Tamangs, two Gurungs, two Chhetris, and one Newar), and ten Darjeeling Sherpas. There have been a total of 1,648 ascents of Everest, by 1195 individuals.

Sherpa success at high altitudes coincided with a surge of interest in things Tibetan after the great publicity given the Dalai Lama's retreat from Lhasa in 1959. Then after the 1962 China-India border war, when India placed severe restrictions on travel by foreigners into the Indian Himalayas and closed such traditional centers of Tibetan culture as Kalimpong to Westerners, Kathmandu became a place not only for foreigners to experience the culture of Tibetan refugees but for Bhutanese, Sikkimese, and Tibetan nobility and entrepreneurs (and, increasingly as time went on, rich Tibetan refugees) to live and work. Being wealthier than most Nepalese, they frequented the more elegant hotels and restaurants in their traditional dress. Thus their costume ceased to be identified only with the lowly Bhotias (Nepali for person of Tibetan culture) and became accepted as the standard apparel of wealthy, sophisticated, influential people.

As all these developments combined to raise the status of Sherpas in the eyes of their countrymen, the female dress of Sherpas or Tibetans changed from an object of scorn, from the Hindu point of view, to high fashion—worn in the fashionable restaurants, hotels, and discotheques of Kathmandu, and on board Royal Nepal Airlines Corporation aircraft (and those of other private airlines) on international and domestic flights by women who would not have dreamed of wearing anything but a sari a few years before. A telling case in point is that of a Namche Sherpani who married a wealthy Newar and moved to Kathmandu in the late 1950s. During her first few years in Kathmandu she wore a sari, trying to blend in with her husband's milieu. By the 1970s she had reverted to her Sherpa dress, although this time with a more modish, tailored cut. By the late 1980s her tastes had become eclectic—sometimes she wore a Sherpa dress, sometimes a sari, sometimes slacks, blue jeans, or a Western dress.

Political Implications

Although Sherpa culture is being intensified rather than adulterated, tourism is nevertheless accelerating the last stage of nation building in what would otherwise still be a remote and inaccessible area. Until 1964, when then Crown Prince Birendra made one of the first landings at Lukla to dedicate the new school at Chaurikharka, no high-level government official had ever visited Khumbu. Now the King and other high officials have visited Khumbu many times. In 1964 the government's presence in Khumbu was represented by a post office and police checkpost in Namche. By 1978 two airstrips had been added along with a meteorological station, a government yak farm, village panchayat secretaries from outside Khumbu, a medical center, a bank providing such services as savings accounts and cashing of travelers' checks, a police checkpost in Thame, and a national park that includes all of Khumbu (excluding, technically, the villages themselves).

Sherpas have viewed most of these institutions as either helpful or harmless. But initially, at least, the primary feeling about Sagarmatha National Park (Sagarmatha is the Nepali word for Everest) was one of fear. The main impact of the park so far has been to enforce strictly the law against cutting green wood for fuel, and since no realistic alternative has been provided, Sherpa concern is understandable. Much of the fear is based on rumors about even worse regulations still to come, such as one that would prohibit Sherpas from gathering leaf litter in the forests.

The traditional forest wardens *(shing nawas)* had ceased functioning by the early 1970s as the astronomical sums tourists paid for firewood had led to massive cutting that systematically undermined the forest wardens' authority. In 1982 honorary forest wardens were appointed from each panchayat ward, but they did not have much effect because they were given no authority to levy fines. All this is in dramatic contrast to 1964, when firewood was free for the asking to any overnight visitor in Solu-Khumbu.

The consumption of wood is strongly influenced not only by numbers of tourists but also by their trekking style. Seventy percent of Khumbu trekkers in 1978 belonged to organized groups, which carry their own tents and food, while 30 percent stayed in local lodges—teahouse trekkers, as they are known in the trade (Bjonness 1979). The big groups use more wood because they are big (there are two or three porters or Sherpas for each tourist) and because their Sherpas make their own, usually inefficient, cooking fires and keep their clients cozy with bonfires. Teahouse trekkers, on the other hand, require fewer support personnel and keep warm inside the lodges. As year-round lodges have sprung up almost all the way to Everest base camp, Khumbu trekkers are increasingly likely to be the individuals and small groups who patronize them. Kerosene is so prohibitively expensive compared with firewood that only hotels and lodges can afford to use it. Moreover, national park officials can monitor fuel use and enforce regulations much more readily in fixed sites than they can among nomadic trekking groups.

Sherpas say that the national park is now their forest warden. The traditional rule that enjoined Sherpas from cutting green trees applied only to forests near the villages, and the fine for breaking it (a bottle of beer) was mild. National park officials attempt to enforce the rule everywhere, far from the villages as well as near them, and punishment for infractions includes heavy fines and imprisonment.

Sagarmatha National Park has an impact even in areas where it does not belong. When the national park dedicated a new trekkers' lodge on the grounds of Tengboche Monastery, a chicken was sacrificed—not as part of the dedication ceremonies but by some Nepalese officials on their own. Officially or unofficially, the sacrifice of an animal near a monastery, of all places, was resented by the lamas, who refuse to kill even insects.

The deterioration of local political institutions cannot be explained by the existence of the national park alone. Even if the local Village Development Committees did not feel preempted by the park, tourist jobs have lured away virtually everyone with leadership abilities. To serve effectively in Village Development Committees, it is generally necessary to reside in the area. But as one influential local leader put it, anybody with any ambition, brains, or ability is off working for tourists most of the time, so there are too few competent people left to serve on the Village Development Committees. The result is that Village Development Committee members are either capable leaders who are often absent from Khumbu, residents with little interest in politics, or, in one case, the wife of a local leader who serves as a surrogate for her politically important but frequently absent husband.

Both factors—the supremacy of the national park and the lack of leaders who stay put in Khumbu long enough to take an active part in political affairs there—have led to a fragmentation of village interests, with different individuals or groups promoting separate aims: the Everest-View Hotel, the trekking companies, the Himalayan Trust, the Village Development Committees, the national park, and so on. Whatever forces united a village politically in the past seem to have weakened in the face of all the external interests that now assert themselves. This fragmentation of interests is reflected in the lack of consensus on the importance of keeping animals out of the fields of Khumjung.

Demographic Consequences

The major demographic consequence of tourism is the large outflow of young men from Khumbu for the better part of the year. There are two reasons for this emigration: one is to avoid the inflated social obligations that bankrupt those not involved in tourism (the "social budget" is now estimated to exceed the "domestic budget.") The other is to earn the money trekking and mountaineering jobs bring in.

One consequence of the long seasonal absences among the Sherpas is a lower birth rate and a concentration of births nine months after the summer monsoon season. Other demographic consequences of tourism and mountaineering include high mortality rates for young men: through spring 2002, 153 Sherpas died on mountaineering expeditions in Nepal, including 59 on Everest (this figure excludes the many Sherpas killed on K2, Nanga Parbat, and elsewhere outside of Nepal.) The great majority of these were Khumbu Sherpas, and the mortality rate among adult males is therefore quite high. But the existence of polyandry (although younger Sherpas now scorn the custom) and the easy remarriage of widows diminish the effects such deaths might have on the birth rate.

A much greater difference in the birth rate has been effected by the family-planning techniques made available through the Khunde Hospital. Contraception has recreated the relatively low fertility conditions that polyandry had produced before; the former results in fewer children per family, the latter in fewer families. Sherpas simultaneously love children and view them as difficult and demanding to raise, an attitude that provides a traditional basis for an interest in family planning.

The practice of family planning measures seems to be influenced by the degree of participation in tourism. In Khunde, with only seven exceptions, all fertile women who had living husbands and two or more living children were practicing some form of birth control. Of these, fourteen had accepted IUDs, and three were taking pills. By contrast, in Phortse not a single woman had accepted a loop, three had received long-lasting injections (Depo-Provera), seven had tried pills but six of these had stopped taking them (some of whom had since become pregnant), and nineteen were not practicing any form of contraception. The fact that only seven women were not practicing contraception in Khunde, compared with nineteen in Phortse (two villages of about the same size) can be explained by the degree to which the inhabitants of each village have been drawn into the modern world through tourism and mountaineering.[4] The economic importance of children declines quickly in an economy based on tourism rather than agriculture or transhumant nomadism.

A final demographic consequence is the dispersal of the population to previously unoccupied areas of Khumbu or to sites once occupied only seasonally and now inhabited permanently. One example is the Syangboche area, site of the airstrip that serves the Everest-View Hotel. Only one family has moved here on a permanent basis (a recently prospering K mi family from Namche), but many other Sherpas stay in Syangboche for longer periods of time at the hotels, lodges, and tea shops that have sprung up there. If a piped-water system is ever devised to supply water to Syangboche (water at present must be carried from Khumjung-Khunde or from a seasonal spring above Namche), the Syangboche settlement will no doubt grow considerably.

With the opening of teahouses and hotels by entrepreneurs in such places as Phungi Tenga (at the bottom of the hill leading to Tengboche), Pheriche, Dingboche, Lobuche, and Gorak Shep—all formerly inhabited only in the summer months but now occupied the year round—the population has further dispersed. A different example of the same phenomenon is the concentration of Sherpas in an area of Kathmandu called Jyatha Tole, now known only half-jokingly as Sherpa Tole. By the late 1980s the more financially successful Sherpas were moving out of the cramped and congested bazaars of the capital to its airier and more fashionable suburbs.

Conclusion

The immediate future promises more of the same. If one or another of the dire events mentioned earlier, such as an oil embargo, were to transpire, most Sherpas would be able to return to their traditional means of livelihood; they even state that they would be happy to do so. Whether they really would be happy cannot be known before the event, but the more important point is that they have not burned their economic or psychological bridges behind them. Those who have been sufficiently educated would have the option of obtaining office jobs in Kathmandu and elsewhere.

According to the law of evolutionary potential, the more general an adaptation of an organism or population to its environment, the greater its potential to evolve into something else; the more specialized the adaptation, the fewer the options available for further growth. Such specialized adaptations are inherently fragile, but Sherpas are fortunate in that their economic options remain open. Unlike inhabitants of other parts of the world heavily involved in tourism, most Sherpas will be able, if necessary, to return to their traditional ecological niche, even if the hotel and shop owners of Namche and along the trails will have useless buildings and facilities on their hands.

There is little scope for the further growth of tourism in Khumbu now, primarily because airlines are severely limited in the number of tourists they can transport to Lukla and Syangboche. The completion of the Lamosangu-Jiri road has probably brought a few more trekkers, but it has not broken the transportation bottleneck. The number of tourists as of the late 1970s was just under 4,000, up from 20 in 1964. In 1985 the number had reached about 5,000; by 1986 it had climbed to 6,909, and by 1999, 22,000. In Namche, hotels keep springing up to accommodate the increasing numbers of teahouse trekkers, but if lodges are overbuilt, profits will be split into an increasing number of shares, or some businesses will prosper at the expense of others.

I have argued that religious belief remains intact, but the population of the monastery at Tengboche has not. By 1978 there were so few monks that the Tengboche rimpoche had to import four from Thame just to have enough personnel to perform Mani-Rimdu, the biggest monastery celebration of the year. By 1985 the pendulum had begun to swing the other way. Substantial contributions from foreigners and increased receipts from tourist lodges owned by the monastery (in such places as Namche and Lobuche) resulted in improved living facilities, which made the monastic life feasible for more monks than it had been when each monk had to be self-supporting.

No carved stones for the *mani* walls have been commissioned for years, and Sherpas say there are fewer readings of sacred texts (a day's reading still costs nine *manas* of rice, but nine manas cost much more now than formerly). Some Sherpas think religion as a belief system is stronger now than in the past. I have yet to find a university-educated or tourist Sherpa who does not believe in reincarnation or prostrate himself before the rimpoche to receive his blessing. If the prolonged absence of Sherpas from their villages continues, a time may come when many of them will have had little experience of Buddhist rituals such as Mani-Rimdu. This could result eventually in a weakening of religious sentiment. But in each of the three years from 1985 to 1987 an elaborate ritual (*boomtso*, literally "one hundred thousand offerings for the well-being of mankind") was held at Tengboche whose costs included NPR300,000 for the performance and NPR75,000 for a helicopter to import a renowned Nyingmapa lama. (NPR is the official international code for Nepal's currency, the rupee. In 1991, US$1.00 = NPR30.80.) These funds, plus donations to the visiting lama, were collected from Khumbu villagers, despite a general feeling that the sums were extravagant and a financial strain on individual villagers.

To flourish, a religion like Buddhism requires full-time practitioners, particularly specialists who can maintain levels of purity and religiosity that lay villagers cannot possibly aspire to. The danger to Buddhism in Khumbu lies not in the threat from other ideologies—indeed none seems to be even faintly competitive. The efforts of Christian missionaries to proselytize Sherpa students in the high schools elsewhere in Nepal have been ineffectual and even resented. The danger to the practice of Buddhism at its present high level (in 1989 there were twenty-five monks at Tengboche along with twenty-five novices in the new school) would lie in the dwindling numbers of monks in the monasteries (if the pendulum were to swing back once again), which could ultimately result in an insufficient critical mass of clergy. There is no guarantee the novices will stay, and three of the eight thawas sent at great expense for further studies at Boudhanath dropped out of the order.

In the short run tourism is enormously popular with the Sherpas of Khumbu. Although an occasional older Sherpa mutters ominously about what the future may bring, even such mutterings in effect acknowledge the blessings that abound. The Tengboche rimpoche told me that tourists are somewhat like the torrents of rain that plague the north Indian states of Bihar and Uttar Pradesh that border Nepal: the floods come every year, and there is not much anyone can do about them. Whatever misgivings exist are overshadowed by the knowledge that most Sherpas have never had it so good. But if it is good, it is good in the way that a political honeymoon is good—the course of subsequent events needs careful attention.

Source: Adapted from *Sherpas: Reflections on Change in Himalayan Nepal*, 1990, University of California Press.

Notes

[1] Perhaps because of the sense of humor of tired trekkers who had hoped to escape from questionnaires in the Himalayas, the book tourists cited most frequently in my 1978 survey was *Tintin in Tibet*.

[2] Goodman reports 22,000 visitors to Khumbu in 1999; the numbers have declined since then due to the Maoist insurgency and the events of "9/11."

[3] See the May 2003 issue of the National Geographic for an unprecedentedly detailed map of Mt. Everest.

[4] The Sherpa medical assistant at Khunde Hospital reports that Phortse women are too shy to ask for loops and are reluctant to ask for any other form of contraception, whereas for Khunde women such devices are accepted as an everyday fact of life. It is true that the hospital is located in Khunde and not in Phortse, but more than mere physical proximity is involved, since for any Phortse woman it is only a two-hour walk to Khunde—no great distance by Khumbu standards. Many Phortse women come within a few minutes of Khunde on their trips to the weekly bazaar at Namche on Saturdays, when the clinic is closed.

References

Bjonness, I. M. 1979. "Impacts on a High Mountain Ecosystem: Recommendations for Action in Sagarmatha (Mount Everest) National Park." Unpublished report.

Fisher, James F., and Edmund Hillary. 1990. *Sherpas: Reflections on Change in Himalayan Nepal*. Berkeley: University of California Press.

Fürer-Haimendorf, Christoph von. 1984. *Sherpas Transformed: Social Change in the Buddhist Society of Nepal*. Bangalore, India: Sterling Publishers.

Goodman, Anthony Richard. 2002. *Away from the Honey-pot: Potential for Redistributing Visitors in Solu-Khumbu District, Nepal*. M.S. thesis in Protected Landscape Management, International Centre for Protected Landscapes, University of Wales, Aberystwyth.

Hillary, Sir Edmund. 1964. *Schoolhouse in the Clouds*. Garden City, NY: Doubleday.

Ortner, Sherry. 1973. "Sherpa: Purity." *American Anthropologist* 75:49–63.

23

Backpacking: Diversity and Change

Erik Cohen

Backpacking is a controversial subject: while often imagining themselves as the "real" travelers as against the mass tourists (e.g. Uriely et al. 2002), backpackers are often condemned for their appearance, conduct—especially sexual freedom and use of drugs—superficiality, stinginess, and seclusion in backpacker enclaves. While tourism officials and the tourist industry picture backpackers as exploiters of poor locals from whom they seek to live on the cheap, researchers have recently highlighted their neglected but significant economic contribution to marginal communities in less-developed parts of the world (Scheyvens 2002). Governments of many developing countries have in the past sought to "upgrade" the tourism services of localities popular with backpackers (e.g., Wilson 1997) or put restrictions on backpacking visits. While some Thais have recently begun to recognize the economic potential of this type of tourism (*The Nation* 2001), the Thai authorities are still averse to backpackers and seek to develop luxury tourism (e.g., Niyamabha 2002).

While research on tourism generally lagged behind the rapidly expanding industry, research on backpacking was particularly tardy to pick up with the growing phenomenon—perhaps since it lacked the support of the tourism industry, which had little interest in its exploration. The earliest articles devoted specifically to the topic appeared in the 1970s (Cohen 1973; Vogt

1976), but the 1980s—the period of a major expansion in tourism studies—saw relatively few publications on backpacking (e.g., Cohen 1982; Riley 1988; Teas 1988). Recently, however, research began to pick up with a growing number of publications (e.g., Loker-Murphy et al. 1995; Murphy 2001; Spreitzhofer 1998; Westerhausen 2002).

The time thus seems appropriate for a more systematic approach to the accumulating knowledge, and for the direction of research beyond the presently prevalent themes of backpackers' motives, conduct, and relationships or of their impact upon host communities (but see Elsrud 1998 and 2001). This paper is intended as a first step in these respects.

From Tramp to Drifter, from Drifter to Backpacker

Youth nomadism, as Judith Adler (1985) reminds us, has been a widespread phenomenon in the pre-modern West. She argues that the lower-class tramp, wandering in quest of employment, became the formative model or trope for the emergent modern middle-class youth traveler, traveling for enjoyment and experiences. While some degree of historical continuity thus apparently exists between tramping of the past and contemporary backpacking, the emergence of the latter as a large-scale touristic phenomenon is, in my view, related to some distinctive traits of modern Western societies (Cohen 1973) and the position of youth within them; these traits, in turn may have engendered the desire to adopt "tramping" as a model for this mode of traveling, which in its aims, style, and consequences differs markedly from all Western precedents. Chief among these traits was the widespread alienation of Western youths from their societies of origin, especially in the United States and Western Europe, which culminated during the 1960s and led to the (failed) "student revolution" and the various attempts to create alternative lifeways. While the extent of alienation may have receded to a significant extent toward the end of the last century, the stresses and uncertainties of late modern life are certainly a disorienting factor which induces young men and women to take a "time out" (Elsrud, 1998:311–3) to gain a new perspective on their own life and future (Noy and Cohen forthcoming), while having a challenging but enjoyable time in the world of others.

I propose to call the earlier, alienated individuals roaming the world alone, common in the 1960s and 1970s, "drifters," and the more recent youth travelers, following well-trodden paths in large numbers, "backpackers." If the model for the drifter was the tramp, the drifter is the model for the backpacker; but I wish to stress that this chronological division is not strict: the *Vermassung* of drifting started already in the 1970s (Cohen 1973); and even today, individual drifters can be found in remote localities as yet untouched by massive "backpacker" tourism. Their very remoteness, indeed, appears to hide them from the fieldworker studying backpackers on the more popular itineraries and enclaves.

My own conceptualization of the original "drifter" was to a significant extent influenced by a personal encounter in the later 1960s. While on field-work in Ayacucho, a town in the central Andes of Peru, I was approached on the street by a tall, athletic young German, a student of chemistry, who asked to lodge in my flat for a day or two. It turned out that he arrived to the central Peruvian Sierra all the way from the Atlantic coast of Brazil by the Amazon River and its tributaries, part of the time traveling alone in a small boat and curing himself from the tropical illnesses he suffered from in the wilderness; his trip took about seven months, during which he was sometimes alone for such a long time that he talked to himself.

This self-reliant individual served as the prototype of the "original drifter" in my article on the "Nomads from Affluence," in which I claimed that in order to preserve the freshness and spontaneity of his experience, the drifter purposely travels without either itinerary or timetable, without a desti-nation or even a well-defined purpose (Cohen 1973:176). However in this rather ideal-typical characterization I overlooked two significant constraints, which impact on even the most independently-minded traveler: on the one hand, there are external constraints on his or her unrestrained freedom of travel, such as temporal restrictions on the validity of visas and passports or of airline tickets, or limitations of access to some countries, or sensitive areas within them imposed by the authorities.

On the other hand, and probably more important, are inward con-straints: drifting, as I have conceived it, appears to take much more compe-tence, resourcefulness, endurance, and fortitude, as well as an ability to plan one's moves, even if they are subject to alteration, than I had originally sur-mised. Not many young travelers have the ability to cure their illnesses in midst of a tropical forest as that German did.

The "original drifter" (Cohen 1973), may have been an ideal to which many youths were attracted, but only very few succeeded. Therefore I already at an early stage qualified the concept and suggested several sub-types of drifters (100–101) emerging as contemporary youth tourism became a mass phenomenon; those would at present be loosely called "backpackers." I also described the alternative tourism infrastructure of itineraries, transpor-tation services, accommodations, and other facilities, which began to emerge in response to the growth of this kind of tourism (95–97).

However, I did not in that early paper relate the concept of the drifter to what has emerged as the dominant paradigm in tourism research from the mid-1970s to the 1990s: MacCannell's (1973, 1976) conceptualization of the tourist as a secular pilgrim in quest of authenticity, which is in turn staged for him or her by his obliging hosts. However, it would follow from my later work on the "phenomenology of tourist experiences" (1979) that drifters—assumedly the most alienated kind of tourists—would tend to the most inten-sive types of experiences, and especially the "experimental" or "existential" ones, as they seek an alternative "elective center," which they could substi-tute for that of their home society. The drifter would thus strive more than the ordinary tourist to reach places and people, which are "really" authentic, and display considerable touristic *angst* that places or events that appear authentic are in fact staged.

It is hard to check this hypothesis regarding the early drifters; and there do not appear to be any systematic studies on the contemporary drifters who seek to set themselves apart from the mass of backpackers, just as the latter seek to distinguish themselves from the mass tourists. Contemporary backpackers tend to embrace the ideology of drifting (Elsrud 2001) and imitate the style or form of travel characteristic of the drifter; but the mode or type of experience they pursue varies widely with only a minority traveling in an existential or experimental mode; many resemble the ordinary tourists in that they seek diversionary or recreational experiences (Uriely et al. 2002). At least Israeli backpackers are rarely alienated from the "center" of their own society (ibid.; Mevorach 1996; Noy and Cohen forthcoming). While the drifter remains the model for the backpacker, few backpackers seek to realize it in practice, or show a great concern for profoundly "authentic" experiences of sites, events, or people on their trip.

This may partly reflect the change in the nature of backpacking, which came with its *Vermassung*—and partly also the broader changes in the nature of tourism in late modernity or "postmodernity," to which I shall yet return.

In my early article, I distinguished between outward- and inward-oriented drifters—those who seek to reach faraway locations and live with the locals, and those who seek out primarily the enclaves of their own kind (Cohen 1973). While this distinction appears to be still significant, it should be used to distinguish different kinds of backpackers' conduct, rather than define types of backpackers. Contemporary backpackers combine, to varying degrees, outward- and inward-directed conduct (Elsrud 1998).

Though we do not possess adequate statistical information, it appears that the great majority of the young contemporary backpackers spend significant periods of their time, perhaps even most of it, in various backpacker enclaves, or on the road from one such enclave to the other—even though these enclaves may serve as bases for trekking, riding, or rafting trips, and for tours or excursions to natural sights, ethnic communities, or various events in the vicinity of the enclaves. There thus exists a parallelism between backpacker and mass tourism, the enclaves fulfilling a function parallel to that of vacationing resorts, in which most mass tourists tend to spend their holidays. Only a minority of backpackers travels off the beaten backpacker tracks, or spend much of their time staying with local people.

Many backpackers travel to remote localities just to reach such enclaves, as for example the district township of Pai (Emmons 2000) on the Chiang Mai-Mae Hong Son road in northern Thailand. Backpackers apparently tend to share "mental maps" of backpacker destinations that are reinforced by way of oral communication in backpacker enclaves, where travel routes and plans are a principal theme of conversation (Murphy 2001), and updated as the popularity of countries and enclaves changes (Teas 1988).

While most backpackers travel alone or in pairs, they seek out primarily the company of other backpackers. However, they do not form lasting groups; rather their enclaves are places of fleeting, spontaneous, but friendly and pleasant—and frequently even intimate—encounters between individuals belonging to a shared, but loosely defined subculture (Murphy 2001). When talking about "people" on the trip, backpackers generally refer to other backpackers, rather than to the locals (Elsrud 2001; Murphy 2001). Though "friendly" local staff is appreciated by backpackers (Murphy 2001), relations with the locals in the enclaves are of secondary importance in comparison to those with other backpackers.

Despite basic similarities between backpackers as well as between their enclaves, some significant differences, not yet systematically documented in the literature, can be discerned:

1. There appear to be significant differences between urban and rural enclaves in the degree of their demarcation, the kinds and quality of services provided, and their functions in the backpackers' trip. Urban enclaves, such as Khao San in Bangkok, are less demarcated than rural ones—such as Pai in the north of Thailand (Emmons 2000)—and much more commercialized (Maneerungsee 2001; Spreitzhofer 1998); they are central nodes at which backpackers arrive to the country, or through which they are forced to pass—rather than destinations of choice as are remote rural enclaves. Urban enclaves therefore serve instrumental purposes: in them the new arrivals orient themselves, organize their travels, and make purchases, activities which are less important in rural enclaves; both kinds of enclaves, however, also serve as meeting places and provide for the hedonistic desires of backpackers for food, drink, drugs, rest, and "having a good time," although the rural ones appear to be preferred to the urban ones for these purposes, and some, like Ko Pangan in southern Thailand, acquired a worldwide reputation as sites of virtually unrestrained hedonism epitomized in the Full Moon Party (Jidvijak 1994).

2. There appear to be differences between backpackers from different countries in the scope of their interactions with other backpackers: while most interact with members of all countries with whom they have a common language, others tend to restrict interaction to their co-nationals; this is particularly the case with Israeli backpackers, as several studies have found (Noy and Cohen forthcoming), and possibly also with Japanese and other Asian backpackers.

3. There appear to exist distinct variants within the general, vaguely defined backpacker subculture, based primarily on the kind and intensity of the use of drugs and on preferred musical fashions; the possibility of subcultural differences between the middle-class backpackers and the growing numbers of backpackers of working-class origins should also be investigated.

4. Finally, there appear to be important differences between young backpackers and those in older age-groups. While the former tend to stay in backpacker enclaves for relatively short periods of time[1] and use them as a basis for short excursions and longer tours, the older ones appear to settle down for prolonged periods of time—up to several months—in local communities that may not be particularly popular with young backpackers (Maoz 1999).

Backpacker Ideology and Practice

It emerges from my presentations that the actual practice of most backpackers is at considerable variance with the predominant image of the young traveler who roams alone the far-off places of the continents. How is this discrepancy between the image or ideology and actual practice of backpacking resolved by the backpackers themselves?

It should be noted that, as Scheuch (1981) pointed out a long time ago, that a discrepancy between the intentions of tourists and their practice is endemic to tourism. This does not appear to be a matter of concern to ordinary tourists. But backpacking, as a traveling practice studiously contrasted to mass tourism, is more ideologically "loaded" and hence necessitates some express mechanisms that may help to maintain the identity of the backpackers in face of the discrepancy between their ideology and their practice.

While these mechanisms have not yet been explicitly addressed in the literature, some recent work, which goes beyond the mere descriptions of backpackers' motives and conduct and looks into the ways in which they themselves emically perceive their trip and construct their identity, helps us to detect them. Important in this respect is Elsrud's recent article on "risk creation" in backpacking tourism, which aims to show "... how the risk and adventure narrative . . . is (still) being manifested and expressed within backpacker communities" (2001:598). Elsrud's approach shows how risk and adventure on the trip are constructed by the backpackers; it thus deflects the focus of research from the question of whether the backpackers have "real" adventures and face "real" risks to the manner in which they perceive and narrate their experiences, narrowing and closing thereby the discrepancy between the model and actual behavior.

The creation of risk and adventure appears to be facilitated by the institutional structure of backpacker tourism, especially by the backpacker-oriented tour companies who represent themselves as alternatives to mass tourism, and advertise their tours in such terms as ecotourism, soft tourism, "green" tourism, or adventure tourism, and the localities and people on their tours as "nontouristic" or "authentic" (Cohen 1989). They thus create the impression of offering "real" adventure in unexplored areas. The "staged authenticity" of such tours is more ingeniously concealed than it is in similar advertisements directed to mass tourism, and appears more credible, precisely because of the allegedly alternative character of such tours. Many backpackers seem to take such representations at face value, hereby gaining external endorsement for the construction of their trip as risky and dangerous.

There thus exists an ironic parallelism between backpacker tourism and ordinary mass tourism: both thrive on fantasy, supported and exploited by different sectors of the tourist industry. But while contemporary, increasingly sophisticated mass tourists often tend to relate skeptically and ludically to the enchanting images offered them in touristic advertisements, (cf. Perkins and Thorns 2001), mass backpackers appear to be more easily taken in by the apparently credible images conjured up for them by the establishments serving this market segment, which presents itself as an alternative to the mainstream tourist industry.

Backpackers—Modern and Postmodern

From the 1990s on, several researchers began to identify a "postmodern" trend in tourism (e.g., Ritzer and Liska 1997; Rojek 1993; Urry 1990), reflecting broader transformative tendencies in contemporary Western society. For present purposes the most important ones among the latter are the devaluation of "origins," the alleged disappearance of "originals," and the concomitant growing salience of "surface" experiences, and the growing legitimation of the quest for "fun" and of a ludic (playful) attitude to the world. Since in the postmodern world there are allegedly no genuine "primitives" anymore (MacCannell 1992) nor "untouched" cultures or environments, it follows that a quest for authenticity would be a futile enterprise.

Under the circumstances, the quest for authenticity loses its primacy as a culturally legitimizing principle of (sightseeing) tourism; hedonistic enjoyment and fun tend to take their place in postmodern tourism. Postmodern tourists or "post-tourists" (Ritzer and Liska 1997) acquiesce with this predicament, turning from the serious quest for experiences of the authentic to a ludic enjoyment of surfaces, irrespective of their genuineness; but they may consciously and reflectively play an "as if" game, imagining that simulated and otherwise contrived attractions are the real thing (Cohen 1995). Contrived attractions such as theme parks, amusement centers, malls, reconstructed environments, and touristic festivals increasingly become the principal attractions of postmodern mass tourism. Rather than seeking the experience of the Other, post-tourists often seek familiar experiences on their trip (Ritzer and Liska 1997), deriving enjoyment from the quality of the offerings, rather than from their strangeness.

These general tendencies raise a question with regard to backpacking: are backpackers immune to the transformations of postmodern tourism or are they amenable to their influence? In other words, are the backpackers the "rear guard" of modern tourism, attached to its ideals in opposition to the postmodern trend in tourism? Or are they, contrariwise, the trendsetters of postmodern tourism, creating a mode of traveling to be followed by more routinized tourism, just as the drifters have served as the spearhead of penetration into new and heretofore marginal "authentic" destinations?

While backpacker studies do not address themselves directly to these questions, an outline of an answer can be formulated on the available information: it appears that backpackers profess to various degrees the ideals of modern tourism, such as the experience of nontouristic, "authentic" sites, but their actual practices are marked by many traits of postmodern tourism.

The quest for authenticity was, according to MacCannell, closely related to the alienation of moderns from their own society (MacCannell 1973); by extension, it can be argued that, the more alienated an individual, the more intensive his or her quest for authenticity will be, motivating the most alienated moderns to seek and attach themselves to an "elective center" beyond the boundaries of the modern world (Cohen 1979:189–191).

Backpackers appear to differ in the degree of their alienation and hence travel in quest of different modes of touristic experiences, as Uriely and his colleagues have recently empirically demonstrated for Israeli backpackers (2002). But, while many may be to different degrees critical of Western civilization (Spreitzhofer 1998), or of their own society, overall their alienation has apparently diminished over time. Few contemporary backpackers will make pronouncements of the kind I heard from a drifter about twenty years ago: "You don't know why you travel until you return home!" The great majority perceive their trip as a "break" or "time bubble" (Elsrud 2001) within their otherwise routine life path: between school and college or university, university and a job, or between jobs. Few see in travel an alternative to a "normal" career or seek an "elective center" abroad. Within this limited period, they are primarily desirous of achieving unlimited freedom to do their own thing, which may include the unrestricted hedonistic quest of enjoyment and fun, which is iconically embodied in the much-maligned Full Moon Parties on Pangan (Jidvijak 1994). At the height of the ecstatic rush of such events the participants may indeed experience "existential authenticity" (Wang 2000:56–71), which, in contrast to the "objective authenticity" allegedly sought by the modern tourist (MacCannell 1973), is basically a postmodern experiential mode: it is a heightened internal state of exaltation or excitement unrelated to any external referent, such as an "authentic" sight, event, or object. "Existential authenticity" is a state of "real living," which may be induced by an appropriate environment, but, unlike "objective authenticity," does not derive from its contemplation.

There is an irony inherent in the backpacker's quest for freedom: while each might seek to do "his own thing," most do very similar things; like the mass tourists, from whom they desire to distinguish themselves, most backpackers pursue highly conventional lifestyles, characteristic of their subculture, following similar itineraries, staying in the same currently popular enclaves, and participating in similar sightseeing, vacationing, and partying activities—though the places that are currently "in" may change over time

(Teas 1988:37). The "freedom" pursued by backpackers does not lead to personal individuation of traveling styles, which has marked the earlier drifter; rather, the freedom most backpackers desire is that of unrestrained permissiveness found in the enclaves, which enables them to pursue similar hedonistic enjoyment, experimentation, and self-fulfillment under relatively simple (and affordable) circumstances. The state of liminality, facilitated by their "out-there-ness" (Lengkeek 2001:179–180), enables them to gain a novel perspective on their own society (Noy and Cohen forthcoming), and to reflect upon their own identity. Several researchers therefore approach backpacking as a contemporary rite of passage (Teas 1988; Mevorach 1997). While the rite of passage is in many respects a useful and adequate model for the interpretation of backpacking, the extent of its applicability ought to be critically examined.

Backpacking as a Rite of Passage

Backpacking is related to life crises and transitions—especially, but not exclusively, the transition from late adolescence to early adulthood in Western societies, characteristic of the 20–30 age group from which originates the great majority of backpackers. The attempt to apply the rite of passage model, as initially formulated by van Gennep (1960) and later elaborated by Victor Turner (Turner 1973; Turner and Turner 1978), to backpackers derives from this affinity between life transitions and the backpacking trip: the backpacking youths can be said to "exit" their normal life, separating themselves from their family and community to enter an unfamiliar, "liminal" situation abroad; they have to prove themselves by resolving the problems encountered on their trip and make independent decisions without the direction, assistance, or advice of parents or other authoritative adults. Their successful resolution of the problems and the eventual accomplishment of their trip can be seen as indicating their competence in managing their own affairs autonomously, a significant marker of adulthood in Western societies; they will thus be reincorporated into their society, after returning from their trip, as "adults."

The case of Israeli backpackers, as analyzed by Mevorach (1997), is a particularly enlightening example of the successful application of this model. It is widely assumed in Israel that the compulsive military service, with its exertions, dangers, and responsibilities, constitutes the formative stage in the transition from adolescence to adulthood for (Jewish) Israeli youths. Mevorach, however, claims that the youths remain closely linked to and supported by their parents throughout their military service. Indeed, the Israeli army purposely fosters the link between the parents and the army by means of a number of institutionalized practices. In contrast, according to Mevorach, on the extended trip abroad, usually engaged upon by the youths after the completion of their military service, they find themselves for the first time in their lives on their own and have to rely on their own wits without the advice or support of parents or other adults. It is under these conditions that they learn to act autonomously, thus achieving one of the principal marks of adulthood.

More recent work by Maoz on older Israeli backpackers indicates that backpacking plays a similar role as a rite of passage in other life crises, especially in the transition from early to late adulthood of individuals who did not have the occasion for a moratorial break earlier in life (1999).

While the model of the rite of passage is a useful heuristic device to interpret the dynamics and function of backpacking, several points should be noted that mitigate its applicability to this phenomenon.

The model of the rite-of-passage, as proposed by Turner, comprises a middle stage between separation from the community and re-entrance into it in a new status: a liminal stage at which the youths lose their individuality and constitute an undifferentiated "communitas" (Turner 1973). Such a complete immersion of backpackers with their co-travelers has not been reported in the literature, nor is it in fact to be expected. Rather, backpackers remain very much egocentrically concerned with their own fun, enjoyment, and experiences, even if they are gregarious, easily approachable, and engage in a superficial camaraderie with the constantly fluctuating membership of their enclaves. While honing their social skills by interacting with many different strangers (Murphy 2001), the fleeting nature of their encounters precludes the emergence of lasting intimate ties, not to speak of an embracing communitas.

Second, the apparent inversion of home on the trip and the need to deal alone with strange and dangerous situations—though highlighted in backpackers' narratives (Elsrud 2001)—has been largely ameliorated by the emergence of an institutional structure serving the needs of the backpackers, which ensconces them in a familiar "environmental bubble," paralleling that characteristic of mass tourism. Hence, contemporary backpackers need to develop fewer skills and invest less effort in their trip than had the earlier drifters (Cohen 1973).

Third, the separation from home, which Mevorach stressed, is presently less severe than it used to be when Mevorach conducted his study. Since then, the cumbersome means of communication at that time, the mails and international calls, have been largely supplanted by cell phones and e-mail; the latter is especially popular among backpackers, who keep in touch with home and friends by means of the "Internet cafes," which have recently proliferated rapidly in most tourist destinations and especially in the backpacker enclaves.

Fourth, the parent-child relationship in contemporary Western societies is very different from that prevailing in tribal or traditional societies where rites of passage were commonly practiced. Adolescents in contemporary society seek independence at an early stage and engage in activities of which the parents are often unaware—especially in the widespread drug subculture and the associated cults of techno, rap, and other musical fashions. The departure on a backpacking trip is decided upon by the youths, often in contradiction to parental wishes, unlike in tribal or traditional societies where the rite of passage was conducted in full concurrence and often with the active participation of the parents.

Fifth, though backpacking may in a sense be a reversal of the ordinary conditions of the youths' life in their society of origin and in that respect resemble the rite of passage in tribal societies, the reversal is not complete. Rather, it is in many respects an extension and intensification of the prevalent youth subcultures widespread in those societies; this is particularly observable in the backpacker enclaves, which—owing to their very remoteness from home and isolation from the local society—make possible a fully fledged blossoming of these subcultures to an extent which, owing to legal restrictions, parental and social controls, and the high prices of drugs and drinks, cannot be as fully realized at home.

Although backpackers may use their freedom to experiment with new experiences while under the prevailing conditions of liminality, such experimentation appears at present to be less oriented to the novel and strange lifeways of the locals at the destinations and more to possibilities offered by the enclaves with which the backpackers have already been aware of from home and that may have constituted a major motive for their trip—like the availability and affordability of a variety of drugs. Even the spiritual quest of some backpackers, which may induce them to spend some time in an Indian *ashram* or a Thai Buddhist temple, appears to be frequently based on a predisposition, deriving from New Age spirituality, which constitutes a significant component of many contemporary Western youth subcultures. The "reversal" at the destination is thus, unlike in rites of passage, not complete.

Finally, the uses backpackers make of their freedom and their experimentation with new experiences—some of which may involve the overstepping of normative boundaries to which they have been committed at home—are formative factors in the constitution or reconstitution of the backpackers' sense of identity, and may, in some cases, influence their view of the world, their attitude to their society, and the choices regarding studies, occupation, and sexual relations made upon their return home. A significant number may adopt a "postmodern," hybrid identity, embracing concomitantly two centers or cultural worlds—that of their own Western society and that of the country of their choice, such as India, Nepal, or Thailand (Uriely et al. 2002). Unlike in the case of the rite of passage, their reaggregation in the home society is thus not necessarily complete; and insofar as the number of such individuals increases over time, their hybrid worldviews may exert an influence on their home society. Backpackers who have returned from the "Orient" thus appear to serve to no small extent as agents of the "Easternization" (Campbell 1999) of the contemporary West.

Diversity of Historical and National Contexts of Backpacking

Up till now I have dealt with (Western) backpacking as an undifferentiated phenomenon, as did most of the literature. Indeed, one of the shortcomings of that literature is that it tends to disregard the particular historical backgrounds within which drifting and backpacking emerged, or the differences between backpackers, engendered by the specific problems and tensions experienced in their various home societies. Most of the current literature takes backpacking for granted and disregards the social forces in the backpackers' societies of origin, which may have motivated them to depart on extended trips.

Contemporary backpacking as a massive movement of youths to the less developed regions of the world started in close association with the major social and political upheavals of the 1960s: the student revolution and the Vietnam War. It could be argued that the failure of the student revolution and the frustrations of the war drove many Western youths to seek personal redemption elsewhere, after their disappointment to achieve social salvation at home.

This historically based resentment against Western society led me at the time to see drifting as grounded in the counterculture (Cohen 1973) and thus as impelled by alienation from the home society. The changing sociocultural circumstances of the contemporary West, associated with the emergence of postmodernism, with its greater openness to multiculturalism, multiple identities, and growing separation of the public and private spheres of life, make it implausible to link contemporary backpacking with alienation.

Student backpacker meets Vietnamese villager near Mai Chau in 2003. (Photo by Sharon Gmelch)

As pointed out above, contemporary backpacking may be a "time-out" from the pursuit of an ordinary career, but it is not a quest for an alternative way of life or of an "elective center." Indeed, none of the Israeli backpackers studied by Uriely et al. (2002) sought to opt out of his or her society. But, as Elsrud (1998) has shown, backpacking is also a "time frame" free of obligations, within which backpackers can "create" their own time, and thus helps to further the process of personal growth and development—one of the principal life goals of contemporary individualistic Western society.

While we can thus discern a general historical trend in Western backpacking, the more specific contextual circumstances prevailing in particular societies, which influence the relative magnitude of the phenomenon and, more significantly, the particular motives and styles of travel of their respective backpackers, remain largely unexplored. Virtually all existing studies do not pay particular attention to the origins of the backpackers studied or to the differences between backpackers of different nationalities. The only case with which I am familiar in which the relationship between the social context and the magnitude and style of backpacking has been extensively investigated is the Israeli one. But this case illustrates exceptionally well the close connection between particular social circumstances and backpacking. Without going into details, a series of studies on Jewish backpackers from Israel (Noy and Cohen forthcoming), demonstrates that an extended trip abroad is usually taken by Israeli youth after the completion of their army service, when they are in their early twenties. The trip is typically both a reversal and a continuation of military service. While it often involves intensive and strenuous activities in which the youths can make use of their skills and stamina acquired during the service, it also offers them relief from the strains of that service—and from the wider strains of their society. They enjoy the freedom to live on their own and make personal decisions rather than follow directions or orders of authoritative adults. As pointed out above, the trip rather than the army can thus be seen as the principal rite of passage for Israeli youth, in which they prove their autonomy and consolidate their identity (Mevorach 1997). This process, however, proceeds under constant preoccupation with Israeli affairs.

In contrast to other Western youths, Israeli backpackers spend most of their time with other Israelis and their conversations revolve to a considerable extent on their military experiences and the complexities of the Israeli society. The trip thus offers them an opportunity to reflect upon their recent past and reevaluate from a distance their perceptions and attitudes regarding their society and their own place and future in it.

While basically committed to their society and not alienated, the Israeli youths are often critical of various aspects of it. However, the studies do not specify the extent to which their criticism is influenced by their encounter with other ways of life on the trip rather than by their reflections and conversations with other Israelis under the unrestrained conditions of backpacker enclaves.

Detailed studies of backpackers from other countries would enable us to formulate a comparative framework relating the crucial experiences of the youths in their different countries of origin—reflecting wider social strains and problems—to the magnitude and style of their backpacking travel. It would also show to what extent the Israeli case is exceptional, or only exemplifies, perhaps in an intensified manner, some general preoccupations current among contemporary Western backpackers.

Future Research Directions

In this paper I have dwelt on three major points, which appear to me important for the formulation of a strategy for future research on backpacking: (1) the dynamic and diverse nature of backpacking phenomena; (2) the difference between the image and the practice of backpacking; (3) the historical and social context, which generates the motivation for backpacking and influences the particular style of travel of backpackers from different backgrounds.

It follows that future research should desist from referring to backpacking as if it were a homogenous phenomenon and pay much more attention to its diverse manifestations in terms of differences in age, gender, origins, and particular subcultures. The complex relationship between the domestic, class, ethnic, national, and cultural background of the backpackers and their trip should be given much more systematic attention than it has received up to now.[2] The simple assumption that backpacking is a consequence of alienation is not borne out by contemporary research—but that does not mean that there do not exist more subtle linkages between stresses in the home society and the motivation and style of backpacking. The application of the model of the rite of passage to backpacking proved more suitable than that of alienation, but, as I have attempted to show, suffers from several limitations; its applicability is further diminished in "postmodern" situations, where owing to their openness to global influences, their hybridities and internal heterogeneity, the concept of "reversal"—central to the model of the rite of passage—does not seem to make much sense any more.

There is also a need for a reorientation of research on backpackers from the currently prevalent concern with their itineraries, traveling style, and interactions to a more emic approach concerned with the manner in which they themselves construct, represent, and narrate their experiences (e.g., Elsrud 2001; Noy 2002); such an approach would help us to understand the gap between the model and practice of backpacking which is at present merely noted as a curious fact.

Studies on backpackers have to a large extent been conducted by researchers who have themselves often had considerable backpacking experience (e.g., Teas 1988; Westerhausen 2002). The researchers' background has doubtlessly colored their orientation to their research and the interpretation of their findings; this is particularly visible in the at least covert desire of most researchers to defend backpacking from its critics in the tourism establishment and to stress its value for the backpackers as well as for their hosts (e.g., Scheyvens 2002). Another consequence of this background of the researchers is that only few, if any, possess any in-depth acquaintance with the host societies and communities popular with backpackers, even if they have conducted fieldwork in those sites and have not just interviewed their subjects after the latter's return home. The focus of most studies is thus almost exclusively on the backpackers, with the locals merely constituting a background—mostly as service personnel (e.g., Murphy 2001); they are usually not studied as subjects in their own right (but see Saldanha 2002). I suspect that this focus on the backpackers has led to an over-estimation of the closure and exclusiveness of the enclaves and overlooked the extent and significance of interaction with the host community.

We therefore need anthropological community studies of popular backpacker destinations in which the researcher will achieve a grasp of the local situation and study the backpacking visitors within its context. Such a turn will not only enhance our understanding of backpackers' interactions with the locals but also give us a better picture of the locals' perceptions and attitudes to the backpackers, which heretofore have been given little systematic attention in the literature. It would also contribute to a direction of research, which I have not dealt with in this paper but which is not merely of academic but also of practical significance: the economic contribution of backpacking to the often marginal and impoverished host communities (Scheyvens 2001).

Until now researchers have focused virtually only on Western backpackers belonging to the middle classes of the white majority of their respective countries. It is therefore necessary to extend the scope of research to the emergent backpacking from non-Western countries—especially from East and Southeast Asia[3] as well as from Latin America—and from the working classes and the ethnic minorities of Western countries. Such an extension would complement a wider effort to expand research on tourism by nationals of non-Western countries and by ethnic minorities, which has until now suffered from considerable neglect in tourism studies. Although the scope of backpacking from non-Western countries (with the exception of Japan) and ethnic minorities is as yet apparently limited, early attention to it would enable us to follow its growth and dynamics in "real time," an opportunity that has been largely missed with respect to backpacking from the West.

Backpacking research is as yet in its early stages. I have outlined some of the directions in which it could profitably develop and some ideas which could advance our theoretical understanding of backpacking phenomena. A more systematic, discerning comparative approach to backpacking is called for, and some progress toward it will hopefully be made in the future. But it should not block alternative approaches; the most important and original ideas in tourism research came from researchers following their own lights, and this was and will probably also remain the case in the study of backpackers.

Source: From *The Global Nomad: Perspectives on Backpacker Tourism*, Greg Richard and Julie Brown (eds.), forthcoming. Reprinted with permission of the authors and Channel View.

Notes

[1] A study of Byron Bay, a popular backpacker enclave in Australia, for example, found that the average stay of backpackers is about 3.5 days (Firth and Hing, 1999).

[2] The domestic context of backpackers before, during, and after the trip, and particularly the changing parent-offspring relationship, is an almost neglected issue in backpacker research. The only study I am aware of in which this topic is extensively dealt with is Mevorach's (1997) dissertation, which is in Hebrew and remains unpublished.

[3] In Thailand, for example, the Thai Youth Hostels Association started "a series of eco-tour programs to overseas destinations" to enable young travelers "traveling by themselves . . . [to] learn how to adapt and live with other people" (Jariyasombat, 2001).

References

Adler, J. 1985. "Youth on the Road; Reflections on the History of Tramping." *Annals of Tourism Research* 12:335–354.

Campbell, C. 1999. "The Easternization of the West," in *New Religious Movements: Challenge and Response*, ed. B. Wilson and J. Cresswell. London: Routledge.

Cohen, E. 1973. "Nomads from Affluence: Notes on the Phenomenon of Drifter-Tourism." *International Journal of Comparative Sociology* 14(1–2): 89–103.

———. 1979. "A Phenomenology of Touristic Experiences." *Sociology* 13:179–201.

———. 1982. "Marginal Paradises—Bungalow Tourism on the Islands of Southern Thailand." *Annals of Tourism Research* 9(2): 189–228.

———. 1989. "Primitive and Remote: Hill Tribe Trekking in Thailand." *Annals of Tourism Research* 16(1): 30–61.

———. 1995. "Contemporary Tourism: Trends and Challenges," in *Change in Tourism*, ed. R. Butler and D. Pearce, pp. 12–29. London: Routledge.

Elsrud, T. 1998. "Time Creation in Traveling." *Time and Society* 7(2): 309–334.

———. 2001. "Risk Creation in Traveling." *Annals of Tourism Research* 28(3): 597–617.

Emmons, R. 2000. "Peaceful Days in Pai." *Bangkok Post, Horizons* (Feb. 24): 12.

Firth, T., and N. Hing. 1999. "Backpacker Hostels and Their Guests: Attitudes and Behaviours Relating to Sustainable Tourism." *Tourism Management* 20:251–254.

Jariyasombat, P. 2001. "Thais on a Shoestring." *Bangkok Post, Horizons* (Aug. 23): 2.

Jidvijak, S. 1994. "Worshipping at the Altar of Hedonism." *Bangkok Post, Horizons* (May 24):25.

Loker-Murphy, L., and P. Pearce. 1995. "Backpackers in Australia: A Motivation-Based Segment Study." *Journal of Travel and Tourism Marketing* 54(4): 23–45.

MacCannell, D. 1973. "Staged Authenticity: Arrangements of Social Space in Tourist Settings." *American Journal of Sociology* 79(3): 589–603.

———. 1976. *The Tourist: A New Theory of The Leisure Class*. New York: Schocken.

———. 1992. "Cannibalism Today," in *Empty Meeting Grounds: The Tourism Papers*, ed. D. MacCannell, pp. 17–73. London and New York: Routledge.

Maneerungsee, W. 2001. "Budget Heaven Lifts Profile." *Bangkok Post* (Jan. 25): 8.

Maoz, D. 1999. *Libi BaMizrach (My Heart is in the East)*. M.A. Thesis, The Hebrew University in Jerusalem (in Hebrew).

Mevorach, O. 1997. *The Long Trip after the Military Service: Characteristics of the Travelers, The Effects of the Trip and Its Meaning*. Ph.D. dissertation, The Hebrew University of Jerusalem (in Hebrew).

Murphy, L. 2001. "Exploring Social Interactions of Backpackers." *Annals of Tourism Research* 28(1): 50–67.

Niyamabha, V. 2002. "Eden at a Price." *The Nation* (Feb. 2): 1C.

Noy, C. 2002. *The Great Journey: Narrative Analysis of Israeli Trekking Stories*. Ph.D. dissertation, The Hebrew University of Jerusalem (in Hebrew).

Noy, C., and E. Cohen, eds. Forthcoming. *Israeli Backpackers and Their Society: A View from Afar*.

Perkins, H. C., and D. C. Thorns. 2001. "Gazing or Performing?" *International Sociology* 16(2):185–204.

Riley, P. 1988. "Road Culture of International Long-Term Budget Travelers." *Annals of Tourism Research* 15:313–328.

Ritzer, G., and A. Liska. 1997. "'McDisneyization' and 'Post-Tourism': Complementary Perspectives on Contemporary Tourism," in *Touring Cultures*, ed. C. Rojek and J. Urry, pp. 96–109. London and New York: Routledge.

Rojek, C. 1993. *Ways of Escape: Modern Transformations in Leisure and Travel*. London: Macmillan.

Saldanha, A. 2002. "Music Tourism and Factions of Bodies in Goa." *Tourist Studies* 2(1): 43–62.

Scheuch, E. K. 1981. "Tourismus," in *Die Psychologie des 20. Jahrhunderts*, pp. 1089–1114. Zurich: Kindler Verlag.

Scheyvens, R. 2002. "Backpacker Tourism and Third World Development." *Annals of Tourism Research* 29(1): 144–164.

Spreitzhofer, G. 1998. "Backpacking Tourism in Southeast Asia." *Annals of Tourism Research* 25(4): 979–983.

Teas, J. 1988. "'I'm Studying Monkeys; What Do You Do?'—Youth and Travelers in Nepal." *Kroeber Anthropological Society Papers*, No. 67/68: 35–41.

The Nation. 2001. "Smelling Better Than Ever." *The Nation* (Nov. 19): 7A.

Turner, V. 1973. "The Center Out There: Pilgrim's Goal." *History of Religions* 12(3): 191–230.

Turner, V., and E. Turner. 1978. *Image and Pilgrimage in Christian Culture*. New York: Columbia University Press.

Uriely, N., Y. Yonay, and D. Simchai. 2002. "Backpacking Experiences: A Type and Form Analysis." *Annals of Tourism Research* 29(2): 520–538.

Urry, J. 1990. *The Tourist Gaze*. London: Sage.

Van Gennep, A. 1960. *The Rites of Passage*. London: Routledge and Kegan Paul.

Vogt, J. 1976. "Wandering Youth and Travel Behavior." *Annals of Tourism Research* 4:25–41.

Wang, N. 2000. *Tourism and Modernity: A Sociological Analysis*. Kidlington, Oxford: Elsevier Science Ltd.

Westerhausen, K. 2002. *Beyond the Beach*. Bangkok: White Lotus.

Wilson, D. 1997. "Paradoxes of Tourism in Goa." *Annals of Tourism Research* 24(1): 52–75.

24

Giving a Grade to Costa Rica's Green Tourism

Martha Honey

Costa Rica is the poster child for ecotourism. This brand of nature-based tourism, which seeks to be low impact and provide tangible benefits for both the environment and host communities, is widely said to be the fastest growing sector of the tourism industry. And tourism, in turn, rivals oil as the world's largest industry. Today, nearly every country in Latin America that is promoting tourism is also promoting some form of ecotourism. In no other country, however, has the experiment with ecotourism been as extensive as in Costa Rica. It seems that every traveler in the United States who is interested in nature has been to, or is heading for, Costa Rica. Costa Rica's ecotourism boom, while largely positive, has not been without a series of problems, conflicts, and conundrums over its direction and its effects.

Beginning in the late 1980s, Costa Rica was transformed from a staging ground for the covert U.S. war against Nicaragua and a testing ground for U.S. free trade and privatization policies into a laboratory for "green" tourism. More than any other event, President Oscar Arias's 1987 receipt of the Nobel Peace Prize for his role as the architect of the Central American Peace Plan propelled Costa Rica onto the world stage, securing its image as a peaceful country and marking the start of the ecotourism boom.

In the 1990s, Costa Rica jumped to the head of the ecotourism queue, surpassing older nature travel destinations such as the Galapagos Islands,

Kenya, and Nepal. In 1992, the U.S. Adventure Travel Society dubbed Costa Rica the "number one ecotourism destination in the world." By 1993, tourism had become Costa Rica's number one foreign exchange earner, surpassing coffee and bananas.

As a journalist based in Costa Rica in the 1980s and early 1990s, I witnessed firsthand Costa Rica's transformation from the southern front for the contras into an ecotourism mecca. Costa Rica illustrates that, most fundamentally, tourism can only thrive in an atmosphere of peace. But while regional peace accords and the dismantling of the contras and local CIA operations improved conditions on the ground in Costa Rica, it can be argued that, as a result, the country changed less than did its international image. Arias's Central American Peace Plan helped the world to view Costa Rica through a different lens—in part because once the region's wars ended, journalists began turning their attention to stories about what made Costa Rica unique. The reality was that Costa Rica had the right stuff—the right political, socioeconomic, infrastructural, geographic, and natural ingredients—to permit it to successfully ride the crest of the ecotourism wave.

Student tourists walk above the forest canopy across a suspended bridge at Sky Walk Monteverde, Costa Rica. (Photo by R. Hays Cummins)

Costa Rica's main building block for ecotourism has been, as in many other countries, its national park system. Officially created in 1969, the national park system grew rapidly so that by 1990 it included 230 different protected areas with varying restrictions and permitted uses, including tourism. Today, more than 25 percent of Costa Rica's territory is under some form of protection. Worldwide, the average is just 3 percent. Some 13 percent of Costa Rica falls under the rubric of national parks and other strictly protected areas. In recent years, national parks and their surrounding buffer areas have been reorganized into nine regional conservation areas or megaparks. These are complemented by hundreds of private nature reserves; more than 110 of these contain "ecolodges" and/or provide tourism activities such as hiking, bird watching, rainforest canopy walks, and butterfly farms. As Amos Bien, a biologist and founder of Costa Rica's first genuine ecolodge, Rara Avis, writes, "This mosaic of large, pristine national parks with smaller private reserves with visitor facilities provided the fertile ground necessary for ecotourism to be born in Costa Rica."

While the country's name—Rich Coast—comes from Christopher Columbus's mistaken belief when he landed in 1502 that the land was full of precious minerals, in recent decades this misnomer has seemed appropriate as scientists, conservationists, and tourists discovered its vast ecological richness. As part of the narrow isthmus joining North and South America, Costa Rica has flora and fauna from both continents as well as its own endemic species. This West Virginia-sized country boasts more bird species (850) than are found in the United States and Canada combined, more varieties of butterflies than in all of Africa, more than 6,000 kinds of flowering plants (including 1,500 varieties of orchids), and over 35,000 species of insects. Costa Rica's extraordinary natural wonders are encapsulated in the statistic that the country contains 5 percent of the world's biodiversity within just 0.035 percent of the earth's surface. Costa Rica is, as former minister of natural resources Alvaro Umana put it, a biological "superpower."

However, Costa Rica's national parks and biodiversity have been supplemented by other ingredients lacking in many developing countries: its longstanding and well-functioning democracy, its political stability, the abolition of its army in 1948, strong social welfare programs, its respect for human rights, and its (generally) welcoming attitude toward foreigners, particularly the gringo variety. Costa Rica has one of the highest standards of living, the largest middle classes, the best public health care systems, the best public education through the university level, and the highest literacy rates in Latin America. The country has produced an outstanding coterie of scientists and conservationists and has for decades attracted scientists and researchers from around the world. More than a hundred local and international environmental NGOs have branches in the country. Costa Rica is physically compact and easy to get around in, with adequate amounts of paved roads, telephones, and electricity. It has a pleasant climate. And it's just a few hours' flight from the United States. The combination of these qualities made Costa Rica uniquely prepared to rapidly move into ecotourism.

On these stable foundations, Costa Rica's ecotourism industry grew. Until the mid-1980s, Costa Rica's tourism sector was modest, largely locally owned, and geared to domestic and regional visitors. Between the mid-1970s and mid-1990s, the number of foreign visitors nearly doubled and gross receipts grew more than 11-fold. By 2000, Costa Rica, with a population of only four million, was receiving over one million visitors a year. Government exit surveys conducted at the airport showed that about 60 percent of tourists were motivated primarily by ecotourism; another 20 percent reported visiting a national park or ecotourism facility during their stay. The country was earning over $600 million from ecotourism and nature-based attractions.

And, propelled by ecotourism, environmentalism has taken root in the national consciousness just as a tradition of nonmilitarism (not having an army) had done earlier. When my family and I first moved to Costa Rica in 1982, environmentalism was confined to a small cadre of scientists and national park officials. I recall, for instance, that buses in San José carried signs saying something like: "Don't litter. Throw your trash out the window." Today, however, ecotourism has become part of "self-identity," as Chris Wille, an official with the Rainforest Alliance puts it. "Ecotourism has helped create the self-image of Costa Ricans. That's tremendously important. There's a lexicon of environmentalism here, right up to the president."

Three decades ago, "ecotourism" was not part of the lexicon in Costa Rica or anywhere else. The origins of ecotourism can be traced to the late 1970s, when conventional, mass, packaged tourism, epitomized by cruise ships and high-rise beach hotels, came under criticism on a number of fronts. Developing countries that had moved into tourism as a way to earn foreign exchange and reduce poverty, found they were gaining little. Most of the profits, particularly from prepaid packaged tours, never entered the country or "leaked out" as foreign investors repatriated their profits, paid high salaries to expatriate managers, and imported luxury goods, vehicles, and building materials to replicate First-World lifestyles in some of the world's poorest locations. An increasing consolidation within the tourism industry made it easier and more convenient for travelers to pay for nearly everything—airline tickets, hotels, car rental, and sometimes meals—before they left home. The smaller and less industrialized a country, the more foreign exchange had to be expended to meet the demands of the international tourism market. In some cases almost everything used in a tourist facility was purchased overseas. The World Bank estimated that the "leakage" of tourism dollars from developing countries averages 55 percent; other studies found the leakage from some areas could run as high as 80 percent to 90 percent.

Parallel with this was the growing realization of the darker side of mass tourism. While tourism has been popularly portrayed as the benign, "smokeless industry," many countries found that poorly regulated mass tourism brought not only environmental destruction and pollution but also social ills such as prostitution, crime, black marketeering, gambling, drugs and, increasingly, sexually transmitted diseases. In the 1970s, social ills associated with mass tourism helped spur the "responsible tourism" movement, supported by Protestant churches and centered in Thailand, with a focus on countering child prostitution.

Ecotourism also grew up in the womb of the worldwide environmental movement that took off in the 1970s. In Latin America, particularly in the Amazon region, scientists and environmentalists were becoming increasingly alarmed about the rapid destruction of the rainforest through logging, ranching, oil drilling, mining, and human encroachment and settlement. The rise of the environmental movement helped increase public awareness that rainforests are vital as both reservoirs of biological diversity and suppliers of oxygen necessary to maintain a balance in the earth's atmosphere. Gradually, ecotourism, along with various forms of sustainable harvesting of trees and plants, was proposed as alternative economic activities to protect the rainforest.

Parallel with this, there was a growing realization among parks officials, scientists, and community development activists that the concept of park management through cordoning off parks—either literally with fences or figuratively with police forces—and barring access to local people was not working. Seeing no tangible benefits from either parks or nature tourism, angry and hungry rural communities, who had often been forcibly expelled to create the parks, turned to poaching of wildlife, particularly elephant and rhino in Africa. Beginning in the late 1970s and early 1980s, some parks officials, scientists, and community activists began to call for a new approach to give local people tangible benefits from parks. They argued that protected areas and wildlife would only survive if there were harmony, not hostility, between people and parks.

In a groundbreaking 1976 article, Costa Rica–based biologist Gerardo Budowski wrote that the relationship between tourism and conservation can be variously one of conflict, coexistence, or symbiosis, and he went on to outline ways in which tourism can be used to support conservation. The emphasis, described in the prolific writings of Mexican architect and ecotourism expert Hector Ceballos-Lascurain, was that the rainforest could be saved in part through low impact, locally run tourism by turning tourists into environmentalists and by building an activist constituency among the traveling public committed to environmental protection. In the mid-1980s, University of Pennsylvania biologist Daniel Janzen, who has worked for decades in Costa Rica, argued that parks would only survive if there were "happy people" living around them. Janzen put this philosophy in practice in Costa Rica's Guanacaste National Park where, as new cattle lands were incorporated into the park, he invited the cattlemen and their herds to remain inside the park. He proposed turning ranchers into rangers and incorporating them as part of the park staff.

Only with time did these various experiments and intellectual strands come together under the ecotourism label. While definitions vary, the most widely accepted is that first promulgated in 1991 by The International Ecotourism Society (TIES): "Responsible travel to natural areas that conserves the environment and improves the welfare of local people." The core tenet is that, done right, ecotourism can, on balance, be positive in its impacts, i.e., it can provide tangible benefits for both conservation and host communities and it can be educational as well as enjoyable for the traveler. Properly understood, ecotourism is not simply a niche market within the tourism industry but rather a set of principles and practices closely linked to the concept of sustainable development.

Over the years, ecotourism proponents have further expanded the definition arguing, for instance, that the architecture of ecotourism sites should be both low impact ("tread lightly on the earth") and should convey a "sense of place," incorporating local customs, culture, styles, and materials. Others stress that ecotourism must also adhere to international norms and conventions regarding human rights and fair labor standards, as well as respect local democratic social movements. This includes honoring calls for tourism boycotts, such as the African National Congress's call for a boycott of apartheid South Africa in the 1970s and 1980s and, today, the call by Burma's pro-democracy movement for a tourism boycott against the ruling military junta.

During the 1990s, propelled in part by the United Nations' 1992 Earth Summit in Rio de Janeiro and a rapidly growing tourism industry, ecotourism exploded. In 2002, the United Nations declared the "International Year of Ecotourism" and staged the World Ecotourism Summit—a signal that this concept had taken on global significance. The significance of ecotourism can be measured in other ways as well: the expansion of university departments and degrees in eco- and sustainable tourism, the dozens of national ecotourism societies and scores of international meetings dealing with this alternative form of tourism, and the hundreds of millions of dollars flowing from the Inter-American Development Bank and other international aid and lending institutions as well as from environmental NGOs into projects with ecotourism components.

More volume and international recognition, both around the globe and within Costa Rica, has not, however, necessarily meant better quality. While ecotourism is described as "win-win" for the environment and conservation, host communities and developing countries, the traveling public and the travel industry, the reality is more complex. Because definitions and standards have been weak, far too much gets put under the big green tent labeled "ecotourism." Instead, what is currently being served up as ecotourism includes a mixture of three rather distinct phenomena: "greenwashing" scams, ecotourism "lite," and real ecotourism. In Costa Rica all three varieties have taken root, jousting to capture pieces of the tourist market.

Costa Rica's ecotourism panorama is marked by both contradictions and potential. Visitors to Costa Rica find an ecotourism industry full of creativity and experimentation as well as crass opportunism, marketing ploys, and downright scams. Although the image is of a country of small ecolodges and beach cabinas, government investment policies have favored larger and foreign-owned hotels.

Beginning in the mid-1980s, Costa Rica passed legislation providing investment incentives for hotels, air and sea transportation companies, car rental agencies, and tour operators. The Costa Rican Institute for Tourism's (ICT) incentives and tax exemptions favored foreign investors and applied only to facilities with more than twenty rooms. "These restrictions often preclude local people from qualifying for incentives," wrote geographer Carole Hill in 1990. Experts estimated that by the early 1990s, 80 percent of the country's beachfront property had been purchased by foreigners. Between 1990 and 1994, 13 new four- and five-star hotels were built, involving investments of nearly $1 billion. While in the early 1980s there were virtually no foreign-owned hotel chains, by early 2000 many international hotel chains, including Sheraton, Holiday Inn, Hampton, Melia, and Barcelo, had either built or bought hotels in Costa Rica.

Some of these big hotel projects have brazenly sought to put on the "eco" mantle. One of the most controversial projects has been Papagayo, a megaresort along a dry and barren peninsula in Guanacaste province. The original developer was Mexico's Group Situr, which laid out plans for a giant resort complex a la Cancún: vacation homes, condos, shopping centers, golf courses, marinas, and hotels for up to 30,000 rooms—more than twice the total number of rooms in the entire country. Despite much public outcry and charges that public officials were being bribed, the Costa Rican government in 1995 gave a "green" light to this $3 billion project, the largest to date in all of Central America. Situr's first hotel was a stucco complex named Caribbean Village, an incongruous choice since it overlooked the Pacific Ocean. Equally inappropriate was the large sign out front reading Ecodesarrollo Papagayo ("Ecodevelopment Papagayo"). In an interview at the site, Arnoldo Estaril, Situr's infrastructure coordinator, told me that the name was fitting because "we're going to plant trees and do an aviary for birds and a butterfly farm." Environmental activist Leon Gonzalez retorted, "Everybody calls themselves 'eco developments,' but Papagayo is a city!"

Around this same time, another near-city masquerading as ecotourism was slated for development along Playa Grande, an important leatherback turtle nesting beach on the Nicoya Peninsula, also in Guanacaste. I became aware of the project through an article in a 1995 architectural magazine entitled "Green Luxury" which bragged, "ecotourism will meet the high life in a luxury beach resort." The project's architect and main developer, Yves Ghiai, an Iranian based in San Francisco, boasted that "environmental considerations are an integral part of the design" including a system of yellow lights designed not to disturb the leatherbacks as they lay their eggs. "[T]esting found the yellow lights to meet reptilian and human needs alike." Nonsense, scientists later told me in Costa Rica: Any lights on a beach will scare away turtles looking for a nesting area. Nonsense, also, said the project's administrator in Costa Rica who admitted he knew nothing about any of the environmental innovations described in the article—solar panels, electric golf carts, etc. And, he added, the yellow lights were intended to keep away mosquitoes, not protect the turtles. He showed me the plans for the project: an enormous beachfront complex with condos, restaurant, shops, a casino and nightclub, hotel, marina, and yacht club. As ecotourism expert Anne Becher, who helped devise Costa Rica's first eco-rating program, put it, "The only thing green about some of these places is the color of the dollars they are earning." Fortunately, the "Green Luxury" project provoked a public outcry and it was shelved. But struggles to block such developments continue at Playa Grande and elsewhere.

Today, everything in Costa Rica seems to carry "eco" in its name. There is, for instance, "Eco-Playa" (a typical beach indistinguishable from other gray-black sand beaches), "Ecological Rent-a-Car" (which rents the same vehicles as Hertz, Budget, or Avis), "eco-gas" (super unleaded), "eco-musica" (songs with environmental themes), and innumerable ecolodges, ecosafaris, and ecological cruises. Many of these tourism enterprises can be categorized as ecotourism "lite," meaning that the company's green rhetoric far outstrips the reality of its adherence to sound ecotourism principles. The classic example of this in Costa Rica as elsewhere is the growing number of major hotel chains that offer guests the "eco-option" of not having their sheets and towels laundered every day. Such sensible but relatively minor environmental innovations are advertised with claims such as "Keep your towels and help save the world!" The reality is that it is the hotels that are saving sizeable sums on their laundry bills.

Or consider the new Four Seasons Hotel, which is scheduled to open as part of the Papagayo complex in early 2004. Billed on the Four Seasons Web site as bringing "casual luxury and unsurpassed service to this pristine jungle setting," it is actually situated on dry and denuded former cattle grazing land. Although still under construction, it is also being billed to the travel press as ecologically responsible because plans for the golf course include using a special type of grass that can be watered with a combination of sea and recycled wastewaters. However, this all-inclusive resort will bring only modest revenue to Costa Rica, with vacationers paying for their packages overseas and not needing to venture into Costa Rica since everything (except a rain forest!) is available at the resort.

Some smaller lodges, too, have little more than the patina of ecotourism. One of the most notorious examples is Villas del Caribe (this one correctly named for its Caribbean coast location), built by Canadian multimillionaire businessman and U.N. official Maurice Strong, the architect of the U.N.'s 1992 Earth Summit. The Rio Summit was opening just as Strong's company, Desarrollos Ecológicos (Ecological Development), was putting the finishing touches on the $35 million, 12-suite beach resort. While billed as environmentally sensitive for its recycling, composting, and nature walks, one researcher who took a close look concluded that it had "very modest offerings of ecotourism." Even more troubling to local residents and Costa Rican environmentalists, Strong did not have clear title to the land: the luxury hotel was built within the Gandoca-Manzanillo Wildlife Refuge, where development is restricted, and the Kekoldi Indian Reserve, where construction must be approved by the Indian association. It was not, and Costa Rican Indian leaders were livid about Strong: "He's supporting Indians and conservation around the world, and here he's doing the complete opposite," declared Demetrio Mayorga, president of the Kekoldi Indian Association.

Despite many hypes and shams the green brush is dragged over, Costa Rica also contains scores of genuine ecotourism businesses that are working to be low impact, good environmental stewards, socially responsible, culturally respectful, and beneficial to the surrounding communities. Costa Rica's original ecolodge, Rara Avis, was built by Amos Bien, a New York biologist and ecotourism expert who, since his arrival in 1977, has put down deep roots in the country. Beginning in 1983, Bien took out a bank loan and built Rara Avis, a modest lodge on a private reserve, with the intent of demonstrating to area farmers that rainforest left intact could be more profitable than clear-cut land. He also has sought to provide tangible benefits to area residents through employment and profit-sharing, purchasing supplies locally, awarding student scholarships, offering free tours for local school children, and making in-kind donations to the local clinic and schools.

As ecotourism has grown, whole rural communities of Costa Rica—Monteverde, Tortuguero, the Osa Peninsula, to name a few—have been converted into ecotourism centers. They include small-scale lodges situated in or near private or public reserves and offer a variety of nature hikes, white water rafting, and other outdoor activities. Costa Rica has also developed some of the world's best naturalist guides who deftly interpret the ecological, cultural, and political panorama. Many middle- and lower-middle-class Costa Ricans have managed to move into auxiliary businesses associated with ecotourism, including opening tour agencies or restaurants featuring local dishes, renting riding horses, or building butterfly "farms" or a few guest cabinas. While there are shortcomings and conflicts in all these communities, on balance, ecotourism has brought more income to many Costa Ricans, raised environmental awareness, and provided more funds for conservation projects, national parks, and private reserves.

The New Key to Costa Rica, the country's oldest and most respected guidebook, has long specialized in highlighting genuine ecotourism businesses. Most are locally owned or owned by longtime foreign residents, thereby ensuring that most of the profits stay within the country. Beginning in 1992, the guide's authors, Beatrice Blake and Anne Becher, began a pioneering "green-rating" system with the aim of helping to protect high standards within nature-based, small-scale, and often locally owned lodges. With input from other environmentalists, academics, lodge owners, and tour operators, they created an eight-page survey to measure environmental, economic, and sociocultural impacts of accommodations. Based on on-site inspections and interviews with hotel managers, workers, and community representatives, the *New Key* authors began awarding eco-logos—one to three "suns"—to those hotels that passed a certain number of the criteria.

In 1997, Costa Rica's tourism ministry, the ICT, unveiled its own certification program. Like the New Key survey, the ICT's Certification for Sustainable Tourism (CST) program grew out of a mounting concern that the "golden goose" of ecotourism was being killed by mass tourism, greenwashing, and ecotourism "lite." Tourism officials as well as sectors of the tourism industry were worried that, unless the government began setting rigorous standards, Costa Rica would lose its ecotourism edge. According to a 1998 evaluation, many of the 104 hotels that had signed up to be assessed were resentful of other facilities that "also use such terminology but do not really put into practice basic environmental principles or contribute to the quality of life in their communities." From the outset, the CST was designed to take in a broader swath of the market than simply ecotourism. Its principle creator, ICT official Eduardo Lizano, felt strongly that tourism in Costa Rica was moving beyond small ecolodges and that if the country were to remain competitive internationally, the new, lamer, more conventional, and often more luxurious hotels also needed to abide by responsible environmental and social principles.

Unlike the homegrown, low-budget *New Key* survey, the CST program has been backed with political muscle and financial resources. A CST audit includes 153 yes/no questions covering the physical-biological environment, hotel facilities, customer satisfaction, and socioeconomic issues, including respect for the surrounding community and nature. Accommodations voluntarily apply for certification, which includes an on-site audit by a team of experts. The first round of audits is free. Certified facilities are awarded logos—one to five leaves—by a seven-member National Accreditation Commission. Although several hundred hotels have applied for certification, political infighting within ICT slowed the process so only 59 hotels so far have been certified. Of these only five have been awarded four leaves; none have yet achieved a top score of five leaves.

In 2002, tourism ministers from the other Central American countries officially accepted CST as the model to be used throughout the isthmus, and currently a number of South American governments, including Brazil, Ecuador, Peru, and Chile are creating certification programs modeled along the lines of the CST. It has also been welcomed by many within Costa Rica: former Costa Rican President Rodrigo Carazo, whose ecolodge in a private reserve features traditional Costa Rican architecture and art, said, "I never thought they could do what they are doing. Tourism ministers always think in terms of number of hotel rooms. When they began to talk about paying attention to the environment, I thought they were going to be rejected by the hotels. But this did not happen and CST is growing bigger and stronger." Even the Four Seasons Papagayo project is being forced to build with an eye on the CST program and incorporate some showcase eco-reforms so that it might be able to get certified.

Despite these obvious successes, there have been problems. In addition to bureaucratic haggling, the CST is poorly marketed, leading some hotels to wonder if it's worth the effort. The CST is, however, working to develop and expand the program to include tours and guides. Finally, there is a longer term and very sensible plan to move CST outside the tourism ministry and set it up as either an NGO or a for-profit entity.

Despite Costa Rica's international reputation, some recent studies are indicating that ecotourism so far has fulfilled only partially its objectives of providing significant resources for national conservation efforts and benefits to local communities. A recent study around the Corcovado National Park by Caroline Stem and a team of Cornell University professors reported "mixed" findings "regarding ecotourism's effectiveness as a conservation and community development tool." The study, to be published in the *Journal of Sustainable Tourism*, concluded that "ecotourism would be most effective as a component of a broader conservation strategy," i.e., if there was stronger and clearer national planning and policies.

When stacked against other land-based, foreign-exchange-generating activities such as cattle ranching, banana growing, and logging, Costa Rica's ecotourism industry does appear more economically and environmentally viable than the others. During the first half of the 1990s, tourism grew at 17 percent per year. While this has slowed considerably due to a combination of internal and external factors, the future still looks relatively bright. Projects such as Papagayo, however, raise the wider question of whether tiny Costa Rica can afford, in the long run, to have it both ways: to promote itself as a leading ecotourism/nature tourism destination sprinkled with small-scale rainforest lodges and beach front cabinas, along with dozens of hotel chains and a growing number of megaresorts catering to mass tourism. In the long run, many Costa Ricans fear, the country's unique ecotourism image will be lost, with other countries, particularly Belize, taking on the ecotourism mantle. The move toward creating a strong certification model is important, but certification is only one tool. The government also needs to work to bring its regulations and legislation into line with its country's international reputation and its innate strengths. Ecotourism, not mass or conventional tourism, is most in keeping with Costa Rica's geographical size, its extraordinary biodiversity, and its political and social history.

Source: From "Giving a Grade to Costa Rica's Green Tourism," *NACLA Report on the Americas*, 2003, 36(6):39–46. Reprinted with permission of the author and the North American Congress on Latin America.

25

Let's Go Europe: What Student Tourists Really Learn

George Gmelch

In a landmark study of American students in Europe, Jerry Carlson and colleagues (1990) found that one of the most valuable activities students engage in while studying abroad is travel. American students do a lot of it. The 400 students from four universities in the Carlson study spent a month on the road during their academic year abroad. Students often spend their weekends and school breaks traveling. Some terms abroad purposely do not schedule classes on Fridays so that students have three-day weekends to devote to tourism and travel.

What do students actually do when they travel? And is it educationally enriching? I spoke with a half dozen directors of study-abroad programs, all of whom believe that traveling is an important part of most students' overseas experience. Yet few could say exactly why. A search through the literature was of little help. Many studies have examined the study-abroad experience, but none have looked specifically at student travel and its impact on students. The first half of this paper describes the travel patterns and daily routines of a group of American students studying in Innsbruck, Austria. It then explores in what sense this travel is educational and why.

Some background to the research is in order, especially since I did not go to Austria with the intention of doing this study. Most research on the impact of foreign study has been done by educational psychologists, while I am a cultural anthropologist. I have been taking students abroad, however, for over twenty years to Barbados, Ireland, and Japan. In 1993 and again in 1996, I taught American students in a six-week summer program at the University of Innsbruck.[1] The students attended class Monday through Thursday and then traveled during their three-day weekends.

In Innsbruck, a colleague and I required our students to keep a daily journal about their experiences.[2] At midterm, when I collected and began reading their journals, I was startled at how shallow their engagement with the people and places they visited seemed to be. Assuming that travel would be an immensely enriching experience, I had made the journals an important part of the course. Yet there was little evidence that the students had learned anything much about the local cultures and countries they visited. Their observations on the whole seemed to me to be naive and simplistic. Nevertheless, there was plenty of evidence, both in the journals and from class discussions, that the time they had spent traveling had not been wasted. It just happened to be important in ways I had not anticipated. In fact, the students told me they learned more from their travels than they did from their academic courses. That notion piqued my curiosity about what was really happening to them on their trips and why they thought of it as being so significant. This is the central issue explored in this paper, although I also wish to describe in ethnographic terms what students actually do when they travel.

Methods

My data comes primarily from the journals of 51 students enrolled in three anthropology classes.[3] Information on the logistics of their trips was obtained from "travel logs" in which the students recorded what they were doing and who they were with at 15-minute intervals during their weekend travels.[4] The use of travel logs, like the journals, was fortuitous since I originally assigned them merely to help the students see and make sense of the patterns in their travel. At the end of the term, I had them fill out a twenty-item open-ended questionnaire to gather additional data about their experiences. I also learned a lot by talking to the students in and outside of the classroom, and especially during afternoon hikes. In fact, hiking proved to be an ideal setting for talking casually with them about a broad range of subjects. I also made a weekend trip to Salzburg mimicking the activities and movements that the students had reported to get a first-hand sense of what they were seeing and doing.

Student Tourism

At the end of classes each Thursday afternoon, the students, packs on their backs, set out for the Innsbruck train station to begin their weekend sojourn. With Eurail passes' unlimited travel they visited countries through-

Innsbruck, Austria. (Photo by George Gmelch)

out Western Europe and parts of Central Europe. They went wherever the trains could conveniently take them, but their preferred destinations were places other students had recommended, which also happened to be the places featured in popular guidebooks like *Let's Go Europe*. The most popular destinations were Venice, Florence, and Rome in Italy; Vienna and Salzburg in Austria; Munich and Berlin in Germany; Budapest, Hungary; and Prague, Czechoslovakia. They also went to resort areas on the Italian and French Rivieras, and to Interlaken in the Swiss Alps, a center of adventure tourism.

They traveled frequently and never stayed long in one place. Their travel logs showed that they visited an average of 1.7 countries and 2.4 cities per weekend.[5] This means that the average student spent slightly over one day in each of the cities he or she visited. (They stayed longest in the resort areas of the French and Italian Rivieras—beaches—and at Interlaken's adventure tourism sites.) Their city-a-day tourism was due to several factors. Many wanted to see as much of Europe as they could during their brief time abroad. They were not sure when, if ever, they would come back. Amanda expressed the sentiments of many when she explained, "I wanted to be able to go home and say that I saw as much as I could in the six weeks that I was here." There was also some competition among the students, especially the men, to see how much of Europe they could cover with their Eurail passes. For many students, getting to know the places well mattered far less than being able to say that they had been there.

The tendency to "map hop," as some students referred to it, was also motivated by their desire to get maximum value from their Eurail passes, for which they each had paid about $500. They traveled hastily despite the program director's advice "not to run up the mileage," but to get to know the places they visited. One consequence of their highly mobile form of tourism was that they spent a lot of time waiting in train stations and sitting on trains. Over an average three-day or 72-hour weekend, the students spent 18.7 hours on trains and 3.0 hours in stations waiting for them. That is, nearly one-third of their time was spent in transit.

Despite all the time in transit, the journey itself was much less important to most students than the destination. Few reported or were observed to spend much time looking out the window. Karen wrote about her traveling companions: "They want to run to the goal and run back." Another student reflected: "I seem to be preoccupied on most train rides, if not sleeping, reading, or writing, just talking or laughing with friends. Now that I look back, I wish that I had paid more attention to the places that we were passing through because I think that probably a lot more would have come out of it." But there were an equal number of students who had no regrets. Michelle, who calculated that she had spent five full days sitting on trains since arriving at Innsbruck, wrote:

> Some of my most striking moments occurred on the trains—the train strike in Milan, sleeping in couchettes with complete strangers, being hot as hell, the French man that molested Betsy and me, the beautiful scenery in Switzerland, random thoughts, open windows, mountains . . . sleeping with Andrew, not knowing what stop to get off.

Decisions about where to go next were often made spontaneously. If students were disappointed with a place once they reached it, they were inclined to return to the train station and pick a new destination. The choice of where to go was often determined by where the next available train was heading. If, for example, they were thinking of going to Florence but the wait for the train to Milan was half as long, they would be just as likely to hop on the train for Milan.

As the term progressed many students slowed down, staying longer in the places they visited. And as they did so, many became critical of those who continued to travel excessively. Betsy, who had visited eight countries in her first three weekends in Innsbruck, commented: "Americans approach their leisure activity like work . . . they exhaust themselves running about trying to get in as much as they can. I am guilty of this too, but I now try to spend some time pondering where I am." And Julia wrote in her journal: "I wonder if we really enjoy the museums and sights that we see. It seems that too often we are too concerned about where to go next, and how we will get there, and that we don't always appreciate where we are at the time."

At the end of the term Julia wrote:

> I need to go back and stay for a longer period of time in each place. Everywhere we went everyone would ask why we only stayed for one

day. And now I am wondering the same thing. For most Americans it seems to be enough to visit a place, take a few pictures and say to their friends and relatives, "Been there, done that."

Traveling Companions

Students were asked to record in their travel logs the number of companions they traveled with. The average group size during journeys was 5.2 students, shrinking to 4.6 once students arrived at their destination. Why such large groups? For most students, this was their first time abroad and they were understandably nervous about traveling alone or even in pairs; they found security in numbers. Over the summer, as the students learned their way around and became more confident, the size of the groups declined by a third. The decline occurred largely as a result of the frustrations the students experienced in looking for accommodation, going to restaurants, and visiting places in large groups. As Stephen wrote: "I've discovered that it is better to travel in small numbers! Not only is it a pain to appease a large crowd, but you have to listen to constant complaining. . . ." Some students saw other liabilities to large groups, as Stephanie wrote while on a train to Amsterdam:

> As I head for the city of 24-hour decadence I have realized that we create our own little culture here and that may not be entirely good. Don't get me wrong. I've had fun. But our student culture isolates us from absorbing and trying to fit in to the cultures that we are visiting. Even in Innsbruck we tend to go out in flocks, mostly to local bars at night and the same bars over and over again. And more often than not, the places we choose are tourist magnets where we don't have any chance of meeting people in the country we are in. I think it will be important for me to come back to Europe with just one or two people.

Other students noted that they often followed the "herd" rather than deciding for themselves how they really wanted to spend their time. A freshman, Ben, wrote about his companions following him during a trip to Munich. He was the only one in the group who had been there before: "I said, 'Let's go to the Hofbrauhaus' and everybody followed. I felt like the Pied Piper." About her stay in Cannes, Andrea wrote: "We ended up at the Miss Cannes pageant. How, I don't know. Sara and Charles were following the music and paid thirty francs to get in, so we all followed along. . . ."

Walking around European cities in groups limits students contact with local people.[6] It also means they spend much of their time interacting with each other and less time observing their surroundings. Their conversations, even when standing before great works of European art, architecture, or scenery, are often about people, places, and events back home rather than where they are at that moment. And local people are less inclined to start a conversation with a group of students than they would be with one or two. Carlson and his colleagues found that "the most important medium for personal experience in the host country was conversation with host nationals" (1991:11).

So, by traveling in small groups, students could enhance the educational value of their trips. Most of my students eventually realized this, but they were still not ready to give up the security of the group, although some said they hoped to do so in the future. Megan, who spent most of the summer traveling with five companions, wrote about the one day on the road when she was away from the group:

> I really enjoyed the Italian Riviera. It was only Jennifer and me, and we met a lot of different people. On the train ride back I was by myself and literally took in everything—the people I saw, how they acted, a baby on the train yelling, everyone annoyed at him, and I was too until the baby made me think of my niece and I laughed. Women talking to a couple and kissing cheeks. A couple leaving one another on the train. They were kissing and it made me so sad that they were leaving each other that I cried. Looking out the window at the gorgeous Mediterranean sea and cliffs. . . . Being by myself I had lots of emotions going on inside of me that I hadn't felt before.

But few students ever traveled alone, and those that did were invariably traveling to meet someone else—a friend, pen pal, or relative who was also in Europe. Being on their own usually made them anxious. Before going to London to visit a college friend, Amanda wrote in her journal, "I'm very excited and nervous. I'll be in Europe all by myself. I'll have to make all the decisions without having to consult anyone. This will be an experience of independence."

Daily Routines of Student Travelers

What do students do once they have arrived at their destination? Most did what the students who preceded them had recommended. They also used their guidebooks and got advice from local tourist offices. In Salzburg, they walked around the old town, climbed the hill to the castle, and took the Sound of Music tour; in Venice they went to St. Mark's Square, rode the canals in a gondola or vaparetto, and visited the glass shops; in Munich they looked at paintings in the Alte Pinakethek or technology in the Deutsches Museum, visited the *Englischer Garten*, and spent an evening in the Hofbrauhaus drinking beer with other tourists; in Florence they went to the Uffizi and the Academic museums (the latter mainly to see the *David*); and in Budapest they visited the castle district, the free museums, and because goods and services are cheaper there than elsewhere, they ate well and the female students went to the spas for massages, pedicures, and facials.

Early in the term the students rushed to the great cities of Western Europe—Paris, Munich, Venice, and Vienna—where they engaged in cultural tourism—visiting museums and galleries and looking at great architecture. Toward the end of the term, the students' interests shifted to places of recreation—the beach resorts of the Italian and French Rivieras, and Interlaken, Switzerland, which offered paragliding, white water rafting, and horseback riding. The number of museums students visited declined by over two-thirds during the last half of the term. When I asked students about this in class, some said, with others nodding or murmuring in agreement, that they had had their fill of museums and churches. Staying on the French Riviera toward the end of the term, Jane wrote: "Laying out seems to be the only incentive these days! Whatever happened to sightseeing?"

Besides going to the prescribed attractions, the students spent their days walking the streets, looking at buildings, stepping into churches to gaze at the art and stained glass windows, sitting on benches watching people go by, resting in parks, and talking amongst themselves. And like tourists everywhere, they took photographs: an average of 16 pictures per weekend. Many of their photos are of themselves and their companions posed in the foreground of the places they visited. When I asked why a postcard wouldn't be as good, one student said: "A photograph is proof that you've been there. You took it and it's got you and your friends in it."

There was nothing remarkable about the students' eating habits, except that 1.5 times per weekend they went to an American-style or franchise restaurant (e.g., McDonalds, NY Bagels, Pizza Hut). Their interest in American franchise restaurants was strongest when they were in countries like Hungary, where none of the students spoke the language and waiters spoke little

College students enjoy their independence. (Photo by Andrea Tehan)

or no English, making it difficult to decipher the menu. In Budapest, a group of students took a thirty-minute taxi ride across the city merely to find a NY Bagels. Food was one of the subjects students were required to write about in their journals and almost invariably it was the women who wrote the most. They wrote not only about the different kinds of foods they saw but often what dishes they ordered for dinner. Women students were more willing and interested in trying new foods. The men were more inclined to write about European beer and how it differed from American beer than about the food they ate.

Time was also spent shopping. Female students set aside time specifically to shop, but students of both sexes made a habit of looking at the goods displayed in shop windows as they walked around European cities. For many women, shopping was an integral part of traveling; most could say what the best buys were in each country or city they visited—leather and jewelry in Italy, Hummel figurines in Germany, etc. Many looked for "bargains," that is, high-quality goods at lower prices than at home. They also shopped for mementos or souvenirs of the places they visited and for presents to take home to parents and friends. The amount of time spent shopping declined over the term as funds ran low, or they had already purchased the requisite number of gifts, or had run out of luggage space.

By late afternoon, students returned to their hotel or hostel to nap. Evenings, after going out to dinner, were spent drinking and fraternizing in bars. The travel logs showed that only 14 percent of the students routinely did something other than go to bars in the evening. The students stayed out late (after midnight), and often reported going to bed drunk and exhausted. In her journal, Elizabeth characterized her companions as "Young students who come to Europe to spend their parents' money by getting drunk in as many different cities as possible." Another wrote about a recurrent dream she had in which she broke down crying from exhaustion: "Sometimes I feel like I just need to stop everything and sleep for several days non-stop. It would probably help if we all just eased up on the drinking and eating poorly."

Personal Development

It should be evident from the descriptions above that most students do not learn much about European history and culture. Certainly not as their parents and professors would hope. As noted earlier, when reading the students' journals I was surprised by the superficiality of their engagement in the cultures they visited and how little meaningful contact they had with local people. A colleague who read my description of what the students did in a draft of this paper suggested that "Europe was for the students a big shopping mall in which to hang out, not a place to challenge one's cultural categories." Perhaps. But there is much evidence that touring and living in Europe for a summer did have a significant positive impact on the students.

At the end of the term, I asked the students to read their own journals imagining they had been written by someone else and then describe how the author had changed, if at all, since arriving in Europe. Two broad areas of change emerged in their accounts. First, a large majority of the students believed that the experience of having gone abroad on their own and then traveling extensively through Europe without the supervision of parents or other adults had given them more self-confidence.[7] Some typical declarations were: "I now have the confidence that I can handle any situation I encounter, in some way, even if I am alone, unable to communicate easily and unsure of the culture . . ." and "I've learned that I don't need any pretenses, that if I just be myself people will still like me." One student referred to her reaction to an incident in London as evidence of her growing self-confidence. She was in Trafalgar Square where she and her companions wanted a picture of themselves sitting on top of a large stone lion:

> I was wearing my navy silk shorts outfit and slippery sandals. I was having difficulty getting up on the lion when a young girl asked me if I would like some help. So here I am flailing about trying to get up on this lion with this girl pushing up on my butt. My silk shorts came totally up my butt and a crowd of people are standing below, right beneath me. I was so embarrassed when I finally got up, but I was psyched. . . . It was not only a physical victory; it was also a mental victory. I might finally be at the period where I can say "this is who I am, you can like me or not like me. . . ." Actually I am probably not at that point yet, but I am getting closer. I am not as paralyzed by my insecurities and fears as I was before this trip.

The other change that many students wrote about was having become more adaptable. They believed they were now better able to cope with the surprises, the inevitable problems that arise when traveling, and doing without the comforts they were accustomed to at home. The terms they used when they wrote and talked about this change in themselves included being able to "survive," "cope," and "deal" with unfamiliar situations and minor adversity. For example, Emily wrote:

> This trip has made me more laid back. I always tended to need things on time and just the way I like it at home or else I became quite agitated. I suppose that is just part of being American. When you learn that things don't always go your way, and that you simply have to go with the flow. Here [Europe] you have to adjust to the differences . . . . Your train isn't always going to be on time; you may not want to go everywhere that your travel companions do; the locals may not speak English or be particularly thrilled to see you; and you will not get ice in your drink. I can deal with that now.

When Emily first arrived in Europe she was angry with the limited hours that stores were open, but five weeks later she noted: "I have learned to accept them . . . I now even think it's great that they close the stores on weekends, as it gives people time to spend with their families."

The students' perceptions of how they had changed were echoed by their parents, who I interviewed later over the telephone. When I asked if they thought their son or daughter had changed while abroad, most talked about how they seemed more "mature" and "independent." Typical of many, one mother said about her daughter: "She was just so self-assured when she got back." The phenomenon the students and their parents described are all part of what developmental psychologists call "personal development." That is, the "unfolding, growth, evolution, expansion and maturation of the individual self" (Kauffmann et al. 1992:124). Personal development is distinguished from "cognitive development" which has more to do with the acquisition of knowledge (e.g., what students actually learn about European cultures and places).

The students' assessments of how they had changed are consistent with the research literature on the impact of international study programs. For example, a study of 1,260 American Field Service students found that they became "less materialistic, more adaptable, more independent in their thinking, more aware of their home country and culture, and better able to communicate with others and to think critically" than a control group that did not go abroad (Hansel 1988:87). A study by Stitsworth (1988) has shown that even a short stay abroad with a home stay family can have a significant effect. Stitsworth administered a psychological inventory to 154 student exchangees before and after their one-month stay in Japan. He found personality changes in three areas, with the student exchangees having less conventional attitudes, being more "adaptable" in their thinking (e.g., they showed more tolerance of uncertainty and ambiguity), and scoring higher on measures of independence and autonomy than a comparison group that stayed at home. He also found that students who paid for most of their trip themselves changed more than those who paid only a small proportion.

But what interested me most was not how the students had changed, but why? After twenty years of taking students abroad, I already knew that cross-cultural experiences had a big impact on my student's development (see Gmelch 1992). But I was never sure what exactly caused this change until an idea came to me while reading the students' journals. The journals showed that from the instant the students left the familiarity of their Innsbruck dorm at the beginning of every weekend trip, they were continuously confronted with problems to solve—where to go, how to get there, where to stay, where best to change money, where to find good but reasonably priced places to eat, what sights were worth seeing given limited time, what places or areas of the city were unsafe and to be avoided, what goods were worth buying and where, and so on. In order to make good decisions, and to satisfy their basic needs, they had to learn how each local "system" worked. They had to learn something about the culture. To do this they had to communicate with local people, asking the right questions and understanding the responses, often in a foreign language. They often had to ask the same questions of different people to assure its reliability. One student, after traveling in Hungary and

Czechoslovakia, said he had become so adept at nonverbal communication and mimicking that he could not wait to get home to play charades. So it is not surprising that many students reported their travels had given them confidence in speaking with strangers, and confidence in collecting information.

Also, traveling is rarely predictable, and I believe students learn much from having to cope with the surprises, unexpected problems, and predicaments—missing a train connection, getting lost, arriving in a town only to discover there is no available accommodation, and so on. A dozen students, for example, found themselves stranded in Italy by a train strike. They had to find a way to let the college administrators in Innsbruck know they were safe, learn about the strike in order to assess how long it might last, and look for alternative ways of getting back to Austria. Here nineteen-year-old Megan describes the problems she and her companions encountered in a single journey across Budapest on public transportation:

> We took the Metro [subway] and trams, which were even more frustrating than the bus system. Along the way, we almost lost Susan, Kelly got her sunglasses stuck in the Metro doors, Susan almost had her purse stolen, and some weirdo put his face in my hair. But we made it to the bagel shop [NY Bagels].

For adolescents traveling on their own in a strange culture, these are challenging life experiences.

Because the students travel in so many different countries and move so frequently—almost a new city every day—the challenges are multiplied. They have to find and arrange for travel, shelter, food, local transportation, and decide how best to spend their free time, not once but several times every weekend. Such challenges, of course, are compounded when the travel takes them across national borders. When students journey from Austria to Czechoslovakia, Hungary, Italy, France, and Spain, they are not just crossing political boundaries but cultural and language barriers, and therefore new social systems, new customs, and new meanings, the basics of which they must learn in order to get by. In some countries, women students face the additional problem of dealing with unwanted sexual advances from local men. Traveling in a foreign country also required a certain level of organization. Students had to remember to bring and keep track of their passport, Eurail pass, student identification, and their money and Travelers Cheques.

I found support for the idea that the students' development was promoted by their having to cope with change and solve problems in the writings of development psychologists, notably Chickering (1969), Bruggemann (1987), and Kauffmann et al. (1992). Kauffmann and his colleagues' research on the growth of logical thinking among adolescents asserts that individual change and maturation occur in "periods of discontinuity, displacement, and disjunction." Put differently, individuals acquire new understandings about life, culture, and self when they deal with changes in their environment and circumstances. This is exactly what happens to student tourists.[8]

Conversely, it is argued that little change occurs when students are in "situations of equilibrium," such as staying at home. In the words of Bruggemann, "personal development is . . . about . . . interaction in which the person is evoked, assaulted, and impinged upon in formative and transformative ways . . ." (1987:9). Of course other factors inherent in studying abroad also contribute to students' personal development. Being in a new school environment, for example, requires the students to develop new social relationships; and the lack of the usual forms of recreation, such as fraternity parties and talking to friends on the telephone, forces them to find new ways to entertain themselves.

Conclusion

First, let's review the major points. When traveling, the American students toured in groups, rarely stayed in any place for more than a day or two, often made decisions about where to go next on the spur of the moment, and had little meaningful contact with local people. Their daily routines varied but usually involved going to recognized tourist attractions, shopping, taking afternoon naps, and staying out late drinking in bars or pubs. Their touring did, however, change over time: they slowed down, becoming less mobile, moved about in slightly smaller groups, did less shopping, and became more interested in recreation than in seeing famous sites. Despite their limited immersion in the cultures they visited, the students' travel seemed to contribute to their personal development—they became more confident, self reliant, and adaptable. It is hypothesized that the primary cause of this change were the daily challenges students faced in having to function and satisfy their basic needs in an ever-changing array of foreign places, each requiring a new set of cultural understandings, often in a foreign language.

One lesson that I learned from doing this research is the importance of encouraging and enabling students to travel on their own. University sponsored and organized study trips are not a substitute for independent travel. But, students should be encouraged to travel in small numbers in order to increase the likelihood of interacting with local people. Smaller groups also mean that individual students have to cope with the challenges of getting information and solving daily problems more directly, with less diffusion of responsibility than is true of larger groups.[9] In any case, whatever the size of the group, there is no doubt that independent travel in a foreign culture is a catalyst for personal growth in students. Hanna speaks for many: "Coming to Europe was a huge experience for me, bigger than anything I've ever done before. I'll never be the same because of it."

Source: Adapted from "Crossing Cultures: Student Travel and Personal Development," *The International Journal of Intercultural Relations* 21(4): 475–89.

Notes

[1] The program is run by the University of New Orleans.

[2] The students were asked to divide their journal into chapters, each dealing with a different broad topic, including customs, food, people, language, stories, etc. It was suggested that the students try to write in several different chapters each day in order to encourage them to observe and write about a range of experiences.

[3] Some psychologists (Biggs 1992; Cloninger, personal communication) assert that journals are a particularly effective means of understanding personal growth in students. Writing about students in cross-cultural situations, Donald Biggs argues that students think about and describe their study abroad experiences with "narrative forms of thought" and not with a logical, abstract and/or context independent mode of thought (1992:7). It is primarily narrative accounts of their experiences that students write in journals. Hence, journals are a conduit to understanding the development of the students' narrative thinking (these narratives or stories about life events influence and guide behavior).

[4] The students recorded, from the time they got up in the morning until they retired at night, what they did—each activity, number of companions involved, and its duration. Each student then calculated, at the end of the weekend, how much time has been spent in each type of activity (e.g., waiting for trains, riding trains, walking around, shopping, eating, etc.).

[5] Over the six-week term the students traveled in an average of 5.5 countries. Two students had gone to fourteen countries, while one middle-aged adult student never left Austria.

[6] The difference between the average group sizes of students when traveling versus when staying in cities is due to some groups, upon arriving at their destination, splitting up into smaller groups to look for accommodation.

[7] Kauffmann et al. (1992:99) discuss the reliability and validity of students self reports, notably the lack of uniformity in the students' responses and the difficulty of comparison between studies. For example, the meaning given to *self-reliance* by one researcher may be the same that other researchers refer to as *independence* or *autonomy*. Similarly, *self-esteem* in some studies means the same as *self-confidence* in others (Kauffmann et al 1992:99). But Kauffmann (1992) and others note that other techniques for measuring personal development can also be problematic and that for some areas self-reports yield better data than standardized tests or questionnaires.

[8] Donald Biggs (1992) arrived at a similar conclusion in his attempt to assess the benefits of study abroad for Cypriot students. He uses the term "surprises" to refer to the differences between the students' home culture and the host culture, which they encounter abroad. It is their exposure to these "surprises," "troubles," or enigmas, and the students' attempts at resolving them that become "potent influences" in their development.

[9] Although large groups dilute the educational benefits of travel, it must be said that they do pose other challenges, including the need to cooperate with others and to make joint decisions.

References

Biggs, D. 1992a. "Psychological Issues in the Cross-cultural Exchange of Expertise and Training," in *Advances in Educational Productivity*, vol. 2, pp. 271–287. Greenwich, CT: JAI Press.

———. 1992b. "The Costs and Benefits of Study Abroad." Mimeograph.

Bruggemann, W. 1987. *Hope within History*. Atlanta: John Knox Press.

Carlson, J. et al. 1990. *Study Abroad: The Experience of American Undergraduates in Western Europe and the United States*. Westport CT: Greenwood Press.

Chickering, A. 1969. *Education and Identity*. San Francisco: Jossey-Bass.

Gmelch, G. 1992. "Learning Culture: The Education of American Students in Caribbean Villages." *Human Organization* 51(3): 245–252.

Hansel, B. 1998. "Developing an International Perspective in Youth through Exchange Programs." *Education and Urban Society* 20(2): 177–195.

Kauffmann, N. et al. 1992. *Students Abroad: Strangers at Home*. Yarmouth, ME: Intercultural Press.

Klineberg, O., and F. Hull. 1979. *At a Foreign University: An International Study of Adaptation and Coping*. New York: Praeger.

Lambert, R. 1989. *International Studies and the Undergraduate*. Washington DC: American Council on Education.

Piaget, J., and B. Inhelder. 1958. *The Growth of Logical Thinking from Childhood to Adolescence*. New York: Basic Books.

Stitsworth, M. 1988. "The Relationship between Previous Foreign Language Study and Personality Change in Youth Exchange Participants." *Foreign Language Annals* 21(2): 131–137.

26

Tourism, Europe, and Identity

John Urry

In this chapter I want to try to think through some of the implications of mass travel and tourism for the forms of social identity by which people organize their day-to-day lives. This is clearly a different concern from the standard impact studies on the one hand and the debates about tourism and international understanding on the other. I want to relate travel and tourism much more generally to the changing forms of culture that characterize contemporary society. Indeed, I want to suggest first that travel and tourism are extremely significant features of the modern world; and second, that debates about the changing nature of "Europe" cannot be undertaken without relating them to possible transformations of social identity that mass mobility brings about. This chapter is unashamedly conceptual and presents no new empirical information.

I begin by examining rather more carefully the concept of the "modern" by quoting from the seminal work on this subject. Marshall Berman says that to be modern is:

> . . . to find ourselves in an environment that promises adventure, power, joy, growth, transformations of ourselves and the world—and, at the same time, that threatens to destroy everything we have, everything we know, everything we are. Modern environments and experiences cut across all boundaries of geography and ethnicity, of class and nationality, of religion and ideology; in this sense, modernity can be said to unite all mankind. (1983:15)

Berman then describes some of the processes integral to modern towns and cities that "pour us into a maelstrom of perpetual disintegration and renewal," as well as some of the strategies that people employ in order 'to make oneself somehow at home in the maelstrom'" (1983:15, 345). And that, as many writers now illuminate, is particularly difficult. The current epoch is one of expanding horizons and dissolving boundaries, of "collapsing space and time" (Brunn and Leinbach 1991), of globalization through transformed informational and communicational flows, and of the erosion of territorial frontiers and clear-cut national and other social identities. Particular identities around place become seriously disrupted by such global change—there is a disengagement of "some basic forms of trust relation from the attributes of local contexts" (Giddens 1990:108).

What, however, this account does not address is one particular set of social practices that are central to the modern experience that Berman discusses in the nineteenth century, and to the recent transformations of space and time that contemporary theorists have analyzed in the late twentieth century, namely, the social practices of travel and tourism. Is it really sensible to consider, as Berman does, that it is pedestrian strollers (flâneurs) who can be taken as emblematic of the modern world? It is surely rather train passengers, car drivers, and jet plane passengers who are the heroes of the modern world. And it is the social organization of such long-distance travel that is the characteristic feature of modernity. In some ways the "social organization of the experience of modernity," beginning of course with Thomas Cook's, is as important a feature of modern Western societies as is the socialized production of manufactured goods.

When Berman for example talks of crossing boundaries of geography and ethnicity, when we anticipate adventure, joy, growth, and so on, these should be seen as centrally bound up with mobility, especially for pleasure. Travel may be enjoyable in its own right; it may involve liminal spaces permitting less structured forms of social interaction and enabling the cultures and environments of many other places to be encountered, consumed, and collected. The scale of this is enormous and has three types of immediate effect. First, on the places that such visitors travel to, which come to be remade in part as objects for the tourist gaze. Their built and physical environments, their economies, and their place-images are all substantially reconstructed. Second, on the places from which visitors come, which effectively export considerable amounts of income, images, social and cultural patterns, and so on. And third, via the construction of often enormous transportation infrastructures, which may have effects not only on the places just mentioned but also on all sorts of intermediate spaces close to runways, motorways, railway stations, and so on.

Thus travel and tourism are important industries and have significant effects on many places. But more significantly they are centrally important to the very nature of modern societies. Such modern societies are unique for the scale of such flows of short-term mobility. In the rest of this paper I want to think through some of the issues involved in investigating the wider cultural impact of such huge flows of visitors, the impact upon the very forms of social identity available in the modern world.

I begin with Morley and Robins, who talk of the "need to be 'at home' in the new and disorientating global space" (1990:3). There are two points to emphasize: first, that the disorientating global space is in part the product of massive global flows of tourists; and second, that such flows disrupt the very sense of what is a person's home. In what sense then can spatial meanings be attached or developed in which: "the space of flows . . . supersedes the space of places" (Henderson and Castells 1987:7)? That space of flows consists in part of tourists and means that many places are constructed around attracting and receiving large numbers of visitors. This is true not just for obvious places such as Brighton and Benidorm, Stratford-upon-Avon, and San Sebastian but also for cities such as London and New York, Paris, and Berlin. When some such cities are described as "cosmopolitan" this means they receive very large numbers of tourists. Their nature as a specific place in part results from their location at the intersection of various global flows, not just of money or capital but of visitors.

Watts notes the importance of investigating how people define themselves, how identities are produced "in the new spaces of a post-Fordist economy" (1992:123). How are identities constructed amidst the processes of globalization and fragmentation, especially when part of the image of place is increasingly produced for actual or potential visitors? Identity almost everywhere has to be produced partly out of the images constructed for tourists.

Furthermore, it is not just that places are transformed by the arrival or potential arrival of visitors. It is also that in an increasing number of societies, particularly in Europe, people are themselves transformed. The right to travel has become a marker of citizenship. It is important to consider what this does to conventional conceptions of citizenship based upon the notion that rights were to be provided by institutions located within territorially demarcated nation-states (see Held 1990). A novel kind of "consumer citizenship" is developing with four main features.

First, people are increasingly citizens by virtue of their ability to purchase goods and services; citizenship is more a matter of consumption than of political rights and duties. Second, people in different societies should have similar rights of access to a diversity of consumer goods, services, and cultural products from different societies. Third, people should be able to travel within all societies as tourists and those countries that have tried to prevent this, such as Albania, China, and some Eastern European countries in the past, have been seen as infringing on the human rights of foreigners to cross their territories. Fourth, people are viewed as having rights of movement across and permanent or seasonal residence in whichever society they choose to visit as a stranger, for whatever periods of time.

Thus citizenship rights increasingly involve claims to consume other cultures and places throughout the world. A modern person is one who is able to exercise those rights and who conceives of him or herself as a consumer of other cultures and places. What though will happen to such notions with the future changes in Europe after 1992 and especially the increased mobility between the formerly relatively separate East and West Europes? Currently about two-thirds of international tourism occurs to or within Europe. In particular what will be the effects of mass mobility, dependent upon such consumerist notions of citizenship, upon the multiple forms of social identity within Europe?

Social identities emerge out of imagined communities, out of particular structures of feeling that bind together three elements—space, time, and memory—often in part in opposition to an imagined "other" such as a neighboring country. However, massive amounts of mobility may transform such social identities formed around particular configurations of space, time, and memory. This can be seen by briefly considering each of these terms.

Visitors may overwhelm the "spaces" of a neighborhood, town, or region such that locals no longer feel it is their space/place anymore. So many visitors pass through, visually appropriating the space and leading locals to feel that they have "lost" their space. Visitors are viewed as the "other." However, it should be recognized that some places only exist because of visitors, that the very place, the particular combination of landscape and townscape, could only exist because of visitors, such as the English Lake District. Visitors are in a sense as much local as are "real" locals.

The second element is time. Tourism normally brings about some striking changes in the organization of time: attractions are here today and gone tomorrow; there are representations of different historical periods placed in unlikely juxtapositions; tourism involves extensive time-travel; and time is speeded up so that sufficient attractions can be accumulated in the prescribed period. Time seems to be organized in terms of the interests of the large leisure companies and of their clients. But two points should be noted: first, that some spaces, like Blackpool, only exist for locals because of the particular emphasis on being modern, being up-to-date, being almost ahead of time; and second, that some tourists increasingly wish to slow down time, to participate in sustainable or responsible tourism, which may not be the kind of time that locals feel is their time.

And finally, memory. One kind of dispute is over history: whose history should be represented and whose history should be packaged and commodified? Visitors are likely to seek a brief comprehensible history that can be easily assimilated—heritage rather than history as it is normally conceptualized. However, it should be noted that social memories are in fact always selective and there is no real memory to counterpose to the supposedly false memory of the visitor. The memories of "locals" will be as selective as those of visitors.

What then can we say about international tourism and social identity? As a general claim the suggestion in the literature that tourism facilitates international understanding seems very dubious. However, international tourism does surely have two relevant effects. First, it produces international familiarization/normalization so that those from other countries are no longer seen as particularly dangerous and threatening—just different. This seems to have happened on a large scale in Europe in recent years. Second, there is the generation of cosmopolitanism amongst at least some travelers. Living in the modern world is taken to a new level with cosmopolitanism, with a willingness of people to open out to others who live elsewhere. Cosmopolitanism involves an intellectual and aesthetic stance of openness toward divergent experiences from different national cultures. There is a search for and delight in contrasts between societies rather than a longing for uniformity or superiority. Hannerz talks of the need for the cosmopolitan to be in "a state of readiness, a personal ability to make one's way into other cultures, through listening, looking, intuiting, and reflecting" (1990:239).

Hebdige likewise argues that a "mundane cosmopolitanism" is part of many people's everyday experience, as they are world travelers, either directly or via the television in their living room. He argues that: "It is part of being 'taken for a ride' in and through late twentieth-century consumer culture. In the 1990s everybody [at least in the 'West'] is more or less cosmopolitan" (1990:20). I would further argue that contemporary societies have initiated a distinctive kind of cosmopolitanism, an aesthetic cosmopolitanism dependent upon certain scopic regimes. The following is a model of such an aesthetic cosmopolitanism:

Aesthetic Cosmopolitanism

1. Extensive patterns of real and simulated mobility in which it is thought that one has the right to travel anywhere and to consume at least initially all environments.

2. A curiosity about all places, peoples, and cultures and at least a rudimentary ability to map such places and cultures historically, geographically, and anthropologically.

3. An openness to other peoples and cultures and a willingness/ability to appreciate some elements of the language/culture of the place that one is visiting.

4. A willingness to take risks by virtue of moving outside the tourist environmental bubble.

5. An ability to locate one's own society and its culture in terms of a wide-ranging historical and geographical knowledge—to have some ability to reflect upon and judge aesthetically between different natures, places, and societies.

6. A certain semiotic skill—to be able to interpret tourist signs, to see what they are meant to represent, and indeed to know when they are partly ironic and to be approached coolly or in a detached fashion.

In the late eighteenth and early nineteenth centuries a similar kind of cosmopolitanism developed amongst the British upper class that was able to expand their repertoire of landscapes for visual consumption. Barrell summarizes the importance of their mobility throughout Europe:

> ... the aristocracy and gentry were not ... bound up in, any particular locality which they had no time, no money, and no reason ever to leave. It meant also that they had experience of more landscapes than one, in more geographical regions than one; and even if they did not travel much they were accustomed, by their culture, to the notion of mobility, and could easily imagine other landscapes. (1972:63; see also Zukin 1992a:224–5)

Overall then I am concerned here with the issues of social identity, of local, regional, national, and European identities, and ask what is the role of mobility and cosmopolitanism in forming and reproducing such identities. In conclusion I briefly consider some possible changes that are likely to take place in Europe in the next few years as a result of changes in mobility.

First, we can note the contemporary importance of Europe within international tourism: in 1990 the world's top ten destinations were: France, United States, Spain, Italy, Austria, Hungary, United Kingdom, Germany, Canada, and Switzerland; in 1991 there were some 429 million international tourist arrivals worldwide of which 275 million occurred in Europe, a 41 percent increase over the decade. Seventy percent of international visits by Europeans were not on inclusive tours but were by so-called "independent travelers"; and 80 percent of leisure travel in Europe is by car. The "richer" countries in the EC dominate the European tourism industry in absolute terms, accounting for about three-quarters of both expenditure and employment. But the "poorer" countries gain disproportionately and tourism is one of the main industries that produce a net flow of resources from north to south in Europe.

The following summarizes the main developments in mobility patterns in Europe in the 1990s:

1. Changes in companies: Europeanization of leisure companies; investment in Eastern Europe; breakdown of nationally regulated and protected travel industries; tour operators to operate more across borders; stricter consumer protection laws.

2. Changes in travel: abolition of internal frontiers; exchange of health provision; Channel Tunnel; high-speed trains in Europe; deregulation of airlines and the weakening of the power of "national carriers"; hub airports in Europe; longer-distance car holidays; moves toward a single currency and savings of foreign exchange dealing; elimination of immigration controls for intra-EC traffic; probable abolition of duty-free sales.

3. Changes in places: spectacular resort development as regions and nations compete for a larger share of the European market; increased

competition by cities to establish themselves as "European"; a greater specialization of place and image; increased marketing of "Europe"; and threats to regional/national identities; importance of "Europe" as signifying "history and culture"; fewer gains for "poorer" Mediterranean Europe.

4. Changes in types of tourism: growth of "globally responsible tourism"; of overseas second homes/timeshare; some more EC support given to peripheral regions especially via a "Europe of the regions"; diversification of rural areas away from agriculture toward tourism, etc.; growth of city center tourism given that international tourists tend to keep inland; further growth of historical/cultural tourism; large increases in tourism amongst the young and the old.

In the current debates about the nature of Europe, we need to consider the following: changing European institutions, such as the apparent weakening of the powers of individual nation-states; a possible Europe of the regions; the relationship of Europe to Islam; the growth of Europe-wide institutions of the media; and the efforts to construct a European homeland. But at the same time we need to investigate the massive and growing patterns of short-term mobility within Europe. It is inconceivable that new or reinforced conceptions of social identity can be formed without both actual and imagined journeys around Europe playing an important role. In his influential book on nationalism, Anderson analyzes the importance of "imagined communities," of investigating the rituals, the media, and patterns of travel by which people came in different supranational territories to imagine themselves as members of a single nation (1983). He argues that nations are: "imagined because the members of even the smallest nation will never know most of their fellow-members, meet them, or even hear of them, yet in the minds of each lives the image of their communion" (15). Anderson notes the importance of travel in this process, quoting Victor Turner on the importance of real and metaphorical journeys between times, statuses, and places as being particularly meaning-creating experiences (55). I want to suggest something similar here: that in the current reworkings of social identity, of the changing relations between place, nation, and Europe, travel is an element that may be of great importance in constructing/reinforcing novel identities. The development of a possible "European identity" cannot be discussed without considering how massive patterns of short-term mobility may be transforming dominant social identities.

Moreover, these mass forms of mobility involve tremendous effects upon the places visited, which almost all become locked into a competitive struggle for visitors. One consequence is the emergence of a new Europe of competing city-states, where local identities are increasingly packaged for visitors. And one way in which such competition between city-states takes place is through the identity of actually "being European." Such a place-image conventionally entails the establishment of various cultural and other "festivals," the designation of artistic quarters, the development of areas of outdoor cafes and restaurants, the preservation of old buildings and street layout, the redevelopment of river and canalside waterfronts, and the use of the term European as standing for "history" and "culture" for marketing that particular place (see Clark 1992 on the tradition of communal celebrations in Europe).

But there is an interesting paradox here. Part of what is involved in towns and cities becoming more European is that places should demonstrate at least some signs of local distinctiveness. Robins refers to this as "the importance of place marketing in placeless times" (1991:38). This will of course often entail the use of an area's heritage: "Even in the most disadvantaged places, heritage, or the simulacrum of heritage, can be mobilized to gain competitive advantage in the race between places" (38). But there are of course competing heritages waiting to be captured by various kinds of organizations. There will be contestation over whose heritage is being conserved and how this relates to local people and their sense of what is important to remember. Robins notes that in northern England there is a struggle taking place between the working-class, industrial image of the region and a new image that emphasizes enterprise and opportunity, proclaiming that "Andy Capp is dead—Newcastle is alive" (39). However, it is clearly impossible to eliminate entirely the industrial history of the area; Robins notes that Beamish in the northeast of England has become a European recognized tourist site while there are numbers of cultural projects designed to recreate the area's working-class heritage and to show how it contributed to a particular regional identity (40–1).

In the reworking of the relationships between a European identity and regional and local identities, the role of travel and its collective forms of organization seem particularly salient and currently underexamined. Mass mobility is probably one of the main factors that will determine whether a European identity will emerge; it is a crucial factor in transforming local identities. Robins clearly summarizes the dilemmas involved here:

> The driving imperative is to salvage centered, bounded, and coherent identities—place identities for placeless times. This may take the form of the resuscitated patriotism and jingoism that we are now seeing in a resurgent Little Englandism. Alternatively . . . it may take a more progressive form in the cultivation of local and regional identities or in the project to construct a continental European identity. (1991:41)

Source: From *Consuming Places*, 2002. Reprinted with permission of the author and Sage Publications.

References

Anderson, B. 1983. *Imagined Communities*. London: Verso.
Barrell, J. 1972. *The Idea of Landscape and the Sense of Place 1730–1840*. Cambridge: Cambridge University Press.

Berman, M. 1983. *All that is Solid Melts into Air: The Experience of Modernity*. London: Verso.

Brunn, S. D., and T. Leinbach, eds. 1991. *Collapsing Space and Time*. London: Harper Collins.

Clark, S. 1992. "Leisure: *Jeux sans FrontiPres* or Major European Industry," in *Social Europe*, ed. J. Bailey. London: Longman.

Giddens, A. 1990. *The Consequences of Modernity*. Cambridge: Polity.

Hannerz, U. 1990. "Cosmopolitans and Locals in World Culture." *Theory, Culture and Society* 7:237–52.

Hebdige, D. 1990. "Fax to the Future." *Marxism Today* (January):18–23.

Held, D. 1990. "Democracy, the Nation-state and the Global System," in *Political Theory Today*, ed. D. Held. Cambridge: Polity.

Henderson, J., and M. Castells, eds. 1987. *Global Restructuring and Territorial Development*. London: Sage.

Morley, D., and K. Robins. 1990. "No Place Like *Heimat*: Images of Home(land) in European Culture." *New Formations* (Autumn):1–23.

Robins, K. 1991. "Tradition and Translation: National Culture in its Global Context," in *Enterprise and Heritage*, ed. J. Corner and S. Harvey. London: Routledge.

Watts, M. 1992. "Spaces for Everything (A Commentary)" *Cultural Anthropology* 7:115–29.

Zukin, S. 1992. "The City as a Landscape of Power," in *Global Finance and Urban Living*, by L. Budd and S. Whimster. London: Routledge.

27

Rethinking Tourism

Deborah McLaren

"Welcome to Paradise . . . before it's gone" is macabre. Do we really want to destroy paradise, make it go? Current high-consumption forms of tourism are *not* sustainable. Realistic information must be made easily available. As we travel, we need to ask ourselves, "Why am I traveling? How can I help change the destructive aspects of the travel industry?"

I asked these questions of several responsible tourism advocates. Virginia Hadsell, founder of the Center for Responsible Tourism, told me that despite the efforts of the worldwide responsible tourism movement that began to emerge in the 1970s, the negative impact of irresponsible tourism has increased. She sees some hopeful signs, however, as the issue of irresponsible tourism is being placed on the agenda in many parts of the world. Increasingly, from many quarters, the rights of indigenous peoples, concern for the deteriorating environment, the homogenization of cultures, and the rights of women and children are being addressed—and often connected with the tourism industry.

Over the past few decades, the world has truly shrunk, in a large part because of tourism. As citizens of the global North, we can fly to Rio de Janeiro tomorrow and float down the Amazon the day after. Our ability to see the world close up has made us more concerned about international problems. News about environmental threats to the rain forests, the plight of the people who live there, human rights abuses around the world, and the increasing poverty and economic gaps between citizens reach us speedily each day.

Issues like the uncontrolled power of corporations and the destruction of the planet have become central in many of our lives. Yet in some ways the rapid rate at which information is being thrown at us makes it almost too much to comprehend. We feel overwhelmed, sometimes jaded, by the surplus of information. We see the problems but remain unsure how to effect change.

Numerous "alternative" types of tourism are evolving, and the real danger is that travelers will simply consume these new products, places, and peoples without recognizing the urgent need for a critical reevaluation of global tourism and their participation in it. To rethink tourism is to challenge the travel industry at every level, including the booming new forms of travel, which, even if well intended, have many of the same detrimental effects as conventional tourism. Olivier Pouillon, a tourism activist who works in Indonesia, warns, "Stop looking for alternatives or technical solutions to tourism. When you scream ecotourism, agritourism, and alternative tourism, it makes people forget to look at what is wrong with tourism." Tourism scholar and activist Shelley Attix asks,

> Why are we "activists" afraid of the "t" word? Tourism industry people aren't. If we are concerned about what tourism is doing and come from different backgrounds—business, indigenous sovereignty, environmental—then we should talk instead of waiting until there is a crisis. It is very difficult, except in strategic boycott situations, to shut down tourism. We have to keep alliances strong and prepare for transitional efforts. We need to train young people to be managers and handle policy decisions during these transitions from mass tourism. We have to make plans in terms of finances and management skills to take over the helm and make big changes. We're making the "t" word so bad that no one wants to talk about it, and that's counterproductive.

The remedy is within tourism itself. To counter tourism's economic, social, and environmental devastation, we must learn to recognize corporate tourism's messages and methods. Tourism has provided us with fantasies. At the same time, it provides potentially free public relations that may help to encourage rethinking of the industry and create alternatives. Tourism provides people-to-people contacts and an opportunity to utilize the ability to communicate with one another, to meet, and to organize. On a global level, this can help foster an appreciation for rich human, cultural, and ecological diversity and can cultivate a mutual trust and respect for one another and for the dignity of the natural world.

You and I are tourists, even if we are traveling to learn about or change the world. Unless we are willing to stay at home, reject the transportation systems, communication lines, and technologies and the tremendous amount of resources that we consume each time we travel, we need to understand not only our participation in the promotion of the global tourism industry but also its importance and potential as a tool for change. Tourism can raise awareness of and action for the global nature of problems like poverty, pollution, and cultural erosion. Close human relationships and activities liberated from preoccupations with profits and bottom lines are crucial to this awareness. In the past three decades, there has been a return to social responsibility and social idealism. This value shift is reflected to a small degree in the tourism industry (in the tourism-for-peace movement, for example) in the consciousness of the cross-cultural impact a travel experience has for both a visitor and the communities visited. The trend in travel is for more tourists and locals in alliance with schools, NGOs, religious groups, the media, cities, and governments to work to stop the paving of paradise.

So where do we start? With ourselves. We can read, learn, make personal changes, be more involved in our own communities, pressure governments and corporations, denounce exploitation, change policies, and investigate the global forces transforming our lives. We can discuss, educate, and organize. I believe that most tourists understand that there are many things wrong with tourism. What we need is a clear outline for change.

The first requirement is for more tourism research and analysis. This can occur as activism goes forward. Travelers from the global North can link with people in other places to make progress on issues that concern us all. By building on experiences and developing relationships and networks, we can challenge international trade and tourism policies, misinformation produced by the travel industry, and exploitative practices. We can make sure that monies from tourism go to the local economy.

Many developing countries are on the brink of abandoning traditional organic practices and moving toward more capital-intensive methods of development. The responsible tourism movement can draw attention to development policies that are undemocratic and promote reliance on the global economy as opposed to local resources. In many places around the world people are building sustainable communities that focus on the well-being of the community, rely more on renewable energy, discourage consumption, and create less pollution.

The Need for Education

While there has been a fair amount of critical analysis of tourism from the academic community, most tourism education focuses on hospitality management, training, and operations. Critical studies in economics, political control, culture, the North-South dichotomy, and the way tourists view themselves have contributed important insights.

According to Luis Vivanco, "Many tourism programs are designed to reproduce the industry, validate its basic capitalist paradigms, and create the next generation of managers. Will they allow for more critical, deconstructive work to happen under their umbrella? My guess is that if it's allowed, truly critical social scientific and political perspectives will be marginalized by the business and technique-focused emphasis of the industry." Real changes in tourism will not be created until people from diverse communities, backgrounds, and disciplines take a more integrated approach. Anthropologists, political scientists, and sociologists must connect with tourism management and training programs to share information, challenge unsustainable practices and unfair labor, and develop critical analysis.

A few programs do exist that are not completely industry-focused. Texas A&M is an example of an interdisciplinary approach to tourism in the United States. The University of Waitago in New Zealand has a very unique program in tourism that is completely interdisciplinary and based in geography, and offers some critical analysis. At the same time it hopes to serve the Maori, the indigenous peoples of New Zealand.

Women of all colors are urgently needed to look at gender issues in tourism and change policies that exploit, discriminate, and cause violence to women. Support for tourism gender studies at universities and colleges will support education for women to work in tourism in areas other than as prostitutes, waitresses, maids, bar attendants, and housekeepers.

There needs to be tremendous support for indigenous students of tourism. While it is necessary to understand Western systems in order to tackle the issues of tourism, it is important to remember that Western education has produced the systems that are threatening the planet. Educational programs must introduce and integrate lessons from indigenous ecological values and traditional and subsistence economics. I encourage students to research tourism, to undertake an analysis of advertising strategies or investigate the corporate responsibility of a tourism company. When educational programs encourage critical thinking and opportunities for people from diverse perspectives, they can create the tools, information, and education for those who are affected to change tourism. The global tourism industry must be persuaded to set aside some of its trillions of dollars in profits to advance the education of young people around the world to rethink tourism.

Tourists as Activists

The Center for Responsible Tourism suggests tourists ask themselves: Is this trip necessary? "Tourism has become a supermarket of illusions, exotic lands promising to satisfy secret desires. Ask yourself, why am I buying this trip? What do I leave behind? How many trips does it take to renew my soul and body? What do I do with my experiences when I return home?"[1] As tourists questioning tourism, the role we play, and the impact of our very presence in destination communities, we can start by considering the amount of natural resources it takes to transport us to our destination, to get us around while we are there (whether the oil used by airplanes and cars or the energy for the lights and air conditioning in the hotel room), where our waste is going, whether the locals have adequate water resources, how much land has been "reconstructed" for the place we stay, and whether residents have been moved to make room for us. Who owns the hotels, and where do our dollars go? We tourists can make some powerful political choices by voting with our feet and our pocketbooks.

As tourists, we must make educated economic choices and support small-scale, locally owned and operated businesses. Get involved in your own community so that when you travel you will have a reason to be involved in other communities and will *stay involved*; acknowledge the modern realities of indigenous and rural communities and learn to respect, not romanticize, other cultures. Support responsible tourism organizations. Subscribe to their magazines and newsletters. Volunteer. Study. Learn about local currency programs and how you can start one in your community. Pressure large tourism companies to do more than greenwash. Organize a "reality tour" of your own community to examine environmental, economic, or social justice issues. Invite teachers, students, local community members, your family, city officials, religious leaders, local businesses (including those in tourism), and others to participate. Make activism a goal of the tour. Contribute funds to support more integrated, diverse critical tourism studies.

Travelers can act responsibly by seeking out accurate information about the places they intend to visit. In the United States and elsewhere, many indigenous organizations will provide a list of recommended readings by authors they believe accurately describe their culture and history. Environmental and social justice groups that work with native and indigenous peoples will have information about important current issues. Indigenous peoples face any number of issues, ranging from health care and uranium mining cleanup to sovereignty rights and free trade agreements. In the United States, travelers can support the protection of sacred religious sites. Many such places have been turned into tourist destinations, rock-climbing walls, and even resorts. Sacred Sites International Foundation advocates for "the preservation of natural and built sacred places. We believe that protecting sacred sites is key to preserving traditional cultures and time-honored values of respecting the earth."[2]

While social activists are developing new tourism strategies, concerned tourists are changing their focus from relaxation to activism. Global Exchange, a San Francisco organization, has been a leader in people-to-people tourism. Their reality tours explore grassroots movements, offering travelers an opportunity to meet people behind the scenes, from Zapatistas in Chiapas and young people in Cuba to women organizers in South Africa and Vietnamese facing injustices created by capitalism. Tourists are now monitoring elections in Mexico, speaking out on behalf of indigenous peoples being forced from their lands by oil companies, and trying to uphold human rights in Bosnia. They are sharing information about fair trade, organic farming, or permaculture, and less consumptive technologies.

Deborah Tull joined a reality tour organized by Bard College:

> I spent nine months traveling, meeting local people and helping out. I still have questions about what we did—did it really make a difference?

Some places I could see that yes, it did. However, in other places I felt we were contributing to problems. Yet, overall, we traveled in a different way—meeting and learning from local people involved in important issues. It certainly changed my perceptions about tourism. It actually changed my life. I will never see tourism in the same light, I will never travel in a conventional way. I've talked to a lot of friends, family, and my teachers about it and believe I have been influential.

Travel Industry Changes

Some segments of the travel industry are more aware of environmental and human rights issues and are actively involved in reform. A growing number of small tour operators are rethinking their industry. Although many alternative ideas claim to benefit local people, we must not lose sight of the fact that tour operators are in the business to make money, and the tourist is the paying consumer they cater to. Tourism researcher Barbara Johnston warns against some tourism ideas that are emerging:

> Alternative tourism represents an industry whose ventures capitalize on the increasing global concern with disappearing cultures, lifestyles and ecosystems. . . . [However], the vision of responsible tourism includes more than this potentially exploitative relationship. Responsible tourism encompasses those ventures that are consciously designed to enhance the socio-environmental milieu of the host while educating and entertaining the guest. These ventures sell the "exotic" to gain money, labor, and/or foreign presence—all in an effort to restore the degraded environment while attacking the roots of social inequity. (Johnston 1990:31)

Many ecotourism projects are extremely misleading and exploitative. Some may be well intentioned but are misguided attempts to sell nature and culture. One example of a tour company that not only follows responsible tourism guidelines but also monitors the global travel industry is The Travel Specialists (TTS). A member of Co-Op America, a fair-trade organization, TTS serves as a link between concerned travelers, tour operators, tour programs, and local community projects. It evaluates other travel programs, promotes responsible tourism, and monitors the impact of tourism on local communities and the environment. TTS established the Eagle Eye Institute, a program to get urban youth out of the cities and into nature for hands-on learning experiences. The group also publishes a newsletter that includes travel opportunities, suggested readings on responsible tourism, and updates about the travel industry.

The Alaska Wilderness Recreation & Tourism Association (AWRTA) is a statewide model of how local business and industry, conservation, and communities—including native communities—come together to improve the tourism industry. AWRTA, a nonprofit trade organization, promotes the recognition and protection of Alaska's recreation and tourism resources and the businesses that rely on them. AWRTA's mission is to support the stewardship

of the wild in Alaska and the development of healthy, diverse travel businesses and communities by linking business, community, and conservation
interests. AWRTA promotes the recognition and protection of Alaska's recreation and tourism resources including scenic qualities, wildlife, fisheries, wilderness, wildlands, and rivers. AWRTA also developed an innovative funding
mechanism for environmental and conservation groups. The *Dollars a Day
for Conservation* program, aimed at tour operators arranging travel to Alaska,
can help clients and the habitat and wildlife they enjoy by putting their
money toward conservation efforts. It is a voluntary program and asks tour
operators to simply introduce the concept to their clients and "passing
through" their donations. AWRTA consists of members from native communities and therefore offers travelers to Alaska more realistic expectations and
connections to native cultures.

More Natural Experiences

The real argument for environmental protection through any form of
tourism requires a departure from the global marketplace economy that
exploits the natural world. It is almost impossible to do this within the context of the global tourism industry, which gobbles up resources. We must
expect to pay for the environments we visit. In the global North, we pay taxes
to keep up our sewer systems, water, and even national parks. In many other
countries, there is no such public support. If you plan to travel, factor in the
cost of the environment and public services into your trip. Better yet, set
aside funds especially for this purpose and donate them to an environmental
organization or community development project. But it is important to understand as well that Western solutions to saving the planet are not always compatible with those of the people who live in wilderness areas. For example,
conservation—a Western concept—is an idea that land should be preserved
in its natural state. Under conservation statutes new parks, wildlife refuges,
wilderness areas, and monuments have become protected lands. The designation of wilderness lands may actually impinge on indigenous ways of life
because limitations are placed on traditional and subsistence activities.
Instead of developing new sites, new destinations, we should consider the
pressing issues related to tourism that are already on our doorstep, investigate
the "corridors" and peripheral areas of protected lands.

Local Action

Local people in destination communities are speaking out and taking
action against exploitative tourism. Some paint murals on walls near tourist
resorts to graphically illustrate their anti-tourism sentiments. Others have
developed educational programs for residents and designed regional tourism
strategies to protect their natural resources and limit the numbers of tourists

and developers who enter their lands. Still others are setting up their own travel companies that promote responsible tourism through people-to-people links, some of which focus on human rights; they are developing tour programs that recruit scientists and volunteers to work directly with them to preserve their environments. Native people are taking over operations of parks—their ancestral homelands—and training others to do the same. While they share the use of these areas with tourists, their own communities are the first priority. They are establishing local currencies that keep dollars within the communities. Some are working with universities and local governments to come up with new policies on land planning and use in their regions. Some programs are even assessing the reasons *why* record numbers of stressed tourists are escaping from urban environments. Many programs examine the impacts of tourism upon their environments, teach tourists about the impact of their mere presence, and invite them to take action to help offset the damage. There are even projects for individuals or organizations in the United States and Europe to help purchase land in the global South to set aside as protected areas for wildlife and for local people.

Indigenous peoples are resisting tourism with increasing strength. The Maasai in Africa, the Mayans in Chiapas, the Quechuas in the Amazon, many Native Americans in the United States, and many others are resisting irrational development of their lands in the name of ecotourism. These groups have organized opposition both from within their own countries and in the international community, and their voices are being heard. Responsible tourism groups, environmentalists, and others have responded by providing support and publicizing injustices. Concerned citizens rallied in 1996 to oppose the construction of a sprawling resort in the heart of India's Nagarhole National Park, one of the world's biological "hot spots" and home to indigenous peoples. The opponents denounced the development, organized locally with tribal people, and called upon responsible tourism organizations around the world to help publicize their plight. In 1997 the Indian courts ruled against the resort, at least for the time being. Unfortunately the hotel continues to press for development and the community members live in a precarious situation. Rural communities are organizing to address conflicts caused by tourism. Chris Beck explains one such project in Alaska.

The Talkeetna Community

Since 1998, visits to the small, end-of-the-road-town Talkeetna increased dramatically. Talkeetna traditionally has been a destination for modest numbers of climbers, anglers, and independent sightseers. These travelers come for spectacular views of the Alaska Range, proximity to Denali National Park and Preserve, and the town's historic and colorful character. In recent years, the opening of two new hotels led to a rapid increase in package tourist visits. Annual visitation is up at least threefold, from about 30,000 to 120,000 annual visitors.

Many townspeople are feeling overwhelmed by the sudden rush of tourism. In a town of less than 700 residents, as many as 1,000 visitors per day has led to congestion, parking problems, and new commercial development. Perhaps most important, many people have the sense that they're losing the things they most like about their town—a sense of contact with history, the natural world and their neighbors.

To respond to these changes, the town is currently in the middle of an ambitious tourism-planning project. One goal of the project is to address the immediate side affects of rapid tourism growth—for example, finding ways to reduce congestion by parking motor coaches and RVs on the edge of town, rather than having them drive through the middle of the community. Another goal of the project is to establish, for the first time, land use controls so future development is compatible with the town's funky/rustic/historic character. Finally, the project is working to build better lines of communication, and improved decision-making capacity, both within the community, and between the community and "outside" interests such as major cruise lines.

It is essential to create links within communities. Foreign-owned or -operated tourism companies could help support local agriculture and more sustainable practices by buying local goods and services such as food and transportation. They could recognize the harm in building cluster sites and make sure broad planning in the area included agricultural lands and other lands used by locals.

The Media

Most travel advertising of destination communities is created in the global North or by private industry and government tourist offices in the global South. This medium dominates the planet and promises paradise while other sectors of the media discuss how backward, poor, and degraded these same locations are. Any argument to rethink tourism must see through this corporate vision and its methods of propaganda. While responsible tourism organizations and tourism scholars have provided the best critiques of global tourism, the mainstream media are taking notice, especially with the growing concern about threats to national parks and protected areas. More travel writers, newspapers, and magazines are responding to the alerts about negative tourism activities and providing more realistic accounts of the life of locals, the dismal conditions that tourism has helped create, and the anti-tourism campaigns launched by grassroots groups everywhere.

Clay Hubbs, an educator, started the alternative travel magazine *Transitions Abroad* in the mid-1970s to provide information on economical, purposeful international travel opportunities—travel that involves learning by living, studying, working, or vacationing alongside the people of the host country. Hubbs describes his magazine's mission:

> A lot of tourists have a consumer attitude—what can I get, instead of what can I learn. We have to put aside our own cultural biases and learn as much as possible from the people we visit. I find that if you stay long enough, learn the language, you get a sense of who locals are as "peo-

ple." Through the magazine we are providing people-to-people links and small-scale programs, and with the numbers of people traveling "independently" mushrooming, it is obvious that people benefit and the travel industry does not.

Indigenous brochures describe cultural taboos and warn tourists from certain areas. Internet services speak to broad issues that affect both travelers and people in local destinations. Ron Mader, who coordinates the Internet service Planeta.com, told me, "It seemed to me that there were all of these groups not talking to each other about 'ecotourism.' I set up Planeta to run both positive and critical articles on ecotourism in the Americas and to hear from many people throughout the hemisphere. Many have been excluded from the governmental arena or the larger circles of powerhouse NGOs."

New and interesting media tools for tourists abound. One is *On This Spot: An Unconventional Map and Guide to Lhasa*, published by the International Campaign for Tibet. It provides uncensored stories behind Lhasa's tourist sites and commemorates dozens of places and events that the Chinese government is trying to hide from tourists and the international community. The map explains the contemporary political situation and gives the exact locations where Tibetan prisoners of conscience are held today. Linking travelers with Tibetan support organizations around the world, this map is a great example of a rethinking tourism tool.

The Green Tourism Association, based in Toronto, is the first such city to offer a written green tourist guide and a companion green map to show people all the best ways to experience a rich and sustainable urban existence. *The OTHER Guide to Toronto: Opening the Door to Green Tourism* (and the accompanying *The OTHER Map of Toronto*) provides resources that links tourism to the environment and celebrate the green city.

What can you do to encourage the media and marketers to present a more realistic image of tourism and its effects? Don't buy travel magazines that are simply advertisements for corporations and reject the "awards" they give themselves. Support the alternative press that does not depend upon corporate funds and offers critical analysis of travel. Educate your local news media. As a tourist, researcher, or activist, you can write about your tourism experiences. Always make sure to include resource information to link people, and illustrate how the issues you learned about on your travels are related to you and your community. For example, a traveler to the Amazon wrote about irresponsible, exploitative oil and gas development and linked her story to increased consumer demand for petroleum in the United States.

Human Rights

On several occasions the United States has sought to use tourism as a political weapon. As Linda Richter, a tourism scholar who has researched politics and tourism in Asia, wrote, "The United States demonstrated opposition to the regimes of the People's Republic of China and Cuba by forbidding travel to those countries for many years. Now it is symptomatic of the desired change in political relationships that the United States has lifted the travel ban on the People's Republic of China (and) allowed some travel to Cuba" (1989:6). By opening the doors of free trade, countries are "rewarded" with an expanding force of superconsumers, the tourists. They are also "rewarded" with expanding infrastructures, technologies, imports and exports, Western homogenization, and all the other tools of capitalism, consumerism, and globalization.

Despite the "rewards," some countries continue to oppress people. Individual tourists, as opposed to tour groups, have played a role in documenting some of the abuses simply by being part of the community. According to tourism analyst Ronald Schwartz, following demonstrations in Tibet in 1987, tourists who witnessed the events "became the principal source of information to journalists denied access to Tibet and gathered material on arrests, torture, and imprisonment for human rights organizations. A loosely knit network that arose in the first few days following the demonstrations continued to function for more than two years, recruiting new volunteers [tourists] to take the place of those who left" (1991:588). They also provided medical treatment to wounded Tibetans who were afraid to go to government hospitals. Yet Schwartz emphasizes that this was a special group of independent travelers who might have been concerned about human rights in Tibet in the first place. Such "engaged" tourists have not simply stepped out of their own societies, leaving behind obligations and seeking relaxation and luxury: "The ease with which travelers from different nationalities, a group of strangers, were able to create a clandestine organization and pool their skills . . . is remarkable. But their ready agreement on goals and tactics suggests a common culture of shared perceptions and values" (589). Engaged tourists share skills and values that belong to a larger social world.

Monitoring Corporations

Some corporations are taking steps to become more responsible, but only after facing tremendous pressure from the public. The public is needed to monitor and challenge corporations at every level. Community resistance to tourism corporations has been mostly unsuccessful. Nevertheless, resistance is increasing, and workers in the tourism industry are also organizing to resist. Any argument to rethink tourism calls for investigation of the power of international tourism corporations in order to get large corporations out of the local planning process and reduce their local political influence and control. In the United States, disclosure laws mean that information about global tourism corporations is fairly easy to obtain. The U.S. Securities and Exchange Commission requires corporations to file quarterly and annual reports. Any environmental liabilities—significant remediation or cleanup—must be reported. It is much more difficult to investigate overseas corporations. The best way is to locate and work with a grassroots group in the destination country. Friends of the Earth publishes the booklet *How to Research Corporations*. Other groups like the Multinational Monitor and Transnational Resource Action Center (TRAC) can also assist in investigating corporate actions and responsibility, and may help publish your own investigative work.

Travelers can learn more about corporate responsibility, oppressive governments, and actions against human rights abusers from the numerous publications that monitor human rights, corporations, the environment, and government actions. *Boycotts in Action* (BAN) provides information about boycotts of corporations, countries, and organizations, including tourism and travel-related corporations. A dedicated hiker told me, "People underestimate the power they wield. I became an environmental activist to save the places I love. It makes me angry to see politicians 'selling' wilderness areas, designing bills with loopholes allowing for construction of roads, power lines, and pipelines. I write about my experiences to encourage others to get involved. There is no doubt it is effective. Public pressure is the only way to make sure politicians don't sell out to private interests."

Tourism Revisited

In rethinking tourism, we must analyze the role we tourists play in promoting current destructive practices. With pressure, the industry can be reshaped so that profits from tourism are distributed more equitably. We must reduce consumption and respect natural limits rather than merely think "green." Technology is not neutral but interacts with society and nature. It is essential to replace environmentally and socially obsolete high technology with more appropriate, less-consuming, and traditional technologies.

This task is enormous. The developed world is in a state of denial about such severe problems. It is unlikely to change voluntarily; it will have to be forced by community groups in the global South and by cross-border organizations everywhere. A more generous spirit and greater volunteerism with respect to tourism issues goes hand in hand with a condemnation of the elitist, materialistic view that tourists are entitled to purchase other environments and cultures. Travelers must be willing to be on equal footing with locals, to try to understand cultures widely disparate from their own, to contribute to the community (perhaps through manual labor or professional expertise).

Those of us in the North who reject the advance of commercialized global culture and those from the South who are victimized by it vociferously oppose the continued devastation of the environment and indigenous populations. We need to take a hard look at the travel industry, at the self-exploitation of communities, and the roles we play as individuals. This inner journey of reevaluation won't be easy, but it is essential.

Some say it is too late. At a conference to rethink current economic directions, a former executive of one of the largest travel companies in the world was asked if he could see an alternative future. He replied, "There is no way to stop economic globalization because tourism and travel have already created globalization." Yet because of global grassroots movements for change, it may be possible to develop a deeper understanding of the course we're on and the role of global tourism. There are alternative strategies and movements, and there are alternatives to tourism.

Tourism has become politicized within global institutions, nations, communities, industry, the environment, and within almost all of us, whether we are tourists or persons affected by tourism in our community. The field begs for more research, monitoring, linking, policymaking, and change. Meanwhile, despite the slowdown caused by the September 11, 2001 terrorist attacks, global tourism is growing at a phenomenal rate—particularly in areas deemed "safe" such as the Arctic. There is an urgent need to rethink tourism and ecotravel and stop the paving of paradise.

It has been almost twenty years since my first trip to Jamaica. My continual journey through "tourism" over those years has been one of learning—sometimes frustrating, always challenging, often delightful, and in many ways transformative. When I think back to the day when I rode horseback among the shantytowns and hills near Montego Bay with a local guide named Joseph, one thing seems clear to me: in many ways we were both searching for dignity and an opportunity for self-realization. Throughout the world, among different cultures and classes, people are looking for self-determination. The world we are now born into and the society we know measures humans in terms of their economic worth. Human potential is enormous and largely unrealized. Western-style capitalism and consumerism have undermined the possibility for people to make their own choices about their lives and to have opportunities for their futures. Tourism continues to play a tremendous role in spreading the corporate empire. However, it is an industry that is different from many others. One of its primary functions is to develop human relationships. I see that as a chance to rethink and change our future. *That* would be paradise.

Source: From *Rethinking Tourism and Ecotravel*, 2003. Reprinted with permission of the author and Kumarian Press.

Notes

[1] Quoted from "Third World Travel—Buy Critically," brochure adapted from a TEN publication and distributed by the Center for Responsible Tourism, Berkeley, CA.
[2] Quoted from Web site for Sacred Sites International Foundation, 1442A Walnut St. #330, Berkeley, CA 94709, 510-525-1304, e-mail sacredsite@aol.com, Web address www.sitesaver.org.

References

Attix, Shelly. 1993. *Ecotourism: A Directory of Marketing Resources*. Pearl City: University of Hawai'i Press.

Hubbs, Clay. Annually. *Alternative Travel Directory*. Amherst, MA: Transitions Abroad
     Publishing.
Johnston, Barbara. 1990. "'Save Our Beach Dem and Our Land Too!' The Problems of
     Tourism in 'America's Paradise.'" *Cultural Survival Quarterly* 14(2):30–37.
Richter, Linda. 1989. *The Politics of Tourism in Asia*. Honolulu: University of Hawai'i Press.
Schwartz, Ronald. 1991. "Travelers Under Fire: Tourists in the Tibetan Uprising." *Annals
     of Tourism Research* 18(4):588–604.

Appendix A: Contributors

JON G. ABBINK is senior researcher at the African Studies Centre, Leiden, the Netherlands, where he heads the research group on culture, politics, and inequality in Africa. He is also professor of African ethnic studies at Vrije Universiteit, Amsterdam. He has carried out field research in Israel and Ethiopia. His research interests are political change and ethnic relations in Africa, culture and violence, and the anthropology and history of Ethiopia. He became interested in tourism research while doing fieldwork in southern Ethiopia, where he was struck by the ambivalent response of local people, seeing tourists as a "necessary evil." His books include *Mytho-légendes et histoire: L'énigme de l'ethnogenèse des Beta Esra'el* (1991), *Meanings of Violence: A Cross-Cultural Perspective* (edited with G. Aijmer, 2000), and *Rethinking Resistance: Revolt and Violence in Africa History* (edited with K. van Walraven and M. de Bruijn, 2003).

CONNIE ZEANAH ATKINSON is the associate director of the Midlo Center for New Orleans Studies, University of New Orleans. She also teaches courses on the history of New Orleans music in the history department at the University of New Orleans. She received her PhD from the Institute of Popular Music, University of Liverpool, England. Her work on tourism and music has appeared in *Dixie Debates* (edited by R. H. King and H. Taylor, 1996), *Tourists and Tourism* (edited by S. Abram, J. D. Waldren and D. V. L. Macleod, 1998), and *Cultural Vistas*. A music journalist in New Orleans for many years, she edited and published *Wavelength*, New Orleans' music magazine, from 1980–1992. In 1994–96, she and colleague Sara Cohen investigated the impact of tourism on two cities renowned for their musical heritage: Liverpool, England and New Orleans, Louisiana.

JEREMY BOISSEVAIN is emeritus professor of social anthropology, University of Amsterdam. Besides his work on tourism, he has published extensively on local politics, ethnic relations, small entrepreneurs, and public celebrations. His recent publications include *Revitalizing European Rituals* (1992), *Saints and Fireworks: Religion and Politics in Rural Malta* (1965/1993), and *Coping with Tourists: European Reactions to Mass Tourism* (1996). He became interested in tourism through personally experiencing its impact on Malta as annual tourist arrivals rose from a few thousand to over a million during the past 45 years.

DENISE BRENNAN is assistant professor of anthropology in the department of sociology and anthropology at Georgetown University. Her book, *What's Love Got to Do with It? Transnational Desires and Sex Tourism in Sosúa, the Dominican Republic*, will be out with Duke University Press in 2004.

EDWARD M. BRUNER is professor emeritus of anthropology and professor emeritus of criticism and interpretive theory at the University of Illinois. He was past president of the American Ethnological Society and the Society for Humanistic Anthropology. He became interested in tourism in the mid-1980s while leading a student group on a round-the-world year abroad program, where he realized that anthropologists and tourists are found together, everywhere. "Tourism haunts the anthropological enterprise," he says. His edited volumes include *Text, Play, and Story* (1988) and *The Anthropology of Experience* (1986). He is currently preparing a book entitled *Tourist Tales: Ethnographies of Travel*.

SO-MIN CHEONG is a visiting assistant professor in the department of geography at Texas A&M University and has published in environmental management, marine policy, and coastal management concerning fishing communities in transition to tourism and community-based resource management. She is currently working on the intersection of tourism and nature.

ERIK COHEN is the George S. Wise professor of sociology (emeritus) at the Hebrew University of Jerusalem. He has conducted sociological and anthropological research in Israel, Peru, the Pacific Islands, and Thailand. His recent publications include *Thai Tourism: Hill Tribes, Islands and Open-ended Prostitution* (1996), *The Commercialized Crafts of Thailand: Hill Tribes and Lowland Villages* (2000), and *The Chinese Vegetarian Festival in Phuket: Religion, Ethnicity and Tourism on a Southern Thai Island* (2001). A collection of his general articles on tourism, *Contemporary Tourism: Diversity and Change*, is in press.

FREDERICK ERRINGTON is distinguished professor of anthropology at Trinity College in Hartford, Connecticut. Together with Deborah Gewertz, he has engaged in anthropological research in four regions of Papua New Guinea and in the state of Montana. In all of these contexts, tourism is an important social fact. In addition to his separately authored books, he has written jointly with Deborah Gewertz *Cultural Alternatives and a Feminist Anthropology* (1987), *Twisted Histories, Altered Contexts* (1994), *Articulating Change in the "Last Unknown"* (1995), and *Emerging Class in Papua New Guinea* (1999).

JAMES F. FISHER is the John W. Nason professor of Asian studies and anthropology, Carleton College, Minnesota. He has published *Sherpas* (1997) and *Living Martyrs* (1998). He became interested in tourism after participating in an expedition in the Himalayas led by Sir Edmund Hillary. "One of our objectives was building the Lukla airstrip in northeast Nepal, which shortened the trip to the Mt. Everest area from two weeks to 45 minutes, thus opening the floodgates to tourists and forever changing the lives of the Sherpas who live there."

DEBORAH GEWERTZ is the G. Henry Whitcomb professor of anthropology at Amherst College, Massachusetts. She has conducted research in four regions of Papua New Guinea and in Montana. She is the author of numerous books, including four with Frederick Errington. Recently, they delivered the Lewis Henry Morgan Lectures at the University of Rochester about their latest work on a Papua New Guinea sugar plantation. Based upon these lectures, the book *As Natural as Life, As Complex as Culture: What a Papua New Guinea Sugar Plantation Teaches about Human History* is forthcoming.

GEORGE GMELCH is professor of anthropology at Union College in upstate New York. He first became interested in tourism while living in rural Barbados where many of his village neighbors worked at the island's resorts. He is the author of nine books, with the most recent being on the culture of professional baseball—*In the Ballpark: The Working Lives of Baseball People* (1998) and *Inside Pitch: Life in Professional Baseball* (2001)—and on Caribbean tourism—*Behind the Smile: The Working Lives of Caribbean Tourism* (2003).

SHARON BOHN GMELCH is professor of anthropology at Union College in upstate New York. She has published five books including *Tinkers and Travellers*, which won Ireland's Book of the Year Award in 1976, and *Nan: The Life of an Irish Travelling Woman* (1986/1991), which was a finalist for the Margaret Mead Award. Her interests include visual anthropology, gender, ethnicity, and tourism. "I became interested in tourism because of its impact on the places I have done research, such as Sitka, Alaska, where cruise ship passengers overrun the town in summer, and Barbados, where white Bajans at one time sported T-shirts proclaiming, 'I'm not a tourist, I live here.'" In *The Parish Behind God's Back: The Changing Culture of Rural Barbados* (with George Gmelch, 1997/2001), she examines some of tourism's impact.

NELSON H. H. GRABURN obtained his BA in the natural sciences and anthropology at Cambridge University, his MA at McGill University, and his PhD at the University of Chicago, both in anthropology. He has taught in the department of anthropology at the University of California, Berkeley since 1964. He has done research among Canadian Inuit on cultural change and the emergence of tourism and commercial arts since 1959 and on Japanese tourism since 1974. His interest in the invention and commoditization of Inuit sculptures and prints led to the publication of *Ethnic and Tourist Arts* (1976) and to his contribution "Tourism: The Sacred Journey" in Valene Smith's *Hosts and Guests* (1977). He is a founding member of the International Academy for the Study of Tourism and of RC-50, the Research Committee on International Tourism of the International Sociological Association.

DAVYDD J. GREENWOOD is the Goldwin Smith professor of anthropology and director of the Institute for European Studies at Cornell University. Elected a corresponding member of the Spanish Royal Academy of Moral and Political Sciences, he has written on agricultural change, ethnic conflict, biological determinist theories, and action research. Among his major publications are *Unrewarding Wealth: Commercialization and the Collapse of Agriculture in a Spanish Basque Town* (1976), *The Taming of Evolution: The Persistence of Nonevolutionary Views in the Study of Humans* (1985), *Industrial Democracy as Process: Participatory Action Research in the Fagor Cooperative Group of Mondragón* (with José Luis González, 1992), and *Introduction to Action Research: Social Research for Social Change* (with Morten Levin, 1998). Greenwood's interest in tourism arose from the direct confrontation in Hondarribia in the Basque Country between tourism development and the agricultural and fishing economies.

MARTHA HONEY is executive director of the International Ecotourism Society and the Center on Ecotourism and Sustainable Development (a joint project of the Institute for Policy Studies and Stanford University), both based in Washington DC. She is author of *Hostile Acts: U.S. Policies in Costa Rica in the 1980s* (University Presses of Florida, 1994), *Ecotourism and Sustainable Development* (Island Press, 1999), and *Ecotourism and Certification: Setting Standards in Practice* (Island Press, 2002).

ORVAR LÖFGREN is professor of European ethnology at the University of Lund, Sweden. His recent books include *On Holiday: A History of Vacationing* (1999) and *Invoking a Transnational Metropolis: The Making of the Öresund Region* (with Per Olaf Berg and Anders Linde-Laursen, 2000). Tourism interests Löfgren "as a laboratory of modernity, an arena where people have been able to experiment with new aspects of their identities and social relations and also develop cultural skills like daydreaming and mindtraveling."

DEAN MACCANNELL is professor of landscape architecture and research sociologist in the experiment station at the University of California at Davis. His book *The Tourist: A New Theory of the Leisure Class* (1976) was one of the earliest contributions to tourism studies. He was a founding member and officer of the International Tourism Research Academy and Research Group 50 (the sociology of tourism) of the International Sociological Association. His work on tourism was the subject of a six-hour BBC miniseries, *The Tourist*, which aired in 1996. MacCannell's current research is at the intersection of tourism, architecture, planning, art, and psychoanalysis.

DEBORAH MCLAREN is the director of Indigenous Tourism Rights International (formerly the Rethinking Tourism Project) in St. Paul, Minnesota. She is the author of *Rethinking Tourism and Ecotravel* (1998/2003). She has an MA in social ecology, with an emphasis and research focus on tourism and globalization. She is concerned about the ability of researchers and academics to adequately disseminate tourism research results to indigenous and rural communities—"often the focus of the research, yet rarely the recipients of the information."

MARC L. MILLER is professor in the school of marine affairs and adjunct professor in the school of aquatic and fishery sciences and the department of anthropology at the University of Washington. His research interests broadly concern social, cultural, ethical, and aesthetic aspects of coastal leisure and marine species management.

LAWRENCE E. MINTZ has been a member of the American studies faculty of the University of Maryland since 1969. He teaches courses and writes on popular culture and American humor and is the director of the Art Gliner Center for Humor Studies. He became interested in tourism watching visitors navigate the tourist voyage during a year living in Paris and by defending his enthusiasm for Walt Disney World and other theme parks against the usual academic criticism.

BRIAN MOERAN is professor of culture and communication at the Copenhagen Business School, Denmark. Irish by nationality, he is by training a social anthropologist who specializes in advertising, media, and Japan. Among his more recent publications are *A Japanese Advertising Agency* (1996), *Asian Media Productions* (edited, 2001) and *Advertising Cultures* (edited with Timothy dewaal Malefyt, 2003). He became interested in tourism through his study of a pottery community (*Folk Art Potters of Japan*, 1997) and watching endless hours of television advertising while nursing his son in the hospital after a diving accident.

POLLY PATTULLO is a British journalist who works for the *Guardian* newspaper in London. She is the author of three books about the Caribbean: *Last Resorts: The Cost of Tourism in the Caribbean* (2003), *The Gardens of Dominica* (1998), and *Fire from the Mountain* (2000). She is particularly interested in so-called ecotourism, having closely observed its impacts—both negative and positive—in Dominica.

PETER PHIPPS is a researcher in the Globalism Institute at RMIT University, Melbourne, Australia. His research has dealt with transnational cultural and intellectual flows, tourism, new religious movements, and the cultural politics of settler-indigenous relations in Australia. He was forced to write about tourism after spending twelve months as a backpacker in India and trying to make sense of what it had turned him into. He continues to be an active (possibly professional) tourist whenever circumstances allow or require it, deliberately embracing fellow tourists with a friendly smile.

DEBORAH PRUITT is on the faculty at Laney College in Oakland, California and the Western Institute for Social Research in Berkeley. She also devotes time to strengthening nonprofit organizations through her consulting practice, Group Alchemy Consulting. Her interest in tourism grew out of her experiences while living in Jamaica and studying grassroots organizing for social change and development. Realizing the dominant role tourism plays in shaping people's hopes for the future and setting the stage for possibilities of local development, she seeks to understand it further.

SUZANNE LAFONT is an assistant professor of anthropology at City University of New York, Kingsborough Community College. She has edited the reader *Constructing Sexualities: Readings in Sexuality, Gender and Culture* (2002). Her related publications include "Very Straight Sex: The Development of Sexual Mores in Jamaica" (*Journal of Colonialism and Colonial History*, 2001); *Women in Transition: Voices from Lithuania* (1998); and *The Emergences of an Afro-Caribbean Legal Tradition in Jamaica* (1996). Her research interests are the interrelations of sexualities, gender, power, and the law.

M. ESTELLIE SMITH is research professor at Union College and professor emerita at the State University of New York at Oswego. She has been interested in tourism since she was a child, when she and her parents endured endless trips to nearby Niagara Falls with a stream of houseguests who had all placed it at the top of their "must see" list. Her interests have broadened since then, but her fascination with tourism has remained. Besides tourism, she has also published on urban anthropology, maritime studies, migration, the European Union, and the Early State. Her most recent book is *Trade and Trade-Offs: Using Resources, Making Choices, and Taking Risks* (2000).

JILL D. SWEET is a professor of anthropology at Skidmore College in upstate New York. She received her PhD in anthropology from the University of New Mexico in 1981 and her MFA in dance from the University of California in 1975. Sweet has published extensively on Pueblo Indian ritual performance and the effects of tourism on this rich expressive form. Currently she is writing a new edition to her book *Dances of the Tewa Pueblo Indians: Expressions of New Life* (1985).

JOHN URRY is professor of sociology at Lancaster University. His recent books in the area of tourism and mobility include *The Tourist Gaze* (1990/2002), *Consuming Places* (1995), *Contested Natures* (with Phil MacNaghten, 1998), *Sociology Beyond Societies* (2000), *Bodies of Nature* (2001), and *Global Complexity* (2003). He became interested in tourism as a result of living near the English lake district, where scenic landscape tourism really began, and to Morcambe, a classic working-class seaside resort.

Appendix B:
Documentary Films about Tourism

CANNIBAL TOURS
Dennis O'Rourke (1987, 77 minutes)
Available from Direct Cinema Limited, Santa Monica, California

Cannibal Tours is two journeys. The first is that depicted—European and American "ethnic" tourists on a luxury cruise up the Sepik River in Papua New Guinea. The second journey (the filmmaker's underlying text) is a metaphysical one—an attempt to discover the place of the Other in the Western popular imagination. Why do "civilized" people want to visit the "primitive"? It is also a powerful film about the role photography plays in tourism.

CONEY ISLAND
Ric Stone, Buddy Squires and Lisa Ades (1991, 60 minutes)
Available from PBS: http://www.shop.pbs.org/

Before there was Disneyland, there was Coney Island. Produced for public television (PBS), the documentary uses archival photographs, newsreel footage, and interviews to reveal the development and appeal of New York's famous tourist playground from its birth in the mid-1800s until its demise after WWII. In addition to its beaches, Coney Island at its peak consisted of three vast amusement parks offering an assortment of rides (it was the birthplace of the roller

coaster) and spectacles including huge moving panoramas showing the creation, the end of the world and Hell, and reenactments of the Boer War and the
fall of Pompeii. There was also a miniature town, known as Lilliputia, inhabited by 300 little people. Good supplemental materials are available through
the PBS Web site (http://www.pbs.org).

GOA UNDER SIEGE
Magic Lantern Foundation (1999, 30 minutes)
Available from Tourism Concern, London, UK; www.tourismconcern.org.uk

The film discusses the many impacts of tourism on Goa's residents, from the
introduction of the drug culture to the stress that tourism places on the local
water supply. The conflict between residents who have mobilized to gain a
voice in the tourism industry and those of governmental officers in India interested in development is apparent. Although the production quality is not as
high as it could be, the video comes with useful supplemental materials (i.e.,
printed film narration and citizen's tourism manifesto).

THE GOOD WOMAN OF BANGKOK
Dennis O'Rourke (1992, 82 minutes)
Available from Direct Cinema Limited, Santa Monica, California

The film, which Dennis O'Rourke labels a "documentary fiction film," explores
sex tourism in Bangkok largely through the experiences and commentary of a
woman named Aoi. It also includes explicit nude scenes of Thai sex workers
dancing, the comments of male sex tourists, and a recurring interview with a
woman relative in Aoi's home village. The nature of O'Rourke's involvement
with Aoi has been the subject of critical commentary. According to O'Rourke,
". . . the film includes a character—'the film maker'—who reflects me and
others of my race and class, gender and profession, *but who is not me* (the person who was/is me was/is very different; because every day and every night I
had to make the film). Through the description of this character, I took the rhetorical but sincere position that 'the film maker' was implicated and guilty
along with the sex tourists." An essay by O'Rourke appears in *The Filmmaker
and the Prostitute*, ed. Chris Berry, Annette Hamilton, and Laleen Jayamanne
(Sydney: Power Publications, 1997).

HOLI-DAYS
Randi Steinberger (2002, 50 minutes)
Available from Tell-Tale Productions, 900 N. Michigan Ave., Suite 2010, Chi-
cago, IL 60611-1542; http://tell-taleprod.com.

Holi-days documents the contradiction between modern travelers' and pilgrims'
expectations and their actual experiences in Jerusalem, Florence, and Las
Vegas. It captures, in the words of one reviewer, "their theme-park similarities.
Jerusalem seems a carnival of religious intensity and Florence a diorama of

Renaissance culture, each retailing its past for the entertainment of visitors; like Vegas, they're tourist towns now." Las Vegas is filled with spectators enjoying its ability to replicate the physical icons of global travel: the Eiffel Tower, the Canals of Venice, and the Statue of Liberty, to name a few. As one tourist in the film happily exclaims, "I'm never going to Paris . . . so I think it's worth it to see it here." *Holi-days* suggests that the change tourists seek can be as profound as a religious epiphany, as superficial as a successful shopping spree, or as life transforming as winning the big jackpot.

IN AND OUT OF AFRICA
Lucien Taylor and Llisa Barbash (1992, 59 minutes)
Available from University of California Extension Center for Media and Independent Learning, Berkeley, California

This film explores authenticity, taste, and racial politics in the transnational African art market. It follows a Nigerian art trader, Gabai Baare, from rural Cote d'Ivoire to Long Island, New York, where he bargains for a sale. As objects change hands, they transform in meaning as well as in economic value. At the core of the film are the stories Baare tells about the art objects as he mediates between the values and aspirations of African producers and American consumers.

INNOCENTS ABROAD
Les Blank (1991, 84 minutes)
See www.lesblank.com; also available from http://picpal.com/lesnhar.html

American filmmaker Les Blank and editor Chris Simon join American tourists on a whirlwind and often funny tour of Europe. A Globus Gateway "European Horizons" tour bus leaves London with 40 mostly retired people in the hands of British tour director Mark Tinny. They cover 3,000 miles and 24 European cities in 14 frantic days. The film's overall impression is one of excited travelers having the adventure of a lifetime while relying on the security provided by an organized tour. The perceptions of Americans looking at Europeans is matched by the varied responses of Europeans they encounter working in popular tourist destinations.

LIFE & DEBT
Stephanie Black (2001, 86 minutes)
Available from New Yorker Films, 85 Fifth Ave., NY 10003 or www.NewYorkerFilms.com

Life & Debt looks at the impact of globalization on Jamaica. Through images and narration by Jamaica Kincaid (based on her book, *A Small Place*), it contrasts the reasons tourists come to Jamaica with what they do not see and know about real conditions on the island. Excellent interviews with former Jamaican Premier Minister Michael Manley, deputy director of the IMF Stanley Fisher, and others reveal the devastating impact free trade, NAFTA, the business practices of multinationals, and lending policies of the IMF and World Bank have had on the country's economy. Reggae soundtrack.

THE TOURED: THE OTHER SIDE OF TOURISM IN BARBADOS
Julie Pritchard Wright (1991, 39 minutes)
Available from University of California Extension Center for Media and Independent Learning, Berkeley, California

This documentary, made by an American anthropology student/filmmaker, shows tourism from the point of view of some of those working in the industry. Bajans talk about the realities of making a living in a tourist economy and witnessing one's traditional culture change under the impact of foreign visitors. The occupation most highlighted is that of the "beach boy" who becomes sexually and "romantically" involved with women tourists. It also includes interesting comments from one of the women.

TREKKING ON TRADITION
Jennifer H. Rodes (1992, 44 minutes)
Available from University of California Extension Center for Media and Independent Learning, Berkeley, CA.

This film explores the effects of mountain tourism or trekking on a small village in rural Nepal. It examines the views of both the trekkers (Europeans and Americans) and the Nepalese, and weaves a complex patchwork of conflicting dreams, aspirations, and frustrations.

Appendix C: Tourist Guidelines

The following guidelines, written for tourists by various NGOs and indigenous peoples, are a few of those available.

Traveler's Code for Traveling Responsibly: Guidelines for Individuals

Cultural Understanding

- Travel with an open mind: cultivate the habit of listening and observing; discover the enrichment that comes from experiencing another way of life.

- Reflect daily on your experiences and keep a journal.

- Prepare: learn the geography, culture, history, beliefs, and some local language; know how to be a good guest in the country or culture.

Social Impacts

- Support the local economy by using locally run restaurants and hotels, buying local products made by locals from renewable resources.

- Interact with local residents in a culturally appropriate manner.

- Make no promises that you cannot keep (photos, college admission).

- Don't make an extravagant display of wealth; don't encourage children to beg.

- Get permission before photographing people, homes, and other sites of local importance.

Environmental Impacts

- Travel in small, low-impact groups. Stay on trails.

- Pack it in, pack it out; assure proper disposal of human waste.

- Don't buy products made from endangered animals or plants. Become aware of and contribute to projects benefiting local environments and communities (a social benefit as well).

Adapted by Tourism Concern (www.tourismconcern.org.uk).

Tourism Concern's Guidelines

- Save precious natural resources. Try not to waste water. Switch off lights and air-conditioning if you go out.

- Support the local tradespeople and artisans. Buy only locally made souvenirs where possible. But do help safeguard nature by avoiding souvenirs made from ivory, skins, or other wildlife.

- Recognize land rights. Tribal peoples' ownership of the lands they use and occupy is recognized in international law. This should be acknowledged irrespective of whether the national government applies the law or not (governments are among the principal violators of tribal rights). When in tribal lands, tourists should behave as they would on private property. (From *Survival International*'s code.)

- Always ask before taking photographs or videotape recordings of people. Don't worry if you don't speak the language—a smile and a gesture will be understood and appreciated.

- Please don't give money or sweets to children—it only encourages begging and demeans the child. A donation to a recognized project, health center, or school is a more constructive way to help. (If you have a guide, ask for details.)

- Respect for local etiquette earns you respect. In many countries, loose and lightweight clothes are preferable to revealing shorts, skimpy tops, or tight-fitting wear. Similarly, kissing in public is often culturally inappropriate.

- Learning something about the history and current affairs of a country helps you understand the attitudes and idiosyncrasies of its people and helps prevent misunderstandings and frustrations.

- Be patient, friendly, and sensitive. Remember—you are a guest.

The Achuar Visitors Behavior Requests

- Though culture and traditions may appear odd, please don't criticize them. Follow the Achuar community rules and learn about their extraordinary culture.

- Ask your Achuar guide if is possible to take photographs or video-tape recordings. Avoid close-up shots and offer people money for a photograph.

- The Achuar feel pleased when you buy their handicrafts. All communities have a fixed price. Avoid purchasing items made from feathers, animal skins, or insects.

- Please avoid any physical contact with community members.

- Do not give money, presents, or sweets to the kids. If you have educational materials that you would like to donate, please give them to the resident manager.

- Do not enter an Achuar house without an invitation.

- The Achuar are jealous people. If you are a man, you should never look directly at a woman's face.

- Because the Achuar house is divided by gender, do not go to the *ekent* or female area on the east side.

- *Nijiamanch,* the manioc beer, is always offered. If you do not like it, you should at least pretend to drink it. Refusing might be considered an insult.

- Please do not take animals or plants out of the reserve area.

- Donations to the FINAE, the Achuar organization, the different projects, or scientific research can be coordinated through the Pachamama Alliance. Please ask the resident manager.

Kapawi Ecolodge and Reserve; www.ecuador-wildlife.com/jungle/kapawi.html

Tourism—Simply . . . a Guide to Better Tourism

- Don't rely on guidebooks. Learn as much as you can from other sources (indigenous writers, independent newspapers, films, and so on). Try to understand the different cultures of the place you're visiting on their own terms and behave appropriately. For example, don't visit religious places semi-clothed.

- Look at your own mindset. Try to understand why people behave differently: concepts of time, for example, vary between cultures. Don't demand special privileges, like better access to transport and services.

- Don't steal pictures. In some cultures it's more than invasive to have your picture taken. Ask if it's okay for you to take someone's photograph and be ready to offer or exchange something you have.

- If you make a promise to send a letter or photograph then keep it.

- Use locally produced goods and services—from your choice of airline to the food you eat.

- Respect the local environment. Try to be a guest rather than a colonizer.

- Don't go somewhere if you think that being a tourist there supports a repressive regime.

- Ask yourself—why am I going? Consider using international networks that can help you to stay with local families rather than in hotels.

New Internationalist 245 (July 1993). Some points adapted from *Guide Notes for Responsive Travel* published by Centre for the Advancement of Responsive Travel (CART).

Treading Softly: A Guide to Eco-Friendly Travel in Vietnam

Dear Traveler,

Welcome to Vietnam—a country that evokes a multitude of images and emotions—a nation small in size but expansive in heart and soul.

Vietnam's contrasts and diversity—its many ethnic groups and its rich cultural, historical, and ecological heritage—attract thousands upon thousands of tourists each year. However, it is a fragile land that has borne the brunt of human and natural disasters. Years of war, subsequent reconstruction of the country, high population growth, poverty, and now the push toward rapid industrialization and a market-oriented economy have had environmental and social consequences.

Tourism, too, has had a negative impact, affecting even the most distant corners of the country with its cultural and environmental footprint. The aim of this guidebook is to show how you, as a visitor, can play a part in helping to protect Vietnam from the negative impacts of tourism.

By treading softly on the country's environment and respecting its people, you can minimize your impact while gaining the maximum enjoyment from your traveling experience, and take home an abundance of happy memories. You will also contribute positively, by thoughtful example, to a more sustainable tourism industry in Vietnam.

Protecting the Future

Tourism, one of the planet's biggest industries, has been a major driving force behind globalization. Every corner of the planet has become a potential tourist destination, and some of the world's most fantastic landscapes are now nationally and internationally protected as a direct result. The idea of sustainable tourism has evolved out of concern about the negative impacts of tourism. Sustainable tourism aims to protect the environment and respect peoples and their cultures while enhancing the socioeconomic benefits of tourism. Importantly, sustainable tourism should contribute to improving the quality of life of host communities. Protecting destinations in your lifetime— so that you, your children, and future generations will also have the opportunity to revisit—is a must. Here's how you can help . . .

Getting You on Side

First and foremost, it is important to realize that what you do makes a difference. By being a responsible and sensitive traveler, you can raise awareness of others in the tourism sector, be they tour operators, guides, or your fellow holidaymakers; be they from the country you are visiting or abroad. It doesn't cost a lot and it doesn't require a revolutionary adjustment. Small changes can add up to a significant overall positive impact.

Vietnam has only comparatively recently opened up to international tourism, which is now a major foreign exchange earner. While Vietnam can learn from the experiences, both positive and negative, of other countries— you can help by showing your support for sustainable tourism. You can vote with your money, choosing to patronize hotels, airlines, resorts, and tour operators that advance energy and environmental conservation and are committed to global principles of sustainability. You are not the only visitor to Vietnam—your impact on the environment is multiplied a millionfold by other people every year.

Every tourist and every host community will have a different concept of crowding, environmental degradation, invasion of privacy, noise, and so on, and a different level of tolerance. If you are aware of being crowded, or of not enjoying your visit due to pollution or noise, then you have touched upon your carrying capacity. Think of others—both tourists and hosts—and the possibility that their tolerance level may be lower than yours.

Temper Your Expectations with Reality

Tourists strive to have "authentic" experiences when they travel. They want to experience "untouched paradise" or "traditional" cultures, while often expecting the same comforts they would have at home. Fantasy often turns to disappointment when tourists arrive at their destination and find it "modernized" or "spoiled." Think about how realistic this expectation is when so many people are traveling with similar expectations.

The truth is, cultures are rarely stagnant, but constantly changing and adapting. Development usually brings increased options for communities, be they in the form of electric pumps, plastic buckets, fluorescent lights, televisions, new concrete toilets, or modern clothing. Unfortunately, when visitors no longer consider a community "authentic," tour operators are forced to move on, taking away valuable income and impacting other areas.

Yet modern life in Vietnam is also fascinating! Accept that you cannot expect to preserve living culture as in a museum. Accept the people you visit as they are, whether they are wearing traditional dress or baseball caps. Culture is more than clothes, crafts, and dances—dig deeper to discover the inner expression of culture and tradition.

It's also worth mentioning that "exotic," "innocent," "graceful," "virginal," "pure," and other such tired stereotypes of Vietnam do not paint a realistic picture and are, in fact, demeaning in their simplicity and connotations. Remember that no society or people is perfect or pure. Each has its shortcomings and foibles, and Vietnam is no exception.

Low-Impact Tourism

Although there are commonsense ways in which you can avoid creating negative impressions and damaging the environment, it's still easy to make mistakes when you are new to a place. Here are some Vietnam-specific guidelines that, if appropriately followed, should make your trip more enjoyable and ensure that you leave behind a positive impression and only the softest of footprints.

Be an Environmental Ambassador

Home to one-tenth of the world's mammal, bird, and fish species, Vietnam has a unique environment. Scattered throughout the country are around 100 protected areas that encompass a huge variety of ecological systems that include coral reefs, islands, beaches and dunes, wetlands, mountains, forests of every description, limestone landscapes and caves, river deltas, and lakes. Among these protected areas are 11 national parks managed by the Forest Protection Department, which represent some of the jewels of Vietnam's natural heritage. Vietnam's 11 national parks are: Ba Be, Ba Vi, Bach Ma, Ben En, Cat Ba, Cat Tien, Con Dao, Cuc Phuong, Tam Dao, Tram Chim, and Yok Don. In addition to these 11 national parks, the country has four UNESCO World Heritage Sites—the Ancient Capital at Hue (December 94), Ha Long Bay (December 94), Hoi An (January 99) and the Cham Monument at My Son (January 99), and one UNESCO/MAB Biosphere Reserve named Can Gio Mangrove.

Numerous flora and fauna species are also unique to Vietnam—40 percent of Vietnam's plants grow nowhere else—while seven of the 12 large mammals that have been described in the last century were discovered in Vietnam. Sadly, the environment is under threat. In 1943, natural forest covered an estimated 43 percent of the country. At the end of 2000, total forest cover, including both natural forest and plantations, had dwindled to 33 percent. Tourism provides an economic reason for conserving natural resources and, if sustainable, can encourage the protection of the country's biodiversity.

Helping to Conserve Vietnam's Precious Biodiversity

Many species of Vietnam's wild fauna and flora are under threat from both domestic consumption and the illegal international trade. Though it may be "an experience" to try wild meat such as bear, muntjac, bat, monkey, and python, ordering these foods will indicate your acceptance of these products and add to their demand.

- Be careful when consuming wild products such as bush meat and traditional medicine, as these may have come from endangered or threatened species. When offered wild meat, be sure that it is derived from sustainable management practices that can, in fact, contribute to the conservation of wild animals and rural development. In case of doubt, however, the best policy is to politely refuse it.

- In the case of tourist souvenirs, do not buy products made from endangered plants or animals, such as elephant ivory, tortoiseshell, and wild animal skins. Again, unless you are certain the species is not endangered, never buy live or stuffed animals, however tempting, and forgo the coral you will no doubt see on sale in the markets. Vietnam's coral and ornamental fishes are being severely depleted by destructive harvesting practices.

- Remember that virtually all countries in the world are parties to the CITES Convention, which regulates the trade in endangered species of wild fauna and flora. Accordingly, importing many wildlife products without special permit is illegal and you could be severely fined in your own country.

Rubbish, Waste, and Energy Use

Environmental awareness in Vietnam is generally low. You can help change this subtly by example—for instance, not dropping litter even if someone tells you it's okay to do so. By setting a quiet example, practicing the 3 Rs—reduce, reuse, recycle—and explaining the reasons for your actions to others, you can play a positive role in protecting the environment and the natural and cultural resources of Vietnam.

- Make sure you properly dispose of any rubbish you generate. There are few public rubbish bins in Vietnam, so this may mean carrying it with you for a while.

- If no toilet is available, make sure you bury your waste, and avoid sites near waterways. Burning or carrying toilet paper and hygienic items out of natural areas is a must.

- Carry a toilet roll and a couple of airtight plastic bags with you in case you need to take your rubbish with you.

- Never use shampoo or soap in rivers, lakes, or the sea. Vietnam's waterways are precious resources, and in some of the country's drier areas water is a very scarce commodity.

- Please turn off your air conditioner, fans, lights, and other electrical appliances when you leave your hotel or guesthouse.

- Try to reduce the use of air conditioners in cars and encourage drivers to turn off the engine when stationary.

Coral Reefs and Limestone Caves

Vietnam is home to a large expanse of stunning limestone landscapes—of which Halong Bay in the north is the most famous—and coral reefs, both of which have suffered severe damage in recent years. Coral reefs in particular have been damaged due to dynamite fishing, boat anchorage, mining for concrete production, and sale to tourists.

- When visiting coral reefs do not touch live coral, as this hinders growth—some species, such as "fire corals" are also able to cause a harmful sting.

- Do not anchor boats on coral reefs. If your tour operator does this, try to convince him or her to anchor in a sandy area. Indicate that you are willing to swim the extra distance to the coral.

- When exploring limestone caves, don't touch the formations, as it hinders growth and turns the limestone black. Never break off stalactites and stalagmites in limestone caves—they take lifetimes to regrow.

Walking and Trekking in Natural Areas

While walking and trekking are preferable to 4WDs as a means of exploring national parks and other protected areas, the constant flow of tourists can still have a negative impact on the fragile ecological balance of these places. Remember that you are just one of thousands who will visit and impact an area.

- Keep to designated trails when out walking, both for your safety and the protection of the environment. There are reasons why certain trails are used.

- Follow the rules and regulations of the protected area you are visiting. For example, never make fires, avoid making unnecessary noise, and do not take samples from nature (flowers, mushrooms, frogs, etc.).

- Pay particular attention to the guidelines for rubbish discussed above. Do not dispose of rubbish or cigarette butts in the wild as they may take many years to break down (if ever).

Culture: A Matter of Etiquette

Traveling in Vietnam is not always relaxing. It can be unpredictable, intense, and frustrating, but it is rewarding. Being demanding and loud, however, will get you nowhere. Remember the importance of "face"—the subtle but important quality of personal dignity in Asian countries.

- Try to learn about the local culture before you travel and broaden your experiences beyond the guidebooks. Guidebooks can make or break a guesthouse or hotel by concentrating people in certain places. Guidebooks are also often out of date by the time they are distributed. Be willing to try alternative options.

- Learn some of the local language. Even basics such as "hello," "goodbye," and "thank you" will be appreciated

- Respect cultural differences and don't look down on or try to change them.

- Be careful when showing affection in public. Relationships in Vietnamese society are fairly traditional, so in general it's best to limit affection to holding hands—especially in rural areas.

- Avoid patting or touching people on the head—it's the symbolic high point in Asia.

- Be aware of the importance of the ancestral shrine in Vietnam. Avoid backing up to, pointing your feet at, or changing your clothing in front of it.

What to Wear

To be sure of not causing offense, it is best to respect local dress standards and dress modestly, especially in the countryside.

- There are no areas where nude or topless swimming or sunbathing is appropriate.

- Women should try to avoid wearing low-cut or tight sleeveless tops and brief, clinging shorts. It is advisable to wear a bra at all times. Men should avoid walking around bare-chested.

- At religious sites, do not wear shorts or sleeveless tops and remember to remove your shoes.

Questions, Privacy, and Humor

Vietnamese concepts of privacy are very different from those of Westerners, as they are accustomed to living and sharing in a close-knit community and in crowded conditions.

- Don't be offended by the (very Vietnamese) fascination with your personal details—How old are you? Are you married? Do you have children? and so on—questions that you may consider private. You may find the answer "not yet" *(chưa)* to the question of marriage or children a useful one.

- Don't be taken aback if people are intrigued by your size, especially if you are tall or well built. The Vietnamese are a small, slight people and may openly display their amazement at Western bulk. Remember this when selecting your clothing!

- Talk to the locals and make friends. The people of Vietnam are friendly and hospitable. They love it when they hear a foreigner try to speak their language.

Snap Happy

Vietnam is a photographer's dream—from the vivid greens of the rice paddies and cloud-shrouded mountains to the bustle of open-air markets and street life, there are endless photographic opportunities. However, nobody enjoys being followed by a camera, so remember to ask permission before taking photographs—and respect a refusal.

- Don't hound men and women in traditional ethnic dress for the "perfect colorful shot" if they appear shy or avoid your camera, and remember that videos are even more intrusive.

- Try not to get into the situation of paying for the right to take photos, as it encourages a begging mentality.

- If you promise to send back a photo, make sure you are sincere in your offer.

Just Say No

It's in your own interests to respect local regulations and practices concerning drugs and alcohol. Drugs are illegal in Vietnam and their possession and usage carry harsh penalties.

- Be careful about alcohol consumption, especially when visiting rural and ethnic minority areas, where as a tourist you may enjoy privileged status.

- Remember that tourism can fuel the demand for alcohol and drugs and lead to increased consumption/use by locals, encouraging social problems.

Getting Personal

Be aware that in some communities it may be taboo to conduct an intimate relationship with a local.

- Don't assume that what is acceptable at home is acceptable everywhere. Vietnam is still a largely traditional society and getting involved with a local may cause offense.

- Remember also that the recipient of a foreigner's attentions can be seriously affected within their local communities in terms of their well-being, social standing, and reputation.

Out and About: Buying Local

By using locally produced goods and services, you can contribute financially to the community you are visiting and help turn tourism to the country's benefit.

- Drink and eat local food when you can.

- Use local transport and local shops.

- Offer to repay hospitality in cash or in kind to avoid exploiting the goodwill of others. At the same time, try to avoid paying for simple acts of kindness in cash—for example, being given directions.

- Hire a local guide when visiting protected areas or historical sites. This way you will contribute to the local economy, learn more about the area, and have the opportunity to meet local people.

Giving Money or Gifts

Giving money away to both children and adults promotes a begging mentality and culture. It also highlights the income gap and strips away people's self-esteem. By avoiding cash handouts you can play a part in discouraging the development of a society that equates every human action as a potential moneymaking scheme.

- Avoid giving children money or gifts; it is better to pay for a postcard, map, or a shoeshine.

- Giving chocolate or sweets is a bad idea, as many people do not have access to dentists and knowledge of dental hygiene is poor.

The Hard Sell

Vietnam is a developing country and one that has experienced a long period of war, so poverty is obvious and unavoidable. Be prepared to be approached by street sellers, shoe shine boys, etc., or followed by empty *cyclos* expectantly awaiting your patronage, especially in Hanoi, Ho Chi Minh City, and other large towns.

- If you are approached by a street seller, be firm but polite and calm in turning them away, even if you are irritated by a day filled with similar approaches.

- Take a *cyclo* when you can, as they are a great way to see a city and view street life at close quarters. *Cyclos* are today losing out to taxis and *xe om* (motorbike taxis), so you'll also be supporting a threatened trade.

- Certain streets have been made off-limits to *cyclos*, so your driver may have to take an indirect route to your destination.

- Negotiate prices in advance before accepting either goods from street sellers or getting on a *xe om* or into a *cyclo*.

The Sex Trade

In Asia, prostitution is an unfortunate fact of life. The link between tourism and prostitution is undisputed. Be aware that prostitution is illegal in Vietnam. Be careful not to act in any way that could be seen as encouraging this, especially where children are concerned.

- Don't buy sexual services; remember that the relationship between tourists and prostitutes is almost always unequal and tends to be exploitative.

- The sexual exploitation of children is a significant problem right across Asia. However, several countries now have laws that enable the trial at home of tourists who have committed crimes of pedophilia abroad. If you observe anyone known to you involved in child prostitution, you might consider reporting him or her to the police when you get home.

Before You Go

As you head off on holiday, it is important to think about the main reason for your trip to Vietnam, whether it's adventure, biodiversity, new cuisine, history, art, and culture, meeting new people, or simply cultivating a golden tan. It's equally important to realize that everything you do while you're away has a consequence for somebody, or something, else.

Enjoying your time in Vietnam will be easy. But by following the *A to G Green Guide*, you'll also be doing something active toward ensuring a long-term future for both tourism and the environment. In return, you'll be rewarded with a richer traveling experience and the respect of the people of this fascinating country.

Treading Softly was produced as part of the "Support to Sustainable Tourism Project" executed by SNV (Netherlands Development Organization) Vietnam together with IUCN (World Conservation Union) Vietnam.